Fundamentals of Criminal Law and Procedure for Paralegals

Fundamentals of Criminal Law and Procedure for Paralegals

Third Edition

Thomas E. McClure
Director of Legal Studies and
Professor
Illinois State University

Thomas E. Eimermann
Emeritus Professor
Illinois State University

ASPEN
PUBLISHING

Cover image credit: Gorodenkoff/stock.adobe.com

To contact Customer Service, e-mail customer.service@aspenpublishing.com, call 1-800-950-5259, or mail correspondence to:

Aspen Publishing
Attn: Order Department
PO Box 990
Frederick, MD 21705

Printed in the United States of America.

1 2 3 4 5 6 7 8 9 0

ISBN 978-1-5438-5860-0

Library of Congress Cataloging-in-Publication Data

Library of Congress Cataloging-in-Publication Data application is in process.

SUSTAINABLE FORESTRY INITIATIVE Certified Sourcing
www.forests.org
SFI-00756

About Aspen Publishing

Aspen Publishing is a leading provider of educational content and digital learning solutions to law schools in the U.S. and around the world. Aspen provides best-in-class solutions for legal education through authoritative textbooks, written by renowned authors, and breakthrough products such as Connected eBooks, Connected Quizzing, and PracticePerfect.

The Aspen Casebook Series (famously known among law faculty and students as the "red and black" casebooks) encompasses hundreds of highly regarded textbooks in more than eighty disciplines, from large enrollment courses, such as Torts and Contracts to emerging electives such as Sustainability and the Law of Policing. Study aids such as the *Examples & Explanations* and the *Emanuel Law Outlines* series, both highly popular collections, help law students master complex subject matter.

Major products, programs, and initiatives include:

- **Connected eBooks** are enhanced digital textbooks and study aids that come with a suite of online content and learning tools designed to maximize student success. Designed in collaboration with hundreds of faculty and students, the Connected eBook is a significant leap forward in the legal education learning tools available to students.
- **Connected Quizzing** is an easy-to-use formative assessment tool that tests law students' understanding and provides timely feedback to improve learning outcomes. Delivered through CasebookConnect.com, the learning platform already used by students to access their Aspen casebooks, Connected Quizzing is simple to implement and integrates seamlessly with law school course curricula.
- **PracticePerfect** is a visually engaging, interactive study aid to explain commonly encountered legal doctrines through easy-to-understand animated videos, illustrative examples, and numerous practice questions. Developed by a team of experts, PracticePerfect is the ideal study companion for today's law students.
- The **Aspen Learning Library** enables law schools to provide their students with access to the most popular study aids on the market across all of their courses. Available through an annual subscription, the online library consists of study aids in e-book, audio, and video formats with full text search, note-taking, and highlighting capabilities.
- Aspen's **Digital Bookshelf** is an institutional-level online education bookshelf, consolidating everything students and professors need to ensure success. This program ensures that every student has access to affordable course materials from day one.
- **Leading Edge** is a community centered on thinking differently about legal education and putting those thoughts into actionable strategies. At the core of the program is the Leading Edge Conference, an annual gathering of legal education thought leaders looking to pool ideas and identify promising directions of exploration.

To our wives for their understanding and support.

Summary of Contents

Contents

PART 2 CRIMINAL PROCEDURE: FROM COMMISSION OF THE OFFENSE TO PLEA BARGAINING

PART 3 CRIMINAL PROCEDURE: TRIALS AND THEIR AFTERMATH

CHAPTER 13 ■ SENTENCING 439

CHAPTER 14 ■ APPEALS 471

List of Illustrations

Preface

This book is designed to be used as a textbook for paralegal courses covering criminal law and procedure. In addition to discussing the organization and function of criminal law, it covers the most common types of criminal offenses and the procedures used to enforce these criminal laws at the federal and state levels.

Because it is **designed specifically for paralegals**, it describes the various roles played by paralegals and focuses on providing the skills and knowledge students will need to function effectively in jobs related to criminal law. It also contains discussions of the role of police and lawyers, the basic principles of criminal law, constitutional limitations, and trial procedures that **can benefit criminal justice majors, government majors, pre-law students, and anyone wishing to know more about criminal law.**

As with all books of this type, the authors have been faced with the challenge of covering both federal law and variations in state laws. We have tended to focus on federal law because it is relevant to readers in all parts of the country, but we have also discussed how state laws and procedures vary. Because there are so many variations among the states, and even between judicial districts within a given state, it is imperative that readers research their own state and local statutes and procedural rules to see how they differ from the ones used as illustrations in this book. This book includes instructions and Application Exercises designed to teach readers how to find and apply the laws and procedures of their own state and local area.

Another feature that sets this book apart from many of its competitors is the extent to which we have included discussions of white-collar crime. Discussions of criminal codes, the exhibits, and the Application Exercises all include references to these types of crimes. References to juvenile law are also included where relevant.

New to this Edition

While covering the same topics and maintaining the same organizational structure, the third edition has expanded discussion of some of these topics and incorporates new, more current examples of how our criminal justice system works.

Some of these additions include expanding coverage of laws dealing with insurrection, rebellion, sedition and hate crimes; and prosecutions of law enforcement personnel for having violated criminal statutes while carrying out their police duties: officer kneeling on George Floyd's neck; officer shooting

Daunte Wright with a service revolver rather than a taser; and officers shooting Breonna Taylor while serving a no-knock warrant. We have also expanded our discussion of "hate crimes" to include a discussion of how it relates to the death of George Floyd and its use in the prosecution of the Georgia jogger case.

In Chapter 7, we have added discussions of the self-defense claims raised by George Zimmerman and Kyle Rittenhouse in their respective prosecutions for murder. The Rittenhouse case raises related issues of vigilantism and gun laws. Chapter 12 now includes a discussion of how court system adopted to the challenges of the Covid-19 pandemic.

Organization of the Book

PART 1: CRIMINAL LAW

This section of the book provides a general overview of the criminal justice system. Chapter 1 discusses the purpose of the law and the differences between criminal law and civil law, as well as the procedural stages of a criminal case. It also explains the distinct roles and responsibilities of the different types of people involved in the day-to-day operation of the system.

Chapter 2 explains the underlying principles and concepts reflected in the criminal law, and Chapter 3 provides an overview of the types of offenses covered by the criminal law. In our discussion of substantive criminal law, we provide a sampling of some of the common offenses included in most criminal codes and examples of charges filed in some highly publicized cases. Special emphasis is placed on learning how to interpret and apply statutory language.

PART 2: CRIMINAL PROCEDURE: FROM COMMISSION OF THE OFFENSE TO PLEA BARGAINING AND DIVERSION

Part 2 shifts from the substance of the criminal law to how violations of those laws are discovered and investigated, how alleged violators are arrested and charged, and what attorneys on both sides do to prepare for criminal trials.

Chapter 4 covers the actions taken by police in investigating alleged criminal behavior and arresting alleged offenders. Chapter 5, in turn, focuses on the prosecutor's role and the charging process, while Chapter 6 explains the role of the defense attorney and the differences between private counsel, appointed counsel, and public defenders.

Chapter 7 covers the potential defenses that attorneys can assert on behalf of their clients. Chapter 8 explores the actions taken by attorneys and paralegals working for the prosecution and defense to learn more about the facts of the case though the discovery and disclosure procedures.

Chapter 9 covers pre-trial motions relating to substitution of judges, joinder and severance, competency, and motions to exclude key pieces of evidence. It then goes on to discuss the plea-bargaining process. It also includes a discussion of diversion into specialized treatment programs.

PART 3: CRIMINAL PROCEDURE: TRIALS AND THEIR AFTERMATH

In the final part of this book, we present the ways in which trials are conducted and how the sentences of those convicted are determined. It also covers appeals and other post-trial actions that defense attorneys can take on behalf of their clients.

Chapter 10 sets the stage for our coverage of trials, sentencing, and preparation for appeals by reviewing constitutional provisions affecting the conduct of criminal trials and discussing how evidence is presented in trials. Chapter 11 then discusses the things that attorneys and paralegals do to prepare for a trial. It includes preparation for jury selection and preparation of exhibits, motions, witnesses, and electronic presentations.

The actual conduct of the trial itself is covered in Chapter 12, where each stage of the trial is discussed in detail, from jury selection to post-verdict motions.

Chapter 13 addresses the sentencing phase of a case.

After discussing the types of punishments that courts can impose, it goes on to examine the amount of discretion judges have and the role of sentencing guidelines. From there, it goes on to cover sentencing procedures and mechanisms for seeking modification of a sentence.

After providing an overview of the appeals process, Chapter 14 discusses the timing of an appeal, the preservation of the record, and alternative methods of challenging criminal convictions. Finally, Chapter 15 deals with collateral remedies ranging from *habeas corpus* actions to state post-conviction relief, civil proceedings in order to expunge or limit access to criminal records, civil recovery of assets that were seized as part of the investigative process, and challenges to summary suspensions of driver's licenses.

Special Features

USE OF LEGAL DOCUMENTS FROM REAL CASES

As in most texts of this type, we will frequently reference statutes and court decisions to explain and illustrate principles of criminal law and criminal procedure. In addition to including excerpts from featured statutes and cases, we include arrest reports, indictments, criminal informations, and other legal documents from cases that have received national attention.

INTEGRATION OF HYPOTHETICAL CASES

Throughout this text, we use five hypothetical cases to illustrate how a number of types of crime are handled at the various stages of the criminal justice process. One case involves a state reckless homicide charge related to an accident involving a driver who had been drinking alcoholic beverages. The second involves charges related to illegal drugs and weapons, and the third involves a white-collar crime, in which a registered securities agent is charged with misappropriation of customer funds. Sexual assault charges brought against the complaining witnesses' employer are presented in the fourth hypothetical case. In the fifth case, a police officer applies force to remove a passenger from a vehicle pulled over for an alleged traffic violation.

These cases are integrated into the appropriate chapters throughout the book, where they are used to illustrate questions of statutory interpretation and criminal procedure. They are also incorporated into some of the Discussion Questions and Application Exercises. Initial facts about the nature of the crimes involved in these cases are presented in a separate section following this Preface, which should be read in conjunction with Chapter 2 and then referred to again when reading most of the following chapters.

PRACTICAL SKILL DEVELOPMENT

This book incorporates a variety of pedagogical techniques for developing analytical and drafting skills. Most chapters will include excerpts from statutes, court opinions, investigative reports, or court filings.

Discussion Questions raise controversial issues that require legal analysis and argumentation. The Application Exercises involve legal research and the drafting of various reports and legal documents as well as legal analysis.

STUDY AIDS

This book includes standard reader aids such as marginal definitions of key terms, a chapter summary, and Review Questions. An instructor's manual includes suggested answers for all the Discussion Questions, Review Questions, and Application Exercises. A computerized test bank is also available to help teachers make the most effective use of this book.

Special Thanks

We would like to thank the staff at Aspen Publishing for the excellent support we have received in the preparation of this book and to the reviewers who gave us such positive feedback and useful suggestions.

We would also like to recognize the contributions of the following research assistants from the Department of Politics and Government at Illinois State University: Trey Georgie, Rhiannon Stringer, Anthony Nigliaccio, Theodore Mason, and Renee Prunty.

Finally, we also wish to thank our spouses for their continued support and understanding of our professional activities.

Thomas E. McClure
Thomas E. Eimermann
January 2023

Acknowledgments

We are grateful to copyright holders for permission to reprint excerpts from the following items:

Model Penal Code, © 1985 by The American Law Institute. Reprinted with permission: All rights reserved.

National Association of Legal Assistants, Code of Ethics and Professional Responsibility. Copyright 2007, NALA, Inc. Reprinted by permission from the National Association of Legal Assistants, 1516 S. Boston, #200, Tulsa, OK 74119, www.nala.org.

NFPA Model Disciplinary Rules © (2006); NFPA Model Code of Ethics and Professional Responsibility and Guidelines for Enforcement © (2006); and "What Is a Conflict of Interest?" © (2019), The National Federation of Paralegal Associations, Inc., www.paralegals.org. Reprinted by permission.

About the Authors

Thomas E. McClure is a professor in the Department of Politics and Government and the director of legal studies at Illinois State University. He teaches Introduction to Paralegal Studies, Introduction to Torts, Investigative Techniques and Evidence, Litigation I and II, and several constitutional law courses. He currently chairs the ABA Standing Committee on Paralegals.

He graduated from Illinois State University in 1976 with a BS in political science. He received his JD from DePaul University, where he served as an editor of the *DePaul Law Review.* In 2001, he earned his MS in political science from Illinois State University.

Following law school, Professor McClure served for two years as a law clerk to an Illinois appellate court justice. He then entered private practice as one of the two principals of Elliott & McClure, a law firm in Kankakee County, Illinois. He specialized in personal injury, criminal defense, family law, and civil rights litigation. In 2009, he left private practice to become a full-time professor at Illinois State University.

He is a member of the Illinois Bar and admitted to practice before three U.S. District Courts, the Seventh Circuit Court of Appeals, and the U.S. Supreme Court. When the death penalty was in effect, he was a member of the Illinois Capital Litigation Bar.

Professor McClure has published journal articles on the Supreme Court's approach to *ex post facto* law analysis, the constitutional rights of disabled applicants for public employment, and the effectiveness of court-connected parenting classes. He has authored book chapters on the Roberts Court's approach to the First Amendment, as well as to its search and seizure jurisprudence. He recently published a trilogy of pieces on the relationship between judicial selection and judges' bar poll impartiality scores. As a co-author, he recently published a law review article concerning preemption of state laws affecting non-Indians on tribal lands and an article analyzing the effect of paralegal education director experience on ABA-approval of the education program.

Thomas E. Eimermann is an emeritus professor of political science at Illinois State University, where he started their paralegal program in 1976 and served as its director until 2004. During those years, he taught the Introduction to Paralegal Studies and the Legal Research and Writing courses, as well as courses on constitutional law and administrative law.

He received his BA in political science at North Central College, and then went on to earn an MA and a PhD in political science from the University of Illinois-Urbana/Champaign.

Professor Eimermann was a member of the American Association for Paralegal Education's board of directors from 1986-1993 and served as president of that organization in 1991-1992. He has also served in the Certification Board and Specialty Task Force of the National Association of Legal Assistants, as a member of the Illinois State Bar Association Committee on the Delivery of Legal Services, and as a member of the Hearing Board, the Inquiry Board, and the Oversight Committee of the Illinois Attorney Registration and Disciplinary Commission. As a consultant for the Illinois Department of Corrections, he designed their Uniform Law Clerk Training Program.

Professor Eimermann's other publications include multiple editions of *Fundamentals of Paralegalism; Introduction to Law for Paralegals* and *The Study of Law* (coauthored with Katherine Currier and Marisa Campbell); and *Introduction to Paralegal Studies* (coauthored with Katherine Currier). He has also published journal articles on paralegals, jury behavior, and free speech issues.

Introduction to Hypothetical Cases

At various points in this text, we will be referring to five hypothetical cases that are used as illustrations and in Application Exercises. Take a moment now to read the facts given in each of these cases, and then record this information in a notebook or a word processing file in a way that will allow you to organize and add to it as you learn more about these cases in the different chapters.

CASE 1: People v. Cook

Bud Cook left a pizzeria at 9:30 P.M. to drive home. He consumed a pitcher of beer with his meal but didn't think it would affect his driving. He drove his pickup truck in the northbound direction in the outermost lane on Sumner Drive.

Several blocks north of the pizza parlor, he came upon a woman wearing a black T-shirt and jeans, riding a black bicycle in the northbound outside lane about two feet from the shoulder of the road. Bud did not notice the bicyclist until the right front fender of his pickup struck the rear of the bike, causing the rider to land on top of the hood and hit the windshield. As she hit the windshield, Bud slammed on his brakes, which in turn threw the rider forward across the pavement.

Bud panicked and raced home without stopping. When he told his wife, Tammy, that he had either struck an animal or a man on a bicycle, she called 911 to report the incident. While driving home, a passerby had called 911 to report that there was a human body on the road. When the police arrived, they found that the victim was dead.

CASE 2: United States v. Turner

At two o'clock in the afternoon, a local police officer, Steve Milner, was on a routine patrol when he saw an automobile run a stop sign. Officer Milner activated his overhead lights on his marked squad car and started to pursue the car.

The driver of the car speeded up and then stopped in front of a sandwich shop. The driver, Brandon Turner, got out of the car and began to walk rapidly toward the restaurant. Officer Milner stepped out of his squad car, blew his horn, and yelled at Turner to halt. Turner did not stop and went into the sandwich shop.

Milner saw Turner go through the restaurant and then into a restroom. He followed Turner into the restaurant and met him at the restroom door when Turner came out after having been in the restroom for less than a minute.

Through a series of searches, police discovered that Turner had hidden a loaded handgun in the restroom, and there was a bag of cocaine in Turner's car.

CASE 3: United States v. Edwards

Bill Edwards is a registered representative for a local broker-dealer. He has many high-net-worth clients and is involved in several local social networks. Many prominent individuals in the community are his clients.

Edwards was also involved in several business ventures outside of his employment as a registered representative. Many of these businesses began having financial troubles and could not maintain their operations without an infusion of capital. Edwards also began having personal problems at home and was having difficulty paying alimony and child support.

To resolve these financial woes, Edwards began diverting customer funds and liquidating customer securities and using the proceeds to help these failing businesses. He did this without getting permission or authority from customers. To help cover up these misappropriations, he issued promissory notes to the customers.

When customers saw that funds or investments were missing from their accounts and asked Edwards what happened, he told them that he had put them in safe investments with guaranteed returns of 12 percent to 20 percent. However, when interest on the promissory notes came due, the entities that issued the notes could not make the payments. To keep these customers from complaining and to cover up the fraud, Edwards began misappropriating funds from other customers to make the interest payments owed to the existing customers.

CASE 4: People v. Marshall

Clay Marshall is the manager of a local office of the Van Buren Insurance Agency. He supervises four female clerks. The clerks rotate working on Saturday mornings. Two of the clerks, Randy Jefferson and Madison Pickering, claim that Clay kissed and groped them on separate Saturdays when no one else was at the office.

Randy is a single mother in her early thirties who continues to work for the agency. She told the police that Clay embraced her and gave her a long kiss. She also claimed that he rubbed her genital area with his hand through her clothes. Randy said nothing at that time. After he stopped, she walked into a different area of the office and avoided him for the remainder of the morning. She never reported the incident to the Van Buren Agency.

Madison is a single college student who worked part time at the insurance agency. She told the police that Clay hugged and kissed her and fondled her through her jeans. She claims that Clay continued after she told him to stop. She quit her job two days later.

Weeks after the alleged incidents occurred, the women spoke to each another and decided to go to the police.

CASE 5: People v. Smith

When a police car pulled up behind a car being driven by Jose Perez and turned on its flashing lights, Jose promptly pulled into an adjacent strip mall parking lot and stopped the car. Police officers John Smith and Paul Jones then exited their car and approached the vehicle (one on each side), which they had stopped for switching lanes without having used a turn signal.

The officers observed two men who appeared to be Hispanic in the front seat, as well as a woman and two children (ages 6 and 11) in the back seat. When Officer Smith asked the front-seat passenger for his driver's license, the passenger, Javier Mendoza, told the officer that he didn't have to produce it since he was just a passenger.

At this point, Smith ordered Mendoza to get out. When Mendoza remained seated, Smith grabbed his arm and tried to pull him out of the car. Because Mendoza was wearing a seat belt and shoulder harness, Smith had difficulty removing him from the vehicle. Because Mendoza was not obeying his order to leave the car, Smith shocked him with a taser 11 times and placed him under arrest.

Fundamentals of Criminal Law and Procedure for Paralegals

PART 1

Criminal Law

Chapter 1

The Criminal Justice System

Chapter Objectives

After reading this chapter, you should be able to:

- Explain why governments enact laws and the differences between criminal law and civil law.
- Discuss the differences between the crime control and the due process models of the criminal justice system and the implications of following one model versus the other.
- Identify and describe the role of the participants in the system of criminal justice.

Introduction

This book is designed to help prepare readers to perform paralegal tasks within the criminal justice system. We begin our exploration of criminal law and procedure with an overview of the criminal justice system and how criminal law differs from civil law.

The **criminal justice system** refers to a collection of institutions and individuals that are typically involved in the processing of criminal cases. These individuals include legislators, law enforcement officers, attorneys, paralegals, judges, court clerks, bailiffs, juries, correctional officers, and probation officers. Criminal justice institutions include law enforcement agencies, the courts, forensics labs, and corrections.

Criminal justice system
A collection of institutions and individuals that are typically involved in the processing of criminal cases.

A. Purpose of Law

Law
A rule of conduct promulgated and enforced by the government.

A **law,** in its most general sense, is defined as "a rule of conduct promulgated and enforced by the government." Rules of conduct can be stated in either positive or negative terms. Hence some laws prohibit people from stealing others' property or driving faster than the posted speed limit, while other laws require people to report their income and pay taxes on it.

Laws can apply to the behavior of individuals, businesses, and even governments themselves. Thus, municipalities may be prohibited from dumping raw sewage into lakes and rivers, and police officers are prohibited from conducting unreasonable searches and seizures.

Although Americans frequently complain about the specific content of some of the staggering number of laws that have been enacted by federal, state, and local governments, most laws are considered essential to the functioning of a modern industrialized society. Indeed, the development and enforcement of these laws are arguably the most important functions of government. As the Task Force on Law and Law Enforcement reported to the National Commission on the Causes and Prevention of Violence:

> Human welfare demands, at a minimum, sufficient order to insure that such basic needs as food production, shelter and child rearing be satisfied, not in a state of constant chaos and conflict, but on a peaceful, orderly basis with a reasonable level of day-to-day security. . . . When a society becomes highly complex, mobile, and pluralistic; the beneficiary, yet also the victim, of extremely rapid technological change; and when at the same time, and partly as a result of these factors, the influence of traditional stabilizing institutions such as family, church, and community wanes, then that society of necessity becomes increasingly dependent on highly structured, formalistic systems of law and government to maintain social order. . . . For better or worse, we are by necessity increasingly committed to our formal legal institutions as the paramount agency of social control.[1]

Some laws, such as restrictions on abortion, cannabis use, and gambling, are heavily influenced by the religious and moral beliefs of various groups in the society. Others, such as traffic regulations and zoning laws, do not reflect any specific moral code. Drivers on two-lane American roads are required to use the right lane. This permits a greater number of vehicles to travel more safely and efficiently. While it is important that everyone drive in the properly designated lanes, there is no moral principle requiring people to drive in the right lane (as is done in the United States), rather than the left lane (as is done in Great Britain).

As this text proceeds, we will discuss the scope of U.S. criminal law and occasionally raise questions about the wisdom of specific laws. For example, to save lives and medical costs, many argue that governments should require drivers and passengers to wear seat belts and motorcyclists to wear helmets. Others argue that such laws infringe on people's individual rights. But while people often disagree about the application of specific laws, all but a very limited number of anarchists accept the idea that we need laws to establish the type of order and predictability that are essential to the functioning of modern society.

---

[1] J. Campbell, J. Sahid, & D. Stang, *Law and Order Reconsidered: Report of the Task Force on Law and Law Enforcement to the National Commission on the Causes and Prevention of Violence* 3, 5 (1970).

B. Criminal Versus Civil Law

Law can be categorized in a number of ways. One of the major divisions is between **criminal law** and **civil law**. Both consist of rules of conduct that have been established by the appropriate legal authorities, but they differ in terms of the consequences to the wrongdoer, as well as the way in which violations are investigated and prosecuted. (*See* Figure 1.1.) Criminal law has been defined as "the body of law defining offenses against the community at large, regulating how suspects are investigated, charged, and tried and establishing punishments for convicted offenders."[2] On the other hand, civil law concerns private rights and obligations.

Criminal law
The body of law defining offenses against the community at large, regulating how suspects are investigated, charged, and tried and establishing punishments for convicted offenders.

Civil law
The body of law defining actions for which individuals can use the courts to seek remedies for violations of their private rights, establishing procedural requirements for using the courts and establishing remedies for violations of those rights.

Damages
The monetary compensation awarded to the wronged party in a civil case.

The government is the dominant participant in criminal cases. When an individual violates a criminal law, society at large is considered to be the offended party, and government agents are responsible for initiating and prosecuting the case. Thus, if Peter Jones burglarizes Sam Smith's home, the criminal law views that act as an offense against the state rather than simply a matter between Smith and Jones. When the case goes to court, it is listed as *People v. Jones* or *State v. Jones* rather than *Smith v. Jones.* Government attorneys prosecute the accused party, and the victim is relegated to the role of a witness. The victim plays no role in how the case is presented at trial.

In civil cases, on the other hand, the aggrieved party is responsible for filing and prosecuting the claim. Thus, when one party defaults on the terms of a contract, for example, the other party must initiate the legal process on an individual basis. Generally, private parties hire their own attorneys to file the suit and present their case in court.

The legal consequences of civil and criminal violations also reflect this difference. Most civil cases are intended to make whole, or compensate, victims for the losses they suffered. Generally, this is accomplished through awards of money **damages**. In contrast, victims of crimes seldom receive any financial compensation from the perpetrator. Although a negotiated resolution of a

	Criminal Law	Civil Law
TYPE OF HARM	Harm to society	Harm to individual interests
PARTIES TO CASE	Government and defendant	Plaintiff and defendant
STANDARD OF PROOF	Beyond a reasonable doubt	Preponderance of the evidence
JUDGMENT GIVEN	Guilty or not guilty	Liable or not liable
SANCTIONS	Fines, incarceration, death	Damages, injunctions

Figure 1.1 Comparison of Civil and Criminal Law

[2]B. Garner, ed., *Black's Law Dictionary* 456 (10th ed. 2014).

criminal case will occasionally contain some provisions for restitution to the victim and/or the community, the fines that are assessed as part of the criminal process are paid to the state rather than the victim. In fact, incarcerating the perpetrator usually actually reduces the likelihood of that person being able to financially compensate the victim.

Plaintiff
The party who initiates a civil lawsuit.

Under the civil law, the individual **plaintiff** benefits directly from the outcome. The party that is found to be at fault can be required to directly compensate the victim for various types of injuries sustained. Even when the damages are punitive (designed to punish the wrongdoer rather than compensate the victim), the plaintiff, rather than the government, receives the damages award. Note, however, there are situations (usually involving antitrust and securities violations) in which the government can seek civil damages rather than criminal penalties for violations of some laws. In these cases, the government takes on the role of the plaintiff and gets any damages that are awarded.

In addition to the contrasting roles of the government and the victim, there are differences in the way that criminal and civil trials are conducted. The most significant is the standard of proof that is applied. In criminal cases, the prosecution is required to prove its case "beyond a reasonable doubt," but in civil actions, the plaintiff need only meet the "preponderance of the evidence" standard. "Preponderance of the evidence" is usually understood to mean that the facts asserted are more likely to be true than not true. On the other hand, "beyond a reasonable doubt" is the degree of doubt that exceeds the doubt that a reasonable person would have after considering all of the evidence.

A study conducted by Rita James Simon and Linda Mahan showed that judges tend to equate "beyond a reasonable doubt" with a median probability of approximately 8.8 out of 10, while jurors averaged approximately 8.6 out of 10. "Preponderance of the evidence" was interpreted by the judges as a median probability of 5.4 out of 10, with 7.1 out of 10 being the median for jurors.[3] While we cannot establish a specific percentage, it is clear that it is more difficult to convict under a "beyond a reasonable doubt" standard than it is to find for the plaintiff under a "preponderance of the evidence" standard.

Defendant
The party who is defending against either a criminal prosecution or a civil lawsuit. In a criminal case, the defendant is the person accused of committing a crime.

It is important to note that a single event could become the basis for both a criminal prosecution and a civil action. For example, the victim of a battery could sue the **defendant** for civil damages at the same time the state is prosecuting the defendant on a criminal charge. The driver of an automobile involved in a traffic accident may receive a traffic ticket from the police and at the same time be sued by someone else involved in the accident. In certain types of antitrust cases, the government can choose between seeking criminal charges and civil damages.

Because civil and criminal proceedings involving the same occurrence are conducted independently of each other, a defendant could be unsuccessful before one court and prevail before the other. One of the most publicized cases of the late twentieth century illustrates this point. The former football star and actor O. J. Simpson was prosecuted for the murders of his ex-wife, Nicole Brown Simpson, and her friend Ronald Goldman. The jury in the criminal case acquitted Simpson, but a civil jury found him liable for the victims' wrongful deaths and entered a multimillion-dollar verdict against him. The essential facts were the same in the civil and criminal cases, and yet the case outcomes were different.

---

[3] R. Simon & L. Mahan, *Quantifying Burdens of Proof*, 5 Law & Soc. Rev. 319 (1971).

Discussion Questions

1. In 1995, a jury found the former star football player O. J. Simpson not guilty of the murders of his ex-wife, Nicole Brown Simpson, and her friend Ronald Goldman, and yet a civil jury found him liable for the victims' wrongful deaths and entered a large monetary verdict against him. How can you reconcile the seemingly inconsistent outcomes in the O. J. Simpson criminal trial and the civil wrongful death case filed against him?

2. Although the criminal law is designed to protect the interests of the community at large, can a successful criminal prosecution further the interests of a private individual? If so, how?

3. Sometimes large monetary awards of punitive damages are imposed against wrongdoers in civil cases who act recklessly or in conscious disregard of the safety of other people. How are civil claims for punitive damages similar to criminal prosecutions? How are they different? Should a criminal offender be subject to suit for punitive damages if he was already prosecuted for the crime that gave rise to the civil suit?

C. Conflicting Models of the Criminal Justice System

The criminal justice system is designed to process people suspected of having violated criminal law. But what is the overall purpose of this system?

In a famous law review article published in 1964, a distinguished law professor named Herbert Packer identified two conflicting views as to what the purpose of the criminal justice system should be.[4] He called one the "crime control model" and the other the "due process model." Each presents different criteria for evaluating the criminal justice system. (*See* Figure 1.2.)

	Crime Control	Due Process
PURPOSE OF CRIMINAL JUSTICE SYSTEM	Suppress criminal conduct	Preserve the integrity of the process
ANALOGY	A conveyor belt, emphasizing speed and efficiency	An obstacle course, emphasizing reliability and eliminating error
UNDERLYING PRESUMPTION	Presumption of guilt	Presumption of innocence
EMPHASIS/FOCUS	Early administrative fact-finding	Integrity of the process and adequacy of appeals

Figure 1.2 Comparisons of the Crime Control and Due Process Models

[4] H. L. Packer, *Two Models of the Criminal Process*, 113 U. PA. L. Rev. 1 (1964).

Crime control model
An approach to evaluating the criminal justice system on the basis of how efficiently it suppresses crime.

Due process model
An approach to evaluating the criminal justice system on the basis of how well it protects people from being charged and/or convicted of crimes they didn't commit.

Due process of law
Legal procedures that enforce basic rights that are considered necessary for fairness and justice.

In the **crime control model**, the purpose of the criminal justice system is to repress criminal conduct in the most efficient way possible. In contrast, the **due process model** asserts that the criminal justice system should focus on protecting innocent people from being falsely convicted. The problem is that actions designed to keep more criminals off the street may increase the number of innocent people who are mistreated by the system, and actions designed to protect the innocent often make it more difficult to convict the guilty.

The application of the due process model raises very important questions about what due process actually involves and how much due process is too much. **Due process** is one of the most ambiguous and difficult-to-explain concepts in our legal system. The term "due process" appears in both the Fifth and Fourteenth Amendments to the U.S. Constitution. The Fifth Amendment, for instance, states:

> nor shall any person . . . be deprived of life, liberty, or property, without **due process of law** . . .

In *Barron v. Baltimore,*[5] the U.S. Supreme Court ruled that the due process protections guaranteed by the Fifth Amendment are applicable only to actions of the federal government, not those of state or local governments. However, the Fourteenth Amendment explicitly expands due process protections to state actions when it declares:

> nor shall any State deprive any person of life, liberty, or property, without due process of law

However, neither amendment explicitly defines what "due process" is. To find out what it actually means, we have to turn to U.S. Supreme Court opinions in which the justices have applied the concept to specific situations.

In a frequently quoted opinion in *Palko v. Connecticut*, the U.S. Supreme Court justice Benjamin Cardozo defined "due process" as rights that were necessary to protect against practices that subjected defendants to "a hardship so acute and shocking that our polity will not endure it," or which violate those "fundamental principles of liberty and justice which lie at the base of all our civil and political institutions."[6] Other justices have defined "due process" as being equivalent to "fundamental fairness."

But language like "a hardship so acute and shocking that our polity will not endure it," "fundamental principles of liberty and justice which lie at the base of all our civil and political institutions," and "fundamental fairness" are subjective concepts rather than objective criteria. Therefore, to really be able to determine whether a particular right or practice is an essential part of due process, it is necessary to do a case-by-case review of court decisions that have specifically involved the right or practice in question.

In Chapter 2, we will look closer at the role of constitutional law, and in Parts 2 and 3 we will examine what the courts have ruled regarding specific rights and procedures. For now, it is sufficient to think of due process as the protections that are provided to people by law when they are involved in legal disputes with the government.

---

[5]32 U.S. 243 (1833).

[6]302 U.S. 319, 328 (1937).

D. Participants in the Criminal Justice System

1. THE LAWMAKERS

The U.S. Congress, in addition to state and local governmental legislative bodies, is the source of most of our criminal law. This means that the largest part of our criminal law is made by elected politicians, who respond to public opinion within their districts. When voters express concerns about rising crime rates, the legislators are likely to react by increasing penalties, mandating longer sentences, creating "three strikes and you're out" laws, and other actions.

While these legislative bodies draft and adopt the statutes that define what is or is not considered criminal behavior, it is important to note that the laws they adopt are limited by the requirements of the U.S. and state constitutions. The U.S. Supreme Court, as well as other courts of review at both the federal and state levels, has the power to invalidate laws and police practices that a majority of their members determine to be unconstitutional.

In Chapter 2, we will discuss the rule of law and other basic principles reflected in our criminal laws. Then, in Chapter 3, we will provide an overview of the types of behavior covered by the criminal law and examples of how these laws are structured.

2. LAW BREAKERS

Unfortunately, not everyone obeys all of our laws. The law breakers who are identified and subsequently prosecuted become defendants. While we will use examples involving criminal defendants who were rich and famous (e.g., O. J. Simpson, Tiger Woods, Mel Gibson, Bill Cosby, and Winona Ryder), most defendants are young males with little or no income and are disproportionately from racial and ethnic minority groups. Whereas the rich and famous can usually get out on bail and can hire high-powered lawyers, "average" defendants often remain incarcerated pending their trials and have to rely on public defenders.

3. VICTIMS OF LAW BREAKERS

The term "victim" is commonly understood as someone who was physically harmed or had valuable possessions stolen from them. In these situations, victims are most likely to participate in the criminal process by reporting the existence of the crime to law enforcement personnel and by serving as a witness for the prosecution. However, there are situations in which criminal proceedings are started without any action being taken by the victim. For example, the crime may have been observed by police or by eyewitnesses. There are also situations in which the victim is either unable or unwilling to testify. In domestic violence cases, it is not unusual for the victim to deny that an offense took place and to refuse to testify against the abuser.

The reason that criminal prosecutions can go on without the participation of the victim is that our criminal law is based on a broader definition of "victim." As pointed out in Part B of this chapter, violations of the criminal law are treated as offenses against society at large. Thus, persons can be prosecuted for prostitution or drug transactions even though all the parties participated voluntarily.

In addition to reporting a crime and testifying in court, victims may play a role in the sentencing process. Indeed, some state victims' rights laws provide for **victim impact statements,** in which the victim describes how the crime affected his or her life and those of family members.

Victim impact statement
A written or oral statement made by the victim of a crime (or the family members of a deceased victim) that is presented at the sentencing hearing for the convicted offender.

4. LAW ENFORCEMENT OFFICIALS

State and local law enforcement officials include local police, sheriff's officers, highway patrols, state police, game wardens, and park rangers. The category also includes Federal Bureau of Investigation (FBI) agents; Immigration and Customs Enforcement agents; Bureau of Alcohol, Tobacco, Firearms and Explosives (ATF) agents; Internal Revenue Service (IRS) agents; U.S. Postal Inspection Service agents; and other federal agents assigned to law enforcement duties.

There is wide variation in the nature of the qualifications and training of the types of law enforcement personnel. Most positions require some minimal level of physical fitness. Some, such as the FBI, have very selective educational background requirements. All have extensive training programs for new agents.

It is these law enforcement agents who usually make the first contact with defendants. Many times, they actually see the crime being committed and immediately make an arrest. Other times, they are assigned to investigate a crime based on information from either a victim (e.g., a business owner reports an overnight break-in) or a third party who discovers evidence of a crime (e.g., neighbors find a dead body in their alley). The subsequent investigation then leads law enforcers to question or arrest a defendant.

5. ATTORNEYS AND PARALEGALS

Attorneys (also called "lawyers") play several key roles in the criminal justice system.[7]

Most serve as advocates for either the governmental unit that is seeking to enforce the law or the defendant that is accused of violating it. The prosecuting attorneys usually carry titles such as District Attorney, State's Attorney, or U.S.

[7]These are professionals who are licensed to practice law in a state or federal jurisdiction. In most jurisdictions, they must have attained a bachelor's degree and a graduate degree in law (JD or LLB) from an American Bar Association-accredited law school and have passed a state bar exam plus a character and fitness check.

Attorney and are employees of a unit of the state, local, or federal government.[8] Those representing the defendants are either in private practice or employees of a government-financed public defender's office.

Typically, the prosecuting attorneys don't get involved in a case until after law enforcement officers have already made an arrest. In these cases, the attorney then reviews the arrest report and decides what (if any) formal charges should be filed with the court. At other times, prosecuting attorneys become involved prior to an arrest if law enforcement officials need a search warrant or decide that it might be useful to bring a case before a grand jury. Much to the frustration of many defense attorneys, they seldom get involved in a case prior to their client's arrest. In most cases, either the defendant doesn't make arrangements to retain an attorney or is unable to have one appointed prior to being arrested. Based on the U.S. Supreme Court's decision in *Miranda v. Arizona*,[9] law enforcement personnel are required to inform criminal suspects of their right to be represented by an attorney (and the right to have one appointed if they cannot afford one) and to remain silent if they are in custody.[10] However, many defendants ignore these warnings and proceed to make incriminating statements prior to having consulted with an attorney.

In this text, we are particularly interested in the role that paralegals[11] play in the criminal justice system. They typically work in prosecuting attorneys' offices, for public defenders' offices, and for private defense attorneys. In these offices, paralegals are usually involved in reviewing police reports and statements of witnesses, drafting documents such as discovery requests and motions, interviewing potential witnesses, researching legal issues, arranging for expert witnesses, helping to evaluate potential jurors, organizing documents for trial, helping to prepare witnesses, keeping witnesses informed as to when they will be called to testify, and taking notes during the trial. When they work for attorneys doing appellate work, they are frequently called upon to digest the record and help draft appellate briefs.

In later chapters of this book, we will go into greater detail regarding the specific tasks that paralegals are typically called upon to undertake in criminal law. It is also important to keep in mind what paralegals *cannot* do. They cannot give legal advice, set fees, or represent clients in court. It is also important to stress that paralegals must work "under the supervision" of a licensed attorney. Note what the New Jersey Supreme Court had to say about the nature of this supervision.

---

[8]In smaller communities, these positions may only be part time and, on occasion, a private attorney may be appointed as a "special prosecutor."

[9]384 U.S. 436 (1966).

[10]The nature of what constitutes custodial interrogation is discussed in more detail on pp. 100-103.

[11]The American Bar Association defines a "paralegal" as a person qualified by education, training, or work experience who is employed by a lawyer, law office, corporation, governmental agency, or other entity who performs specifically delegated substantive legal work for which a lawyer is responsible. Although some states have authorized paralegals with additional training to become limited licensed legal technicians, no state permits them to participate as advocates in criminal proceedings.

In Re Opinion No. 24 of the Committee on the Unauthorized Practice of Law
Supreme Court of New Jersey
128 N.J. 114 (1992)

The opinion of the Court was delivered by JUSTICE GARIBALDI.

The New Jersey Supreme Court Committee on the Unauthorized Practice of Law (the "Committee") concluded in Advisory Opinion No. 24, 126 *N.J.L.J.* 1306, 1338 (1990), that "paralegals functioning outside of the supervision of an attorney-employer are engaged in the unauthorized practice of law." Petitioners are several independent paralegals whom attorneys do not employ but retain on a temporary basis. They ask the Court to disapprove the Advisory Opinion.

Like paralegals employed by attorneys, independent paralegals retained by attorneys do not offer their services directly to the public. Nonetheless, the Committee determined that independent paralegals are engaged in the unauthorized practice of law because they are performing legal services without adequate attorney supervision. We agree with the Committee that the resolution of the issue turns on whether independent paralegals are adequately supervised by attorneys. We disagree with the Committee, however, that the evidence supports a categorical ban on all independent paralegals in New Jersey.

The Committee received inquiries from various sources regarding whether independent paralegals were engaged in the unauthorized practice of law. Pursuant to its advisory-opinion powers under *Rule* 1:22-2, the Committee solicited written comments and information from interested persons and organizations.

* * *

The Committee characterized the information that it received in two ways: first, the material expressed positive views on the value of the work performed by paralegals; second, all of the materials expressly or implicitly recognized that the work of paralegals must be performed under attorney supervision. None distinguished between paralegals employed by law firms and those functioning as independent contractors offering services to attorneys. Several recurring themes played throughout the submissions:

1. One need not be a full- or part-time employee of a single attorney to be under the direct supervision of an attorney and independent paralegals in particular work under the direct supervision of attorneys.
2. Independent paralegals provide necessary services for sole practitioners and small law firms who cannot afford to employ paralegals on a full-time basis.
3. Independent paralegals confer an invaluable benefit on the public in the form of reduced legal fees.
4. Independent paralegals maintain high standards of competence and professionalism.
5. Rather than exacting a per se prohibition, the Committee should consider regulations or standards or other alternative forms of guidance, such as licensure and certification.
6. A blanket prohibition on independent paralegals would work a disservice to the paralegals and the general public.

After receiving those submissions, the Committee held a hearing at which four independent paralegals, three employed paralegals, and three attorneys testified. All the independent paralegals testifying before the Committee were well qualified. One independent paralegal noted that as an NALA [National Association of Legal Assistants] member she is bound by both the *ABA Model Code of Professional Responsibility* and the ABA *Model Rules of Professional Conduct*. The independent paralegals stated that although they had worked with many attorneys during their careers, they had worked solely for those attorneys and only under their direct supervision.

The independent paralegals gave several reasons for being retained by attorneys. First, attorneys may be understaffed at any time and may need to devote additional resources to one case. Second, attorneys may need paralegal assistance but be unable to afford a full-time paralegal. Third, attorneys may hire independent paralegals who have expertise in a given field.

. . .

After the hearing, the Committee issued Advisory Opinion No. 24, 26 *N.J.L.J.* 1306 (1990), in which it compared the amount of supervision attorneys exercise over employed paralegals and retained paralegals. It concluded that attorneys do not adequately supervise retained paralegals.

. . .

Based on those findings, the Committee concluded that attorneys are currently unable to supervise adequately the performance of independent paralegals, and that by performing legal services without such adequate supervision those paralegals are engaging in the unauthorized practice of law. *Ibid.*

We granted petitioners' request for review, and the Chairperson of the Committee granted their motion to stay the enforcement of Opinion No. 24.

No satisfactory, all-inclusive definition of what constitutes the practice of law has ever been devised. None will be attempted here. That has been left, and wisely so, to the courts when parties present them with concrete factual situations. Essentially, the Court decides what constitutes the practice of law on a case-by-case basis.

. . .

There is no question that paralegals' work constitutes the practice of law. *N.J.S.A.* 2A:170-78 and 79 deem unauthorized the practice of law by a nonlawyer and make such practice a disorderly-persons offense. However, *N.J.S.A.* 2A:170-81(f) excepts paralegals from being penalized for engaging in tasks that constitute legal practice if their supervising attorney assumes direct responsibility for the work that the paralegals perform. *N.J.S.A.* 2A:170-81(f) states:

> Any person or corporation furnishing to any person lawfully engaged in the practice of law such information or such clerical assistance in and about his professional work as, except for the provisions of this article, may be lawful, but the lawyer receiving such information or service shall at all times maintain full professional and direct responsibility to his client for the information and service so rendered.

Consequently, paralegals who are supervised by attorneys do not engage in the unauthorized practice of law.

Availability of legal services to the public at an affordable cost is a goal to which the Court is committed. The use of paralegals represents a means of achieving that goal while maintaining the quality of legal services. Paralegals enable attorneys to render legal services more economically and efficiently. During the last twenty years the employment of paralegals has greatly expanded, and within the last ten years the number of independent paralegals has increased.

Independent paralegals work either at a "paralegal firm" or freelance. Most are employed by sole practitioners or smaller firms who cannot afford the services of a full-time paralegal. Like large law firms, small firms find that using paralegals helps them provide effective and economical services to their clients. Requiring paralegals to be full-time employees of law firms would thus deny attorneys not associated with large law firms the very valuable services of paralegals.

The United States Supreme Court, in upholding an award of legal fees based on the market value of paralegal services, stated that the use of paralegal services whenever possible "encourages cost-effective legal services . . . by reducing the spiraling cost of . . . litigation." *Missouri v. Jenkins.*

The Court further noted:

> It has frequently been recognized in the lower courts that paralegals are capable of carrying out many tasks, under the supervision of an

> attorney, that might otherwise be performed by a lawyer and billed at a higher rate. Such work might include locating and interviewing witnesses; assistance with depositions, interrogatories, and document production; compilation of statistical and financial data, checking legal citations, and drafting correspondence. Much such work lies in a gray area of tasks that might appropriately be performed either by an attorney or a paralegal. To the extent that fee applicants under §1988 are not permitted to bill for the work of paralegals at market rates, it would not be surprising to see a greater amount of such work performed by attorneys themselves, thus increasing the overall cost of litigation.

. . .

We also note that the American Bar Association ("ABA") has long given latitude to attorneys to employ non-lawyers for a variety of tasks. For example, Ethical Consideration 3-6 of the ABA *Model Code of Professional Responsibility* provides as follows:

> A lawyer often delegates tasks to clerks, secretaries, and other lay persons. Such delegation is proper if the lawyer maintains a direct relationship with his/her client, supervises the delegated work, and has complete professional responsibility for the work product. This delegation enables a lawyer to render legal services more economically and efficiently.

The ABA has further stated, in Formal Opinion 316, that "we do not limit the kind of assistance that a lawyer can acquire *in any way* to persons who are admitted to the Bar, so long as the non-lawyers do not do things that lawyers may not do or do the things that [only] lawyers[] may do." (emphasis added)

No judicial, legislative, or other rule-making body excludes independent paralegals from its definition of a paralegal. For example, the ABA defines a paralegal as follows:

> A person qualified through education, training or work experience; is employed or *retained* by a lawyer, law office, government agency, or other entity; works under the *ultimate* direction and supervision of an attorney; performs specifically delegated legal work, which, for the most part, requires a sufficient knowledge of legal concepts; and performs such duties that, absent such an assistant, the attorney would perform such tasks. (emphasis added)

The ABA definition expands the role of a legal assistant to include independent paralegals, recognizing that attorneys can and do retain the services of legal assistants who work outside the law office.

. . .

Under both federal law and New Jersey law, and under both the ABA and New Jersey ethics Rules, attorneys may delegate legal tasks to paralegals if they maintain direct relationships with their clients, supervise the paralegal's work and remain responsible for the work product.

Neither case law nor statutes distinguish paralegals employed by an attorney or law firm from independent paralegals retained by an attorney or a law firm. Nor do we. Rather, the important inquiry is whether the paralegal, whether employed or retained, is working directly for the attorney, under that attorney's supervision. Safeguards against the unauthorized practice of law exist through that supervision. Realistically, a paralegal can engage in the unauthorized practice of law whether he or she is an independent paralegal or employed in a law firm. Likewise, regardless of the paralegal's status, an attorney who does not properly supervise a paralegal is in violation of the ethical Rules. Although fulfilling the ethical requirements of *RPC* 5.3 is primarily the attorney's obligation and responsibility, a paralegal is not relieved from an independent obligation to refrain from illegal conduct and to work directly under the supervision of the attorney. A paralegal who recognizes that the attorney is not directly supervising his or her work or that such supervision is illusory because the attorney knows nothing about the field in which the paralegal is working must understand that he or she is engaged in the unauthorized practice of law. In such a situation an independent paralegal must withdraw from representation of the client. The key is supervision, and that supervision must occur regardless of whether the paralegal is employed by the attorney or retained by the attorney.

We were impressed by the professionalism of the paralegals who testified before the Committee. They all understood the need for direct attorney supervision and were sensitive to potential conflict-of-interest problems. Additionally, they all recognized that as the paralegal profession continues to grow, the need to define clearly the limits of the profession's responsibilities increases.

. . .

We recognize that distance between the independent paralegal and the attorney may create less opportunity for efficient, significant, rigorous supervision. Nonetheless, the site at which the paralegal performs services should not be the determinative factor. In large law firms that have satellite offices, an employed paralegal frequently has less face-to-face contact with the supervising attorney than would a retained paralegal. Moreover, in this age of rapidly-expanding instant communications (including fax tele-transmissions, word processing, computer networks, cellular telephone service and other computer-modem communications), out-of-office paralegals can communicate frequently with their supervising attorneys. Indeed, as technology progresses, there will be more communication between employers and employees located at different sites, even different states. That arrangement will be helpful to both the paralegal and the attorney. Parents and disabled people, particularly, may prefer to work from their homes. Sole practitioners and small law firms will be able to obtain the services of paralegals otherwise available only to large firms.

Moreover, nothing in the record before the Committee suggested that attorneys have found it difficult to supervise independent paralegals. Indeed, the paralegals testified that the use of word processing made an attorney's quick review of their work possible. Most of the independent contractors who testified worked under the supervision of attorneys with whom they had regular communication.

. . .

Nonetheless, we recognize that because independent paralegals are retained by different firms and lawyers, a potential conflict exists. For example, the Advisory Committee on Professional Ethics has noted that "[h]iring a paralegal formerly employed by a firm with which the prospective employer presently is involved in adversarial matters would clearly be improper." In re Opinion No. 546 of the Advisory Committee on Ethics, 114 *N.J.L.J.* 496 (1984). Opinion No. 546 is extremely brief, however, and does not detail the circumstances under which such employment would be improper.

The ABA, however, has also considered whether an employing firm can be disqualified by a change in employment of a non-lawyer employee, specifically a paralegal, in Informal Ethics Opinion 88-1526 (June 22, 1988). The ABA determined that such firms can be disqualified unless they thoroughly screen the paralegal and ensure that the paralegal reveals no information relating to the representation of the client at the former firm to any person in the employing firm. The ABA also noted its concern that paralegals could potentially lose the ability to earn a livelihood if they were prevented from working for different law firms:

> It is important that nonlawyer employees have as much mobility in employment opportunities as possible consistent with the protection of clients' interests. To so limit employment opportunities that some nonlawyers trained to work with law firms might be required to leave the careers for which they are trained would disserve clients as well as the legal profession. Accordingly, any restrictions on the nonlawyer's employment should be held to the minimum necessary to protect the confidentiality of client information.

We again conclude that regulations and guidelines can be drafted to address adequately the conflict-of-interest problem. For example, a surged by paralegal associations, there could be a requirement that paralegals must keep records of each case, listing the names of the parties and all counsel. Before undertaking new employment, paralegals would check the list. Likewise, attorneys should require the paralegals to furnish them with such a list. The attorney could thus examine whether such matters would conflict with the attorney's representation of a client before retaining that paralegal. Regulation can also remedy any problems resulting from the attendant problem of paralegals sending correspondence directly to clients without the attorney's review and approval.

. . .

Regulation and guidelines represent the proper course of action to address the problems that the work practices of all paralegals may create. Although the paralegal is directly accountable for engaging in the unauthorized practice of law and also has an obligation to avoid conduct that otherwise violates the Rules of Professional Conduct, the attorney is ultimately accountable. Therefore, with great care, the attorney should ensure that the legal assistant is informed of and abides by the provisions of the Rules of Professional Conduct.

Although an attorney must directly supervise a paralegal, no rational basis exists for the disparate way in which the Committee's opinion treats employed and independent paralegals. The testimony overwhelmingly indicates that the independent paralegals were subject to direct supervision by attorneys and were sensitive to potential conflicts of interest. We conclude that given the appropriate instructions and supervision, paralegals, whether as employees or independent contractors, are valuable and necessary members of an attorney's team in the effective and efficient practice of law.

Subsequent to the issuance of the Committee's decision, the State Bar Association forwarded a resolution to this Court requesting the establishment of a standing committee on paralegal education and regulation. We agree that such a committee is necessary, and will shortly establish it to study the practice of paralegals and make recommendations. The committee may consider guidelines from other states, bar associations, and paralegal associations in formulating regulations for New Jersey paralegals. Any such regulations or guidelines should encourage the use of paralegals while providing both attorneys and paralegals with a set of principles that together with the Rules of Professional Conduct can guide their practices. The guidelines drafted will not be static but subject to modification as new issues arise.

We modify Opinion No. 24 in accordance with this opinion.

Case Discussion Questions

1. What court decided this case?
2. Who were the petitioners in this case?
3. What were the petitioners asking the court to do?
4. What was the legal issue that the court was being asked to decide?
5. What does the court cite as the underlying justification for using paralegals?
6. What is the difference between an "independent paralegal" and a paralegal who is an employee of a law firm?
7. Why did the New Jersey Supreme Court Committee on the Unauthorized Practice of Law consider the distinction between independent paralegals and paralegals who are employees of law firms important?
8. What are the primary reasons for using independent paralegals?
9. What constitutes "the practice of law"?
10. Do paralegals who are supervised by attorneys engage in the unauthorized practice of law? Why or why not?
11. What official action did the New Jersey Supreme Court take?

6. JUDGES

A **judge** is a public official who presides over various types of legal proceedings and is authorized to take specified types of legal action. Within the various state and federal court systems, there are different types of judges, serving on different courts, with different powers and responsibilities. The judges who preside over trials are known by various names, such as "circuit judges" or "district court judges." Some lower-level trial judges may be called "magistrates," "justices of the peace," "court commissioners," or "associate judges." Higher-level judges who review trial court proceedings are appellate judges. Judges on supreme courts are typically called justices.

Judge
A governmental official who presides at legal proceedings and is authorized to decide specified types of legal cases.

Judges are either elected or appointed to positions on designated courts. In the federal system, they are appointed by the president, with the consent of the Senate. At the state level, some judges are elected, some are appointed by the governor, and some are appointed by other judges. Although neither the U.S. Constitution nor federal statutes require it, standard practice has been to appoint only licensed attorneys to serve as judges. Most states have laws requiring judges to be attorneys.

In handling criminal cases, judges issue search warrants, determine the terms of any pre-trial release (e.g., set bail or issue personal recognizance bonds), arraign defendants on charges brought by the prosecutor's office, rule on pre-trial motions, preside at criminal trials, empanel and instruct juries, and sentence convicted defendants. In **bench trials**, judges also serve as the sole finder of fact and determine whether a defendant is guilty or not guilty.

Bench trial
A non-jury trial at which the judge decides all questions of fact.

7. OTHER COURT PERSONNEL

In performing their functions, judges are assisted by a number of other non-attorney personnel, including court clerks, bailiffs, court reporters, sheriffs, and marshals.

Court clerks are responsible for maintaining court files in proper order, as well as accepting for filing the motions submitted by lawyers and ensuring that the actions taken by judges are accurately docketed. A head clerk of the courts is usually responsible for running the central records section of the courthouse; his or her assistants may be assigned to sit in on the actual courtroom proceedings.

Bailiffs are responsible for maintaining order in the courtrooms. They are also responsible for watching over the juries when they are in recess or when they have been sequestered. When a jury is sequestered, the members sleep at a hotel and are kept isolated from the public and their families to prevent them from being exposed to prejudicial publicity, threats, bribes, or any other improper influences.

The court reporter prepares verbatim transcripts of courtroom proceedings. Most reporters use a stenotype machine rather than shorthand. Some courts are beginning to use audio recording in place of court reporters who are present in the courtroom during the proceedings. In either case, the proceedings can be transcribed. Because doing so is expensive, court reporters typically prepare a written transcript only if the case is being appealed.

Finally, deputy sheriffs and marshals also serve as officers of the court. They serve summonses and other court documents, collect money as required by court judgments, and otherwise help in carrying out the court's orders. They also may provide security for the courthouse.

8. JURORS

The jury system originated in England as a check on the powers of the government and became an important part of the U.S. judicial system. Among other things, the Sixth Amendment to the U.S. Constitution creates a right to a public trial by an impartial jury in federal criminal cases. The U.S. Supreme Court has ruled that the due process clause of the Fourteenth Amendment applies the right to a trial by jury to defendants in state criminal actions when they face possible incarceration of six months or more.

9. CORRECTIONS PERSONNEL

Correctional personnel are responsible for carrying out the punishments that are handed out by the courts. In addition to employing people to serve as prison guards, correctional facilities employ counselors and therapists, medical staff, and librarians. Probation and parole officers are employed to check on the whereabouts and activities of people who have been convicted of crimes and have either been placed on probation (rather than being incarcerated) or on parole (after having been conditionally released from their incarceration).

E. Juvenile and Other Specialized Criminal Courts

Juvenile
An individual who has not yet attained the age at which persons are legally considered to be adults under criminal law.

Juvenile courts
Special courts established to deal with juveniles who commit acts that are violations of criminal law or who are adjudged to be abused or neglected.

Juvenile delinquent
A juvenile who has been adjudicated to have committed acts that are violations of criminal law.

Over the years, many states have created special courts for handling selected types of defendants. The most common of these specialized courts involve juveniles.

Rather than convicting a **juvenile** of a crime and punishing the juvenile as they would an adult, **juvenile courts** adjudicate the individual to be a **juvenile delinquent** and require the juvenile to participate in various types of treatment options, such as counseling or incarceration.

Under the federal Juvenile Delinquency Act, a person is classified as a juvenile if that person has not attained his or her eighteenth birthday. Some states define it as being under age seventeen.

In cases where older juveniles commit very serious crimes, such as rape or murder, the juvenile court can waive its jurisdiction and authorize adult criminal prosecutions. In *Kent v. United States*,[12] the U.S. Supreme Court ruled that juvenile courts could not waive their jurisdiction and authorize adult criminal prosecution without a hearing at which the minor has access to the records on which the juvenile court waived jurisdiction.

Some juvenile courts also deal with situations in which adults have been accused of the abuse or neglect of a juvenile victim. In these situations, the

---

[12]383 U.S. 541 (1966).

court can assign custody of the child to the state department of child services and establish criteria for the child's return to biological or adoptive parents.

Some state and local governments have also developed specialized courts to address a variety of social problems, such as drug addiction, domestic violence, and mental health. See Chapter 9 for further discussion of these specialty courts.

SUMMARY

This chapter has provided an overview of the criminal justice system. It explained how the law prohibits or requires certain types of behaviors to protect and improve our society. Criminal law differs from civil law in the types of sanctions imposed and the role of the government in enforcement.

The criminal justice system is a very complex set of people and institutions that make criminal laws, identify and process alleged violators, and punish those who have been found guilty of having violated these laws. It includes legislators and administrative officials, law enforcement authorities (police, FBI, and others), attorneys (and their staffs), judges (and other court officials), jurors, and corrections officials.

There are, however, two conflicting views as to how the criminal justice system should operate. Those who support the crime control model believe that the system should suppress criminal conduct in the most efficient manner possible; supporters of the due process model believe that the system should focus on protecting innocent people from being falsely convicted. You should keep these conflicting goals in mind as you learn more about how the criminal justice system operates in the chapters that follow.

In the next two chapters, we will explore the substance of our criminal laws. Chapter 2 will discuss the rule of law and other basic principles reflected in our criminal laws. Then, in Chapter 3, we will provide an overview of the types of behavior covered by the criminal law and examples of how these laws are structured. In Parts 2 and 3 of this book, we will go into greater detail about which participants do what at each stage of the criminal justice process. Throughout, special attention will be given to what paralegals do and how they go about performing these tasks.

INTERNET RESOURCES

General Information on the Criminal Justice System

- National Criminal Justice Reference Service: **http://www.ncjrs.gov**
- National Institute of Justice: **https://www.nij.gov/Pages/welcome.aspx**
- Office of Justice Programs: **http://www.ojp.usdoj.gov/**
- National Center for State Courts: **http://www.ncsc.org**
- U.S. Courts: **http://www.uscourts.gov/Home.aspx**
- Directory of state and local websites: **http://www.statelocalgov.net/**

Participants in the Criminal Justice System

- Attorneys: U.S. Bureau of Labor Statistics, **https://www.bls.gov/oes/current/oes231011.htm**
- Corrections Personnel:
  U.S. Bureau of Labor Statistics, **https://www.bls.gov/oes/current/oes333012.htm**
  U.S. Bureau of Labor Statistics, **https://www.bls.gov/oes/current/oes333011.htm**

- Law Enforcement:
  The Balance Careers, **http://legalcareers.about.com/od/careerprofiles/tp/Law-Enforcement-Careers.htm**
  U.S. Bureau of Labor Statistics, **https://www.bls.gov/oes/current/oes333051.htm**
  Federal Bureau of Investigation, **http://www.fbi.gov/**
- Paralegals: **https://www.bls.gov/oes/current/oes232011.htm**

The Juvenile Justice System

- National Center for Juvenile Justice (NCJJ): **http://www.ncjj.org/default.aspx**
- Office of Juvenile Justice and Delinquency Prevention (OJJDP): **http://www.ojjdp.gov/**
- The Gault Center: **https://njdc.info/**

REVIEW QUESTIONS

1. What is a law?
2. Why do governments enact laws?
3. What are the basic differences between criminal law and civil law?
4. What are the crime control and due process models of the criminal justice system?
5. What governmental bodies are most responsible for the enactment of criminal laws?
6. Because victims of crime are not formal parties to a criminal action, how can they help bring offenders to justice?
7. Identify five types of law enforcement officials at each level of government.
8. What roles do defense attorneys and prosecutors play in the criminal justice system?
9. What rights does the U.S. Supreme Court case of *Miranda v. Arizona* afford to persons taken into custody by law enforcement officers?
10. What tasks do paralegals undertake in the field of criminal law?
11. What functions do judges carry out in criminal cases?
12. How does the juvenile justice system differ from the criminal justice system that serves adults?

Chapter 2

Basic Principles of Criminal Law

Chapter Objectives

After reading this chapter, you should be able to:

- Explain what the "rule of law" is and why it is such an important part of our legal system.
- List the primary sources of federal and state laws and explain how they differ.
- Describe the major classifications used for identifying different types of criminal law.
- Distinguish between *actus reus* and *mens rea*.
- Explain the differences between a principal, an accomplice, and an accessory, and why it matters.

Introduction

Before jumping into the details of criminal law and criminal procedure, we need to examine some of the basic concepts upon which our criminal law is based. One of the most important principles is adherence to the rule of law.

A. Rule of Law

The rule of law is a collection of legal principles that all relate to the placement of limitations on the exercise of political power and the operation of government. These principles include: (1) government must follow its own rules; (2) government must apply the law impartially; and (3) government must provide due process for those accused of breaking the rules.

To achieve the rule of law, the laws must:

- Be enacted in accordance with preexisting legal rules (e.g., be constitutionally authorized)
- Be made public
- Be reasonably clear in meaning
- Be capable of being followed
- Be applied prospectively, not retroactively
- Be applied in an impartial manner consistent with their meaning
- Remain in force for a reasonable period of time

B. Sources of Law

Law
A rule of conduct promulgated and enforced by the government.

Statutory law
A form of law that is created by legislative bodies in the form of statutes and ordinances.

Statutes
A form of written law that is enacted by federal and state legislative bodies.

Code
A compilation of statutes, ordinances, or administrative regulations that is organized by subject matter rather than by the date of its enactment.

Ordinance
A form of law that is created by local legislative bodies such as city councils.

Administrative law
Rules and regulations created by administrative agencies.

Constitutional law
Laws and legal principles derived from constitutions through judicial interpretation.

You probably remember something from a high school civics class about the legislature making the law, the executive branch enforcing the law, and the courts applying it. The truth, however, is that the legislative, executive, and judicial branches are all involved in creating the **law**. Their specific roles depend in part upon the type of law that is being promulgated.

When people think about a law, they usually envision what is formally classified as **statutory law**. **Statutes** appear as you would expect a law should appear. They spell out rules that apply to general categories of people, businesses, etc. Statutes are enacted by a majority of an official legislative body, such as the U.S. Congress or a state legislature. These laws are given specific names and citations and are usually incorporated into an official code. (A **code** is a compilation of statutes, ordinances, or regulations that is organized by subject matter rather than by the date of its enactment.) When local governmental units such as county boards, city councils, and sanitary districts pass laws, they are usually called **ordinances** rather than statutes but are still categorized as a type of statutory law.

If all of these statutes were written in such a way that their meaning was clear to everyone, we could apply the conventional wisdom that the legislative branch makes the law, the executive branch enforces it, and the judicial branch applies it. However, statutes and ordinances frequently contain ambiguous language and therefore are not clear to all who read them. In these situations, the executive branch has some degree of discretion over how it chooses to interpret statutes. Similarly, a judge cannot reach a decision as to whether someone is guilty of breaking the law without clarifying what behavior the law actually requires or prohibits. In these situations, the executive branch and the judicial branch are clearly involved in "making" the law.

Administrative law is similar to statutory law in that it usually consists of fairly specific regulations that are written in a form similar to statutes. In effect, the legislative branch intentionally leaves it to the executive branch and to independent regulatory agencies to "fill in the details" of the law within a general structure set down by the legislature. Through the process of filling in these details, the executive branch, rather than the legislature, is crafting the exact wording of the law. And to the extent that there is some degree of ambiguity in these administrative regulations, the courts are drawn into the lawmaking process when they are called upon to resolve that ambiguity.

A third major category of law is **constitutional law**. This type of law is based on the texts of the constitutions of the United States and of the 50 states.

Because constitutions include provisions that speak in general and broad language, the judicial branch has to interpret the meaning of these terms in the context of the facts of the case. Therefore, one cannot understand what a constitution requires without reviewing how it has been applied in the written opinions of the U.S. Supreme Court and of those of the highest courts of the states. These decisions are published in **court reporters**.

Constitutions define how the government is organized and the powers given to the various governmental institutions. Most also contain a "Bill of Rights" section that enumerates specific rights of the government's citizens. Constitutional law is therefore frequently used to challenge a statute or administrative regulation on the basis that it is prohibited by one or more provisions in the constitution.

While the U.S. Constitution is pretty clear about things like the age requirements for representatives, senators, and the president, it contains many broad, sweeping phrases, such as "interstate commerce," "establishment of religion," "freedom of speech and press," and "unreasonable searches and seizures." These somewhat ambiguous phrases open the door for the judicial branch to play a key role in the development of constitutional law. Based on the principle of **judicial review** as it was enunciated by Chief Justice John Marshall in *Marbury v. Madison*,[2] the judicial branch has the power to strike down statutes and void other government actions that are not consistent with the Court's interpretation of the Constitution. State courts also employ judicial review to invalidate statutory and administrative laws that conflict with state constitutions.

A fourth source of law is what is referred to as the common law. **Common law** is the body of law derived from judges' decisions rather than from the other three sources of law. The common law, which originated in England and continues to evolve in the United States, applies to legal disputes involving subjects that are not addressed by the other three types of law. In other words, in the absence of pronouncements from the constitution or a legislative or administrative body, the judge looks to the earlier decisions of other judges in similar circumstances. An earlier judicial decision relied upon in deciding a case is called **judicial precedent**.

Over time, statutory law has superseded much of the common law. This is especially true in the area of criminal law, which is now almost entirely statutory. However, while Section 1.05(1) of the **Model Penal Code** of the American Law Institute (ALI) states: "No conduct constitutes an offense unless it is a crime or violation under this Code or another statute of this State,"[3] there are still a few states that recognize some common law crimes. For instance, as recently as 1999, the Rhode Island Supreme Court upheld convictions on the basis of common law crimes.[4] The common law continues to play its most prominent role in the area of tort law.

In addition to classifying law based on its being found in constitutions, statutes, administrative regulations, or past court decisions, it can also be classified as to whether it is federal, state, or local law. Federal laws consist

Court reporters (books)
Books that contain decisions and opinions of courts.[1]

Judicial review
The legal doctrine that courts have the power to strike down statutes and void other government actions that are not consistent with the court's interpretation of the constitution.

Common law
Legal principles that have evolved over time from the analyses of court decisions made in the absence of constitutional, statutory, and administrative law.

Judicial precedent
An earlier judicial decision that is relied upon by judges in deciding a case.

Model Penal Code
A model criminal code prepared by the American Law Institute (ALI) to promote improvements in and greater consistency among state criminal codes.

---

[1]The term "court reporter" can also refer to people who prepare transcripts of legal proceedings.

[2]5 U.S. (1 Cranch) 137 (1803).

[3]In 1956, the ALI assembled a group of law professors and practicing attorneys to develop a model criminal code to be used to seek legal reform and greater uniformity among the states. While the Model Penal Code has been highly influential, states have not adopted all sections as it was written or as it has been revised in later years.

[4]*State v. Rodriguez*, 731 A.2d 726 (R.I. 1999).

of laws made by Congress, federal executive agencies, and the rulings of federal courts. State laws are created by state legislatures, state executive agencies, and state court rulings. Local laws are made by local legislative bodies such as city councils and county boards, by local administrative agencies, and by courts interpreting those laws. Whereas federal laws apply nationwide, state laws pertain only to the state in which they were made, and local laws apply only to selected local areas. It is left to the state courts to settle any conflicts between state and local laws and to the federal courts to resolve conflicts between federal and state laws. In some cases, the federal law preempts the state law; in others, both federal and state laws may be enforced simultaneously.

Executive order
A directive issued by the president or a governor, enforceable by members of the executive branch of government, that has the force of law.

The **executive order** is not technically considered a law but has the same effect as law. At the federal level, this is a directive from the president that is enforceable by members of the executive branch of government. Although there is no specific provision in the U.S. Constitution authorizing the issuance of executive orders, the president has general authority to issue these directives as the commander-in-chief and as the official charged with taking care that the laws be faithfully executed. Governors may also issue executive orders at the state level. Executive orders do not criminalize conduct but rather may give direction on enforcement of statutory laws.

While most criminal law comes from state statutes, certain types of crimes are found only in federal statutes. State and federal regulations can also play a role in criminal prosecutions. Federal and state statutes, regulations, court rules, and constitutional law are also involved in questions of criminal procedure. Constitutional guarantees such as protection against double jeopardy, the right to counsel, the privilege against self-incrimination, the right to confront witnesses, and the right to a jury trial also play a key role in the criminal law.

Although the common law does not play much of a role in criminal law, one frequently needs to refer to case law interpreting constitutional rights and the statutes being applied.

Figure 2.1 summarizes the sources of criminal law; Figure 2.2 lists rights guaranteed to criminal defendants by the U.S. Constitution.

C. Classifications of Crimes

Felony
A major crime that is punishable by a year or more in prison.

Misdemeanor
A crime that is punishable by less than a year of incarceration.

Crimes are generally classified as either felonies or misdemeanors. **Felonies** are considered to be "major crimes," such as murder, rape, armed robbery, and aggravated assault. The key is that crimes classified as felonies generally carry sentences of a year or more in prison. **Misdemeanors**, on the other hand, involve crimes like disorderly conduct and criminal damage to property. When incarceration is called for in these cases, it usually is for less than one year in a county jail.

In addition to the length and location of incarceration, the consequences of being convicted of a felony versus a misdemeanor often include loss of the right to vote and hold public office. Under federal law, anyone convicted of a felony in any jurisdiction loses the right to possess a firearm.

While there are many similarities from one state to another, there are also many differences. What is treated as a felony in one state may be only

	Constitutional	Statutory	Administrative	Common Law
FEDERAL GOVERNMENT	U.S. Constitution and federal court decisions interpreting it	U.S. Code (U.S.C.) enacted by Congress and federal court decisions interpreting it	Code of Federal Regulations (C.F.R.) adopted by agencies and federal court decisions interpreting it	Federal court interpretations in limited body of federal law
STATE GOVERNMENT	State constitution and state court decisions interpreting it	State Code enacted by legislature and state court decisions interpreting it	Administrative Code adopted by state agencies and state court decisions interpreting it	State court decisions interpreting common law principles
LOCAL GOVERNMENT	None	Ordinances enacted by municipalities and state court decisions interpreting them	Ordinarily none	None

Figure 2.1 Sources of Criminal Law

Protected Right	Constitutional Provision
Bills of attainder prohibited	Article I, §9
No ex post facto laws	Article I, §10
No unreasonable searches and seizures	Fourth Amendment
Indictment by grand jury	Fifth Amendment
No self-incrimination	Fifth Amendment
No double jeopardy	Fifth Amendment
Due process of law	Fifth and Fourteenth Amendments
Speedy and public trial	Sixth Amendment
Informed of charge	Sixth Amendment
Confrontation of witnesses	Sixth Amendment
Compulsory process of witnesses	Sixth Amendment
Assistance of counsel	Sixth Amendment
Jury trial	Sixth Amendment
No excessive fines or bail	Eighth Amendment
No cruel and unusual punishment	Eighth Amendment
Equal protection of law	Fourteenth Amendment

Figure 2.2 Rights Guaranteed to Criminal Defendants Under the U.S. Constitution

a misdemeanor in another. Indeed, it may not even be considered a crime in another state. Gun laws provide a good illustration. A failure to register a firearm may be a felony in some states and a misdemeanor in others. In some states it is illegal to carry a concealed weapon without a special permit, while it is perfectly legal in others. Each legislative body decides what will or will not be legal and whether it will be considered a felony or a misdemeanor.

Capital offense
A special type of felony that is punishable by death.

Many states further subdivide felonies and misdemeanors into subcategories on the basis of the degree of harm done and/or the length of the sentence imposed. **Capital offenses** are a special type of felony in which the offense could be punished by death.[5] In addition to having a special category for capital offenses, some states further divide their felonies and misdemeanors to reflect the variations of the punishments that are authorized. For example, Illinois categorizes most felonies as Class 1, Class 2, Class 3, or Class 4; misdemeanors as Class A, Class B, or Class C; Petty Offenses; and the most serious felonies as Class X. The statute defining the crime also specifies its class.[6] A separate part of the state code lists minimum and maximum sentences for first- and second-degree murder, habitual criminals, and each of these classes of felonies and misdemeanors.[7]

Petty offense
A violation of the law that is considered less serious than a misdemeanor.

In addition to felonies and misdemeanors, there are some other types of laws that are often called **petty offenses** and are sometimes referred to as being "quasi-criminal." Traffic offenses such as speeding or failure to obey a traffic signal are commonly classified as petty offenses and do not carry the same stigma as do violations of the regular criminal law. Nevertheless, the judicial proceedings used to enforce these types of laws are criminal in nature. The state takes it on itself to prosecute offenders, who in turn must be found guilty "beyond a reasonable doubt." Some juvenile proceedings are also criminal in nature. Local ordinances for matters like garbage disposal and barking dogs are additional examples of petty offenses. Petty offenses are not punishable by incarceration.

Crimes can also be classified on the basis of the nature of the harm done and the type of victim involved. For example, the previously mentioned Model Penal Code is divided into five categories: Offenses Involving Danger to the Person, Offenses Against Property, Offenses Against the Family, Offenses Against Public Administration, and Offenses Against Public Order and Decency. Figure 2.3 provides examples of the types of crimes that fall into each of these categories.

White-collar crime
A non-violent crime characterized by deceit, concealment, or violation of trust that is committed by individuals in the course of their occupation or by a company in the course of its business.

Street crime
A crime that usually involves violence.

Crimes can also be categorized on the basis of the nature of the criminal and the context in which they take place. For example, people will sometimes distinguish between **white-collar crime** and **street crime**. The term "white-collar crime" was introduced by a prominent sociologist named Edwin Sutherland in 1939. In his book *White-Collar Crime,* he defined it as "a crime committed by a person of respectability and high social status in the course of his occupation."[8] Sutherland argued that white-collar crime was largely ignored

[5]See the discussion of the death penalty in Chapter 13.

[6]730 ILCS 5/5-5-1.

[7]730 ILCS 5/5-8-1 and 5/5-8-3. See Chapter 13 for a more extended discussion of sentencing.

[8]E. Sutherland, *White Collar Crime* (New York, Dryden Press 1949).

Category	Types of Crimes Included
Offenses involving danger to person	Homicide; assault; criminal endangerment; false imprisonment; kidnapping; sexual assault
Offenses against property	Destruction of property (e.g., arson); intrusions of property (burglary and trespass); fraud; forgery
Offenses against the family	Bigamy and incest
Offenses against public administration	Bribery; obstruction of government; perjury; treason
Offenses against public order and decency	Alcohol and drug offenses; disorderly conduct; obscenity; prostitution

Figure 2.3 ALI Model Criminal Code Classifications

because the press and law enforcement agencies focused on the more violent street crimes carried out by people in the lower economic classes.

Whereas Sutherland focused on the social status of the criminal, the Federal Bureau of Investigation (FBI) defines white-collar crime in terms of the methods used. A 1983 Department of Justice report noted that "white-collar criminals occupy positions of responsibility and trust in government, industry, the professions, and civic organizations."[9] The FBI website provides that white-collar crimes are "characterized by deceit, concealment, or violation of trust and are not dependent on the application or threat of physical force or violence. The motivation behind these crimes is financial—to obtain or avoid losing money, property, or services, or to secure a personal or business advantage."[10] Typical white-collar crimes involve some type of fraud in the context of business activities, banking, insurance, or the Internet. Other examples include bribery, tax evasion, antitrust violations, and violations of environmental protection regulations.

Whereas state criminal codes are generally very inclusive, the federal criminal law tends to focus on criminal activities that take place in the context of interstate commerce, immigration, national security, and interference with the activities of federal agents and employees. Some of the best-known sections of federal criminal law cover crimes like kidnapping, bank robbery, illegal transportation and sale of drugs and firearms, pornography, and sexual exploitation of children. Thanks to the public attention given to National Football League (NFL) football player Michael Vick, many sports fans also know that federal statutes prohibit "buying, selling, delivering, or transporting animals for

[9]E. Podgor & J. Isreal, *White Collar Crime* (2, St. Paul, MN, West Group 1997).

[10]https://www.fbi.gov/investigate/white-collar-crime (website last visited 7/6/19).

participation in animal fighting venture(s)."[11] Less familiar to the layman are federal laws involving bank and securities fraud, bribery, and influence peddling.

D. Elements of a Crime

Actus reus
A Latin term referring to a person's wrongful conduct that resulted in an illegal act.

Mens rea
A Latin term referring to what was going on in someone's mind at the time he or she committed an illegal act.

In order to determine if a crime has taken place, one must analyze not only what the person did but what was going on in that person's mind at the time he or she committed this act and what the results of that act were. The Latin terms ***actus reus*** (translated as "guilty act" or "wrongful conduct") and ***mens rea*** (translated as "guilty mind" or "criminal intent") are frequently used in this context. For example, if Mr. Jones shoots a gun, the existence of a crime will depend upon whether Mr. Jones was authorized to possess the weapon, why he shot it, where he shot it, and the nature of the damage caused by the bullet he fired.

Application Exercises

1. Based on the facts presented in the discussion of the Cook case (*see* hypothetical cases information presented on p. xxxvii):
   a. Identify the types of criminal laws Cook may have violated.
   b. Which of these laws are likely to be federal, state, or local laws?
   c. What, if any, civil actions might also arise out of these facts?
2. Based on the facts presented in the discussion of the Turner case (*see* hypothetical case information presented on pp. xxxvii-xxxviii):
   a. Identify the types of criminal laws Turner may have violated.
   b. Which of these laws are likely to be federal, state, or local laws?
   c. What, if any, civil actions might also arise out of these facts?
3. Based on the facts presented in the discussion of the Marshall case (*see* hypothetical case information presented on pp. xxxviii-xxxix):
   a. Identify the types of criminal laws Marshall may have violated.
   b. Which of these laws are likely to be federal, state, or local laws?
   c. What, if any, civil actions might also arise out of these facts?
4. Based on the facts presented in the discussion of the Smith case (*see* hypothetical case information presented on p. xxxix):
   a. Identify the types of criminal laws Smith may have violated.
   b. Which of these laws are likely to be federal, state, or local laws?
   c. What, if any, civil actions might also arise out of these facts?
   d. What, if anything, is significant about the fact that Smith is a police officer?

We will focus on *actus reus* first. If Mr. Jones was not authorized to possess or shoot a firearm, he could be guilty of violating a number of possible

[11] 7 U.S.C. §2156(b).

Offense	Criminal Intent
Murder	Purposely; knowingly; reckless disregard for human life
Manslaughter	Recklessly; influenced by extreme mental or emotional disturbance
Negligent homicide	Negligently

Figure 2.4 Model Penal Code *Mens Rea* for Criminal Homicide

state and federal laws regulating firearms. If the bullet damaged someone's house or automobile, he could be guilty of such crimes as criminal damage to property or disorderly conduct. If the bullet injured someone, the potential crimes could include first degree homicide, second degree homicide, involuntary manslaughter, reckless homicide, assault, aggravated assault, battery, aggravated battery, and reckless conduct.

As previously mentioned, *mens rea* translates as "guilty mind." Here the focus is on what a person's intentions were. Why did Mr. Jones shoot the gun? What did he think was going to happen to the bullet? Although it is difficult to prove what was going on in someone's mind when a crime was committed, the courts allow judges and juries to infer the defendant's state of mind from both statements made and actions undertaken at that time. Furthermore, the law assumes that people know the probable consequences of their acts. A person who strikes another person may be presumed to have intended the infliction of harm in that such a result naturally flows from hitting another.

The defendant's intent is also important in distinguishing one potential crime from another. For example, murder, voluntary manslaughter, involuntary manslaughter, and reckless homicide all involve causing the death of another human being. They differ on the basis of the *mens rea*. Compare the way in which the following offenses are defined in the ALI Model Penal Code. *See* Figure 2.4.

OFFENSES INVOLVING DANGER TO THE PERSON
j Article 210. Criminal Homicide

Section 210.1 Criminal Homicide

(1) A person is guilty of criminal homicide if he purposely, knowingly, recklessly or negligently causes the death of another human being.

(2) Criminal homicide is murder, manslaughter or negligent homicide.

Section 210.2 Murder

(1) Except as provided in Section 210.3(1)(b), criminal homicide constitutes murder when

(a) it is committed purposely or knowingly; or

(b) it is committed recklessly under circumstances manifesting extreme indifference to the value of human life. Such recklessness and indifference are presumed if the actor is engaged or is an accomplice in the commission of, or an attempt to commit, or flight after committing or attempting to commit robbery, rape or deviate sexual intercourse by force or threat of force, arson, burglary, kidnapping or felonious escape.

Section 210.3 Manslaughter

(1) Criminal homicide constitutes manslaughter when:

(a) it is committed recklessly; or

(b) a homicide which would otherwise be murder is committed under the influence of extreme mental or emotional disturbance for which there is reasonable explanation or excuse. The reasonableness of such explanation or excuse shall be determined from the viewpoint of a person in the actor's situation under the circumstances as he believes them to be.

(2) Manslaughter is a felony of the second degree.

Section 210.4 Negligent Homicide

(1) Criminal homicide constitutes negligent homicide when it is committed negligently.

(2) Negligent homicide is a felony of the third degree.

Section 210.5 Causing or Aiding Suicide

(1) A person may be convicted of criminal homicide for causing another to commit suicide only if he purposely causes such suicide by force, duress or deception.

(2) A person who purposely aids or solicits another to commit suicide is guilty of a felony of the second degree if his conduct causes such suicide or an attempted suicide, and otherwise of a misdemeanor.

To constitute the crime of murder, the action that caused the death must have been committed "purposely," "knowingly," or "recklessly under circumstances manifesting extreme indifference to the value of human life." To be considered manslaughter, on the other hand, the action that caused the death must have been committed "recklessly" or "under the influence of extreme mental or emotional disturbance for which there is reasonable explanation or excuse." Negligent homicide requires the action that caused the death to have been committed "negligently." But what do the terms "purposely," "knowingly," "recklessly," and "negligently" mean?

Purposeful
Intending to cause a specific harm.

Acts are categorized as **purposeful** when the defendant specifically intended to cause the harm that resulted. So, Mr. Jones would meet the purposeful element needed to establish murder if he shot the gun at someone with the intent to kill that person.

Knowingly
Not intending to cause a specific harm, but being aware that such harm would be caused.

He could also be convicted of murder if he acted **knowingly**. This requires a showing that the defendant knew or had reason to know that harm would be caused by the actions taken even if the specific harm was not the objective of the defendant. So, if Mr. Jones fired his gun at a group of people, he could be found guilty of murder even if he did not intend to kill a specific individual.[12]

[12]In *United States v. Jewell*, 532 F. 2d 697, 704 (9th Cir. 1976), the court stated that the term "knowingly" includes a mental state in which the defendant is aware that the fact in question is highly probable but consciously avoids enlightenment.

It could also be murder if Mr. Jones acted **recklessly** "under circumstances manifesting extreme indifference to the value of human life." Acting recklessly is defined in terms of disregarding a substantial and unjustifiable risk that harm will result from the action a person is taking. In Jones's case, the judge or jury would have to consider the number of people in the area and what Jones knew about guns.

Recklessness
Disregarding a substantial and unjustifiable risk that harm will result.

The murder section of the Model Penal Code states that recklessness and indifference are presumed "if the actor is engaged or is an accomplice in the commission of, or an attempt to commit, or flight after committing or attempting to commit robbery, rape or deviate sexual intercourse by force or threat of force, arson, burglary, kidnapping or felonious escape." Mr. Jones could be found guilty of murder without proof that he disregarded a known risk if he shot the gun in the context of committing or attempting to commit one of the listed crimes.

Notice that recklessness is also a factor in defining the crime of manslaughter. To be convicted of manslaughter, if the defendant's actions must either be reckless or have been committed under the influence of "extreme mental or emotional disturbance for which there is reasonable explanation or excuse."

Negligent homicide occurs when the defendant acted **negligently**. This occurs when one simply fails to be aware of a substantial and unjustifiable risk. To be convicted of negligent homicide, the judge or jury would have to find that Mr. Jones neither knew nor should have known that someone could be killed when he fired his gun.

Negligence
A failure to act reasonably under the circumstances.

So far, we have discussed how the law defines a criminal act and different types of criminal intent. But what happens when a person intends to commit a crime but stops short of actually carrying it out? It could be that the person "saw the light" and had a change of heart, or it could be that some intervening event prevented the person from completing the crime. In either case, there would be criminal intent but no criminal act.

A special category of crimes called **inchoate crimes** addresses this situation. Inchoate means "imperfect," "partial," or "unfinished." Thus, an inchoate crime is one that was planned but not completed. The crimes of attempted murder, attempted robbery, attempted sexual assault, etc., are examples of these inchoate crimes. To satisfy the *actus reus* requirement or an attempted crime, the state must prove that the defendant did some overt act in furtherance of his or her intent that went beyond mere preparation. Other examples are the crimes of solicitation and conspiracy. **Solicitation** involves requesting or encouraging someone to commit a crime. For example, if a wife encourages her boyfriend to kill her husband, she could be found guilty of the crime of solicitation. **Conspiracy** involves an agreement between two or more persons to commit an unlawful act. The state must show that they intended to enter into an agreement and that they had the specific intent to commit some crime. Unlike an attempt, where mere preparation is not enough of an overt act to satisfy the *actus reus* requirement, in many states the defendant's preparation is sufficient to prove conspiracy. In others, the defendants must take substantial overt steps to be found guilty.

Inchoate crimes
A crime that was planned but not completed.

Solicitation
The crime of encouraging someone to commit a crime.

Conspiracy
An agreement between two or more persons to commit an unlawful act.

APPLICATION EXERCISES

5. How is the concept of *mens rea* relevant to the Cook case (*see* hypothetical case on p. xxxvii)?
6. If you were a prosecuting attorney operating under the Model Penal Code, what charges would you file in Cook's case?
7. In the Turner case (*see* hypothetical case on pp. xxxvii-xxxviii), if Turner's actions took place in a non-strict liability state where mens rea is required, what would be the *mens rea* and *actus reus* elements for disobeying a stop sign?
8. Why do you think that states have eliminated the *mens rea* requirement for traffic cases?
9. What would be the *mens rea* for the crime of illegal drug possession? What if the vehicle Turner was driving was registered to another person and he denied that the crack cocaine was his? Should the crime of possession of contraband be a strict liability offense? Why or why not?
10. Suppose that when he originally accepted his clients' money, Edwards had every intention to provide a better-than-average rate of return on the money they invested with him. It was only when his personal financial situation deteriorated that he misappropriated their funds. If this is true, how would it affect a potential criminal prosecution (*see* hypothetical case on pp. xxxviii-xxxix)?
11. What would be the *actus reus* in any crimes Smith may have committed (*see* hypothetical case on p. xxxix)?
12. Did Smith commit a crime when his subjective intent was simply to carry out his job as a law enforcement officer)?

E. DOUBLE JEOPARDY

In the preceding section you have seen how the same act, such as causing the death of another person, can result in being charged with several different crimes. It is the *mens rea* rather than the act that distinguishes murder from manslaughter or negligent homicide. It is not unusual for a prosecutor to charge a defendant with multiple offenses and then let the jury sort out which one is supported by the evidence presented at the trial. Stop and consider how these types of multiple charges relate to the concept of double jeopardy.

The Fifth Amendment to the U.S. Constitution provides in part: "nor shall any person be subject for the same offence to be twice put in jeopardy of life or limb." But what constitutes an offense, and what does it mean to be "put in jeopardy of life or limb"?

Jeopardy is usually defined as a danger or a peril, and *jeopardy of life or limb* refers to being subject to criminal punishment. Being subject to criminal punishment goes beyond being incarcerated or fined, however, and includes being either convicted or acquitted by a court of competent jurisdiction.

A defendant is placed in **double jeopardy** when he is prosecuted or punished twice for the same crime.[13] Therefore, the government may not appeal a verdict or institute a second prosecution for the same offense.[14] Jeopardy generally attaches once a jury has been selected. However, if the trial ends in a mistrial, due to something like a hung jury, the double jeopardy clause does not prevent the state from prosecuting the defendant in a second trial.[15]

Double jeopardy The Fifth Amendment prohibition against prosecuting or punishing a defendant twice for the same crime.

Determining what constitutes the same offense is far more complicated. Take a few minutes to read the following excerpts from *Ashe v. Swenson.*

Ashe v. Swenson
Supreme Court of the United States
397 U.S. 436 (1970)

MR. JUSTICE STEWART delivered the opinion of the Court.

In *Benton v. Maryland,* 395 U.S. 784, the Court held that the *Fifth Amendment* guarantee against double jeopardy is enforceable against the States through the *Fourteenth Amendment.* The question in this case is whether the State of Missouri violated that guarantee when it prosecuted the petitioner a second time for armed robbery in the circumstances here presented.

Sometime in the early hours of the morning of January 10, 1960, six men were engaged in a poker game in the basement of the home of John Gladson at Lee's Summit, Missouri. Suddenly three or four masked men, armed with a shotgun and pistols, broke into the basement and robbed each of the poker players of money and various articles of personal property. The robbers—and it has never been clear whether there were three or four of them—then fled in a car belonging to one of the victims of the robbery. Shortly thereafter the stolen car was discovered in a field, and later that morning three men were arrested by a state trooper while they were walking on a highway not far from where the abandoned car had been found. The petitioner was arrested by another officer some distance away.

The four were subsequently charged with seven separate offenses—the armed robbery of each of the six poker players and the theft of the car. In May 1960 the petitioner went to trial on the charge of robbing Donald Knight, one of the participants in the poker game. At the trial the State called Knight and three of his fellow poker players as prosecution witnesses. Each of them described the circumstances of the holdup and itemized his own individual losses. The proof that an armed robbery had occurred and that personal property had been taken from Knight as well as from each of the others was unassailable. The testimony of the four victims in this regard was consistent both internally and with that of the others. But the State's evidence that the petitioner had been one of the robbers was weak. Two of the witnesses thought that there had been only three robbers altogether, and could not identify the petitioner as one of them. Another of the victims, who was the petitioner's uncle by marriage, said that at the "patrol station" he had positively identified each of the other three men

[13] "[T]he Double Jeopardy Clause protects against three distinct abuses: a second prosecution for the same offense after acquittal; a second prosecution for the same offense after conviction; and multiple punishments for the same offense." *United States v. Halper,* 490 U.S. 435 (1989).

[14] The prohibition against government appeals only applies to an initial appeal of the trial court's verdict. It does not prevent the state from appealing an appellate court ruling that overturns the trial court where the appeal was brought by the accused.

[15] *United States v. Perez,* 22 U.S. 579 (1824).

accused of the holdup, but could say only that the petitioner's voice "sounded very much like" that of one of the robbers. The fourth participant in the poker game did identify the petitioner, but only by his "size and height, and his actions."

The cross-examination of these witnesses was brief, and it was aimed primarily at exposing the weakness of their identification testimony. Defense counsel made no attempt to question their testimony regarding the holdup itself or their claims as to their losses. Knight testified without contradiction that the robbers had stolen from him his watch, $250 in cash, and about $500 in checks. His billfold, which had been found by the police in the possession of one of the three other men accused of the robbery, was admitted in evidence. The defense offered no testimony and waived final argument.

The trial judge instructed the jury that if it found that the petitioner was one of the participants in the armed robbery, the theft of "any money" from Knight would sustain a conviction. He also instructed the jury that if the petitioner was one of the robbers, he was guilty under the law even if he had not personally robbed Knight. The jury—though not instructed to elaborate upon its verdict—found the petitioner "not guilty due to insufficient evidence."

Six weeks later the petitioner was brought to trial again, this time for the robbery of another participant in the poker game, a man named Roberts. The petitioner filed a motion to dismiss, based on his previous acquittal. The motion was overruled, and the second trial began. The witnesses were for the most part the same, though this time their testimony was substantially stronger on the issue of the petitioner's identity. For example, two witnesses who at the first trial had been wholly unable to identify the petitioner as one of the robbers, now testified that his features, size, and mannerisms matched those of one of their assailants. Another witness who before had identified the petitioner only by his size and actions now also remembered him by the unusual sound of his voice. The State further refined its case at the second trial by declining to call one of the participants in the poker game whose identification testimony at the first trial had been conspicuously negative. The case went to the jury on instructions virtually identical to those given at the first trial. This time the jury found the petitioner guilty, and he was sentenced to a 35-year term in the state penitentiary.

The Supreme Court of Missouri affirmed the conviction, holding that the "plea of former jeopardy must be denied." A collateral attack upon the conviction in the state courts five years later was also unsuccessful. The petitioner then brought the present habeas corpus proceeding in the United States District Court for the Western District of Missouri, claiming that the second prosecution had violated his right not to be twice put in jeopardy. Considering itself bound by this court's decision in *Hoag v. New Jersey,* 356 U.S. 464, the District Court denied the writ, although apparently finding merit in the petitioner's claim. The Court of Appeals for the Eighth Circuit affirmed, also upon the authority of *Hoag v. New Jersey, supra.* We granted certiorari to consider the important constitutional question this case presents.

The question is not whether Missouri could validly charge the petitioner with six separate offenses for the robbery of the six poker players. It is not whether he could have received a total of six punishments if he had been convicted in a single trial of robbing the six victims. It is simply whether, after a jury determined by its verdict that the petitioner was not one of the robbers, the State could constitutionally hale him before a new jury to litigate that issue again.

After the first jury had acquitted the petitioner of robbing Knight, Missouri could certainly not have brought him to trial again upon that charge. Once a jury had determined upon conflicting testimony that there was at least a reasonable doubt that the petitioner was one of the robbers, the State could not present the same or different identification evidence in a second prosecution for the robbery of Knight in the hope that a different jury might find that evidence more convincing. The situation is constitutionally no different here, even though the second trial related to another victim of the same robbery. For the name of the victim, in the circumstances of this case, had no bearing whatever upon the issue of whether the petitioner was one of the robbers.

In this case the State in its brief has frankly conceded that following the petitioner's acquittal, it treated the first trial as no more than a dry run for the second prosecution: "No doubt the prosecutor felt the state had a provable case on the first charge and, when he lost, he did what every good attorney would do—he refined his presentation in light of the turn of events at the first trial." But this is precisely what the constitutional guarantee forbids.

The judgment is reversed, and the case is remanded to the Court of Appeals for the Eighth Circuit for further proceedings consistent with this opinion.

Case Discussion Questions

1. What court wrote this opinion?
2. Who is Mr. Ashe, and what is he alleged to have done?
3. Who is Mr. Swenson, and why is his name part of the title of the case?
4. Is this a civil case or a criminal one? Why?
5. What charges were brought against Mr. Ashe?
6. Who brought these charges and in what court were they filed? Why were they filed in that court?
7. What was the outcome of Ashe's first trial?
8. What happened after Ashe's first trial?
9. What was the outcome of the second trial?
10. How did the case get before the U.S. Supreme Court?
11. Which side won in the U.S. Supreme Court?
12. What, if any, issues of state statutory law were decided in this opinion?
13. What, if any, issues of federal statutory law were decided in this opinion?
14. What, if any, issues of state constitutional law were decided in this opinion?
15. What, if any, issues of federal constitutional law were decided in this opinion?
16. What legal principle (rule of law) did the U.S. Supreme Court use to explain its decision?

It is important to note that in situations where both the state and federal governments criminalize the same act, it does not violate the Double Jeopardy Clause when one government tries the accused after the one has already either acquitted or convicted that person.[16] For example, an act that is prosecuted as a homicide in state court may also be prosecuted as a violation of civil rights in federal court. Furthermore, double jeopardy does not prevent a civil action for damages based on the same set of facts presented in a criminal prosecution. Indeed, the trial in the O. J. Simpson civil case commenced after Simpson was acquitted in the criminal jury trial.

F. Parties to the Crime

When more than one person is involved in committing a crime, the people involved can be classified as a principal, an accomplice, or an accessory. The person who commits a criminal act is a **principal** in the first degree. A principal in the second degree, also referred to as an **accomplice**, assists the principal in the first degree during the commission of the crime. That person could literally be standing next to the principal in the first degree or be waiting in a getaway car.

Principal
A person who actually commits the crime.

Accomplice
A person who assists the principal with the crime or with the preparation of the crime.

[16]Under the dual-sovereignty doctrine, two offenses are not the same offense for double jeopardy purposes if prosecuted by separate sovereigns. *Gamble v. United States*, 139 S. Ct. 1960 (2019).

Accessory
A person who assisted in the preparation of the crime but was not present when it was actually carried out.

Accessory after the fact
A person who first aided the principal after the commission of the crime.

An **accessory**, on the other hand, is someone who assisted in the preparation of the crime but was not present when it was actually carried out. An **accessory after the fact** is someone who first aided the principal after the commission of the crime.

When it comes to punishment, principals of any degree and accessories are all treated the same. However, accessories after the fact are not punished as severely as are principals and accomplices.

G. Punishments for Crimes

As pointed out earlier in this chapter, one of the significant differences between criminal law and civil law is the nature of the sanctions involved. Criminal law is enforced through fines, incarceration, and, in some cases, even death.

The range of sanctions for specific crimes is determined by the legislature when it passes the statute or ordinance making certain behavior a crime. In Chapter 13, we will examine how judges determine what the sentences will be in specific cases. In this section we will take a quick look at the alternative justifications that are given for implementing these punishments. The five major justifications for administering punishment are summarized in Figure 2.5. Each provides a different type of justification for punishing criminal offenders.

Deterrence is the most frequently cited justification for punishment. The idea is that fear of punishment will deter people from committing crimes. The difference between general and specific deterrence is that specific deterrence applies to the person who has already committed a crime, and general deterrence is directed at others who might be tempted to commit a similar crime. Both versions of deterrence theory rely on the assumption that, prior to committing a crime, would-be perpetrators will weigh the benefits of committing

Theory of Punishment	Rationale
Specific deterrence	The perpetrator is punished to deter this individual from committing future crimes.
General deterrence	The perpetrator is punished to deter others from committing future crimes.
Incapacitation	The perpetrator is prevented from committing future crimes by removing the opportunity or means to commit crime.
Rehabilitation	Treatment is given to the perpetrator to eliminate need and/or desire to commit future crimes.
Retribution	The perpetrator is punished to exact revenge on behalf of the victim or the victim's family.

Figure 2.5 Justifications for Punishment

the crime against the punishment they would receive if they are caught. If the punishment is perceived to outweigh the benefits of the crime, the person will have been successfully deterred.

Under deterrence theory, criminals are sent to prison as punishment. With the incapacitation approach, criminals are incarcerated to prevent them from being able to commit new crimes. As long as criminals are kept behind bars, they will not be in a situation in which they are able to victimize the public. Another application of the incapacitation approach would be in cases where people have argued for castration of rapists.

Rehabilitation involves changing the perpetrators of crime so that they will have no need or desire to commit crimes in the future. This approach usually involves providing offenders with the education and job skills they need to get the kinds of jobs they need to support themselves and their families through legal employment. Rehabilitation programs may also include psychological counseling to help the criminals understand the difference between right and wrong and to appreciate the harm their crimes produce. It is argued that if people are able to legally earn a good income, they will not need to engage in criminal behavior.

The final theory is called "retribution." It validates people's desire for revenge and cites the biblical admonition that punishment should involve "an eye for an eye, a tooth for a tooth." The theory is that it is better to have the government administer retribution than to leave it up to victims to seek their own vengeance, thereby starting a cycle of retaliation involving friends and relatives.

Each of these theories of punishment has its critics. Furthermore, the actions suggested by one theory frequently undercut the effectiveness of measures taken on the basis of other theories.

Critics of the deterrence theories are quick to point out that they are based on the assumption that the would-be criminals will stop and think about the punishment before committing the crime. In so-called crimes of passion, however, the perpetrator acts instinctively based on emotion rather than stopping to think through the consequences. Another problem with this approach is that it only works if the potential criminal believes he or she is likely to get caught and to receive a punishment that is severe enough to deter the criminal act. Most criminals expect to get away with their crime and not be caught. If they are caught, they may believe they can "beat the rap," or get away with "a slap on the wrist." Young "gangbangers" may think their juvenile status will insulate them from serious punishment.

Critics of the incarceration approach point out that the logic behind it could justify lifetime incarceration for relatively minor crimes. Conversely, in situations involving very personal "crimes of passion," no incarceration would be needed. For example, in situations where an abused spouse kills the abusive spouse, there is little reason to believe that the perpetrator will kill again.

Critics of rehabilitation argue that it doesn't work and that these programs take away from punishment needed to deter criminals. Critics of retribution point out that the "eye for an eye" concept cannot really be applied in situations involving multiple murders and argue that it is uncivilized to torture the criminal when the criminal tortured the victim.

SUMMARY

This chapter has tried to lay the theoretical and organizational groundwork for a better understanding of what is to come in later chapters. Before jumping into the details of criminal law, it is important to understand the basic concepts behind criminal law and the role it plays in the larger context of our American legal system.

Most laws are created by federal and state legislative bodies as statutes and ordinances. Administrative regulations are enacted by executive agencies and are similar to statutes in form and function. Constitutional law is based on the texts of the constitutions of the United States and of the individual states. The meaning of statutory, administrative, and constitutional law ultimately is determined by the courts interpreting it. Although the common law has been superseded by statutes in most states, there are still a few examples where it has force in criminal matters. Like other forms of the common law, it is found in court decisions and commentaries. In addition to classifying law on the basis of its documentary source, we often break law down into federal, state, and local laws.

Besides classifying law on the basis of its source, it can also be categorized on the basis of the type of the punishment. After splitting criminal law off from civil law, it can be divided into felonies, misdemeanors, and petty crimes. Felonies are often further subdivided into capital crimes and different classes of felonies on the basis of the type of sentence. Misdemeanors can also be further divided.

Finally, crimes can be classified on the basis of the nature of the harm done and the type of victim involved. Common classifications are: Offenses Against Persons, Offenses Against Property, Offenses Against the Family, Offenses Against Public Administration, and Offenses Against Public Order and Decency.

In order to determine if a crime has taken place, one must analyze not only what the person did but what was going on in that person's mind at the time the act was committed and what the results of that act were. *Actus reus* refers to the nature of the act and *mens rea* relates to what was going on in the criminal's mind when the act was committed. This criminal intent is usually classified as purposeful, knowing, reckless, or negligent. Crimes like attempted murder, solicitation, and conspiracy are called inchoate crimes because they are planned but not completed.

When more than one person is involved in committing a crime, the people involved can be classified as a principal, an accomplice, or an accessory. The person who commits a criminal act is a principal. An accomplice assists during the commission of the crime, and an accessory is someone who assisted in the preparation of the crime but was not present when it was actually carried out. An accessory after the fact is someone who first aided the principal after the commission of the crime.

We ended with a discussion of the theories used to justify various forms of punishment: specific deterrence, general deterrence, incapacitation, rehabilitation, and retribution.

While most criminal law comes from state statutes, certain types of crimes are only found in federal statutes. State and federal regulations can also play a role in criminal prosecutions. Federal and state statutes, regulations, court rules, and constitutional law are also involved in questions of criminal procedure. Constitutional guarantees such as protection against double jeopardy, the right to counsel, privilege against self-incrimination, and the right to a jury trial also play a key role in the criminal law. On rare occasions you might have to consult the common law, but in the federal system and in most states, the common law has been completely superseded by statutory law.

INTERNET RESOURCES

General Legal Information

- Legal Information Institute at Cornell University Law School: **http://www.law.cornell.edu/**
- U.S. Law: **https://www.justia.com/**

Federal Statutes

- United States Code: **http://uscode.house.gov/**
- U.S. Statutes at Large: **https://www.loc.gov/law/help/statutes-at-large/**
- Federal Administrative Regulations, Code of Federal Regulations: **https://www.govinfo.gov/help/cfr**
- U.S. Constitution Online: **http://www.usconstitution.net/const.html**

Federal Court Decisions

- Supreme Court of the United States: **http://www.supremecourt.gov/**
- About Federal Courts: **http://www.uscourts.gov/FederalCourts.aspx**

State and Local Information

Use these links to find official state websites and then follow links on the state website to find statutes, administrative regulations, etc.

- State, Local, and Tribal Governments: **http://www.usa.gov/Agencies/State_and_Territories.shtml**
- National Conference of State Legislators: **http://www.ncsl.org/?tabid=17173**

REVIEW QUESTIONS

1. Which branches of government are involved in making the law, and what is the branch's respective role?
2. Name and explain the four sources of law.
3. Can a local governing body, such as a city council, pass statutory law? If so, what types of statutory law can a locality enact?
4. How do executive orders differ from criminal laws enacted by the legislature?
5. What role does case law play in criminal procedure?
6. What are the basic differences between criminal law and civil law?
7. What is the difference between a felony and a misdemeanor?
8. What are the five major categories of crime set forth in the Model Penal Code?
9. What is white-collar crime? How does it differ from street crime?
10. What are the two general elements required of most crimes?
11. Define *inchoate crimes* and give examples of these types of offenses.
12. What is *double jeopardy,* and what provision of the U.S. Constitution protects persons from being subjected to double jeopardy?
13. What are the roles of a principal, an accomplice, an accessory, and an accessory after the fact?
14. What are the five major justifications for punishment?

Chapter 3

Types of Offenses

Chapter Objectives

After reading this chapter, you should be able to:

- Discuss the purpose of the Model Penal Code and explain how it relates to state criminal law statutes.
- Identify the major categories used to classify different types of criminal laws and give examples of the crimes included in each classification.
- Explain the process judges use when they interpret criminal statutes.

Introduction

Chapters 1 and 2 provided a brief overview of the criminal justice system, the people who participate in that system, and the basic principles upon which the system is based. In this chapter, we take a closer look at some of the most common types of criminal offenses.

A. The Model Penal Code

Model Penal Code
A model criminal code developed by the American Law Institute.

Although there are many similarities among the criminal codes of the states and that of the federal government, there are also many differences. In this chapter, we utilize the **Model Penal Code**[1] to illustrate the type of behaviors

[1]1956, the American Law Institute assembled a group of law professors and practicing lawyers to simplify U.S. criminal law by creating the Model Penal Code, which they hoped would be adopted in all 51 jurisdictions. While this hoped-for uniformity was never achieved, many of the provisions of the Model Penal Code have been adopted and incorporated into the laws of some states.

that are classified as crimes by most states. You need to compare these provisions with those that have been adopted in the state in which you will be working. Criminal codes are divided into subsections that identify and differentiate specific crimes and related punishments.

B. Offenses Involving Danger to the Person

The Model Penal Code and many state criminal codes start with a listing of offenses involving danger to people. They typically include various types of homicides, assaults, rape, kidnapping, and false imprisonment.

1. HOMICIDE

"Thou shalt not kill" is perhaps the most frequently referenced section of the Ten Commandments. But who does it refer to, and what does it actually mean? Does it mean that slaughterhouses can't kill cattle to provide steaks or hamburgers? Does it mean that the police cannot shoot to kill a terrorist trying to drive a tanker truck into a high-rise building? Does it mean that a soldier cannot fire a missile at an enemy artillery site? Does it mean that a pilot cannot drop a bomb in an area that may include civilians? Does it mean that a doctor cannot administer a fatal drug to a prisoner who was convicted of multiple murders? The point is that although it represents a noble ideal, "Thou shalt not kill" is too ambiguous to serve as an enforceable criminal statute.

Contrast the wording of the commandment with the language of Section 210.1(1) of the Model Penal Code, which states: "A person is guilty of criminal **homicide** if he purposely, knowingly, recklessly, or negligently causes the death of another human being."

Homicide
An act by one human being that causes the death of another human being. To be considered a crime, the act must have been done purposely, knowingly, recklessly, or negligently.

Unlike the biblical command, this provision explicitly requires the victim be a "human being." It is thus clear that slaughterhouse employees are not subject to the statute when they kill cattle. But what about a situation in which someone causes the death of a fetus while it is still in the womb? That question is addressed in Section 210.0 of the Model Code, which defines a human being as "a person who has been born and is alive."[2] However, some states, such as Illinois (a state in which abortion is legal), have created special crimes such as intentional homicide of an unborn child,[3] voluntary manslaughter of an unborn child,[4] and involuntary homicide manslaughter and reckless homicide of an unborn child,[5] to fill this gap.

---

[2]The Supreme Court in *Dobbs v. Jackson Women's Health Organization*, 142 S.Ct. 2228 (2022) reversed *Roe v. Wade*, 410 U.S. 114 (1973), holding that the Constitution does not prohibit the states from regulating or prohibiting abortions. In response, several states have enacted anti-abortion laws. Readers should check to see their laws since there is a large variation among the states.

[3]720 ILCS 5/9-1.2.

[4]720 ILCS 5/9-2.1.

[5]720 ILCS 5/9-3.

Criminal codes also are divided into subsections that identify defenses to criminal charges. For example, Section 2.10 of the Model Penal Code states: "It is an affirmative defense that the actor, in engaging in the conduct charged to constitute an offense, does no more than execute an order of his superior in the armed services which he does not know to be unlawful," and Section 3.03(d) relieves people of criminal responsibility when they are following "the law governing the armed services or the lawful conduct of war." Other parts of Section 3.03 release police and official executioners of criminal responsibility when their conduct is required or authorized by "(a) the law defining the duties or functions of a public officer or the assistance to be rendered to such officer in the performance of his duties; or (b) the law governing the execution of legal process; or (c) the judgment or order of a competent court or tribunal; . . . or (e) any other provision of law imposing a public duty." We will discuss these and other defenses in greater detail in Chapter 7.

Most criminal codes subdivide homicide into crimes with labels such as murder, manslaughter, and negligent homicide. The primary difference between them is typically related to the state of mind of the perpetrator. (See the discussion of *mens rea* in Chapter 2.) **Murder** generally requires that the act has been committed purposefully or knowingly, but it may also include some situations where it can be shown the person acted recklessly "under circumstances manifesting extreme indifference to the value of human life."[6] **Manslaughter** usually applies where the act was committed recklessly or "under the influence of extreme mental or emotional disturbance for which there is reasonable explanation or excuse."[7] Then, as the name implies, **negligent homicide** involves negligent acts that result in someone's death.

Under federal law, there are two types of homicide: murder and manslaughter. Murder is defined as the "unlawful killing of a human being with **malice aforethought**,"[8] whereas manslaughter is the "unlawful killing of a human being without malice."[9] This is the same approach that was taken at common law.

The term "malice aforethought" is a technical legal term. "Malice" does not mean hatred or ill will toward the victim; rather, it refers to the conscious desire to cause serious injury or death. "Aforethought" includes both a premeditated, planned killing and a homicide in which the perpetrator's intent existed immediately prior to the commission of the act. Thus, malice aforethought is the level of intent shown by the actor's premeditation, the cruelty or conscious disregard for the safety of others, or the demonstrated intent to commit another felony. Because the term "malice aforethought" appears to be ambiguous, most modern criminal codes do not employ it and instead use an approach similar to that of the Model Penal Code in defining the specific intent element of first-degree murder.

Federal law further subdivides homicides into subcategories. Manslaughter is divided into two different offenses. Voluntary manslaughter is the killing of a

Murder
A homicide that was committed purposefully, knowingly, or where the person acted recklessly with extreme indifference to the value of human life.

Manslaughter
A homicide where the act was committed recklessly or under the influence of extreme mental or emotional disturbance.

Negligent homicide
A homicide based on a negligent act.

Malice aforethought
The level of intent shown by the actor's premeditation, the cruelty or conscious disregard for the safety of others or the intent to commit another felony.

---

[6] ALI Model Penal Code, §210.2(1)(b).

[7] ALI Model Penal Code, §210.3(1)(b).

[8] 18 U.S.C. §1111(a).

[9] 18 U.S.C. §1112(a).

human being upon a sudden quarrel or in the heat of passion. Involuntary manslaughter is the killing in "the commission of an unlawful act not amounting to a felony, or in the commission in an unlawful manner, or without due caution and circumspection, of a lawful act which might produce death."[10]

Murder is likewise divided into two degrees. Murder in the first degree is a homicide (a) that is willful, deliberate, malicious, and premeditated; (b) committed in the perpetration of one of a list of other crimes (e.g., arson, escape, murder, kidnapping, treason, espionage, sabotage, aggravated sexual abuse, sexual abuse, child abuse, burglary, robbery, or child torture); or (c) a premeditated design to kill a different human being than the actual victim. Murder in the second degree is "[a]ny other murder that is not murder in the first-degree."[11]

Felony murder
The unintended killing of a human being that occurs during the commission of another felony. The intent to commit the felony transfers to the killing to give rise to first-degree murder.

Transferred intent doctrine
The concept of transferring the *mens rea* from one crime to another.

In essence, first-degree murder under federal law is any murder that is either premeditated or a specific type of **felony murder**. Felony murder is the unintended killing of a human being that occurs during the commission of another felony. The intent to commit the felony transfers to the killing, giving rise to the offense of first-degree murder. The concept of transferring the *mens rea* from one crime to another is called the **transferred intent doctrine**. Most jurisdictions recognize this doctrine and include felony murder as a basis for first-degree murder.

Two highly publicized cases from Minnesota illustrate the relationship between murder and manslaughter. The first, involved the death of George Floyd in May 2020. In responding to a complaint that Floyd had passed a counterfeit $20 bill, four Minneapolis policemen found him sitting in his car across the street from the store in which he had supposedly used the counterfeit bill. After questioning Floyd, police handcuffed him and instructed him to get into the back of a police car. When he refused to do so, police officer Derek Chauvin forced him to the ground and knelt on the back of Floyd's neck. Another officer knelt on Floyd's legs to make it harder for him to move while Chauvin's knee was pressing against his neck. For over eight minutes, the two officers continued to kneel on Floyd, even though Floyd protested that he couldn't breathe, civilian bystanders pleaded for Chauvin to let him up, and a third police officer at the scene urged Chauvin to stop and check Floyd's pulse. When the two officers finally got off him, Floyd was no longer breathing and had no pulse. The medical examiner testified that Floyd died from asphyxia from the pressure on his neck.

The Minnesota Attorney General's Office charged Chauvin and the three other policemen with both murder and manslaughter. The charges in the criminal complaint against Officer Tou Thao appears in Exhibit 3.1. Chauvin's trial was separated from the trial of the other three policemen, and a jury convicted him of both murder and manslaughter. The judge sentenced him to 22 years in prison.[12] Prosecutors dropped the murder charges for the other three officers, but proceeded toward a trial on the manslaughter charges, on the basis that they had not intervened to stop Chauvin from kneeling on Floyd's neck.[13]

---

[10] 18 U.S.C. §1112(a).

[11] 18 U.S.C. §1111(a).

[12] Chauvin pleaded guilty to a federal charge of violating Floyd's civil rights and was sentenced to 21 years.

[13] The three other officers were convicted in federal court and were sentenced to 2-1/2 to 3-1/2 years. One pleaded guilty to state charges and was sentenced to 3 years while the other two are awaiting a state court trial.

Exhibit 3.1: Charge Against Officer in Connection with George Floyd's Death

State of Minnesota
County of Hennepin

District Court
4th Judicial District

Prosecutor File No. 33.EC55.0227
Court File No. 27-CR-20-12949

State of Minnesota,
Plaintiff,
vs.
TOU THAO DOB: 01/02/1986
1311 130th Lane NW
Coon Rapids, MN 55448
Defendant.

COMPLAINT
Warrant

The Complainant submits this complaint to the Court and states that there is probable cause to believe Defendant committed the following offense(s):

COUNT I

Charge: Aiding and Abetting Second Degree Murder - Unintentional - While Committing A Felony
Minnesota Statute: 609.19.2(1), with reference to: 609.05.1
Maximum Sentence: Imprisonment of not more than 40 years.
Offense Level: Felony

Offense Date (on or about): 05/25/2020

Control #(ICR#): 20200338

Charge Description: That on or about May 25, 2020, in Hennepin County, Minnesota, Tou Thao intentionally aided, advised, hired, counseled, or conspired with or otherwise procured the other to commit the crime, namely causing the death of a human being, George Floyd, without intent to effect the death of any person, while committing or attempting to commit a felony offense other than criminal sexual conduct in the first or second degree with force or violence or a drive-by shooting, namely assault in the third degree.

COUNT II

Charge: Aiding and Abetting Second Degree Manslaughter - Culpable Negligence Creating Unreasonable Risk
Minnesota Statute: 609.205(1), with reference to: 609.05.1
Maximum Sentence: Imprisonment of not more than 10 years, or payment of a fine of not more than $20,000, or both.
Offense Level: Felony

Offense Date (on or about): 05/25/2020

Control #(ICR#): 20200338

Charge Description: That on or about May 25, 2020, in Hennepin County, Tou Thao intentionally aided, advised, hired, counseled, or conspired with or otherwise procured the other to commit the crime, namely caused the death of another, George Floyd, by his culpable negligence, creating an unreasonable risk and consciously took the chances of causing death or great bodily harm to another, George Floyd.

The second high-profile case occurred in a Minneapolis suburb later that same year, when a Brooklyn Park police officer, Kimberly Potter, shot and killed 20-year-old Daunte Wright when he jumped into his car and tried to drive away during a traffic stop. Potter, a 26-year veteran police officer, claimed that she had intended to use her taser rather than her service revolver, but mistakenly drew and fired her gun instead. Film from body cameras worn by the police officers revealed that Potter was yelling "Taser, taser, taser" while she was firing her gun.

Potter was charged with first- and second-degree manslaughter.[14] Testimony at her trial established that she had undergone extensive training on use of both her service revolver and her taser; and that the revolver and the taser were made of different materials, had different weights, and were kept on different sides of her belt. The jury convicted her of both first- and second-degree manslaughter.[15]

2. SUICIDE

Suicide
The deliberate termination of one's own life.

Although it makes little sense to bring criminal charges against a dead person who successfully committed **suicide**, the Model Penal Code has a crime designated as "Causing or Aiding Suicide." Section 210.5 creates a felony when a person purposely causes another to commit suicide by "force, duress or deception," and a misdemeanor where "force, duress or deception" was not present. States have taken a variety of approaches to address this issue. For instance, the Illinois law on suicide requires either coercion or "with knowledge that another person intends to commit or attempt to commit suicide, intentionally (i) offers and provides the physical means by which another person commits or attempts to commit suicide, or (ii) participates in a physical act by which another person commits or attempts to commit suicide."[16]

In contrast, Oregon became the first state to legalize assisted suicide when voters approved a 1994 referendum enacting the Oregon Death with Dignity Act.[17] This law exempts from civil or criminal liability state-licensed physicians who dispense or prescribe a lethal dose of drugs upon the request of a terminally ill patient.

---

[14]In Minnesota, first-degree manslaughter requires that the defendant commits or attempts to commit an offense where death or great bodily harm was "reasonably foreseeable." Second-degree manslaughter requires that "culpable negligence" that creates an "unreasonable risk" of causing death or great bodily harm."

720 ILCS 5/12-31.

Ore. Rev. Stat. §§127.800 *et seq.* (2003).

[15]Kimberly Potter was sentenced to two years in prison.

[16]720 ILCS 5/12-31.

[17]Ore. Rev. Stat. §§127.800 *et seq.* (2003).

APPLICATION EXERCISES

After reviewing the facts of the Bud Cook Hypothetical Case (*see* p. xxxvii), answer the following questions:

1. Setting aside questions of drunk driving and leaving the scene of an accident, was Cook guilty of any of the homicide-related provisions in the Model Penal Code?
2. Which, if any, of these crimes would a prosecutor be most likely to file? Why?
3. What additional information would the prosecutor want to have before deciding on the charges?
4. After you locate and read the section of your own state's criminal code that covers these types of crimes, answer the following:
   a. What are the citations for these sections?
   b. How do your state's laws on homicide differ from those of the Model Penal Code?
   c. How do your state's laws on homicide differ from federal law?

3. ASSAULT AND BATTERY

A second category of offenses involving danger to the person focuses on bodily harm that doesn't involve death. It includes crimes such as assault, battery, intimidation, stalking, and reckless endangerment.

Although charges of assault and battery often arise from a single incident, assault and battery involves different types of actions. At common law, **assault** was defined as a willful attempt or threat to inflict injury upon another person, while **battery** involved intentional physical contact that was either offensive or harmful. The physical contact can be direct, person-to-person contact, or contact with an object that is held or thrown by another person.

Assault
An act that causes or attempts to cause serious bodily harm to another individual.

Battery
An act of intentional physical contact that is either offensive or harmful to another person.

At common law assault and battery were considered both crimes and torts. In other words, the offender could be prosecuted criminally and, if found guilty, be punished by fine or imprisonment. Alternatively, the victim could sue the perpetrator in civil court for damages. Some state criminal codes classify assault and battery as separate crimes, whereas other state codes, federal laws, and the Model Penal Code include battery as a type of assault. For instance, in the State of New York, conduct known at common law as a battery is characterized as an assault. See Exhibit 3.2 for a sample of an assault charge brought in New York.

In most states, simple assault and battery are classified as misdemeanors, and aggravated assault and battery are felonies. Note how the Model Penal Code defines simple and aggravated assault:

Exhibit 3.2: New York Assault Charge

Actor Russell Crowe was charged with assault for hitting a hotel employee with a telephone and unlawfully possessing a firearm. Crowe pleaded guilty to reduced misdemeanor charges and was fined $160. The judge placed Crowe on conditional discharge, thereby requiring that the actor not be arrested for one year. The criminal complaint follows:

CRIMINAL COURT OF THE CITY OF NEW YORK
COUNTY OF NEW YORK

Page 1 of 1

THE PEOPLE OF THE STATE OF NEW YORK -against- 1. Russell Crowe (M 41) 549751 Defendant.	FELONY ADA SJOQUIST [redacted]

Police Officer Malika Simmons, shield 12871 of the 001 Precinct, states as follows:

On June 6, 2005, at about 04:20 hours at 147 Mercer Street in the County and State of New York, the Defendant committed the offenses of:

1. PL120.05(2) Assault in the Second Degree (1 count)
2. PL265.01(2) Criminal Possession of a Weapon in the Fourth Degree (1 count)

the defendant, with intent to cause physical injury to another person, caused such injury to another person by means of a dangerous instrument; and the defendant possessed a dangerous or deadly instrument with intent to use it unlawfully against another.

The offenses were committed under the following circumstances:

Deponent states that she is informed by an individual whose name and address are known to the District Attorney's Office that informant is a concierge at the Mercer Hotel and that defendant picked up a telephone and threw it at informant, hitting him in the face and causing a laceration and substantial pain.

Deponent states that she observed informant's injury and that defendant admitted that he picked up the phone and threw it at informant because he was angry.

False statements made herein are punishable as a class A misdemeanor pursuant to section 210.45 of the penal law.

Deponent ____________________ Date and Time ____________________

§211.1 (1) Simple Assault

A person is guilty of assault if he:

(a) attempts to cause or purposely, knowingly or recklessly causes bodily injury to another, or

(b) negligently causes bodily injury to another with a deadly weapon; or

(c) attempts by fear or menace to put another in fear of imminent serious bodily injury.

§211.1(2) Aggravated Assault

A person is guilty of aggravated assault if he:

(a) attempts to cause serious bodily injury to another, or causes such injury purposely, knowingly or recklessly under circumstances manifesting extreme indifference to the value of human life; or

(b) attempts to cause or purposely or knowingly causes bodily injury to another with a deadly weapon.

Under Illinois law, persons are guilty of aggravated battery if they intentionally or knowingly causes "great bodily harm, or permanent disability or disfigurement." Persons are also guilty of aggravated battery if they know the person harmed to be a peace officer, fireman, teacher, or other specified types of public service workers.[18] The Illinois statutes go further to create separate crimes for aggravated battery with a firearm, aggravated battery with a machine gun or a gun with a silencer, aggravated battery of a child, aggravated battery of a person with intellectual disability, aggravated battery of an unborn child, and aggravated battery of a senior citizen.[19]

Throughout this chapter, we will provide you with examples of situations in which people have been charged with violating these types of crimes. Exhibit 3.2 is a copy of the assault charge filed against actor Russell Crowe.

4. INTIMIDATION, STALKING, AND ENDANGERMENT

Notice that part (c) of the Model Code's definition of simple assault includes "attempts by fear or menace to put another in fear of imminent serious bodily injury." This wording is designed to cover the concept of **intimidation**, which involves putting someone in fear of something bad happening to them, their loved ones, or their property. Synonyms for "intimidation" are *coercion*, *extortion*, and *duress*.

Intimidation
An act which involves putting someone in fear of something bad happening to them, their loved ones, or their property. Sometimes referred to as "coercion," "extortion," or "duress."

Many states have a separate statute making intimidation a crime. Take note of how it is defined in the following excerpt from the Illinois Criminal Code:

5/12-6 Intimidation

(a) A person commits intimidation when, with intent to cause another to perform or to omit the performance of any act, he or she communicates to

---

[18] 720 ILSC 5/12-4.

[19] 720 ILSC 5/12-4.2, 5/12-4.2-5, 5/12-4.3, 5/12-4.4, & 5/12-4.7.

another, whether in person, directly or indirectly, a threat to perform without lawful authority any of the following acts:

(1) Inflict physical harm on the person threatened or any other person or on property; or

(2) Subject any person to physical confinement or restraint; or

(3) Commit a felony or Class A misdemeanor; or

(4) Accuse any person of an offense; or

(5) Expose any person to hatred, contempt or ridicule; or

(6) Take action as a public official against anyone or anything, or withhold official action, or cause such action or withholding; or

(7) Bring about or continue a strike, boycott or other collective action.[20]

Illinois goes on to define aggravated intimidation as committing the above defined crimes in furtherance of organized gang activities or where the person being intimidated is a peace officer, firefighter, correctional official, or community policing volunteer.[21]

Stalking
The act of harassing another person in a manner that would cause a reasonable person to fear for his or her own safety, the safety of another person, or suffer other emotional distress.

Consider also the crime of **stalking**. At one time, this offense was limited to situations in which the perpetrator by surveilling another person created a reasonable apprehension in that person of physical harm. The scope of this offense has broadened. For instance, Illinois now defines stalking as a course of conduct directed at a specific person when "he or she knows or should know that this course of conduct would cause a reasonable person to fear for his or her own safety or the safety of a third person; or suffer other emotional distress."[22] It can become aggravated stalking if it violates an order of protection, involves actual confinement of the victim, or causes bodily harm to the victim.[23]

In California, persons are guilty of stalking when they harass another person and "make a credible threat with the intent to place that person in reasonable fear for his or her safety, or the safety of his or her immediate family."[24] Repeated stalking episodes involving the same victim or violations of a court order result in greater penalties.[25] While many stalking cases involve defendants that have had relationships with their victims, it is not uncommon for the California statute to be enforced against celebrity stalkers. A woman pleaded no contest in 2005 to stalking and threatening the actress Catherine Zeta-Jones. That same year, an Idaho man who obsessively followed Mel Gibson claimed that he was on a mission from God to pray with the movie star. He was convicted under the California stalking law.

Another type of application of the intimidation concept can be found in Section 211.3 of the Model Penal Code:

[20] 720 ILSC 5/12-6.

[21] 720 ILSC 5/12-6.2

[22] 720 ILSC 5/12-7.3.

[23] 720 ILSC 5/12-7.4.

[24] Cal Pen Code §646.9(a).

[25] Cal Pen Code §646.9(b).

§211.3 Terroristic Threats

A person is guilty of a felony of the third-degree if he threatens to commit any crime of violence with purpose to terrorize another or to cause evacuation of a building, place of assembly, or facility of public transportation, or otherwise to cause serious public inconvenience, or in reckless disregard of the risk of causing such terror or inconvenience.

As was the case with homicides, assaults and batteries are usually prosecuted by local law enforcement officials. Federal law enforcement officials would be more likely to get involved where threats were related to federal officials or terrorism and where intimidation was related to organized crime or civil rights activities. Section 245 of Title 18 of the U.S. Code prohibits force or threat of force that injures, intimidates, or interferes with any person exercising their federal civil rights, and the Racketeer Influence and Corrupt Organizations Act (RICO)[26] covers various organized crime activities. A federal jury convicted Dzhokhar Tsarnaev with using a "weapon of mass destruction" and maliciously destroying property, resulting in death, in the 2013 Boston Marathon bombings. Tsarnaev received a death sentence.[27]

5. KIDNAPPING AND FALSE IMPRISONMENT

Crimes such as kidnapping, unlawful restraint, forcible detention, false imprisonment, and child abduction all involve seizing someone or detaining someone against their will. False imprisonment is also a common law tort. Therefore, the offender may not only be prosecuted in the criminal justice system but also be sued for damages in a state court action brought by the victim. Note how the crimes of kidnapping, felonious restraint, and false imprisonment are defined in the Model Penal Code:

§212.1 Kidnapping

A person is guilty of kidnapping if he unlawfully removes another from his place of residence or business, or a substantial distance from the vicinity where he is found, or if he unlawfully confines another for a substantial period in a place of isolation, with any of the following purposes:

(a) to hold for ransom or reward, or as a shield or hostage; or

(b) to facilitate commission of any felony or flight thereafter; or

(c) to inflict bodily injury on or to terrorize the victim or another; or

(d) to interfere with the performance of any governmental or political function.

---

[26]18 U.S.C. §§1961 *et seq.*

[27]The Supreme Court upheld the death sentence in this case. See *United States v. Tsarnaev*, 142 S. Ct. 1024 (2022). However, it is questionable whether Tsarnaev will actually be put to death. Before the Supreme Court heard oral argument in Tsarnaev's case, President Joe Biden ordered a moratorium on carrying out federal death sentences. Even though as a presidential candidate Biden had pledged to end the federal death penalty, the President did not direct the Department of Justice to reverse its position on capital punishment in this case.

§212.2 Felonious Restraint

A person commits a felony of the third degree if he knowingly:

(a) restrains another unlawfully in circumstances exposing him to risk of serious bodily injury; or

(b) holds another in a condition of involuntary servitude.

§212.3 False Imprisonment

A person commits a misdemeanor if he knowingly restrains another unlawfully so as to interfere substantially with his liberty.

As most people know from newspapers and television, the federal government often gets involved in kidnapping cases where there is reason to believe the victim may have been taken across state lines. A notable example is the Elizabeth Smart case, involving the kidnapping and repeated sexual assault of a 14-year-old girl. In 2013, a federal jury found the perpetrator, Brian David Mitchell, guilty of one count of kidnapping and one count of illegally transporting a minor across state lines for sexual purposes. He was sentenced to life imprisonment without the possibility of parole. Mitchell's wife, Wanda Barzee, pleaded guilty to state and federal charges and was sentenced to concurrent terms of 15 years in federal and state prison.

6. SEX OFFENSES

Many criminal codes have a separate section on sex-related crimes ranging from rape and sexual assault to prostitution and public indecency. While acts of sexual assault clearly cause physical and mental harm to the victim, crimes such as prostitution may involve willing participants who do not see themselves as being victimized. When this argument is made, the laws in question are often justified on the basis that they protect against criminal elements that force vulnerable people into participating in sexual acts, and that they preserve the "moral values" of the community.[28]

Common law rape
Non-consensual sexual intercourse between a male and a female.

Statutory rape
An act of sexual intercourse (even if consensual) with a person under a certain age.

Sexual assault and sexual exploitation of children are usually considered the most heinous sex crimes. At common law, **rape** was defined as non-consensual sexual intercourse between a male and a female who was not his wife.

Statutory rape was created to outlaw sexual intercourse with a person under a certain age, even if it was *consensual.*

The Model Penal Code follows the common law tradition of defining the crime of rape in terms of males having non-consensual sexual intercourse with females who are not their wives.[29] It then goes on to define a crime called "Deviate Sexual Intercourse by Force or Imposition" that is gender-neutral and does not exclude spouses,[30] and another crime, labeled "Sexual Assault," that covers other forms of non-consensual sexual contact (but still excludes

---

[28] See the discussion on victimless crimes on pp. 78-81.

[29] ALI Model Penal Code, §213.1.

[30] ALI Model Penal Code, §213.2.

spouses).[31] The concept of statutory rape is incorporated into the Model Code by expanding the definition of rape to include consensual intercourse with a female who is less than ten years old[32] and by creating a crime called "Corruption of Minors and Seduction."[33]

While the Model Code continues to define rape in terms of a male having intercourse with a female and it doesn't apply to a husband forcing himself on his wife, in recent years, many states have revised their rape laws to make them sex-neutral and to remove the exemption for having non-consensual sex with a spouse. Illinois, for example, has replaced the crime of rape with criminal sexual assault and aggravated criminal sexual assault. Notice how it covers female perpetrators as well as males and how it incorporates age limitations found in statutory rape laws.

720 ILCS 5/11-1.50 Criminal Sexual Abuse

(a) A person commits criminal sexual abuse if that person:

(1) Commits an act of sexual conduct by the use of force or threat of force; or

(2) Commits an act of sexual conduct and knows that the victim is unable to understand the nature of the act or is unable to give knowing consent.

(b) A person commits criminal sexual abuse if that person is under 17 years of age and commits an act of sexual penetration or sexual conduct with a victim who is at least 9 years of age but under 17 years of age.

(c) A person commits criminal sexual abuse if that person commits an act of sexual penetration or sexual conduct with a victim who is at least 13 years of age but under 17 years of age and the person is less than 5 years older than the victim.

720 ILCS 5/11-1.20 Criminal Sexual Assault

(a) Accused person commits criminal sexual assault if that person commits an act of sexual penetration and:

(1) uses force or threat of force; or

(2) knows that the victim is unable to understand the nature of the act or is unable to give knowing consent; or

(3) is a family member of the victim, and the victim is under 18 years of age; or

(4) is 17 years of age or over and holds a position of trust, authority or supervision in relation to the victim, and the victim who is at least 13 years of age but under 18 years of age.

Acts of criminal sexual assault become aggravated criminal sexual assault when a weapon is displayed or use of a weapon is threatened, when the act causes bodily harm, when the victim is age 60 or older, or several other listed

---

[31] ALI Model Penal Code, §213.4.

[32] ALI Model Penal Code, §213.1(1(d)).

[33] ALI Model Penal Code, §213.3.

factors are present.[34] Criminal sexual abuse is likewise elevated to the more serious offense of aggravated criminal sexual abuse when certain aggravating factors are present.[35] One count of an Illinois multicount indictment for aggravated criminal sexual assault appears in Exhibit 3.3.

Other laws involving sexual behavior are designed to protect children and young adults from sexual exploitation. In addition to prohibiting direct sexual activity with minors, these laws prohibit the production and distribution of child pornography and the recruitment of children to work in the sex industry.

Exhibit 3.3: Illinois Aggravated Criminal Sexual Abuse Indictment (Count 2)

In February 2019, a Cook County, Illinois, grand jury charged the Grammy-winning R & B artist R. Kelly with 10 counts of aggravated criminal sexual abuse. One count of the indictment appears below. Please note that this is the format used in Illinois. Other jurisdictions may use a different style. Although Kelly has been tried in federal criminal cases since then, this case had not yet gone to trial when this book went to press.

The Grand Jurors chosen, selected and sworn, in and for the County of Cook, in the State of Illinois, in the name and by the authority of the People of the State of Illinois, upon their oath present that between May 01, 2009 and January 31, 2010 at and within the County of Cook

Robert Kelly

Committed the offense of AGGRAVATED CRIMINAL SEXUAL ABUSE

IN THAT HE KNOWINGLY COMMITTED AN ACT OF SEXUAL PENETRATION UPON J.P. TO WIT: CONTACT BETWEEN ROBERT KELLY'S PENIS AND J.P.'S SEX ORGAN, AND J.P. WAS A LEAST THIRTEEN (13) YEARS OF AGE BUT UNDER SEVENTEEN (17) YEARS OF AGE, AND ROBERT KELLY WAS AT LEAST FIVE (5) YEARS OLDER THAN J.P.,

AND THE STATUTE OF LIMITATIONS FOR THIS PROSECUTION IS EXTENDED PURSUANT TO 720 ILLINOIS COMPILED STATUTES ACT 5 SECTION 3-6(J) (2003) IN THAT J.P. WAS UNDER THE AGE OF EIGHTEEN (18) AT THE TIME OF THE COMMISSION OF THE OFFENSE, AND THIS PROSECUTION WAS COMMENCED WITHIN TWENTY (20) YEARS OF J.P.'S EIGHTEENTH BIRTHDAY.

IN VIOLATION OF CHAPTER 720 ACT SECTION 12-16(D) OF THE ILLINOIS COMPILED STATUTES 1992 AS AMENDED AND

Contrary to the Statute and against the peace and dignity of the same People of the State of Illinois.

COUNT NUMBER 2
CASE NUMBER 19CR-2760
CHARGE ID CODE: 0999700

---

[34] 720 ILSC 5/11-1.30.

[35] 720 ILSC 5/11-1.60 (formerly 720 ILSC 5/12-16).

These child exploitation situations received a good deal of public attention with the prosecutions of R. Kelly[36] and Jeffrey Epstein. The U.S. Attorney charged Epstein, a wealthy money manager, of multiple counts of sex trafficking, alleging that Epstein and Ghislaine Maxwell, an adult female friend, lured underage young girls into having sexual relations with him and his friends. Epstein committed suicide before his case went to trial. A federal jury found Maxwell guilty in December 2021 on charges of (1) conspiracy to entice minors to travel to engage in illegal sex acts; (2) conspiracy to transport minors with intent to engage in criminal sexual activity; (3) transportation of a minor with intent to engage in criminal sexual activity; (4) sex trafficking conspiracy; and (5) sex trafficking of a minor.

APPLICATION EXERCISES

After reviewing the facts of the Clay Marshall Hypothetical Case (*see* pp. xxxviii-xxxix), answer the following questions:

5. Are there any significant factual differences between the facts alleged in Count 2 of the R. Kelly indictment and Marshall's case? If so, what are the key differences?

6. Assuming that the Marshall hypothetical case occurred in Illinois, identify the criminal statute that applies.

Pop icon Michael Jackson was charged with and acquitted of statutory rape.[37] The felony complaint against him alleged multiple violations of the following statute:

Cal Pen Code §288 Lewd or Lascivious Acts Involving Children

Any person who willfully and lewdly commits any lewd or lascivious act, including any of the acts constituting other crimes provided for in Part 1, upon or with the body, or any part or member thereof, of a child who is under the age of 14 years, with the intent of arousing, appealing to, or gratifying the lust, passions, or sexual desires of that person or the child, is guilty of a felony and shall be punished by imprisonment in the state prison for three, six, or eight years.

Whereas crimes against prostitution and obscenity are often classified as crimes against public order and decency, laws against child pornography are usually justified in terms of protecting children from being harmed in the making and distribution of these materials. Over a decade before he was indicted for aggravated criminal sexual abuse, Cook County prosecutors charged R. Kelly with 21 counts of child pornography, alleging that he videotaped himself having

[36] A New York federal jury convicted Kelly of racketeering and sex trafficking. A Chicago federal jury found him guilty of producing child pornography and enticing a minor to engage in sexual activity. Kelly faces similar charges filed in Illinois and Minnesota. He is serving a 30-year sentence in the New York case and awaits sentencing in the Chicago case.

[37] *People v. Jackson* (Superior Court of California, Santa Barbara County Case No. 1133603).

sex with an underaged girl. Neither the girl appearing on the tape nor her parents testified at trial. In 2008, a jury found him not guilty. In 2019, federal prosecutors in Chicago charged with creating and receiving child pornography, enticing minors into illegal sexual activity, and obstruction of justice in the Illinois 2008 child pornography case. In 2022, a federal jury found Kelly guilty of producing child pornography as well as enticing a minor to engage in sexual activity and acquitted him of the obstruction charge.

7. VIOLATION OF CIVIL RIGHTS, HATE CRIMES, AND TERRORISM

The federal criminal code includes two key provisions designed to protect people's civil rights. These laws were first passed in 1909 and then revised several times. These statutes proved to be very important tools in the civil rights movement in the 1960s and 1970s, when some local law enforcement officials turned their back on violent crimes that were being committed against African Americans and civil rights advocates.[38]

18 U.S.C.S. §241 Conspiracy Against Rights

If two or more persons conspire to injure, oppress, threaten, or intimidate any person in any State, Territory, Commonwealth, Possession, or District in the free exercise or enjoyment of any right or privilege secured to him by the Constitution or laws of the United States, or because of his having so exercised the same; or

If two or more persons go in disguise on the highway, or on the premises of another, with intent to prevent or hinder his free exercise or enjoyment of any right or privilege so secured—They shall be fined under this title or imprisoned not more than ten years, or both; and if death results from the acts committed in violation of this section or if such acts include kidnapping or an attempt to kidnap, aggravated sexual abuse or an attempt to commit aggravated sexual abuse, or an attempt to kill, they shall be fined under this title or imprisoned for any term of years or for life, or both, or may be sentenced to death.

Hate crime
A prejudice-motivated crime in which the offender intentionally targets the victim because of the victim's membership in a particular social or demographic group.

Hate crimes laws are designed to place additional criminal responsibility on offenders who commit crimes that are motivated by hatred toward the victim on the basis of prejudice against a group to which the victim belongs. Examples include burning a cross in front of the home of an African American family, assaulting someone because of the victim's sexual orientation, or setting fire to a mosque. The Kentucky hate crime statute provides, in part, as follows:

KRS 532.031 Hate crimes—Finding—Effect—Definitions

(1) A person may be found by the sentencing judge to have committed an offense specified below as a result of a **hate crime** if the person intentionally because of race, color, religion, sexual orientation, or national origin of another individual or group of individuals . . . , violates a provision of any one (1) of the following: . . .

Not only do the states have hate crime statutes, but the federal government has enacted hate crime legislation as well.[39]

[38]The movie *Mississippi Burning* deals with how these laws were used by the Federal Bureau of Investigation (FBI) and federal prosecutors in Mississippi in the 1960s.

[39]18 U.S.C. § 249.

In 2020, a father, his adult son, and their neighbor, William Bryan, attempted to stop and question Ahmaud Arbery, a 25-year-old African American man who was jogging through their upscale neighborhood in a coastal area of Georgia. When the jogger failed to stop, they chased and fatally shot him.

Following their homicide convictions in state court, the three white men were tried in federal court for committing a federal hate crime.[40] The federal prosecutors introduced evidence of the defendants' racially biased postings on social media to establish that their actions had been motivated by racial bias. A portion of the federal indictment against Bryan appears in Exhibit 3.4.

Exhibit 3.4: Federal Hate Crime Indictment (Count Two)

COUNT TWO
Interference with Rights
18 U.S.C. § 245(b)(2)(B) and § 2

On or about February 23, 2020, in Glynn County, in the Southern District of Georgia, defendant **WILLIAM "RODDIE" BRYAN**, while aiding and abetting Travis and Gregory McMichael, did willfully, by force and threat of force, injure, intimidate, and interfere with Ahmaud Arbery, an African American man, because of Arbery's race and color, and because he was and had been enjoying a facility provided and administered by a state and subdivision thereof; specifically, as Arbery was running on a public street in the Satilla Shores neighborhood of Brunswick, Georgia, **WILLIAM "RODDIE" BRYAN** got into a truck and chased Arbery through the public streets of the neighborhood, and used his truck to cut off Arbery's route.

The offense:

a. Included the use, attempted use, and threatened use of a dangerous weapon (a truck); and

b. Included an attempt to kidnap, in that **WILLIAM "RODDIE" BRYAN** attempted to forcibly hold and detain Arbery against his will.

All in violation of Title 18, United States Code, Sections 245(b)(2)(B), and 2.

[40]Although the defendants were sentenced to life imprisonment for homicide, they were eligible for parole after 10 years. The U.S. Attorney's Office brought charges to increase the period of imprisonment.

As was the case in the death of the Georgia jogger, federal prosecutors brought hate crime charges against the Minneapolis police officers involved in George Floyd's death. Derek Chauvin, the officer who had been kneeling on Floyd's neck, pleaded guilty to the federal charges following his state conviction for murder. The other three officers were tried and convicted of violating the federal hate crimes act prior to being tried on state manslaughter charges.[41]

Penalty enhancement statute
A law providing for a stiffer penalty for the violation of a criminal statute due to the presence of an aggravating factor, such as the age or race of the victim, the heinous nature of the offense, or other circumstances.

Penalty enhancement statutes provide another tool that prosecutors can use to increase the punishment for hate crimes. These statutes provide for a stiffer penalty if the jury finds that the crime victim had been specifically selected on the basis of race, religion, color, disability, sexual orientation, national origin, or ancestry.[42] Penalty enhancement statutes also are employed in other circumstances besides hate crimes. We will explore the general concept of penalty enhancement when we discuss sentencing in Chapter 13.

Following the September 11, 2001, terrorist attacks on the World Trade Center and the Pentagon, Congress amended the U.S. Code to include the crime of "international terrorism," defined as "violent acts or acts dangerous to human life that are a violation of the criminal laws of the United States or of any State, or that would be a criminal violation if committed within the jurisdiction of the United States or of any State . . . intended (i) to intimidate or coerce a civilian population; (ii) to influence the policy of a government by intimidation or coercion; or (iii) to affect the conduct of a government by mass destruction, assassination, or kidnapping."[43]

Discussion Questions

1. The Model Penal Code requires proof of some degree of fault to convict someone of homicide. Do you think that a person who causes the death of another should be punished even if he or she did not act in a purposeful, knowing, reckless, or negligent manner?

2. Based on what you read about the death of George Floyd:

a. Do you think Officer Chauvin committed murder? Why or why not?

b. Do you think any of the other three officers involved in Floyd's arrest were guilty of manslaughter? Which ones and why?

3. Based on what you read about the death of Daunte Wright:

a. Do you think Officer Potter committed manslaughter?

b. What crime, if any, would she have committed if she knowingly fired her revolver at him to prevent his escape?

4. During the Vietnam conflict, President Richard Nixon authorized the secret bombing of Cambodia. Critics argued that this action was unconstitutional. Under Section 2.10 of the Model Code, would soldiers carrying out the directives of the president have a defense to homicide charges for the deaths of civilian casualties?

---

[41]The state court judge had approved a motion (filed by the three other officers) to be tried separately from Chauvin, and the federal prosecutors went ahead with their trial before the state trial was ready to begin.

[42]Such statutes were upheld by the U.S. Supreme Court in *Wisconsin v. Mitchell*, 508 U.S. 476 (1993).

[43]18 U.S.C. § 2331(1).

5. If an Illinois physician travels to the state of Oregon for the sole purpose of assisting her terminally ill Illinois patient to commit suicide, should the physician be held accountable under Illinois criminal law for "causing or aiding suicide"?

6. During a bank robbery, a security guard is killed by one of the robbers. If the robbery takes place in a jurisdiction that recognizes the felony murder doctrine, will the getaway car driver be accountable for the homicide? Could the prosecutor charge the people who harbor the robbers a week after the robbery with homicide?

7. The felony assault charge against Russell Crowe was resolved following an amicable resolution of the victim's tort claim. Do you think that it is appropriate for a crime victim to receive compensation for injuries from the defendant when criminal charges remain pending?

8. Sometimes both participants in a fight are charged with assault and battery. Should both participants be charged with crimes? If so, how will the prosecution prove its case?

9. A college football team is particularly rough against its rival during a game, thereby causing injuries to several opposing players. Are they guilty of battery? If a fistfight between the teams breaks out after the game, is there a battery?

10. Celebrities seem to be targets for stalkers. Should a starstruck fan be subjected to criminal penalties simply because he wants to get an autograph and photograph of his favorite actor or singer? Should the paparazzi be arrested for doing their job just because a celebrity doesn't appreciate the invasion of privacy? At what point should there be criminal consequences?

11. In the aftermath of the 9/11/2001 terrorist attacks, should all statements suggesting a terroristic threat be criminal? Is this the case even if the statement was made as a joke? Should there be criminal responsibility if an actor makes what appears to be a terroristic threat to the audience during a performance of a play?

C. Crimes Against Property

The second major category of Model Penal Code crimes is "Offenses Against Property." They include offenses such as arson, criminal damage to property, burglary, trespass, robbery, extortion, forgery, and fraud.

1. ARSON AND OTHER TYPES OF DESTRUCTION OF PROPERTY

Arson occurs when someone "starts a fire or causes an explosion with the purpose of (a) destroying a building or occupied structure of another; or (b) destroying or damaging any property, whether his own or another's, to collect insurance for such loss."[44] Lesser, related offenses include reckless burning or exploding[45] and failure to control or report dangerous fire.[46] The offense of

Arson
An act of starting a fire or causing an explosion with the purpose of destroying or damaging the property of another; or to collect insurance for such loss.

[44] ALI Model Penal Code, §220.1(1).

[45] ALI Model Penal Code, §220.1(2).

[46] ALI Model Penal Code, §220.1(3).

criminal mischief covers damage to property by means that go beyond the use of fire or explosives.[47]

2. TRESPASS AND BURGLARY

Trespass
An unauthorized intrusion onto private land or into a building that belongs to someone else.

In the common law, **trespass** is an unauthorized intrusion onto private land or into a building that belongs to someone else. It is a concept that involves issues of civil liability, as well as potential criminal penalties.

The Model Penal Code defines two types of criminal trespass.

§221.2 Criminal Trespass

(1) *Buildings and Occupied Structures.* A person commits an offense if, knowing that he is not licensed or privileged to do so, he enters or surreptitiously remains in any building or occupied structure, or a separately secured or occupied portion thereof.

(2) *Defiant Trespasser.* A person commits an offense if, knowing that he is not licensed or privileged to do so, he enters or remains in any place as to which notice against trespass is given by:

(a) actual communication to the actor; or

(b) posting in a manner prescribed by law or reasonably likely to come to the attention of intruders; or

(c) fencing or other enclosure manifestly designed to exclude intruders.

Burglary
An act of entering into a building for the purpose of committing a crime.

Whereas trespass is treated as a misdemeanor in the Model Penal Code, burglary is a felony. **Burglary** differs from trespass in that it involves entering for the purpose of committing a crime. Under the common law, the entry had to take place at night and the crime being committed had to be a felony. However, the Model Penal Code and most state statutes are broader than the common law.

§221.1 Burglary

A person is guilty of burglary if he enters a building or occupied structure, or separately secured or occupied portion thereof, with purpose to commit a crime therein, unless the premises are at the time open to the public or the actor is licensed or privileged to enter. It is an affirmative defense to prosecution for burglary that the building or structure was abandoned.

Lesser included offense
A crime whose elements are all included among the elements of the more serious crime being charged.

Note that all of the elements of trespass are included within the offense of burglary. Thus, by definition, a burglar always is a trespasser. A **lesser included offense** is a crime whose elements are all included among the elements of the more serious crime being charged. Under the Model Penal Code, a defendant cannot be convicted of both the serious crime and the lesser included offense for the same conduct.[48]

---

[47]ALI Model Penal Code, §220.3.

[48]ALI Model Penal Code, §1.07(1)(a).

3. THEFT, LARCENY, ROBBERY, AND FRAUD

In the common law, the crime of **larceny** was defined as taking away the goods or property of another without the consent and against the will of the owner or possessor and with a criminal intent to convert the property to the use of someone other than the owner.

Larceny
A crime that involves taking away the goods or property of another without the consent and against the will of the owner or possessor and with a criminal intent to convert the property to the use of someone other than the owner.

The Model Penal Code contains separate offenses for **theft** by unlawful taking or disposition; theft by deception; theft by extortion; theft of property lost, mislaid, or delivered by mistake; and theft of services. Some state statutes list separate offenses for retail theft, library theft, theft of coin-operated machines, unlawful use of recorded sounds or images, and identity theft. There are also laws against falsely reporting a theft, receiving stolen property, and commercial bribery.

Theft
A crime involving taking property without the owner's consent.

A **robbery** occurs when someone uses force or fear to take something of value from the possession of another against that person's wishes. In the Model Penal Code, it is defined as follows:

Robbery
A crime in which someone uses force or fear to take something of value from the possession of another against that person's wishes.

§221.1 Robbery

A person is guilty of robbery if, in the course of committing a theft, he:

(a) inflicts serious bodily injury upon another; or

(b) threatens another with or purposely puts him in fear of immediate serious bodily injury; or

(c) commits or threatens immediately to commit any felony of the first or second degree.

An act shall be deemed "in the course of committing a theft" if it occurs in an attempt to commit theft or in flight after the attempt or commission.

The Model Penal Code contains separate offenses for theft by unlawful taking or disposition; theft by deception; theft by extortion; theft of property lost, mislaid, or delivered by mistake; and theft of services. Some state statutes list separate offenses for retail theft, library theft, theft of coin-operated machines, unlawful use of recorded sounds or images, and identity theft. There are also laws against falsely reporting a theft, receiving stolen property, and commercial bribery.

A sample retail theft complaint appears in Exhibit 3.5. Note how the format of this complaint differs from the New York charging instrument that appears in Exhibit 3.2 and the Illinois indictment appearing in Exhibit 3.3. Each state has its own style of drafting charging instruments. Make sure that you check the format of your state when you draft a criminal law document.

Fraud involves theft through deception. It is an intentional perversion of the truth to induce someone to part with something of value. Rather than physically stealing someone else's property, the offender illegally obtains the victim's property through embezzlement, forgery, false billing, misrepresentation, and other deceptive practices. Fraud is the key component in most forms of white-collar crime.[49] Examples include mail fraud, insurance fraud, identity theft, money laundering, and investment Ponzi schemes like the one run by

Fraud
An act of using deception to commit a theft.

---

[49]See the distinction between white-collar crime and street crime on pp. 26-27.

Exhibit 3.5: California Felony Shoplifting Complaint

The Los Angeles County District Attorney charged actress Winona Ryder with several felonies arising from a shoplifting arrest. Investigators claimed that Ryder cut security tags off merchandise valued at more than $4,000. Ryder was convicted of grand theft and felony vandalism and acquitted of commercial burglary. She was originally sentenced to three years' probation, 480 hours community service, and a court-prescribed counseling program. She was ordered to pay more than $10,000 in fines and restitution. Seven months later, the sentencing judge reduced the charges to misdemeanors and placed her on unsupervised probation. The felony complaint reads, in part, as follows:

SUPERIOR COURT OF THE STATE OF CALIFORNIA
FOR THE COUNTY OF LOS ANGELES

THE PEOPLE OF THE STATE OF CALIFORNIA, Plaintiff, v. 01 WINONA RYDER (10/29/1971) Defendant(s).	CASE NO. SA044291 *FELONY COMPLAINT*

The undersigned is informed and believes that:

COUNT 1

On or about December 12, 2001, in the County of Los Angeles, the crime of SECOND DEGREE COMMERCIAL BURGLARY, in violation of PENAL CODE SECTION 459, a Felony, was committed by WINONA RYDER, who did enter a commercial building occupied by SAKS FIFTH AVE with the intent to commit larceny and any felony.

COUNT 2

On or about December 12, 2001, in the County of Los Angeles, the crime of GRAND THEFT OF PERSONAL PROPERTY, in violation of PENAL CODE SECTION 487(a), a Felony, was committed by WINONA RYDER, who did unlawfully take money and personal property of a value exceeding Four Hundred Dollars ($400), to wit merchandise in excess of Four Hundred Dollars ($400.00) the property of SAKS FIFTH AVE.

COUNT 3

On or about December 12, 2001, in the County of Los Angeles, the crime of VANDALISM OVER $400 DAMAGE, in violation of PENAL CODE SECTION 594(a), a Felony, was committed by WINONA RYDER, who did unlawfully and maliciously damage and destroy personal property, to wit, Clothing, not his or her own, belonging to SAKS FIFTH AVE, the amount of said damage being over $400.00.

* * * * *

I DECLARE UNDER PENALTY OF PERJURY THAT THE FOREGOING IS TRUE AND CORRECT AND THAT THIS COMPLAINT, CASE NUMBER SA044291, CONSISTS OF 4 COUNT(S).

Executed at BEVERLY HILLS, County of Los Angeles, on February 1, 2002.

____

DECLARANT AND COMPLAINANT

Bernard Madoff.[50] Like assault and battery, fraud is a common law concept that can be pursued as either a tort or a crime.

On the other hand, **extortion** involves using illegal means to obtain someone else's property or to force the victim to take actions that he or she would not otherwise take.

Extortion
The practice of obtaining money, property, or services from an individual or institution, through coercion.

§223.4 of the Model Penal Code defines Theft by Extortion as follows:

A person is guilty of theft if he purposely obtains property of another by threatening to:

(1) Inflict bodily injury on anyone or commit any other criminal offense; or

(2) Accuse anyone of a criminal offense; or

[50] In 2009, Bernard Madoff pled guilty to orchestrating a massive fraud that bilked investors out of more than $65 billion.

(3) Expose any secret tending to subject any person to hatred, contempt or ridicule, or to impair his credit or business repute; or

(4) Take or withhold action as an official, or cause an official to take or withhold action; or

(5) Bring about or continue a strike, boycott or other collective unofficial action, if the property is not demanded or received for the benefit of the group in whose interest the actor purports to act; or

(6) Testify or provide information or withhold testimony or information with respect to another's legal claim or defense; or

(7) Inflict any other harm which would not benefit the actor.

Wealthy companies and public figures often are the victims of extortion schemes. For instance, the journalist Robert Halderman was convicted for trying to extort $2 million from David Letterman by threatening to expose his sexual affairs with female staff employees.[51] In 2021, a federal jury convicted the celebrity attorney Michael Avenatti of trying to extort about $25 million from Nike by threatening to publicize claims that the company authorized payments to the families of high school basketball players.[52]

Application Exercises

After reviewing the facts of the Bill Edwards Hypothetical Case (*see* p. xxxviii), answer the following questions:

7. By diverting customer funds and liquidating customer securities without permission or authority from customers, Edwards appears to be guilty of some form of fraud. He then compounded his crime when he began misappropriating funds from other customers to make the interest payments owed to the existing customers. If Edwards operated in your state, what, if any, statutes might he have violated?

8. Since Edwards was a registered representative for a local broker-securities dealer, he may have violated federal statutes and regulations of the Securities and Exchange Commission (SEC). Which, if any, of these regulations might he have violated? Although Schroeder was not a registered securities agent, could he still be subject to federal securities laws by virtue of his representation of Amalgamated Industries?

---

[51] Halderman was charged in state court with attempted grand larceny. Section 155.30 of the New York Penal Law says, "A person is guilty of grand larceny in the fourth-degree when he steals property and when: . . . 6. The property, regardless of its nature and value, is obtained by extortion."

[52] In 2022, a different federal jury found Avenatti guilty of stealing nearly $300,000 from porn actor Stormy Daniels. He was sentenced to four years imprisonment.

Discussion Questions

12. If a camper in a national park causes a fire that develops into a major wildfire, has the camper committed arson? If a firefighter loses his life in combating the fire, is the camper guilty of homicide under the felony murder doctrine?

13. A photographer for a weekly magazine enters the property of a celebrity to take a candid picture. Is the photographer a trespasser? Is the photographer a burglar?

14. Suppose that a private investigator is hired by a celebrity's spouse to check up on his activities. Is the private eye a trespasser? Is the private eye a burglar?

15. Is there a good policy reason not to convict a defendant of the lesser included offense if he or she is convicted of the more serious one? Why shouldn't a burglar also be convicted of trespassing for the same conduct?

16. A shoplifter steals $200 worth of merchandise on Monday, and on Tuesday takes items worth $400 from the same store. The jurisdiction classifies retail theft of $500 or more as a felony and theft of less than $500 as a misdemeanor. If the offender admits that she committed both thefts, should she be charged with one felony or two misdemeanors? Why?

17. In 2019, Jeff Bezos, the chief executive officer (CEO) of Amazon and owner of the *Washington Post,* accused David Pecker, CEO of American Media, Inc. (the company that publishes the tabloid newspaper *The National Enquirer*) and a close friend and supporter of President Donald Trump, of threatening to print nude photos of Bezos, as well as a woman with whom he was having an extramarital affair, unless Bezos agreed to stop investigating how the *Enquirer* acquired Bezos's private messages and pictures and publicly declare that the *Enquirer*'s coverage of him had not been politically motivated. Assuming that these accusations are true, do you think Pecker's actions constituted a violation of §223.4?

D. Crimes Against Public Order

1. MOTOR VEHICLE CODES

Regulating the proper side of the road on which to drive, as well as requiring drivers to observe speed limits, stop signs, stop lights, and other traffic signs, enhances public order by moving traffic more efficiently and safely. Violations of most traffic laws concern minor infractions resulting in fines. Other traffic offenses are classified as misdemeanors and, in some cases, as felonies. These violations can result in the offenders losing their driving privileges or even being incarcerated.

Two of the most serious motor vehicle code violations are the offenses of **driving under the influence** of alcoholic beverages or drugs[53] and leaving the scene of an accident without reporting it to police authorities.

---

[53]DUI laws are discussed in greater detail in Section H: Crimes Concerning Alcohol and Drugs on pages 75-78.

In recent years, many states added laws against talking on a cell phone or texting while driving. These laws are based on the assumption that drivers using their cell phones to talk or text take their attention off of the road and at least one hand off the steering wheel. Both are hazardous to passengers and other vehicles. It is a traffic infraction in the state of Washington "to drive dangerously distracted." Under this law, a driver is considered "dangerously distracted" when he or she "engages in any activity not related to the actual operation of a motor vehicle in a manner that interferes with the safe operation of such motor vehicle on any highway."[54]

Discussion Question

18. Would changing the radio volume be considered "distracted driving" under the Washington law? What about drinking a cup of coffee or eating a sandwich?

2. PERMIT REQUIREMENT AND DISPERSAL OF CROWDS

Although the First Amendment guarantees the right to freedom of speech and the right to assemble, these rights are not absolute. Federal, state, and local governments can enact and enforce laws against trespass on property that is not open to the public, such as the offices of public officials and correctional facilities. To ensure public safety, governments can also require citizens to obtain permits to conduct demonstrations and rallies. When permits are not secured, the police may order demonstrators to disperse and arrest them for crimes such as failure to disperse, disorderly conduct, and disturbing the peace.

Some examples of the definitions of these crimes in the Model Penal Code are:

§250.1 Riot; Failure to Disperse

(1) *Riot.* A person is guilty of riot . . . if he participates with [two] or more others in a course of disorderly conduct

(a) with purpose to commit or facilitate the commission of a felony or misdemeanor;

(b) with purpose to prevent or coerce official action; or

(c) when the actor or any other participant to the knowledge of the actor uses or plans to use a firearm or other deadly weapon.

(2) *Failure of Disorderly Persons to Disperse Upon Official Order.* Where [three] or more persons are participating in a course of disorderly conduct likely to cause substantial harm or serious inconvenience, annoyance or alarm, a peace officer or other public servant engaged in executing or enforcing the law may order the participants and others in the immediate vicinity to disperse. . . .

---

[54]46.61.673 RCW.

§250.2 Disorderly Conduct

(1) *Offense Defined.* A person is guilty of disorderly conduct if, with purpose to cause public[55] inconvenience, annoyance or alarm, or recklessly creating a risk thereof, he:

(a) engages in fighting or threatening, or in violent or tumultuous behavior; or

(b) makes unreasonable noise or offensively coarse utterance, gesture or display, or addresses abusive language to any person present; or

(c) creates a hazardous or physically offensive condition by any act which serves no legitimate purpose of the actor.

§250.6 Loitering or Prowling

A person commits a violation if he loiters or prowls in a place, at a time, or in a manner not usual for law-abiding individuals under circumstances that warrant alarm for the safety of persons or property in the vicinity. Among the circumstances which may be considered in determining whether such alarm is warranted is the fact that the actor takes flight upon appearance of a peace officer, refuses to identify himself, or manifestly endeavors to conceal himself or any object . . .

Crimes such as disorderly conduct and loitering typically are not classified as felonies. However, sometimes a conviction for such an offense can have serious ramifications for the offender. For instance, in 2007, U.S. Senator Larry Craig (a Republican from Idaho) was arrested as part of a sting directed at homosexual conduct in the Minneapolis–St. Paul International Airport men's restroom. The senator was charged with the misdemeanors of peeping and disorderly conduct. Craig pleaded guilty to the disorderly conduct charge and paid a $1,000 fine. Although he avoided jail time, the publicity surrounding the arrest ended his political career.

Discussion Questions

19. While these statutes are intended to preserve public order, their use can sometimes conflict with the First Amendment to the U.S. Constitution and other basic principles of democratic government. In what type of circumstances could a disorderly conduct or loitering law be used to restrict free expression? How should the courts resolve these conflicts?

20. Should police be allowed to use "non-lethal" weapons such as tear gas and "rubber bullets" to break up large crowds when they are not following orders to leave the area?

21. When large crowds come to protest actions taken by police or other public authorities, member of the press usually also arrive to film and report what is going on. Should police be able to require them to leave the area as well?

[55]"Public" here means affecting or likely to affect persons in a place to which the public or a substantial group has access; among the places included are highways, transport facilities, schools, prisons, apartment houses, places of business or amusement, or any neighborhood.

E. Crimes Against the Family

Domestic violence
Physical abuse, harassment, or intimidation of a victim by a family or household member.

Order of protection
A court order entered to forbid an individual from harassing, abusing, or otherwise interfering with the liberty of a particular person. Typically, the order protects a victim from a household or family member.

This section of the criminal code is designed to protect families by criminalizing things such as bigamy, polygamy, incest, and failure to provide child support.

In addition to having general laws for battery and aggravated battery, some states have special laws against domestic battery that apply to actions taken against other family or household members. These types of laws can either be grouped with others involving danger to a person or in the category of those affecting the family. In recent times, states increasingly have relied on assault and battery laws to fight domestic violence. Generally, **domestic violence** means physical abuse, harassment, or intimidation of a victim by a family or household member.

The federal government has enacted the Violence Against Women Act. Under this law, it is a crime for anyone to cross state lines with the intent to injure his or her partner or to violate a state **order of protection.**[56] Despite the federal government's involvement in combating domestic violence, the vast majority of assault and battery prosecutions are brought by local authorities under state law. Typically, women are the victims of domestic battery, although there are times when men are the subjects of physical abuse (see Exhibit 3.6).

Exhibit 3.6: Domestic Violence Police Report Excerpt

Men can be victims of domestic violence. This excerpt from a Las Vegas Metropolitan Police Department incident report describes an altercation involving actor Christian Slater and his wife.

Narratives

Entered date/time:	11/12/2003 10:01	Narrative type:	INCIDENT CRIME REPORT
Subject:	BATTERY/DOMESTIC VIOLENCE	Author:	DOSCH, M 7907

CHRISTIAN SLATER AND RYAN SLATER AREA MARRIED, COHABITANTS AND HAVE TWO CHILDREN IN COMMON. CHRISTIAN SLATER WAS THE VICTIM OF BATTERY DOMESTIC VIOLENCE WHEN CHRISTIAN SLATER AND RYAN SLATER WERE INVOLVED IN AN ARGUMENT. DURING THE ARGUMENT, RYAN SLATER STRUCK THE LEFT SIDE AND EAR AREA OF CHRISTIAN SLATER'S HEAD WITH A GLASS WHICH WAS IN HER RIGHT HAND. RYAN SLATER WAS ARRESTED AT 0830 HOURS. THE BATTERY OCCURRED AT APPROXIMATELY 0600 HOURS. THE BATTERY CAUSED A ONE INCH VERTICAL LACERATION TO APPEAR JUST BEHIND THE EAR.

PERSON #1 VISIBLE INJURY
PERSON #2 NERVOUS, CRYING

PERSONS INVOLVED ARE: SPOUSE, COHABITANTS, HAVE CHILD IN COMMON. NO PHOTOS TAKEN. VICTIM DID NOT REQUEST TEMPORARY HOUSING. NO TPO IN EFFECT. VICTIM GIVEN DOMESTIC VIOLENCE INFO CARD. WEAPON: GLASS. EVIDENCE: BROKEN GLASS. 911 CALLED BY SECURITY.

SUSPECT ARRESTED. PRIMARY AGGRESSOR DETERMINED BY SEVERITY OF INJURIES INFLICTED.

[56] 18 U.S.C. §§2261(a)(2), 2262(a)(1),(2).

F. Crimes Against Government

The Model Penal Code also contains laws designed to protect the ability of federal, state, and local government agencies and officials to perform their assigned functions. This category ranges from crimes such official misconduct and bribery to treason, espionage, and terrorism.

1. TREASON AND ESPIONAGE

Treason is the only crime specifically mentioned in the U.S. Constitution. Article III, Section 3, states that "treason against the United States shall consist only in levying War against them, or in adhering to their Enemies, giving them Aid and Comfort." It goes on to specify that "No Person shall be convicted of Treason unless on the Testimony of two Witnesses to the same overt Act, or on Confession in open Court," and that "Congress shall have Power to declare the Punishment of Treason, but no Attainder of Treason shall work Corruption of Blood, or Forfeiture except during the Life of the Person attainted."

Treason
An attempt to overthrow the government of one's country or to assist its enemies in war.

In addition to this constitutional provision, Section 2381 of Title 18 of the U.S. Code declares:

> "Whoever, owing allegiance to the United States, levies war against them or adheres to their enemies, giving them aid and comfort within the United States or elsewhere, is guilty of treason and shall suffer death, or shall be imprisoned not less than five years and fined under this title but not less than $10,000; and shall be incapable of holding any office under the United States."

Espionage, the act of disclosing information with intent to interfere with the operation or success of the U.S. armed forces or to promote the success of enemies of the United States, may also be punished by the death penalty.

Espionage
The act of disclosing information with intent to interfere with the operation or success of the U.S. armed forces or to promote the success of enemies of the United States.

Section 793 of Title 18 of the U.S. Code prohibits gathering, transmitting, or losing specified types of defense information. Section 794 covers gathering or delivering defense information to aid a foreign government. While there have been espionage prosecutions involving classical spy operations in which an agent steals secrets and then turns them over to a foreign government, there are other cases in which citizens disclose confidential information for political reasons. For instance, the 2010 prosecution of U.S. Army private Chelsea Manning (formerly Bradley Manning) involved a situation in which a member of the U.S. military turned over classified government documents to WikiLeaks[57] to develop political support for changing U.S. policies she found objectionable. The government charged her with 22 counts of espionage, theft of military records or property, and aiding the enemy. In 2013, she was acquitted of aiding the enemy, but she was convicted of the other charges and given a 35-year prison sentence.[58]

---

[57]WikiLeaks is a non-governmental organization that posts confidential and classified materials on its public website. This is the organization that released hacked emails from the Democratic National Committee and Hillary Clinton's private email servicer during the 2016 Presidential campaign.

[58]President Barack Obama commuted the remainder of her sentence in 2017.

About the time Manning was tried, the United States also prosecuted a former Central Intelligence Agency (CIA) employee for similar crimes. Edward Snowden was charged with theft of government property, unauthorized communication of national defense information, and willful communication of classified communications of intelligence information to an unauthorized person. Like Manning, Snowden disclosed government documents to WikiLeaks to expose what he believed were unethical practices of the U.S. intelligence community. In 2022, Russia granted Snowden citizenship.

2. INSURRECTION, REBELLION, AND SEDITION

The previous two editions of this book did not mention insurrection, rebellion, or sedition. But on January 6, 2021, the invasion of the U.S. Capitol brought these crimes to national attention.

The U.S. Justice Department has successfully prosecuted numerous individuals (identified from videos and social media postings) who had assaulted police, vandalized Capitol offices, and threatened to do bodily harm to various members of Congress and to Vice President Mike Pence.

Section 18 U.S. Code §2383: states that:

Insurrection/rebellion
An organized, and usually violent, act of revolt against an established governmental entity or its leaders.

> "Whoever incites, sets on foot, assists, or engages in any **rebellion** or **insurrection** against the authority of the United States or the laws thereof, or gives aid or comfort thereto, shall be fined under this title or imprisoned not more than ten years, or both; and shall be incapable of holding any office under the United States."[59]

Inciting others to participate in an insurrection is the crime of **sedition.**

Sedition
Conduct or speech that incites individuals to violently rebel against the authority of the government.

18 U.S.C. §2384. Seditious Conspiracy

> If two or more persons in any State or Territory, or in any place subject to the jurisdiction of the United States, conspire to overthrow, put down, or to destroy by force the Government of the United States, or to levy war against them, or to oppose by force the authority thereof, or by force to prevent, hinder, or delay the execution of any law of the United States, or by force to seize, take, or possess any property of the United States contrary to the authority thereof, they shall each be fined under this title or imprisoned not more than twenty years, or both.

The U.S. Justice Department rarely brings sedition charges. However, federal grand juries in the District of Columbia have indicted members of the far-right groups the Proud Boys and the Oath Keepers with seditious conspiracy in connection with the January 6 attack of the Capitol.[60]

---

[59]In addition to the punishment authorized in the U.S. Criminal Code, Section 3 of the 14th Amendment to the U.S. Constitution prohibits senators, representatives, and other public officials from holding public office if they have "engaged in insurrection or rebellion" against the United States.

[60]Currently, these cases have not yet gone to trial.

Discussion Question

22. Based on the findings of the investigation of the House of Representative's Special Committee on the January 6 insurrection, do you think Donald Trump committed the crime of seditious conspiracy? Why or why not?

3. PERJURY AND OBSTRUCTION OF JUSTICE

Other crimes against the government include **perjury** and **obstruction of justice.** Both involve activities that interfere with the ability of government agencies to enforce laws. Perjury focuses on knowingly providing false information under oath, whereas obstruction of justice covers a variety of other actions (including failure to answer specific questions) when those actions interfere with police and other government officials carrying out their lawful duties. The House of Representatives alleged the commission of both crimes in their bills of impeachment against presidents Bill Clinton[61] and Donald Trump.[62]

Perjury
The act of lying or knowingly making false statements while under oath in court or in affidavits or depositions.

Obstruction of justice
An act that intentionally interferes with the work of police, prosecutors, and other governmental officials.

Section 1001 of Title 18 of the U.S. Code prohibits **making false statements to federal investigators.** Unlike perjury, this offense is not limited to statements made under oath. Rather, it is designed to punish anyone who gives false statements meant to pervert or undermine the functions of governmental bodies.

Making false statements to federal investigators
The act of lying to or concealing information from a federal official.

§1001 Statements or Entries Generally

(a) Except as otherwise provided in this section, whoever, in any matter within the jurisdiction of the executive, legislative, or judicial branch of the Government of the United States, knowingly and willfully—

(1) falsifies, conceals, or covers up by any trick, scheme, or device a material fact;

(2) makes any materially false, fictitious, or fraudulent statement or representation; or

(3) makes or uses any false writing or document knowing the same to contain any materially false, fictitious, or fraudulent statement or entry. . .

While the Fifth Amendment gives people the right to refuse to answer an investigator's questions based on a claim of self-incrimination, it does not provide immunity for giving false statements to authorities.[63]

---

[61]The House of Representatives alleged in one article of its bill of impeachment that President Clinton perjured himself in a deposition he gave concerning his relationship with a White House intern. A second article of impeachment alleged obstruction of justice relating to an investigation into his law practice in Arkansas being conducted by Independent Counsel Kenneth Starr. The Senate did not convict him of either charge.

[62]President Trump was impeached twice. In 2019, he was charged with abuse of power and obstruction of Congress for threatening to cut military aid to Ukraine unless it investigated the business activities of a political opponent's son. In 2021, he was impeached for inciting an insurrection for his actions leading up to the January 6 uprising at the Capitol. The Senate did not convict him in either trial.

[63]*United States v. Wong*, 431 U.S. 174 (1977).

It is also a crime to make false statements to state or local authorities. Although some offenders make false statements to avoid revealing incriminating information to law enforcement officials, there are situations in which an offender purposely gives false statements to police for other reasons.

The case involving the actor Jussie Smollett is an example of this type of illegal behavior. Smollett filed a false report with the Chicago Police Department claiming to have been attacked by two men who made racist and homophobic comments while they wrapped a rope around his neck and poured an "unknown substance" on him. After a police investigation revealed that Smollett had hired the two men to stage the event, a grand jury returned a 16-count indictment against him for making false police reports. He was found guilty of several counts of felony disorderly conduct and was sentenced to five months in jail. He was also fined $25,000 and ordered to pay $120,000 to reimburse the Chicago Police Department for their efforts.

Prosecutors also may charge individuals for obstruction of justice for altering or destroying physical evidence—even if they had no legal obligation to produce the evidence at the time it was destroyed. For instance, when Martha Stewart was being investigated for insider trading, she falsified some documents to create an explanation for a suspicious-looking trade of a pharmaceutical company stock owned by a friend. Although it was ultimately determined that her trades had not violated SEC regulations on insider trading, her falsification of her trading records had made it more difficult for the government to develop its case against the company's CEO.

In addition to criminalizing attempts to obstruct a law enforcement investigation, state and federal laws also make it illegal for government officials to misuse their legal authority. A prime example of this is the following:

18 U.S.C.S. §242. Deprivation of Rights Under Color of Law

> Whoever, under color of any law, statute, ordinance, regulation, or custom, willfully subjects any person in any State, Territory, Commonwealth, Possession, or District to the deprivation of any rights, privileges, or immunities secured or protected by the Constitution or laws of the United States, or to different punishments, pains, or penalties, on account of such person being an alien, or by reason of his color, or race, than are prescribed for the punishment of citizens, shall be fined under this title or imprisoned not more than one year, or both; and if bodily injury results from the acts committed in violation of this section or if such acts include the use, attempted use, or threatened use of a dangerous weapon, explosives, or fire, shall be fined under this title or imprisoned not more than ten years, or both; and if death results from the acts committed in violation of this section or if such acts include kidnapping or an attempt to kidnap, aggravated sexual abuse, or an attempt to commit aggravated sexual abuse, or an attempt to kill, shall be fined under this title, or imprisoned for any term of years or for life, or both, or may be sentenced to death.

As part of an investigation into possible Russian interference in the 2016 presidential election, Special Counsel Robert Mueller investigated claims that President Trump's firing of James Comey as director of the Federal Bureau of Investigation (FBI) constituted obstruction of justice. Although it is widely accepted that a president has the legal authority to fire an FBI director, Trump's opponents argued that the discharge of Comey amounted to obstruction of justice because it was motivated by a desire to stop an ongoing investigation into Russian influence in Trump's election campaign.[64]

Discussion Questions

23. Politicians who use their influence to assist their contributors in obtaining governmental contracts are sometimes prosecuted for official misconduct. In response, some critics argue that this is simply business as usual. For instance, former Illinois governor George Ryan was convicted of fraud and racketeering after a six-month jury trial. Should law enforcement use its finite resources to investigate and prosecute government officials simply because political supporters receive a contractual benefit?

24. Illinois requires state employees to take an online ethics exam every year to maintain their governmental employment. Should an employee's failure to take the exam result in criminal penalties? Should the employee be charged with a crime if he completes the examination in less time than it would take a normal person to simply read all of the questions (based on the assumption that if the person finished the exam that quickly, he or she must have cheated)?

25. In most civil lawsuits that go to trial, there is conflicting testimony between the witnesses. Should the prosecuting authorities charge the witnesses whose testimony isn't believed with perjury?

26. Because President Bill Clinton, who admitted to giving a false statement under oath, was not convicted of the impeachment charges brought against him, is there any situation in which a perjury prosecution is the appropriate course of action by law enforcement authorities?

27. When a police officer falsely arrests a citizen or physically abuses a suspect, few would claim that the officer should be immune from prosecution for misuse of power. Should the police be prosecuted for helping a friend by "unofficially" running another person's license plates or arrest record?

G. Crimes Involving Firearms

Regulation of who can possess and use firearms is a very controversial issue of public policy in the United States, and great variation exists among the states. Since the passage of the National Firearms Act in 1934,[65] the federal government has regulated the possession and sale of certain types of firearms like machine guns and firearm silencers. In 1993, Congress amended the Gun Control Act of 1968[66] by enacting the Brady Handgun Violence Prevention Act.[67] These acts mandated

---

[64]In his report, Mueller stated that he could not establish that the campaign conspired or coordinated with the Russian government in his election efforts. Mueller did not draw a conclusion as to whether Trump's conduct constituted obstruction of justice. Although the Special Counsel's report did not conclude that the president's actions were criminal, it did not exonerate him either. U.S. attorney general William Barr and deputy attorney general Rod Rosenstein decided that the evidence presented in the report was insufficient to charge the president with a crime.

[65]26 U.S.C. §1132c.

[66]18 U.S.C. §§921 *et seq.*

[67]18 U.S.C. §922.

the establishment of a national system for instant criminal background checks of proposed handgun transferees. In 2019, the Department of Justice amended the regulations of the Bureau of Alcohol, Tobacco, Firearms, and Explosives (ATF) to classify bump stocks, a firearm attachment that allows a semiautomatic gun to shoot almost as rapidly as an automatic weapon, as machine guns.[68]

State laws typically regulate how firearms are to be transported, the circumstances under which they can be concealed, and where they can be discharged (e.g., not in urban areas, not within a set number of feet from a public road). There are significant differences in how the states regulate guns. For instance, New Jersey requires owners to register their handguns and limits the size of the magazine on their firearms. In contrast, West Virginia does not impose these constraints on gun owners. Most states prohibit the unlawful use or possession of weapons and often increase the level of punishment when a firearm is used in connection with a crime like robbery or assault. For example, in Illinois an act of criminal sexual assault becomes aggravated criminal sexual assault when a weapon was displayed or use of a weapon was threatened.[69]

720 ILCS 5/12-14 Aggravated Criminal Sexual Assault

> The accused commits aggravated criminal sexual assault if he or she commits criminal sexual assault and any of the following aggravating circumstances existed during . . . the commission of the offense: . . .
>
> (8) the accused was armed with a firearm, . . .

Many other crimes concerning firearms do not include the element of intent. Hence, mere possession of a weapon in some situations may violate a statute even if the person with the firearm had lawful intentions.

However, the constitutionality of many of these laws was brought into question in 2008 when the U.S. Supreme Court *in District of Columbia v. Heller* struck down two key provisions of a District of Columbia ban on handguns on the basis that they violated the Second Amendment right to bear arms.[70] While the *Heller* decision only applied to federal actions, the Supreme Court followed it up with a ruling in *McDonald v. City of Chicago,* stating that the right to bear arms was among those rights protected from state interference by the Fourteenth Amendment due process clause.[71] The Supreme Court also has ruled that a state law prohibiting the possession of stun guns was inconsistent with the *Heller* opinion.[72] In 2022, the Supreme Court in *New York State Rifle & Pistol Association, Inc. v. Bruen,*[73] struck down a New York "concealed carry" statute on the basis that it violated the Second Amendment. It is important to note, however, that these decisions do not preclude all forms of government regulation. The right to bear arms is not unlimited. Laws such as those prohibiting convicted felons and mentally ill persons from possessing firearms are likely to be found to be valid.[74]

---

[68] 27 CFR 447.11, 478.11, & 479.11.

[69] 720 ILSC 5/12-14.

[70] 554 U.S. 570 (2008).

[71] 561 U.S. 742 (2010).

[72] *Caetano v. Massachusetts*, 136 S. Ct. 1027 (2016) (per curiam).

[73] 142 S. Ct. 2111 (2022).

[74] In *New York State Rifle & Pistol Association, Inc. v. Bruen*, the Court stated, "Properly interpreted, the Second Amendment allows a 'variety' of gun regulations. As Justice Scalia wrote

H. Crimes Involving Alcohol and Drugs

Approximately 100 years ago, the activities of the Women's Christian Temperance Union and other well-intentioned religious groups led to the passage of the Eighteenth Amendment, which prohibited the manufacture, sale, or transportation of intoxicating liquors within, the importation thereof into, or the exportation thereof from the United States. They were motivated by a desire to eliminate all the evil effects of drinking alcoholic beverages.[75]

However, due to the increase in organized crime,[76] law enforcement abuses,[77] and the fact that so many people did not want to give up consumption of these beverages, it was repealed by the Twenty-First Amendment in 1933. The repeal left it to state and local governments to pass their own statutes and ordinances regulating who could sell alcoholic beverages, the minimum age people could drink, and the days and hours during which alcohol could be sold.[78]

Because drug and alcohol use can affect a person's ability to drive safely, the courts have upheld provisions making it a crime to drive "while intoxicated" (DWI) or "under the influence" (**DUI**). We will discuss the methods used for determining whether a driver was in fact "under the influence" in Chapter 4.

DUI
The offense of driving under the influence of alcoholic beverages. Some states refer to this violation as DWI (driving while intoxicated).

The California Vehicle Code contains the following provisions:

§23152. Driving Under the Influence

(a) It is unlawful for any person who is under the influence of any alcoholic beverage or drug, or under the combined influence of any alcoholic beverage and drug, to drive a vehicle.

(b) It is unlawful for any person who has 0.08 percent or more, by weight, of alcohol in his or her blood to drive a vehicle.

An actual DUI complaint, based upon §23152 of the California Vehicle Code, is displayed in Exhibit 3.7. Notice how the style of this complaint closely tracks the felony shoplifting complaint set forth in Exhibit 3.5. Contrast the style of these two complaints with the New York charging instrument (Exhibit 3.2) and the Illinois indictment (Exhibit 3.3).

---

in his opinion for the Court in *Heller*, and Justice ALITO reiterated in relevant part in the principal opinion in *McDonald*: 'Like most rights, the right secured by the Second Amendment is not unlimited. . . . [N]othing in our opinion should be taken to cast doubt on longstanding prohibitions on the possession of firearms by felons and the mentally ill, or laws forbidding the carrying of firearms in sensitive places such as schools and government buildings, or laws imposing conditions and qualifications on the commercial sale of arms." 142 S. Ct. at 2162.

[75]This included domestic violence, failure to keep a job, etc.

[76]Although prohibition didn't create organized crime, it greatly increased its size and scope.

[77]Overzealous police and federal agents often violated civil rights while searching for and destroying the paraphernalia of alcohol production.

[78]Many states did not allow sales on Sundays, and some did not allow alcohol to be sold in restaurants. However, the Twenty-First Amendment does not authorize the states to impose a two-year durational-residency requirement on retail liquor store license applicants. *Tennessee Wine & Spirits Retailers Association v. Thomas*, 139 S. Ct. 2449 (2019).

Exhibit 3.7: California DUI Complaint

Mel Gibson is one of a horde of celebrities who has been charged with driving under the influence. Gibson pleaded no contest to a misdemeanor drunken-driving charge and was sentenced to three years' probation. Counts 1 and 3 of the complaint were dismissed, and Gibson volunteered to do public-service announcements on the hazards of drinking and driving and to immediately enter rehabilitation. The judge ordered Gibson to attend Alcoholics Anonymous meetings five times a week for 4 1/2 months, three AA meetings per week for another 7 1/2 months and enroll in an alcohol-abuse program for three months. He was fined $1,300 and had his license restricted for 90 days.

SUPERIOR COURT OF THE STATE OF CALIFORNIA
FOR THE COUNTY OF LOS ANGELES

THE PEOPLE OF THE STATE OF CALIFORNIA, Plaintiff, v. MEL C. GIBSON (01/03/1956), Defendant(s).	CASE NO. MAL 6MB01891 *MISDEMEANOR COMPLAINT*

The undersigned is informed and believes that:

COUNT 1

On or about July 28, 2006, in the County of Los Angeles, the crime of DRIVING UNDER THE INFLUENCE OF ALCOHOL OR DRUGS, in violation of VEHICLE CODE SECTION 23152(a), a Misdemeanor, was committed by MEL C. GIBSON, who did unlawfully, while under the influence of an alcoholic beverage, drive a vehicle.

COUNT 2

On or about July 28, 2006, in the County of Los Angeles, the crime of DRIVING WHILE HAVING A 0.08% OR HIGHER BLOOD ALCOHOL, in violation of VEHICLE CODE SECTION 23152(b), a Misdemeanor, was committed by MEL C. GIBSON, who did unlawfully, while having 0.08 percent and more, by weight, of alcohol in the blood, drive a vehicle.

COUNT 3

On or about July 28, 2006, in the County of Los Angeles, the crime of POSSESSION OF OPEN CONTAINER WHILE DRIVING, in violation of VEHICLE CODE SECTION 23223(a), an Infraction, was committed by MEL C. GIBSON, who did unlawfully have in his possession an open alcoholic beverage container while driving in a motor vehicle upon a highway.

* * * * *

I DECLARE UNDER PENALTY OF PERJURY THAT THE FOREGOING IS TRUE AND CORRECT AND THAT THIS COMPLAINT CONSISTS OF 3 COUNT(S).

Executed at MALIBU, County of Los Angeles, on August 2, 2006.

Det. PETE SANZONE
DECLARANT AND COMPLAINANT

For many of the same reasons that people opposed the use of alcoholic beverages, they have also opposed the use of various "recreational drugs." And in recent years, a number of states have overhauled their laws that previously had criminalized the use and possession of marijuana (also known as "cannabis"). A substantial majority of the states, in addition to the District of Columbia, now allow the use of marijuana for specified medical conditions,[79] and others now have even legalized recreational use. Still other states have either reduced or eliminated criminal penalties associated with possession or use.[80] Washington's statute provides:

RCW 69.50.4013 Possession of controlled substance. . .

(1) It is unlawful for any person to possess a controlled substance unless the substance was obtained directly from, or pursuant to, a valid prescription or order of a practitioner while acting in the course of this or her professional practice, or except as otherwise authorized by this chapter.

. . .

(3)(a) The possession, by a person twenty-one years of age or older, of useable marijuana, marijuana concentrates, or marijuana-infused products in amounts that do not exceed those set forth in RCW 69.50.360(3) is not a violation of this section, this chapter, or any other provision of Washington state law.

Even though an increasing number of states have changed their statutes to legalize marijuana for medical and in some cases recreational use, the federal government has not changed its drug laws.[81] It still classifies marijuana as a Schedule 1 drug, putting it in the same category as heroin, which

---

[79]Modern research suggests that marijuana is a valuable aid in the treatment of a wide range of clinical applications, including pain relief, nausea, spasticity, glaucoma, and movement disorders. It is also a powerful appetite stimulant, and emerging research suggests that its medicinal properties may protect the body against some types of malignant tumors and are neuroprotective.

[80]Internet sites such as disa.com and Vox.com have a summary of the current marijuana laws in the various states.

[81]The federal government regulates drugs through the Controlled Substances Act, 21 U.S.C. §811, which does not distinguish between medical and recreational use of marijuana. In *Gonzales v. Raich*, 545 U.S. 1 (2005), the U.S. Supreme Court held that the Commerce Clause gave the federal government power to regulate local growth and use of marijuana.

places it in a more restrictive category than drugs like cocaine, fentanyl, and methamphetamine.

Even if marijuana is legal at the state level, the Schedule I classification at the federal level creates problems for the cannabis industry, as well as for users. For example, many state-legal marijuana businesses function on a cash-only basis because federally insured banks might be fined by their regulators if they conduct business with customers operating a business that violates federal law. Likewise, attorneys who use marijuana may be subject to professional discipline because they are committing a crime.

As the state legalization movement has grown, federal enforcement of cannabis laws has declined, but it varies from administration to administration. The Obama Justice Department took a relaxed approach and generally let states do as they wanted, so long as they met certain criteria, such as not letting legal marijuana fall into children's hands or crossing state lines. Although the Trump administration's initial attorney general permitted local U.S. Attorneys to decide whether to enforce the law in states where marijuana is legal, his successor, William Barr, pledged not to go after cannabis companies that complied with state laws.

Laws prohibiting the use of "recreational drugs" are far more controversial because their focus is more on protecting the user from harming himself or herself than on protecting the public at large. Opponents of these laws cite the philosophical writings of John Stuart Mill and the nation's experience with Prohibition in their arguments against such laws. Mill rejected the concept of paternalism[82] and argued that the government should use the coercive power of the law only to prevent harm to others. He argued that individuals are in a better position to know what is best for them than is the government, and people can develop their intellect best when they learn from their own mistakes. Mill and his followers thus oppose laws designed to prevent people from gambling, smoking, taking drugs, using prostitutes, and other activities.

While the marijuana legalization movement may suggest that the public is moving in the direction of Mill's philosophy, this has not the case for other recreational drugs. Indeed, federal and state prosecutors continue to seek serious penalties for sellers and suppliers of heroin and other opioids, crack cocaine, lysergic acid diethylamide (LSD), and other street drugs. Penalties are increased based on the quality of the product, when firearms are involved, the location of the trafficking, age of the purchasers, and other factors.

I. "Victimless Crimes" That Challenge Community Standards

1. GAMBLING

Like consumption of alcoholic beverages, gambling traditionally has been either banned or regulated under state law. At the beginning of the twentieth century,

---

[82]Paternalism is defined as the practice of restricting an individual's liberty for his or her own good.

all states outlawed gambling. In 1931, Nevada became the first state in modern times to legalize it. In 1978, New Jersey became the second state to permit casino gambling. Ten years later, the federal government adopted the Indian Gaming Regulatory Act (IGRA),[83] which provides the "statutory basis for the operation of gaming by Indian tribes as a means of promoting tribal economic development, self-sufficiency, and strong tribal governments."[84] A number of states have authorized riverboat casinos, and in the 1960s New Hampshire and New York started lotteries. Currently, forty-four states and the District of Columbia sponsor lotteries, and nearly all jurisdictions permit gambling in some form, through casinos, pari-mutuel betting facilities, or lotteries.

Given the popularity of legalized gambling, you might think that law enforcement would legislate against it. However, this has not been the case, although most state criminal codes prohibit some types of gambling and the federal authorities have targeted Internet gambling with several statutes, including RICO, the Wire Act,[85] and the Unlawful Internet Gambling Enforcement Act.[86] Although Congress has attempted to limit the spread of gambling, the U.S. Supreme Court struck down a federal law that prohibited states from authorizing and licensing sports betting.[87]

2. CONSENSUAL SEXUAL PRACTICES AND PORNOGRAPHY

Prior to the latter half of the twentieth century, many states had a variety of laws criminalizing various sexual activities, even when those activities involved consenting adults. These "sodomy laws" were struck down in 2003 by the U.S. Supreme Court in *Lawrence v. Texas*.[88]

It is important to note, however, that the activities involved in this case took place in a private setting rather than in public view. Most states have statutes, like the following law enacted in Illinois.

720 ILCS 5/11-30 Public Indecency

(a) Any person of the age of 17 years and upwards who performs any of the following acts in a public place commits a public indecency:

(1) An act of sexual penetration or sexual conduct as defined in section 12-12 of this Code; or

(2) A lewd exposure of the body done with intent to arouse or to satisfy the sexual desire of the person.

Breast feeding of infants is not an act of public indecency.

(b) "Public place" for purposes of this Section means any place where the conduct may reasonably be expected to be viewed by others.

---

[83] 25 U.S.C. §2701 *et seq.*

[84] 25 U.S.C. §2702

[85] 18 U.S.C. §1084

[86] 31 U.S.C. §§5361-5367.

[87] *Murphy v. National Collegiate Athletic Association*, 38 S. Ct. 1461 (2018).

[88] 539 U.S. 558 (2003).

At one time, the states prohibited the distribution of sexually explicit materials to anyone. Prior to the development of the Internet, most sexually explicit magazines, books, and videos were distributed through specialized "adult bookstores," and it was relatively easy to bring criminal charges against the seller for violations of obscenity laws. On the other hand, getting convictions for creating or distributing sexually explicit materials was much more challenging and led to a series of U.S. Supreme Court cases in which the justices grappled with the challenge of defining which materials were protected by the First Amendment and which were not.[89]

While adults now have free access to sexually explicit materials, there are a number of key restrictions involving minors. See, for example, the following Illinois statute:

720 ILCS 5/11-21 Harmful Material

(b) A person is guilty of distributing harmful material to a minor when he or she:

(1) knowingly sells, lends, distributes, exhibits to, depicts to, or gives away to a minor, knowing that the minor is under the age of 18 or failing to exercise reasonable care in ascertaining the person's true age:

(A) any material which depicts nudity, sexual conduct or sado-masochistic abuse, or which contains explicit and detailed verbal descriptions or narrative accounts of sexual excitement, sexual conduct or sado-masochistic abuse, and which taken as a whole is harmful to minors.

In 1982, the U.S. Supreme Court upheld state laws criminalizing the production or sale of any visual depiction of children under 16 engaging in sexual acts.[90]

Discussion Questions

28. Based on John Stuart Mill's philosophy, the government should allow consenting adults to engage in any form of sexual activities, so long as all parties involved are adults who have knowingly consented to participate. Do you agree? If not, why not?

29. Disorderly conduct under the Model Penal Code makes it a crime for someone to make an "offensively coarse utterance, gesture or display, or [address] abusive language to any person present." Does this mean that swearing in public is a crime? Should it be?

30. In a case that got national news coverage, a carpenter in Oakland, California, was charged with indecent exposure after he was spotted building cabinets in the buff at a home where he had been hired to work. He told the judge that he liked to work in the nude because it was more comfortable and helped him keep his clothes clean. His attorney pointed out that he was

---

[89]*See Roth v. United States*, 354 U.S. 476 (1957); *Jacobellis v. Ohio*, 378 U.S. 184 (1964); *Miller v. California*, 413 U.S. 15 (1973).

[90]*New York v. Ferber*, 458 U.S. 747 (1982).

not acting lewdly or seeking sexual gratification. How do you think the judge would rule, and why?

31. Because people respond to alcohol in different ways, should a driver be conclusively presumed to be in violation of a DUI statute simply because she has a blood alcohol content (BAC) of 0.08? Would a general prohibition of driving under the influence without a set BAC be more appropriate?

32. If paternalism is not good public policy, should recreational drugs be legal? If so, should marijuana be available in vending machines? Should a retailer be allowed to sell opioids through vending machines?

33. If paternalism is good public policy, should the government impose greater criminal sanctions and restrictions on the use of guns?

34. The phrase "war on drugs" was popularized by the media shortly after a press conference given by President Nixon in the context of promoting legislation on drug abuse prevention and control. Do you think he won this "war"? Why or why not?

J. Interpreting Criminal Statutes

In reading the excerpts from the statutes and ordinances we included in this chapter, you have seen the extent to which they frequently contain ambiguous language. Take, for example, the words "causes," "knowingly," "recklessly," and "negligently," which are used in defining the crime of homicide. Many, but not all, statutes contain a separate section of definitions of key terms. However, the definitions given in the statute may themselves be somewhat ambiguous.

In situations like these, it is necessary to research how the terms in question have been interpreted and applied by judges in previous cases involving the same or similar statutes. The following excerpt from the U.S. Supreme Court's opinion in *Smith v. United States* provides an example of how judges interpret ambiguous language in statutes. Take a few minutes to read the Court's decision in the box that follows and then develop answers to the Discussion questions that follow it.

Smith v. United States
Supreme Court of the United States
508 U.S. 223 (1993)

JUSTICE O'CONNOR delivered the opinion of the Court in which REHNQUIST, C.J., and WHITE, BLACKMUN, KENNEDY, and THOMAS, J.J., joined.

We decide today whether the exchange of a gun for narcotics constitutes "use" of a firearm "during and in relation to . . . [a] drug trafficking crime" within the meaning of *18 U.S.C. §924(c)(1)*. We hold that it does.

Petitioner John Angus Smith and his companion went from Tennessee to Florida to buy cocaine; they hoped to resell it at a profit. While in Florida, they met petitioner's acquaintance, Deborah Hoag. Hoag agreed to, and in fact did, purchase cocaine for petitioner. She then accompanied petitioner and his friend to her motel room, where they were joined by a drug dealer. While Hoag listened, petitioner and the dealer discussed petitioner's MAC-10 firearm, which had been modified to operate as an automatic. The MAC-10 apparently is a favorite among criminals.

It is small and compact, lightweight, and can be equipped with a silencer. Most important of all, it can be devastating: A fully automatic MAC-10 can fire more than 1,000 rounds per minute. The dealer expressed his interest in becoming the owner of a MAC-10, and petitioner promised that he would discuss selling the gun if his arrangement with another potential buyer fell through.

Unfortunately for petitioner, Hoag had contacts not only with narcotics traffickers but also with law enforcement officials. In fact, she was a confidential informant. Consistent with her post, she informed the Broward County Sheriff's Office of petitioner's activities. The Sheriff's Office responded quickly, sending an undercover officer to Hoag's motel room. Several others were assigned to keep the motel under surveillance. Upon arriving at Hoag's motel room, the undercover officer presented himself to petitioner as a pawnshop dealer. Petitioner, in turn, presented the officer with a proposition: He had an automatic MAC-10 and silencer with which he might be willing to part. Petitioner then pulled the MAC-10 out of a black canvas bag and showed it to the officer. The officer examined the gun and asked petitioner what he wanted for it. Rather than asking for money, however, petitioner asked for drugs. He was willing to trade his MAC-10, he said, for two ounces of cocaine. The officer told petitioner that he was just a pawnshop dealer and did not distribute narcotics. Nonetheless, he indicated that he wanted the MAC-10 and would try to get the cocaine. The officer then left, promising to return within an hour.

Rather than seeking out cocaine as he had promised, the officer returned to the Sheriff's Office to arrange for petitioner's arrest. But petitioner was not content to wait. The officers who were conducting surveillance saw him leave the motel room carrying a gun bag; he then climbed into his van and drove away. The officers reported petitioner's departure and began following him. When law enforcement authorities tried to stop petitioner, he led them on a high-speed chase. Petitioner eventually was apprehended.

Petitioner, it turns out, was well armed. A search of his van revealed the MAC-10 weapon, a silencer, ammunition, and a "fast-feed" mechanism. In addition, the police found a MAC-11 machine gun, a loaded .45 caliber pistol, and a .22 caliber pistol with a scope and homemade silencer. Petitioner also had a loaded 9 millimeter handgun in his waistband.

A grand jury sitting in the District Court for the Southern District of Florida returned an indictment charging petitioner with, among other offenses, two drug trafficking crimes—conspiracy to possess cocaine with intent to distribute and attempt to possess cocaine with intent to distribute in violation of *21 U.S.C. §§841(a)(1)*, *846*, and *18 U.S.C. §2*. App. 3-9. Most important here, the indictment alleged that petitioner knowingly used the MAC-10 and its silencer during and in relation to a drug trafficking crime. *Id.*, at 4-5. Under *18 U.S.C. §924(c)(1)*, a defendant who so uses a firearm must be sentenced to five years' incarceration. And where, as here, the firearm is a "machinegun" or is fitted with a silencer, the sentence is 30 years. See *§924(c)(1)* ("If the firearm is a machinegun, or is equipped with a firearm silencer," the sentence is "thirty years"); §921(a)(23), *26 U.S.C. §5845(b)* (term "machinegun" includes automatic weapons). The jury convicted petitioner on all counts.

On appeal, petitioner argued that *§924(c)(1)*'s penalty for using a firearm during and in relation to a drug trafficking offense covers only situations in which the firearm is used as a weapon. According to petitioner, the provision does not extend to defendants who use a firearm solely as a medium of exchange or for barter. The Court of Appeals for the Eleventh Circuit disagreed. *957 F.2d 835 (1992)*. The plain language of the statute, the court explained, imposes no requirement that the firearm be used as a weapon. Instead, any use of "the weapon to facilitate *in any manner* the commission of the offense" suffices. *Id., at 837* (internal quotation marks omitted).

Shortly before the Eleventh Circuit decided this case, the Court of Appeals for the District of Columbia Circuit arrived at the same conclusion. [H]owever, the Court of Appeals for the Ninth Circuit held that trading a gun in a drug-related transaction could not constitute use of a firearm during and in relation to a drug trafficking offense within the meaning of *§924(c)(1)*. We granted certiorari to resolve the conflict among the Circuits. We now affirm.

Section 924(c)(1) requires the imposition of specified penalties if the defendant, "during and in relation to any crime of violence or drug trafficking crime[,] uses or carries a firearm." By its terms, the statute requires the prosecution to make two showings. First, the prosecution must demonstrate that the defendant "use[d] or carrie[d] a firearm." Second, it must prove that the use or carrying was "during and in relation to" a "crime of violence or drug trafficking crime."

Petitioner argues that exchanging a firearm for drugs does not constitute "use" of the firearm within the meaning of the statute. He points out that nothing in the record indicates that he fired the MAC-10, threatened anyone with it, or employed it for self-protection. In essence, petitioner argues that he cannot be said to have "use[d]" a firearm unless he used it as a weapon, since that is how firearms most often are used. See *957 F.2d at 837* (firearm often facilitates drug offenses by protecting drugs or protecting or emboldening the defendant). Of course, [HN4] *§924(c)(1)* is not limited to those cases in which a gun is used; it applies with equal force whenever a gun is "carrie[d]." In this case, however, the indictment alleged only that petitioner "use[d]" the MAC-10. App. 4. Accordingly, we do not consider whether the evidence might support the conclusion that petitioner carried the MAC-10 within the meaning of *§924(c)(1)*. Instead we confine our discussion to what the parties view as the dispositive issue in this case: whether trading a firearm for drugs can constitute "use" of the firearm within the meaning of *§924(c)(1)*.

When a word is not defined by statute, we normally construe it in accord with its ordinary or natural meaning. Surely petitioner's treatment of his MAC-10 can be described as "use" within the everyday meaning of that term. Petitioner "used" his MAC-10 in an attempt to obtain drugs by offering to trade it for cocaine. Webster's defines "to use" as "to convert to one's service" or "to employ." . . . Black's Law Dictionary contains a similar definition: "to make use of; to convert to one's service; to employ; to avail oneself of; to utilize; to carry out a purpose or action by means of." . . . Petitioner's handling of the MAC-10 in this case falls squarely within those definitions. By attempting to trade his MAC-10 for the drugs, he "used" or "employed" it as an item of barter to obtain cocaine; he "derived service" from it because it was going to bring him the very drugs he sought.

In petitioner's view, *§924(c)(1)* should require proof not only that the defendant used the firearm, but also that he used it *as a weapon*. But the words "as a weapon" appear nowhere in the statute. Rather, *§924(c)(1)*'s language sweeps broadly, punishing any "use" of a firearm, so long as the use is "during and in relation to" a drug trafficking offense. . . .

Language, of course, cannot be interpreted apart from context. The meaning of a word that appears ambiguous if viewed in isolation may become clear when the word is analyzed in light of the terms that surround it. Recognizing this, petitioner and the dissent argue that the word "uses" has a somewhat reduced scope in *§924(c)(1)* because it appears alongside the word "firearm." Specifically, they contend that the average person on the street would not think immediately of a guns-for-drugs trade as an example of "us[ing] a firearm." Rather, that phrase normally evokes an image of the most familiar use to which a firearm is put—use as a weapon. Petitioner and the dissent therefore argue that the statute excludes uses where the weapon is not fired or otherwise employed for its destructive capacity. . . . Indeed, relying on that argument—and without citation to authority—the dissent announces its own, restrictive definition of "use." "To use an instrumentality," the dissent argues, "ordinarily means to use it for its intended purpose." . . .

There is a significant flaw to this argument. It is one thing to say that the ordinary meaning of "uses a firearm" *includes* using a firearm as a weapon, since that is the intended purpose of a firearm and the example of "use" that most immediately comes to mind. But it is quite another to conclude that, as a result, the phrase also *excludes* any other use. Certainly that conclusion does not follow from the phrase "uses . . . a firearm" itself. As the dictionary definitions and experience make clear, one can use a firearm in a number of ways. That one example of "use" is the first to come to mind when the phrase "uses . . . a firearm" is uttered does not preclude us from recognizing that there are other "uses" that qualify as well. In this case, it is both reasonable and normal to say that petitioner "used" his MAC-10 in his drug trafficking offense by trading it for cocaine; the dissent does not contend otherwise.

The dissent's example of how one might "use" a cane, suffers from a similar flaw. To be sure, "use" as an adornment in a hallway is not the first "use" of a cane that comes to mind. But certainly it does not follow that the *only* "use" to which a cane might be put is assisting one's grandfather in walking. . . . In any event, the only question in this case is whether the phrase "uses . . . a firearm" in *§924(c)(1)* is most reasonably read as *excluding* the use of a firearm in a gun-for-drugs trade. The fact that the phrase clearly *includes* using a firearm to shoot someone, as the dissent contends, does not answer it.

. . .

In any event, the "intended purpose" of a firearm is not that it be used in any offensive manner whatever, but rather that it be used in a particular fashion—by firing it. The dissent's contention therefore cannot be that the defendant must use the firearm "as a weapon," but rather that he must fire it or threaten to fire it, "as a gun." Under the dissent's approach, then, even the criminal who pistol-whips his victim has not used a firearm within the meaning of *§924(c)(1)*, for firearms are intended to be fired or brandished, not used as bludgeons. It appears that the dissent similarly would limit the scope of the "other use[s]" covered by *USSG §2B3.1(b)(2)(B)*. The universal view of the courts of appeals, however, is directly to the contrary. . . .

To the extent there is uncertainty about the scope of the phrase "uses . . . a firearm" in *§924(c)(1)*, we believe the remainder of *§924* appropriately sets it to rest. Just as a single word cannot be read in isolation, nor can a single provision of a statute. . . . Here, Congress employed the words "use" and "firearm" together not only in *§924(c)(1)*, but also in *§924(d)(1)*, which deals with forfeiture of firearms. . . . Under *§924(d)(1)*, any "firearm or ammunition intended to be used" in the various offenses listed in *§924(d)(3)* is subject to seizure and forfeiture. Consistent with petitioner's interpretation, *§924(d)(3)* lists offenses in which guns might be used as offensive weapons. See *§§924(d)(3)(A)*, *(B)* (weapons used in a crime of violence or drug trafficking offense). But it also lists offenses in which the firearm is *not* used as a weapon but instead as an item of barter or commerce. For example, any gun intended to be "used" in an interstate "transfer, sale, trade, gift, transport, or delivery" of a firearm prohibited under *§922(a)(5)* where there is a pattern of such activity, see *§924(d)(3)(C)*, or in a federal offense involving "the exportation of firearms," *§924(d)(3)(F)*, is subject to forfeiture. In fact, none of the offenses listed in four of the six subsections of *§924(d)(3)* involves the bellicose use of a firearm; each offense involves use as an item in commerce. Thus, it is clear from *§924(d)(3)* that one who transports, exports, sells, or trades a firearm "uses" it within the meaning of *§924(d)(1)*—even though those actions do not involve using the firearm as a weapon. Unless we are to hold that using a firearm has a different meaning in *§924(c)(1)* than it does in *§924(d)*—and clearly we should not, . . .—we must reject petitioner's narrow interpretation.

* * *

The dissent suggests that our interpretation produces a "strange dichotomy" between "using" a firearm and "carrying" one. *Post*, at 246. We do not see why that is so. Just as a defendant may "use" a firearm within the meaning of *§924(c)(1)* by trading it for drugs *or* using it to shoot someone, so too would a defendant "carry" the firearm by keeping it on his person whether he intends to exchange it for cocaine or fire it in self-defense. The dichotomy arises, if at all, only when one tries to extend the phrase "'uses . . . a firearm'" to any use "'for any purpose whatever.'" *Ibid*. For our purposes, it is sufficient to recognize that, because *§924(d)(1)* includes both using a firearm for *trade* and using a firearm as a *weapon* as "us[ing] a firearm," it is most reasonable to construe *§924(c)(1)* as encompassing both of those "uses" as well.

* * *

Both a firearm's use as a weapon and its use as an item of barter fall within the plain language of *§924(c)(1)*, so long as the use occurs during and in relation to a drug trafficking offense; both must constitute "uses" of a firearm for *§924(d)(1)* to make any sense at all; and both create the very dangers and risks that Congress meant *§924(c)(1)* to address. We therefore hold that a criminal who trades his firearm for drugs "uses" it during and in relation to a drug trafficking offense within the meaning of *§924(c)(1)*. Because the evidence in this case showed that petitioner "used" his MAC-10 machine gun and silencer in precisely such a manner, proposing to trade them for cocaine, petitioner properly was subjected to *§924(c)(1)*'s 30-year mandatory minimum sentence. The judgment of the Court of Appeals, accordingly, is affirmed.

Case Discussion Questions

1. What did John Smith do that got him arrested?
2. With what crime was he charged? Was it a federal or a state crime?
3. What was the outcome of his trial?
4. What is the basis for Smith's appeal?
5. What, if any, issues of state statutory law were decided in this opinion?
6. What, if any, issues of federal statutory law were decided in this opinion?
7. What, if any, issues of state constitutional law were decided in this opinion?
8. What, if any, issues of federal constitutional law were decided in this opinion?
9. Which side won in the U.S. Supreme Court?
10. What principle of "statutory construction" was utilized in this case?
11. Briefly summarize how this principle was applied in this case.

Now go back and review the Illinois statutes on public indecency and harmful materials that were reproduced in the preceding section. When does exposure become "lewd," and what constitutes "harmful" materials? Although the indecency statute explicitly exempts the breastfeeding of infants, questions can be raised as to how long a child is considered an infant. It defines "public place" as "any place where the conduct may reasonably be expected to be viewed by others," but how clear is this definition? Does it apply if the conduct takes place in your backyard at night? What if the backyard is fenced in such a way that something going on there could be viewed only by a neighbor looking out of a second-story window?

To seek answers to these types of questions, an attorney will first look to see if the legislature provided definitions for some of these terms in the statute. (Note that these definitions may be found in a different part of the statute.) The Illinois legislature defined harmful materials as follows:

720 ILCS 5/11-21 Harmful Material

(b)(1) Material is harmful if, to the average person, applying contemporary standards, its predominant appeal, taken as a whole, is to prurient interest, that is a shameful or morbid interest in nudity, sex, or excretion, which goes substantially beyond customary limits of candor in description or representation of such matters, and is material the redeeming social importance of which is substantially less than its prurient appeal.

Do you think they did a good job? Does this section provide reasonable guidelines for determining what is or is not harmful material? It refers to the outlook of the average person, but how do you know what that is? How do you determine what the contemporary standards are? What is a prurient interest? When does an interest in nudity, sex, or excretion become shameful or morbid? How do you identify customary limits of candor or determine if the material has redeeming social importance?

When faced with these kinds of somewhat vague and ambiguous statutory definitions, attorneys will usually look for court cases that have applied the statute to similar types of circumstances. This can be very useful if you find cases that cover identical materials in the same setting, but many times no such cases can be found. When these types of judgments are left to a jury to decide, the outcome may depend on the luck of the draw as to the makeup of the jury in that particular case.

Constitutional challenges can be mounted when criminal statutes are deemed to be either too vague or too broad or when they place unconstitutional restraints on freedom of expression. The **void for vagueness doctrine** is a fundamental part of the Due Process Clause of the U.S. Constitution. It requires that penal statutes fairly inform ordinary people as to what is commanded or prohibited.[91] If a statute is vague, it might also be challenged on the basis of the **chilling effect doctrine** in First Amendment jurisprudence. Under this doctrine, a statute violates rights of free expression if it makes people fearful of engaging in legitimate, constitutionally protected activities.

Void for vagueness doctrine
A principle of constitutional law that requires penal statutes be written so that they fairly inform ordinary people as to what is commanded or prohibited.

Chilling effect doctrine
A principle of constitutional law that invalidates statutes that are worded in such a way as to makes people fearful of engaging in legitimate, constitutionally protected First Amendment activities.

Another fundamental principle of constitutional law is reflected in the **overbreadth doctrine.** Based on the First Amendment, any regulation of expression must be narrowly tailored to meet the government's legitimate objectives. A law can be struck down as overbroad if it restricts constitutionally protected free expression.

Overbreadth doctrine
A principle of constitutional law that any regulation of expression must be narrowly tailored to meet the government's legitimate object.

Statutes might also be challenged on the basis that they violate the Equal Protection Clause by discriminating on the basis of race, sex, religion, sexual orientation, etc. A law affecting freedom of expression can be struck down if it discriminates on the basis of viewpoint (e.g., applies to speech activities supporting a war but not those criticizing it).

K. Enforcement of Criminal Codes

State and local police departments investigate violations of state criminal codes. Then district attorneys (or state's attorneys) prosecute the cases.[92] Violations of the federal criminal code are typically investigated by the FBI and then

---

[91] In *United States v. Davis*, 139 S. Ct. 2319 (2019), the Supreme Court held that a federal law that provides enhanced penalties for using a firearm during a "crime of violence" is unconstitutionally vague. Although this principle has traditionally been used in the criminal law context, the Supreme Court used this doctrine to strike down the Immigration and Nationality Act's removal provisions that defined "violent felony." *Sessions v. Dimaya*, 138 S. Ct. 1204 (2019).

[92] District attorneys and state's attorneys are usually elected. They hire the assistant district attorneys who work for them.

prosecuted by U.S. Attorneys.[93] In highly controversial cases, such as the trial of the Minneapolis police officers involved in the death of George Floyd, the state police and the state attorney general's office may take over the investigation and prosecution. Likewise, when local prosecuting attorneys have conflicts of interest, state-level law enforcement officers and attorneys investigate and prosecute the case.

SUMMARY

This chapter presented an overview of the scope of criminal law at both the state and federal levels. Most criminal codes are organized into sections that cover topics such as offenses involving danger to people, offenses involving harm to property, offenses against the family, offenses against the government, and offenses against public order and decency.

Since it is not possible to cover every crime, and since there are many variations among the states, we could provide only a sampling of some of the most common offenses included in most criminal codes. The details of all of these offenses will vary from one state to another, so you will always need to check your own state's statutes to see how they define these same types of crimes and what additional offenses they may include.

Statutes often contain terms that are not part of your everyday language or are open to a wide variety of meanings. When this occurs, you should first check for a listing of definitions that may be included in another section of the code. You also need to research court cases that have applied the statute in similar situations. If the statute is too vague, interferes with First Amendment rights, or discriminates against some classes of people, it might be open to a constitutional challenge.

In Part 2 of this book, we will discuss how police and prosecutors decide with what crimes they plan to formally charge the accused criminals. We will also cover how defense attorneys go about developing their defense strategy.

INTERNET RESOURCES

General Search Engines for Statutes, Cases, and Regulations

- LawCrawler (at FindLaw): **http://lawcrawler.findlaw.com/**
- FindLaw: **http://www.findlaw.com**

Statistical Information on Crimes

- Bureau of Justice Statistics: **http://bjs.ojp.usdoj.gov/**
- Federal Bureau of Investigation (FBI): Uniform Crime Reports: **https://www.fbi.gov/services/cjis/ucr**

Most state and many local governments have a link to crime statistics for their area posted on their websites.

[93]U.S. Attorneys are nominated by the president and confirmed by the senate.

REVIEW QUESTIONS

1. How does the Model Penal Code define homicide?
2. What jobs or official duties permit individuals to cause the death of another human being without being guilty of homicide?
3. What are the three typical categories of homicide recognized in most criminal codes? How do these categories differ from one another?
4. Define *malice aforethought.*
5. List and define the two different types of manslaughter recognized under federal law.
6. Felony murder is a form of transferred intent. What is felony murder? Can arson be the basis for a felony murder charge? If it can form such a basis, how does it do so?
7. How do criminal assault and criminal battery differ from one another?
8. The offenses of stalking, assault, and terroristic threats are encompassed in a general category of crime. State the name and explain this category of crime.
9. Distinguish common law rape from statutory rape.
10. What are "hate crimes"?
11. For what felony is trespass a lesser included offense? Why is this?
12. How does larceny differ from robbery?
13. What is domestic violence and how does it differ from battery?
14. What classification of crime includes bribery, concealing or aiding a fugitive, and obstruction of justice?
15. DUI and BAC are abbreviations for what terms?
16. What is the concept of paternalism, and why did the philosopher John Stuart Mill reject it?
17. Is the overbreadth doctrine more like the doctrine of void for vagueness or the chilling effect doctrine?

PART 2

Criminal Procedure: From Commission of the Offense to Plea Bargaining

Chapter 4

Investigation of Criminal Behavior

CHAPTER OBJECTIVES

After reading this chapter, you should be able to:

- Explain the importance of due process of law and to illustrate how it affects the work of police and prosecutors.
- Describe how police go about discovering and investigating criminal behavior.
- Explain when and why search warrants are sometimes needed, as well as when and why they aren't.
- Describe how law enforcement personnel gather and preserve physical and documentary evidence.

INTRODUCTION

In Part 1 of this book, we discussed the purpose, organization, and major principles that underlie our criminal justice system. These topics are typically referred to as "substantive criminal law" because they relate to what the general public can or cannot legally do. In Parts 2 and 3, on the other hand, we explore the procedural side of criminal law, where the focus is on the various stages involved in criminal prosecutions and the tasks performed by participants in the criminal justice system.

In reading this and the chapters that follow, you should find it helpful to refer to the overview of the various stages of the criminal justice process that is shown in Figure 4.1. Note, however, that some of these details vary from one jurisdiction to another. For example, only about half the states have a mandatory grand jury system. Also, be aware that the stages may be accelerated

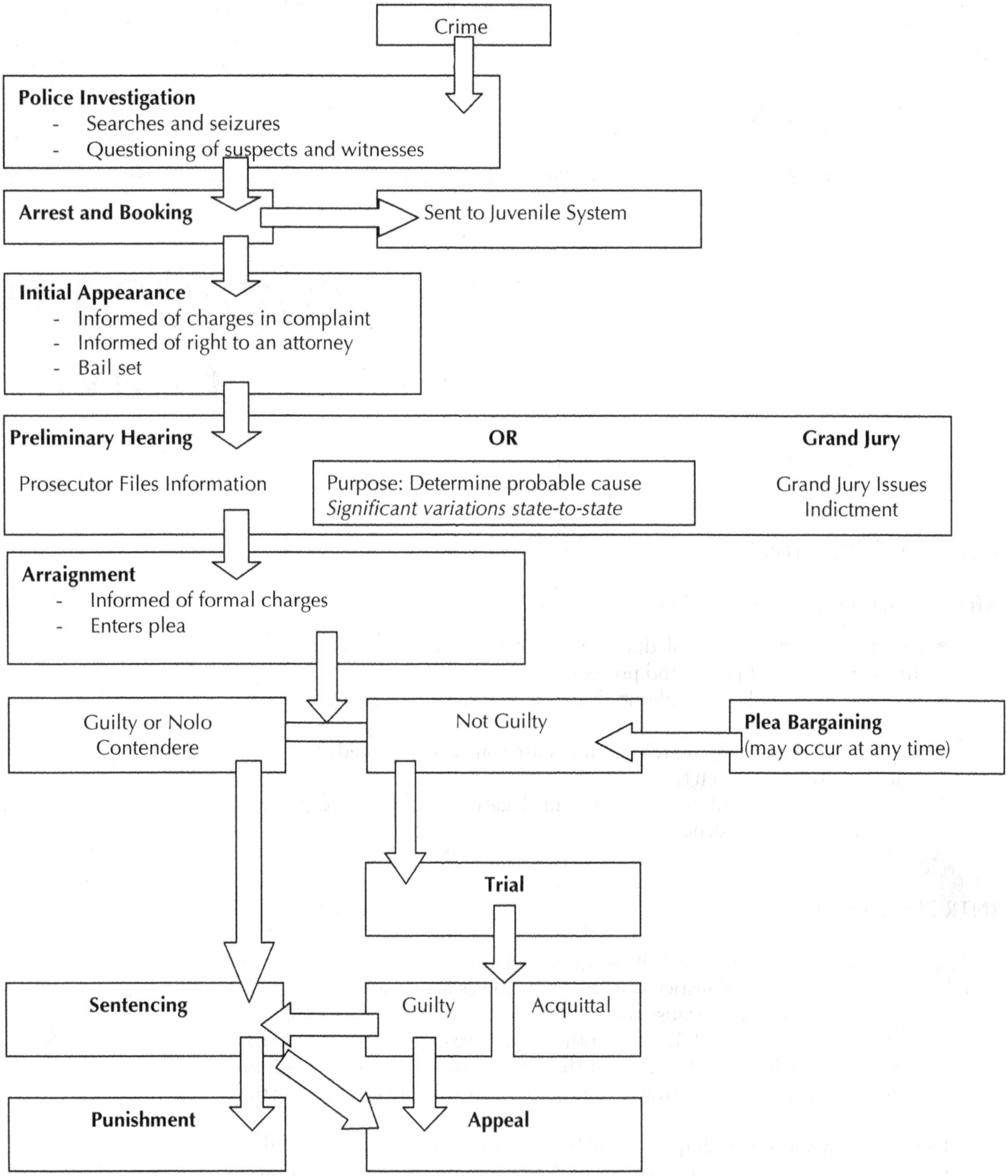

Figure 4.1 Stages of the Criminal Justice Process

or even combined in certain types of situations.[1] Additionally, note that there are many shortcuts and diversions built into the criminal justice system, and charges can be dropped at any time along the way. Where plea bargains are involved, the trial stage is skipped and the case moves directly to the corrections stages of the criminal justice process.

This chapter concentrates on the role played by police and other law enforcement personnel in identifying the people who commit crimes, gathering the evidence required to justify prosecuting them, and placing them under arrest. The other chapters in this section will focus on the roles played by prosecution and defense attorneys in preparing cases for trial.

It is also important to understand that in performing their duties, law enforcement officials must act in ways that are consistent with the due process requirements of the U.S. and state constitutions.

A. Constitutional Principles of Due Process

The investigation and prosecution of criminal behavior must be conducted in ways that do not violate basic constitutional rights set forth in the Fourth, Fifth, and Fourteenth Amendments to the U.S. Constitution.

1. Fifth and Fourteenth Amendments: Due Process of Law

The Fifth Amendment to the U.S. Constitution states, "No person shall . . . be deprived of life, liberty, or property, without due process of law"; and the Fourteenth Amendment states, ". . . nor shall any State deprive any person of life, liberty, or property, without due process of law. . . ." However, since the Constitution does not define what "due process" means, the justices of the U.S. Supreme Court determine its meaning. "Due process" usually refers to the series of procedures that governments must follow before they can deprive anyone of life, liberty, or property. This is called **procedural due process**. However, there is another type of due process, called **substantive due process**, which refers to the requirement that government cannot deprive anyone of life, liberty, or property where the law being violated is found to be arbitrary or unreasonable.

The Pennsylvania Supreme Court overturned the sexual assault conviction of actor/comedian Bill Cosby on due process grounds. As you read the following excerpts from the court's opinion in the *Cosby* case, compare the rights of the defendant to the interests of the prosecution and victim.

Procedural due process The series of procedures that federal and state government are constitutionally required to follow before they can deny anyone life, liberty, or property.

Substantive due process The constitutional limitation placed on the federal and state governments barring the deprivation of anyone's life, liberty, or property by means of a law found to be arbitrary and/or unreasonable.

[1] This is especially true for misdemeanors.

Commonwealth of Pennsylvania v. William Henry Cosby, Jr.
Supreme Court Pennsylvania
252 A.3d 1092 (PA 2021)

OPINION

In 2005, Montgomery County District Attorney Bruce Castor learned that Andrea Constand had reported that William Cosby had sexually assaulted her in 2004 at his Cheltenham residence. Along with his top deputy prosecutor and experienced detectives, District Attorney Castor thoroughly investigated Constand's claim. In evaluating the likelihood of a successful prosecution of Cosby, the district attorney foresaw difficulties with Constand's credibility as a witness based, in part, upon her decision not to file a complaint promptly. D.A. Castor further determined that a prosecution would be frustrated because there was no corroborating forensic evidence and because testimony from other potential claimants against Cosby likely was inadmissible under governing laws of evidence. The collective weight of these considerations led D.A. Castor to conclude that, unless Cosby confessed, "there was insufficient credible and admissible evidence upon which any charge against Mr. Cosby related to the Constand incident could be proven beyond a reasonable doubt."

Seeking "some measure of justice" for Constand, D.A. Castor decided that the Commonwealth would decline to prosecute Cosby for the incident involving Constand, thereby allowing Cosby to be forced to testify in a subsequent civil action, under penalty of perjury, without the benefit of his Fifth Amendment privilege against self-incrimination. Unable to invoke any right not to testify in the civil proceedings, Cosby relied upon the district attorney's declination and proceeded to provide four sworn depositions. During those depositions, Cosby made several incriminating statements.

D.A. Castor's successors did not feel bound by his decision and decided to prosecute Cosby notwithstanding that prior undertaking. The fruits of Cosby's reliance upon D.A. Castor's decision—Cosby's sworn inculpatory testimony—were then used by D.A. Castor's successors against Cosby at Cosby's criminal trial. We granted allowance of appeal to determine whether D.A. Castor's decision not to prosecute Cosby in exchange for his testimony must be enforced against the Commonwealth.

. . .

Nearly a decade after D.A. Castor's public decision not to prosecute Cosby, the Commonwealth charged Cosby with three counts of aggravated indecent assault stemming from the January 2004 incident with Constand in Cosby's Cheltenham residence. On January 11, 2016, Cosby filed a petition for a writ of habeas corpus seeking dismissal of the charges based upon the former D.A. Castor's purported promise—made in his representative capacity on behalf of the Commonwealth—that Cosby would not be prosecuted. . . .

From February 2-3, 2016, the trial court conducted hearings on Cosby's habeas petition, which it ultimately denied. . . .

For the reasons detailed below, we hold that, when a prosecutor makes an unconditional promise of non-prosecution, and when the defendant relies upon that guarantee to the detriment of his constitutional right not to testify, the principle of fundamental fairness that undergirds due process of law in our criminal justice system demands that the promise be enforced. Prosecutors are more than mere participants in our criminal justice system. [P]rosecutors inhabit three distinct and equally critical roles: they are officers of the court, advocates for victims, and administrators of justice. As the Commonwealth's representatives, prosecutors are duty-bound to pursue "equal and impartial justice," and "to serve the public interest." Their obligation is "not merely to convict," but rather to "seek justice within the bounds of the law." . . .

Considered together, these authorities obligate courts to hold prosecutors to their word, to enforce promises, to ensure that defendants' decisions are made with a full understanding of the circumstances, and to prevent fraudulent inducements of waivers of one or more constitutional rights. Prosecutors can be bound by their assurances or decisions under principles of contract law or by application of the fundamental fairness considerations that inform and undergird the due process of law. The law is clear that, based upon their unique role in the criminal justice system, prosecutors generally are bound by their assurances, particularly when defendants rely to their detriment upon those guarantees. . . .

[W]hen a defendant relies to his or her detriment upon the acts of a prosecutor, his or her due process rights are implicated. The Fourteenth Amendment to the United States Constitution and Article I, Section 9 of the Pennsylvania Constitution mandate that all interactions between the government and the individual are conducted in accordance with the protections of due process. We have explained that review of a due process claim "entails an assessment as to whether the challenged proceeding or conduct offends some principle of justice so rooted in the traditions and conscience of our people as to be ranked as fundamental and that defines the community's sense of fair play and decency." . . .

As a reviewing court, we accept the trial court's conclusion that the district attorney's decision was merely an exercise of his charging discretion. As we assess whether that decision, and the surrounding circumstances, implicated Cosby's due process rights, former D.A. Castor's *post-hoc* attempts to explain or characterize his actions are largely immaterial. The answer to our query lies instead in the objectively indisputable evidence of record demonstrating D.A. Castor's patent intent to induce Cosby's reliance upon the non-prosecution decision. . . .

D.A. Castor's press release, without more, does not necessarily create a due process entitlement. Rather, the due process implications arise because Cosby detrimentally relied upon the Commonwealth's decision, which was the district attorney's ultimate intent in issuing the press release. There was no evidence of record indicating that D.A. Castor intended anything other than to induce Cosby's reliance. Indeed, the most patent and obvious evidence of Cosby's reliance was his counseled decision to testify in four depositions in Constand's civil case without ever invoking his Fifth Amendment rights.

The Fifth Amendment to the United States Constitution, which is applicable to the States via incorporation through the Fourteenth Amendment, commands that "[n]o person . . . shall be compelled in any criminal case to be a witness against himself." U.S. Const. amend. V. The right to refuse to incriminate oneself is an "essential mainstay" of our constitutional system of criminal justice. The privilege constitutes an essential restraint upon the power of the government, and stands as an indispensable rampart between that government and the governed. The Fifth Amendment's self-incrimination clause "is not only a protection against conviction and prosecution but a safeguard of conscience and human dignity and freedom of expression as well." . . .

It is indisputable that, in Constand's civil case, Cosby was entitled to invoke the Fifth Amendment. No court could have forced Cosby to testify in a deposition or at a trial so long as the potential for criminal charges remained. Here, however, when called for deposition, Cosby no longer faced criminal charges. When compelled to testify, Cosby no longer had a right to invoke his right to remain silent.

Cosby was forced to sit for four depositions. That he did not—and could not—choose to remain silent is apparent from the record. When Cosby attempted to decline to answer certain questions about Constand, Constand's attorneys obtained a ruling from the civil trial judge forcing Cosby to answer. Most significantly, Cosby, having maintained his innocence in all matters and having been advised by a number of attorneys, provided critical evidence of his recurring history of supplying women with central nervous system depressants before engaging in (allegedly unwanted) sexual activity with them—the very assertion that undergirded Constand's criminal complaint. . . .

In accordance with the advice of his attorneys, Cosby relied upon D.A. Castor's public announcement that he would not be prosecuted. His reliance was reasonable, and it resulted in the deprivation of a fundamental constitutional right when he was compelled to furnish self-incriminating testimony. Cosby reasonably relied upon the Commonwealth's decision for approximately ten years. When he announced his declination decision on behalf of the Commonwealth, District Attorney Castor knew that Cosby would be forced to testify based upon the Commonwealth's assurances. Knowing that he induced Cosby's reliance, and that his decision not to prosecute was designed to do just that, D.A. Castor made no attempt in 2005 or in any of the ten years that followed to remedy any misperception or to stop Cosby from openly and detrimentally relying upon that decision. In light of these circumstances, the subsequent decision by successor D.A.s to prosecute Cosby violated Cosby's due process rights. No other conclusion comports with the principles of due process and fundamental fairness to which all aspects of our criminal justice system must adhere.

Having identified a due process violation here, we must ascertain the remedy to which Cosby is entitled. . . .

Here, only full enforcement of the decision not to prosecute can satisfy the fundamental demands of due process. In light of the extent and duration of Cosby's reliance, induced as intended by then-District Attorney Castor, no other remedy will do. Anything less under these circumstances would permit the Commonwealth to extract incriminating evidence from a defendant who relies upon the elected prosecutor's words, actions, and intent, and then use that evidence against that defendant with impunity. . . .

For these reasons, Cosby's convictions and judgment of sentence are vacated, and he is discharged.

Case Discussion Questions

1. Did the Pennsylvania Supreme apply substantive or procedural due process?
2. Is it just to the alleged victim in the case to bar the government from retrying Cosby on the charges?
3. Would justice be served if the government were allowed to retry the case, but without using the statements Cosby made in his depositions?

Through a process that constitutional scholars call "selective incorporation," the Supreme Court has ruled that most, though not all, provisions of the Bill of Rights are applicable in state criminal prosecutions.[2] They include protection against unreasonable search and seizure, double jeopardy, and

[2]Throughout the years, various justices have used a variety of standards for determining whether a particular practice was, or was not, required by the Fourteenth Amendment. The most famous and widely used standard was announced in 1937 in *Palko v. Connecticut,* 302 U.S. 319 (1937), a case in which Justice Benjamin Cardozo announced that the standard for what does or does not violate the Due Process Clause of the Fourteenth Amendment is whether the challenged practice violates "fundamental principles of liberty and justice which lie at the base of all our civil and political institutions." Other tests have included "case by case fairness," whether the right was "fundamental to ordered liberty," and whether it reflected the "fundamental principles of liberty and justice which lie at the base of all our civil and political institutions." Even in the twenty-first century, the Supreme Court continues to incorporate provisions of the Bill of Rights through the Fourteenth Amendment. For instance, in *Timbs v. Indiana,* 139 S. Ct. 682 (2019), the Court held that the Eighth Amendment's excessive fines clause is an incorporated protection applicable to the states under the Fourteenth Amendment's Due Process Clause.

self-incrimination, as well as the right to a speedy public trial, trial by jury, confrontation of accusers, the compulsory process for obtaining witnesses, and effective assistance of counsel.

2. FOURTH AMENDMENT: "UNREASONABLE" SEARCHES AND SEIZURES

The Fourth Amendment to the U.S. Constitution states:

> The right of the people to be secure in their persons, houses, papers, and effects, against unreasonable searches and seizures, shall not be violated, and no Warrants shall issue, but upon probable cause, supported by Oath or affirmation, and particularly describing the place to be searched, and the persons or things to be seized.

Although the entire amendment consists of only one sentence, it contains two distinct clauses. The first explains that the prohibition against unreasonable searches and seizures is designed to protect a right of the people to be "secure" in their "persons, houses, papers, and effects." The second part limits the circumstances under which warrants can be issued and describes what must be contained in the way they are worded. It declares that warrants can only be issued "upon probable cause" and where they are "supported by oath or affirmation." The content of the warrant must "particularly describe" the place to be searched and the "persons or things" to be seized.

Although the amendment doesn't define "unreasonable," the context of its use implies that a search would not be unreasonable if it were based on a warrant that had been issued upon probable cause, supported by oath or affirmation, and particularly described the place to be searched and/or the persons or things to be seized. Note, however, that this doesn't mean that other types of searches without a warrant are necessarily prohibited by the Fourth Amendment. Indeed, the courts have approved warrantless searches and seizures in a wide variety of situations, including consent searches, searches incident to arrest, inventory searches, searches in "exigent circumstances," and "plain view" seizures. Fundamentally, Fourth Amendment jurisprudence requires that searches must either be consensual or be based on probable cause to believe that it will lead to the discovery of contraband materials or other evidence that a crime was committed.

Note also that the amendment doesn't specify the penalty for violating this right. Based on historical and contextual factors, the courts have ruled that it is a limitation on the actions of governmental agents, not the actions of private citizens. The means for enforcing this amendment and other provisions of the Bill of Rights are discussed in Chapter 7.[3]

---

[3] See the discussion of the exclusionary rule on pp. 229-233.

3. FIFTH AMENDMENT: PROTECTION AGAINST SELF-INCRIMINATION

The Fifth Amendment to the U.S. Constitution states:

> No person . . . shall be compelled in any criminal case to be a witness against himself, nor be deprived of life, liberty, or property, without due process of law; . . .

Courts have interpreted the phrase about not being compelled to be a witness against oneself to apply to police interrogations as well as formal testimony presented in court. The Fifth Amendment also protects defendants from being placed in "double jeopardy," which will be covered in Chapter 7.

4. SIXTH AMENDMENT: RIGHT TO COUNSEL

The Sixth Amendment to the U.S. Constitution states:

> In all criminal prosecutions, the accused shall enjoy the right . . . to have the assistance of counsel for his defence.[4]

The provisions in this amendment relate to procedural safeguards available to defendants before and during their trials. We will discuss the right to counsel in Chapter 6. The Sixth Amendment also grants defendants the rights to a speedy trial, an impartial jury, and compulsory process, as well as the right to confront and cross-examine witnesses, will be discussed in Chapter 10.

Discussion Question

1. Note the frequent use of inherently ambiguous terms such as "liberty," "due process," and "unreasonable" in the abovementioned amendments to the Constitution.

a. Why do you think the drafters used such vague language? Why weren't they more specific?

b. How should a judge go about determining if a specific search is, or is not, "reasonable"?

B. Investigating Crimes

1. LOCATING AND QUESTIONING VICTIMS AND WITNESSES

The first stage of a criminal investigation typically involves interviewing witnesses to learn more about what happened and who was involved. However, it is not always easy to identify and locate these people. Police often go door to door in the area of the crime scene inquiring as to what neighbors know about

---

[4]The drafters of the Constitution used the British spelling of "defense."

the victims or possible perpetrators. Sometimes witnesses turn out to be suspects. Some witnesses may not be able or willing to cooperate with law enforcement authorities. The victim may have died, and some witnesses may refuse to cooperate for fear of retribution or of incriminating themselves.

2. IDENTIFICATION OF SUSPECTS

One of the most valuable pieces of information that a victim or witness can provide is the identification of persons involved in the crime. Many times, they can provide a name, an address, or other information that will help law enforcement officials find the alleged perpetrator. In situations in which victims and witnesses don't remember having seen the suspect before, the police may ask them to look through mug books (collections of photos of people who have been arrested in connection with other crimes) or to view a police lineup.[5]

3. INTERROGATIONS

a. *The Right to Question*

As pointed out at the beginning of this chapter, the Fifth Amendment's protection against self-incrimination gives people the right to refuse to answer questions from law enforcement agents. Indeed, except for the very limited privilege to briefly detain people and require them to identify themselves, police cannot even make someone stop and listen to their questions. This is because the term *seizure*, as it is used in the Fourth Amendment, has been interpreted as applying to seizing a person as well as a physical object. Therefore, government agents cannot detain people beyond the time it takes to have them identify themselves without having probable cause to believe they were involved in a crime.

Reasonable suspicion
A reasonable belief in the context of the specific facts of the situation. This standard is greater than a mere hunch, but less than a probable cause.

***Terry* stop**
A law enforcement officer's stop of a person for a brief period of time to ask a few questions when the officer has "reasonable suspicion" that the person has committed, is in the process of committing, or is about to commit a crime.

Two key U.S. Supreme Court cases have defined what police can and cannot do in these types of situations. In *Terry v. Ohio*,[6] the justices ruled that police are entitled to stop (detain) an individual for a brief period of time, to ask a few questions where they have a **reasonable suspicion** that the person being stopped has committed, is in the process of committing, or is about to commit a crime. This short detention is referred to as a "***Terry* stop.**" According to *Terry*, reasonable suspicion must be based on "specific and articulable facts which, taken together with rational inferences from those facts, reasonably warrant that intrusion."[7] In this case, the police officer thought that a group of individuals was hanging around a street corner to plan a stickup. He asked the men to identify themselves. (The *Terry* case also involved a "pat-down search," which we will discuss in Section C of this chapter.)

---

[5]When police place a suspect in a formal lineup, they are required to make sure that there are other participants of a similar age, race, hairstyle, and other characteristics as the suspect and to provide an opportunity for the suspect's attorney to be present.

[6]392 U.S. 1 (1968).

[7]392 U.S. at 21.

But what if those individuals do not wish to identify themselves? That question was answered by the Supreme Court in *Hiibel v. Nevada*,[8] a case in which a Nevada police officer was responding to a call reporting that a man had assaulted a woman. The officer observed a man standing outside a parked truck that matched the description the police had been given and saw a woman inside the truck. The officer asked the suspect to identify himself. When he refused, the police arrested him. Nevada had a statute requiring suspects to identify themselves to the police. The Supreme Court ruled that the officer had reasonable suspicion to stop the suspect and was justified in arresting him. The Court held that a statute requiring suspects to disclose their names during a valid *Terry* stop does not violate the Fourth or Fifth Amendment.[9]

b. The Rights to Have Attorney Present and to Refuse to Answer

Miranda v. Arizona[10] is one of the most frequently referenced decisions in the history of the U.S. Supreme Court. Not only have most people in the United States heard of it, many have seen enough TV cop shows to be able to recite the *Miranda* warnings from memory. But, in case you need a quick refresher, the essence of *Miranda* warnings are:

> You have the right to remain silent;
> Anything you say can be used against you in a court of law;
> You have the right to have an attorney present during questioning; and
> If you cannot afford an attorney, one will be appointed for you.

After notifying suspects of these rights, law enforcement personnel are not supposed to question them until they waive these rights. In many jurisdictions, the suspect must sign and initial the *Miranda* waiver form before any interrogation begins.

As you read the following excerpts from the Court's Opinion in the *Miranda* case, focus on the justifications given for requiring these warnings.

Miranda v. Arizona
Supreme Court of the United States
384 U.S. 436 (1966)

MR. CHIEF JUSTICE WARREN delivered the opinion of the Court.

The cases before us raise questions which go to the roots of our concepts of American criminal jurisprudence: the restraints society must observe consistent with the Federal Constitution in prosecuting individuals for crime. More specifically, we deal with the admissibility of statements obtained from an individual who is subjected to custodial police interrogation and

[8]542 U.S. 177 (2004).

[9]In many states, it is considered obstruction of justice to give police a false identity.

[10]384 U.S. 436 (1966).

the necessity for procedures which assure that the individual is accorded his privilege under the Fifth Amendment to the Constitution not to be compelled to incriminate himself.

. . .

We start here . . . with the premise that our holding is not an innovation in our jurisprudence, but is an application of principles long recognized and applied in other settings

. . .

Our holding will be spelled out with some specificity in the pages which follow but briefly stated it is this: the prosecution may not use statements, whether exculpatory or inculpatory, stemming from custodial interrogation of the defendant unless it demonstrates the use of procedural safeguards effective to secure the privilege against self-incrimination. By custodial interrogation, we mean questioning initiated by law enforcement officers after a person has been taken into custody or otherwise deprived of his freedom of action in any significant way. As for the procedural safeguards to be employed, unless other fully effective means are devised to inform accused persons of their right of silence and to assure a continuous opportunity to exercise it, the following measures are required. Prior to any questioning, the person must be warned that he has a right to remain silent, that any statement he does make may be used as evidence against him, and that he has a right to the presence of an attorney, either retained or appointed. The defendant may waive effectuation of these rights, provided the waiver is made voluntarily, knowingly and intelligently. If, however, he indicates in any manner and at any stage of the process that he wishes to consult with an attorney before speaking there can be no questioning. Likewise, if the individual is alone and indicates in any manner that he does not wish to be interrogated, the police may not question him. The mere fact that he may have answered some questions or volunteered some statements on his own does not deprive him of the right to refrain from answering any further inquiries until he has consulted with an attorney and thereafter consents to be questioned.

The constitutional issue we decide in each of these cases is the admissibility of statements obtained from a defendant questioned while in custody or otherwise deprived of his freedom of action in any significant way. In each, the defendant was questioned by police officers, detectives, or a prosecuting attorney in a room in which he was cut off from the outside world. In none of these cases was the defendant given a full and effective warning of his rights at the outset of the interrogation process. In all the cases, the questioning elicited oral admissions, and in three of them, signed statements as well which were admitted at their trials. They all thus share salient features—incommunicado interrogation of individuals in a police-dominated atmosphere, resulting in self-incriminating statements without full warnings of constitutional rights.

An understanding of the nature and setting of this in-custody interrogation is essential to our decisions today. The difficulty in depicting what transpires at such interrogations stems from the fact that in this country they have largely taken place incommunicado. From extensive factual studies undertaken in the early 1930's, including the famous Wickersham Report to Congress by a Presidential Commission, it is clear that police violence and the "third degree" flourished at that time. In a series of cases decided by this Court long after these studies, the police resorted to physical brutality—beating, hanging, whipping—and to sustained and protracted questioning incommunicado in order to extort confessions. The Commission on Civil Rights in 1961 found much evidence to indicate that "some policemen still resort to physical force to obtain confessions," . . . .

[*The opinion then quotes at length from police interrogation manuals to show how police also are encouraged to use various psychological pressures and tricks to obtain confessions.*]

. . .

In these cases, we might not find the defendants' statements to have been involuntary in traditional terms. Our concern for adequate safeguards to protect precious Fifth Amendment rights is, of course, not lessened in the slightest.

In each of the cases, the defendant was thrust into an unfamiliar atmosphere and run through menacing police interrogation procedures. The potentiality for compulsion is forcefully apparent, for example, in *Miranda*, where the indigent Mexican defendant was a seriously disturbed individual with pronounced sexual fantasies, and in *Stewart*, in which the defendant was an indigent Los Angeles Negro who had dropped out of school in the sixth grade. To be sure, the records do not evince overt physical coercion or patent psychological ploys. The fact remains that in none of these cases did the officers undertake to afford appropriate safeguards at the outset of the interrogation to insure that the statements were truly the product of free choice.

. . .

Today, then, there can be no doubt that the Fifth Amendment privilege is available outside of criminal court proceedings and serves to protect persons in all settings in which their freedom of action is curtailed in any significant way from being compelled to incriminate themselves. We have concluded that without proper safeguards the process of in-custody interrogation of persons suspected or accused of crime contains inherently compelling pressures which work to undermine the individual's will to resist and to compel him to speak where he would not otherwise do so freely. In order to combat these pressures and to permit a full opportunity to exercise the privilege against self-incrimination, the accused must be adequately and effectively apprised of his rights and the exercise of those rights must be fully honored.

. . .

The Fifth Amendment privilege is so fundamental to our system of constitutional rule and the expedient of giving an adequate warning as to the availability of the privilege so simple, we will not pause to inquire in individual cases whether the defendant was aware of his rights without a warning being given. . . .

The circumstances surrounding in-custody interrogation can operate very quickly to overbear the will of one merely made aware of his privilege by his interrogators. Therefore, the right to have counsel present at the interrogation is indispensable to the protection of the Fifth Amendment privilege under the system we delineate today. Our aim is to assure that the individual's right to choose between silence and speech remains unfettered throughout the interrogation process. A once-stated warning, delivered by those who will conduct the interrogation, cannot itself suffice to that end among those who most require knowledge of their rights. . . . Even preliminary advice given to the accused by his own attorney can be swiftly overcome by the secret interrogation process. . . . Thus, the need for counsel to protect the Fifth Amendment privilege comprehends not merely a right to consult with counsel prior to questioning, but also to have counsel present during any questioning if the defendant so desires.

The presence of counsel at the interrogation may serve several significant subsidiary functions as well. If the accused decides to talk to his interrogators, the assistance of counsel can mitigate the dangers of untrustworthiness. With a lawyer present the likelihood that the police will practice coercion is reduced, and if coercion is nevertheless exercised the lawyer can testify to it in court. The presence of a lawyer can also help to guarantee that the accused gives a fully accurate statement to the police and that the statement is rightly reported by the prosecution at trial.

. . .

If the interrogation continues without the presence of an attorney and a statement is taken, a heavy burden rests on the government to demonstrate that the defendant knowingly and intelligently waived his privilege against self-incrimination and his right to retained or appointed counsel. . . .

. . .

A recurrent argument made in these cases is that society's need for interrogation outweighs the privilege. . . .

. . .

Over the years the Federal Bureau of Investigation has compiled an exemplary record of effective law enforcement while advising any suspect or arrested person, at the outset of an interview, that he is not required to make a statement, that any statement may be used against him in court, that the individual may obtain the services of an attorney of his own choice and, more recently, that he has a right to free counsel if he is unable to pay. A letter received from the Solicitor General in response to a question from the Bench makes it clear that the present pattern of warnings and respect for the rights of the individual followed as a practice by the FBI is consistent with the procedure which we delineate today. . . .

The practice of the FBI can readily be emulated by state and local enforcement agencies. The argument that the FBI deals with different crimes than are dealt with by state authorities does not mitigate the significance of the FBI experience. . . .

The experience in some other countries also suggests that the danger to law enforcement in curbs on interrogation is overplayed. . . .

* * *

It is so ordered.

Case Discussion Questions

1. Which constitutional rights are involved in this case?
2. How are the *Miranda* warnings related to these constitutional rights?
3. What is the Court's justification for requiring that the *Miranda* warnings be given?
4. What is the Court's response to the argument that society's needs to convict criminals outweighs the enforcement of the defendant's constitutional rights?

As Republican presidents like Richard Nixon, Ronald Reagan, and the Bushes replaced liberal Warren Court justices with conservative ones, many observers thought that *Miranda* would eventually be overruled. Although that has not occurred,[11] the more conservative Burger, Rehnquist, and Roberts Courts rendered decisions that limited the situations in which the warnings had to be given. Examples include:

- *Beckwith v. United States.*[12] The Court held that Internal Revenue Service (IRS) agents were not required to give *Miranda* warnings when they questioned a taxpayer in his home,
- *Oregon v. Mathiason.*[13] The Court held that police were not required to give *Miranda* rights when an individual voluntarily came to the station.
- *Berkemer v. McCarty.*[14] The Court held that police were not required to give *Miranda* rights when they questioned a motorist at the scene of a stop for a traffic offense.
- *Howe v. Fields.*[15] The Court held that police were not required to give *Miranda* warnings when they questioned a prisoner in private about events occurring outside the prison.

[11]In *Dickerson v. United States*, 530 U.S. 428 (2000), the Supreme Court struck down a federal statute providing that voluntary confessions were to be admissible even if *Miranda* warnings are not given.

[12]425 U.S. 341 (1976).

[13]429 U.S. 492 (1977).

[14]468 U.S. 420 (1984).

[15]565 U.S. 499 (2012).

- *Salinas v. Texas.*[16] The Court held that the Fifth Amendment self-incrimination clause does not protect a defendant's refusal to answer questions in a non-custodial police interview when he was not given his *Miranda* rights.

However, not every post–Warren Court decision involving the failure to give *Miranda* warnings favors the prosecution. For example, in *Missouri v. Seibert*, a plurality of the Court ruled that *Miranda* warnings given mid-interrogation, after the suspect gave a confession, were ineffective, and thus the Fifth Amendment self-incrimination clause rendered the confession, repeated after warnings were given, inadmissible at trial.[17]

c. *Consequences of Questioning Suspects Without Having Given the Miranda Warnings*

There is a popular misconception that a police officer's failure to read defendants their *Miranda* rights invalidates their arrests. This is not the case. It is not uncommon for police not to give warnings to defendants charged with misdemeanors. *Miranda* established that "the prosecution may not use statements, whether exculpatory or inculpatory, stemming from custodial interrogation of the defendant unless it demonstrates the use of procedural safeguards effective to secure the privilege against self-incrimination." It did not prohibit police from asking general questions of people at the scene of a crime or in circumstances in which a suspect was not in custody.

Take special note of the fact that the penalty for failure to give the *Miranda* warnings, when they are required, is a ban against using the statements gained in the interrogation against the person in criminal court proceedings. It doesn't mean that the person couldn't still be prosecuted with other evidence that wasn't gained as a result of statements made by the defendant during the interrogation. This means that neither an arrest nor a criminal charge is invalid simply because the officer failed to give the suspect the *Miranda* warnings.

Brewer v. Williams[18] presents an interesting example of how people can be convicted even though police failed to give the appropriate *Miranda* warnings. In this case, police attempted to trick a suspect into making incriminating statements while transporting him in the back seat of their squad car. They did so by talking to each other, in front of the suspect, about the need to find the alleged victim's body so she could receive a proper Christian burial. When the suspect eventually told them where it could be found, the prosecution used this information and evidence found on the body against the suspect. Although the Supreme Court overturned the conviction on the grounds that *Miranda* warnings had not been given, Williams was again convicted of first-degree murder at a second trial. This time, evidence concerning the body's location and condition was admitted based on the doctrine of "inevitable discovery."[19] The Supreme Court affirmed this second conviction.

---

[16] 570 U.S. 178 (2013).

[17] 542 U.S. 600 (2004).

[18] 430 U.S. 387 (1977).

[19] Inevitable discovery is a principle that this type of evidence can be admitted if the state proves that it would have been discovered in essentially the same condition even if the defendant had not been improperly induced to reveal its location.

d. Effectiveness of Interrogations

Movies and television shows often feature dramatic police interrogations that result in suspects either confessing or making surprising admissions that help police make their case. In real life, police interrogations rarely yield these types of results, and in situations where suspects do confess, there is usually sufficient physical and testimonial evidence to convict even without the confession.

What is even more surprising to many people is that so many suspects waive their right to remain silent and answer police questions without consulting with an attorney. Part of the reason why this happens is that police will often "egg them on" by making comments to the effect that they don't need a lawyer unless they have something to hide. Many times, it is because the suspects think they can come up with answers that will make police think they didn't commit any crime.

In the process of trying to talk their way out of their situation, suspects often make the mistake of making inconsistent or contradictory statements that later come back to haunt them when they are used at trial. Exhibit 4.1 contains

Exhibit 4.1: Excerpts of Transcript of Kobe Bryant Interrogation

Detective Winters: Okay. Um, I'll be blunt and ask you. Did you have sexual intercourse with her?

Bryant: No.

Detective Winters: Okay. Uh, what, okay, Kobe here's, here's what I'd like to do okay. Um, yet there is an allegation that it was an unconsensual intercourse that occurred last night, okay. All right. Hang on, okay, hang on, I understand you have every right to be upset, okay, but, you know, but, I'm giving you an opportunity to tell the truth if something did happen, because I'm gonna tell you right now, um, we're gonna find out.

* * *

Detective Loya: Just be straight up, we're not gonna tell your wife or anything like that. Did you have sexual intercourse with her?

Bryant: Uh, this is what I need to know because uh, I did have sexual intercourse with her. Cause I was ...(inaudible whisper).

Detective Winters: And I understand.

Detective Loya: Okay, was it consensual?

Bryant: It was totally consensual.

excerpts of the police interview with the basketball star Kobe Bryant when he was being investigated for sexual assault. Notice how Bryant changed his story as the interview progressed.

Discussion Questions

2. What limits, if any, *should* there be on the right of law enforcement personnel to stop and question individuals to determine if they have any involvement in, or even know anything about, any criminal behavior?

3. Under what circumstances, if any, *should* law enforcement personnel be able to require someone to identify themselves and present proper documentation (such as a driver's license or other form of identification) to prove that they are who they claim to be? Should this extend to a requirement to show documentation that the person is not an illegal immigrant?

4. Under what circumstances, if any, *should* law enforcement personnel be able to take a person to another location in order to interrogate that individual?

5. Under what circumstances, if any, *should* law enforcement personnel be required to inform individuals they are questioning about their rights to counsel and their privilege against self-incrimination?

6. Under what circumstances, if any, *should* principals or teachers be required to inform students of their rights to counsel and their privilege against self-incrimination when they are questioning them about school related matters?

4. USE OF GRAND JURIES TO INVESTIGATE CRIMES

Immunity
An exemption from prosecution given to a witness so that the witness can be compelled to give self-incriminating testimony.

Transactional immunity
Prosecutorial immunity that protects a witness from prosecution for the offense revealed in his or her testimony.

Use immunity
Prosecutorial immunity that bars the government from using the testimony in the prosecution of the witness, except on charges of perjury. Use immunity is also known as "derivative use immunity."

Since grand juries are most closely associated with the activities of prosecuting attorneys, we will wait until Chapter 5 before we go into more detail about their origin and current use. At this point in the text, we simply wish to mention that at the federal level and in some states, these juries present an additional investigative tool, whereby reluctant witnesses can be required to testify in secret about information they may have about criminal activity.

Due to the secretive nature of grand jury proceedings and their power to subpoena witnesses, grand juries are especially useful in investigating governmental corruption, organized crime, and situations involving undercover operatives. Witnesses can be forced to reveal information that incriminates others without the subjects of the inquiry knowing that they are being investigated and without undercover agents having to publicly reveal their identity. This is why federal grand juries played a major role in Special Counsel Robert Mueller's investigation into links between the Donald Trump presidential campaign and Russian interference in the 2016 presidential election.

Although grand jury witnesses can still claim the self-incrimination protections of the Fifth Amendment, they do not have the right to have their attorney in the hearing room with them. Furthermore, prosecutors often grant either transactional or use **immunity** to compel a witness's testimony. **Transactional immunity** protects a witness from prosecution for the offense revealed in his or her testimony, and **use immunity**, also known as "derivative use immunity," bars the prosecution from using the testimony in any prosecution of the witness, except on charges of perjury.

C. Gathering of Physical and Documentary Evidence

Although victims and witnesses can often provide essential information about what took place and may think they can identify the perpetrator, eyewitness identification has often proved to be quite unreliable. In recent years, there have been several well-publicized cases in which people convicted on the basis of eyewitness testimony were later proved, by deoxyribonucleic acid (DNA) testing and/or confessions by others, to have been innocent. For instance, the Northwestern University's Center on Wrongful Convictions reports:

> In the quarter century between restoration of the Illinois death penalty and Governor George Ryan's blanket clemency order, 298 men and women were sentenced to death in Illinois. Of those, 20 have been exonerated—a rate of 6.7%.[20]

Therefore, much greater weight is now placed on the gathering of physical evidence.

As part of their investigation, the police typically take measurements and pictures of the crime scene, retrieve samples of fluids found at the scene, and carry out some of the other things you typically see on *CSI*-type television shows.

In addition to evidence found at the scene of the crime, law enforcement often can locate other incriminating evidence in a suspect's home, business, or automobile. Such searches may locate the fruits of crime (such as stolen property), the instruments of crime (such as burglary tools or weapons), or contraband items (such as illegal drugs or weapons). Letters, notes, e-mails, and financial records can also provide important evidence in criminal trials. This is especially true in cases involving white-collar crimes.

However, in gathering this type of evidence, criminal investigators must be careful to collect it in a manner that does not violate the Fourth Amendment's prohibition against "unreasonable searches and seizures." In other words, it must either be authorized by a proper search warrant or fall into one of the exceptional situations in which a search warrant is not required.

1. SEARCHES THAT DO NOT REQUIRE A WARRANT

While a complete discussion of all exceptions to the warrant requirement is beyond the scope of this chapter, you should become familiar with each of the major types of searches discussed in this section.

a. *Consent Searches*

Consent is perhaps the most common situation in which law enforcement personnel do not need a search warrant. Defendants cannot claim a violation of their Fourth Amendment rights if they consented to the search. But what are

[20] http://www.law.northwestern.edu/legalclinic/wrongfulconvictions/exonerations/deathpenalty/.

the requirements for a search to be considered consensual, and who is authorized to give consent to property that is shared by more than one person?

The courts have ruled that to be a valid consent search, the permission to search must have been given voluntarily and by someone who is authorized to do so. Thus, to be valid consent, it cannot have been obtained through coercion (actual or threatened) or trickery. In *Bumper v. North Carolina*,[21] for example, the Supreme Court invalidated a search where police claimed to have a search warrant but in fact did not.

The question of who is authorized to consent to a search is more complicated. If the owner of a house lives in the house, he or she has authority to consent to a search, but if the house or apartment is leased, the consent must be given by the tenant rather than the owner. Where tenants share a dwelling, the general principle is that a single tenant, who is present, can give consent to search the common areas, but not to search other tenants' bedrooms, chests, and other items that are used exclusively by the other tenants. If other tenants are also present and refuse to consent, police are not allowed to search either the common areas or the personal areas of the others.[22] However, a tenant's refusal to consent does not indefinitely remain in effect. The police may conduct a warrantless search of a suspect's apartment following his arrest when his co-occupant consents to the search.[23] Officers do not need to tell suspects that they do not have to consent to a search.[24]

Most state motor vehicle statutes contain an "implied consent" provision that requires licensed drivers to consent to having their blood, breath, and/or urine tested as a condition for keeping their driving privileges.[25]

b. Exigent Circumstances

Exigent circumstances Conditions that excuse an officer from obtaining a warrant in order to protect a life, preserve evidence, or prevent a suspect from escaping, or rendering emergency aid.

Exceptions to the requirement for a search warrant are also made in situations where there are "**exigent circumstances.**" In situations where it is impractical to get a warrant, law enforcement personnel are allowed to conduct limited searches without one. Ordinarily, the conditions that excuse an officer from obtaining a warrant are the protection of life, the preservation of evidence, or the prevention of a suspect's escape or the rendering of emergency aid.

A common example is a situation in which police are in "hot pursuit" (e.g., physically chasing a suspect who they see run into a private residence). Under these circumstances, the police are allowed to enter the residence without a warrant for the purpose of detaining the suspect and preventing him or her from destroying evidence. However, once the suspect has been detained and the premises secured, the police are expected to obtain a warrant before conducting further searches of the area.

---

[21] 391 U.S. 543 (1968).

[22] *See Georgia v. Randolph*, 547 U.S. 103 (2006).

[23] *Fernandez v. California*, 571 U.S. 292 (2014).

[24] *United States v. Drayton*, 536 U.S. 194 (2002).

[25] The penalty for not taking these tests is typically suspension of their driver's license for a year.

Similarly, law enforcement officers may enter a home without a warrant when they have an objectively reasonable basis for believing that an occupant is seriously injured or imminently threatened with serious injury.[26]

The natural metabolization of alcohol in the bloodstream does not present a *per se* exigency that justifies an exception to the Fourth Amendment's search warrant requirement for nonconsensual blood testing in all drunk-driving cases.[27] Thus, police officers must obtain a search warrant before requiring a conscious drunk-driving suspect to submit to a blood draw. The exigent circumstances exception, however, allows the police to draw blood from an unconscious drunk-driving suspect without first securing a warrant.[28]

c. Plain View Doctrine

The **plain view doctrine** holds that law enforcement officials have the right to seize contraband items or evidence of a crime when they see such items "in plain view" in public or from a location where there is no reasonable expectation of privacy. It is based on the assumption that Fourth Amendment restrictions apply only to searches that invade spaces for which there is a reasonable expectation of privacy.

Plain view doctrine
The legal theory that law enforcement officials have the right to seize contraband items or evidence of a crime when they see such items in public or from a location where there is no reasonable expectation of privacy.

For example, if a police officer walking down the sidewalk or driving down the street happens to spot what appears to be marijuana plants growing in a window box or in a planter on someone's front porch, the officer can walk up to take a closer look and then seize the plants if they still seem to be marijuana. Similarly, if an officer spots what appears to be an illegal drug in an automobile stopped for a minor traffic offense, that police officer can seize it and charge the driver with possession of an illegal substance.[29]

Arizona v. Hicks[30] provides an example of an overreach of the plain view doctrine. In this case, law enforcement officers entered Hicks's apartment after a bullet was reported as being fired into the apartment below his. Once in the apartment, they noticed two sets of expensive stereo equipment that they thought were inconsistent with the "squalor" of the apartment. They then proceeded to move some of the components in order to read and record their serial numbers. When, after phoning the numbers into headquarters, it was confirmed that the equipment had been taken in an armed robbery, the officers seized the equipment, and Hicks was subsequently indicted for robbery. However, the Supreme Court upheld the suppression of the evidence on the basis that the officers' moving of the equipment constituted a separate "search" that was unrelated to the search for the shooter, victims, and weapons that was the lawful objective of their entry, and thus the officers lacked probable cause to search for serial numbers.

---

[26] *Brigham City v. Stuart*, 547 U.S. 398 (2006).

[27] *Missouri v. McNeely*, 569 U.S. 141 (2013).

[28] *Mitchell v. Wisconsin*, 139 S. Ct. 2525 (2019).

[29] This is assuming that the stop was legitimate and the drugs were visible to anyone looking in the window.

[30] 480 U.S. 321 (1987).

d. "Stop and Frisk" and Searches Incident to Arrest

In our discussion about the right to stop and question possible suspects in Section B.3, we talked briefly about *Terry v. Ohio*. In addition to authorizing police to stop and question, this case authorized police to conduct a brief pat-down search for weapons in situations where the officers had legitimate concerns about their personal safety. The officers are not allowed to search the inside clothing or pockets of the suspect unless their initial pat down revealed an object that might be a dangerous weapon.

We need to emphasize that the police cannot stop and frisk individuals whenever they feel like it. Individuals may be stopped only when the officer has a reasonable suspicion that the individual has committed, is in the process of committing, or is about to commit a crime. According to *Terry*, that reasonable suspicion must be based on "specific and articulable facts which, taken together with rational inferences from those facts, reasonably warrant that intrusion."[31]

On the other hand, when police actually arrest someone, as opposed to just questioning a suspect, they are allowed to conduct a more thorough warrantless search of the person and the area immediately surrounding that person. The courts have justified these "searches incident to a valid arrest" on the grounds that they are necessary to protect the safety of the officer (to remove or prevent the acquisition of potential weapons) or the destruction of evidence.

The Supreme Court has developed a body of law governing the tests customarily administered to suspects placed under arrest for driving while intoxicated. In *Birchfield v. North Dakota*, the Court held that the police may not administer non-consensual blood tests but may require drivers to submit to breathalyzer tests. Motorists cannot be deemed to have consented to a blood test if they face criminal prosecution for their refusal.[32]

As part of the booking process, the police will remove the arrested person's personal items, such as watches, billfolds, notes, etc., and place them in marked, sealed envelopes in order to secure them while the person is incarcerated. Any contraband materials or evidence of a crime that is found during this process would be admissible in court under the in plain view doctrine.

A similar inventory process takes place when a motor vehicle is impounded by police. In order to protect themselves from claims that the vehicle was damaged or that goods were stolen from the vehicle while it was in police custody, they are allowed to make a detailed inventory of its contents. Whatever they find during this inventory process falls under the in plain view exception.

e. Special Rules Governing Border Searches, Airline Flights, and Public Venues

As you probably know, special rules apply to searches conducted at border crossings and when boarding commercial airlines. Likewise, security personnel at public venues, such as courthouses and office buildings, may conduct searches of persons entering the facilities. In these types of situations, authorities do not need to establish probable cause to be able to conduct warrantless searches.

---

[31] 392 U.S. 1, 21 (1968).

[32] 136 S. Ct. 216 (2016).

2. APPLICATION REQUIREMENTS AND PROCEDURES FOR OBTAINING A SEARCH WARRANT

In situations where the above exceptions do not apply, law enforcement authorities must get a judge to issue a formal **search warrant** that specifies the area to be searched and the type of evidence that can be seized. Generally, the search warrant application process involves both police and prosecutors. Experienced law enforcement officers may prepare the initial paperwork and then hand it on to the prosecutors to present a formal **application for a search warrant** to the judge.

The application is typically in affidavit form or accompanied by an **affidavit**. An affidavit is a voluntarily written declaration of facts signed under oath or under penalty of perjury. The person who signs the affidavit is referred to as the **affiant**. In some jurisdictions, a notary public, judge, or clerk of the court administers an oath to the affiant. Other states permit an affiant to verify that he or she is telling the truth by signing the affidavit under penalty of perjury. Before you draft an affidavit, research the law of your jurisdiction to determine the proper method of attestation.

An application for a search warrant must make two showings. First, it must demonstrate probable cause that a specific crime was committed. The key to demonstrating this probable cause is to identify the crime at issue, along with the evidence that establishes the crime. You should use precise language that fully describes the evidence. Every application for a warrant is unique in that it is based on the particular facts that give rise to the investigation of a specific crime.

Second, the application must give the specific location (street address, apartment number, and other information) and specifically designate the type of physical evidence that is expected to be found at a particular location. This latter requirement, to specifically identify the types of items being sought, is designed to prevent police from just looking around to see if they can find anything that might be incriminating. The application must also show probable cause to believe that the items they are seeking are connected to criminal activity. For example, if police are looking for stolen television sets, the application should list specific brands and model numbers (if they are known).

Although there are boilerplate templates that are routinely used to draft applications, you would be remiss to simply adopt a form without regard to the peculiarities of your case. Moreover, you should check your jurisdiction's court rules and statutes to see if there is any provision that governs applications for search warrants. Some jurisdictions give detailed instructions as to what should be included in the application. For instance, in Pennsylvania, **Rule 206 of the Criminal Code** provides:

> Each application for a search warrant shall be supported by written affidavit(s) signed and sworn to or affirmed before an issuing authority, which affidavit(s) shall:
>
> 1. state the name and department, agency, or address of the affiant;
> 2. identify specifically the items or property to be searched for and seized;
> 3. name or describe with particularity the person or place to be searched;
> 4. identify the owner, occupant, or possessor of the place to be searched;
> 5. specify or describe the crime which has been or is being committed;

Search warrant
A written court order that authorizes an officer to search a specific place for specific objects. A neutral judge must determine that there is probable cause in order to issue a search warrant.

Application for search warrant
A motion presented to the court that specifies the reasons that a search warrant should be issued. The application for search warrant is typically in affidavit form or accompanied by an affidavit.

Affidavit
A voluntarily written declaration of facts signed under oath or under penalty of perjury.

Affiant
The person who signs an affidavit under oath or under penalty of perjury.

6. set forth specifically the facts and circumstances which form the basis for the affiant's conclusion that there is probable cause to believe that the items or property identified are evidence or the fruit of a crime, or are contraband, or are otherwise unlawfully possessed or subject to seizure, and that these items or property are located on the particular person or at the particular place described;
7. if a "nighttime" search is requested (i.e., 10 p.m. to 6 a.m.), state additional reasonable cause for seeking permission to search in nighttime; and
8. when the attorney for the Commonwealth is requesting that the affidavit(s) be sealed pursuant to Rule 211, state the facts and circumstances which are alleged to establish good cause for the sealing of the affidavit(s). (234 Pa. Code Rule 206.)

There are a variety of resources available to assist law enforcement officers and prosecutors' offices in drafting these documents. Handbooks for law enforcement officers, as well as prosecutor training materials, provide helpful instruction on how to prepare the application for a particular type of case. For example, Susan S. Kreston, a senior attorney with the American Prosecutors Research Institute's National Center for Prosecution of Child Abuse, gives a step-by-step approach for preparing warrant applications to retrieve computers on which child pornography is stored:

> Affidavits should contain the following information and be specifically incorporated by reference into the warrant:
>
> 1. Introductory paragraph with a recitation of affiant's training and experience, particularly in this area. . . . .
> 2. Identification of the statute that is being alleged to be violated, by both statute number (title and section) and content. . . . .
> 3. Description of the premises to be searched, with as much particularity as possible. . . . .
> 4. Definition of terms used in the application. . . . .
> 5. Background information. . . . .
> 6. Description of the investigation in as much detail as possible. . . . .
> 7. General description of individuals who are sexually interested in children, including only those characteristics that apply to the suspect in the case. . . . .
> 8. Request for search and seizure of computer and computer-related equipment. . . . .
> 9. List of items to be seized. . . . .
> 10. Summary paragraph stating why there is probable cause to believe the items to be seized will be found at the subject premises.[33]

Probably the best guide for preparing applications for warrants are applications prepared by your office that resulted in the issuance of search warrants. These documents should be helpful in understanding what your supervisor and judges expect. An example of a successful application used in a Louisiana terrorism case is depicted in Exhibit 4.2. It appears that the person who prepared

[33] S. S. Kreston, Search and Seizure in Cases of Computers and Child Pornography, www.ndaa.org/publications/newsletters/apri_update_vol_12_no_9_1999.

Exhibit 4.2: Application for Search Warrant

In May 2007, Richard Wargo, a Louisiana State college student, was charged with threatening the life of Senator Hillary Clinton. Before he was arrested the university police secured a warrant to search Wargo's dormitory room. The application for the warrant was based upon the statements that Wargo made to another student.

APPLICATION FOR SEARCH WARRANT

W05-07-0051

STATE OF LOUISIANA
PARISH OF EAST BATON ROUGE

BEFORE ME, The Honorable Michael Irwin, Judge of the Nineteenth Judicial District Court in and for the State and Parish aforesaid, personally appeared Officer Patrick McCarty, LSU Police Officer in and for East Baton Rouge Parish and the state of Louisiana, who, being duly sworn by me, deposed and said:

THAT probable cause does exist for the issuance of a search warrant authorizing the search of the premises at Louisianan State University's Herget Hall, room 233, located in Baton Rouge, LA: further described as a multi-story dormitory with a light tan brick exterior: including Richard Ryan Wargo's personal closet, trash bin, assigned dormitory desk, and common space shared with his roommate located therein where certain fruits of a crime, to wit:

LRS 14:40.1 - Terrorizing

Namely:

> Materials, writings, computers (desktop and/or laptop), any digital audio, video recording devices and vehicle (a 2002 Toyota 4runner, silver in color, Louisiana Lic OXK186, VIN JT3GN87R320240721) that would suggest any intent to execute an arson or any act of terrorism

> Is (are) believed to be secreted or concealed, and such probable cause is based upon the following:

On May 3, 2007, your affiant met with Daniel Demetrios Morgan, a classmate of Richard Ryan Wargo. Morgan stated that on April 20th 2007, Richard Ryan Wargo asked him if he had an interest in committing any arson. According to Morgan, on April 23rd, 2007, Wargo indicated that he was interested in committing an act of terrorism, and that it would be a "national event". Morgan asked "it's political, isn't it?" Morgan stated that Wargo shook his head yes and said "Hillary Clinton". Morgan assumed that Wargo was referencing using a form or arson against Clinton's Headquarters and stated: "You know that that's only going to make her more popular?" to which Morgan stated that Wargo said "True, but have you ever heard of a dead president?" Morgan further advised your affiant that Wargo stated that he would commit this act when Hillary Clinton came to Baton Rouge for the primary, to which Wargo nodded his head yes.

THAT writ to search the aforesaid dormitory room is requested, and when the thing to be searched is a dwelling or other structure, that the writ to search include all other structures, vehicles and places of concealment on the premises where the thing(s) may be found.

THAT it may become necessary to conduct the search during the nighttime or on Sunday, and affiant(s) request(s) that the writ so provide.

SWORN to and subscribed before me on this 3rd day of May 2007

[signature] 1589
AFFIANT

[signature]
EX-OFFICIO NOTARY PUBLIC AND DEPUTY CLERK OF COURT

19TH JUDICIAL DISTRICT
EAST BATON ROUGE PARISH, LA
2007 MAY -4 AM 9:14
DEPUTY CLERK OF COURT

the document was using a form. Although some of the language of the second-to-last paragraph does not seem to apply to the facts, the application does set forth with sufficient particularity the pertinent facts that would give the judge a sound basis to conclude that a search warrant should be issued.

The warrant typically incorporates language from the application that identifies the property to be inspected. Thus, the application and the proposed warrant can be prepared at the same time. If the court grants the application for search warrant, it will then sign the warrant. Federal Rules of Criminal Procedure, 41(e)(2)(A) sets forth the required contents of a search warrant for physical property and to seize a person as follows:[34]

> [T]he warrant must identify the person or property to be searched, identify any person or property to be seized, and designate the magistrate judge to whom it must be returned. The warrant must command the officer to:
> (i) execute the warrant within a specified time no longer than 10 days;
> (ii) execute the warrant during the daytime, unless the judge for good cause expressly authorizes execution at another time; and
> (iii) return the warrant to the magistrate judge designated in the warrant.

3. EXECUTING SEARCH WARRANTS

Execution of a warrant
Police, or other law enforcement officers searching for the objects identified in the warrant in the locations specified in the warrant.

Once the search warrant has been issued, it must be **executed**—that is, the police search must actually be carried out—within a specific period of time. In keeping with the underlying Fourth Amendment values of preserving the security and privacy of one's home, police are normally required to serve the warrant during daylight hours and to announce their presence. However, with special permission from the judge, they can serve the warrant at night without knocking on the door first and, unless the warrant specifically allows other arrangements, execute the warrant during daytime hours.

No-knock warrant
A special type of search warrant that authorizes police to break into a house/apartment without first knocking on the door and waiting to be let in.

Under special conditions, the courts will sometimes issue **no-knock warrants**, which allow the police to enter without announcing their presence in advance. These special types of search warrants are issued where law enforcement authorities convince the judge that evidence is likely to be destroyed or that the police administering the warrant will be in danger.[35] Criminal justice experts estimate that police carry out tens of thousands of no-knock raids every year.[36]

However, the executions of these no-knock warrants have sometimes led to the tragic deaths of innocent civilians. A highly publicized example of this occurred in 2020 in Louisville, Kentucky, when the execution of one of these types of warrants resulted in the death of Breonna Taylor, a 26-year-old Black

---

[34]The form used for federal search warrants is located online at https://www.uscourts.gov/sites/default/files/ao093.pdf.

[35]The Supreme Court expressly approved the use of no-knock warrants in *Richards v. Wisconsin,* 520 U.S. 385 (1997). For further discussion of no-knock warrants, see the discussion of *Hudson v. Michigan,* 547 U.S. 586 (2006) in Chapter 7, pp. 232-233, in the section on the exclusionary rule.

[36]"What to Know About No-Knock Warrants," Courtney Kan, Nicole Dungca, and Jenn Abelson, *The Washington Post* (May 27, 2022), https://www.washingtonpost.com/investigations/2022/04/06/no-knock-warrants/.

woman who lived in an apartment that she shared with her boyfriend. In the incident, while executing a no-knock warrant to search for illegal drugs, police used a battering ram to break through their apartment's entrance door to search for evidence that her boyfriend was dealing drugs. No drugs were found in the search. When the boyfriend heard the crash of the door being rammed, he grabbed a gun and fired at the invaders. In response, the police returned fire; their bullets not only killed Taylor but went through the walls into another apartment in the building. No one was killed in the adjacent apartment, and the officer who fired the shots was charged with wanton endangerment and found not guilty.

Three months later, the Louisville Metro Council passed "Breonna's Law," prohibiting no-knock warrants and requiring officers to turn on their body cameras before and after every search. Although Brett Hankison, a former Louisville police detective, was indicted on charges of reckless endangerment for his role in the raid, a jury found him not guilty.

In August 2022, the U.S. Attorney brought charges against four police officers connected to Breonna Taylor's death. Charges included civil rights violations, conspiracy, use of excessive force offenses and obstruction. One of the officers pleaded guilty to falsifying the search warrant and is awaiting sentencing. The other three cases remain pending.

A somewhat similar situation arose in Minneapolis in 2022, when a SWAT team shot and killed Amir Locke, a 22-year-old Black man who was sleeping on a couch in a cousin's apartment when police burst into the apartment during the execution of a no-knock search warrant. Body camera footage showed that Locke had a pistol in his hand, but at the time he was shot, he was still lying on the couch and the gun was pointed at a 45-degree angle to the floor with his index finger extended straight along the side of it, not on the trigger.[37] No charges were brought against the police officers, but two months later, the City of Minneapolis banned no-knock warrants and revised its protocol for the execution of search warrants.

It is the responsibility of those executing the warrant to prepare an inventory of the items seized in the search. This information is then included in a **return of the warrant** (a court document, signed by the law enforcement officer who conducted the search, specifying when the warrant was executed and listing the items seized). Exhibit 4.3 is the return of the search warrant served in the Louisiana terrorism case that was referenced in Exhibit 4.2.

Return of search warrant
A court document that specifies when a search warrant was executed and lists the items of the property seized.

4. SPECIAL RULES FOR ELECTRONIC SURVEILLANCE

Electronic surveillance involves using sophisticated electronic devices to hear, view, and record people's activities and messages. These devices include such gadgets as hidden cameras and microphones, parabolic microphones that can hear through walls, thermo-imaging cameras that can see through walls, and devices that can intercept cell phone transmissions and e-mail messages. They are most likely to be used in investigations of organized crime, government corruption, and espionage.

[37]This is a textbook grip for safely handling a gun that one does not intend to shoot.

Exhibit 4.3: Return of Search Warrant

In addition to seizing items specified in the search warrant, the university police officer seized suspected illicit drugs and drug paraphernalia. If this contraband were out in the open, the officer had the right to seize it in accordance with the plain view doctrine.

RETURN TO SEARCH WARRANT

To the Honorable Michael Erwin. Judge of the Nineteenth Judicial Court:

I hereby certify that I received the attached Search Warrant on the 3 day of May, 2007 at the hour of 1035 PM. and that I executed the said warrant on the 3 day of May, 2007 at the hour of 1058 PM. and made a diligent search as ordered. The following property was found and seized:

1. Dell Espiron Laptop Computer Model:Ei505 Service Tag #:CB3DKB1
2. Two Sertralin HCL 50 Mg Pill Bottles containg unknown medication
3. Three Plastic Bags Containing Suspected marijuana
4. Nokia Cell Phone Model 6102j
5. 20GB IPOD
6. Assorted CD's in Black Case
7. Assorted Paperwork
8. Cingular Cell Phone
9. 3 1/2 Black floppy disk
10. Plastic Bottle Containing Suspected marijuana
11. Glass Pipe
12. Dell Computer Bag

A copy of the said search warrant and a receipt (if seizure of property is indicated above) were given to: Richard R. Wargo

2007 MAY -4 AM 9:14

Respectfully Submitted,

0589

When hidden microphones and cameras were first used for eavesdropping, the courts developed an important distinction between devices that were located within a private building and those that were outside the building. So, while a warrant is needed to hide a bug in someone's bedroom, one would not be needed to listen in on telephone calls where the phone lines were "tapped" outside the house. However, in *Kyllo v. United States*, the Supreme Court held that the use of thermo-imaging cameras that allow government agents to "see" through walls was an unreasonable search and violated the Fourth Amendment. Although some of the earlier Supreme Court cases ruled that searches that did not penetrate the walls of a room were not protected by the Fourth Amendment, Congress and many state legislatures have passed antieavesdropping statutes that provide much greater protections. Some of these statutes impose stricter standards for obtaining an electronic interception order than for getting a traditional search warrant. Unlike the search warrants application process, which may be initiated by a law enforcement officer, only specifically designated prosecuting attorneys or their designees may apply for orders permitting wiretaps or other electronic surveillance. Moreover, judges may enter electronic interception orders for the investigation of only certain crimes.

The Foreign Intelligence Surveillance Act (FISA) establishes the Foreign Intelligence Surveillance Court.[38] This special court is composed of 11 federal district court judges, appointed by the Chief Justice of the United States, who serve one week at a time on a rotating basis. The court acts on applications submitted by the U.S. Justice Department seeking to conduct electronic surveillance and other investigative actions relating to foreign intelligence. Most of the court's work is kept secret due to the need to protect classified national security information.

At the federal level, the application for the electronic eavesdropping order must be made by the U.S. Attorney General, Associate Attorney General, or specifically designated Assistant Attorneys General in the Criminal Division.[39] Such requests at the state level must be brought by the state or county prosecutor or their authorized representatives.[40] Judges are authorized to enter an interception order only when certain stringent criteria are met. In federal court, for instance, there must be a showing that normal investigative procedures have been tried or reasonably appear to be unlikely to succeed if tried, or to be too dangerous. Exhibit 4.4 displays an application for an interception order that could have been presented to a judge in the Brandon Turner hypothetical case for drug trafficking. Note that the events cited in the petition are different from the activities giving rise to the sample case.

---

[38] 50 U.S.C. §§1801 *et. seq.*

[39] 18 U.S.C. §2516(1).

[40] 18 U.S.C. §2516(2).

Exhibit 4.4: Application for Use of Eavesdropping Device

PETITION FOR ORDER AUTHORIZING USE OF EAVESDROPPING DEVICE

Petitioner, D. TRACY, a police officer with the City of Anytown, currently assigned to the Watterson County Drug Enforcement Unit, being duly authorized by the State's Attorney of Watterson County, requests the issuance of an order authorizing the use of an eavesdropping device. In support thereof he states as follows:

1. Petitioner has reasonable cause to believe that a felony has been or is about to be committed as follows: between the months of November 2019 into December 2019, specifically included but not limited to solicitation, conspiracy, unlawful delivery of a controlled substance, unlawful delivery of cocaine, unlawful delivery of a look-alike substance, unlawful possession of a controlled substance with intent to deliver, unlawful possession of cocaine, unlawful possession of cocaine with the intent to deliver, and or possession of a controlled substance and hereby states as follows in support thereof the following under oath:

2. Petitioner is a police officer with the city of Anytown. As a regular part of petitioner's duties, he regularly works with other law enforcement officers investigating sales and distribution of illegal drugs in the Watterson County area. During the course of an ongoing investigation, petitioner has been involved in working with a confidential source regarding illegal drug sales and distribution in the Watterson County area. The confidential source utilized in this investigation has been designated as Confidential Source 857 (hereinafter referred to as "CS 857").

A. On October 30, 2019, petitioner [and affiant] interviewed CS 857 about illegal drug activity in Watterson County involving the sale of crack cocaine. Specifically, CS 857 advised petitioner that CS 857 knows of an African American male who sells crack cocaine who is known to CS 857 as well, "Brandon Turner." CS 857 has bought crack cocaine from "Brandon Turner" a lot of times. CS 857 subsequently positively identified "Brandon Turner" from an EJS photograph. See attached Exhibit 1 incorporated by reference. CS 857 indicated to petitioner that Brandon Turner supplies crack cocaine and that CS 857 could buy any amount of crack cocaine from Brandon Turner but CS 857 usually buys 4 rocks at a time. See attached Exhibit 2 incorporated by reference for the report relating to the October 30, 2019 interview.

B. Specifically, on November 11, 2019, CS 857 made a FIRST CONTROLLED BUY of about 1.1 grams of crack cocaine (5 rocks) directly from Brandon Turner at 999 West First Street in the City of Anytown, Watterson County for the sum of $200.00. A subsequent field test indicated positive for the presence of cocaine. See attached Exhibits 3–6 herein incorporated by reference for the reports containing details relating to said November 11, 2010 FIRST CONTROLLED BUY.

3. CS 857 has agreed to permit the use of an overhear device during in-person and/or telephone conversations with Brandon Turner and/or any unknown others/associates as CS 857 may be directed by said suspects are working with petitioner and the Anytown Police Dept.

4. Petitioner has reasonable cause to believe that a conversation relating to a felony will be overheard as follows: CS 1857 has agreed to participate in arrangements for controlled buys of illegal drugs involving Brandon Turner and any unknown other associates as CS 857 may be directed by said suspects. Said controlled buys with petitioner or the Anytown Police Department will be conducted pursuant to standard law enforcement practice for such buys and in accordance with the aforementioned background, history, and information set forth in this petition.

5. The nature and approximate location of the facilities from which, or the place where the conversation is to take place or to be monitored, is via telephone or in-person conversations with Brandon Turner and/or any other unknown associates or co-conspirators as CS 857 may be directed in Watterson County and any other locations/individuals as CS 857 may be directed.

6. The type of communication to be monitored is by telephone and/or in person.

7. CS 857 is the party to the expected conversations consenting to the use of the eavesdropping device.

8. The parties and locations, whose conversations are to be overheard by the eavesdropping device requested are as follows: CS 857, Brandon Turner, and/or any possible unknown other associates or co-conspirators as CS 857 may be directed are the parties whose conversations are to be overheard by the eavesdropping device.

9. The time period for the use of the eavesdropping device is from 2:00 p.m. on November 13, 2019 to 2:00 p.m. on December 13, 2019.

10. Petitioner knows of no other previous application requesting permission to use an eavesdropping device involving the same persons or circumstances as in the instant application referred to above by the court.

11. The nature of this investigation is such that any authorization granted pursuant to this petition should not terminate automatically in the event that calls or transactions are necessary in order to obtain needed statements within the 30-day scope of the said order.

____

D. Tracy, Affiant/Petitioner

The Supreme Court generally requires law enforcement to obtain search warrants before using new technologies to conduct surveillance. For instance, in *United States v. Jones*, the Court held that the Fourth Amendment requires that a warrant is necessary for law enforcement to attach a global positioning system (GPS) tracking device to a motorist's vehicle to monitor its movements on public streets.[41] *Riley v. California* holds that the Fourth Amendment does not permit a warrantless search of digital information on a cell phone seized from an individual who has been arrested.[42] And in *Carpenter v. United States*, the Court held that the warrantless search of historical cell-phone records revealing the location and movements of a cell-phone user over the course of 127 days is not permitted by the Fourth Amendment.[43] In contrast, the Supreme Court permits law enforcement personnel to take and analyze a cheek swab of a defendant's DNA as part of the booking procedure of defendants accused of felonies who are in custody.[44]

[41] 565 U.S. 400 (2012).

[42] 573 U.S. 373 (2014).

[43] 138 S. Ct. 2206 (2018).

[44] *Maryland v. King*, 569 U.S. 435 (2013).

Discussion Questions

7. Under what circumstances, if any, do you think a roommate *should* be able to give permission to law enforcement authorities to conduct a search of an apartment that the roommate shares with someone else?

8. Under what circumstances, if any, *should* principals and teachers be able to search students' clothing and personal effects when they are on school property?

9. Under what circumstances, if any, *should* one private person be able to make a video or audio recording of a conversation or an activity with someone else without notifying the other person that it is being recorded?

10. Under what circumstances, if any, *should* law enforcement officials be able to conduct "no-knock" searches?

5. PRESERVATION OF EVIDENCE

Chain of custody
A record of who possessed an object being presented as evidence from the time it came into possession of government agents until it is presented in court.

Arrest
The act of physically apprehending and taking into custody a person who is suspected of committing a crime.

Suspect
A person that law enforcement officials think may have committed a crime.

Arrest warrant
A court order issued at the request of the prosecutor and/or law enforcement that authorizes the arrest and detention of an individual.

Probable cause
A reasonable belief based on specific facts that a person committed a crime or that something will be found in a specific location.

In addition to collecting evidence in a manner that does not violate the Fourth Amendment, law enforcement authorities are responsible for properly identifying and preserving that evidence. This means that physical objects (like guns or drugs) must be properly "tagged" and stored in a secure location prior to trial. It also means that an appropriate record must be kept of who had access to the evidence from the time it was first collected until the time it is introduced in court. This permits the prosecuting attorney to establish the "chain of custody" of the evidence.

Chain of custody is the chronological documentation of the whereabouts of evidence beginning at the time it comes into the possession of law enforcement authorities. The reason for keeping this record is to show that specific evidence is related to the offense in question. When tight controls are maintained, claims of evidence tampering are less likely to succeed.

Maintaining a proper chain of custody is particularly important in illegal drug cases. Attorneys prosecuting drug cases will present chain of custody documentation and testimony to show that the substance in evidence was indeed in the possession of the defendant. In preparation for trial, paralegals often prepare a synopsis of the chain of evidence to aid the prosecutor in laying the foundation for the admission of exhibits into evidence. The paralegal's synopsis of the chain of evidence in the Brandon Turner sample case is depicted in Exhibit 4.5.

6. ARRESTING SUSPECTS AND DEFENDANTS

An **arrest** is the act of physically apprehending and taking into custody a person who is suspected of committing a crime. The difference between a **suspect** and a defendant is that a suspect is a person that law enforcement officials think may have committed a crime, whereas a defendant is a person that has been formally charged with committing a crime.

Since the Fourth Amendment applies to the seizure of people, as well as things, law enforcement officers are either required to have an **arrest warrant** or be able to prove independently that there is **probable cause** to believe the

Exhibit 4.5: Chain of Evidence Synopsis

MEMORANDUM

To: Grant Manchester, ASA
From: Paula Paralegal

RE: Brandon Turner Chain of Custody

Exhibit #1: (Lab No. M10-0001857) approximately 1.2 grams of purported crack cocaine in plastic sandwich bag:

11/08/19	Steve Milner to locked evidence drop chute at Illinois State Police Department Task Force Fifteen Unit Office
11/08/19	Task Force Fifteen drop chute to Watterson Forensic Science Lab via Special Agent Stevenson
11/18/19	Special Agent Stevenson to Scientist Denise Felmley

Exhibit #2: Vehicle title retrieved from car driven by Brandon Turner:

11/08/19	Steve Milner to locked evidence drop chute at Illinois State Police Department Task Force Fifteen Unit Office

Exhibit #3: Miscellaneous papers retrieved from car driven by Brandon Turner:

11/08/19	Steve Milner to locked evidence drop chute at Illinois State Police Department Task Force Fifteen Unit Office

Exhibit #4: One disc containing photos of the car driven by Brandon Turner:

11/08/19	Detective Gina DeGarmo created Exhibit #4.
11/08/19	Gina DeGarmo to locked evidence drop chute at Illinois State Police Department Task Force Fifteen Unit Office

Exhibit #5: (Lab No. M10-0001858) Smith & Wesson Model 10 revolver 160125, 38 Special:

11/08/19	Detective Gina DeGarmo to locked evidence drop chute at Illinois State Police Department Task Force Fifteen Unit Office
11/08/19	Task Force Fifteen drop chute to Watterson Forensic Science Lab via Special Agent Stevenson
11/18/19	Special Agent Stevenson to Scientist Wesley Horton

Exhibit #6: One disc containing photos of dining area and restroom located at the Normal Eatery, 857 Normal St., Anytown, Illinois:

11/08/19	Detective Gina DeGarmo created Exhibit #6.
11/08/19	Gina DeGarmo to locked evidence drop chute at Illinois State Police Department Task Force Fifteen Unit Office

person committed a crime before they can arrest someone. To determine probable cause, the police can rely on their knowledge of the suspect as well as information provided by witnesses and victims.

The process for getting an arrest warrant usually involves the prosecuting attorney's office and will be covered in Chapter 5. In situations in which the police catch the offender in the act of committing the crime or where there is legitimate concern that the offender will flee during the time that it would take to get a warrant, police are allowed to make the arrest without a warrant.

a. Example of an Arrest Based on an Officer's Observations

DUI cases are common situations in which law enforcement officers make an arrest based on their personal observations. After approaching a vehicle that has been pulled over for some routine traffic violation such as speeding or improper lane usage, the officer observes the driver behaving in a manner indicating that the driver is under the influence of alcohol or drugs. The forms generated from a Florida police officer's traffic stop of pro golfer Tiger Woods are examples of the type of documents that accompany an arrest in this type of case. See Exhibits 4.6-4.9.

Exhibit 4.6 is an affidavit that describes what the police officer observed when he approached a car that was stopped in the right lane of the roadway. Note how the officer described Wood's physical condition and his slurred speech. As is commonly done in this type of situation, the officer conducted a series of roadside sobriety tasks and recorded the results. Exhibit 4.7 is the list of questions that are frequently asked in this type of situation. On the basis of his performance on these roadside tests, Woods was taken to a special testing facility, where he took a breathalyzer test and gave a urine sample. Exhibit 4.8 is the testing facility's task report. The police then made an arrest and served Woods with a notice to appear, which is presented in Exhibit 4.9.

Discussion Questions

11. Based on these exhibits do you think police had probable cause to arrest Woods for DUI? Why or why not?

12. Do you think the police violated Woods's constitutional right to counsel or his constitutional privilege against self-incrimination? Why or why not?

13. Do you think the police violated Woods's constitutional right to be free from unreasonable searches and seizures by taking blood, breath, and/or urine samples from him?

b. Use of Force in Making Arrests

When making an arrest, police are allowed to use "**reasonable force.**" This is the amount of force necessary for the police to protect themselves or their property when they carry out the arrest. Anything beyond that is considered "**excessive force**" and is impermissible. This means, for example, that they cannot purposely bang the arrested person's head on the top of the car door when placing him or her in their squad car, but they can tackle someone who is trying to run away. State laws differ as to the circumstances under which law enforcement personnel can use "**deadly force**" to effectuate an arrest.

Reasonable force
The amount of force necessary to protect oneself or one's property.

Excessive force
Any force greater than the level of force that a reasonable and prudent law enforcement officer would use under the circumstances.

Deadly force
The amount of force which could reasonably be expected to cause death or grave bodily harm.

Exhibit 4.6: DUI Probable Cause Affidavit – Tiger Woods

D.U.I. PROBABLE CAUSE AFFIDAVIT

ON THE 29th DAY OF May 20 17 , AT 0203 AM ✓ PM

SUBJECT: Eldrick Tiger Woods CASE NUMBER: 17-002626

AGENCY: JUPITER POLICE DEPARTMENT ARRESTING OFFICER: Ofc. C. Fandrey

PERSONAL CONTACT

DRIVING PATTERN: ACTUAL PHYSICAL CONTROL (PHYSICAL EVIDENCE OR STATEMENTS PUTTING DEF. BEHIND WHEEL OF VEHICLE)

Ofc. Palladino #362 observed a black Mercedes bearing FL tag ECNY70 stopped in the roadway in the right lane. Ofc. Palladino made contact with the driver and sole occupant of the vehicle B/M Eldrick T. Woods (12/30/1975) who had his seat belt on and was seated in the drivers seat. It should be noted the Woods was asleep at the wheel and had to be woken up. The vehicle was running and brake lights were illuminated as well as the right blinker flashing.

See Ofc. Palladino #362 supplement for further.

OBSERVATION OF DRIVER:

Upon my arrival after speaking to officers on scene I made contact with the sole occupant of the vehicle who was later positively identified as B/M Eldrick T. Woods (12/30/1975) was seated in the driver seat of the vehicle. Woods had extremely slow and slurred speech.

DRIVER'S STATEMENTS:

Woods stated that he was coming from LA California from golfing. Woods stated that he did not know where he was. Woods had changed his story of where he was going and where he was coming from. Woods asked how far from his house he was. It should be noted that Woods was heading south bound away from Hobe Sound. Takes several prescriptions.

ODORS:

None

GENERAL OBSERVATIONS

SPEECH: **Extremely slow and slurred, mumbled, confused**

ATTITUDE: **Cooperative, confused,**

CLOTHING: **White shirt, black shorts, black/white shoes**

MEDICAL/OTHER: **Stated takes several prescriptions.**

STATE OF FLORIDA
COUNTY ~~OF PALM BEACH~~

340

(Signature of Arresting/Investigating Officer)

The foregoing instrument was sworn to or affirmed and subscribed before me this 29th day of May 20 17 by Ofc. C. Fandrey

(Print name of Arresting/Investigative Officer), who is personally known to me and/or produced identification. Type of identification produced Personally Known

Sue Owen

Notary Public, Clerk of Court, Officer (F.S.S. 117.10)

B. SUE OWEN
State of Florida-Notary Public
Commission # FF093160
My Commission Expires
May 30, 2018

SCANNED
MAY 30 2017

SUBJECT: Eldrick Tiger Woods **CASE NUMBER** 17-002626

ROADSIDE TASKS

HORIZONTAL GAZE NYSTAGMUS:

- ☐ LT EYE-LACK OF SMOOTH PURSUIT
- ☐ RT EYE-LACK OF SMOOTH PURSUIT
- ☐ LT EYE-DISTINCT & SUSTAINED NYSTAGMUS AT MAX. DEVIATION
- ☐ RT EYE-DISTINCT & SUSTAINED NYSTAGMUS AT MAX. DEVIATION
- ☐ LT- EYE-ONSET OF NYSTAGMUS PRIOR TO 45 DEGREES
- ☐ RT- EYE-ONSET OF NYSTAGMUS PRIOR TO 45 DEGREES

Other Observations:
Did not follow stimulus and was not able to conduct HGN.

WALK & TURN

Could not maintain starting position. Missed heel to toe each time. Stepped off line several times. Used arms for balance. Did not return. Re explained instructions and again did not maintain starting position, stepped off line, used arms for balance, also stopped walking to steady self.

ONE LEG STAND:

Did not maintain starting position did not raise leg off the ground six inches, placed foot down several times

FINGER TO NOSE:

Did not maintain starting position, reexplained instructions multiple times to which he stated he understood, did not return arms to side after touching nose,

ROMBERG ALPHABET:

When asked if he understood directions he stated "yes, recite entire national anthem backwards". After several times of explaining instructions he completed the task correctly.

BREATH TEST RESULTS: .000 .000

STATE OF FLORIDA
COUNTY OF PALM BEACH

340

(Signature of Arresting/Investigative Officer)

The foregoing instrument was sworn to or affirmed and subscribed before me this 29th day of May 20 17 by Ofc. C. Fandrey

(Print name of Arresting/Investigative Officer), who is personally known to me and/or produced identification. Type of identification produced Personally Known

Sue Owen

Notary Public, Clerk of Court, Officer (F.S.S 117.10)

B. SUE OWEN
State of Florida-Notary Public
Commission # FF093160
My Commission Expires
May 30, 2018

SCANNED
MAY 3 0 2017

Exhibit 4.7: Standard Questions – Tiger Woods

SUBJECT: ____________ CASE NUMBER: ____________

QUESTIONS AND ANSWERS

I AM NOW GOING TO ASK YOU SOME QUESTIONS. WITH THESE RIGHTS IN MIND, YOU MAY ANSWER SOME OF, ALL OF, OR NONE OF THE FOLLOWING QUESTIONS AS YOU LIKE.

WERE YOU OPERATING A MOTOR VEHICLE AT THE TIME OF THE STOP/ACCIDENT? ____________

WHERE WERE YOU GOING? ____________

WHAT STREET OR HIGHWAY WERE YOU ON? ____________

DIRECTION OF TRAVEL? ______ WHERE DID YOU START? ____________

WHAT TIME DID YOU START? ______ WHAT TIME IS IT NOW? ____________

WHAT IS TODAY'S DATE? ______ WHAT DAY OF THE WEEK IS IT? ____________

WHAT COUNTY AND CITY ARE YOU IN NOW? ____________

WHEN DID YOU LAST EAT? ______ WHAT DID YOU EAT? ____________

WHAT HAVE YOU BEEN DOING FOR THE LAST THREE HOURS? ____________

HOW MUCH DO YOU WEIGH? ______ HAVE YOU BEEN DRINKING? ______ WHAT? ____________

HOW MUCH? ______ WHERE? ______ WITH WHOM? ____________

WHEN DID YOU HAVE YOUR FIRST DRINK? ______ AND YOUR LAST DRINK? ____________

HOW DID YOU CONSUME YOUR LAST TWO DRINKS? ____________

CAN YOU FEEL THE EFFECTS OF THE ALCOHOL? ______ ARE YOU UNDER THE INFLUENCE? ____________

HAVE YOU CONSUMED ANY ALCOHOL SINCE THE ACCIDENT? ______ HOW MUCH? ____________

WHAT? ______ WHERE? ______ WHEN? ____________

WHAT LINE OF WORK ARE YOU IN? ______ WHEN DID YOU LAST WORK? ____________

DO YOU HAVE ANY PHYSICAL DEFECTS OR INJURIES? ______ WHAT? ____________

ARE YOU SICK OR INJURED? ______ WHAT'S WRONG? ____________

DO YOU LIMP? ______ DID YOU RECEIVE A BUMP ON THE HEAD RECENTLY? ____________

WERE YOU IN AN ACCIDENT TODAY? ____________

HAVE YOU TAKEN ANY DRUGS OR SMOKED ANY MARIJUANA TODAY? ______ WHEN? ____________

HAVE YOU SEEN A DOCTOR OR DENTIST TODAY? ______ WHO? ______ WHY? ____________

ARE YOU TAKING ANY PRESCRIPTION MEDICINES? ______ WHAT? ______ WHEN? ____________

DO YOU HAVE:
- EPILEPSY? ______
- GLASS EYE? ______
- FALSE TEETH? ______
- EAR INFECTION? ______
- INNER EAR TROUBLE? ______
- DIABETES? ______

DO YOU HAVE ANY PROBLEMS WITH YOUR EYES THAT ARE NOT CORRECTED BY GLASSES? ____________

DO YOU TAKE INSULIN? ______ IF SO, WHEN WAS YOUR LAST INJECTION? ____________

HAVE YOU EVER HAD A DRIVER'S LICENSE IN ANY OTHER STATE? ______ WHERE? ____________

INTERVIEWER: ____________

WHITE - STATE ATTY. YELLOW - DHSMV PINK - CENTRAL RECORDS GOLD - JAIL

Exhibit 4.8: Testing Facility Report – Tiger Woods

TESTING FACILITY TASK REPORT

AGENCY: Jupiter P.D.

SUBJECT: Woods, Elorick Tiger CASE NUMBER: 17-083484

DATE: 5/29/17 VIDEO TAPE NUMBER: 62714

BEGINNING TIME: 0422 ENDING TIME: 0434

BREATH TESTS RESULTS: 1) .000 TIME 0428 A.M./P.M. 2) .000 TIME 0431 A.M./P.M.

3) ______ TIME ______ A.M./P.M. 4) ______ TIME ______ A.M./P.M.

BREATH OPERATOR: S. Owen #3184

MAINTENANCE TECHNICIAN: J. Karlecke #6467

TESTING OFFICER'S OBSERVATIONS

SPEECH: slow, sluggish, very slurred

ATTITUDE: sluggish, sleepy, unable to walk alone

CLOTHING: black athletic shorts, white athletic shirt

MEDICAL CONDITIONS: Soloxex, vicodin, torix, viox (Not taken This year)

MEDICATIONS: 4 left Knee surgeries, 4 achilles

OTHER: Co-operative as much as possible very doopy extremely sleepy hard to keep eyes open & hard to walk.

COMMENTS: A/O & Δ arrived at 0402 hrs
A/O observed 20 minutes
A/O requested breath test, Δ agreed
No problem with test, Tech explained results
Δ blew .000's A/O requested urine, Δ agreed
A/O read C/W Δ understood rights
Refused Q&A Urine drawn at 0440 hrs
Ofc Borrows JPD did DRE

WHITE · STATE ATTY. YELLOW · DHSMV PINK · CENTRAL RECORDS GOLD · JAIL

PBSO #0129A REV.11/02

Exhibit 4.9: Notice to Appear – Tiger Woods

0488422 N|H ARREST / NOTICE TO APPEAR 2017CT9620 1513

OBTS Number

1. Arrest 2. N.T.A. 3. Request for Warrant 4. Request for Capias — 1 — JUVENILE

ADMINISTRATION

Agency ORI Number: 0501700 — Agency Name: Jupiter Police Department — Agency Report Number (N.T.A.'s only): 5 4 17-002626

Charge Type: Check as many as apply: ☐ 1. Felony ☐ 2. Traffic Felony ☐ 3. Misdemeanor ☒ 4. Traffic Misdemeanor ☐ 5. Ordinance ☐ 6. Other — If Weapon Seized Enter Type: NONE — Multiple Clearance Indicator

Location of Arrest (Including Name of Business): 2999 MILITARY TRL/INDIAN CREEK PARKWAY

Location of Offense (Business Name, Address): 2999 MILITARY TRL/INDIAN CREEK PKWY, JUPITER, FL

Date of Arrest: 05/29/2017 — Time of Arrest: 02:49 — Booking Date — Booking Time — Jail Date — Jail Time — Location of Vehicle

DEFENDANT

Name (Last, First, Middle): WOODS, ELDRICK TIGER — Alias (Name, DOB, Soc. Sec. #, Etc.) Alias:

Race (W - White, B - Black, I - American Indian, O - Oriental/Asian): B — Sex: M — Date of Birth: 12/30/1975 — Height: 6'00 — Weight: 185 — Eye Color: BROWN — Hair Color: BLACK — Complexion: DARK — Build: Medium

Scars, Marks, Tatoos, Unique Physical Features (Location, Type, Description) — Marital Status: D — Religion: OTHER — Indication of: Alcohol Influence / Drug Influence: Yes ☐ No ☒ Unk. ☐ / Yes ☐ No ☐ Unk. ☒

Local Address (Street, Apt. Number) (City) (State) (Zip): 462 S BEACH RD, HOBE SOUND, FL 33455 — Phone: (407) 421-1888 — Residence Type: 1. City 2. County 3. Florida 4. Out of State: 3

Permanent Address (Street, Apt. Number) (City) (State) (Zip): 462 S BEACH RD, HOBE SOUND, FL 33455 — Phone: (407) 421-1888 — Address Source: FL DL

Business Address (Name, Street) (City) (State) (Zip) — Phone — Occupation: Athlete

D/L Number, State: W320218754700 / FL — Soc. Sec. Number: [redacted] — INS Number — Place of Birth (City, State): LONG BEACH, CA, — Citizenship: US

CO-DEFENDANT

Co-Defendant Name (Last, First, Middle) — Race — Sex — Date of Birth — ☐ 1. Arrested ☐ 2. At Large ☐ 3. Felony ☐ 4. Misdemeanor ☐ 5. Juvenile

Co-Defendant Name (Last, First, Middle) — Race — Sex — Date of Birth — ☐ 1. Arrested ☐ 2. At Large ☐ 3. Felony ☐ 4. Misdemeanor ☐ 5. Juvenile

JUVENILE

☐ Parent ☐ Other: ☐ Legal Custodian — Name (Last, First, Middle) — Residence Phone

Address (Street, Apt. Number) (City) (State) (Zip) — Business Phone

Notified by: (Name) — Date — Time — JUVENILE DISPOSITION: 1. Handled/Processed within Department and Released 2. TOT JAC 3. Incarcerated

Released To: (Name) — Relationship — Date — Time

The above address was provided by ☐ defendant and/or ☐ defendant's parents. The child and/or parent was told to keep the Juvenile Court Clerk's Office (Phone 355-2526) informed of any change of address. ☐ Yes, by: ☐ No: — School Attended — Grade

Property Crime? ☐ Yes ☒ No — Description of Property — Value of Property

CODE

Drug Activity: N. N/A, P. Possess, S. Sell, B. Buy, T. Traffic, R. Smuggle, D. Deliver, E. Use, K. Dispense/Distribute, M. Manufacture/Produce/Cultivate, Z. Other — Drug Type: N. N/A, A. Amphetamine, B. Barbiturate, C. Cocaine, E. Heroin, H. Hallucinogen, M. Marijuana, O. Opium/Deriv., P. Paraphernalia/Equipment, S. Synthetic, U. Unknown, Z. Other

CHARGE

Charge Description: DUI - DRIVING WHILE UNDER INFLUENCE — Statute Violation Number: 316.193(1) — Violation of ORD #

Drug Activity — Drug Type: N — Amount / Unit: / — Offense #: 17-002626 — Counts: 1 — Domestic Violence: ☐ Y ☒ N — Warrant / Capias Number — Bond

CHARGE

Charge Description — Statute Violation Number — Violation of ORD #

Drug Activity — Drug Type — Amount / Unit: / — Offense # — Counts — Domestic Violence: ☐ Y ☐ N — Warrant / Capias Number — Bond

CHARGE

Charge Description — Statute Violation Number — Violation of ORD #

Drug Activity — Drug Type — Amount / Unit: / — Offense # — Counts — Domestic Violence: ☐ Y ☐ N — Warrant / Capias Number — Bond

INTAKE

Health / Apparent Physical Condition of Defendant — Any knowledge of the following: ☐ Mental ☐ Escape Risk ☐ Medication ☐ Deformities ☐ Injuries — Explain:

Check which applies: ☐ Released O.R. ☐ Posted Bond ☐ Released to Parent/Guardian ☐ South County Mental Health ☐ T.O.T. County Jail — PROPERTY - Received By — Released By — Released To

Transported By — Date Transported — Time Transported — Other

NOTICE TO APPEAR

☒ INSTRUCTION NO. 1 - Mandatory appearance in court
☐ INSTRUCTION NO. 2 - You need not appear in Court but must comply with instructions on Page 2.

Location (Court, Room): North County PALM BEACH GARD — Court Date and Time: 07/05/2017 08:30:00

No Photo Available

I AGREE TO APPEAR AT THE TIME AND PLACE DESIGNATED TO ANSWER THE OFFENSE CHARGED OR TO PAY THE FINE SUBSCRIBED. I UNDERSTAND THAT SHOULD I WILLFULLY FAIL TO APPEAR BEFORE THE COURT AS REQUIRED BY THIS NOTICE TO APPEAR, THAT I MAY BE HELD IN COMTEMPT OF COURT AND A WARRANT FOR MY ARREST SHALL BE ISSUED.

X [signature] — Signature of Defendant (or Juvenile and Parent/Custodian) — SCANNED — Date Signed — 2017 MAY 30 AM 5:35

ADMIN

HOLD for Other Agency: ☐ Dangerous ☐ Suicidal ☐ Resisted Arrest ☐ Other — Signature of Arresting Officer: [signature] 340 — MAY 3 0 2017 — Name Verification (Printed by Arrestee): (PRINT) Eldrick Wood — #38

Name of Arresting Officer (Print): FANDREY, CHRISTOPHER — I.D. #: 1182 — PAGE 1 OF 1

Intake Deputy: DTS Willingham 7141 — Pouch # — Transporting Officer: C Fandrey — I.D. #: 340 — Agency: JPD — Witness here if subject signed with an X — MAY 29 AM 7:30

NOT A CERTIFIED COPY

News coverage of the 2014 riots in Ferguson, Missouri, brought the issue of police shootings to national attention. However, the 2020 police killing of George Floyd in Minneapolis was the catalyst for a nationwide movement against police violence toward African Americans. Within a year of Floyd's death, 25 states and the District of Columbia enacted legislation addressing at least one of three issues directly related to Floyd's killing: (1) use of force; (2) duty for officers to intervene, report, or render medical aid in instances of police misconduct; and (3) policies related to law enforcement misconduct reporting and decertification of law enforcement officers.[45]

For instance, in early 2021, Illinois adopted a series of police reform laws in response to concerns about police misconduct. Among other things, these reforms include prohibiting the police from using chokeholds, requiring all officers to wear body cameras by 2025, and creating new guidelines for the decertification of police officers. Section 7-16(a) of the Code of Criminal Procedure, 720 ILSC 5/7-16(a), imposes a duty on officers to intervene when one of their colleagues uses excessive force.

§ 7-16 (a) Duty to Intervene

> A peace officer, or any other person acting under the color of law who has an opportunity to intervene, shall have an affirmative duty to intervene to prevent or stop another peace officer in his or her presence from using any unauthorized force or force that exceeds the degree of force permitted, if any, without regard for chain of command.

Discussion Questions

14. What, if anything, should a law enforcement officer be allowed to do when a person being arrested:
    a. punches the officer;
    b. spits on the officer;
    c. swears at the officer;
    d. sits down or goes limp rather than following the officer's directions?
15. At what point should an officer be required to intervene in situations in which another officer uses excessive force:
    a. When the arresting officer pulls a suspect's arms behind his or her back?
    b. When the arresting officer strikes a suspect who threw the first punch?
    c. When the arresting officer strikes a suspect who just spit in his face?

[45]Ram Subramanian and Leily Arzy, Brennan Center for Justice, *State Policing Reforms Since George Floyd's Murder* (May 21, 2021), https://www.brennancenter.org/our-work/research-reports/state-policing-reforms-george-floyds-murder.

Application Exercises

1. In the Cook case (*see* Introduction to Hypothetical Cases, p. xxxvii):
   a. What type of law enforcement official would most likely have been sent out to follow up on the passerby's 911 call?
   b. When authorities arrived at the location at which the phone caller had reported seeing the body, they found that the body was that of someone who appeared to have been struck by a motor vehicle while riding a bicycle. What would typically be done to preserve and investigate the scene of the "accident"?
   c. Police also received a phone call from Cook's wife. What type of law enforcement official would most likely have been sent out to follow up on this call? What do you think that officer would do?
2. In the Turner case (*see* Introduction to Hypothetical Cases, pp. xxxvii-xxxviii), a police officer followed Turner into a restaurant and met him at the restroom door when Turner came out after having been in the restroom for less than a minute.
   a. What do you think Officer Milner should do at this point? Why?
   b. Could the officer place Turner under arrest? If so, for what crimes?
   c. What, if any, types of searches could he conduct at this point?
   d. Suppose that Officer Milner had placed Turner under arrest and as he was escorting him out of the restaurant, someone from inside the restaurant called out to him that there was a gun in the restroom. What actions might Officer Milner take in light of this information about a gun being found in the restroom?
3. In the Edwards case (*see* Introduction to Hypothetical Cases, p. xxxviii):
   a. Suppose that you were one of Bill Edwards's brokerage clients who began to get suspicious about some of the explanations he was giving you about transactions in your account. Other than simply moving your account to another financial advisor, what actions could you take to follow up on your suspicions?
   b. Now suppose that you are an investigator with the Securities and Exchange Commission (SEC). What types of things might you do to follow up on a complaint from one of Edwards's clients?
4. In the Smith case (*see* Introduction to Hypothetical Cases, p. xxxix):
   a. Did the police have a valid reason for stopping the car that Mendoza was driving? If so, what was that reason?
   b. Did the police have a legal right to require Perez to exit the vehicle? If so, what was that reason?
   c. Did Officer Smith use excessive force in attempting to extract Mendoza from his seat? Why or why not?
   d. If Officer Smith's arrest of Mendoza occurred in Illinois, did 720 ILCS 5/7-16 (the Duty to Intervene law) require his partner, Officer Jones, to intervene?

5. What should Officer Smith have done differently? Research the statutes and court rules in your state to find out if they set out requirements for search warrants. Then provide a brief summary (with citations) of what you found.
6. Using the federal form entitled "Search and Seizure Warrant," located online at *https://www.uscourts.gov/sites/default/files/ao093.pdf,* prepare a search warrant and return for a federal case based on the information set forth in the Louisiana terrorism case featured in Exhibits 4.2 and 4.3.

SUMMARY

This chapter focused on the role played by police and other law enforcement personnel in identifying the people who commit crimes and in gathering sufficient evidence to warrant their arrest and prosecution.

In carrying out their duties, law enforcement officers understand and comply with the provisions of the due process requirements established in the U.S. and state constitutions. Particularly relevant to this chapter are the Fourth Amendment prohibition against unreasonable searches and seizures and the Fifth Amendment right of individuals accused of a crime to not be required to incriminate themselves.

Once authorities learn that a possible crime has been committed, officers interview victims, witnesses, and suspects to piece together how it occurred. When these investigators question suspects, they must first give the *Miranda* warnings to ensure that the suspect statements are voluntary so that they can be used in court. Grand jury subpoenas can be used in a criminal investigation to compel reluctant witnesses to give testimony.

Following their initial investigations, police may arrest a suspect. For an arrest to be proper, the officer must either have an arrest warrant or probable cause to believe that the suspect committed the offense. Police can use reasonable force to carry out an arrest but are not permitted to use excessive force. When officers engage in excessive force, their colleagues must intervene.

When a search warrant is issued by the court, officers execute it and file a return of the warrant. Law enforcement agents are excused from obtaining a search warrant when the search is consensual, the seized item is in plain view, there are exigent circumstances, or the seized item is discovered during the course of a *Terry* stop and frisk. If prosecutors want to conduct electronic surveillance, they must first apply to the court for the entry of an eavesdropping order.

Once evidence is retrieved from a search, it is inventoried and securely stored so that a chain of evidence can be established at trial.

INTERNET RESOURCES

Government Investigative Agencies

- Federal Bureau of Investigation: **http://www.fbi.gov/**
- Federal Bureau of Alcohol, Tobacco, Firearms, and Explosives: **http://www.atf.gov/**

- Interpol: **http://www.interpol.int/**
- U.S. Border Patrol: **https://www.cbp.gov/**
- U.S. Drug Enforcement Administration: **https://www.dea.gov/**
- U.S. Immigration and Customs Enforcement: **http://www.ice.gov/**
- U.S. Marshal's Service: **http://www.justice.gov/marshals/**

Crime Scene Investigations

- Crime Scene Investigator Network: **http://www.crime-scene-investigator.net/csi-photo.html**
- How Stuff Works: **http://science.howstuffworks.com/csi.htm**
- Child Welfare Information Gateway: **http://www.childwelfare.gov/responding/iia/investigation/**

Victim Assistance Services

- Online Guide from Office for Victims of Crime (OVC): **https://ovc.ncjrs.gov/HelpVictim.aspx**

REVIEW QUESTIONS

1. How does procedural due process differ from substantive due process?
2. What are the Fourth Amendment requirements for the issuance of warrants?
3. Under what circumstances do government authorities typically learn that a crime has been committed?
4. As used in the Fourth Amendment, to what types of matters does a "seizure" apply?
5. What is a *Terry* stop? Under what set of circumstances can the police carry it out?
6. What constitutional provision gives individuals the right not to identify themselves when asked to do so by the police?
7. What are the *Miranda* warnings?
8. What effect does the failure to give the *Miranda* warnings have on a defendant's case?
9. Compare transactional immunity with derivative use immunity.
10. What's the difference between a suspect and a defendant?
11. Name and explain the level of force the police are permitted to use when making an arrest.
12. What are the two alternative bases that law enforcement officers need to make an arrest under the Fourth Amendment?
13. What is a search warrant? How can a prosecutor obtain a search warrant?
14. What are the general showings that must be included in an application for a search warrant?
15. What is the name of the voluntarily written declaration of facts signed under oath or under penalty of perjury? What do you call the person signing this document?
16. What are the required contents for a search warrant issued in federal court?
17. What information would you expect to find in a return of a search warrant?
18. Explain the "plain view" and "exigent circumstances" exceptions to the requirement of a search warrant.
19. Why is maintaining a proper chain of evidence important in an illicit drug prosecution?

Chapter 5

The Prosecutor's Role in Initiating Cases

Chapter Objectives

After reading this chapter, you should be able to:

- List the various titles given to prosecuting attorneys at the federal, state, and local levels, in addition to describing the role that they play in the criminal justice system.
- Discuss the ethical obligations imposed on prosecuting attorneys.
- Explain the various ways in which prosecuting attorneys can be involved in investigations into potential criminal behavior.
- Identify the various ways in which people can be charged with crimes and the role played by prosecuting attorneys in drafting criminal complaints, indictments, and informations.

Introduction

This chapter focuses on the activities of **prosecuting attorneys** ("**prosecutors**") and the paralegals who work for them during the investigative and charging stages of criminal cases. We will turn our attention to **defense attorneys** in Chapter 6. Before you read further, it would be good to go back and review Figure 4.1 on page 92 to familiarize yourself with the stages of the criminal justice system that occur between an arrest and the start of a trial.

Prosecutor
The lawyer authorized to represent a particular unit of government in criminal court.

Defense attorney
The lawyer who represents a criminal defendant in court.

A. Who They Are and Where They Work

Depending upon which governmental unit employs them, prosecuting attorneys have titles such as U.S. Attorney, State's Attorney, District Attorney, or City Attorney, as well as Assistant U.S. Attorney, Assistant District Attorney, and other positions. While their powers differ, they are all attorneys who are employed (either full or part time) to represent the public at large in court proceedings involving violations of the criminal code.[1]

The primary duties of prosecuting attorneys are to supervise and advise law enforcement agencies and grand juries in criminal investigations, decide whether to charge a suspect with a crime, determine the appropriate charge, and present the government's case in court proceedings.

1. FEDERAL PROSECUTORS

United States Attorney (U.S. Attorney)
The chief federal law enforcement officer for a specific judicial district. The U.S. Attorney is responsible for prosecuting persons accused of committing federal crimes.

United States Attorneys prosecute violations of federal law.[2] They are federal employees of the U.S. Department of Justice who report to the U.S. Attorney General. They are appointed by the president with the advice and consent of the senate and continue in office at the pleasure of the president. Currently, there are 93 U.S. Attorneys who are assigned to 94 specific judicial districts over which they serve as the chief federal law enforcement officer.[3] They have a support staff of Assistant U.S. Attorneys, paralegals, and clerical workers.

The number of attorneys in their offices and the scope of their geographic authority vary greatly. For instance, the U.S. Attorney's Office for the Southern District of New York has more than 220 Assistant U.S. Attorneys in its Criminal Division.[4] It has authority over seven counties, plus the boroughs of the Bronx and Manhattan in New York City. In contrast, the Criminal Division for the District of Wyoming consists of a criminal chief and 13 Assistant U.S. Attorneys.[5] This office is responsible for federal law enforcement for the entire state of Wyoming.

2. STATE AND LOCAL PROSECUTORS

While their titles differ, states have similar types of prosecuting attorneys enforcing violations of criminal law. They are known as district attorneys,[6] prosecuting attorneys,[7] state's attorneys,[8] state attorneys,[9] county

---

[1]In the states, the "public at large" is referred to as either "the People" or "the Commonwealth." In federal cases, the U.S. Attorney represents the United States.

[2]The U.S. Attorneys have three statutory responsibilities under 28 U.S.C. §547: the prosecution of criminal cases brought by the federal government, the prosecution and defense of civil cases in which the United States is a party, and the collection of debts owed the federal government that are administratively uncollectible.

[3]One U.S. Attorney is assigned to each of the judicial districts, with the exception of Guam and the Northern Mariana Islands, where a single U.S. Attorney serves in both districts.

[4]U.S. Department of Justice Southern District of New York website, https://www.justice.gov/usao-sdny/about (last checked June 5, 2022).

[5]U.S. Department of Justice District of Wyoming website, https://www.justice.gov/usao-wy/office (last checked June 5, 2022).

[6]The following states designate their chief local prosecutors as district attorneys: Alabama, Alaska, California, Colorado, Georgia, Louisiana, Maine, Massachusetts, Mississippi, Nevada, New Mexico, New York, North Carolina, Oklahoma, Oregon, Pennsylvania, and Wisconsin.

[7]The following states designate their chief local prosecutors as prosecuting attorneys: Arkansas, Hawaii, Idaho, Michigan, Missouri, Ohio, Washington, and West Virginia.

[8]The following states designate their chief local prosecutors as state's attorneys: Connecticut, Illinois, Maryland, North Dakota, South Dakota, and Vermont.

[9]Florida is the only state that designates its chief local prosecutors as "state attorneys."

prosecutors,[10] county attorneys,[11] commonwealth's attorneys,[12] solicitors,[13] and attorneys general.[14] In addition, some municipalities have city prosecutors who litigate local ordinance violations. Attorney generals, district attorneys, and states' attorneys are usually elected officials. They then appoint their assistants. Municipal attorneys are usually appointed by local government officials. Depending on the type of governmental unit, state and local prosecutorial positions may be full time or part time.

State and local prosecutors' offices vary in the size and scope of their geographic authority. Most state prosecutors' offices have divisions for handling certain types of cases, such as felony, misdemeanor, traffic, and juvenile. Many larger offices have specialized units for such matters as drug prosecutions, high-tech crime, gang activity, asset forfeiture, auto theft, and arson. Small, rural offices are staffed by the supervising public official, a few deputy attorneys, and clerical staff. Because of staffing limitations, these offices typically do not have divisions or specialized units.

APPLICATION EXERCISES

1. Research the number and locations of the federal district courts in your state to find out how many districts are in your state, the cities where the courthouses are located, and the name and background of the current U.S. Attorney for each district.
2. Research the titles and locations of the different types of prosecuting attorneys in your state. Are they elected or appointed? If they are appointed, who appoints them?

B. ETHICAL RESTRICTIONS APPLICABLE TO PROSECUTING ATTORNEYS

All attorneys, regardless of the nature of their practice, are subject to ethical rules established and enforced by state supreme courts or bar associations. Although the format and content of these ethical rules vary from state to state, they typically follow the general principles set out in the American Bar Association (ABA)'s **Model Rules of Professional Conduct.**

Model Rules of Professional Conduct A set of recommended ethics standards for attorneys promulgated by the American Bar Association (ABA). Most of the states have adopted some or all of the model rules.

---

[10]Indiana and New Jersey use the title of "county prosecutor." Delaware's county prosecutors are part of the Attorney General's Office. Texas refers to its chief local prosecutors as "county attorney" and/or "district attorney."

[11]The following states designate their chief local prosecutors as county attorneys: Arizona, Iowa, Kansas, Minnesota, Montana, Nebraska, New Hampshire, Utah, and Wyoming.

[12]Kentucky and Virginia refer to their chief local prosecutors as "commonwealth's attorneys."

[13]South Carolina is the only state that refers to its chief local prosecuting official as "solicitor."

[14]Rhode Island and Tennessee conduct local prosecutions through their attorney general offices.

In the preface to these model rules, the ABA states that they are designed to ensure the highest standards of professional competence and ethical conduct within the legal profession. The rules impose ethical limitations on how prosecuting attorneys can obtain convictions.

Ethical Obligations Specific to Prosecuting Attorneys

All attorneys are expected to be effective advocates for the interests of their clients, but what does that mean when, as in the case of prosecuting attorneys, the client is the people of the state or the people of the United States? Is it necessarily in the people's interest to prosecute every crime, regardless of the cost, or to seek the maximum sentence for everyone convicted of a crime?

Even if prosecutors had enough budgetary resources to seek as many convictions as possible, the Model Code imposes various ethical limitations on the means by which they can obtain those convictions. Rule 3.8 of the Model Code lists a number of "special responsibilities" that go with being a prosecutor. These ethical duties include:

- Not prosecuting charges that are unsupported by probable cause;
- Making reasonable efforts to ensure that defendants have been advised of their constitutional rights;
- Making timely disclosures to the defense of information known to the prosecutor that tends to "negate the guilt of the accused or mitigates the offense";
- Not making extrajudicial comments that are prejudicial to the defendant unless they serve a "legitimate law enforcement purpose."

Section (g), which applies in situations where a prosecutor knows of new, credible, and material evidence creating a reasonable likelihood that a convicted defendant did not commit an offense of which the defendant was convicted, and section (h), which applies when a prosecutor knows of clear and convincing evidence establishing that a defendant in the prosecutor's jurisdiction was convicted of an offense that the defendant did not commit, will be discussed in Chapter 14, which covers the subject of appeals.

The ABA Model Rules of Professional Conduct can be found on the ABA website at https://www.americanbar.org/groups/professional_responsibility/publications/model_rules_of_professional_conduct/model_rules_of_professional_conduct_table_of_contents/.

C. The Role of Prosecuting Attorneys in Investigations

1. GENERAL INVESTIGATIVE RESPONSIBILITIES

Prosecutors are responsible for the overall coordination of criminal investigations. They must establish good working relationships with local police agencies and give them legal advice as to how they should go about gathering and preserving evidence. When they discover holes or weak points in their cases, prosecutors need to give directions to police or in-house investigators as to the types of additional evidence they need to gather. When physical evidence is sent to crime labs, the prosecutor's office is responsible for making sure that the right tests are performed and determining what the results really mean.

2. APPLICATIONS FOR SEARCH WARRANTS

In Chapter 4, we discussed the function of search warrants and how they were prepared. Although there is wide variation as to the roles played by police, prosecutors, and paralegals in drafting some of these documents, the prosecuting attorney is ultimately responsible for presenting them to the court.

3. COORDINATION OF GRAND JURY ACTIVITIES

Grand juries are part of our common law tradition. The Fifth Amendment to the U.S. Constitution requires that "[n]o person shall be held to answer for a capital, or otherwise infamous crime, unless on a presentment or indictment of a Grand Jury." Unlike most other sections of the Bill of Rights, the grand jury provision of the Fifth Amendment does not apply to the states.[15] However, a substantial minority of states require a grand jury indictment to pursue serious criminal charges.[16] However, in a majority of states, indictment by a grand jury is optional; and two states use grand juries only to conduct investigations into criminal activity, but not to indict.[17]

Like citizens serving on trial juries (also known as "petit juries"), grand jurors are made up of local residents who are randomly selected from voter registration rolls or driver's license registration records. Unlike service on a trial jury, which takes place on consecutive business days, people serving on a grand jury typically meet one day a week over a period of several months.

Grand jury
A court-appointed panel composed of sixteen to twenty-three citizens that considers evidence presented by prosecutors and determines whether there is probable cause to bring formal criminal charges.

Grand juries usually consist of between 16 and 23 persons who review the prosecutor's recommendations regarding whether specific individuals should be forced to stand trial for alleged criminal offenses and who initiate independent investigations of criminal activities.[18] Since grand juries are typically made up of ordinary citizens who do not have a legal background, they naturally look to

---

[15] *Hurtado v. California*, 110 U.S. 516 (1884).

[16] Twenty-three states and the District of Columbia require an indictment issued by a grand jury to enable a prosecutor to bring serious criminal charges. For a display of the various approaches taken by the individual states concerning grand juries. see National Center for State Courts, *Reforming the Grand Jury Indictment Process: Recent Efforts to Improve Public Confidence in Cases Involving Police Use of Lethal Force* (2021), p. 2 (https://www.ncsc-jurystudies.org/__data/assets/pdf_file/0019/5851/grand-jury-report_rev-2021.pdf).

[17] Twenty-seven states give prosecutors the option to indict serious crimes without a grand jury. Connecticut and Pennsylvania abolished the indictment requirement but continue to use grand juries to conduct investigations. *Id.*

[18] The size of a grand jury varies from jurisdiction to jurisdiction. Thirteen states and the District of Columbia have the largest size of 23 members. Virginia permits 5-member grand juries. *Id* at p. 4.

the prosecutor's staff for guidance on interpreting the law, as well as the procedures they should follow.

In the federal system and in most states, grand juries provide prosecutors with a powerful avenue to conduct investigations. This is because a grand jury can subpoena witnesses and question them under oath in secrecy. As a practical matter, the prosecutor's office directs the grand jury's activities so it not only determines the crimes being investigated, but also the evidence that the grand jury will consider. Ordinarily, the prosecutor provides the grand jury only with **inculpatory evidence**—that is, evidence tending to show that the person being investigated committed a crime. Thus, the prosecutor has tremendous influence as to whether a suspect will be indicted by the grand jury.

Inculpatory evidence
Evidence tending to show that a person committed a crime.

As a paralegal in a prosecutor's office, you may be asked to prepare a subpoena to compel a witness to appear before a grand jury. This is a relatively simple task to perform. Most subpoenas are fill-in-the-blank forms, which are usually available from the clerk's office and often available online.[19] Your supervising attorney will give you the name of the witness, along with the documents or other items that the witness must bring to the grand jury proceedings.

Special Counsel Robert Mueller's investigation of Russian interference in the 2016 presidential election provides a good example of using grand juries as an investigative tool. Individuals who were thought to have knowledge of important events were questioned under oath and indicted for perjury if they gave false answers. Some of these witnesses received immunity from prosecution or promises of reduced charges or lesser sentences in return for their cooperation. In the aftermath of the January 6, 2021, attack of the U.S. Capitol, the U.S. Attorney for the District of Columbia impaneled several separate grand juries to look into activities behind and during President Donald Trump's rallies, Trump attorneys, and Trump associates. The U.S. Attorney's letter that accompanied a federal grand jury subpoena directed to Peter Navarro, one of President Trump's advisors, is displayed in Exhibit 5.1.

D. The Role of the Prosecutors in Charging Defendants

As discussed in Chapter 4, law enforcement officers can make arrests without first consulting a prosecutor when, based on their own observations, they have probable cause to believe that the person being arrested has violated a provision of the criminal law.

1. THE DECISION TO CHARGE

The arresting police officer, without prosecutorial input, can prepare a charge against a suspect for traffic infractions, petty offenses, and misdemeanors. In these situations, the "initial charge" is determined by the police. The prosecutor's office usually screens these "initial charges" before they are filed with

---

[19]The federal subpoena to appear before a grand jury is available online at *https://www.uscourts.gov/sites/default/files/ao110.pdf.*

Exhibit 5.1: United States Attorney's Letter Accompanying Grand Jury Subpoena

In late 2021, a grand jury convened by the U.S. Attorney for the District of Columbia issued a subpoena to Peter Navarro, one of President Trump's top White House advisors. Navarro filed suit seeking to declare the grand jury subpoena and a congressional subpoena invalid. The cover letter accompanying the grand jury subpoena appears below.

U.S. Department of Justice

Matthew M. Graves
United States Attorney

District of Columbia
Patrick Henry Building
601 D Street N.W.
Washington, D.C. 20530

May 26, 2022

VIA Hand Delivery

Peter K. Navarro

Re: Grand Jury Subpoena #GJ2022052590979
USAO #2022R00631

Dear Peter K. Navarro:

Pursuant to a criminal investigation being conducted by the United States Attorney's Office, it is required that you furnish the requested records as described in the attached subpoena.

In lieu of personally appearing before the Grand Jury on the date indicated, you may comply with this grand jury subpoena by promptly providing the agent designated in the attachment with the requested records. If you choose to provide the requested records voluntarily, please provide them in a non-proprietary electronic format via FedEx, UPS or DHL. Also enclosed please find a blank "Declaration of Custodian of Records" form. It may save time and costs if an appropriate person at your business could complete the form and return it with the records. A properly completed "Declaration of Custodian of Records" form will make it more likely that we could present the records at trial without requiring you or another employee to come to court and testify.

Although you are not required to do so, you are requested not to disclose the existence of this subpoena. Any such disclosure could impede the investigation being conducted and thereby interfere with the enforcement of the law. Thank you for your cooperation in this matter.

Sincerely,

Matthew M. Graves
United States Attorney

By: Elizabeth Aloi
Elizabeth Aloi
Assistant United States Attorney

the court. In rural areas, prosecutors generally screen all criminal cases before charges are filed; in large urban areas, the police may file misdemeanor charges without prosecutorial review.[20] A designated attorney in the prosecutor's office typically screens misdemeanor cases, whereas either a single prosecutor or a committee screens felonies.

Some prosecutors, as a matter of policy, decline to prosecute certain categories of cases. For instance, when President Barack Obama held office, the U.S. Justice Department took the position that it would not enforce the federal marijuana prohibition in states that legalized marijuana if the state had established effective regulatory and enforcement systems in place except in limited circumstances. Similarly, the Biden administration's attorney general, Merrick Garland, has announced that the Department of Justice does not prioritize prosecuting marijuana use. Further, in 2020, in response to the enactment of antiabortion legislation shortly before the U.S. Supreme Court overturned *Roe v. Wade,* 68 state and local prosecutors promised not to charge women or medical providers for activities having to do with abortions.[21]

In conducting their review of potential criminal charges, screeners examine the reports prepared by the investigating police officer, as well as the offense stated when the accused was booked. Following the screening process, the prosecutor's office can either adopt the charge determined by the arresting officer, modify the charge to better reflect the facts, or drop the charges completely.

Situations in which police officers shoot civilians pose one of the most difficult decisions for prosecutors. This is especially true when the shooting occurs while the officer is on duty.[22] For now, we simply note that these types of cases typically receive considerable media coverage and often lead to public demonstrations and racial tension. Police shootings (especially those involving white officers and minority race civilians) often generate great public pressure to prosecute the police officers. However, it is usually very difficult for prosecutors to obtain convictions in these types of cases because of inconsistent accounts as to what police claim to have seen and what other witnesses observed. This is in part due to the "code of silence"[23] within police departments, as well as the nature of self-defense and the law enforcement defense.[24]

Since many chief prosecuting attorneys are elected and regularly work closely with the police, they will sometimes use the grand jury to provide political cover in deciding whether to prosecute a police officer. An example of this occurred in 2014, when a Ferguson, Missouri, policeman fired 12 times at an

---

[20] W. LaFave, J. Isreal & N. King, *Criminal Procedure* (4th ed., West Publishing 2004), at 13.

[21] Route Fifty, "The Prosecutors Not Planning to Enforce Post-Roe Abortion Laws." https://www.route-fifty.com/health-human-services/2022/05/prosecutors-who-wont-enforce-post-roe-v-wade-state-abortion-trigger-laws/367244/ (last examined June 5, 2022).

[22] From 2005 until 2013, authorities brought murder or manslaughter charges against 56 officers involved in off-duty slayings versus 41 officers involved who killed someone while on duty and obtained a higher percentage of convictions against the off-duty defendants. Philip M. Stinson, "The Federal Government Doesn't Track Police Violence—But I Do," *The Atlantic,* September 11, 2013. https://www.theatlantic.com/ideas/archive/2018/09/amber-guyger-fallout-how-common-is-police-crime/569950/.

[23] The code of silence, also referred to as the "Blue Code," is the unwritten custom among police of not reporting fellow officers' errors, misconduct, or crimes.

[24] See the discussion of self-defense and the law enforcement defense in Chapter 7, pp. 217-223.

18-year-old Black youth who was alleged to have been walking toward the police officer with his empty hands held up over his head. When rioting started after the youth died from his wounds, the local prosecutor took the matter to a grand jury. After watching videos and hearing from 50 witnesses, the grand jury declined to indict the officer.

That same year, Eric Garner died from a chokehold applied by a New York policeman making an arrest for the crime of selling loose cigarettes. The local prosecutor also took the case to a grand jury that declined to indict the officer. However, when a video from a bystander's cell phone (showing that the policeman continued to apply the chokehold while Garner gasped for breath while calling out that he couldn't breathe) became public, it sparked protests by the activist group Black Lives Matter and others.

The Missouri and New York cases were each referred to the U.S. Department of Justice to investigate whether the officers' actions violated federal civil rights laws. In both cases, the Justice Department decided not to indict the policemen. In both cases, the department determined that there was insufficient support to prove that either officer willfully used excessive force to violate federal civil rights.

This trend appears to be reversing. In 2015, a Cook County, Illinois, grand jury returned an indictment of first-degree murder against Jason Van Dyke, a Chicago policeman, for killing Laquan McDonald, a 17-year-old Black youth. A jury found Van Dyke guilty on one count of second-degree murder and 16 counts of aggravated battery.

In 2019, Elijah McClain, a 23-year-old Black man, died after police officers restrained him with a chokehold. After a local prosecutor declined to bring charges, the Colorado attorney general appointed a special prosecutor, who opened a grand jury investigation. In 2021, the grand jury indicted three police officers and two paramedics on charges of negligent homicide and manslaughter. In July 2022, a judge found the evidence against these defendants strong enough to proceed.[25]

Shortly after George Floyd's death in 2020, the Minnesota attorney general and the Hennepin county attorney filed murder charges against Officer Derek Chauvin and aiding and abetting murder charges against the three police officers with Chauvin during the incident (who have since left the force). A federal grand jury indicted the four men on federal charges of violating Floyd's civil rights.[26]

Discussion Question

1. After reviewing the laws of your state for homicide, manslaughter, and negligent homicide, determine what crime, if any, would apply to a situation like the one described in Eric Garner's death. What, if any, charges would you bring against the officer if you were a prosecuting attorney? Why?

[25]The case remains pending as of now.

[26]For further discussion of the Floyd criminal proceedings, see pages 44-45 and 58 in Chapter 3.

2. INITIAL APPEARANCE AND BOND HEARING

Initial appearance
A court proceeding at which the judge informs the defendant of the charges and the right to be represented by an attorney and also determines bail. This is also called a **first appearance**.

Bail
Security paid on behalf of the accused that is pledged to guarantee that the accused will appear in court for scheduled proceedings. This is also referred to as **bond**.

Own recognizance
The defendant's promise to appear in court without posting a bond. This is also referred to as **O.R.** and **personal recognizance**.

Officers are allowed to detain suspects in custody for a "reasonable amount of time" as the investigation continues before formal charges must be filed.

The first time a suspect in custody appears before a judge is the **initial appearance** (also called **first appearance**). In this proceeding, the judge gives defendants a copy of charge(s), informs them of the right to be represented by an attorney, and determines the conditions under which the defendant can be released pending the eventual trial. Specifically, the judge decides whether the defendant should be released from custody on **bail** (also known as **bond**) or their **own recognizance** (also known as **O.R.** and **personal recognizance**). The prosecutor's recommendation can have a major influence on this decision.

In most felony cases, the judge determines the amount of bail at the initial hearing. However, for lesser crimes, some jurisdictions have adopted a fixed schedule and allow defendants to post their bonds immediately after being booked at police headquarters. In traffic cases, it is customary for alleged offenders to post their driver's license in lieu of a predetermined cash amount. On any given day in the United States, about a half million defendants are in custody pending trial.[27]

Depending upon the jurisdiction involved, bail can be posted in the form of cash, a bond posted by a professional bail bondsman, or deeds to real estate property. If the defendant fails to appear, the judge will issue a bench warrant and the prosecutor will petition to revoke bail. If the petition is granted, bail is forfeited.

The practice of depositing money or pledging property to secure a defendant's release pending trial is firmly established in our legal history. However, it has a discriminatory impact on low-income defendants who lack the financial resources to come up with the amount of bail that was set in their cases. The Eighth Amendment prohibits the setting of excessive bail. However, the contours of what amount is "excessive" is unclear. Therefore, the trial judge has a great deal of discretion in establishing the amount. The California Supreme Court recently reexamined the use of money bail as a means of pretrial detention, as the following case demonstrates.[28] The Illinois General Assembly adopted legislation, effective in 2023, that eliminated cash bail for defendants charged in a large proportion of offenses as part of a major criminal justice reform act.

---

[27]Isabella Jorgensen and Sandra Susan Smith, *The Current State of Bail Reform in the United States* (2021), https://research.hks.harvard.edu/publications/getFile.aspx?Id=5111 p.1.

[28]Similarly, the Nevada Supreme Court ruled that the state must provide clear and convincing evidence that bail is necessary "to ensure the defendant's presence at future court proceedings or to protect the safety of the community" and held that substantive due process mandates that bail can be imposed only when necessary to ensure a defendant's appearance or to protect the community. *Valdez-Jimenez v. Eighth Judicial District Court in and for County Clerk*, 136 Nev. 155 (2020).

In re Humphrey
Supreme Court of California
11 Cal.5th 135 (2021)

Opinion of the Court by Cuéllar, J.

An arrestee's release pending trial is often conditioned on whether the arrestee can make bail. To do so, an arrestee posts security—in the form of cash, property, or (more often) a commercial bail bond—which is forfeited if the arrestee later fails to appear in court. Those who can't afford to satisfy the bail condition remain in jail until the end of the criminal proceedings.

Underlying this arrangement is a major premise: that the state has a compelling interest in assuring the arrestee's appearance at trial and protecting the safety of the victim as well as the public. Yet those incarcerated pending trial—who have not yet been convicted of a charged crime—unquestionably suffer a "direct 'grievous loss'" of freedom in addition to other potential injuries. In principle, then, pretrial detention should be reserved for those who otherwise cannot be relied upon to make court appearances or who pose a risk to public or victim safety. But it's a different story in practice: Whether an accused person is detained pending trial often does not depend on a careful, individualized determination of the need to protect public safety, but merely—as one judge observes—on the accused's ability to post the sum provided in a county's uniform bail schedule.

Petitioner Kenneth Humphrey, joined by the Attorney General, challenges this system with a claim as simple as it is urgent: No person should lose the right to liberty simply because that person can't afford to post bail. His claim joins a "clear and growing movement" that is reexamining the use of money bail as a means of pretrial detention.

We find merit in Humphrey's claim. The common practice of conditioning freedom solely on whether an arrestee can afford bail is unconstitutional. Other conditions of release—such as electronic monitoring, regular check-ins with a pretrial case manager, community housing or shelter, and drug and alcohol treatment—can in many cases protect public and victim safety as well as assure the arrestee's appearance at trial. What we hold is that where a financial condition is nonetheless necessary, the court must consider the arrestee's ability to pay the stated amount of bail—and may not effectively detain the arrestee "solely because" the arrestee "lacked the resources" to post bail.

In unusual circumstances, the need to protect community safety may conflict with the arrestee's fundamental right to pretrial liberty—a right that also generally protects an arrestee from being subject to a monetary condition of release the arrestee can't satisfy—to such an extent that no option other than refusing pretrial release can reasonably vindicate the state's compelling interests. In order to detain an arrestee under those circumstances, a court must first find by clear and convincing evidence that no condition short of detention could suffice and then ensure the detention otherwise complies with statutory and constitutional requirements.

Detention in these narrow circumstances doesn't depend on the arrestee's financial condition. Rather, it depends on the insufficiency of less restrictive conditions to vindicate compelling government interests: the safety of the victim and the public more generally or the integrity of the criminal proceedings. Allowing the government to detain an arrestee without such procedural protections would violate state and federal principles of equal protection and due process that must be honored in practice, not just in principle.

Because the trial court here failed to consider Humphrey's ability to afford $350,000 bail (and, if he could not, whether less restrictive alternatives could have protected public and victim safety or assured his appearance in court), we agree with the Court of Appeal: Humphrey was entitled to a new bail hearing.

What brought Humphrey, 66 years old, to this point was his arrest on May 23, 2017, for first degree residential robbery and burglary against an elderly victim, inflicting injury on an elder adult, and misdemeanor theft from an elder adult. The criminal complaint also charged that Humphrey had suffered four prior strike convictions and four prior serious felony convictions, all for robbery or attempted robbery.

. . .

At arraignment on May 31, 2017, Humphrey sought release on his own recognizance (OR) without any condition of money bail. He cited his advanced age, his community ties as a lifelong resident of San Francisco, and his unemployment and financial condition. He also noted the minimal value of the property he was alleged to have stolen, the remoteness of his prior strike convictions (the most recent of which was in 1992), the lack of any arrests over the preceding 14 years, and his history of complying with court-ordered appearances. Humphrey invited the court to impose an appropriate stay-away order regarding the victim, who lived on a different floor of the senior home in which they both resided. The prosecutor requested bail in the amount of $600,000, as recommended by the bail schedule, as well as a criminal protective order directing Humphrey to stay away from the victim.

The trial court denied Humphrey's request for OR release and, acceding to the People's request, set bail at $600,000. After acknowledging Humphrey's ties to San Francisco and the age of his prior convictions, the court buttressed its decision by citing "the seriousness of the crime, the vulnerability of the victim, as well as the recommendation from pretrial services." The court also ordered Humphrey to stay away from the alleged victim, including the victim's floor in the senior home.

Humphrey challenged this ruling. He did so by filing a motion for a formal bail hearing and an accompanying request for OR release. . . .

At the hearing, the prosecutor pointed out the trial court would need to find unusual circumstances to justify a deviation from the bail schedule because Humphrey was charged with robbery, a serious and violent felony, and asserted there were no such circumstances here. He also argued that Humphrey's substance abuse and inability to address it constituted "a great public safety risk" and that Humphrey was a flight risk because he faced a lengthy prison sentence based on his prior strike convictions.

The trial court once again denied OR and supervised release, but did find unusual circumstances warranting a reduction of bail to $350,000. The court characterized the current charges as "serious" and similar to those Humphrey had committed in the past, "so that continuity is troubling to the court." Although "little was taken," "that's because the person whose home was invaded was poor [and] I'm not [going to] provide less protection to the poor than to the rich." The court elected to deviate from the bail schedule because of Humphrey's "willingness to participate in treatment, and I do commend that"—but only to a limited extent, citing "public safety and flight risk concerns." The court included an additional condition of bail: that Humphrey participate in the residential treatment program he had identified.

The public defender cautioned that Humphrey was too poor "to make even $350,000 bail" and would therefore be unable to participate in the required residential treatment program. The court did not comment on Humphrey's inability to afford bail. Nor did the court consider whether nonfinancial conditions of release could meaningfully address public safety concerns or flight risk.

Humphrey filed a petition for writ of habeas corpus in the Court of Appeal. . . .

The Court of Appeal granted habeas corpus relief, reversed the bail determination, and directed the trial court to conduct a new bail hearing. . . .

No party petitioned for review. On remand, the superior court conducted a new bail hearing and ordered Humphrey released on various nonfinancial conditions, including electronic monitoring, an order to stay away from the victim and his residence, and participation in a residential substance abuse treatment program for seniors. A few weeks later, upon request by several entities (including the District Attorney of the City and County of San Francisco, which had not been designated a party in the Court of Appeal), we granted review on our own motion to address the constitutionality of money bail as currently used in California as well as the proper role of public and victim safety in making bail determinations.

. . .

Twice, the superior court granted Humphrey bail—and on both occasions, the trial court set bail at sums Humphrey couldn't afford. Initially set at $600,000, bail was then reduced, after a formal bail hearing, to the still substantial sum of $350,000. At no point did the court inquire into Humphrey's ability to pay such an amount. As it turned out, Humphrey could not post bail so he remained in custody, even though a person facing similar charges, but with greater means, would've been able to post bail and be released.

The United States Supreme Court "has long been sensitive to the treatment of indigents in our criminal justice system." So have we. Humphrey asks whether it is constitutional to incarcerate a defendant solely because he lacks financial resources. We conclude it is not.

Neither this court nor the United States Supreme Court has yet held that a judge must consider what an arrestee can pay when fixing the amount of money bail. But from cases resolving analogous questions, we can perceive a theme. Consider *Georgia v. Bearden* (1983), 461 U.S. 660, which examined the permissibility of imprisoning a probationer for failing to satisfy the balance due on a court-ordered fine and restitution. Bearden argued that it violated the federal Constitution to imprison him "solely because" he lacked the ability to make these payments—a proposition that garnered agreement from the Supreme Court. *Bearden*'s analysis proves illuminating in our assessment of whether it likewise violates the state and federal Constitutions to hold an arrestee in custody solely because the arrestee cannot afford bail.

. . .

Principles of equal protection and substantive due process likewise converge in the money bail context. The accused retains a fundamental constitutional right to liberty. Further, the state's interest in the bail context is not to punish—it is to ensure the defendant appears at court proceedings and to protect the victim, as well as the public, from further harm.

Yet if a court does not consider an arrestee's ability to pay, it cannot know whether requiring money bail in a particular amount is likely to operate as the functional equivalent of a pretrial detention order. Detaining an arrestee in such circumstances accords insufficient respect to the arrestee's crucial state and federal equal protection rights against wealth-based detention as well as the arrestee's state and federal substantive due process rights to pretrial liberty.

. . .

What we must therefore conclude is that pretrial detention is subject to state and federal constitutional constraints. Consistent with the aforementioned principles, we hold that such detention is impermissible unless no less restrictive conditions of release can adequately vindicate the state's compelling interests.

. . .

We therefore affirm the judgment of the Court of Appeal.

Case Discussion Questions

1. At what amount did the trial court originally set Humphrey's bail?
2. What two constitutional principles form the bases of the California Supreme Court's decision?
3. Under what circumstances is a California trial court justified in placing an arrestee into pre-trial detention?
4. What factors did Humphrey present to argue for release on his own recognizance?
5. What factors did the trial court cite in denying Humphrey's request for release on his own recognizance?

Factors that are considered in setting the amount of bail include the seriousness of the crime charged, the strength of the prosecution's evidence, the defendant's prior criminal record, the likelihood the defendant will appear in court, their ties to the community, their employment, and their financial circumstances.

Paralegals working for the prosecutor's office and for defense attorneys are often asked to research the defendant's prior record and organize key police reports in anticipation of the hearing. Paralegals employed by defense attorneys often gather information from the accused and family members regarding their family situation and financial resources.

If the defendant has a steady job and "ties to the community," the judge may agree to release the person on their own recognizance. In these situations, the defendants are released based on their promise to appear. In recent years, it has become more common to require defendants released on their own recognizance to wear ankle bracelets with electronic transmitters in them so that they can be monitored. A defendant released on bail or on recognizance may be subject to certain conditions, such as non-contact with the alleged victim and witnesses, denial of the right to possess a firearm, and prohibition from violating the law.

The federal Bail Reform Act of 1984[29] creates the procedure that the federal courts follow to determine whether the defendant should be released or detained prior to trial. The federal government may keep an accused in custody for three days by seeking detention and a continuance of the detention hearing.[30]

Under the Act, the court initially determines the propriety of pretrial release on the defendant's own recognizance or on an unsecured bond. If these options are inappropriate, then the court decides whether it should release the defendant under restrictions or with conditions. Only if the court concludes after a hearing that no condition or combination of conditions of release will reasonably ensure the defendant's appearance in court or protect the safety of others can the court hold the defendant in pretrial detention. In essence, there is a presumption in favor of pretrial release of federal defendants. There also is authority to release a defendant temporarily to the custody of a third person when the court finds that release is necessary for preparation of the defense.[31]

After a defendant is arrested and before the initial court appearance, a pretrial services officer interviews the defendant and attempts to verify the information provided. The Pretrial Services Agency works for the court.[32] Usually the pretrial services officer contacts persons familiar with the defendant for verification. The officer prepares a report for the court and makes a recommendation as to pretrial release.

In most states, when a defendant cannot afford bail, a bail bond agent may post the bond. Generally, a bail agent will charge the defendant 10 percent of the bail amount and require them to post collateral. However, if the defendant fails to appear in court, the bail bond agent is responsible for the full amount of the bail. A copy of a commercial bail bond is displayed in Exhibit 5.2.

---

[29] 18 U.S.C. §§3141 *et seq.*

[30] 18 U.S.C. §3142(f).

[31] 18 U.S.C. §3142(i).

[32] 18 U.S.C. §3152.

Exhibit 5.2: Commercial Bail Bond

Brooklyn Park police officer, Kimberly Potter, was charged with first- and second-degree manslaughter for killing a Black man. After she was arrested, she posted a $100,000 commercial bail bond while awaiting trial. A copy of the bond appears below.

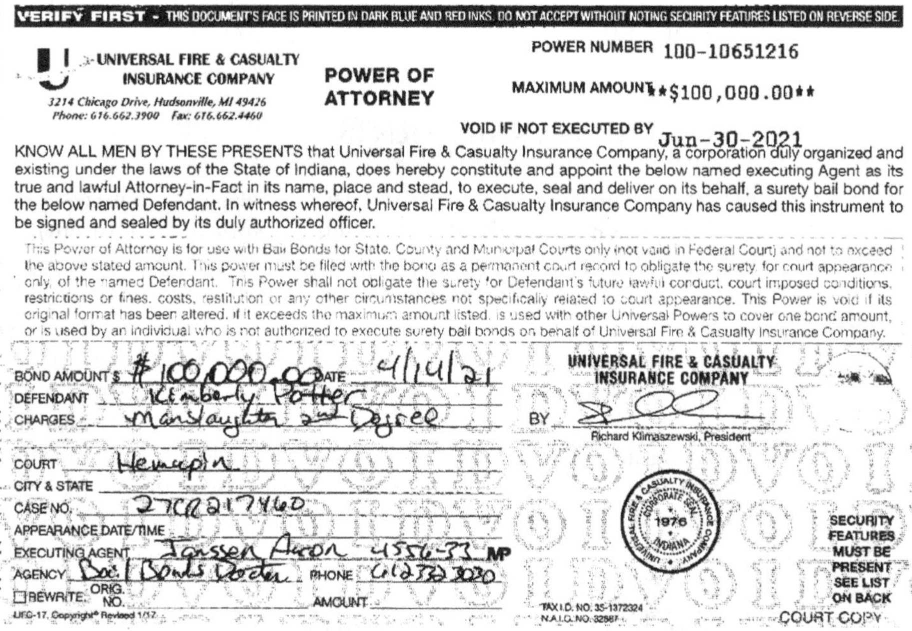

VERIFY FIRST - THIS DOCUMENT'S FACE IS PRINTED IN DARK BLUE AND RED INKS. DO NOT ACCEPT WITHOUT NOTING SECURITY FEATURES LISTED ON REVERSE SIDE.

UNIVERSAL FIRE & CASUALTY INSURANCE COMPANY
3214 Chicago Drive, Hudsonville, MI 49426
Phone: 616.662.3900 Fax: 616.662.4460

POWER OF ATTORNEY

POWER NUMBER 100-10651216

MAXIMUM AMOUNT **$100,000.00**

VOID IF NOT EXECUTED BY Jun-30-2021

KNOW ALL MEN BY THESE PRESENTS that Universal Fire & Casualty Insurance Company, a corporation duly organized and existing under the laws of the State of Indiana, does hereby constitute and appoint the below named executing Agent as its true and lawful Attorney-in-Fact in its name, place and stead, to execute, seal and deliver on its behalf, a surety bail bond for the below named Defendant. In witness whereof, Universal Fire & Casualty Insurance Company has caused this instrument to be signed and sealed by its duly authorized officer.

This Power of Attorney is for use with Bail Bonds for State, County and Municipal Courts only (not valid in Federal Court) and not to exceed the above stated amount. This power must be filed with the bond as a permanent court record to obligate the surety, for court appearance only, of the named Defendant. This Power shall not obligate the surety for Defendant's future lawful conduct, court imposed conditions, restrictions or fines, costs, restitution or any other circumstances not specifically related to court appearance. This Power is void if its original format has been altered, if it exceeds the maximum amount listed, is used with other Universal Powers to cover one bond amount, or is used by an individual who is not authorized to execute surety bail bonds on behalf of Universal Fire & Casualty Insurance Company.

BOND AMOUNT $ #100,000.00 DATE 4/14/21
DEFENDANT Kimberly Potter
CHARGES Manslaughter 2nd Degree
COURT Hennepin
CITY & STATE
CASE NO. 27CR217460
APPEARANCE DATE/TIME
EXECUTING AGENT Janssen Aaron 4556-33 MP
AGENCY Bail Bonds Doctor PHONE 6123323030
☐ REWRITE ORIG. NO. AMOUNT
UFC-17, Copyright® Revised 1/17

UNIVERSAL FIRE & CASUALTY INSURANCE COMPANY
BY
Richard Klimaszewski, President

UNIVERSAL FIRE & CASUALTY INSURANCE COMPANY CORPORATE SEAL 1976 INDIANA

TAX I.D. NO. 35-1372324
N.A.I.C. NO. 32867

SECURITY FEATURES MUST BE PRESENT SEE LIST ON BACK

COURT COPY

There is a growing trend of bail reform across the country. Since 2017, several prosecutors have announced that their offices will no longer seek cash bail for certain crimes.[33] Some state legislatures have enacted legislation creating a presumption of release and/or non-monetary bond.[34] A number of states adopted risk assessments as part of bail reform.[35]

Some jurisdictions have adopted their own risk assessment tools.[36] Others use established tools, such as the Public Safety Assessment (PSA), which has been implemented in 4 states and is being used in communities in at least 15 other states.[37]

---

[33]Examples include Los Angeles County, CA, Cook County, IL, Hennepin County, MN, Prince George's County, MD, Brooklyn, NY, Manhattan, NY, and Chittenden County, VT. Isabella Jorgensen and Sandra Susan Smith, *The Current State of Bail Reform in the United States* (2021), https://research.hks.harvard.edu/publications/getFile.aspx?Id=5111 p.2.

[34]E.g., Illinois, Kentucky, Nebraska, New Hampshire, New Jersey, and West Virginia. *Id.* at 5.

[35]E.g., Delaware, Hawaii, Illinois, Kentucky, Maryland, Montana, and New Jersey. *Id.* at 6.

[36]E.g., Colorado, Virginia, and Washington, D.C. *Id.* at 23.

[37]*Id.*

Discussion Questions

2. In 2008, when a nationally prominent financier named Bernard Madoff was arrested for directing a Ponzi scheme that allegedly defrauded investors of something between $13 billion and $65 billion, his bail was set at $10 million. Do you think the amount set for bail was excessive? Why or why not?

3. In addition to posting the $10 million bail, Madoff was placed under house arrest and required to wear an electronic monitoring device. Does this additional information affect your view about the appropriateness of the amount of bail?

3. GRAND JURY INDICTMENTS

Bill of indictment
The formal written document returned by a grand jury finding that the evidence presented to it constituted probable cause that an individual committed a crime. It is also referred to as **a true bill** or **indictment.**

No bill
The grand jury's determination finds that there is no probable cause that an individual committed a crime.

After having heard testimony from witnesses, grand juries may issue a **true bill** (also known as a **bill of indictment** or simply **indictment**), which signifies that the evidence presented to it constituted probable cause that an individual committed a crime. Alternatively, it may vote a **no bill,** which means that it finds that there is no probable cause to conclude that the person committed a crime. Although grand juries have the inherent power to indict (or refuse to indict) anyone they wish, the reality is that grand jurors typically have no legal background and are very likely to follow the directions they get from the prosecuting attorney. When a grand jury decides to return a true bill, the prosecutor's office drafts the document that lists the crimes involved and the facts supporting the charges.

4. INDICTMENT AND INFORMATION JURISDICTIONS

Indictment jurisdictions
Jurisdictions in which defendants accused of committing felonies have the right to be indicted by a grand jury.

Information jurisdictions
Jurisdictions in which prosecutors are authorized to initiate felony charges by either indictment or information.

In federal court, the general rule is that the government must obtain and file an indictment from a grand jury within 30 days of the defendant's arrest unless the court extends the time.[38] Although the Fifth Amendment requires a grand jury indictment for all felonies prosecuted by the federal government, U.S. Attorneys are not required to prosecute misdemeanors by indictment.

Most states, on the other hand, do not require indictment by a grand jury for persons accused of committing felonies.[39] **Indictment jurisdictions** follow the approach taken in the federal system of justice and require indictments for all felony charges. Five states require indictments only for serious felonies ("limited indictment jurisdictions").[40] The majority of states are categorized as **information jurisdictions.** In these states, prosecutors are authorized to initiate felony charges by either indictment or information.

---

[38] 18 U.S.C. §3161(b).

[39] The U.S. Supreme Court has ruled that the grand jury clause of the Fifth Amendment does not apply to the states. *Hurtado v. California*, 110 U.S. 516 (1884).

[40] National Center for State Courts, *Reforming the Grand Jury Indictment Process: Recent Efforts to Improve Public Confidence in Cases Involving Police Use of Lethal Force* (2021), p. 2 (https://www.ncsc-jurystudies.org/__data/assets/pdf_file/0019/5851/grand-jury-report_rev-2021.pdf).

Discussion Questions

4. Do you think the grand jury is an effective check on prosecutorial discretion?

5. What are the pros and cons of continuing to use grand juries at either the federal or state levels?

5. ARRAIGNMENTS AND PRELIMINARY HEARINGS

Whereas the initial appearance focuses on the conditions under which someone charged with a crime can be released pending trial, arraignments focus on the crimes for which the person is charged with having committed. At an **arraignment,** the judge informs the accused of the specific charges brought by the prosecution and elicits the defendant's plea (response) to those charges (e.g., guilty, not guilty, or *nolo contendere*[41]). With a ***nolo contendere*** plea, the defendant neither admits nor denies the charges but concedes that if the case went to trial, the prosecution would have sufficient evidence to prove its case beyond a reasonable doubt. Because it is not considered an admission of guilt, this plea cannot be used later against the defendant at a civil trial. However, for the purposes of the arraignment, the case proceeds as though the defendant had pleaded guilty.

Arraignment
A court proceeding at which the judge informs the defendant of the charges filed by the government.

Nolo contendere
A "no contest" plea in which the defendant neither admits nor denies the charges but concedes that if the case went to trial, the prosecution would have sufficient evidence to prove its case beyond a reasonable doubt.

If the accused is unable to afford an attorney and the prosecutor is seeking incarceration, the court will appoint a defense lawyer. We will discuss the role of public defenders and other types of appointed counsel in Chapter 6.

In many courts, the judge also enters a scheduling order at this time. The schedule for upcoming steps in the trial process often includes a date for a **preliminary hearing** at which the judge determines whether there is sufficient evidence to show probable cause that the defendant committed the offense charged.[42] If the court concludes that the evidence presented at the preliminary hearing does not establish probable cause, the case is dismissed, and the defendant is discharged.

Preliminary hearing
The initial hearing by a judge to determine whether there is probable cause for the charge against the defendant.

The U.S. Constitution does not guarantee the right to a preliminary hearing, but a federal felony defendant who has not yet been indicted has a statutory right, under FRCrP 5.1(a), to a preliminary hearing. Likewise, states that are classified as indictment jurisdictions have statutes that require preliminary hearings for unindicted defendants who are charged with felonies.[43] Almost all of the information jurisdictions provide for preliminary hearings. In most of these states, the prosecutor can bypass the preliminary examination by indicting the defendant.[44] In many jurisdictions, the defendant's right is premised upon a timely demand for the hearing.[45] Defendants can waive their right to a

---

[41]This is a Latin phrase meaning "no contest."

[42]Probable cause is evidence sufficient to cause a person of ordinary prudence and caution to conscientiously entertain a reasonable belief of the defendant's guilt. *Beck v. Ohio*, 379 U.S. 89 (1964).

[43]W. LaFave, et al., *Criminal Procedure,* at 721.

[44]*Id.* at 722.

[45]*Id.* at 723.

preliminary hearing, but in many jurisdictions, the prosecutor can insist upon a preliminary hearing even if the defendant waives it.[46]

U.S. Magistrate Judge
A federal trial judge appointed by the life-tenured federal judges of a district court. Magistrates often try misdemeanor and petty offense cases and handle felony preliminary proceedings.

Under Rule 5.1(a) of the Federal Rules of Criminal Procedure, if the defendant is charged with a crime other than a petty offense, the **U.S. Magistrate Judge** must conduct a preliminary hearing unless the defendant waives the hearing, the defendant is indicted, the defendant waives prosecution by indictment, the government charges the defendant with a misdemeanor, or the defendant is charged with a misdemeanor and consents to a trial by the magistrate. If the magistrate finds that probable cause was not shown and dismisses the case, the U.S. Attorney can file a complaint or present the case to a grand jury for indictment. This procedure is the same in state court.

Unlike a grand jury proceeding, the accused is afforded significant rights at the preliminary hearing. Procedural protections include the right to an attorney and to challenge the rulings of the magistrate at the time of the hearing. Defendants are also afforded limited rights to cross-examine witnesses and to present defense witnesses.

These differences create opportunities for discovering information that will help the attorneys develop their cases and provide both sides an opportunity to assess the credibility of the witnesses. Additionally, both sides can use the statements made by witnesses at this stage for impeachment at trial. From the perspective of the defendant, the preliminary hearing also offers an opportunity to gain insight into the government's theory of the case and its evidence. Moreover, the hearing may permit the perpetuation of testimony of a witness who later becomes unavailable.

At preliminary hearings, paralegals can serve the same functions they do during formal trials. We will discuss these duties in greater detail in Chapter 12. As part of the trial preparation process, paralegals are often called upon to summarize or prepare abstracts of the testimony that was given at the preliminary hearing. These abstracts are helpful in preparing cross-examination questions and impeaching witnesses. Furthermore, it can be used to prepare opening statements.

6. PREPARATION OF CHARGING DOCUMENTS

Paralegals are often involved in drafting and filing the charging documents. Depending upon the types of charges and the jurisdiction, these charging documents can be criminal complaints, indictments, or informations. Following attorney review in the office, the original is filed with the clerk of the court, and copies are provided to the defendants and their attorneys.

a. *Format*

Like most other documents filed in court, these charging documents typically include the following components:

- Caption
- Introductory paragraph

[46]*Id.* at 724.

- Body
- Signature section
- Address block/preparer's data

The **caption** of a case includes the name of the court,[47] the party names, the file number, and the name of the document. Because there are variations from court to court, you should look at other filed documents in your jurisdiction as a guide to local custom and practice.

Caption
The heading of a court document containing the name of the court, the names of the parties, a case number, and the name of the document.

The title of the case consists of the names of the prosecuting authority versus the defendant. The document name identifies the purpose of the document (e.g., criminal complaint, indictment, information). There are different styles of captions based on the custom of the local court in question. You should find out the appropriate style in your legal community before you draft court documents. An example of a caption is depicted in Exhibit 5.3.

The name of the court is placed at the line at the top of the page. In federal court, the name of the court includes the district and division. For instance, Chicago is in the Northern District of Illinois, Eastern Division. In state court, the court name includes the name of the state and may include the district or circuit, as well as the county or parish. For example, a Chicago suburban court caption may reference the State of Illinois, the Nineteenth Judicial Circuit, and Lake County.

Exhibit 5.3: Sample Caption

THE UNITED STATES DISTRICT COURT
FOR THE NORTHERN DISTRICT OF ILLINOIS,
EASTERN DIVISION

UNITED STATES OF AMERICA	)	
	)	
vs.	)	Case No. 22 CR XXX
	)	
BRANDON TURNER,	)	
Defendant.	)	

BILL OF INDICTMENT

[47] E.g., United States District Court for the Northern District of Illinois; Circuit Court of Cook County, Illinois.

The title of the action includes the full names of all of the parties, in all capital letters. The title is presented on the left side of the caption. The party initiating the federal criminal prosecution will always be listed as "UNITED STATES OF AMERICA." In state court, the prosecuting authority is often listed as the "PEOPLE OF THE STATE [or COMMONWEALTH] OF [Name of State]." Following the designation of the prosecuting authority, a line is skipped and the word "versus" or its abbreviation is centered under the government's name. Then next line is skipped, and the name of person accused of the crime is set forth. The term "Defendant" appears on the next line. This designation is presented in lowercase type.

The case number appears on the right side of the page opposite the title of the action. This number is assigned by the court. The first document filed in a case, such as a complaint, does not have a number when it is initially presented to the clerk of the court. When the clerk accepts the document, the clerk will affix a case number in the caption. Once assigned, the case number must be included in the caption of future documents filed in the case. The case number usually includes a reference to the year in which a document is filed, the type of case, and the chronological order of filing. For instance, in a downstate Illinois county, the 150th criminal felony case filed in the year 2022 would be identified as 22 CF 150. Other jurisdictions may include a reference to the division of a court in the case number. A vertical line divides the title. Usually, the line is formed by a series of closed parentheses marks [)] placed under each other.

In most court documents, an introductory paragraph appears directly under the caption. This is ordinarily a one- or two-sentence paragraph that identifies the party who authored the document and succinctly explains the purpose of the document. For criminal charges, the introductory paragraph may simply be an attestation by the officer who is verifying the contents of the document, as follows: "I, the undersigned complainant being duly sworn, state the following is true and correct to the best of my knowledge and belief." An introductory paragraph of a bill of indictment might read: "The Grand Jurors of the State of [Name of State] and of the County of [Name of County], attending the Court aforesaid, upon their oaths present the following true bill of indictment against the Defendant [Name]."

The next component of a court document is the body, the most important part. It presents the basis for the relief sought in motions, the information requested in discovery, and the substance of an accusation in a charging document. In charging documents, this section sets out the specific actions the accused is alleged to have done, and the specific provisions of the criminal code that were violated by having taken those actions. In most jurisdictions, this information should be presented in concise numbered paragraphs. However, there are some states where the body is presented as a narrative.

Address block
The portion of a court document that identifies the attorney responsible for the preparation of the document, the party that the attorney represents, the address, and the telephone number. The address block is also known as the **preparer's data**.

After the signature section is the **address block**, also known as the **preparer's data**. The address block identifies the attorney responsible for the preparation of the document, the party that the attorney represents, the address, and the telephone number. In many jurisdictions, the attorney's signature appears on the right side of the page and the address block is on the left side. In other venues, the address block may appear immediately after the attorney's name. A sample of the signature section and address block can be seen in Exhibit 5.4. The charging documents typically close with a signature and an address block.

Exhibit 5.4: Sample Signature and Address Block

Respectfully submitted,

BRANDON TURNER,

Defendant

By ______________

CHARLES HOVEY,
his attorney

CHARLES HOVEY
Attorney for Defendant
1857 Bone Street
Normal, IL 61761
(309) 555-1857

For bills of indictment, the foreperson of the grand jury may provide the signature. In many jurisdictions, the person who signs a charging document must do so under oath or under penalties of perjury.

b. Criminal Complaints, Indictments, and Informations

The **criminal complaint** is a charge, made under oath, alleging that the defendant committed a crime. Criminal complaints are prepared by the prosecutor's office and signed under oath by the **complainant** (typically the investigating officer or the victim) but can also be signed by the prosecutor. If the complainant does not have firsthand knowledge, he or she will declare the information contained in the document is true "on information and belief." In most cases, the complaint is a brief document that simply alleges that the accused committed specific acts in violation of a particular statute at a specified time and place. Take a couple of minutes to look over examples of federal and state criminal complaints in Exhibits 5.5 and 5.6.

Criminal complaint
A charge of the commission of a crime, made under oath.

Complainant
The person who signs a criminal complaint under oath, attesting that the allegations of the complaint are true.

In some jurisdictions, a criminal complaint on felony charges must be presented to a judge or **magistrate** before an arrest warrant is issued. In most jurisdictions, a felony complaint will be replaced by an indictment or information before the case goes to trial. Misdemeanor complaints typically remain the charging instruments throughout the proceedings. An example of a misdemeanor complaint filed in federal court is depicted in Exhibit 5.7.

Magistrate
A judicial officer vested with limited authority to administer and enforce the law.

For any of the three types of charging documents, the body must set forth information specific enough to adequately apprise the defendant of the offense

Exhibit 5.5: Federal Criminal Complaint

This is a federal complaint filed in the Northern District of Illinois charging Rod Blagojevich (then governor of Illinois) with wire fraud and solicitation arising out of an alleged "pay to play" scheme. Even though Blagojevich was the target of a grand jury probe for many months, the United States Attorney cited the importance of expeditiously charging the defendant even though an investigation continued. The filing of this complaint was accompanied by an affidavit of over 70 pages.

UNITED STATES DISTRICT COURT

NORTHERN DISTRICT OF ILLINOIS, EASTERN DIVISION

UNITED STATES OF AMERICA

V.

ROD R. BLAGOJEVICH, and

JOHN HARRIS

UNDER SEAL

CRIMINAL COMPLAINT

I, the undersigned complainant being duly sworn state the following is true and correct to the best of my knowledge and belief.

Count One

From in or about 2002 to the present, in Cook County, in the Northern District of Illinois, defendants did conspire with each other and with others to devise and participate in a scheme to defraud the State of Illinois and the people of the State of Illinois of the honest services of ROD R. BLAGOJEVICH and JOHN HARRIS, in furtherance of which the mails and interstate wire communications would be used, in violation of Title 18, United States Code, Sections 1341,1343, and 1346; all in violation of Title 18 United States Code, Section 1349.

Count Two

Beginning no later than November 2008 to the present, in Cook County, in the Northern District of Illinois, defendants ROD R. BLAGOJEVICH and JOHN HARRIS, being agents of the State of Illinois, a State government which during a one-year period, beginning January 1, 2008, and continuing to the present, received federal benefits in excess of $10,000, corruptly solicited and demanded a thing of value, namely, the firing of certain Chicago Tribune editorial members responsible for widely-circulated editorials critical of ROD R. BLAGOJEVICH, intending to be influenced and rewarded in connection with business and transactions of the State of Illinois involving a thing of value of $5,000 or more, namely, the provision of millions of dollars in financial assistance by the State of Illinois, including through the Illinois Finance Authority, an agency of the State of Illinois, to the Tribune Company involving the Wrigley Field baseball stadium; in violation of Title 18, United States Code, Sections 666(a)(1)(B) and 2.

I further state that I am a Special Agent of the Federal Bureau of Investigation and that this complaint is based on the following facts:

SEE ATTACHED AFFIDAVIT

Continued on the attached sheet and made a part hereof: __X__ Yes ____ No

____

Daniel W. Cain, Special Agent
Federal Bureau of Investigation

Sworn to before me and subscribed in my presence,

December 7, 2008 at Chicago, Illinois
Date City and State

MICHAEL T. MASON, United States Magistrate Judge
Name & Title of Judicial Officer Signature of Judicial Officer

being charged against him or her. For example, in Illinois, a criminal charge must include the following information:

- Name of the offense
- Statute alleged to have been violated
- Nature and elements of the charged offense
- Date and county of the offense
- Name or a detailed description of the accused[48]

You should refer to your jurisdiction's statutes to find the requirements for your state.

If the government claims that the defendant committed more than one offense, the body of the charging document should include a separate **count** for each alleged offense. Each count is designated with subtitles such as "Count I," "Count Two," or "Third Count." If only one charge is alleged, do not use a count subtitle. Consult your supervisor to learn the appropriate style for your office. Exhibits 5.8 and 5.9 depict state court misdemeanor and felony indictments. Exhibit 5.10 displays the first page of a federal felony indictment.

Count
A subsection of the body of a charging document that alleges the defendant's commission of a crime, which sets out all of the required elements of an offense.

c. *Document Drafting Considerations*

Most prosecuting attorneys' offices rely on law enforcement agencies to conduct the initial investigation before opening a case file. Accordingly, the prosecutor

[48] 725 ILCS 5/111-3.

Exhibit 5.6: State Criminal Complaint

This is the first page of a criminal complaint charging a 17-year-old, Kyle Rittenhouse, with two counts of homicide and five other counts. Rittenhouse fatally shot two men and wounded a third in Kenosha, Wisconsin, during the protest and riots that followed a white police officer shooting of a Black man. A jury acquitted the defendant.[49]

Case 2020CF000983 Document 2 Filed 08-27-2020 Page 1 of 5

FILED
08-27-2020
Clerk of Circuit Court
Kenosha County
2020CF000983
Honorable Bruce E. Schroeder
Branch 3

STATE OF WISCONSIN CIRCUIT COURT KENOSHA COUNTY

STATE OF Wisconsin
Plaintiff,

vs.

KYLE H. RITTENHOUSE
286 Anita Terrace, #10
Antioch, IL 60000-2
DOB: 01/03/2003
Sex/Race: M/W
Eye Color: Green
Hair Color: Brown
Height: 5 ft 8 in
Weight: 150 lbs
Alias:
Defendant.

CRIMINAL COMPLAINT

DA Case #: 2020KN003907

Agency Case #: KPD 2020-00047360

For Official Use

The undersigned, being first duly sworn, states that:

Count 1: FIRST DEGREE RECKLESS HOMICIDE, USE OF A DANGEROUS WEAPON

The above-named defendant on or about Tuesday, August 25, 2020, in the City of Kenosha, Kenosha County, Wisconsin, did recklessly cause the death of Joseph D. Rosenbaum, under circumstances which show utter disregard for human life, contrary to sec. 940.02(1), 939.50(3)(b), 939.63(1)(b) Wis. Stats., a Class B Felony, and upon conviction may be sentenced to a term of imprisonment not to exceed sixty (60) years.

And further, invoking the provisions of sec. 939.63(1)(b) Wis. Stats., because the defendant committed this offense while using a dangerous weapon, the maximum term of imprisonment for the felony may be increased by not more than 5 years.

Count 2: FIRST DEGREE RECKLESSLY ENDANGERING SAFETY, USE OF A DANGEROUS WEAPON

The above-named defendant on or about Tuesday, August 25, 2020, in the City of Kenosha, Kenosha County, Wisconsin, did recklessly endanger the safety of Richard McGinnis, under circumstances which show utter disregard for human life, contrary to sec. 941.30(1), 939.50(3)(f), 939.63(1)(b) Wis. Stats., a Class F Felony, and upon conviction may be fined not more than Twenty Five Thousand Dollars ($25,000), or imprisoned not more than twelve (12) years and six (6) months, or both.

And further, invoking the provisions of sec. 939.63(1)(b) Wis. Stats., because the defendant committed this offense while using a dangerous weapon, the maximum term of imprisonment for the felony may be increased by not more than 5 years.

[49] See the discussion of self-defense in Chapter 7.

Exhibit 5.7: Federal Misdemeanor Information

The U.S. Attorney for the Eastern District of New York charged a man with the theft of Theodore Roosevelt's Colt revolver that was on display at a federal historical museum. The defendant pleaded guilty. He was fined and sentenced to probation.

CR 06 746

MJL:LTG
F.#2006R01134

FILED
IN CLERK'S OFFICE
U.S. DISTRICT COURT E.D.N.Y.
★ NOV 13 2006 ★
LONG ISLAND OFFICE

UNITED STATES DISTRICT COURT
EASTERN DISTRICT OF NEW YORK

- - - - - - - - - - - - - - - - - - X

UNITED STATES OF AMERICA

- against -

ANTHONY TULINO,

Defendant.

- - - - - - - - - - - - - - - - - - X

M I S D E M E A N O R
I N F O R M A T I O N

Cr. No. ________
(T. 16, U.S.C., § 433;
T. 18, U.S.C., §§ 3551 et seq.)

TOMLINSON, M

THE UNITED STATES ATTORNEY CHARGES:

In and about April 1990, within the Eastern District of New York, the defendant ANTHONY TULINO knowingly and intentionally, without the permission of the Secretary of the United States Department of the Interior, appropriated an object of antiquity, to wit: an 1895 Colt revolver (the "revolver") bearing serial number 334 and inscriptions stating that the revolver was recovered "from the sunken Battleship Maine," and that on "July 1, 1898, San Juan, [the revolver was] carried and used by Colonel Theodore Roosevelt," which revolver had been situated on lands owned and controlled by the Government of the United States, to wit: Sagamore Hill National Historical Site, Oyster Bay, New York.

(Title 16, United States Code, Section 433; Title 18, United States Code, Sections 3551 et seq.)

ROSLYNN R. MAUSKOPF
UNITED STATES ATTORNEY
EASTERN DISTRICT OF NEW YORK

Exhibit 5.8: State Court Indictment for Animal Cruelty

The Virginia attorney general secured indictments against Bhagavan "Doc" Antle, the owner of a roadside zoo in South Carolina who was featured in the Netflix docuseries *Tiger King* on one felony count of wildlife trafficking, one felony count of conspiracy to wildlife traffic, four misdemeanor counts of conspiracy to violate the Endangered Species Act, and nine misdemeanor counts of animal cruelty.

VIRGINIA: IN THE CIRCUIT COURT OF FREDERICK COUNTY

COMMONWEALTH OF VIRGINIA **Case No.** CR20-827

COUNTY OF FREDERICK, to-wit

INDICTMENT

The Grand Jury of Frederick County, Virginia, attending the Circuit Court of said County at its October Term, 2020, charges that:

On or about July 27, 2017, BHAGAVAN ANTLE did unlawfully: willfully set on foot, instigate, engage in, or in any way furthered any act of cruelty to any animal (to wit: one lion cub); or carried or caused to be carried by any vehicle, vessel or otherwise any animal (to wit: one lion cub) in a cruel, brutal, or inhumane manner, so as to produce torture or unnecessary suffering in violation of Sections 3.2-6570(A)(vi) and (vii) of the Code of Virginia (1950) as amended.

VCC: ANM-3302-M1 (VCC CODE)

A TRUE BILL

[signature]
Foreman

10-8-2020
Date

The following witnesses were sworn in open Court and sent before the Grand Jury to testify:

[signature]
Amy K. Taylor 10/8/20

[signature]
Richard Samuels

Exhibit 5.9: State Court Indictment for Rape

In 2017, over 80 women accused Academy Award–winning film producer Harvey Weinstein of sexual assault. This led to the #MeToo social media campaign that fostered similar accusations of sexual abuse against other powerful men, phenomena which came to be known as the "Weinstein effect." In 2018, a New York grand jury indicted him on accusations concerning two different women.

SUPREME COURT OF THE STATE OF NEW YORK
COUNTY OF NEW YORK

THE PEOPLE OF THE STATE OF NEW YORK

-against-

HARVEY WEINSTEIN ,

Defendant.

THE GRAND JURY OF THE COUNTY OF NEW YORK, by this indictment, accuses the defendant of the crime of **CRIMINAL SEXUAL ACT IN THE FIRST DEGREE**, in violation of Penal Law §130.50(1), committed as follows:

The defendant, in the County of New York, during the period from on or about June 1, 2004 to on or about September 1, 2004, engaged in oral sexual conduct by forcible compulsion with a person known to the Grand Jury, to wit, contact between defendant's penis and the mouth of a person known to the Grand Jury.

SECOND COUNT:

AND THE GRAND JURY AFORESAID, by this indictment, further accuses the defendant of the crime of **RAPE IN THE FIRST DEGREE**, in violation of Penal Law §130.35(1), committed as follows:

The defendant, in the County of New York, on or about March 18, 2013, engaged in sexual intercourse by forcible compulsion with a second person known to the Grand Jury.

THIRD COUNT:

AND THE GRAND JURY AFORESAID, by this indictment, further accuses the defendant of the crime of **RAPE IN THE THIRD DEGREE**, in violation of Penal Law §130.25(1), committed as follows:

The defendant, in the County of New York, on or about March 18, 2013, engaged in sexual intercourse with a second person known to the Grand Jury without said person's consent, where such lack of consent was by reason of some factor other than incapacity to consent.

CYRUS R. VANCE, JR.
District Attorney

has the benefit of the investigating officer's reports plus witness statements and summaries when a case is presented. The information contained in these documents is usually sufficient to prepare a charging document.

If you are requested to prepare the charge, you should carefully read the officer's report and materials and make note of the charge that the officer thought was appropriate. Before drafting the charge, you should refer to the criminal code of your jurisdiction to determine whether the conduct reported satisfies all of the elements of the offense suggested by the officer or any other offense. You also should consult charges filed in other cases to familiarize you with the customary drafting style used in your office. Most prosecutors' offices have form books that contain examples of complaints, informations, and indictments for most offenses in their jurisdiction. In addition, most offices keep examples of charging documents they have filed. Use these examples wisely to prepare your assignment. After you have prepared your draft, carefully proofread it for accuracy. Be especially mindful of dates and the spelling of proper names. Careless draftsmanship may result in dismissal of the charge.

Once the court document is in final form, it is filed with the clerk of the court. Traditionally, this has meant that the original of the document was accepted by the clerk and placed in the individual file of the case. At the time of acceptance, the clerk's office would have stamp-filed the document to show the date and time of receipt. The filer would also have presented one or more copies of the document to the clerk so that that they could also be date- and time-stamped. The filer would retain the copy to document the filing.

The federal courts and many state courts now require that documents be e-filed. In the federal system, the U.S. District Clerk accepts PDF documents

Exhibit 5.10: Federal Felony Indictment for Child Pornography Production

In mid-2019, while Illinois statutory rape charges were pending against him, R. Kelly was indicted by federal grand juries in the Eastern District of New York and Northern District of Illinois on charges including producing child pornography, sex-trafficking, racketeering, crossing state lines for sex with underage girls, and obstruction of justice. Count one of the Illinois indictment appears below.

Case: 1:19-cr-00567 Document #: 1 Filed: 07/11/19 Page 1 of 25 PageID #:1

FILED

JUL 11 2019

THOMAS G. BRUTON
CLERK, U.S. DISTRICT COURT

UNITED STATES DISTRICT COURT
NORTHERN DISTRICT OF ILLINOIS
EASTERN DIVISION

UNITED STATES OF AMERICA	UNDER SEAL
v.	No. 19CR 567
ROBERT SYLVESTER KELLY, also known as "R. Kelly," DERREL MCDAVID, and MILTON BROWN, also known as "June Brown"	Violations: Title 18, United States Code, Sections 371, 2251(a), 2252A(a)(2), 2252A(b)(1), and 2422(b)

JUDGE LEINENWEBER

MAGISTRATE JUDGE KIM

COUNT ONE

The SPECIAL MAY 2019 GRAND JURY charges:

In or around 1998 or 1999, at Chicago, in the Northern District of Illinois, Eastern Division,

ROBERT SYLVESTER KELLY, also known as "R. Kelly,"

defendant herein, did knowingly employ, use, persuade, induce, entice, and coerce a minor, namely Minor 1, to engage in sexually explicit conduct for the purpose of producing a visual depiction of such conduct, namely, Video 1, and defendant knew or had reason to know that such visual depiction would be transported in interstate or foreign commerce or mailed, or such visual depiction was actually transported in interstate or foreign commerce or mailed.

PACER
The acronym for Public Access to Court Electronic Records, an online public-access service that permits users to retrieve case and docket information from the federal courts and the U.S. Party/Case Index.

Return of service
The written verification establishing that a document has been served.

Proof of service
A sworn statement by a member of the attorney's office attesting to the service of the document on the opposing side by mail, personal delivery, or other means.

for online filing. Filed documents are available to the public through a service known as Public Access to Court Electronic Records (**PACER**) offered by the Administrative Office of the U.S. Courts. This is an online public-access service that permits users to retrieve case and docket information from the federal courts and the U.S. Party/Case Index.[50]

For both traditional and e-filing jurisdictions, the filer must also present to the court proof of service of a copy of the document to the opposing party. If the document is the first paper filed in the case, the prosecutor typically files a **return of service**. This is a sworn statement from the person who personally served the document on the defendant. For all other documents, the parties file a **proof of service**, sometimes referred to as a "certificate of service." This is a sworn statement by a member of the attorney's office attesting to the service of the document on the opposing side by mail, personal delivery, or other means.[51] You can use the language of proofs of service filed in prior cases as a guide for the format used in your jurisdiction. A sample proof of service is displayed in Exhibit 5.11.

Like the criminal complaint, an indictment alleges that the accused committed specific acts in violation of a particular statute at a specified time and place. Exhibits 5.8 and 5.9, earlier in this chapter, depict examples of indictments. Although an indictment officially comes from the members of the grand jury, the content of the document is prepared by a representative of the prosecutor's office and then presented to the grand jury for its approval.

Exhibit 5.11: Sample Proof of Service

PROOF OF SERVICE

UNDER PENALTIES OF PERJURY and pursuant to the provisions of [citation], the undersigned hereby certifies that he/she served the [name of document] by depositing a copy thereof into a U.S. Post Office mailbox in [city and state] in an envelope, postage fully prepaid, addressed to:

[Name of Opposing Counsel]

[Address of Opposing Counsel]

on the ______ day of ______, 20 ______ at or about the hour of ______ p.m.

[S] ________________

[50]An overview of PACER and information as to registration for this service is available at https://pacer.uscourts.gov/.

[51]Although service by facsimile is allowed in some circumstances, not all jurisdictions permit it, and those that permit it may limit its use.

It is not unusual for the federal government to join misdemeanor charges with felony counts in a single indictment. In contrast to federal criminal complaints, federal indictments tend to be lengthy. Unlike state court indictments, federal indictments customarily recite detailed information that chronicles the defendant's alleged criminal conduct.

There is little difference between an information and a felony criminal complaint.[52] Both involve a prosecutor filing criminal charges with the proper court. Whereas a complaint is a sworn statement charging a person with an offense punishable by law, an information is the formal written charge presented by the prosecutor's office without a grand jury indictment. It is used for most misdemeanor charges in all jurisdictions. U.S. Attorneys and other indictment jurisdiction prosecutors may not charge felony defendants by information unless the accused waives the right to be indicted. Rule 7(b) of the Federal Rules of Criminal Procedure provides that a defendant may opt to be prosecuted by information by waiving indictment "in open court and after being advised of the nature of the charge and of the defendant's rights." The federal system and 11 of the states in indictment and limited indictment jurisdictions do not permit waiver in capital cases.[53]

The body of an information is virtually identical to the body of an indictment. Thus, federal felony informations tend to be lengthy, reciting the details of the defendant's alleged misconduct. On the other hand, federal misdemeanor informations as well as many state court informations are simply concise recitations of the alleged facts giving rise to an offense along with the citation to the applicable statutes. In this respect, the body portions of many state court informations resemble the bodies of criminal complaints. Earlier in this chapter, Exhibit 5.6 displays the first page of a state criminal complaint, and Exhibit 5.10 displays the first page of a federal felony indictment. Most state prosecutors' offices have standard forms that are used for each offense. Although the forms can be a tremendous time saver, be mindful of the fact that a form may have to be tailored to the circumstances of a particular case. Use the form as an aid; do not feel compelled to follow portions of the form that do not apply to your case. When in doubt, ask your supervising attorney for guidance.

APPLICATION EXERCISES

3. Prepare a caption, introductory paragraph, signature section, and address block/preparer's data for an indictment that would be filed in the Bill Edwards case (*see* hypothetical case on page xxxvii). Assume that the case is to be filed in the federal district in which your school is located and that the current U.S. Attorney for the district is the prosecutor.
4. Draft the caption, introductory paragraph, signature section, and address block/preparer's data (not the body) for a state criminal complaint against

[52] Police officers often prepare complaints for misdemeanors, traffic, and petty offenses.

[53] FRCrP 7; W. LaFave et al., *Criminal Procedure*, at 746.

Bill Edwards. Assume that he is being prosecuted for criminal fraud and embezzlement under the law of your state, that the prosecuting authority for the locality (county, parish, etc.) where your school is located is filing the complaint, and that you are the complainant.

5. Draft the body of a drunk driving criminal complaint to be filed in your state based on the facts given in the Bud Cook sample case (*see* hypothetical case on page xxxvii). Assume that the incident took place in the community in which your school is located and that the offense occurred on the 5th day of last month.
6. Draft the body of a criminal complaint against Bud Cook for the applicable homicide charge for your state (e.g., reckless homicide, involuntary manslaughter). Assume that the incident took place in the community in which your school is located and that the offense occurred on the 5th day of last month.
7. Prepare a one-count state complaint charging Brandon Turner with the lowest grade of felony for possession of crack cocaine. Assume that the incident took place in the community in which your school is located and that the offense occurred on the 13th day of last month. The top local prosecutor for your community is bringing the charge.
8. Prepare a two-count federal complaint charging Turner with (a) the felony of possession of crack cocaine with intent to deliver and (b) the felony of possession of a firearm by a convicted felon. Assume that the incident took place in the community in which your school is located and that the offense occurred on the 13th day of last month. It will be filed by the U.S. Attorney for the district in which your school is located.

7. Role of Prosecuting Attorneys in Issuing Arrest Warrants and Summonses

When a formal charge is issued against an individual who is not already in police custody, the prosecutor's office will prepare an arrest warrant or a criminal summons to be presented to a judge. Typically, these documents are "fill-in-the-blank forms." Hard copies of forms are usually available at the office of the clerk of the court. Many courts also make forms available online.[54]

Arrest warrant
A court order issued at the request of the prosecutor and/or law enforcement that authorizes the arrest and detention of an individual.

An **arrest warrant** is an order issued by a court that authorizes the arrest and detention of an individual. Ordinarily, the court issues the warrant at the request of the prosecutor and/or a law enforcement officer. There must be probable cause in order for the court to have authority to issue the warrant. Many times, an arrest warrant is served on the defendant with the formal criminal charge. In some jurisdictions, law enforcement officers must first present an affidavit before a warrant is issued. An example of an affidavit for an arrest warrant is depicted in Exhibit 5.12.

---

[54]The federal warrant for arrest form may be found at https://www.uscourts.gov/sites/default/files/ao442.pdf. The federal criminal summons is available at https://www.uscourts.gov/forms/law-enforcement-grand-jury-and-prosecution-forms/summons-criminal-case.

Exhibit 5.12: State Court Affidavit for Warrant and Detention

Actor Shia LeBeouf has a history of being charged with misdemeanors involving public intoxication and disturbing the peace. In 2015, City of Austin, Texas, police officers secured an arrest warrant for LeBeouf for public intoxication.

CAUSE NUMBER: ______________

THE STATE OF TEXAS	§	IN THE MAGISTRATE COURT
	§	CITY OF AUSTIN
COUNTY OF TRAVIS	§	IN TRAVIS COUNTY, TEXAS

AFFIDAVIT FOR WARRANT OF ARREST AND DETENTION

The undersigned Affiant, who after being duly sworn by me, on oath, makes the following statement:
I have good reason to believe and do believe that:

Shia LaBeouf W/M 6/11/86

On or about the 9th day of October, 2015, in the incorporated limits of the City of Austin, County of Travis, Texas, did then and there commit the offense of:

Public Intoxication – Class C Misdemeanor

On October 9, 2015 at approximately 19:31:07 hours Sergeant Jelesijevic 3462 advised me, Officer Muchnikoff 7299, that he was on his regular assigned patrol in the Downtown Austin area wearing the uniform of his profession to include shoulder patches and a badge. Sgt. Jelesijevic was driving a clearly marked Austin Police Department patrol unit equipped with emergency lights and the word "Police" on the vehicle. Sgt. Jelesijevic was driving West bound on E 6th St. after dark and was stopped in the middle of three lanes at the red light at the intersection of E 6th St and San Jacinto Blvd, a public place. The E 6th St West bound light turned green at 19:31:07 hours and at 19:31:12 hours a group of one male and two females began crossing the intersection from the South West corner to the North West corner against the clearly lit crossing signal. The subjects entry into the roadway obstructed the flow of traffic, including Sgt. Jelesijevic, and was acknowledged by the subjects when the male subject lifted his hand in the internationally recognized sign for stop when directing traffic as they crossed. Sgt. Jelesijevic conducted a probable cause subject stop on the three crossing against signal by activating his emergency lights and repositioning his vehicle to be pointed directly at them. Sgt. Jelesijevic later identified the subjects as: Shia LaBeouf W/M 6/11/86; Grace Alayna W/F 11/9/94; and Daytona Stanga W/F 6/2/97.

After Sgt. Jelesijevic activated his overhead lights LaBeouf visually acknowledged him, looking straight at him, and raised his hands waist high while taking six backward steps followed by three more while turning away from Sgt. Jelesijevic as he exited his patrol vehicle and ordered LaBeouf to stop. LaBeouf returned next to Stanga and Alayna and a strong odor of an alcoholic beverage was immediately apparent to Sgt. Jelesijevic as emanating from LaBeouf. Sgt. Jelesijevic stated that LaBeouf's speech was slurred and thick tongued and his eyes were glassy and dilated.

While speaking with Sgt. Jelesijevic, LaBeouf stated that if stopped by Los Angeles Police Department he typically walks away because Police had killed a friend of his and he became increasingly confrontational, aggravated, profane, and verbally aggressive with Sgt. Jelesijevic throughout the stop, calling him a "silly man" three times. While interacting with Sgt. Jelesijevic, an unidentified third party began filming the encounter which is common on E 6th St. LaBeouf reacted very hostile to this stranger by puffing his chest and walking in an aggressive and threatening manner at the male, prompting Sgt. Jelesijevic to intervene and stop LaBeouf from potentially assaulting the stranger. LaBeouf then continued his verbal tirade towards Sgt. Jelesijevic and began to bow up or puff his chest, a sign of prepatory resistance, out at Sgt. Jelesijevic, within two feet of Sgt. Jelesijevic's face and staring intently at him. During this time LaBeouf began stating he was a member of the National Guard and that Sgt. Jelesijevic needed to "do whatever the fuck you gotta do!"

Sgt. Jelesijevic stated he determined that LaBeouf was a danger to himself and others due to his complete disregard for vehicular traffic who had the right of way when he walked into oncoming traffic. LaBeouf then acknowledged he was walking into traffic when he attempted to unlawfully direct traffic at night in his highly intoxicated state. By stopping the oncoming traffic LaBeouf acknowledged through his hand signal that vehicles had the right of way and he did not. LaBeouf's complete disregarded that traffic might have to suddenly stop causing a potential collision to avoid hitting him, or worse a vehicle may have struck his party highlighting his reckless and dangerous behavior. LaBeouf's escalating aggressive behavior towards by standers and Sgt. Jelesijevic further demonstrated LaBeouf's poor decision making and that he was a danger to others. Sgt. Jelesijevic determined that LaBeouf was a danger to himself and others due to his level of intoxication and placed him under arrest for Public Intoxication.

[signature] 7299 10/10/15
Affiant

Sworn and subscribed to before me by the said Affiant on this 10 day of OCT, 2015.
[signature] R R Muñoz #3029
Peace Officer in the State of Texas

On this, the 12 day of OCTOBER, 2015, I hereby acknowledge that I have examined the foregoing affidavit and have determined that probable cause exists for the issuance of an arrest warrant for the individual accused therein.

MAC
Magistrate, Magistrate Court, Austin, Travis County, Texas

$____________
Bond

Austin Police Incident #: 152821579   Officer: Muchnikoff 7299   Call Sign: C504

Bench warrant
A court order that authorizes the arrest of someone for failing to show for a court appearance.

Criminal summons
A document issued under a court order that directs the accused to appear in court to answer the charges made against him or her.

A **bench warrant** is a special type of arrest warrant that authorizes the arrest of someone for failing to show up for a court appearance. It can be entered in civil as well as criminal cases and may be issued against parties as well as witnesses. Because a bench warrant is a judicial instrument imposed in response to a person's disobedience to a court order, it need not be accompanied by a criminal charge.

A **criminal summons** is a less intrusive means of obtaining jurisdiction over a person in a criminal case. As part of the arrest process, the individual is taken into custody, where he or she is searched, fingerprinted, photographed, and interviewed for demographic information. When a criminal summons is used, on the other hand, the accused party is simply directed to appear in court at a set date and time to answer the charges made against him or her. The summons and a copy of the charges are delivered to the accused at the same time.

E. Extradition of Fugitives

Extradition
The procedure by which one state formally requests another state to turn over the custody of a fugitive for criminal prosecution or punishment.

Fugitive (fugitive from justice)
A person who has fled a jurisdiction to escape criminal prosecution or punishment.

Sometimes prosecutors charge individuals with crimes who are not located within the judication in which the charges are filed. At other times, a defendant may flee a jurisdiction after being charged. To move forward with the case in either scenario, the prosecutor must take formal steps to have the defendant extradited to the prosecutor's venue. This process is referred to as **extradition**, and the defendant being sought is called the "**fugitive**" or "fugitive from justice."

Federal law governs this procedure. Article IV, Section 2 of the U.S. Constitution (the Extradition Clause) provides that:

> A person charged in any State with Treason, Felony, or other Crime, who shall flee from Justice, and be found in another State, shall on Demand of the executive Authority of the State from which he fled, be delivered up, to be removed to the State having Jurisdiction of the Crime.

The federal extradition law[55] implements the Extradition Clause by setting forth the following steps:

- The executive authority from one state ("the demanding state") makes a formal demand to the state to which a fugitive from justice has fled ("the asylum state").
- The formal demand must be accompanied by a copy of an indictment found or an affidavit made before a magistrate of any state or territory.
- This document must charge the fugitive demanded with having committed treason, felony, or other crime. It must be certified as authentic by the governor or chief magistrate of the state or territory from whence the person so charged has fled.
- The executive from the receiving state must cause the fugitive to be arrested and secured, and notify the demanding state's executive authority or agent to receive the fugitive.

[55] 18 U.S.C §3182.

- An agent of the demanding state's executive must appear to receive the prisoner within 30 days from time of arrest or the prisoner may be released.
- Cases of kidnapping by a parent to another state automatically involve the U.S. Marshal.

Although the extradition process is governed by state law, there is uniformity across the United States due to the Uniform Criminal Extradition Act (UCEA).[56] First, the demanding state issues an arrest warrant when either the defendant failed to appear in court or the prosecuting authorities have reason to believe that the defendant has fled. The prosecutor will enter the arrest warrant's information into the National Crime Information Center, an electronic clearinghouse of crime data that is accessible to every criminal justice agency across the nation. Next, the demanding state's executive authority, usually the governor, makes a formal demand for the fugitive. Many times, the prosecuting authority does not seek extradition of the fugitives charged with non-violent felonies, misdemeanors, or petty offenses. Third, the asylum state conducts a judicial hearing to determine whether the demanding state followed the legal requirements of extradition.[57] Fourth, the demanding state sends personnel to the asylum state to take custody of the fugitive within 30 days.

If the demanding state does not follow the requirement set forth in federal extradition law, the governor from the asylum state may refuse the demanding state's request for extradition. Additionally, the governor may decline to extradite when the fugitive is serving a sentence in the asylum state.

SUMMARY

This chapter examined the role that prosecuting attorneys play in investigations into criminal activities and the process of bringing formal criminal charges against those thought to have committed criminal offenses.

These prosecuting attorneys are divided along federal and state jurisdictional lines, and they have different job titles. Some are elected and some are appointed. Larger offices are usually organized into separate divisions.

Although most of the investigative work is typically done by police, prosecutors typically draft and present applications for search warrants, arrest warrants, and direct grand jury investigations. They are the key gatekeepers when it comes to determining who will be brought to trial and with which offenses they will be charged.

Paralegals who work for prosecutors may also be involved in these investigations and are often involved in drafting the various documents that need to be filed with the court. These documents include criminal complaints, indictments, informations, arrest warrants, and summons. Paralegals also assist prosecuting attorneys with initial appearances, bail settings, arraignments, and preliminary hearings.

[56]The Uniform Criminal Extradition Act has been adopted by almost all of the states. Illinois' UCEA is codified at 725 ILCS 225/1 *et seq.*

[57]The fugitive often will waive extradition before the case is called for hearing.

INTERNET RESOURCES

Participants in the Criminal Justice System

- Offices of the United States Attorneys: **http://www.justice.gov/usao/**
- Directory of Prosecuting Attorneys in Each State: **https://www.justice.gov/usao/us-attorneys-listing**
- National District Attorneys Association: **http://www.ndaa.org/**
- Handbook for Grand Jurors for Maryland: **https://mdcourts.gov/sites/default/files/import/juryservice/pdfs/grandjury service.pdf**
- Model Rules of Professional Conduct: **http://www.abanet.org/cpr/mrpc/mrpc_toc.html**

REVIEW QUESTIONS

1. How do the basic functions of attorneys employed by each U.S. Attorney's office differ from those of state prosecutors?
2. In what ways are prosecutors involved in the investigation of crimes?
3. What are the two alternative methods for a person signing an affidavit to verify that he or she is being truthful?
4. What are the two basic matters that must be shown in an application for search warrant?
5. What process must be carried out before an officer files a return of a search warrant with the court?
6. What is the original purpose of the grand jury?
7. What is meant by a grand jury issuing a true bill?
8. By what method can a grand jury require a knowledgeable yet reluctant witness to provide testimony?
9. What is the difference between transactional immunity and use immunity?
10. What are arrest warrants and bench warrants?
11. How does an arrest warrant differ from a criminal summons?
12. What are the five major components of a court document?
13. What information is included in the caption of a case?
14. List and describe the three types of charging documents.
15. What are indictment jurisdictions and information jurisdictions?
16. What is bail? What factors does the court consider in setting bail?
17. How does the arraignment differ from the preliminary hearing?
18. What is extradition, and when is it used?

Chapter 6

Legal Representation for the Accused

Chapter Objectives

After reading this chapter, you should be able to:

- Compare and contrast the adversarial and the inquisitorial systems of law.
- Discuss the Sixth Amendment right to counsel and the ways in which it has been implemented.
- Explain the role of defense attorneys and the ethical rules that govern their activities.
- Discuss the differences between attorney-client privilege and the duty of confidentiality.

Introduction

In the previous chapters, we focused on the activities of law enforcement officers and prosecutors' offices as they relate to investigating criminal activities, as well as identifying, detaining, and arresting suspected perpetrators. We also discussed the lawyers and paralegals who prosecute people accused of committing violations of the criminal code. Now we turn our attention to the lawyers and paralegals who defend the people against whom those prosecutors have brought charges in our criminal courts.

A. Adversarial Versus Inquisitorial Legal Systems

Defense attorney The lawyer who represents a criminal defendant in court.

To fully understand the importance of **defense attorneys** in the U.S. legal system, it is necessary to understand the differences between adversarial and inquisitorial legal systems. The U.S. legal system is such a basic part of our popular culture that most readers have no knowledge of how our **adversarial system** differs from the **inquisitorial systems** used in many other nations around the world.

Adversarial system
A judicial system in which judges are supposed to act as passive, neutral decision-makers, while the attorneys for the litigants are responsible for presenting the evidence and arguments that favor their clients. It is also referred to as the **adversary system**.

Inquisitorial system
A judicial system in which judges are supposed to play an active role in bringing out all relevant information related to reaching the appropriate decision in a case.

In the **adversary system**, judges are focused on keeping the trial going smoothly and do not ensure that all potential witnesses are called to the stand or that the lawyers ask all the questions that should be asked.

In contrast, judges in the **inquisitorial system** take an active role in determining who should be called as witnesses and ask their own questions of the witnesses. Whereas the primary criticism of the inquisitorial system is that it puts too much power in the hands of judges, thereby creating an imbalance of power between the individual and the government; the adversarial system is criticized for making the outcome too dependent upon the skills and dedication of the attorneys.

Discussion Question

1. Would you rather live in a country that uses the adversarial system or the inquisitorial system? Why?

B. The Right to Counsel

1. SOURCE OF THE RIGHT

Because attorneys play such a key role in our adversary system, the Sixth Amendment was ratified to establish a right to counsel in criminal cases. It states that "[i]n all criminal prosecutions, the accused shall enjoy the right to . . . the assistance of counsel for his defense."

2. SCOPE OF THE RIGHT

The broad language of the amendment raises many important questions:

- What constitutes "assistance of counsel"?
- Does it really apply to "all" criminal prosecutions, or is it limited to some subset of more serious charges?
- At what stage in a criminal prosecution does this right begin to apply? Does it apply to appeals?
- Does it require the government to provide you with an attorney if you cannot afford one on your own, or is it simply a provision to prevent the government from consulting the attorney you hired with your own money?
- Does the assistance of counsel have to be effective? If so, how should courts determine if the assistance was effective?

In various cases involving the Sixth Amendment right to counsel, the U.S. Supreme Court has answered some of these question by ruling that:

- The right to counsel applies to anyone facing possible incarceration if he or she is convicted of federal, state, or local criminal charges, as well as to minors involved in juvenile proceedings.[1]
- As soon as a defendant retains a private attorney, that attorney can begin immediate representation of the defendant. When the government is providing an attorney for an indigent defendant, however, the right to counsel attaches at the initial appearance before a judicial officer. This first time in court is when the judge or the magistrate informs the defendant of the charge in the complaint and of various rights in further proceedings, in addition to determining the conditions for pretrial release.[2]
- While the right to have assistance from a private attorney extends through as many appeals as the defendant is qualified to make, the right to assistance of an appointed counsel applies only to the first level of appeal.[3]
- In order to have one's conviction reversed on the basis of ineffective assistance of counsel, a defendant must prove both that the defendant's attorney made major errors and that the errors were serious enough to have deprived the defendant of a fair trial.[4]

3. IMPLEMENTATION OF THE RIGHT

Although a defendant has a right to have attorney representation in a criminal proceeding in which a sentence of incarceration may be imposed, in most cases it is up to the defendant to find and pay for the services of a private attorney.[5] In situations in which defendants, facing possible jail time, cannot afford to pay for the services of a defense attorney, they typically are able to get representation from a **public defender**'s office or an assigned counsel program, which will be discussed next.

a. *Public Defenders' Office*

In metropolitan areas, there is usually a separate, publicly funded **public defenders'** office that is primarily staffed by attorneys who represent low-income individuals charged with criminal offenses. The attorneys who work in these offices are usually full-time, salaried employees. In rural areas, public defenders are often part-time employees who also maintain their own legal practices.

Public defender
An attorney who is employed by a governmental unit to defend low-income persons accused of committing crimes.

In addition to having full- and part-time attorneys, these offices employ paralegals, clerical staff, and investigators. Attorneys and paralegals in these offices specialize in criminal law and can easily consult with experienced colleagues when appropriate to do so.

Federal defenders are the federal equivalent of state public defenders. They are the primary representatives for defendants who are unable to afford private counsel in prosecutions initiated by the U.S. Attorney's Office. Like their state

Federal defender
An attorney appointed to represent persons who are unable to afford private counsel in federal prosecutions.

[1] *Gideon v. Wainwright, 372 U.S. 335 (1963)*; *In re Gault,* 387 U.S. 1 (1967).

[2] *Rothgery v. Gillespie County,* 554 U.S. 191 (2008).

[3] *Ross v. Moffitt,* 417 U.S. 600 (1974); *Halbert v. Michigan,* 545 U.S. 602 (2005).

[4] *Strickland v. Washington,* 466 U.S. 668 (1984).

[5] Attorneys who get paid directly by individuals or corporations are referred to as being "in private practice."

counterparts, federal defender offices in urban areas are staffed by full-time attorneys.

b. Assigned Counsel System

Assigned counsel
An attorney in private practice who is appointed by a judge to defend low-income persons accused of committing crimes.

Private Practice
A form of legal practice in which attorneys charge clients fees for the legal services being provided.

Pro bono
A Latin term translated as "for the good," this is used to identify legal work performed for free or at a reduced rate.

CJA panel attorney
An attorney in private practice who is appointed in federal cases pursuant to the Criminal Justice Act ("CJS"), to represent indigent defendants for a fixed hourly fee.

As an alternative to using a public defender system, some smaller communities use an **assigned counsel** system, in which judges assign local attorneys in **private practice** to defend people who are accused of a crime who are unable to pay to have a lawyer defend them. In these assigned counsel appointments, the attorney may either receive a set fee paid by the local government or take the case on a ***pro bono*** basis.[6]

The Criminal Justice Act (CJA)[7] authorizes U.S. district court judges to appoint attorneys to represent low-income clients when there is no federal defender's office or when the federal defender has a conflict of interest. **CJA panel attorneys** are criminal defense lawyers in private practice who are appointed to represent indigent defendants in federal cases for a fixed hourly fee.

Discussion Question

2. List what you think the pros and cons are of each type of defense attorney. Which type would you want to have defend you if you could not afford to hire a private attorney? Why?

Application Exercise

1. What type of system is used in the state courts in the area in which you currently reside for providing representation to persons accused of a crime who cannot afford to hire an attorney? What steps does an indigent defendant have to take to get an attorney to represent him or her? Where did you find this information?
2. Obtain a copy of the financial affidavit used in your local court system to determine whether a defendant qualifies for a court-appointed defense attorney. Fill in the form as you would if you were the one applying for representation.

---

[6]Rule 6.1 of the ABA Model Code of Professional Conduct provides that all attorneys owe a professional duty to provide legal services to individuals of limited means at a reduced fee. Rule 6.2 declares that a lawyer shall not seek to avoid appointment to represent a person except for good cause.

[7]18 U.S.C. §3006A.

4. ATTORNEY'S DECISION TO DECLINE TO REPRESENT A CLIENT

a. *Conflict of Interest*

The American Bar Association (ABA)'s Model Rules 1.6 and 1.7 prohibit an attorney from representing a client who has conflicting interests with either a current or former client of either the particular attorney or other attorneys in the same office.

Before a case is accepted, the attorney's office runs a **conflicts check** on the client to ensure that there is no conflict of interest in representing the client. The staff member conducts this check by verifying whether the client is an adverse party in another case handled by the attorney or if the attorney represents one of the witnesses against the client. The person conducting the check may manually review a list of clients or use a software application designed for this purpose. In general, a conflict for one lawyer in the firm creates a conflict for other attorneys. Attorneys shifting from defense to prosecution or vice versa must refrain from accepting representation that jeopardizes confidences learned in their prior employment.

Conflicts check
The process of verifying whether the acceptance of a new case would result in a conflict of interest for the attorney.

Likewise, paralegals must be careful to avoid their own conflicts of interest. Paralegals are ethically required to disclose to their employers any preexisting client or personal relationship that may conflict with the interests of the employer or prospective clients.[8] The National Federation of Paralegal Associations offers the following advice for preventing conflicts of interest:

- "On your first day of employment (if it has not been done during the interview process), ask the supervising attorney or other appropriate person for a list of legal cases or matters that the firm or employer is handling. Review that list to identify the names of clients, parties in litigation, acquaintances, friends, or family members that you recognize.
- "Compare your list of all legal cases or matters on which you have worked against the new employer's list. If you work in litigation, also review the names of attorneys representing the various parties.
- "Advise the employer of any matters in which you suspect you may have a conflict of interest. Provide only enough information about the matter for the employer (or a firm or corporation conflicts committee) to determine whether there is a conflict of interest. Usually, the client or matter name is sufficient to assess this.
- "As new clients and legal matters come into the office, or if new parties are added to cases already underway, check their names against your list as described above.
- "Despite your best efforts, a matter or client in which you have a possible conflict of interest may slip through. If this happens, bring it to the attorney's attention as soon as you become aware of it.
- Maintain your list of matters on which you work throughout your paralegal career."[9]

---

[8]National Association of Legal Assistants (NALA) Code of Ethics and Professional Responsibility, Canon 8; *see also* National Federation of Paralegal Associations (NFPA) Model Code of Ethics and Professional Responsibility and Guidelines for Enforcement, Canon 8.

[9]See the NFPA website, http://www.paralegals.org/displaycommon.cfm?an=1&subarticlenbr=390.

ETHICAL CONSIDERATIONS RELATED TO CONFLICTS OF INTEREST

ABA Model Rule of Professional Conduct Rule 1.7 prohibits most types of "concurrent conflicts of interest." These types of conflicts are defined as situations in which:

- The interests of one current client directly conflict with those of another current client.
- There is a "significant risk" that the attorney's representation will be limited by his or her past or present representation of another client or by a "personal interest of the lawyer."

ABA Model Rules 1.8–1.10 go into more detail as to what types of situations are considered to be conflicts of interest. See the ABA website: http://www.americanbar.org/groups/professional_responsibility/publications/model_rules_of_professional_conduct/model_rules_of_professional_conduct_table_of_contents.html.

b. Belief That the Defendant Is Guilty

One of the most common questions asked of lawyers is, "How can you defend a guilty client?" A common response to this question is to point out that guilt is a legal concept that is determined by a judge or a jury, not the lawyer. Therefore, a person cannot be considered guilty until after the trial has been completed.

The more philosophical justification is that the legitimacy of the adversary system depends upon having lawyers representing the "guilty" as well as the "innocent." If criminal defendants cannot find attorneys willing to represent them, "the foundation of the judicial system is eroded, and the lawyers become the judges of guilt or innocence by their very decision to accept or reject those criminal clients."[10]

Despite the importance of a defendant's right to have competent counsel in criminal proceedings, some attorneys representing unpopular defendants are rebuked for their choice of clients. For example, Harvard University ended its agreement with law professor Ronald Sullivan to serve as faculty dean of an undergraduate house after the university received pressure from students who felt uncomfortable with Sullivan's position as a member of the movie producer Harvey Weinstein's legal team. Many students claimed that the professor's decision to represent a person accused of abusing women disqualified him from serving in a role of mentorship to students.

---

[10] Stephen Jones, A Lawyer's Ethical Duty to Represent the Unpopular Client, 1 CHAP. L. REV. 105, 107 (1998).

Ethical Considerations Related to the Attorney-Client Relationship

Several of the ABA's Model Rules and the state rules that closely resemble them spell out the nature of an attorney's ethical obligations to clients.

Model Rule 1.3 contains a general admonition that a lawyer should act with "reasonable diligence and promptness" when representing a client. Complaints about lack of diligence and promptness are among the most frequent complaints filed with disciplinary committees by disgruntled clients. Model Rule 1.4 elaborates on Rule 1.3 and adds a requirement that a lawyer "explain a matter to the extent reasonably necessary to permit the client to make informed decisions regarding the representation."

Model Rule 1.2 (d) covers one of the most controversial topics in criminal law by attempting to draw a line between helping a client determine the validity, scope, meaning, or application of the law and assisting a client to engage in conduct that the lawyer knows is criminal or fraudulent. Attorneys have an obligation to fully explain what the law does or does not require and the defenses that a defendant might assert, but they are not supposed to allow a client to present what the attorneys know to be perjured testimony.

See the ABA website: http://www.americanbar.org/groups/professional_responsibility/publications/model_rules_of_professional_conduct/model_rules_of_professional_conduct_table_of_contents.html.

An attorney can in good faith represent a defendant that the attorney believes committed an illegal act by challenging the evidence against the client and arguing that the government has not proved guilt beyond a reasonable doubt. Defense counsel also can present case-dispositive motions and raise defenses such as statute of limitations. However, ethical rules bar an attorney from lying or making misrepresentations to the judge or jury. Likewise, canons of ethics prohibit lawyers from either inducing perjury or knowingly permitting their client to give false testimony. The lawyer is allowed to withdraw from a case if the client persists in committing perjury.

Application Exercise

3. Your supervising attorney, Charles Hovey, informs you that he has agreed to represent Brandon Turner in any criminal matters relating to the events reported in Exhibit 6.1. He further informs you that Turner and Dennis Watterson were co-owners of the car in which the crack cocaine was discovered by the police, and both have been charged with illegal possession of drugs. Draft a memorandum to Mr. Hovey addressing whether the applicable state ethics rules allow him to also represent Mr. Watterson. (Your memorandum should quote your state's statute or rule governing conflicts of interest.)

Exhibit 6.1: Incident Report #1 in *Turner* Case: Case File No. 19-0857

At 2:01 p.m. July 29, I was northbound on Bloomington Avenue at Normal Street. I saw a red sedan traveling west on Bloomington Street and fail to stop at the intersection of Bloomington Avenue at Normal Street. I signaled to the driver of the red sedan to pull over and stop. The vehicle began to accelerate and then came to an abrupt stop. The vehicle stopped partially on the roadway at 857 Normal Street. The driver of the vehicle, Brandon Turner, exited the vehicle. I blew the horn of the patrol car three times and then called out to Turner to stop. Turner walked towards the entrance of the business at 857 Normal Street. Turner entered the business and ran into a bathroom in the southwest corner of the business. I removed him from the bathroom and handcuffed him. I patted Turner down and removed him from the business.

As I was securing Turner in my car, I heard someone say, there was a gun under the sink. Located in a sink cabinet in the bathroom was a Taurus 9 mm semi-automatic handgun. The slide of the gun was pulled back and the magazine was loaded with 15 rounds of ammunition. I removed the gun, and locked it in the trunk of the patrol car.

Looking through the front driver's side window of Turner's car, I could see a plastic sandwich bag containing a white granular substance. The substance had the appearance of cocaine. I unlocked Turner's car and retrieved the substance. Upon further examination, I could see that there were two sandwich-type bags. Each bag contained several smaller bags which contained a white substance. The openings of the bags were tied closed. I secured the bag containing the substance in the breast pocket of my jacket. Turner's car was secured by Troopers S. Wright (number 123) and A. Hamilton (number 456). Troopers Wright and Hamilton conducted a search of the Turner car with the assistance of K-9s. Turner was taken to the Municipal Detention Center. A field test on the white substance found in Turner's car was conducted. The substance tested positive for cocaine. The substance was weighed. It weighed 34.5 grams.

Discussion Question

3. Would you be willing to defend persons who you know to be guilty of the crime with which they are being charged? Why?

5. RIGHT OF THE ACCUSED TO REJECT COUNSEL AND ACT AS OWN ATTORNEY

There is an old saying that "he who acts as his own lawyer has a fool for a client." Intelligent people who are not schooled in the law do not have the knowledge necessary to effectively defend themselves in court. Not only do attorneys have legal knowledge, but they also are trained to analyze cases in an objective, dispassionate manner. In contrast, criminal defendants are personally invested and cannot unemotionally assess their cases. Attorneys understand this. So, when they are accused of a crime, they almost always retain another lawyer to serve as their defense counsel.

Pro se party
A party who represents him/herself in court without legal counsel.

Nonetheless, some defendants act as their own attorney. Individuals who represent themselves in court are referred to as *pro se* parties. In this situation, the judge typically will try to talk the defendant out of the decision to act *pro se*, not only because it is in the defendant's best interest to have a lawyer, but also it makes the judge's job much easier and decreases the likelihood of having a conviction overturned on appeal. In serious felonies, judges may appoint a public defender to serve as an advisor but not the legal representative for the defendant.

Discussion Question

4. Do you think defendants should have the right to decline assistance from a lawyer and be able to serve as their own lawyer during a trial? Why or why not?

C. Attorney-Client Relationship

Whether the defendant is represented by private counsel, a court-appointed attorney, or a public defender, the role of the defense counsel is the same. It is to provide the client with the opportunity to attain the most favorable *realistic* resolution of the case. In many situations, this will be a negotiated plea agreement in which the defendant pleads guilty to a lesser offense, in return for having other charges dropped or lighter sentence.

1. PROTECTING THE CLIENT FROM SELF-INCRIMINATION

Once the attorney has agreed to represent the client and the client has agreed to be represented by the attorney, an attorney-client relationship has been formed. At their initial client meeting, criminal defense attorneys will advise their clients regarding what they should be doing to help prepare for trial, and tell them that they should not talk to anyone about the charges filed against them. It is especially important for clients to decline to speak to police officers. When interviewed by the police, suspects frequently present a biased account that they think casts them in a favorable light. After the officer confronts them with the discrepancies between their version and contradictory facts, suspects typically revise their story. Whenever a suspect makes a statement, the probability of contradicting a prior statement increases, and these internal inconsistencies come back to haunt them at trial. When placed under the stress of a police interrogation, even innocent persons become confused.

Besides advising the client not to speak to anyone about the charges, the attorney should instruct the client not to discuss the case in telephone calls, faxes, emails, or social media. When clients contact your office through any of these methods, they should limit their comments to discussing scheduling or other clerical matters and not talk about the facts of the case. Defense counsel should let incarcerated clients know that their telephone calls are being recorded.

2. ETHICAL DUTIES TO CLIENTS

State codes of professional responsibility impose a number of ethical duties that attorneys owe to their clients. Of particular importance are the duties of due diligence and confidentiality.

a. Due Diligence

ABA Model Rule of Professional Conduct 1.3 requires the lawyer to pursue a matter on behalf of a client despite opposition, obstruction, or personal inconvenience to the lawyer, and take whatever lawful and ethical measures are required to vindicate a client's cause or endeavor without the use of offensive tactics that violate the responsibility to treat all persons involved in the legal process with courtesy and respect.

Along the same vein, an attorney is obligated to maintain effective communication with clients. Model Rule 1.4 requires lawyers to keep the lines of communication open by a number of means. Specifically, they must inform the client of decisions requiring the client's informed consent, confer with the client about the method of reaching the client's objectives, keep the client posted as to the progress of the case, abide by the client's reasonable requests for information, discuss all limitations to the attorney's representation of the client when the client expects assistance that is prohibited by professional ethical rules or other law, and provide the client with sufficient information so that the client can make informed decisions concerning the representation.

b. Confidentiality

Confidentiality is essential to the establishment of a good working relationship between the attorney and the client, and to the extent that paralegals become involved in assisting the attorney, they too must vigorously protect the confidentiality of that relationship.

Unless the client gives informed consent, Model Rule 1.6 forbids a lawyer from revealing information relating to the client's representation unless it is necessary to carry out the representation or the information falls into one of the express exceptions to the rule. Lawyers must make reasonable efforts to prevent disclosure of or unauthorized access to information relating to representing a client.

Lawyers may disclose confidential client information to prevent the following events from occurring, death, substantial bodily harm, the client's commission of a crime, or the client's perpetration of fraud. A lawyer may also reveal confidences to obtain legal advice about the lawyer's compliance with the rules of professional responsibility, comply with the law and court orders, to prepare for claims or defenses between the lawyer and the client, to establish defenses to civil or criminal proceedings in which the lawyer's representation of the client are at issue, and to respond to allegations regarding the lawyer's representation of the client. To the extent necessary to identify and resolve conflicts of interest created by the lawyer's change of employment or changes in the makeup or ownership of a firm, the lawyer may disclose confidential client information, so long as the disclosure does not compromise the attorney-client privilege or otherwise prejudice the client.[10]

As you can see, the Model Rules contain several exceptions to the attorney's ethical obligations to protect a client's confidential information. One of the most controversial exceptions is the one regarding situations in which the attorney has knowledge that the client plans a criminal act. The Model Rules specify a criminal act as one "that the lawyer believes is likely to result in the imminent death or substantial bodily harm." This exemption applies only to *future* crimes.

Ethical Duties of Paralegals Related to Confidentiality

NALA Ethical Canon 7: A paralegal must protect the confidences of a client and must not violate any rule or statute now in effect or hereafter enacted controlling the doctrine of privileged communications between a client and an attorney. [National Association of Legal Assistants Code of Ethics and Professional Responsibility[11]]

NFPA Model Disciplinary Rule 1.5: A paralegal shall preserve all confidential information provided by the client or acquired from other sources before, during, and after the course of the professional relationship. [National Federation of Paralegal Associations, Inc.[12]]

The safest course for a paralegal who becomes aware of situations involving any of these exceptions is to notify the supervising attorney so that the attorney can determine the proper course of action.

It is important to note that this ethical **duty of confidentiality** extends to the attorney's employees and law firm staff, including paralegals. Paralegals regularly receive this type of information and must, at all times, resist the temptation to disclose it. You must refrain from discussing the particulars of a client's situation as interesting gossip with friends or family. Even when names are not used, these confidences cannot be revealed if the disclosure violates the client's privacy interests. The duty of confidentiality protects the private information of potential clients and current clients as well as past clients. This obligation even prohibits revealing the identities of the firm's clients. In most jurisdictions, an attorney may reveal confidential client information only (1) after full disclosure and with the client's written consent, or (2) when required by law or court order, or (3) when necessary to prevent the client from committing an act that could result in death or serious bodily harm.

Duty of confidentiality
An attorney's ethical duty to maintain the confidences of the client.

Discussion Question

5. Assume that you are an attorney who represents a defendant in a felony matter where the client is charged with pouring acid on a car and repeatedly bashing it with a baseball bat. Based on information you learned from reading his rap sheet, you have concluded that your client has violent tendencies. What should you do if the defendant's wife approaches you in the courthouse and tells you that your client had threatened to kill her when he gets out of jail?

---

[11]https://nala.org/certification/nala-code-ethics-and-professional-responsibility/ (last checked September 10, 2022).

[12]https://www.upcounsel.com/lectl-nfpa-model-code-of-ethics-and-professional-responsibility(last checked September 10, 2022).

Application Exercises

4. Your friend Bill Edwards has retained your supervisor, Charles Hovey, to represent him in a state securities fraud case involving the events described on p. xxxviii. When you see Bill at a social function, he takes you off into a corner where no one else can overhear your conversation and then shares some incriminating information about his case with you.
   a. Under the terms of the ABA Model Rules of Professional Conduct, what are your ethical duties regarding the sharing of this information with your supervising attorney?
   b. Under the terms of NALA's Ethical Canon 7, what are your ethical duties regarding the sharing of this information with your supervising attorney?
   c. Under the terms of NFPA's Model Disciplinary Rule 1.5, what are your ethical duties regarding the sharing of this information with your supervising attorney?
   d. Under the terms of the ethical code adopted by the state bar or supreme court in your state, what are your ethical duties regarding the sharing of this information with your supervising attorney?

5. You go to a party also attended by Clay Marshall, a client represented by your firm in a sexual abuse case. You step into a walk-in closet to pick up your jacket, where you observe Clay kiss a woman who responds by slapping him and immediately leaving the party. The woman is not one of the complaining witnesses identified in the charges against Clay. Answer the questions presented in paragraphs a through c of Application Exercise 4.

c. Attorney-Client Privilege

Attorney-client privilege
The rule of evidence that forbids an attorney, or the attorney's employees, from testifying about communications with the client.

While attorney-client privilege is technically not an ethical duty, it is important to understand the difference between the ethical obligation to protect the confidentiality of attorney-client communications and the invoking of **attorney-client privilege**. Whereas the former is an ethical rule about what attorneys and paralegals should keep confidential, the latter is an evidentiary rule about the admissibility of confidential information in court proceedings.

Court rules relating to the admissibility of evidence specifically forbid an attorney, *or the attorney's staff*, from testifying in court about confidential communications with the client. Thus, they both are obligated to protect confidential information about the client. This privilege applies in situations where a client seeks legal advice from a lawyer in his or her professional capacity, when the communications are made in confidence, and when the communications relate to the purpose of receiving legal advice.

There is a four-part test used to determine whether a client disclosure is privileged information: (1) a client's oral or written statement (2) made to the attorney or staff (3) while seeking legal advice (4) given in confidence. The client does not have to pay a fee to have the protection of the privilege. A client can waive the attorney-client privilege. Similar to the duty of confidentiality, a third party's presence can waive the privilege. You must make sure that no third party is present when you interview a client. Unlike the duty of confidentiality, the identity of the client is not protected by the privilege. Thus, the duty of confidentiality is much broader in scope than the attorney-client privilege.

Take a few minutes to read the following excerpts from decisions reached by the Montana and Indiana supreme courts dealing with the question as to whether the attorney-client privilege protected a statement made to a friend who was a paralegal.

Montana v. Ingraham
290 Mont. 18 (1998), appeal after remand, 302 Mont. 39 (2000)
Supreme Court of Montana

JUSTICE JIM REGNIER delivered the opinion of the Court.

Gregory Lloyd Ingraham appeals from a judgment and commitment of the Twentieth Judicial District Court, Lake County, based on a jury verdict convicting him of negligent homicide, criminal endangerment, and criminal trespass to property. We affirm in part, reverse in part, and remand for further proceedings consistent with this opinion.

In the early morning hours of October 13, 1995, Ingraham was driving north on Highway 93 near St. Ignatius, in Lake County, Montana. Roughly two miles north of town, Ingraham's vehicle crossed the center line and struck an oncoming Ford Ranger pickup truck, driven by Cynthia Harriman-Larson. Harriman-Larson died in the collision, and her passenger, Delbert Adams, suffered severe injuries.

Sometime after 5:00 p.m. on the day following the accident, Jeanne Windham, a paralegal and friend of Ingraham's, picked Ingraham up at the hospital. After first stopping at his house to retrieve some clothing, she drove them to the scene of the accident at Ingraham's request. At trial, Windham offered testimony regarding her conversation with Ingraham at the scene of the accident. Windham recollected Ingraham telling her that his dogs began playing in the back seat and that, as he attempted to keep them from jumping into the front seat, his car swerved to the left just prior to colliding with Harriman-Larson's vehicle.

Did the District Court err in admitting testimony by paralegal Jeanne Windham? Ingraham argues the District Court erred in permitting paralegal Jeanne Windham to testify as to statements Ingraham made to her about the accident. Ingraham asserts that Windham was one of his law firm's employees, and argues the content of his conversations with her about the accident was protected by the attorney-client privilege and constituted privileged work product. Moreover, Ingraham asserts the court erred in admitting rebuttal testimony regarding additional conversations overheard by Windham, but which did not tend to counteract new matter introduced by the defense.

The State, in contrast, argues that neither the attorney-client privilege nor the work product rule apply to protect the content of conversations between Ingraham and Windham in the aftermath of the accident. The State additionally asserts that Windham's testimony on rebuttal was proper, and urges the court did not err in overruling Ingraham's objections to its admission.

Ingraham first asserts the content of his conversations with Windham was protected by the attorney-client privilege, and that the

District Court thus erred in overruling his objections to Windham's proposed testimony. Ingraham argues that, upon making the telephone call to his father on the night of the accident, he became a client of the Ingraham Law Office. Ingraham asserts that, because Windham worked as a paralegal for the Ingraham Law Office at the time of the accident, the attorney-client privilege extends to her and protects any statements he made to her regarding the accident.

In support of his argument, Ingraham points to §26-1-803(1), MCA, pursuant to which "an attorney cannot, without the consent of his client, be examined as to any communication made by the client to him or his advice given to the client in the course of professional employment." Ingraham asserts his disclosures to Windham were made "in the course of professional employment," and thus fall within the protection afforded by the attorney-client privilege.

Over Ingraham's objection, the District Court permitted Windham to testify, concluding that it did not believe that the communication that took place between the Defendant and Ms. Windham on October 13th, 1995. . . at approximately six o'clock p.m., can reasonably be construed as communication made by a client to the attorney, as the statute defines in the course of professional employment.

There are several factors that lead me to that conclusion. The first one is that there's no indication that Greg Ingraham had retained Ingraham Law Office as his counsel with regard to this accident. There certainly is no indication, even if that had happened, that Ms. Windham had any reason, whatsoever, to believe that that had happened. And I have no reason to believe that Greg Ingraham believed that that had happened.

Even if it had, Ms. Windham left her professional employment when she left that office at five o'clock that day, on her own volition, to visit the Defendant as a friend. The only reason she received communications from the Defendant that night is because she agreed, as a friend, to transport him to her house so that she could take care of him. And it's inconceivable to me that that can be construed to be in the course of professional employment. The Defendant then requested her, during that visit, to go to the accident scene, apparently, and said certain things to her. That doesn't necessarily become an attorney-client communication just because Ms. Windham happens to have been an independent contractor for the Defendant at that time. I think it's a factor that she wasn't paid for that time that she spent with him. . . . And so I don't believe that this could reasonably have been construed by the Defendant as a conversation by a client with an attorney or a member of his attorney's office. And so I'm going to deny the motion to exclude her testimony.

Windham testified in chambers that, although she worked for Gregory Ingraham as an independent contractor, she performed no paralegal services for Lloyd Ingraham. She also testified that she had done nothing to assist Gregory Ingraham in defending this case, and that to her knowledge, there was no file on this case at the Ingraham Law Firm. Our review of the pertinent testimony indicates that Ingraham's conservations with Windham were purely personal and not in the course of a professional relationship. Having reviewed the record, we conclude the District Court did not abuse its discretion in concluding that the content of Ingraham's conversations with Windham on the day of the accident were not protected by attorney-client privilege and in admitting her testimony.

Mayberry v. Indiana
670 N.E.2d 1262 (Ind.1996)
Supreme Court of Indiana

SULLIVAN, JUSTICE.

We affirm defendant Elizabeth Mayberry's conviction for the murder of minister Roland Phillips, committed as he concluded his Sunday sermon at the North Salem United Methodist Church.

Background

In May, 1992, defendant met Phillips, a student pastor at the North Salem United Methodist Church, at a singles retreat sponsored by the United Methodist Church. Defendant and Phillips dated for several months after the retreat. During the course of their relationship, defendant, then 35 years old, claims that Phillips encouraged her to allow him to kiss her using his tongue, engage in consensual, mutual, oral sex with him, fondle and kiss her breasts, and digitally penetrate her vagina. Defendant had never before had intimate physical contact with a man. Phillips would later deny to church officials that he had ever engaged in oral sex with defendant. Defendant's relationship with Phillips took a turn for the worse in August of 1992. In an attempt to salvage the relationship, defendant wrote Phillips letters inquiring into the status of their relationship. In one of these letters, she asked Phillips to attend counseling with her. In November, 1992, defendant received a letter from Phillips in which he stated that their relationship was over. This letter deeply hurt defendant and made her angry.

In a hearing outside the presence of the jury, defense witness Jennie Maretto, a friend of Phillips and a paralegal for a law firm in Fishers, Indiana, testified that Phillips contacted her at work to obtain legal advice regarding a letter he wrote to the UMC in response to the complaint that defendant had filed. Maretto testified that she felt that she was not legally able to give Phillips legal advice but would have to consult with an attorney. Maretto stated that Phillips asked her to consult an attorney. Maretto also testified that she gave a statement regarding her conversations with Phillips to Officer Danny Williams. When defense counsel inquired about the letter Phillips asked Maretto to look over, the State asserted the attorney-client privilege on Maretto's behalf as to any communication between Maretto and the victim. The trial court sustained the State's objection to the admission of Maretto's testimony.

In an offer to prove, the defense introduced into evidence a police report prepared by Officer Williams. In the report, Officer Williams states that when he spoke with Maretto she informed him that Phillips had contacted her to obtain legal advice. The report also states that Maretto advised the officer that Phillips stated that Phillips and defendant had engaged in consensual, mutual oral sex.

Defendant contends that the trial court erroneously determined that the attorney-client privilege attached to comments Phillips made to Maretto because Maretto did not adequately establish that Phillips contacted her in an effort to employ an attorney for professional advice or aid. In *Colman v. Heidenreich*, 269 Ind. 419, 381 N.E.2d 866 (1978), this court made the following observations:

> The attorney-client privilege is a very important provision in our law for the protection of persons in need of professional legal help. It makes provision for a person to give complete and confidential information to an attorney, so that the attorney may be fully advised in his services to the client. At the same time, it assures the client that these confidences will not be violated.

Colman, 269 Ind. at 421, 381 N.E.2d at 868, Indiana Code §34-1-14-5 (1993) provides that attorneys shall not be competent witnesses "as to confidential communications made to them in the course of their professional business, and as to advice given in such cases." This "attorney-client privilege not only plays a role in our law of evidence but is also fundamental to our rules of professional conduct which forbid attorneys from revealing 'information relating to representation of a client unless the client consents after consultation.' See Ind. Professional Conduct Rule 1.6." *Corll v. Edward D. Jones & Co.*, 646 N.E.2d 721, 724 (Ind. Ct. App. 1995). As long as an attorney is consulted on business within the scope of the attorney's profession, "it is of no moment to the privilege's application that there is no pendency or expectation of litigation. Neither is it of any moment that no fee has been paid." *Colman*, 269 Ind. at 423, 381 N.E.2d at 869 (citations omitted). Rather, the essential prerequisites to invocation of the privilege are to establish by a preponderance of the evidence (i) the existence of an attorney-client relationship and (ii) that a confidential communication was involved. *See Colman*, 269 Ind. at 423, 381 N.E.2d at 869. To meet the burden of showing that an attorney-client relationship existed, the State had to, at the very least, establish that the communication at issue occurred in the course of an effort to obtain legal advice or aid, on the subject of the client's rights or liabilities, from a professional legal advisor acting in his or her capacity as such. *Id.*; *United States v. Demauro*, 581 F.2d 50, 55 (2nd Cir. 1978).

Defendant suggests that Phillips's communications with his friend Maretto are privileged "only if his asking her to have an attorney look over his papers can be construed to be an attempt by Phillips to employ legal counsel." Defendant also states that the State failed to meet its burden of establishing that Maretto's communications with Phillips were privileged because she did not testify that Phillips intended to or sought to employ her firm to represent him concerning his difficulties with the complaint defendant filed with the church. Defendant misstates the State's burden. Although Maretto and Phillips were social friends, the record reveals that Phillips approached Maretto at the law firm where she worked as a paralegal/office manager and asked her to consult an attorney regarding his legal concerns. We believe these facts can be read to establish that the communications at issue occurred in the course of an effort to obtain legal advice or aid from a professional legal advisor in his capacity as such. *Colman*, 269 Ind. at 423, 381 N.E.2d at 869; *Demauro*, 581 F.2d at 55. Therefore, we cannot say that the trial court erred in determining that the State met its burden of showing the existence of an attorney-client relationship. And if the communications at issue occurred during an attempt to procure professional legal aid, confidential communications were involved here. See *Colman*, 269 Ind. at 423, 381 N.E.2d at 869. Therefore, the trial court did not abuse its discretion in determining that the communications between Maretto and Phillips were subject to the attorney-client privilege.

[W]e think Williams's testimony was properly excluded because Phillips's statement to Maretto was subject to the attorney-client privilege. Information subject to the attorney-client privilege retains its privileged character until the client has consented to its disclosure. *Key v. State*, 235 Ind. 172, 175, 132, N.E.2d 143, 145 (1956). Phillips did not consent to Maretto's disclosures to Williams. Therefore, the information possessed by Williams was privileged. In short, privileged information does not cease to be privileged merely because it is subject to the statement against interest hearsay exception. We conclude that the trial court properly excluded Williams's testimony.

Case Discussion Questions

1. What are the factual similarities between the *Ingraham* and *Mayberry* cases?
2. What are the factual differences between the *Ingraham* and *Mayberry* cases?
3. Does the application of attorney-client privilege depend on whether the person making the statement is a party to the case? Why or why not?
4. What are the holdings of the courts in *Ingraham* and *Mayberry*?
5. How can you reconcile the *Ingraham* and *Mayberry* holdings?
6. In light of the *Ingraham* and *Mayberry* decisions, what precautions should you take to ensure that the attorney-client privilege protects statements clients make to you?

3. FEE-RELATED ISSUES[13]

If there is no conflict of interest in accepting the case, the attorney will discuss the fee with the client. *Paralegals are not ethically allowed to set the fee.*

There are several fee arrangement models used when private counsel is hired in a criminal case. The first model is the **hourly fee.** Under this approach, the law office bills the client for the time devoted to the case by the attorneys and paralegals. Rates are based on the experience and the local market. Although public defenders are typically salaried, assigned attorneys are usually paid on an hourly basis.

Hourly fee
The rate of compensation earned by an attorney based on the time devoted to the case.

When a client hires a private attorney on an hourly fee basis, the client usually makes an advanced payment, referred to as a retainer, at the beginning of the representation. This amount is deposited into an account administered by the lawyer or the law firm called the **attorney's trust fund.**

Attorney's trust fund
A special account administered by the lawyer or law firm holding money belonging to clients.

The trust fund is an account holding money belonging to the attorney's clients. The rules governing attorney ethics forbid the lawyer from comingling the attorney's personal or business funds in this account. As the attorneys and paralegals bill for their services, funds from the advance payment are paid to the law office. If any portion of the retainer remains when the case comes to a conclusion, it is refunded to the client. When the funds on deposit are depleted, the lawyer will require that an additional sum be paid into the trust account for payment of future fees.

The second model is the **flat fee,** a pre-established amount that the client pays for all of the services the lawyer is to perform in the case. Both the client and the attorney have the certainty of knowing the amount of the fee before any work is done. The amount of work, however, is not known. A case that

Flat fee
A pre-established amount that the client pays for all of the services the lawyer is to perform in the case.

ETHICAL DUTIES OF ATTORNEYS RELATED TO CLIENT TRUST ACCOUNTS

Unfortunately, many attorneys get in trouble by misusing the special trust fund accounts that are established to hold money that belongs to the client but is held by the attorney for specified purposes. The rules governing the use of these client trust funds are spelled out in the ethics codes adopted by state supreme courts and bar associations. Most establish requirements that are similar to those contained in **ABA Model Rule of Professional Conduct Rule 1.15.**

See http://www.americanbar.org/groups/professional_responsibility/publications/model_rules_of_professional_conduct/rule_1_15_safekeeping_priority.html.

[13]These are fees charged by criminal attorneys in private practice. Indigent defendants do not pay fees to public defenders or assigned counsel.

languishes in the court system for months or even years will dramatically reduce the attorney's profits. On the other hand, the client may be paying an unusually high amount for representation that concludes after a few court appearances.

If the funds used to pay the attorney's fee were acquired by the client in an illegal transaction, such as the sale of illicit drugs, the government may seize the funds. We will discuss civil asset forfeiture in Chapter 15. So the attorney must be careful to make sure the funds used to pay for fees come from legitimate sources. Payment of the fee in $10,000 cash or more requires the attorney to report the transaction to the federal government.

Unlike personal injury cases where attorney's fees are not paid unless there is a successful conclusion of the case, it is unethical for an attorney to enter into a contingent fee agreement in a criminal case. A **contingent fee** is a lawyer's fee owed by the client if the attorney is successful. There is no payment if the client does not prevail.

Contingent fee
The lawyer's fee owed by the client if the attorney is successful. There is no fee if the client does not prevail. It is also referred to as a **contingency fee.**

D. Paralegal Involvement in the Defense of the Accused

There are a variety of ways that paralegals can contribute to the defense of individuals accused of criminal offenses.

1. INTERVIEWING CLIENTS

Many defense attorneys, especially those in a private practice, conduct the initial client interview themselves to get a feel for the potential client's personality and to persuade the client to retain their services. On the other hand, public defender offices or assigned counsel may delegate this task to paralegals. When these interviews are delegated to paralegals, the interviewers are typically given client information sheets and checklists.

When you, as a paralegal, have contact with clients, you should carry out your duties in a responsible and professional manner. Be courteous, considerate, and warm, but don't be too chummy. Minimize waiting to help the client feel that the case is important and reduce the client's general anxiety. Focus on the client by avoiding interruptions so you give the client your undivided attention. Treat the client with dignity, regardless of the client's lot in life. Do not be judgmental.

Meetings with clients should take place at a place that is conducive to open communication and privacy. The law office and a client's home ordinarily provide good settings. In some cases, these meetings take place in special private interview rooms at the jail. To maintain client confidentiality and to protect the attorney-client privilege, these meetings should not be in a public location where other people might overhear the conversation. Neither children nor friends should be present during these client meetings.

APPLICATION EXERCISES

6. After reviewing the facts of the Cook case (*see* Introduction to Hypothetical Cases, p. xxxvii) and reading the investigating officer's police report in Exhibit 6.2, use the full disclosure model of questioning to prepare a set of questions for the initial client interview. (Be sure to include questions that elicit the defendant's contact information.)
7. After reviewing the facts of the Turner case (*see* Introduction to Hypothetical Cases, pp. xxxvii-xxxviii) and reading the investigating officer's police report in Exhibit 6.1, use the limited disclosure model of questioning to prepare a set of questions for the initial client interview. (Be sure to include questions that elicit the defendant's contact information.)

2. INTERVIEWING WITNESSES

The tips on locations for and how to conduct client interviews also apply to interviewing witnesses.

a. Identifying Potential Witnesses

Prior to starting an interview, the paralegal should review relevant charging documents[14] as well as the police report to determine what happened at the scene and who witnessed these events. Exhibit 6.2 provides an example of the type of witness information included in these reports. Law enforcement officer reports usually provide many details of an investigation. A copy of a Miami-Dade police officer's incident report, depicted in Exhibit 6.3, is an example of the kinds of information officers record in their reports.

b. Types of Witnesses

Police reports will reveal the identities of witnesses who may be called to testify against the defendant. Many of these individuals are hostile witnesses. A **hostile witness** is a witness holding a favorable outlook toward the opposing party. Hostility arises from the witness's relationship with the defendant. Hence, the investigating officers and the victim are hostile toward the defendant. Moreover, a large segment of the general public is hostile to persons accused of crimes. Hostile witnesses are not voluntarily likely to be helpful to the client.

Hostile witness
A witness holding a favorable outlook toward the opposing party.

[14]There are three types of documents generated in most criminal cases: charging documents, officer reports, and witness statements. The charge is provided to the defendant at the arraignment. The other documents are furnished to the defense as discovery documents.

Exhibit 6.2: Incident Report #1 in *Cook* Case: Case File No. 19-1857

On Sunday evening, 5/15, at approximately 2031 hrs, this officer arrived at Route 185 near Normal Street to assist in the investigation of a serious personal injury accident involving a bicyclist and a motor vehicle. Shortly after arrival to the scene, I learned that the driver had left the scene and the bicyclist had been pronounced dead at Municipal Hospital at 2221 hrs. The driver then called the sheriff's police to report the crash. Local police were dispatched to the location where they then transported him to the local police station. This officer cleared the accident scene at 2252 hrs.

At approximately 2310 hrs this officer met with a Bud Cook in the booking area of the station. As this officer started the interview of Mr. Cook, a strong odor of alcohol could be detected coming from his breath. His eyes were bloodshot and watery. Mr. Cook was given a Miranda warning at 2315 hrs. At first, he became very upset, saying that he should never have reported the accident because he was going to be blamed for getting someone he did not even see. I explained to him that the reason I was reading him the Miranda warning was to protect his rights. He calmed down, and this officer then read him his rights which he advised that he understood and signed the waiver. Mr. Cook had advised that he knew he struck something but did not know what it was. He advised that for all ne knew, somebody could have thrown something at his car. Mr. Cook had reported that he drove home, very fast going about 80 to 85 miles an hour. The more he thought about the damage and he started to think that he hit something larger than an animal, and it was probably a person. He arrived home and told his wife to immediately call the police. He was informed of the alcohol odor that I was detecting and asked if he had had anything to drink since the accident occurred. He replied "no, all I did was drive straight home, tell my wife to call the cops and two minutes later the cops were at my house."

This officer requested Mr. Cook to perform a field sobriety text, which he did. The first test requested and performed was a finger to note test. He was hesitant and touched underneath his nose and above his upper lip. He tried again and completely missed his nose, again touching below the tip of the nose.

The next test requested was the heel to toe test. On this test, he attempted to take his first step and lost his balance. He regained his balance and attempted the second step and again stumbled.

This officer then brought Mr. Cook back to the police department where he was processed—fingerprinting and photographs. At approximately 0225 hrs on 5/16 this officer again gave Mr. Cook his Miranda warning and told him that I wanted to obtain a typewritten statement from him concerning the events of the evening leading up to the accident. Mr. Cook gave this officer a two-page typewritten statement that this officer prepared and Mr. Cook reviewed.

Friendly witness
A fact witness who knows something about the underlying occurrence and holds a favorable impression of the client.

Not all witnesses identified in police reports, however, are hostile. A **friendly witness** is a fact witness who knows something about the underlying occurrence and holds a favorable impression of the client. The friendly witness usually has a relationship with the client that goes beyond simply being present during events involved in the case. Friends, family members, co-workers, and neighbors usually are friendly witnesses. Persons criminally charged in the same occurrence sometimes, but not always, are friendly witnesses. Some may

Exhibit 6.3: Police Incident Report in Vick Case (Page 1)

In 2007, airport screeners seized a water bottle from NFL star Michael Vick at a security checkpoint. Screeners discovered the bottle included a "concealed compartment" that they believed contained a small amount of marijuana. Laboratory test results revealed no evidence of drugs in the bottle. The State Attorney did not charge Vick. Excerpts of the police incident report follow:

OFFENSE-INCIDENT REPORT

MIAMI-DADE POLICE DEPARTMENT PD070117030397 1

Wed 01-17-07 0715 0830 1100 1100

Wed 01-17-07 0715

#1 1 Found Property C 7

#2

M.I.A. Concourse "G", TSA screening point Miami 7 1154

0 0

21

01 01 01 00 00 00

1 W 01 3 Joseph, Gertrude

8300 NW 36 St, Miami FL 33172 305-526-2893

TSA Screener who discovered hidden compartment

B F 25 01 01 00 00 00 01

1 W 02 03 Rodriguez, Hector

8300 NW 36 St Miami FL 33172 305-526-2893

"G" Supervisor

W M 30 01 01 00 00 00 01

1 S 01 Vick, Michael

B M

See Narrative

Det. Kevin C. Kozak 2268 A6222 01-17-07

Kozak Lageyre 01-17-07

O/P

1 of

NARRATIVE CONTINUATION

MIAMI-DADE POLICE DEPARTMENT

Agency Report Number	PD070117-030397
Page	2

Original Date Reported	Original Primary Offense Description	Victim #1 Name	Original NCIC/UCR Code
01-17-07	Found Property	State of Fl.	

Original Off/Inc Location	Primary Offense Changed To	A - Attempted C - Committed	New Violation Number	New NCIC/UCR Code
MIA "G"				

I was contacted by **Det. Sgt. R. Lageyre** at approx. 0845 hrs. He advised me that a water bottle with a hidden compartment had been found at Concourse "G" screening point and had been taken to the TSA Operations Center at Miami International Airport. He asked that I impound the bottle and initiate an investigation. Upon arrival at the Ops. Center I made contact with TSA screener **M. Salazar** who signed a property receipt for the bottle. The bottle was a 20 oz. "**Aquafina**" water bottle. The bottle's label concealed a seam which separated the top and the bottom of the bottle. Both ends were sealed by clear partitions and what appeared to be silicone sealant. The concealed compartment contained a small amount of dark particulate and a pungent aroma closely associated with Marijuana. The lower half of the bottle was almost completely full of a clear liquid. The top half contained a small amount of clear liquid. When held upright the bottle appeared to be half full of water.

I next made contact with TSA screening Supervisor for Concourse "G". **Mr. Hector Rodriguez** advised me that a B/M "**AirTran**" airlines passenger had been reluctant to turn over his water bottle during the screening process. Subsequently he surrendered the bottle which was placed in the recycle bin by TSA screener **Gertrude Joseph**. The passenger completed his screening through Concourse "G" and was allowed to go to his gate. The passenger's reluctance to relinquish a simple water bottle aroused the suspicions of TSA screener **Gertrude Joseph. Joseph** retrieved the bottle and upon further investigation found the concealed compartment. She notified her supervisor, **Mr. Rodriguez**. The bottle was taken to the TSA Ops center by **M. Salazar**.

I received the written statements from **Joseph** and **Rodriguez** by FAX at approx. 1035 hrs. At approx. 1130 hrs I returned to the "G" Screening point and met with **Joseph**. I asked her specifically how she would have known that the bottle belonged to **Michael Vick**. She advised me that **Mr. Bernard Lee**, another TSA screener had identified the B/M as **Vick**, a Professional football player for the **Atlanta Falcons**. Further, she stated that the "**Aquafina**" bottle was the only item in the recycle bin. I also obtained a written statement from **Mr. Bernard Lee** stating that he had recognized **Vick** as a professional football player. Refer to his written statement for details.

I obtained flight reservation information which indicated that a **Mr. Michael Vick** was a passenger on AirTran flt. 338 to Atlanta, GA.

I later reviewed digital surveillance video of the incident which substantiated the incident as reported by Rodriguez and **Joseph**. The bottle will be transported to **MDPD** lab for analysis.

Officer(s) Reporting	ID Number(s)/Locator Code	Unit	Date
Det. Kevin C. Kozak	2268	A2622	01-17-07

Officer Reviewing (If Applicable)	ID Number	Routed To	Referred To	Assigned To	By	Date
				Kozak	Lageyre	01-17-07

Page 3 of 3

not favor either side. **Neutral witnesses** are witnesses who do not have a relationship with either the defense or the prosecution.

Neutral witness
A witness who has no relationship with either the defense or prosecution.

These differences are important because friendly and hostile witnesses' conscious or unconscious biases may affect their perception of the events on which they are reporting. The attorneys need to keep this distinction in mind as they prepare and present their client's case.

It is best to interview neutral witnesses before speaking to the hostile witnesses. Because if they are not aligned with either side, neutral witnesses have the potential to have a great impact on the jury. As these witnesses do not have a relationship with the parties, the events that they observed will not have a lasting impact. It is, therefore, important to conduct an interview as soon as possible.

To prepare for an interview with a neutral witness, you should gather background information to determine whether the witness is truly neutral or connected to the victim or law enforcement. If possible, try to ascertain how this individual came to be a witness. You should also prepare by orienting yourself to the crime scene and creating an outline or interview checklist.

Application Exercises

8. After reviewing the *People v. Turner* case on pages xxxvii-xxxviii and reading the Incident Report in Exhibit 6.4, prepare a set of interview questions to ask Ms. Haney, based on the assumption that she is a neutral witness.
9. After reviewing the *People v. Cook* case on page xxxvii and reading the Incident Report in Exhibit 6.5, prepare a set of interview questions to ask Officer Terry Atkin, based on the assumption that he will be a hostile witness.

c. *Taking Witness Statements*

When you contact the witness, identify yourself as a paralegal. Disclose your supervising attorney's name and the name of the client. Let the witness know that you would like to ask him or her about the incident and schedule a time and place for the interview. Some witnesses will not want to come to an attorney's office. A public location or the witness's home may be suitable. You should defer to the witness's choice of location.

When you conduct the interview, approach it as if you are questioning a friendly witness by asking open-ended questions. If the witness is hesitant to respond, adapt by asking direct questions (e.g., who, what, where, why, when, and how). If this does not work, ask for particular information through short, one-fact-at-a-time inquiries. At the conclusion of your questioning, prepare a written statement for the witness's signature.

Exhibit 6.4: Incident Report #2 in Turner Case: Case File No. 19-0857

On July 31 at 1:10 P.M. Reporting Agent (RA) interviewed RITA HANEY, W/F, DOB 2/29/52, 909 Beauford, Normal. HANEY is currently employed at the Normal Eatery, 857 Normal St. HANEY was interviewed to determine the last time anyone had been inside the cabinet located under the sink of the bathroom inside the restaurant prior to the arrest of Brandon Turner on July 29.

She provided the following information: she worked the evening of July 28 and cleaned the bathroom after she closed the restaurant at 8:00 P.M. HANEY said there was a full roll of toilet paper on the spindle so she did not open the storage cabinet under the sink to obtain a new roll. According to HANEY, there is no reason for any employee to go into the storage cabinet unless there is a need to replace the toilet paper. HANEY said it would be very unlikely that anyone, employee or customer, would have known the contents of the cabinet interior any time prior to Turner's arrest on July 29.

HANEY saw Turner enter the restaurant and enter the bathroom on July 29. HANEY saw Turner enter the bathroom, shut the door, and exit the bathroom within the few seconds. She thought it was unusual that Turner spent only a few seconds in the bathroom.

HANEY said her fellow employee Sue Williams had observed him enter the bathroom with a gun. Williams later found the gun inside the sink's cabinet interior.

Exhibit 6.5: Cook Case Incident Report #2: Case File No. 19-1857

On Sunday, May 15 at 2159 Reporting Officer (R/O) and Ptm Z. Whitten were dispatched to the scene of a personal injury accident on Route 185 and Normal Street. On arrival, north of the intersection, R/O located a bicycle which had been heavily damaged along the east (northbound curb). Farther north, along the same curb, R/O found a white female lying on her back. The body appeared lifeless. R/O observed her left foot to be near completely severed above the ankle. There was blood pooling on the roadway below the victim's head. Her eyes were open and appeared fixed and she made no response to my oral calls. Municipal Ambulance arrived at the scene within seconds off my assessment and elected to transport her in a "load and go" response.

R/O then began to scour the area, looking for witnesses. None of those present witnessed the accident. It was then determined to be an apparent hit and run. Ptm Whitten began photographing the scene. R/O summoned assistance from state investigators and Detective Colby responded to the scene. While conferring with Det. Colby, R/O learned that the driver of the suspect vehicle had contacted the County Sheriff's office from his residence and acknowledged involvement in the accident. R/O asked the sheriff's office to dispatch a unit to pick up the driver and provide transportation to the police station. Jack's Towing was summoned to retrieve and transport the vehicle to the station for processing.

R/O learned that state accident reconstruction officers were on their way and that the scene was to be secured until their arrival. Detective Colby then responded to the police station for follow-up investigation with the driver of the automobile unit.

R/O then gathered information to complete accident report. Items of evidence were secured by both Ptm Whitten and Detective Colby. Those items include the damaged bicycle remains, two pieces of blocked plastic, fragmented window glass, and broken reflector lens.

After completing the evidence recovery, R/O and reconstruction personnel proceeded to the police station to examine the suspect's vehicle. R/O observed the vehicle's plastic wind/bug deflector to be missing a piece which corresponded with the plastic fragments found at the scene. The unit was photographed by Sergeant Walker of the state police. At approximately 0500 R/O and Det. Colby returned to the scene where we secured hair samples which had been found on the roadway along the victim's action path in addition to cloth fiber samples. Det. Colby recovered the hair while R/O secured the cloth fibers. Items were maintained by Det. Colby.

Prepared by Officer Terry Atkin.

When interviewing articulate clients or witnesses, the interviewer should use broad, open-ended questions with more pointed questions when needed for clarification. For shy clients, the interviewer may need to encourage them to elaborate on their answers. When interviewing overbearing clients, you should gently lead them back to the matter at hand if they go astray. It is especially important to use understandable language, not to talk down to the client, and to elicit information in an objective, dispassionate manner. It is important to find out everything you can about the occurrence, including facts that might be harmful to the client's defense.

Following any contacts with the client or potential witnesses, the paralegal should create a written memorandum that explains the purpose of the meeting, where it took place, and what information was exchanged at the meeting. That memo should then be added to the client's official file in the law office. Traditionally, witnesses are interviewed in person. This allows the interviewer to get a sense of how the witness will appear at trial. This also affords the opportunity to have the witness review and sign a statement prepared by the questioner at the time of the interview. This is the approach typically take by investigating law enforcement officers. Statements may be handwritten or typed. Examples of typed and handwritten witness statements about the hunting accident involving former Vice President Dick Cheney appear in Exhibits 6.6 and 6.7.

Statements also can be recorded electronically. Recorded statements are the most persuasive means of presenting a prior inconsistent statement in court. There are several methods of recording statements. Audio recordings can be made of in-person and telephone interviews, and video recordings can also be made of in-person and Internet interviews.

If you use either of these methods, you need to elicit the witness's consent at the outset of the interview. At the beginning of the recording, introduce

Exhibit 6.6: Handwritten Witness Statement

In February 2006, U.S. Vice President Dick Cheney accidentally shot Harry Whittington, a 78-year-old Texas attorney, while quail hunting on a Texas ranch. The Kenedy County Sheriff's deputies secured several witness statements during the investigation. The statement of Gerado Medellin, a member of the hunting party, follows.

My name is Gerardo Medellin and I live on the Armstrong Ranch, Armstrong TX. My mailing address is P.O. Box 395 Armstrong TX 78338 and I am 45 years of age.

On Saturday February 11, 2006 at approximately 5:30 or 5:45 the dog handlers dog found a covey facing west. We flushed the covey and everyone shot and Mr. Whittington had a double. After that I worked the lab dog to find one of the birds of the double ~~shot~~ GM Mr. Whittington assisted me in finding the first bird. After finding the fist bird, Mr. Whittington asked me if I saw where the second bird had fallen. I told him yes and went to find it. As I was looking for the second bird Mr. Whittington went back to the hunting jeep. It took me approximately 5 minutes to locate the second bird. At that time, I saw Mr. Whittington walking towards the other hunters I yelled to him that I had found his other bird.

Shortly after that the outrider (Oscar) pointing where the other covey was at. At this time I was walking towards them also, to join them.

When I was walking towards the hunters a single bird flew behind the Vice President towards Mr. Whittington. That is when Vice President shot towards the bird and Mr. Whittington was in the line of fire.

[illegible]

Exhibit 6.7 Typewritten Witness Statement

The owner of the ranch where the Cheney accidental shooting incident occurred signed a written statement for the Kenedy County Sheriff's Office.

I, Katharine Armstrong, am one of the owners of the Armstrong Ranch in Kenedy County, Texas and was present and an eye witness to the hunting accident that occurred on Feb. 12th, at approximately 5:30pm in the Comal pasture of the Armstrong Ranch. Although it was late in the afternoon and the sun was low, there was plenty of sunlight. All three shooters were wearing blaze orange gear and to the best of my knowledge there was no alcohol involved.

After being alerted by an outrider our hunting vehicle pulled up to the location where a covey of quail had been found. When the Vice President, Harry Whittington and Pam Willeford got out of the vehicle to work the covey they were told that there was a second covey ahead and to the left. They moved forward on the first covey and Mr. Whittington shot two birds that fell to his right in some tall grass and brush. Mr. Whittington, with the assistance of Gerry Medellin and a Labrador went to the spot where the birds and fallen to find them. The two men and the dog had difficulty finding one of the birds and spent several minutes attempting to find it in the tall grass. While Mr. Whittington stayed behind to look for his bird, the Vice President and Ambassador Willeford moved towards the second covey that was located further ahead and to the left of the first covey. In the meantime, Mr. Whittington returned briefly to the car then went back to look again for his lost bird. A short time later I noticed that Harry was moving forward to rejoin the Vice President and Ambassador Willeford. As he was moving forward I did not hear him announce himself or call to them to let them know he was approaching from behind and to their right. A single bird flushed in front of the Vice President and Ambassador Willeford. TheVice President swung through to his right and shot at the bird. Mr. Whittington fell to the ground about 30 yards away from the Vice President with his head facing towards the hunting vehicle. I saw the Vice President rush towards Mr. Whittington and almost in the same instant the Vice President's security detail was rushing to his side as well. My sister, Sarita Hixon, Ambassador Willeford and I remained out of the way a short distance from Mr. Whittington until the ambulance arrived about 20 to 25 minutes later.

Katharine Armstrong   Feb. 15, 2006

yourself and the name of your employer. Then identify the witness by name and ask the witness to acknowledge that the interview is being recorded with his or her consent. You should identify others who are present, as well as the date and time. You should follow the same protocol at the close of the interview. During the questioning, be careful not to interrupt the witness's answers.

Another way of recording a witness's statement is through the use of a court reporter. You either should elicit the witness's consent on the record or have the witness sworn by the court reporter at the outset.

d. Cell Phone Evidence

When interviewing a client or witness, ask them if there is anything on their cell phone to support their testimony. The most obvious data are photographs or videos. It is not unusual for people to use their phones to take pictures and film events that are out of the ordinary. For instance, Darnella Frazier, a teenage bystander, recorded the George Floyd murder by a police officer in Minneapolis on her cell phone.[15]

For a photograph or video to be admissible in a court, it must be authenticated. Thus, if the person you interview was not present when the video or photo were made, you need to learn who was there so you can verify its legitimacy. Also, other information that can corroborate a statement, such as Google Maps, text messages, and e-mails, can be useful. If the defendant is raising the alibi defense, it is incumbent upon the defense to provide corroboration of their story that they were somewhere other than the scene of the crime.

e. *Witness Interview Summary*

After you interview a witness, you should prepare a witness summary. This is a stand-alone document separate from the signed witness statement. The attitudes and background of a witness are almost as important as the statement itself. Therefore, your witness interview summary should evaluate the witness from the standpoints of accuracy, truthfulness, and personal appeal. One style of witness summary contains the following components:

- Preliminary information, including the name of the witness, date of the interview, file name, and number
- Background and personal information
- Factual information in chronological or topical order
- Evaluation of the witness's demeanor and credibility, along with the specific reasons for your conclusions
- List of documents signed by the witness.
- List of documents produced by the witness, along with the location of the originals.
- Conclusions and recommendations for next steps.[16]

3. DEFENSE PREPARATION FOR INITIAL COURT APPEARANCES

a. *Bail and Detention Hearings*

As mentioned in Chapter 5, in determining whether a person accused of a crime should be released on bond, the judge will consider factors such as the defendant's prior record, ties to the community, prior failures to appear in court, and employment. If the judge finds the defendant to be a danger to the community or a flight risk, the defendant will remain in jail. To prepare for these hearings, the defense attorney needs to be able to present information about the client's family, employment, financial circumstances, and background. Paralegals are frequently checking and documenting these facts. They

---

[15]Frazier was awarded a Pulitzer Prize Special Citation in 2021. This was a rare instance of the board acknowledging the journalistic achievement of a non-professional.

[16]S. Parsons, *Interviewing and Investigating, Essential Skills for the Paralegal* (3d ed., Wolters Kluwer 2008), 322.

also help identify property that could be used to secure a bond. If witnesses are needed at the hearing, the paralegal may be assigned to help prepare them.

APPLICATION EXERCISE

10. Draft a client questionnaire to gather bond hearing information. The initial questions should elicit the defendant's contact information.

A growing number of jurisdictions are using pretrial risk assessment tools to lower pretrial jailing and decrease the use of monetary bail. It is estimated that 25 percent of people in the United States live in a jurisdiction that requires pretrial assessment for bail determinations.[17] Hence, defense attorneys and their staffs need to research and document the historical information necessary for the client's assessment, including the following:

- Client's birth date
- Current employment
- Current student in the community
- Past and current alcohol or drug problems
- Prior arrests (including dates and charges)
- Prior failures to appear in court (including dates and charges)
- Charges pending (at the time of the current arrest)
- Active warrants (at the time of the current arrest)
- Having a home (owners, lease, or other)
- Contributing to residential expenses
- Past or current mental health treatment
- Past jail sentences (including dates and charges)
- Past prison sentences (including dates and charges)
- Currently on probation, supervision, or parole
- History of revoked or suspended bonds (including dates and charges)[18]

You should check with your supervising attorney to find out whether your jurisdiction using a pretrial risk assessment. If it does, familiarize yourself with the criteria used in making the assessment before you prepare for a client's bond hearing.

b. Preparation for Arraignment

To prepare for the arraignment, the defense attorney will draft an appearance. This is a document filed in court identifying the attorney representing

[17]Brandon Buskey and Andrea Woods, "Making Sense of Pretrial Risk Assessments," *The Champion* (June 2018), 18, https://www.nacdl.org/Article/June2018-MakingSenseofPretrialRiskAsses

[18]Victoria A. Terranova and Kyle C. Ward, *Colorado Pretrial Assessment Tool Validity Study Final Report* (2020), 12 and 13, https://www.nacdl.org/getattachment/18510570-e0eb-4d40-b737-5aafb30c1085/terranovaward_cpat-validation-study_final-report.pdf.

Exhibit 6.8: Defense Counsel's Appearance

THE UNITED STATES DISTRICT COURT FOR THE NORTHERN DISTRICT OF INDIANA
HAMMOND DIVISION

UNITED STATES OF AMERICA	)	
vs.	)	Case No. 20 CR XXX
WILLIAM EDWARDS,	)	
Defendant.	)	

APPEARANCE

The undersigned hereby enters his appearance on behalf of the Defendant, WILLIAM EDWARDS.

Respectfully submitted,
WILLIAM EDWARDS,

Defendant

By ______________________

CHARLES HOVEY, his attorney

Charles Hovey
Attorney for Defendant
1857 Bone Street
Normal, IL 61617
(309) 555-1857

a party in the case. The appearance also identifies the attorney's address and telephone number. In some jurisdictions, an attorney identification number is also included. Exhibit 6.8 depicts an appearance. Some judges require pro se defendants to file an appearance. The original of the appearance is filed with the clerk of the court and a copy is provided to the prosecutor.

Note on Drafting Court Documents

In Chapter 5, we discussed the format of charging documents filed by the prosecution. Just as paralegals working in the prosecutor's office frequently participate in the preparation of these documents, so, too, paralegals working for defense attorneys may also be involved. Both sides use the same general format

Exhibit 6.9: Body of Jury Demand

Now comes the Defendant BUD COOK, by CHARLES HOVEY, his attorney, and demands trial by jury.

Exhibit 6.10: Body of Jury Waiver

I, Defendant BUD COOK, hereby waive a jury trial in the above-entitled cause and consent to trial before the court.

of caption, introductory paragraph, body, signature, and address block with information about who prepared it.

In addition to the appearance, the defense also may file a jury demand or jury waiver, a demand for a speedy trial, and a discovery motion. Under the Sixth Amendment, a criminal defendant has a right to be tried by a jury. In some courts, defendants will be tried by a jury unless there is a waiver by both sides. In other jurisdictions, the defendant must expressly demand trial by jury. The body of a sample jury demand is presented in Exhibit 6.9. In jurisdictions in which the defendant must demand a jury, the defendant can waive this right as well. The waiver must be made in writing. An example of the body of a jury waiver is set forth in Exhibit 6.10.

In some states, the defendant may file a demand for a speedy trial at the time of arraignment. The Sixth Amendment and virtually all state constitutions grant defendants the right to a speedy trial. The United States and many states also have adopted statutes specifically granting protections beyond the constitutional guarantees. For instance, the Illinois Speedy Trial Act provides that the trial for defendants not in custody must be commenced within 160 days, provided that they make "a clear and unequivocal" demand for a speedy trial.[19] Thus, a defense attorney files a speedy trial demand to start the clock running. A sample demand for speedy trial is presented in Exhibit 6.11.

In jurisdictions in which the parties must ask the court to order discovery, the defendant may file at arraignment a motion for leave to conduct discovery. Discovery will be discussed in detail in Chapter 8.

[19] 725 ILCS 5/103-5(b).

Exhibit 6.11: Demand for Speedy Trial

IN THE CIRCUIT COURT OF
THE 12th JUDICIAL CIRCUIT
WILL COUNTY, ILLINOIS

PEOPLE OF THE	)	
STATE OF ILLINOIS	)	
v.	)	Case No. 20 CF XXXX
BRANDON TURNER,	)	
Defendant.	)	

DEMAND FOR SPEEDY TRIAL

The undersigned, as attorney for the Defendant, BRANDON TURNER, pursuant to Section 103-5(b) of the Code of Criminal Procedure, 725 ILCS 5/103-5(b), hereby demands a speedy trial.

Respectfully submitted,

____
CHARLES HOVEY,
Attorney for Defendant

CHARLES HOVEY
Attorney for Defendant
1857 Bone Street
Normal, IL 61761
(309)-555-1857

Application Exercises

11. Draft an appearance for defense counsel using the following information:
- Court: State the court for the community in which your school is located
- Defendant: Name yourself as the defendant for the purposes of this exercise
- Case number: The fiftieth misdemeanor case of this year
- Defense attorney: The public defender for your community

To complete the form, you may need to contact the clerk's office or research the court's website for the name, address, and telephone number of the public defender's office.

12. Using the federal form located online at https://www.uscourts.gov/sites/default/files/ao458.pdf and the following information, prepare an appearance for the defendant in the Edwards case (p. xxxviii):
    - Defense attorney: Judith R. Manchester
    - Defense attorney's address and phone number: Your school's address and main telephone number; defense attorney's fax number (same as the office number)
    - Defense attorney's bar number: 1234
    - Venue: U.S. district and division for the community in which your school is located

13. Draft a jury demand using the following information:
    - Court: State the court for the community in which your school is located
    - Defendant: Brandon Turner
    - Case number: Leave blank
    - Defense attorney: Charles Hovey, 1857 Bone Street, Normal, IL 61761, (309)-555-1857

SUMMARY

This chapter examined the constitutional right to counsel, its source, what it entails, and the ethical duties associated with it.

Attorneys defending persons accused of committing crimes may be in private practice, employed in government service as public defenders, or paid by the government as appointed counsel. Private attorneys are paid on an hourly basis, by a flat fee, or by a combination of these two methods.

When the client initially meets with the defense attorney, the client is instructed to refrain from discussing the case with anyone, especially law enforcement officers. Information disclosed to the attorney by the client is protected by the attorney-client privilege and the duty to maintain confidentiality. Before the case is accepted by the attorney, a conflicts check is run to make sure that the representation does not violate the interests of another client.

Paralegals may assist defense attorneys by interviewing fact witnesses. Witnesses' accounts should be memorialized by preparing statements for them to sign or making audio or audio/video recordings of their statements.

They typically are also involved in the preparation of various documents that need to be filed with the court. These documents include: the appearance, jury demand, jury waiver, demand for speedy trial, and discovery motions. In addition to knowing what they contain, paralegals should be able to prepare drafts for attorneys to review.

INTERNET RESOURCES

Criminal Defense Attorneys

- National Association of Criminal Defense Lawyers: **https://www.nacdl.org/**
- American Bar Association (ABA)'s Criminal Justice Standards for the Defense Function: **https://www.americanbar.org/groups/criminal_justice/standards/DefenseFunctionFourth Edition/**

Legal Ethics

- Model Rules of Professional Conduct: **https://www.abanet.org/cpr/mrpc/mrpc_toc.html**

REVIEW QUESTIONS

1. When does the right to counsel apply, and what does it entail?
2. What systems are in place for providing indigent defendants with access to attorneys? What determines which system is used?
3. Under what circumstances can an attorney refuse to take on a potential client?
4. What is the reason that defense attorneys instruct their clients not to give statements to the police?
5. What are appropriate locations for a client interview? Why is a public place inappropriate?
6. When is an attorney permitted to reveal confidential client information?
7. How does attorney-client privilege differ from the duty of confidentiality?
8. How can you demonstrate professionalism when you carry out a client interview?
9. What is a conflict of interest? What can you do to avoid your own conflicts of interest?
10. List and explain the major fee models used by private criminal defense attorneys.
11. What is the difference between a fact witness and an expert witness?
12. What steps should you follow when interviewing a hostile witness?
13. What information must be gathered to prepare for a bond hearing?
14. What types of documents do criminal defense attorneys prepare for the defendant's arraignment?

Chapter 7

Legal Defenses

Chapter Objectives

After reading this chapter, you should be able to:

- Identify and explain the differences among the categories of legal defenses that are available to people who have been accused of crimes.
- Explain status defenses and discuss the controversies surrounding their use.
- Compare and contrast *actus reus* and *mens rea*.
- Identify the types of reactive defenses and discuss the types of situations where they apply.
- Discuss the justification for the insanity defense, how it differs from one state to another, and its relationship to a defendant's competence to stand trial.
- Explain how a reactive defense relates to police shootings.
- Identify and discuss the provisions of the U.S. Constitution that are most often invoked by defense attorneys.

Introduction

Legal defense
A set of facts or legal arguments that, if accepted by the court, relieves a person of criminal liability for having committed an act that is defined as a crime.

At the arraignment, the prosecution presents a document that specifies the formal legal charges being brought, and the defendant enters an initial plea of either guilty or not guilty to these charges. At this point in the process, the defendant will almost always plead not guilty.

Based on what these formal charges are, defense attorneys will focus on collecting the information they will need to determine which potential **legal defenses** they might raise on behalf of their clients. The initial client interview and the discovery process, discussed in Chapter 8, provide some indications of which defenses might apply to the client's situation.

Defense attorneys need to have a pretty good idea of what actually happened, why it happened, the specific charges being filed, and the nature of the evidence the prosecutor can present at trial before evaluating which legal defenses might be appropriate to present in the client's case. In analyzing some of the examples used in this chapter, you may find it useful to go back and review the discussions of various offenses in Chapter 3.

A. Denial of the Facts or Elements

A common defense is to deny the acts the prosecution claims the defendant carried out. For example, the defendant may dispute he fired the gun that killed the victim or may deny that the illegal drugs found in her car were hers.

1. ALIBI DEFENSE

Alibi defense
A defense requiring proof that the defendant could not have been at the scene of the crime.

An **alibi defense** is a type of denial defense in which is the defense claims that the defendant could not have committed the crime because the accused was not at the location of the crime when it was committed. For example, a man charged with robbery might claim that he was playing poker at a friend's home at the time the robbery was taking place on the other side of town.

Although it seems obvious that defendants could not have committed a crime in one location while they were doing something else in a different part of town, or even in a different state, it is often difficult to prove the alibi defense is valid. Most judges and juries will not give any weight to a defendant's claim that he was home sleeping or at a movie if there are no eyewitnesses to back up the alibi. Even when there are alibi witnesses, they are frequently friends or family of the accused—people who may appear to have a motive to lie.

Because the term *alibi* has such a negative connotation, defense attorneys do not use it when they are before the jury, and sometimes present motions *in limine* to bar the use of this term at the trial. (We will discuss motions *in limine* in Chapter 11.)

Perhaps one of the most well-known successful uses of the alibi defense can be found in the criminal prosecution of O. J. Simpson for the murder of his wife, Nicole, and her friend Ronald Goldman. At his trial, defense attorney Johnnie Cochran claimed that Simpson never left his house on the evening of the killings and he was alone in the house packing to fly to Chicago. Cochran also maintained that Simpson went outside to hit some golf balls in his yard. The jury acquitted Simpson of the murder charges.

Another example of a high-profile defendant successfully using an alibi defense involved the prosecution of actor Robert Blake for fatally shooting his wife, Bonnie Lee Bakley, outside a restaurant where they had just eaten dinner. Blake's attorneys claimed that he left his wife at the car when he went back to the restaurant to get a handgun that he had forgotten in the booth where they ate and she was shot while he was gone. Blake was found not guilty of Bakley's murder and of one of two counts of solicitation of murder. A third count was dropped after it was revealed that the jury was deadlocked 11–1 in favor of acquittal.

In federal court, the defense must disclose its intent to raise an alibi defense and must identify all alibi witnesses during the discovery phase of a criminal prosecution. Rule 12.1(a) requires the defendant to give notice of intent to assert the alibi defense within 14 days of the prosecutor's demand. The defense must name the specific place where the defendant claims to have been when the crime was allegedly committed, along with the names, addresses, and telephone numbers of the alibi witnesses. On request, the defendant must also furnish the government with their alibi witnesses' written statements after their direct examination at trial.[1]

Once the defendant has served notice on the prosecution, the prosecutor is obligated to furnish the defense with the names, addresses, and telephone numbers of the witnesses who can establish the accused's presence at the scene of the crime in addition to information about other witnesses it intends to call to rebut the alibi witnesses' testimony.[2] The defendant does not need to request the information. Instead, 12.1(b)(1) requires the government to disclose its alibi witness information within 14 days of service of the notice of intent to raise the alibi defense.

If either side fails to provide alibi information within their respective 14-day time limits, the court may exclude the testimony of undisclosed witnesses.[3] However, courts have discretion to impose less drastic remedies, such as continuing the case so that the surprised party can contact the newly disclosed witnesses and otherwise prepare for their testimony.

More than 40 states mandate that the defense give advance notice of the defendant's intent to raise the alibi defense.[4] Most alibi provisions are similar to the federal requirements found in Rule 12.1.[5] You should check the requirements of your state for the procedures for requesting and disclosing alibi information.

Interviewing Alibi Witnesses

If you, as a paralegal, are involved in interviewing alibi witnesses, it is particularly important to pay close attention to details of their stories and to elicit information that can be compared with the defendant's story. For instance, if the accused maintains that he was at a movie, have the witness give a detailed account of everything that took place in the defendant's presence before and after the show. Also have witnesses relate the plot of the movie, actors' names, previews shown, the time the movie ended, and other key information. If they have any written documents, such as ticket stubs or charge card receipts, request that they produce them for you.

---

[1]FRCrP 12.1(a)(2)(B).

[2]FRCrP 12.1(b)(1).

[3]FRCrP 12.1(e).

[4]W. LaFave, J. Isreal & N. King, *Criminal Procedure* 953 (4th ed., Thomson West 2004).

[5]*Id.*

2. ADMITTING SOME, BUT NOT ALL, OF THE ELEMENTS

Sometimes the accused will admit some of the elements of the charge but deny others. The hypothetical cases in this textbook illustrate how the denial of certain elements of the charges can be an effective defense. In Hypothetical Case 1, Bud Cook could admit to driving his pickup truck but deny that the element that he caused the death of another person. If the bicyclist caused his own death by riding in a reckless manner, Bud would not be criminally responsible for his death. Note, however, this admission might make it easier for the state to convict him of driving under the influence (DUI). In Hypothetical Case 2, Brandon Turner can admit that he drove a car that contained a weapon and illegal drugs but claim that the drugs and the gun were not his. If a jury accepted this defense, he would be acquitted. If Officer Smith (in Hypothetical 5) claimed that Mendoza yelled profanities and threatened to hurt the officer, the prosecution would have to refute Smith's claims.

A defendant charged with crimes connected to the storming of the U.S. Capitol on January 6, 2021, successfully took this approach. The U.S. Attorney charged Matthew Martin with (1) entering and remaining in a restricted building, (2) disorderly and disruptive conduct in a restricted building, (3) violent entry and disorderly conduct in the Capitol building, and (4) parading, demonstrating or picketing in the Capitol building. Martin denied that he engaged in criminal activity and testified in his own defense. In a bench trial, the U.S. District judge acquitted him of all four charges. The evidence included a video showing two police officers standing near the rotunda doors and allowing people to enter as Martin approached. One officer appeared to lean back before Martin placed a hand on the officer's shoulder as a possible sign of gratitude. The judge said that it was not unreasonable for the defendant to believe that the officers were allowing him to enter the Capitol, even though alarms were blaring and broken glass was strewn about the floor. The judge found Martin's testimony to be credible.

At one time, this was a common approach taken by the defense in sexual assault cases. Defendants would acknowledge the conduct while claiming that there was consent. This scenario requires the jury to decide whether to believe the accused or the alleged victim. If it wasn't clear whose testimony was most believable, the jury would find the defendant not guilty because the prosecution did not prove its case beyond a reasonable doubt. In recent times, it appears this has changed. For instance, in 2020, a jury found the former movie mogul Harvey Weinstein guilty of rape and another criminal sexual act. Weinstein did not deny his actions but claimed that his encounters were consensual.

Sometimes an alleged sexual assault victim remains silent, even though she does not want to engage in sex. The alleged perpetrator may view the victim's silence as an acknowledgment of consent. To eliminate this ambiguous situation that is to the detriment of the victim, the #MeToo movement has advocated for reforming the law to establish "affirmative consent." This means that the victim willingly and expressly states consent to participate in sexual activity. Before this reform gained traction, Illinois included the following definition in its criminal code:

720 ILCS 5/11-0.1. Definitions

"Consent" means a freely given agreement to the act of sexual penetration or sexual conduct in question. Lack of verbal or physical resistance or submission by the victim resulting from the use of force or threat of force by

> the accused shall not constitute consent. The manner of dress of the victim at the time of the offense shall not constitute consent.[6]

A few states now require public colleges and universities to adopt "affirmative consent" in their codes of conduct but have not incorporated this definition into their criminal codes. Compare Colorado's definition of "consent" required for higher learning institutions with the definition in its criminal code:

C.R.S.A. § 22-1-128. Comprehensive human sexuality education—legislative declaration—definitions—guidelines and content standards.

> (2) (b.5) "Consent" means the affirmative, unambiguous, voluntary continuous, knowing agreement between all participants in each physical act within the course of a sexual encounter or interpersonal relationship."

C.R.S.A. § 18-3-401. Definitions

> As used in this part 4 [of the Criminal Code], unless the context otherwise requires: . . . (1.5) "Consent" means cooperation in act or attitude pursuant to an exercise of free will and with knowledge of the nature of the act. A current or previous relationship shall not be sufficient to constitute consent under the provisions of this part 4. Submission under the influence of fear shall not constitute consent.

APPLICATION EXERCISES

Review the facts of the Clay Marshall Case (*see* hypothetical case on pages xxxviii-xxxix). A grand jury has indicted Marshal on two counts of criminal sexual abuse, alleging that his actions towards his two employees amounted to the commission of acts of "sexual conduct by the use of force or threat of force."

1. If the incident took place in the state of Colorado:
   a. How can defense counsel show that Randy Jefferson consented to Clay Marshall's sexual advances?
   b. What argument could the prosecution make to claim that Randy Jefferson did not consent to Clay Marshall's sexual advances?
2. If the incident took place in the state of Illinois:
   a. How can defense counsel show that Randy Jefferson consented to Clay Marshall's sexual advances?
   b. What argument could the prosecution make to claim that Randy Jefferson did not consent to Clay Marshall's sexual advances?
3. What can the defense attorney do to discredit the accusers?
4. How can the prosecution prepare the two accusers so that their testimony seems believable?

---

[6]Illinois also revised its definition of "unable to give knowing consent" to include "when the victim has taken an intoxicating substance or any controlled substance causing the victim to become unconscious of the nature of the act, and this condition was known or reasonably should have been known by the accused, but the accused did not provide or administer the intoxicating substance." 720 ILSC 5/11-01.

Similarly, some defense attorneys representing police officers have had success in explaining why the facts presented by the prosecution do not amount to the commission of a crime.

During the execution of the no-knock warrant that resulted in the death of Breonna Taylor (see pp. 114-115), the former Louisville police officer Brett Hankison was charged with three counts of wanton endangerment for having fired bullets that entered a neighboring apartment. Prosecutors argued that Hankison shot blindly into a window from outside the apartment in a direction perpendicular to where the shot originated. The officer testified that he was unaware of the presence of another unit directly behind Taylor's apartment, and the jury returned a not guilty verdict.

In another case, a police officer in Duluth, Minnesota, Tyler Leibfried, was charged with second-degree assault and intentional discharge of a firearm that endangered the public. The defendant testified that he was responding to a call about a domestic disturbance when he fired his service revolver through the closed door of an apartment. Officer Leibfried testified that he was responding to a call about a domestic argument, and when he heard a pounding sound coming from inside the apartment, he fired six bullets into the door. Even though a search of the apartment revealed no evidence of either a firearm or ammunition, the jury acquitted Leibfried of all the charges.

Application Exercises

Review the facts of *People v. Smith* (*see* hypothetical case on page xxxix). A grand jury has indicted Officer John Smith on charges of misdemeanor assault and battery charges for using the taser on Javier Mendoza 11 times. Smith's body camera shows Mendoza's refusal to exit the car, as well as Smith shocking him with the taser. Assume that this occurred in a community which is experiencing a high rate of crime.

5. What approach can the defense attorney take to demonstrate that Officer Smith did not commit a crime?
6. How can the prosecution convince jurors who are concerned about the local crime rate that the officer should be found guilty?

B. Ignorance or Mistake

Although it is generally true that "ignorance of the law is no excuse," there are a limited number of circumstances in which ignorance or a mistaken understanding of the facts can be used as a legal defense. The Model Penal Code places the following conditions on the use of the defense of ignorance or mistake:

Section 2.04 Ignorance or Mistake

(1) Ignorance or mistake as to the matter of fact or law is a defense if:

(a) the ignorance or mistake negatives the purpose, knowledge, belief, recklessness or negligence required to establish a material element of the offense. . . .

(3) A belief that conduct does not legally constitute an offense is a defense to a prosecution for that offense based upon such conduct when:

(a) the statute or other enactment defining the offense is not known to the actor and has not been published or otherwise reasonably made available prior to the conduct alleged; or

(b) he acts in reasonable reliance upon an official statement of the law, afterward determined to be invalid or erroneous. . . .

When presenting this defense, it must be shown that the defendant's ignorance or mistake negated the *mens rea* element of the crime. You will recall from our discussion in Chapter 2 that *mens rea* means "guilty mind" and refers to the fact that crimes require different degrees of "criminal intent." Therefore, whereas homicide requires a mental state of purposely or knowingly causing someone's death, manslaughter requires only that the death result from a reckless or negligent action.

Now, take a couple of minutes to review the Model Penal Code's definition of the crime of criminal trespass as it is stated on page 60 in Chapter 3. Note that it requires proof that the accused entered or occupied someone else's property "knowing" that he was not authorized to do so. Therefore, if a defendant entered your neighbor's house because you had asked him to let your dog out over the lunch hour and he mistook the neighbor's house for your house, he would not be guilty of criminal trespass because he mistakenly thought that he was authorized to enter the property.

At first blush, it would appear that "mistake of age" would fit the conditions necessary to show a mistake of fact. However, this is not so in many jurisdictions. For instance, states differ as to whether mistake of age is a defense to the illegal sale of alcoholic beverages to minors.[7] Likewise, there is a similar divide as to cases involving sexual relations with minors. Indeed, California permits a defendant to assert mistake of age in statutory rape cases, whereas Maryland views this offense as a strict liability crime and thus rejects the defense.[8] Most states do not allow the mistake of age defense to statutory rape.

---

[7]Compare *City of West Allis v. Megna*, 26 Wis. 2d 545 (1965) (finding a bar's good-faith defense irrelevant because providing alcohol to minors is a strict liability crime) with *State v. Niesen*, 415 N.W.2d 326 (Minn. 1987) (holding that the bartender did not commit a crime because he acted in good faith by asking a nineteen-year-old woman for identification before serving her).

[8]Compare *People v. Hernandez*, 61 Cal. 2d 529 (1964) with *Garnett v. Maryland*, 332 Md. 571 (Md. 1993).

APPLICATION EXERCISES

7. Based on the wording of the Model Penal Code, evaluate the extent to which an ignorance of the law/mistake defense might be used successfully in defending Brandon Turner (*see* hypothetical case on pages xxxii-xxxviii) against charges that he was in unlawful possession of drugs.
8. Based on the wording of the Model Penal Code, evaluate the extent to which an ignorance of the law/mistake defense might be used successfully in defending Bill Edwards (*see* hypothetical case on page xxxviii) against charges that he committed fraud.
9. Based on the wording of the Model Penal Code, evaluate the extent to which an ignorance of the law/mistake defense might be used successfully in defending Clay Marshall (*see* hypothetical case on pages xxxviii-xxxix) against charges that he committed fraud.

C. Status of Defendant

The status defenses involve excusing people from the criminal consequences of their actions because their status or condition renders them incapable of formulating the required element of *mens rea*.[9] The status defenses include being too young to form criminal intent, being legally insane, and being intoxicated.

1. INFANCY

Under the common law, children under the age of 7 were conclusively presumed to be incapable of forming criminal intent, and there was a rebuttable presumption that those between the ages of 7 and 14 were not capable of forming such intent. The juvenile court system was created to provide a non-criminal alternative for processing juveniles who are accused of acts that are considered crimes if they had been committed by adults. In recent years, however, especially with the increase in violent, gang-related crimes, there has been a movement to waive juvenile court jurisdiction and apply adult standards to the criminal prosecution of these juvenile offenders. All states have laws that either allow or require juvenile offenders to be prosecuted for more serious offenses regardless of their age.[10]

---

[9] See the discussion of *mens rea* in Chapter 2, on pp. 28-29.

[10] Juvenile Age of Jurisdiction and Transfer to Adult Court Laws, National Conference of State Legislatures, 1/11/19 located at http://www.ncsl.org/research/civil-and-criminal-justice/juvenile-age-of-jurisdic-tion-and-transfer-to-adult-court-laws.aspx (accessed May 15, 2022).

2. INSANITY

Insanity defense
A defense that relieves people who are legally insane from criminal responsibility for their actions.

Although the **insanity defense** has gotten a lot of publicity over the years, it is hard to prove and rarely used. Studies have shown that defendants allege insanity in less than 1 percent of all criminal cases, and of these cases, less than half involve murder charges. When the insanity defense is raised, it proves to be successful in only 1 out of 4 cases. So, out of every 1,000 criminal cases, the insanity defense is raised in approximately 9 and is successful in 2.[11] Further, in a majority of the cases in which insanity was raised and used successfully, it was as the result of an agreement between the prosecution and the defense.

Like the infancy defense, the insanity defense is also based on the assertion that the defendant was incapable of formulating the required element of *mens rea*. Furthermore, many people believe that it is not appropriate to punish someone for actions over which the individual had no control, and insane individuals have no control over their actions. Although the rationale for the insanity defense is relatively clear, the operational standards are not. To begin with, we have to emphasize that "insanity" is a legal term rather than a psychiatric term. Having a mental disorder is not the same as being legally insane.

Over the years, the federal and state courts have developed different tests for determining whether a person was legally insane at the time the crime was committed. The three most common standards are the M'Naghten test, the irresistible impulse test, and the Model Penal Code Substantial Capacity test. These tests are summarized in Figure 7.1.

M'Naghten or "Right from Wrong" Test

"[T]o establish insanity sufficient to relieve the defendant of guilt, it must be proved that, at the time of the commission of the act, the defendant was laboring under such a defect of reason, from disease of the mind as not to know the nature and quality of the act he was doing, or if he did know it, that he did not know that what he was doing was wrong." *M'Naghten's Case,* 8 Eng. Rep. 718, 722 (1843).

Irresistible Impulse Test

One is not guilty by reason of insanity if it is determined that the defendant has a mental disease that kept the defendant from controlling his or her conduct.

Substantial Capacity Test (Model Penal Code)

(1) A person is not responsible for criminal conduct if at the time of such conduct, as a result of mental disease or defect, he or she lacks substantial capacity to appreciate the criminality (wrongfulness) of his or her conduct or to conform that conduct to the requirements of law.

(2) The terms *mental disease* and *mental defect* do not include an abnormality manifested only by repeated criminal or otherwise antisocial conduct.

Figure 7.1 Major Insanity Tests

[11]For a full discussion of this issue, *see* G.H. Morris, *Placed in Purgatory: Conditional Release of Insanity Acquittees*, 39 Ariz. L. Rev. 1061 (1997).

M'Naghten test
A test that provides that the defendant is not guilty due to insanity if, at the time of the killing, the defendant suffered from a defect or disease of the mind and could not understand whether the act was right or wrong.

Irresistible impulse test
A test that provides that the defendant is not guilty due to insanity if, at the time of the killing, the defendant could not control his or her actions.

Substantial capacity test
Part of the Model Penal Code, a test that provides that the defendant is not guilty due to insanity if, at the time of the killing, the defendant lacked either the ability to understand the act was wrong or the ability to control the behavior.

The oldest of the standards, the **M'Naghten test**, originated in the 1840s, in an English case where Daniel M'Naghten was tried for killing the secretary to the prime minister of England. M'Naghten mistook the secretary for the prime minister, whom M'Naghten thought to be engaged in a plot to kill him. The court found M'Naghten not guilty due to insanity because, at the time of the killing, he suffered from a defect or disease of the mind and could not understand whether the act was right or wrong. This test, or standard, is commonly known as either the "M'Naghten test" (sometimes also spelled "McNaughten," "M'Naughten," or "M'Naughton") or the "right from wrong" test.

Under this test, a defendant is not considered guilty of the crime if, at the time of committing the *actus reus*,[12] the defendant was suffering from a defect or disease of the mind and could not understand whether the act was right or wrong. However, the court did not define what constituted a disease or defect of the mind. Under the M'Naghten test, defendants will be found sane if they knew that a certain action was wrong but could not stop taking that action. Therefore, some jurisdictions use both the M'Naghten standard and a variation of what is commonly known as the **irresistible impulse test**. With this test, the focus is on the defendant's ability to control his or her own actions. If a mental disease robs the individual of control over his or her conduct, the person is not guilty by reason of insanity.

The drafters of the Model Penal Code of the American Law Institute (ALI) developed a third test, which combines elements of the other two. This ALI test is known as the **substantial capacity test**. It requires that the defendant "appreciate," rather than "know," the wrongfulness of his or her actions. Under the two options provided in this test, defendants can lack either the ability to understand their acts were wrong or the ability to control their behavior.

The 1982 trial of John Hinckley, Jr., for his attempted assassination of then President Ronald Reagan is one of the most highly publicized cases dealing with an insanity plea. The defense presented three psychiatrists who diagnosed Hinckley as psychotic—and legally insane—at the time of the shooting. They told of his obsession with the actress Jodie Foster and the wild plans[13] he thought up for getting her attention. One of Hinckley's letters to Foster is shown in Exhibit 7.1. Although he was under the care of a psychiatrist, his mental health continued to deteriorate. After being told he could not return home to live with his wealthy parents, Hinckley flew to Washington, D.C., and wrote a letter to Foster a few hours before his failed assassination attempt.

As in most insanity defense cases, the prosecution found other psychiatrists who testified that although he was psychologically disturbed, Hinckley was legally sane because, at the time of the shooting, he appreciated the wrongfulness of his act. Thus, it was left to a jury of laypersons to choose among contradictory psychiatric opinions. In this case, they agreed with the defense experts and found Hinckley not guilty by reason of insanity.[14]

---

[12]See the discussion of *actus rea* in Chapter 2, on pp. 28 and 31.

[13]Hinckley developed plots such as hijacking an airplane and committing suicide in front of her to gain her attention. Eventually, he settled on a scheme to win her over by assassinating the president.

[14]In 2016, the court granted him convalescent leave from the mental hospital, allowing Hinckley to live with his mother. However, the court imposed several conditions on his release and required regular court appearances. In June 2022, a U.S. District judge unconditionally released Hinckley from custody.

Exhibit 7.1: Transcribed Letter from John Hinckley to Jodie Foster

3/30/81
12:45 P.M.
Dear Jodie,

There is a definite possibility that I will be killed in my attempt to get Reagan. It is for this very reason that I am writing you this letter now.

As you well know by now I love you very much. Over the past seven months I've left you dozens of poems, letters and love messages in the faint hope that you could develop an interest in me. Although we talked on the phone a couple of times I never had the nerve to simply approach you and introduce myself. Besides my shyness, I honestly did not wish to bother you with my constant presence. I know the many messages left at your door and in your mailbox were a nuisance, but I felt that it was the most painless way for me to express my love for you.

I feel very good about the fact that you at least know my name and know how I feel about you. And by hanging around your dormitory, I've come to realize that I'm the topic of more than a little conversation, however full of ridicule it may be. At least you know that I'll always love you.

Jodie, I would abandon this idea of getting Reagan in a second if I could only win your heart and live out the rest of my life with you, whether it be in total obscurity or whatever.

I will admit to you that the reason I'm going ahead with this attempt now is because I just cannot wait any longer to impress you. I've got to do something now to make you understand, in no uncertain terms, that I am doing all of this for your sake[[[exlamat]]] By sacrificing my freedom and possibly my life, I hope to change your mind about me. This letter is being written only an hour before I leave for the Hilton Hotel. Jodie, I'm asking you to please look into your heart and at least give me the chance, with this historical deed, to gain your respect and love.

I love you forever,
John Hinckley

This not-guilty verdict aroused so much controversy in some segments of the public that it led the Congress and a number of states to rewrite their laws covering the insanity defense. The old Model Penal Code test was replaced by one that shifted the burden of proof of insanity from the prosecution to the defense. In addition to shifting the burden in insanity cases, Congress narrowed the defense itself. Legislation passed in 1984 states that a person accused of a crime can be judged not guilty by reason of insanity if "the defendant, as a result of a severe mental disease or defect, was unable to appreciate the nature and quality or the wrongfulness of his acts."[15]

Unlike other affirmative defenses, the defendant has the burden of proving the elements of the insanity defense by clear and convincing evidence.[16] The

[15]The Insanity Defense Reform Act of 1984, 18 U.S.C. §17.

[16]18 U.S.C. §17(a)(b).

defense must give the prosecution written notice of its intention to raise the insanity defense. In federal court, notice must be provided within the time allotted for filing pretrial motions.[17] Likewise, the defense must also give the government notice that it intends to call expert witnesses to testify to the defendant's mental disease or defect.[18] Upon request, each side must provide the opponent with the identities of their experts along with a written summary of the expert testimony on the issue of the defendant's mental health.[19]

Once the defendant has expressed an intent to raise the insanity defense, the court may order the defendant to submit to a psychiatric or psychological evaluation.[20] When it orders a mental examination, the court has discretion to determine whether the defendant remains free on pretrial release for an outpatient exam or be committed to the attorney general.[21] The report on the evaluation is filed with the court and provided to the parties.

In federal court, when the defense is asserted, there are three possible outcomes at trial: guilty, not guilty, and not guilty only by reason of insanity.[22] If the defendant is found not guilty only by reason of insanity, the court must commit the defendant to a facility for a mental examination and order the preparation of the report prior to a hearing to determine the defendant's eligibility for release. (This is known as a "dangerousness hearing."[23]) The purpose of the hearing is to determine whether the defendant's release poses a substantial risk to another person or serious damage to another's property because of a present mental disease or defect.[24] If the court finds that release poses such risks, the court remands the defendant to the attorney general, who in turn arranges for placement in a hospital or institution.[25]

Within three years after the Hinckley verdict, two-thirds of the states placed the burden on the defense to prove insanity, eight states adopted a separate verdict of "guilty but mentally ill," and one state (Utah) abolished the defense altogether.[26] So while most jurisdictions have some form of an insanity defense available to criminal defendants, there is disagreement among the states and the federal circuits over the standard that should be used for determining when the insanity defense should apply.

Another highly publicized insanity defense case involved Andrea Yates, a Texas mother who confessed to drowning her five children in a bathtub because she heard voices telling her to kill her children to "save them from Satan."[27] Both the prosecution and the defense agreed that the defendant was mentally

---

[17]FRCrP 12.2(a).

[18]FRCrP 12.2.

[19]FRCrP 16(a)(1)(G) &16(b)(1).

[20]FRCrP 12.2(c)(1).

[21]18 U.S.C. §4243(e).

[22]18 U.S.C. §4242(b).

[23]18 U.S.C. §4246(a)&(b).

[24]18 U.S.C. §4246(d).

[25]18 U.S.C. §4243(e).

[26]D. Linder, *The Trial of John W. Hinckley, Jr.* (2008). http://law2.umkc.edu/faculty/projects/ftrials/hinckley/hinckleytrial.html.

[27]*Jury to Decide Yates' Sentence*, USA Today 3A (March 14, 2002).

ill, but they disagreed as to whether she was aware that what she was doing was wrong. In a three-week-long trial, the defense called psychiatrists, relatives, and friends to testify that Yates suffered from severe postpartum depression. The prosecution countered by arguing that Yates's prompt action in reporting the drowning to the police established that she did know what she had done was wrong. The jury members apparently agreed with the prosecution and convicted her of murder. She was sentenced to life in prison and then sent to a prison psychiatric ward to receive treatment for her mental illness while serving her sentence.[28]

A comparison of the Hinckley and Yates cases illustrates the fact that mentally ill defendants typically end up in secured mental institutions regardless of whether they are found **not guilty only by reason of insanity** or **guilty but mentally ill**. Even though he was found not guilty, John Hinckley ended up being civilly committed to a large-scale, federally run psychiatric hospital. According to the American Psychiatric Association, "studies show that persons found not guilty by reason of insanity, on average, are held at least as long as—and often longer than—persons found guilty and sent to prison for similar crimes."[29] While a finding of guilt will result in a fixed sentence, a finding of not guilty by reason of insanity can result in defendants being committed for an indefinite term, potentially for life, until they are deemed no longer a threat to themselves or society. In fact, Daniel M'Naghten's trial in 1843, which resulted in the creation of the M'Naghten test, also resulted in his commitment to a mental institution, where he remained until his death.[30]

Not guilty only by reason of insanity A verdict finding that the defendant carried out the actions constituting a crime but lacked the mental capacity to have intended to commit the crime.

Guilty but mentally ill A verdict finding that the defendant is guilty of a crime but lacking the mental capacity to commit it.

Another related concept is the notion of temporary insanity. The **temporary insanity** defense asserts that a defendant was insane at the time the criminal act was committed but has since recovered from this temporary condition. A famous example involved a U.S. congressman who killed his wife's lover in 1859. If this defense is successful, it relieves the defendant of both criminal penalties and involuntary commitment to a mental institution. However, it is seldom successful because it is extremely difficult to convince a jury of the validity of this defense.

Temporary insanity The defense that the accused was momentarily insane when the crime was committed and therefore was incapable of understanding the nature of his or her actions.

3. INTOXICATION

In some jurisdictions and under limited circumstances, being under the voluntary influence of drugs or alcohol is considered a valid defense. The rationale is that the intoxicating substance interfered with the defendant's ability to form the required *mens rea*. This defense is applicable to specific-intent crimes, such as murder or burglary.

Voluntary intoxication is not a defense to general intent or strict liability offenses. For general-intent crimes, the prosecution does not have to show

Voluntary intoxication The knowing and voluntary consumption of alcohol and/or drugs.

---

[28] Later, a Texas appeals court reversed Yates's conviction based on improper expert testimony and ordered a retrial. Currently, Yates remains in a Texas prison psychiatric ward.

[29] American Psychiatric Association, *The Insanity Defense,* www.psych.org/publicinfo/insanity.cfm (last updated September 2003).

[30] G. H. Morris, *Placed in Purgatory: Conditional Release of Insanity Acquittees*, 39 ARIZ. L. REV. 1062 (1997).

that a defendant intended to violate the law. Instead, the government need only prove the commission of an unlawful act (*actus reus*) and the defendant's intent to carry out that act (*mens rea*). Although voluntary intoxication can generally be used as a defense for major crimes requiring a specific intent, it cannot be used as a defense to charges involving reckless behavior.

Involuntary intoxication The consumption of alcohol and/or drugs without knowledge or consent.

In many jurisdictions, **involuntary intoxication** can be raised as a defense to both general- and specific-intent crimes. When it is asserted, the defendant must show intoxication without knowledge or consent. An unwitting victim of a spiked drink could present this as a defense to a general-intent crime.

4. COMPETENCY AND MITIGATING FACTORS

Whereas infancy, insanity, and intoxication relate to a defendant's condition at the time the alleged criminal act took place, competency focuses on the defendant's condition at the time that charges are filed, as well as when the trial is to be held. Whereas the former relates to determining legal responsibility for criminal behavior, the latter relates to whether defendants are able to adequately assist their attorneys in preparing a defense, whether they can make informed decisions about trial strategy, and whether they should plead guilty or accept a plea agreement. Even if someone's mental illness or intoxication does not meet the standards necessary to relieve him or her of criminal responsibility, they may still be used as a mitigating factor for reducing the charge to a less serious offense or getting a more lenient sentence.

D. Reactive Defenses

This next category of defenses involves circumstances in which people find themselves in unusual situations requiring actions that, while ordinarily considered to be bad, are justified by the special circumstances existing at that particular time.

1. DURESS AND NECESSITY

Duress A defense requiring proof that force or a threat of force was used to cause a person to commit a criminal act.

Necessity A defense requiring proof that the defendant was forced to take an action to avoid a greater harm.

Duress and necessity both involve situations in which people are forced to violate the law because of the unusual circumstances facing them. Whereas **duress** involves using force or the threat of force to cause someone to commit a criminal act, **necessity** involves situations in which circumstances require people to break the law in order to avert some greater harm from taking place. The rationale for both defenses is that people shouldn't be punished for involuntary acts and that in these situations breaking the law was their only acceptable course of action.

Section 2.09 of the Model Penal Code defines duress as coercion through "the use of, or a threat to use, unlawful force against his person or the person of another, which a person of reasonable firmness in his situation would have been unable to resist." Therefore, if someone held a gun to your head and forced you to commit a criminal act, you would be entitled to use the defense of duress.

To assert this defense, you must prove that you reasonably believed that you were threatened with your death, the death of another person, or serious injury to yourself or others unless you committed the crime. In a highly publicized case in the mid-1970s, Patty Hearst, the daughter of a millionaire newspaper publisher, was placed on trial for bank robbery. Approximately a year before the robbery took place, she had been kidnapped by a radical group calling itself the Symbionese Liberation Army. When members of this same group robbed a bank, Hearst appeared to be a willing participant. At her trial, attorney F. Lee Bailey argued that Hearst had been "brainwashed" by her Symbionese Liberation Army kidnappers and had been coerced into participating in the robbery. The state countered with evidence showing that Hearst had passed up opportunities to flee and call police and argued that this showed she was a willing participant who was acting voluntarily. The jury agreed with the prosecution and convicted her of armed robbery.

Whereas duress involves someone else purposely threatening the life of the defendant (or some innocent third party), under the necessity defense, the defendant broke the law to avoid a harm (either to himself or others) due to special circumstances resulting from natural causes (like floods) or from the actions of another person that were not specifically intended to affect the defendant. For example, you may be forced to trespass across a neighbor's yard to escape a fire in your home. In addition, this defense may be used in a more general way to exonerate otherwise criminal conduct when a person believes that such conduct is necessary to avoid a greater injury. An example would be a motorist choosing to crash an automobile into a building in order to avoid hitting a child who runs into the street. The necessity defense has been asserted by seriously ill patients charged with the possession of marijuana. In these cases, the defendants have claimed that the medical use of cannabis was a necessity because no other drugs were available to address their symptoms. Although this claim has been successful in a few cases, this application of the necessity defense has been rejected by most courts.[31]

2. SELF-DEFENSE

Self-defense is an action utilizing force that is legally justified to protect oneself or others from being injured. It allows people to take actions that would ordinarily violate the law if it was not being done in reaction to special circumstances, such as defending oneself or others from criminal actions by someone who puts you or someone else in danger of losing your life or suffering serious bodily injury.

Self-defense
The justified use of force to protect oneself or others from being injured.

Note, however, that state laws vary as to the type of force that people can use in various situations, as well as when they are required to retreat rather than use force. Generally, however, this right to use force is valid only if the following conditions are met:

[31]See generally, A. J. LeVay, *Urgent Compassion: Medical Marijuana, Prosecutorial Discretion and the Medical Necessity Defense*, 41 B.C.L. Rev. 699 (2000).

- The person claiming self-defense must not have been the initiator of the violence.
- The threat of bodily harm must be immediate.
- The amount of force used must be no more than is reasonably necessary to repel the attack.
- Once the threatening party ceases the threatening behavior, the right to self-defense no longer applies.

a. *Use of Deadly Force*

Deadly force
A force that would cause serious bodily injury or death.

When exercising one's right of self-defense, the amount of force necessary to repel an attack will depend on the physical characteristics of both the attacker and the person attempting to fend off the attack, as well as the weapons being used by both the attacker and the defender. Furthermore, many state laws attach special conditions to the use of **deadly force**, which is usually defined as a force that would cause serious bodily injury or death and is usually limited to situations in which the danger faced includes fear of serious bodily injury or death.

One of the most highly publicized self-defense cases involved Kyle Rittenhouse, a 17-year-old male who drove from his home in northern Illinois to Kenosha, Wisconsin, to help protect local merchants from people who were protesting the police shooting of a Black man. He was motivated to go to Kenosha by social media posts and came equipped with a first aid kit and an AR-15-style assault rifle.[32] On the evening in question, while the downtown streets were crowded with protesters, Rittenhouse fatally shot two men and wounded a third.

At his trial, Rittenhouse claimed that he shot them in self-defense because he felt they were trying to injure him. He testified that the first man he killed was trying to grab his rifle, and the second was attacking him with a skateboard while he was trying to flee to his car.

A jury of five men and seven women deliberated more than 25 hours over four days before returning not guilty verdicts on all the charges against Rittenhouse.

Discussion Questions

The Rittenhouse case raises important questions about vigilantes (civilians who undertake law enforcement without legal authority). Police killings of members of minority races often trigger mass demonstrations that sometimes get out of hand, leading to riots.

1. Should police allow civilians to bring weapons to demonstrations protesting police misconduct?

2. Should private persons who bring guns to police protests be allowed to use their weapons if they put themselves in danger by intermingling with demonstrators holding opposing viewpoints?

---

[32]Rittenhouse was too young to legally purchase this type of weapon, but he convinced his sister's boyfriend to purchase the gun and resell it to him.

b. Retreat Exception

To further complicate the doctrine of self-defense, most jurisdictions include a **retreat exception** in their statutes. This exception generally requires a person in danger to get away from the danger or give up possessions before resorting to the use of deadly force. If the victim can avoid danger but chooses instead to use deadly force, the victim may be prosecuted for any crime committed. Potential victims need not retreat if they are in their own homes or if retreating would create additional danger for them. Potential victims using non-deadly force need not retreat. Only rarely can deadly force be applied to protect property because the law values human life over property, even when the human life in question is trying to steal the property. The key is whether the potential victim of a burglary or robbery can convince a jury that there was reason to believe that the thief was attempting to do great bodily harm to the person using the deadly force.

Retreat exception
The rule that in order to claim self-defense there must have been no possibility of retreat.

Some states, however, do authorize the use of deadly force to protect property. For instance, §776.013(1) and (2) of the Florida "Stand Your Ground" law provides:

> (1) A person who is in a dwelling or residence in which the person has a right to be has no duty to retreat and has the right to stand his or her ground and use or threaten to use:
>
> (a) Nondeadly force against another when and to the extent that the person reasonably believes that such conduct is necessary to defend himself or herself or another against the other's imminent use of unlawful force; or
>
> (b) Deadly force if he or she reasonably believes that using or threatening to use such force is necessary to prevent imminent death or great bodily harm to himself or herself or another or to prevent the imminent commission of a forcible felony.
>
> (2) A person is presumed to have held a reasonable fear of imminent peril of death or great bodily harm to himself or herself or another when using or threatening to use defensive force that is intended or likely to cause death or great bodily harm to another if:
>
> (a) The person against whom the defensive force was used or threatened was in the process of unlawfully and forcefully entering, or had unlawfully and forcibly entered, a dwelling, residence, or occupied vehicle, or if that person had removed or was attempting to remove another against that person's will from the dwelling, residence, or occupied vehicle; and
>
> The person who uses or threatens to use defensive force knew or had reason to believe that an unlawful and forcible entry or unlawful and forcible act was occurring or had occurred.[33]

Notice that the wording used in (1)(a) not only covers situations in which the force was used against a person who was "*in the process of* unlawfully and forcibly entering . . ." but also applies in situations where the person "*had* unlawfully and forcibly entered a dwelling, a residence, or occupied vehicle." In a recent Florida case, a man who was being prosecuted for having fatally shot

---

[33]Fla. Stat. §776.013(1) & (2).

a man who had forced his way into a car in which he was a passenger raised a self-defense claim even though the man he shot was retreating from the scene when the shooting took place. A Florida appeals court ruled that the wording of the state statute in question granted the shooter immunity even though the original aggressor had been in retreat at the time he was shot.[34]

c. Battered Spouse Syndrome

Battered woman's or spouse's syndrome
A syndrome of being the victim of repeated attacks; self-defense is sometimes allowed to the victim even when the victim is not in immediate danger.

Another variation on the self-defense exception is the **battered woman's or spouse's syndrome**. This defense allows a person who has been the victim of repeated attacks the right to self-defense even when there may not be immediate danger at the exact moment that the right to self-defense is exercised. Experts believe that, especially for battered women, the fear of immediate harm extends beyond individual episodes of violence and becomes a part of everyday life. It is therefore argued that because the fear of immediate harm is always present, the doctrine of self-defense should apply to such situations as killing a spouse while he sleeps.

It is important to note that the application of the battered spouse defense is problematic. Not all states have been willing to accept this defense—especially when the woman's actions were not taken in the face of "imminent" death or great bodily harm. The effects of the battered woman's syndrome may be used, however, to reduce the charge from murder to manslaughter or as a mitigating factor in sentencing.

Probably the most publicized of the battered woman's cases was the Bobbit case. In 1993, Lorena Bobbit was charged with aggravated assault for cutting off more than half of her husband John's penis with a carving knife. At trial, Lorena testified that John sexually, physically, and emotionally abused her during their marriage. Other witnesses corroborated her story. However, rather than make a self-defense argument, Lorena's attorneys presented an insanity defense. They argued that her husband's abuse caused her to "snap" because she was suffering from clinical depression, as well as post-traumatic stress disorder caused by the abuse. The jury found Lorena not guilty due to insanity causing an irresistible impulse to assault her husband.

d. Law Enforcement

Finally, it should be noted that law enforcement and military personnel are given special exemptions from the law to take actions that are required as part of their official duties. The killing of enemy soldiers by soldiers in battle and the killing of escaping felons by police officers both fall under the category of justifiable homicide.

As discussed in Chapter 5, numerous police shootings in recent years have received national attention. Many of these publicized shootings involved African American young men or adults with mental problems. Because it is difficult to obtain a conviction, prosecutors are reluctant to bring criminal charges against police officers for their use of excessive force. In most of these cases, officers

[34]*Hair v. State of Florida*, 17 So. 3d 804 (Fla. App., 2009).

claimed they shot the victims in self-defense because they believed the victim was armed and was about to shoot them or others.

When a police officer faces criminal charges, the prosecution must prove that more force was used than was reasonably necessary for the officer to arrest or gain control of the victim. The "reasonableness" of the force used is "judged from the perspective of a reasonable officer on the scene, rather than with the 20/20 vision of hindsight."[35] A police officer may use deadly force only if there is probable cause to believe that the suspect poses a significant threat of death or serious physical injury to the officer or others. Even if the decision to use deadly force was mistaken, the officer is given the benefit of the doubt if the decision was reasonable under the circumstances known at the time of the event.

Another type of excessive force claim against law enforcement officers involves high speed pursuits that lead to injuries to the suspect or to innocent bystanders. The U.S. Supreme Court spoke to this issue in *Scott v. Harris*,[36] where the Court ruled that it was not unreasonable for a deputy sheriff to end a high-speed chase by applying his "push bumper" to the rear of the fleeing vehicle.

Investigative Tips for Paralegals

As a paralegal working for the defense, you need to conduct a thorough investigation if the client is claiming self-defense. Specifically, you should gather information regarding the physical characteristics of the parties, such as height, weight, physical health, and mental condition. You also should explore the parties' cultural backgrounds and possible gang membership. Further, you also should find out the accused's propensity for violence, as well as what the client knew about the accuser's violent tendencies before the altercation. Along this line, you should conduct a criminal background search on the accuser and the client. WestLaw and NexisLexis offer criminal background checks as part of their extended software packages. If you do not have access to these services, you can research criminal backgrounds in your venue by conducting a search at the office of the clerk of the court. Likewise, you can use PACER for researching prior federal charges. Don't overlook evidence of the accuser's violent nature that was unknown to the defendant. Some courts permit this evidence to be presented when self-defense is asserted.[37]

Discussion Questions

3. In a 2018 trial in Minneapolis, a former police officer was found guilty of third-degree murder and manslaughter for fatally shooting a woman in the alley behind her home. The woman had made the 911 call to report what she thought was the sound of a woman being assaulted. When the squad car came slowly down the alley, she approached the driver's side to talk to the two police officers. The officer in the front passenger seat was startled by her movement

---

[35]*Graham v. Connor*, 490 U.S. 386, 396–97 (1989).

[36]550 U.S. 372 (2007).

[37]*People v. Lynch*, 104 Ill. 2d 194 (1984).

and shot her with his service revolver. The officer was Black, and the victim was white.

a. Do you think the officer should have been charged with a crime? Why or why not? With what crime should he have been charged?

b. Both officers had turned their body cameras on and off at the scene. Do you think the verdict would have been different if they had had their body cameras on the whole time? Why?

c. Do you think the verdict would have been different if the woman who was shot had been Black instead of white? Why?

d. Do you think the verdict would have been different if the officer who shot her had been white instead of Black? Why?

4. In 2018, a Caucasian Chicago police officer was found guilty of murder in the 2014 shooting death of an African American 17-year-old male who allegedly lunged at him with a knife. Testimony at the trial indicated that the youth had been struck by 16 bullets fired by the defendant.

a. Do you think the verdict would have been different if the youth's gunshot wounds had been on the front side of his body rather than at his back? Why?

b. Do you think the verdict would have been different if the officer had fired only once or twice? Why?

c. Do you think the verdict would have been different if one of the two other officers with him had also fired at the victim? Why?

d. Do you think the verdict would have been different if the victim had been white rather than Black? Why?

e. Do you think the verdict would have been different if the officer had been Black rather than white? Why?

5. The Florida statute concerning abuse of children[38] makes it a crime for a "person responsible for a child's welfare" to fail "to make a reasonable effort to protect a child from abuse, neglect, or exploitation by another person." The statute also states that the offense "may be based on repeated conduct, or on a single incident or omission that results in . . . serious physical or mental injury or a substantial risk of death to a child." A county prosecutor charged a deputy sheriff, serving as the school resource officer, with violating this statute for failing to intervene as a gunman attacked and killed 17 victims at a Parkland, Florida, high school. The charges allege that rather than entering the building of the shootings, the officer hid at the base of a stairwell after the first shots were fired.

a. Do you think the alleged behavior of the school resource officer violated this statute?

b. What arguments do you think the defense could use in this case?

c. Is the statute violated if a lifeguard chose not to enter the water to rescue an unsupervised child swimmer caught in a rip tide because she thought it would put her own life at too great a risk?

d. Is there a violation of the Florida law when a fireman chooses not to enter a burning building to rescue a child because he thinks the fire reached the point that the building was about to collapse? Is law violated if the fireman believes that there was insufficient oxygen left in his breathing tank?

---

[38] F.S.A. §§827.01 *et seq.*

6. Based on the facts presented in the DOJ Report Regarding Criminal Investigation into Shooting Death (Exhibit 7.2 at pages 224-225), is there a good faith basis to charge the officer with a crime in the state where your school is located? What crime?

7. What facts presented in Exhibit 7.2 are helpful to the officer's defense?

Forensic evidence revealed the following:

- Brown's hand was within inches of the muzzle of Wilson's gun during one of the times it was fired.
- Bruising on Wilson's jaw and scratches on his neck.
- The presence of Brown's DNA on Wilson's collar, shirt, and pants as well as inside the SUV.
- The presence of Wilson's DNA on Brown's palm.
- The presence of a bullet in the side panel of the driver's door just above Wilson's lap.

8. How does the forensics evidence help the prosecution? How does it assist the defense?

DOJ interviews disclosed some witnesses stated that Brown reached into the SUV through the open driver's window and punched and grabbed Wilson. However, other individuals stated that Wilson reached out of the SUV and grabbed Brown by the neck, and Brown's arms were never inside the SUV.

9. How do these witness contradictory statements impact the prosecution and defense's cases?

In its report of the Brown shooting, the DOJ concluded that because Officer Wilson did not act with the requisite criminal intent, it cannot be proven beyond reasonable doubt to a jury that he violated federal law when he fired his weapon at Brown. In its companion report, the Justice Department recommended that the City of Ferguson completely revamp its criminal justice system, finding that the City had engaged in multiple constitutional violations.

E. Entrapment

Entrapment
A defense requiring proof that the defendant would not have committed the crime but for police trickery.

The defense of **entrapment** arises when law enforcement personnel trick or encourage the defendant to commit a crime that the defendant would not have committed without the government's enticement. In other words, the government cannot encourage people to break the law and then turn around and prosecute them for having done so. However, it is not considered entrapment when government agents simply provide an opportunity to commit a crime that the person was already contemplating.

So, for example, the entrapment defense would apply to a situation where a sexily dressed undercover police officer approached a man at a bar and offered to have sex with him for money. On the other hand, if that same sexily dressed undercover officer sat down next to the defendant and struck up a conversation about the weather or the music, it would not be entrapment if the defendant first broached the idea of paying to have sex with her. The key factor in using an entrapment defense is the determination of whether the defendant had a predisposition to commit the crime before the government agents contacted the defendant.

However, the entrapment defense is rarely successful because most juries believe that people should be held responsible for their actions when they chose to follow a suggestion, even though they knew it was illegal.

Exhibit 7.2: DOJ Report Regarding Criminal Investigation into Shooting Death

In 2014, a white police officer shot and killed Michael Brown, an unarmed Black teenager in Ferguson, Missouri, a St. Louis suburb. After a state grand jury chose not to indict the officer, the U.S. Department of Justice began its own investigation of the Brown shooting. Selected excerpts of the DOJ report appear below:

> The encounter between [Officer] Wilson and Brown took place over an approximately two-minute period of time at about noon on August 9, 2014. Wilson was on duty and driving his department-issued Chevy Tahoe SUV westbound on Canfield Drive in Ferguson, Missouri, when he saw Brown and his friend, Witness 101, walking eastbound in the middle of the street. Brown and Witness 101 had just come from Ferguson Market and Liquor ("Ferguson Market"), a nearby convenience store, where, at approximately 11:53 a.m., Brown stole several packages of cigarillos. As captured on the store's surveillance video, when the store clerk tried to stop Brown, Brown used his physical size to stand over him and forcefully shove him away. As a result, an FPD dispatch call went out over the police radio for a "stealing in progress." The dispatch recordings and Wilson's radio transmissions establish that Wilson was aware of the theft and had a description of the suspects as he encountered Brown and Witness 101.
>
> As Wilson drove toward Brown and Witness 101, he told the two men to walk on the sidewalk. According to Wilson's statement to prosecutors and investigators, he suspected that Brown and Witness 101 were involved in the incident at Ferguson Market based on the descriptions he heard on the radio and the cigarillos in Brown's hands. Wilson then called for backup, stating, "Put me on Canfield with two and send me another car." Wilson backed up his SUV and parked at an angle, blocking most of both lanes of traffic, and stopping Brown and Witness 101 from walking any further. Wilson attempted to open the driver's door of the SUV to exit his vehicle, but as he swung it open, the door came into contact with Brown's body and either rebounded closed or Brown pushed it closed.
>
> Wilson. . . stated that Brown then reached into the SUV through the open driver's window and punched and grabbed Wilson. . . .
>
> Wilson told prosecutors and investigators that he responded to Brown reaching into the SUV and punching him by withdrawing his gun because he could not access less lethal weapons while seated inside the SUV. Brown then grabbed the weapon and struggled with Wilson to gain control of it. Wilson fired, striking Brown in the hand. . . . [According to Wilson] during the struggle, Brown used his right hand to grab and attempt to control Wilson's gun. According to three autopsies, Brown sustained a close range gunshot wound to the fleshy portion of his right hand at the base of his right thumb. . . witness accounts [establish] that Wilson fired at least one shot from inside the SUV. . . .
>
> After the initial shooting inside the SUV, the evidence establishes that Brown ran eastbound on Canfield Drive and Wilson chased after him. The autopsy results confirm that Wilson did not shoot Brown in the back as he was running away because there were no entrance wounds to Brown's back. The autopsy results alone do not indicate the direction Brown was facing when he received two wounds to his right arm, given the mobility of the arm. . . .
>
> Brown ran at least 180 feet away from the SUV, as verified by the location of bloodstains on the roadway, which DNA analysis confirms was Brown's blood. Brown

then turned around and came back toward Wilson, falling to his death approximately 21.6 feet west of the blood in the roadway. . . .

. . . Wilson stated that he feared Brown would again assault him because of Brown's conduct at the SUV and because as Brown moved toward him, Wilson saw Brown reach his right hand under his t-shirt into what appeared to be his waistband. . . .

Ballistics analysis indicates that Wilson fired a total of 12 shots, two from the SUV and ten on the roadway. Witness accounts and an audio recording indicate that when Wilson and Brown were on the roadway, Wilson fired three gunshot volleys, pausing in between each one. According to the autopsy results, Wilson shot and hit Brown as few as six or as many as eight times, including the gunshot to Brown's hand. Brown fell to the ground dead as a result of a gunshot to the apex of his head. With the exception of the first shot to Brown's hand, all of the shots that struck Brown were fired from a distance of more than two feet. As documented by crime scene photographs, Brown fell to the ground with his left, uninjured hand balled up by his waistband, and his right, injured hand palm up by his side. Witness accounts and cellular phone video prove that Wilson did not touch Brown's body after he fired the final shot and Brown fell to the ground. . . .

While credible witnesses gave varying accounts of exactly what Brown was doing with his hands as he moved toward Wilson—i.e., balling them, holding them out, or pulling up his pants up—and varying accounts of how he was moving—i.e., "charging," moving in "slow motion," or "running"—they all establish that Brown was moving toward Wilson when Wilson shot him. Although some witnesses state that Brown held his hands up at shoulder level with his palms facing outward for a brief moment, these same witnesses describe Brown then dropping his hands and "charging" at Wilson.

F. Constitutional Defenses

Another category of defenses involves constitutional challenges to either the substance of the criminal statute, the manner in which it was enforced, or the way in which the evidence was gathered. If a statute is found to be unconstitutional, a defendant cannot be legally convicted or punished for having violated it, and if constitutional rights were violated during the investigative stage, it may be possible to prevent that evidence from being used at the trial.

Bill of attainder
A law that imposes criminal penalties on a single person or small, select group of people.

Ex post facto law
A law that imposes criminal penalties for actions that were taken prior to the passage of the law.

1. CHALLENGING THE CONSTITUTIONALITY OF THE LAW

a. *Ex Post Facto and Bill of Attainder Restrictions*

Article I, Section 9 of the U.S. Constitution declares, "No Bill of Attainder or ex post facto law shall be passed." A **bill of attainder** is defined as a law that imposes criminal penalties on a single person or small, select group of people. An **ex post facto law** is one that imposes criminal penalties for actions that were taken prior to the passage of the law. In *Calder v. Bull*,[39] Justice Chase wrote:

[39] 3 U.S. 386 (1798).

> 1st. Every law that makes an action done before the passing of the law, and which was innocent when done, criminal; and punishes such action. 2d. Every law that aggravates a crime, or makes it greater than it was, when committed. 3d. Every law that changes the punishment, and inflicts a greater punishment, than the law annexed to the crime, when committed. 4th. Every law that alters the legal rules of evidence, and receives less, or different, testimony, than the law required at the time of the commission of the offense, in order to convict the offender.

Although this section of the U.S. Constitution is applicable only to laws passed by the U.S. Congress, most states have similar provisions in their state constitutions.

In late 2008, the Illinois legislature adopted legislation, dubbed "Drew's Law," that changed the rules of evidence on the admission of hearsay statements made by a murder victim when the murder was intended to cause the unavailability of the person making the statements.[40] The prosecutor, who was investigating the death of the former police officer Drew Peterson's third wife and the disappearance of Peterson's fourth wife, drafted the law. Five months after passage, the same prosecutor secured the indictment of Peterson and announced that he would be using the new hearsay law in his prosecution of Peterson. Peterson's attorney has challenged the hearsay law as being an unconstitutional ex post facto law.

Application Exercises

1. Is Drew's Law an ex post facto law? Why or why not?
2. Does your state's constitution prohibit the passage of ex post facto laws or bills of attainder? If so, what are the citations for these prohibitions?

b. Vagueness and Overbreadth

Void for vagueness defense
A claim that a criminal charge should be dismissed because the statute being applied fails to fairly inform ordinary people as to what is commanded or prohibited.

One of the most common challenges to a criminal statute is the claim that it is "void for vagueness" or "overbroad." Both are based on the Due Process Clauses of the Fifth and Fourteen Amendments. The **void for vagueness** concept is based on the principle that "fundamental fairness requires that criminal statutes have to be written in such a way that a person of average intelligence has notice as to what is or is not prohibited by the law."

Consider, for example, a Texas stalking statute that made it illegal to engage in conduct that is "reasonably likely to harass, annoy, alarm, abuse, torment, or embarrass" someone. Because terms such as "annoy," "alarm," and "embarrass" are ambiguous and susceptible to different meanings, the highest Texas criminal appellate court struck down the statute on the basis that it was unconstitutionally vague on its face.[41]

---

[40] 725 ILCS 5/115-10.6.

[41] *Long v. State*, 931 S.W.2d 285 (Tex. 1996).

The courts also require criminal statutes to be narrowly drawn so that they don't prohibit more than they are constitutionally permitted to limit. Therefore, if a statute goes too far and can reasonably be interpreted as prohibiting some constitutionally protected behavior, it is said to be "**overbroad.**" For example, a law designed to prevent destruction of public property cannot include a ban on all protests or mass gatherings, and an obscenity statute must define the type of material that it prohibits narrowly enough so that it does not also prohibit sexually explicit materials that are not legally obscene.

Overbreadth
A reason for invalidating a statute that criminalizes constitutionally protected activities along with those that it can legally prohibit.

Another example of a successful challenge based on vagueness and overbreadth can be found in the federal prosecution of former Enron chief executive Jeffrey Skilling on charges that he defrauded Enron stockholders in violation of the provisions of 18 U.S.C. §1341 and §1346. §1341 declares:

> Whoever, having devised or intending to devise any scheme or artifice to defraud, or for obtaining money or property by means of false or fraudulent pretenses, representations, or promises, or to sell, dispose of, loan, exchange, alter, give away, distribute, supply, or furnish or procure for unlawful use any counterfeit or spurious coin, obligation, security, or other article, or anything represented to be or intimated or held out to be such counterfeit or spurious article, for the purpose of executing such scheme or artifice or attempting so to do, places in any post office or authorized depository for mail matter, any matter or thing whatever to be sent or delivered by the Postal Service, or deposits or causes to be deposited any matter or thing whatever to be sent or delivered by any private or commercial interstate carrier, or takes or receives therefrom, any such matter or thing, or knowingly causes to be delivered by mail or such carrier according to the direction thereon, or at the place at which it is directed to be delivered by the person to whom it is addressed, any such matter or thing, shall be fined under this title or imprisoned not more than 20 years, or both. . . .

§1346 states:

For the purposes of this chapter [18 USCS §§1341 *et seq.*], the term "scheme or artifice to defraud" includes a scheme or artifice to deprive another of the intangible right of honest services.

But what does "honest services" mean? Skilling's attorneys attacked the law in question as being vague and overbroad and in June of 2010, the U.S. Supreme Court declared:

> Congress intended at least to reach schemes to defraud involving bribes and kickbacks. Construing the honest-services statute to extend beyond that core meaning, . . . would encounter a vagueness shoal. We therefore hold that §1346 covers only bribery and kickback schemes."[42]

Because Skilling's alleged misconduct entailed no bribe or kickback, the Supreme Court ruled that it does not fall within §1346's proscription.

[42]*Skilling v. United States*, 561 U.S. 358 (2010). Prior to the Supreme Court's ruling in this case, U.S. Attorneys had convicted dozens of state and local governmental officials for violating this "honest services" provision. The list of convictions included the former Illinois governor George Ryan.

c. Challenges Based on Violations of Civil Liberties

Criminal statutes can also be challenged on the ground that they violate constitutionally based civil liberties, such as the First Amendment rights of freedom of religion or freedom of speech or the Equal Protection Clause of the Fourteenth Amendment.

When freedom of religion is used as a basis for challenging a statute, the government must show that the law in question is neutral on its face and of general applicability. If this standard is met, the statute is valid, even though it may have the incidental effect of burdening a particular religious practice.[43] For example, the U.S. Supreme Court upheld the constitutionality of a statute prohibiting polygamy, even though the Mormon defendant argued that polygamous marriage was part of his religion.[44] However, more recently, the Supreme Court invalidated a city ordinance prohibiting the ritual sacrifice of animals, on the grounds that it was neither neutral on its face nor of general applicability.[45] It was not neutral because it was directed at a specific religious group, the Santerias, and it was not of general applicability because it applied only to the killing of animals in the context of a religious service. If the city had been motivated by legitimate public health concerns, the ordinance would have been applicable to all situations in which animals are killed.

Content neutrality
Laws may not limit free expression on the basis of whether the speech's content supports or opposes any particular position.

The First Amendment protection of freedom of speech can also form the basis for a constitutional challenge. The concept of **content neutrality** plays a critical role in First Amendment cases. For example, in *Texas v. Johnson*,[46] the Supreme Court determined that the state of Texas could not punish someone for symbolic speech (in that case, the burning of an American flag) simply because it disagreed with the message being sent. Similarly, the government cannot grant or deny a permit for a rally or parade on the basis of which political party is sponsoring the event. The Court held that the Village of Skokie could not prevent a neo-Nazi group from marching in its town, even though their presence would be offensive to the 60 percent of its residents who were Jewish, 10 percent of whom were survivors of the Holocaust.[47]

Hate crime
A crime where the selection of the victim is based on that person's membership in a protected category, such as race, sex, or sexual orientation.

Hate speech
Speech directed at a particular group or classification of people that involves expressions of hate or intimidation.

Content neutrality also plays a role in the Court's treatment of **hate crime** laws. Hate crimes are offenses that are motivated by a hatred of a specific group or category of people, such as racial or religious minorities or homosexuals. In analyzing these types of laws, one needs to distinguish between those prohibiting certain types of **hate speech** and those that enhance the punishment of another, underlying crime.

The contrast between these two approaches can be seen in two recent Supreme Court cases. In a case dealing with a form of hate speech, the Court was asked to consider whether a state statute that outlawed cross burning unconstitutionally infringed on protected symbolic speech. The Court held that cross burning by itself could be protected speech. However, if the intent behind

---

[43] *Employment Division, Department of Human Resources of Oregon v. Smith*, 494 U.S. 872, (1990).

[44] *Reynolds v. United States*, 98 U.S 145 (1879).

[45] *Church of the Lukumi Babalu Aye Inc. v. City of Hialeah*, 508 U.S. 520 (1993).

[46] *Texas v. Johnson*, 491 U.S. 397 (1989).

[47] *National Socialist Party v. Skokie*, 432 U.S. 43 (1977).

the cross burning was to intimidate, the state could constitutionally criminalize that behavior.[48] Therefore, the Court reversed the conviction of a man who had led a Ku Klux Klan rally during which a cross was burned but affirmed that the state could prosecute those who used a cross burning to intimidate, as was done by two men who placed a burning cross in the yard of an African American family.

In contrast to hate speech laws, the penalty enhancement statutes simply provide for stiffer penalties in situations where the defendant has been found guilty of another crime, such as robbery, but it is proven that the defendant selected the specific victim because of that person's race, religion, or other specified factors. The Supreme Court upheld the validity of such a statute in *Wisconsin v. Mitchell*.[49]

Criminal statutes can also be challenged on the ground that they violate the Equal Protection Clause by treating people differently on the basis of their race, sex, age, sexual orientation, and religionwithout having a legally acceptable basis for doing so.[50] For example, several criminal statutes have been challenged on the basis that they discriminated on the basis of sex in the way the offense was defined or the nature of the punishment that was attached to the crime.[51]

2. CHALLENGING THE CONSTITUTIONALITY OF PROCEDURES USED

In this section, we discuss how these procedural rights can be used to advance the defendant's interests in criminal cases. Before continuing, we recommend that you go back and review Section A in Chapter 4, where we highlighted the portions of the Bill of Rights relating to criminal prosecutions. Note that some, such as the Fourth Amendment prohibition against "unreasonable searches and seizures," relate to how evidence is gathered, and others, such as the Sixth Amendment right to confront witnesses, relate to how trials must be conducted.

Motion to suppress
A request that the court prohibit specified material from being admitted into evidence at a trial because it was gathered in an illegal manner.

a. *The Exclusionary Rule*

Defense attorneys usually address violations of constitutional rights related to the gathering of evidence by filing a **motion to suppress** the evidence involved. We will discuss the mechanics of filing and opposing these motions to suppress in Chapter 9; we focus our attention here on the justification for granting them.

Exclusionary rule
The doctrine that evidence obtained in violation of a defendant's constitutional rights cannot be used against the defendant in a criminal prosecution.

When judges grant motions to suppress based on alleged violations of constitutional rights, they are applying what is commonly referred to as the **exclusionary rule**. If a judge concludes that evidence was collected in a manner

[48] *Virginia v. Black*, 538 U.S. 343 (2003).

[49] 508 U.S. 476 (1993).

[50] The standard for determining what constitutes a legally acceptable basis differs according to the type of group that is experiencing discrimination.

[51] See, e.g., *Craig v. Boren*, 429 U.S. 190 (1976); *Michael M. v. Superior Court of Sonoma County*, 450 U.S. 464 (1981).

that violated the defendant's fundamental constitutional rights, the judge is expected to prevent that evidence from being used at trial.

Use of the exclusionary rule has long been one of the most controversial topics in criminal law because it can sometimes result in a situation in which guilty men and women go free. If the murder weapon was suppressed because there was an illegal search of the defendant's house, or if a confession is thrown out because the defendant wasn't Mirandized before the police began a custodial interrogation, prosecutors may no longer have enough evidence to meet the "beyond a reasonable doubt" standard of the judge or the jury.

Fruit of the poisonous tree doctrine
Evidence that is derived from an illegal search or interrogation is inadmissible.

A critical part of the operation of the exclusionary rule is what is known as the **fruit of the poisonous tree doctrine**. This doctrine holds that evidence that is pawned by or directly derived from an illegal search or illegal interrogation is inadmissible against the defendant by virtue of being tainted by the original illegality. If the tree (the primary evidence) has been poisoned from the illegal search, then all the fruit (collateral or additional evidence) must also be suppressed. It is important to note, however, that the application of this doctrine does not invalidate the arrest or prevent the defendant from being convicted on the basis of independent evidence. Nor does it prohibit officers from later conducting legal searches and gathering additional evidence as long as that evidence was gathered without the aid of knowledge gained from the tainted evidence that was suppressed.

The following excerpts from *Mapp v. Ohio* explain why the Supreme Court chose to apply the exclusionary rule in both federal and state criminal cases.

Mapp v. Ohio
Supreme Court of the United States
367 U.S. 643 (1961)

MR. JUSTICE CLARK delivered the opinion of the Court.

Appellant stands convicted of knowingly having had in her possession and under her control certain lewd and lascivious books, pictures, and photographs in violation of §2905.34 of Ohio's Revised Code. As officially stated in the syllabus to its opinion, the Supreme Court of Ohio found that her conviction was valid though "based primarily upon the introduction in evidence of lewd and lascivious books and pictures unlawfully seized during an unlawful search of defendant's home. . . ."

On May 23, 1957, three Cleveland police officers arrived at appellant's residence in that city pursuant to information that "a person [was] hiding out in the home, who was wanted for questioning in connection with a recent bombing. . . ." Miss Mapp and her daughter by a former marriage lived on the top floor of the two-family dwelling. . . . When Miss Mapp did not come to the door immediately, at least one of the several doors to the house was forcibly opened and the policemen gained admittance. . . . It appears that Miss Mapp was halfway down the stairs from the upper floor to the front door when the officers, in this highhanded manner, broke into the hall. . . . Running rough-shod over appellant, a policeman "grabbed" her, "twisted [her] hand," and she "yelled [and] pleaded with him" because "it was hurting." Appellant, in handcuffs, was then forcibly taken upstairs to her bedroom where the officers searched a dresser, a chest of drawers, a closet and some suitcases. They also looked into a photo album and through personal papers belonging to the appellant. The search spread to the rest of the second floor including the child's bedroom, the living room, the kitchen and a dinette. The basement of the building and a trunk found therein were also searched. The obscene materials for possession of which she was ultimately convicted were discovered in the course of that widespread search.

At the trial no search warrant was produced by the prosecution, nor was the failure to produce one explained or accounted for. . . .

The State says that even if the search were made without authority, or otherwise unreasonably, it is not prevented from using the unconstitutionally seized evidence at trial, citing *Wolf v. Colorado*, 338 U.S. 25 (1949), in which this Court did indeed hold "that in a prosecution in a State court for a State crime the Fourteenth Amendment does not forbid the admission of evidence obtained by an unreasonable search and seizure." At p. 33. On this appeal, of which we have noted probable jurisdiction, it is urged once again that we review that holding.

[T]his Court, in *Weeks v. United States*, 232 U.S. 383 (1914), stated that

> the Fourth Amendment . . . put the courts of the United States and Federal officials, in the exercise of their power and authority, under limitations and restraints [and] . . . forever secure[d] the people, their persons, houses, papers and effects against all unreasonable searches and seizures under the guise of law . . . and the duty of giving to it force and effect is obligatory upon all entrusted under our Federal system with the enforcement of the laws.

Specifically dealing with the use of the evidence unconstitutionally seized, the Court concluded:

> If letters and private documents can thus be seized and held and used in evidence against a citizen accused of an offense, the protection of the Fourth Amendment declaring his right to be secure against such searches and seizures is of no value, and, so far as those thus placed are concerned, might as well be stricken from the Constitution. The efforts of the courts and their officials to bring the guilty to punishment, praiseworthy as they are, are not to be aided by the sacrifice of those great principles established by years of endeavor and suffering which have resulted in their embodiment in the fundamental law of the land.

Finally, the Court in that case clearly stated that use of the seized evidence involved "a denial of the constitutional rights of the accused." At p. 398. Thus, in the year 1914, in the *Weeks* case, this Court "for the first time" held that "in a federal prosecution the Fourth Amendment barred the use of evidence secured through an illegal search and seizure." . . .

Since the Fourth Amendment's right of privacy has been declared enforceable against the States through the Due Process Clause of the Fourteenth, it is enforceable against them by the same sanction of exclusion as is used against the Federal Government. Were it otherwise, then just as without the *Weeks* rule the assurance against unreasonable federal searches and seizures would be "a form of words," valueless and undeserving of mention in a perpetual charter of inestimable human liberties, so too, without that rule the freedom from state invasions of privacy would be so ephemeral and so neatly severed from its conceptual nexus with the freedom from all brutish means of coercing evidence as not to merit this Court's high regard as a freedom "implicit in the concept of ordered liberty." . . .

Moreover, our holding that the exclusionary rule is an essential part of both the Fourth and Fourteenth Amendments is not only the logical dictate of prior cases, but it also makes very good sense. There is no war between the Constitution and common sense. Presently, a federal prosecutor may make no use of evidence illegally seized, but a State's attorney across the street may, although he supposedly is operating under the enforceable prohibitions of the same Amendment. Thus the State, by admitting evidence unlawfully seized, serves to encourage disobedience to the Federal Constitution which it is bound to uphold. . . .

There are those who say, as did Justice (then Judge) Cardozo, that under our constitutional exclusionary doctrine "the criminal is to go free because the constable has blundered." In some cases this will undoubtedly be the result. But, as was said in *Elkins*, "there is another consideration—the imperative of judicial integrity." The criminal goes free, if he must, but it is the law that sets him free. Nothing can destroy a government more quickly than its failure to observe its own laws, or worse, its disregard of the charter of its own existence. As Mr. Justice Brandeis, dissenting, said in *Olmstead v. United States* (1928): "Our Government is the potent, the omnipresent teacher. For good or for ill, it teaches the whole people by its example. . . . If the Government becomes a lawbreaker, it breeds contempt for law; it invites every man to become a law unto himself; it invites anarchy." . . .

Case Discussion Questions

1. According to the Supreme Court, what is the main justification for the exclusionary rule?
2. What negative consequences arise out of application of the exclusionary rule?
3. What problems would be created by having one set of rules for the federal courts and a separate set of rules for the state courts?

Although *Mapp v. Ohio* has not been overruled, the more conservative Supreme Courts of the last 40 years have limited its applicability. In *United States v. Leon*,[52] for example, the Supreme Court carved out a major exception to the exclusionary rule in situations in which the police seized illegal drugs while administering a search warrant that they thought was valid. Later, Leon's defense attorney filed a motion to suppress the drug evidence, based on the theory that the affidavit on which the warrant was based was insufficient to establish the probable cause needed to justify its issuance, and the trial judge found that the affidavit had in fact been insufficient. However, the judge rejected the motion to suppress the evidence because the officer who filed it had done so in good faith. In upholding the trial judge's ruling, the Supreme Court cited the "substantial social costs . . . exacted by the exclusionary rule."[53]

Typical of the manner in which the Supreme Court has been chipping away at many of the most famous precedents of the Warren Court era, a recent John Roberts Court ruling held that the Fourth Amendment did not require the exclusion of evidence that was obtained in a search that violated Michigan's "knock-and-announce" rule. Writing for the majority, Justice Antonin Scalia stated:

> Whether that preliminary misstep had occurred *or not*, the police would have executed the warrant they had obtained, and would have discovered the gun and drugs inside the house. . . . What the knock-and-announce rule has never protected . . . is one's interest in preventing the government from seeing or taking evidence described in a warrant. Since the interests that *were* violated in this

[52] 468 U.S. 897 (1984).

[53] *Id.* at 907.

case have nothing to do with the seizure of the evidence, the exclusionary rule is inapplicable.[54]

Application Exercise

3. Review what you have learned so far about the *Turner* case and then answer these questions.
   a. List what, if any, evidence might be challenged based on the exclusionary rule.
   b. How do you think the judge would rule on these challenges?

b. Double Jeopardy

Double jeopardy The Fifth Amendment prohibition against prosecuting or punishing a defendant twice for the same crime.

Double jeopardy is another type of constitutional defense based on the process being used to obtain a criminal conviction. The **Double Jeopardy** Clause of the Fifth Amendment was designed to prevent a situation in which the government could keep retrying the defendant over and over for the same crime until the prosecutor got the conviction and/or the sentence he wanted, but the wording used—"no person shall be subject for the same offense to be twice up in jeopardy of life or limb"—raises some key questions. What constitutes being put "in jeopardy," and when is something considered the "same offense," as opposed to different offenses related to the same act?

Based on decisions of the U.S. Supreme Court, "jeopardy" attaches once a jury has been selected.[55] If charges are dropped prior to the start of the trial, they can be reinstated at a later date unless they were dismissed "with prejudice." If the trial concludes with either a conviction or acquittal, a defendant cannot be tried again for the same offense. However, if the trial ends in a mistrial because of a hung jury, for example, the Double Jeopardy Clause will not prevent the state from prosecuting the defendant in a second trial.

Although the Double Jeopardy Clause prohibits being tried twice for the same offense, it does not prohibit separate prosecutions for different offenses arising out of the same action. For example, an act that is prosecuted as a homicide in state court may also be prosecuted as a violation of civil rights in federal court.[56] Furthermore, double jeopardy does not prevent a civil action for damages based on the same set of facts presented in a criminal prosecution.

---

[54] *Hudson v. Michigan*, 547 U.S. 586 (2006). Note also the discussion of *Brewer v. Williams* on p. 104, where evidence that was excluded on the basis of an unconstitutional interrogation was allowed on the basis of the inevitable discovery doctrine.

[55] In bench trials, jeopardy attaches when the trial begins with opening statements.

[56] In *Gamble v. United States*, 139 S. Ct. 1960 (2019), the Supreme Court reaffirmed the dual-sovereignty doctrine, which provides that two offenses are not the "same offence" for double jeopardy purposes if prosecuted by the state and federal governments. The Supreme Court also held that the double jeopardy clause does not bar a single sovereign's successive prosecutions of distinct offenses arising from a single act. *Denezpi v. United States*, 142 S.Ct. 1848 (2022).

Finally, if the defendant successfully appeals a conviction, the appellate court may remand the case for a new trial without violating the Double Jeopardy Clause.

G. Statute of Limitations and Speedy Trial Acts

Statute of limitations
A law that sets forth a maximum time limit between the occurrence or discovery of a crime and the date at which formal charges must be filed.

Many crimes, like civil actions, are covered by **statutes of limitations.** Under these statutes the government cannot prosecute an individual after a designated number of years have passed since either the date of the crime or the discovery of the crime. However, there are some crimes, such as murder, for which there usually is no time limit on when charges may be brought.

The Speedy Trial Act of 1974[57] requires that defendants in federal court be brought to trial within 100 days of their being charged with a crime. Many state legislatures have also established specific time limits. Defendants can usually waive these time limits if added time is needed to prepare for the trial, but prosecutors cannot claim the same privilege. Speedy trial statutes may require that the charges be dismissed if defendants are not brought to trial within a given number of days. Therefore, as is true with statutes of limitations, failure to comply with these dates can become a basis for having the charges dismissed.

Application Exercise

4. Review the facts of the Cook case (*see* hypothetical case on page xxxvii) and then read the Traffic Crash Reconstruction Report in Exhibit 7.3 at page 235. Based on these materials, what defenses might Cook assert?

H. Proof Beyond a Reasonable Doubt

Even when defendants do not have a formal defense available, they can still successfully defend the case by convincing the jury (or judge in a bench trial) that the prosecution has failed to meet its burden of proving guilt beyond a reasonable doubt. When this approach is used, the defense usually challenges the credibility of the prosecution's witnesses.

A noteworthy example of this defense strategy was presented by defense counsel in R. Kelly's 2008 trial on child pornography charges. Kelly was accused of appearing in a sex tape with an underage girl. The woman who was allegedly videotaped did not testify, but 14 witnesses identified the woman and several others testified that he was the other person depicted in the tape. One witness testified that she had participated in a threesome with him and the young woman from the video. The defense argued that the witnesses were not

[57] 18 U.S.C. §3161 (2009).

Exhibit 7.3: Police Report in *Cook* Case

STATE POLICE DISTRICT 18 TRAFFIC CRASH RECONSTRUCTION REPORT

FINDINGS

- Route 185 is a four lane asphalt roadway accommodating two lanes northbound and two lanes southbound with 4-foot paved shoulders on both sides.
- The speed limit on Route 185 at the crash site was posted in both directions as 45 mph.
- There is no overhead lighting at the immediate vicinity of the crash.

CONCLUSIONS

Environment

- Visibility for the motorist approaching the rear of the bicycle was limited due to the lack of overhead lighting in the area of the crash.

Unit #1 Schwinn Bicycle

- The Schwinn bicycle was black in color and was not equipped with a headlight or rear taillight as required by state statute. The bicycle was equipped with rear yellow reflectors on both sides of both panels and a white reflector mounted below the seat to the rear.
- The bicyclist was not wearing any type of reflective clothing.
- The bicycle was struck in the rear end approximately 2 feet west of the east side of the northbound driving lane of the roadway.
- At impact, the bicycle struck the left front bumper of the Blazer approximately 8 inches inward from the passenger side of the vehicle.
- The bicyclist struck the front hood area of the Blazer causing the hood to be pushed inward 2 inches.
- The bicyclist continued rearward striking the front passenger side windshield of the Blazer.
- The driver of the Blazer then applied the brakes, without leaving any evidence of skid marks, causing the bicyclist to be thrown forward onto the pavement.
- The bicyclist traveled 82′9″ in a northerly direction on the roadway before coming to final rest.
- County Coroner tests show the bicyclist had a blood alcohol concentration (BOC) of 0.121.

Unit #2 Chevrolet Blazer

- The Chevrolet Blazer was traveling a minimum of 38 mph when it struck the bicyclist.
- The front passenger's side headlamp was pushed inward, causing it to point toward the passenger's side of the vehicle. It is unknown if the headlamp was misaligned prior to the crash.
- Bud Cook, the driver of the Blazer, had a BOC of 0.178.

believable and were testifying for notoriety and money, not for justice. The jury acquitted Kelly because it was not convinced the girl appearing in the tape was underage.

SUMMARY

The most common defense usually involves denial that the defendants did what they are accused of committing, such as, "The light wasn't red when my car entered the intersection" or "I never gave anyone any inside information about our company's plan to introduce a new drug." A specialized version of this denial approach is the alibi defense, which claims that the defendant could not have committed the crime because he or she was someplace else at the time the criminal act took place. In these cases, the prosecution has the burden of presenting enough evidence to convince the judge or jury to reject the defendant's denial. Similarly, some defendants argue that the facts presented by the prosecution do not amount to a crime.

In a limited number of situations, ignorance or mistakes can be raised as a defense when the ignorance relates to *mens rea* or the defendant relied on incorrect official statements about the application of the law.

Another group of defenses is related to the status of the accused at the time the crime was committed. In situations where the defendant is under a certain age, has certain types of mental disorders, or is under the influence of drugs or alcohol, it may be possible for these individuals to establish that they were incapable of formulating the required *mens rea*. Although the insanity defense receives a lot of attention in the media, the legal definition of insanity is very restrictive and difficult to establish. Whereas a "not guilty by reason of insanity" verdict relieves the defendant of all criminal responsibility, the person might still be committed to a mental health facility. With a "guilty but mentally ill" verdict, the defendant has a criminal conviction on record but is sent to a mental treatment facility rather than to a regular prison.

Duress, necessity, and self-defense are reactive defenses. These defenses are based on the recognition that in some situations the crime committed was justified because it was the "lesser of two evils." Therefore, a person *may* (depending on the state and the circumstances) be able to shoot a home invader without committing a crime.

Entrapment, statutes of limitations, and constitutional defenses are all based on the idea that the agents of the government have done something wrong and that these actions have invalidated some part of the criminal prosecution. So, the government cannot prosecute someone when a government agent talked the defendant into taking the illegal action. It cannot prosecute someone after certain time limits have run out, and it cannot use evidence that was illegally obtained. It also cannot prosecute someone for actions that did not constitute a crime until after they were performed or based on laws that were vague and overly broad.

Even when formal defenses are not raised, the defense can argue that the prosecution did not meet its burden to prove the defendant's guilt beyond a reasonable doubt.

REVIEW QUESTIONS

1. Define the alibi defense and explain the role that alibi witnesses play in a case.
2. In federal court, what duties of disclosure do the defense attorneys owe when the alibi defense is raised?
3. In federal court, what duties of disclosure do the prosecuting attorneys owe when the alibi defense is raised?
4. What defense can be raised when a defendant charged with statutory rape claims that the victim lied when she told him that she was 18 when in fact she was 15? Is this defense likely to prevail? Explain why or why not.
5. Explain why the status of a defendant can be raised as a defense. Name three status defenses.
6. List and describe the three major models of the insanity defense.
7. If a federal jury makes a finding of not guilty by reason of insanity, what happens to the defendant?
8. Which intoxication defense is limited to specific-intent crimes? Why is the defense so limited?
9. Compare and contrast the insanity defense and the concept of the defendant's competency to stand trial.
10. What must a defendant show to prove that the commission of the crime occurred under duress?
11. What potential defense can be raised by a person accused of possession of marijuana when the accused was using it to treat his condition of glaucoma? Explain this defense.
12. What conditions must be met to raise self-defense?
13. How does the "retreat exception" affect a person's right to use deadly force to protect property?
14. What defense allows a person who has been the victim of repeated attacks the right to self-defense, even when there may not be immediate danger at the exact moment that the right to self-defense is exercised? What is the rationale for this defense?
15. What is the defense based upon government agents simply providing the defendant an opportunity to commit a crime that the person was already contemplating?
16. What constitutional attacks can be raised to challenge a retroactive statute designed to criminalize the conduct of a single individual?
17. Under what circumstances can hate speech, such as cross burning, be criminalized? When would such hate crime legislation be considered unconstitutional?
18. How does the "fruit of the poisonous tree" doctrine relate to the exclusionary rule?
19. What limitations are imposed on the prosecution in retrying a defendant on the same charge after the first trial resulted in a hung jury?
20. How many days do federal prosecutors have to put the defendant on trial? What is the statutory basis for this requirement?

Chapter 8

Discovery and Disclosure

Chapter Objectives

After reading this chapter, you should be able to:

- Explain why discovery is an essential part of the U.S. legal system.
- Compare and contrast the following terms: "discovery," "disclosure," "depositions," "exculpatory evidence," and "impeachment evidence."
- Discuss the ways in which the Due Process Clause and the Self-Incrimination Clauses impact the discovery process.
- Explain how judges deal with discovery disputes and the standards they use in deciding whether specific types of materials must be disclosed.
- Explain what e-discovery is and how it differs from traditional discovery.
- Prepare documents related to discovery requests and responses.
- List and explain the use of the types of depositions taken in criminal cases.
- Explain what paralegals can do to prepare a witness for a deposition.
- Compare and contrast the use of deposition summaries and abstracts.
- Compare and contrast a written discovery request and subpoena *duces tecum*.

Introduction

Up to this point, we have covered the actions taken by law enforcement officials (i.e., police and prosecutors) as they investigate crimes and prosecute them in the court system. We have also discussed the role of the defense attorney and the responsibilities involved in representing a person accused of a crime. This chapter focuses on the procedures used to acquire and exchange information that is vital to both sides in assessing the strength of the case and preparing for trial. It is an aspect of criminal litigation in which paralegals can play an active role.

In everyday usage, "discovery" is used either to identify something that a person didn't know or hadn't seen before, or as a process used to find something new. In the legal system, **discovery** is a legal procedure by which a party in the case can obtain information about the case from parties or other sources prior to the start of the trial. As part of the discovery process, parties to a case **disclose** to the other side relevant information involved in the litigation.

Discovery
A legal procedure by which a party in the case can obtain information about the case from other parties prior to the start of the trial.

Disclosure
The revealing of information.

The discovery process is somewhat analogous to gold mining. Initially, a miner performs an exploratory drilling to find out whether gold is even present at the site. If it is there, the miner taps into this area. He will continue to focus on sites rich with gold ore as long as it is economically feasible to retrieve it. Ultimately, the mineral that is recovered is processed into a polished product. As in gold mining, formal discovery may yield some, much, or no helpful material. A skilled criminal law practitioner will react to the initial disclosures to determine whether it makes sense to seek additional information and what type should be sought. Once all of the raw data are retrieved and organized, the attorney uses this information to design an appropriate approach to the case.

While there are many variations in the rules of criminal procedure among the states and federal government, there are two basic models of formal discovery in criminal cases. Both models will be discussed in this chapter. You will need to check your jurisdiction's criminal procedural rules to see which model applies to your state and the scope of disclosure.

A. JUSTIFICATIONS FOR DISCOVERY

Discovery is an essential part of the adversary system because it is designed to provide both sides with the evidence needed to present their cases to the judge or jury deciding the matter. Justice would not be done if one side did not know what the opposing side was going to present at trial.

Discovery eliminates the element of surprise. Surprise witnesses make for good movies and television shows, but they do not always lead to just results. Through discovery, each side learns the identities of opposition witnesses and their likely testimony. This knowledge gives each side more time to investigate the background of adverse witnesses, find expert witnesses, etc.

In addition to making trials fairer and more efficient, discovery often encourages out-of-court settlements, which save time and money. If the defense knows that there were several eyewitnesses to the crime or that the defendant's fingerprints were found on the murder weapon, the defendant is far more likely to plead guilty to a lesser crime in return for a reduced sentence. On the other hand, if the defense knows that the only witness has poor eyesight and a longstanding grudge against the defendant, the defense is more likely to either go to trial or hold out for a better plea bargain. The trial will be more efficient because the information gained through discovery allows the attorneys to fight over various evidentiary issues before the trial begins. By resolving these issues before trial, some potential witnesses may not have to appear, or witnesses will spend less time on the stand. Indeed, the judge's rulings on some of these pretrial motions may also encourage a plea-bargained alternative to the trial.

To represent their clients effectively, defense attorneys have a duty to collect information to investigate the case. They might gather information that can be used to impeach police officers, the alleged victim, and other prosecution witnesses. If their trial theory is that a third party committed the crime, defense counsel will seek information about the third-party suspect. When the defendant asserts the alibi defense, counsel will assemble evidence to establish the client's whereabouts when the crime was committed as well as information that may be used to impeach eyewitnesses.

B. Constitutional Issues Involved in Discovery

Before reading further, go back to pages 92-97 in Chapter 4 to review what we had to say about due process of law and the provisions of the U.S. Constitution that protect the rights of criminal defendants. The two main constitutional issues arising in the context of discovery are (1) whether it is a violation of the Due Process Clause to withhold evidence from the other side and (2) whether it is a violation of the privilege against self-incrimination to force the defense to turn over materials that may tend to incriminate the accused.

In 1963, in *Brady v. Maryland*,[1] the U.S. Supreme Court made it clear that the Due Process Clause requires prosecutors to turn over relevant exculpatory evidence to the defense. **Exculpatory evidence** is evidence that either tends to establish the defendant's innocence or is favorable to the accused on the question of punishment.[2] In *Giglio v. United States*, the U.S. Supreme Court held that the prosecution's *Brady* obligations included the affirmative duty to provide the defense with **impeachment evidence.**[3] In either case, the government's duty to disclose is limited to **material evidence.** Evidence is material "if there is a reasonable probability that had the evidence been disclosed to the defense, the result of the proceeding would have been different."[4] In *Kyles v. Whitley*,[5] the Supreme Court expressly stated that the individual prosecutor has an affirmative duty to learn of any favorable evidence known to the other people and agencies acting on the government's behalf on the case, including the police.

In 2020, the United States enacted the Due Process Protections Act to provide defendants with greater protection under *Brady* by adding the following subparagraph to Rule 5 of the **Federal Rules of Criminal Procedure (FRCrP)**:

(f) **Reminder of Prosecutorial Obligation.**

(1) **In General.** In all criminal proceedings, on the first scheduled court date when both prosecutor and defense counsel are present, the judge shall issue an oral and written order to prosecution and defense counsel that

Exculpatory evidence
Evidence that either tends to establish the defendant's innocence or is favorable to the accused on the question of punishment.

Impeachment evidence
Evidence that tends to undermine the credibility of the opponent's witnesses.

Material evidence
For the purposes of determining the prosecution's disclosure obligations under *Brady v. Maryland*, evidence is material if there is a reasonable probability that had the evidence been disclosed to the defense, the result of the proceeding would have been different.

Federal Rules of Criminal Procedure (FRCrP)
The rules that govern the procedure in all criminal proceedings in the U.S. District Courts, the U.S. Courts of Appeals, and the U.S. Supreme Court.

[1] 373 U.S. 83 (1963).

[2] *United States v. Bagley*, 473 U.S. 667 (1985).

[3] 405 U.S. 150 (1972). Impeachment evidence includes evidence that tends to undermine the credibility of the government's witnesses.

[4] *United States v. Bagley*, 473 U.S. 667, 682 (1985).

[5] 514 U.S. 419 (1995). In *Pennsylvania v. Ritchie*, 480 U.S. 39 (1987), the Supreme Court implied that the prosecution may have a duty to examine the files of other government agencies in order to find out whether they contain exculpatory material.

confirms the disclosure obligation of the prosecutor under *Brady v. Maryland*, 373 U.S. 83 (1963) and its progeny, and the possible consequences of violating such order under applicable law.

Subparagraph (f)(2) of Rule 5 requires the U.S. District Courts to develop a model order to implement the change. A model order entered by a District Court Judge in the Southern District of New York appears in in Exhibit 8.1.

Exhibit 8.1: Model Order Entered by a District Court Judge in the Southern District of New York

<u>**United States v. Shalon**</u>
United States District Court for the Southern District of New York
Entered 11/23/2020
[Citations omitted]

ORDER ISSUED PURSUANT TO FEDERAL RULE OF CRIMINAL PROCEDURE 5(F)

LAURA TAYLOR SWAIN, United States District Judge

The parties are directed, pursuant to Federal Rule of Criminal Procedure 5(f) as amended by the Due Process Protections Act of 2020, to take notice of the following:

Brady v. Maryland, and the decisions that have built upon it establish that, in order to assure protection of the defendant's constitutional rights to due process and a fair trial, the prosecution (i.e., the Government) has an affirmative duty to seek out and provide to the defense all material evidence that is favorable to the accused and that is known to the Government or to federal, state, and local law enforcement personnel and officers who are or have been involved in the investigation or prosecution of the case. Evidence is material if there is a reasonable probability that, had the evidence been disclosed to the defense, the result of the proceeding would have been different. Because this is a backward-looking standard, a "prudent prosecutor will resolve doubtful questions in favor of disclosure."

This duty applies to evidence that affirmatively tends to exculpate the defendant, as well as information that impeaches the credibility of the Government's witnesses at both the guilt and sentencing phases. Even inadmissible evidence may be material if it could lead to the discovery of admissible evidence.

The Government must disclose such evidence to the defense promptly after its existence becomes known to the Government, so as to enable the defense to have an opportunity to make effective use of the evidence in preparing its case and at trial, including a reasonable opportunity to investigate the information. This is a continuing obligation and applies to materials that become known to the Government in the future. Additionally, if information is otherwise subject to disclosure, it must be disclosed regardless of whether the Government credits it. As used here, the term "Government" includes all federal state, and local law enforcement officers and other officials who have participated in the investigation and prosecution of the offense or offenses with which the defendant is charged.

In the context of a guilty plea, Brady evidence is material where there is a reasonable probability that, but for the failure to produce such information, the defendant would not have entered the plea but instead would have insisted on going to trial. However, the Government is not required to disclose impeachment material prior to a guilty plea.

In the event the Government believes that a disclosure under this Order would compromise witness safety, victim rights, national security, a sensitive law-enforcement technique, or any other substantial government interest, it may apply to the Court for a modification of its obligations, which may include in camera review and/or withholding or subjecting to a protective order all or part of the information otherwise subject to disclosure.
If the Government fails to comply with this Court's Rule 5(f) Order or the obligations imposed by Brady and its progeny, the Court, in addition to ordering production of the information, may:

(1) specify the terms and conditions of such production;
(2) grant a continuance;
(3) impose evidentiary sanctions;
(4) impose sanctions on any responsible lawyer for the Government;
(5) dismiss charges before trial or vacate a conviction after trial or a guilty plea; or
(6) enter any other order that is just under the circumstances.

SO ORDERED.

Because the prosecution may seek discovery from the defendant or subpoena materials from third parties, the Fifth Amendment privilege against self-incrimination may limit the information that must be disclosed, even though pretrial disclosure of information may make the trial fairer and more efficient. The applicable section of the Fifth Amendment reads: "nor shall any person . . . be compelled in any criminal case to be a witness against himself." In *United States v. Hubbell,*[6] the Supreme Court held that the Fifth Amendment privilege against compelled self-incrimination protects a witness from being forced to disclose the existence of incriminating documents that the government is unable to describe with reasonable particularity.

Another application of the Fifth Amendment self-incrimination clause arises in situations where the government may be conducting parallel civil and criminal investigations. Consider the situations involved in the Edwards sample case (*see* hypothetical case on page xxxviii). Bill Edwards engaged in behavior that might have violated federal securities regulations, as well as state or federal criminal laws. In situations like these, it is not unusual for the Securities and Exchange Commission (SEC) to coordinate its investigation with the U.S. Department of Justice (DOJ). If, as is often the case, the underlying facts are relevant to both a civil enforcement suit and a criminal action, materials that are subpoenaed for a civil suit might be incriminating in a criminal trial.

---

[6] 530 U.S. 27 (2000).

In *United States v. Kordel*[7] the Supreme Court rejected the argument that the government should have to decide whether to pursue a criminal prosecution before commencing a civil proceeding. It further stated that the Due Process Clause did not require government agents to inform witnesses in civil litigation that they might also be prosecuted in criminal court. An individual cannot be forced to make incriminating statements in civil proceedings, but, if the person does make incriminating disclosures, the individual is treated as having invoked the privilege against self-incrimination.

Dicta
Statements made in a court's opinion that go beyond the facts necessary to decide the case and therefore are not binding legal precedent in subsequent cases.

In **dicta**, the *Kordel* opinion suggested that it might reach a different conclusion if it were shown that the civil action was undertaken solely to obtain evidence for a criminal prosecution.[8] SEC policy now mandates that targets of civil enforcement proceedings be made aware of the possibility of criminal prosecution based on information obtained by the SEC from their testimony.[9] In *United States v. Scrushy*[10] and *United States v. Stringer,*[11] federal district courts ruled that in cases where there was extensive cooperation between the SEC and DOJ, the government had an obligation to inform witnesses that criminal prosecution was "probable" rather than just "possible."

In summary, we have seen that the Due Process Clause requires the prosecution to disclose certain types of information, while the privilege against self-incrimination protects defendants from having to reveal some types of information through discovery. It is important to note, however, that while *Brady* ruled that the Due Process Clause prohibits the prosecution from concealing evidence favorable to the accused, the Supreme Court also stated that there is no general constitutional right to discovery in criminal cases[12] and has remarked that "the Due Process Clause has little to say regarding the amount of discovery which the parties must be afforded."[13]

C. Procedural Rules Governing Discovery

American Bar Association (ABA)
The largest voluntary association of attorneys in the United States. As the national representative of the legal profession, the ABA's stated mission is to serve the public and the profession by promoting justice, professional excellence and respect for the law.

The federal government and all of the states have procedural rules that provide for significant discovery in criminal cases. We begin with an analysis of the FRCrP since they apply to all federal courts and illustrate one of the two general approaches to formal discovery that have emerged. The alternative approach we will illustrate by referencing the **American Bar Association (ABA)** standards on criminal discovery.

Rule 16 of the FRCrP provides that *upon the defendant's request*, the government must furnish the defense the following information:

> (A) *Defendant's Oral Statement* ["the substance of any relevant oral statement made by the defendant, before or after arrest, in response to

[7]397 U.S. 1 (1970).

[8]*Id.* at 12.

[9]SEC, Division of Enforcement, *Enforcement Manual* (January 13, 2010), Section 3.2.3.1, Forms 1661 and 1662. http://www.sec.gov/divisions/enforce/enforcementmanual.pdf, at p. 52.

[10]366 F. Supp. 2d 1134 (N.D. Ala. 2005).

[11]408 F. Supp. 2d 1083 (D. Or. 2006).

[12]*Weatherford v. Bursey*, 429 U.S. 545 (1977).

[13]*Wardius v. Oregon*, 412 U.S. 470, 474 (1973).

interrogation by a person the defendant knew was a government agent if the government intends to use the statement at trial"]

(B) *Defendant's Written or Recorded Statement* ["(i) any relevant written or recorded statement by the defendant if: the statement is within the government's possession, custody, or control; and the attorney for the government knows—or through due diligence could know—that the statement exists"][14]

(C) *Organizational Defendant's Representative's Statements* [if the defendant is an organization, the government must disclose to the defendant binding oral, written, or recorded statements made by its representative][15]

(D) *Defendant's Prior Record* ["the defendant's prior criminal record that is within the government's possession, custody, or control if the attorney for the government knows—or through due diligence could know—that the record exists."]

(E) *Documents and Objects* [Under certain specified circumstances, "books, papers, documents, data, photographs, tangible objects, buildings or places, or copies or portions of any of these items"][16]

(F) *Reports of Examinations and Tests* [Under specified circumstances, "the results or reports of any physical or mental examination and of any scientific test or experiment"][17]

(G) *Expert Witnesses* [Under specified circumstances, the government must give to the defendant a written summary of any expert testimony that the government intends to use under Rules 702, 703, or 705 of the **Federal Rules of Evidence (FRE)**.][18]

Federal Rules of Evidence (FRE)
The rules of evidence that govern proof in all civil and criminal proceedings in the U.S. district courts.

Rule 16 discovery is considered restrictive for several reasons. It is not self-executing. Unlike federal civil discovery, criminal discovery under Rule 16 must be initiated by the parties. Also, in contrast to the federal civil rules, there are no predetermined timelines that establish when disclosures must be made.[19]

---

[14]In addition, the government must disclose to the defendant: "(ii) the portion of any written record containing the substance of any relevant oral statement made before or after arrest if the defendant made the statement in response to interrogation by a person the defendant knew was a government agent; and (iii) the defendant's recorded testimony before a grand jury relating to the charged offense." FRCrP 16(a)(1)(B).

[15]FRCrP 16(a)(1)(C) requires disclosure of "any statement described in Rule 16(a)(1)(A) and (B) if the government contends that the person making the statement: (i) was legally able to bind the defendant regarding the subject of the statement because of that person's position as the defendant's director, officer, employee, or agent; or (ii) was personally involved in the alleged conduct constituting the offense and was legally able to bind the defendant regarding that conduct because of that person's position as the defendant's director, officer, employee, or agent."

[16]The item must be "within the government's possession, custody, or control and: (i) the item is material to preparing the defense; (ii) the government intends to use the item in its case-in-chief at trial; or (iii) the item was obtained from or belongs to the defendant." Rule 16(a)(1)(E).

[17]Disclosure is required when "(i) the item is within the government's possession, custody, or control; (ii) the attorney for the government knows—or through due diligence could know—that the item exists; and (iii) the item is material to preparing the defense or the government intends to use the item in its case-in-chief at trial." Rule 16(a)(1)(F).

[18]FRE 702 concerns testimony by experts; FRE 703 relates to basis of opinions by experts; and FRE 705 regards disclosure of facts or data underlying expert opinions.

[19]See Rule 26 of the Federal Rule of Civil Procedure (FRCP), which imposes mandatory disclosure of information and tangible objects at several stages of a case. The time for each disclosure is referenced to specific events in the case.

From the defense point of view, one of the most problematic aspects of Rule 16 is that the government is not required to disclose a list of witnesses or the statements of co-defendants prior to trial.[20] About a dozen states take the federal rules approach.[21]

In contrast, the ABA has encouraged greater disclosure of information. In guidelines adopted in 1994 and updated in 1996,[22] it declared that "within a specified and reasonable time prior to trial," the prosecution should disclose the following types of information to the defense:

- Written and oral statements of the defendant or of any co-defendant that are within the possession or control of the prosecution
- The names and addresses of persons known to the prosecution to have information concerning the offense charged
- Written statements of witnesses; the relationship, if any, between the prosecution and any witness it intends to call at trial
- The nature and circumstances of any agreements between the prosecution and the witness that constitutes an inducement for the cooperation or testimony of the witness
- Reports or written statements of experts made in connection with the case; tangible objects such as books, papers, documents, photographs, and models that pertain to the case; information about prior criminal convictions, pending charges, or probationary status of the defendant, co-defendant, or witness information relating to lineups, show-ups, and picture or voice identifications
- Any material or information within the prosecutor's possession or control that tends to negate the guilt of the defendant as to the offense charged or that would tend to reduce the punishment of the defendant.

Standard 11-2.1 also requires the government to make additional disclosures to the defense if (1) it intends to use character, reputation, or other act of evidence; (2) the defendant's conversations or premises have been subjected to electronic surveillance in connection with the case; or (3) any tangible object that the object the prosecutor intends to offer at trial was obtained through a search and seizure.[23]

---

[20]FRCrP 26 provides for a method that a party can use to obtain a witness's statement *after* the witness has testified on direct examination.

[21]The Justice Project, *Expanded Discovery in Criminal Cases: A Policy Review* 8 (2007). http://www.thejusticeproject.org/solution/Discovery/discovery-lr.pdf.

[22]*ABA Standards for Criminal Justice: Discovery and Trial by Jury* (3d ed., American Bar Association 1996).

[23]Standard 11-2.1 provides in part:

> (a) If the prosecution intends to use character, reputation, or other act of evidence, the prosecution should notify the defense of that intention and of the substance of the evidence to be used.
>
> (c) If the defendant's conversations or premises have been subjected to electronic surveillance (including wiretapping) in connection with the investigation or prosecution of the case, the prosecution should inform the defense of that fact.
>
> (d) If any tangible object which the object which the prosecutor intends to offer at trial was obtained through a search and seizure, the prosecution should disclose to the defense any information, documents, or other material relating to the acquisition of such objects."

A number of states take the ABA approach, including California, New Jersey, Illinois,[24] and Michigan. States that don't fall squarely into either the ABA or the Rule 16 model generally lie somewhere between the two standards.[25] For a comparison of the primary prosecution's pretrial disclosure obligations under the two models, see Figure 8.1. Check your own state's rules of criminal procedure to see how they compare. Note also that the *Brady* obligations (see pp. 241-244) have not been incorporated into the rules of criminal procedure for all states. Accordingly, in a number of state and local jurisdictions, exculpatory evidence is not defined by rule and there is no established timetable for *Brady* material disclosure.

In contrast, some local court rules include the *Brady* requirements, as well as disclosure deadlines, even though the general rule for the jurisdiction is silent as to these matters.

For example, the policy of the Los Angeles County District Attorney's Office on the prosecution's duties under *Brady* states that the prosecution must disclose

Information to Be Disclosed	Rule 16	11-2.1(a)
Defendant's oral, written, or recorded statements	Duty	Duty
Co-defendant statements	No duty	Duty
Identification of all persons with knowledge	No duty	Duty
Identities of trial witnesses	No duty	Duty
Relationship between prosecution and its witness	No duty	Duty
Expert curriculum vitae, a written description of proposed testimony, expert's opinions, and basis of opinions	Limited duty	Duty
Reports of examinations and tests	Duty	Duty
Relevant tangible objects and documents	Duty	Duty
Identification of all objects it intends to offer as evidence at trial	No duty	Duty
Record of prior criminal convictions of defendant	Duty	Duty
Record of prior criminal convictions of co-defendant and any witness a party intends to present at trial	No duty	Duty
Information relating to lineups, showups, and picture or voice identifications	No duty	Duty

Figure 8.1 Prosecution Pretrial Disclosure Duties Under Rule 16 of the Federal Rules of Criminal Procedure and ABA Standard 11- 2.1(a)

[24]Although Illinois, New Jersey, and Michigan have liberal disclosure policies, the parties must formally request discovery.

[25]The Justice Project, *Expanded Discovery in Criminal Cases: A Policy Review.*

information that undermines the credibility of a prosecution witness. The policy lists the following examples of impeachment evidence of material witnesses:

1. Felony convictions involving moral turpitude
2. Misdemeanor or other conduct that reflects on believability
3. Misconduct involving moral turpitude
4. False reports by a prosecution witness
5. Pending criminal charges against a prosecution witness
6. Parole or probation of a prosecution witness
7. Evidence contradicting a prosecution witness's statements or reports
8. Evidence undermining a prosecution witness's expertise (e.g., inaccurate statements or expert opinions)
9. Evidence of misconduct by a Board of Rights or Civil Service Commission that reflects on a prosecution witness's truthfulness, bias, or moral turpitude
10. Evidence that a prosecution witness has a reputation for untruthfulness
11. Evidence that a prosecution witness has a racial, religious, or personal bias against the defendant individually or as a member of a group
12. Promises, offers, or inducements to a prosecution witness, including a grant of immunity[26]

It is important, therefore, to carefully check all criminal discovery rules in your jurisdiction. Local rules may establish disclosure requirements that may not be immediately apparent. On the other hand, if there are no rules governing *Brady* evidence, the defense should make a written request for this discovery at the outset of the case.

APPLICATION EXERCISES

1. Find the part of your state's code of criminal procedure or the court rules that govern discovery in criminal cases. What is the citation for where they appear?
2. Under your state's criminal discovery rules, which of the following is the prosecution required to furnish to the defendant?
   - Defendant's oral, written, or recorded statements
   - Co-defendant statements
   - Identification of all persons with knowledge
   - Identities of trial witnesses
   - Relationship between prosecution and its witness
   - Expert curriculum vitae, written description of proposed expert's testimony, opinions, and basis of opinions

[26]Los Angeles District Attorney's Office, Disclosure of Exculpatory and Impeachment Information, Chapter 14—Legal Policy Manual, https://da.lacounty.gov/sites/default/files/policies/Brady-Chapter14-2020.pdf at page 262.

- Reports of examinations and tests
- Relevant tangible objects and documents
- Identification of all objects the prosecution intends to offer as evidence at trial Record of prior criminal convictions of defendant
- Record of prior criminal convictions of co-defendants and any witness whom a party intends to present at trial
- Information relating to lineups, show-ups, and picture or voice identifications

3. What type of duty, if any, is imposed on the prosecution in your state's rules of procedure to provide the defense with exculpatory evidence?
4. Are the rules of criminal procedure in your state more like the federal rules of criminal discovery or the ABA standards? In what ways?
5. Review all rules for criminal discovery for both the state and federal districts where your school is located. How do these rules attempt to implement the requirements of *Brady v. Maryland*? What time limits for discovery compliance are set forth in these rules?

D. Discovery Requests and Responses

In many jurisdictions, the parties must initiate the request for discovery. Generally, the material that the parties are entitled to receive consists of statements, the defendant's criminal record, the grand jury transcript, documents and tangible items, scientific reports, and *Brady* material. Depending on the jurisdiction, the parties may also get a list of witnesses, as well as the witnesses' statements.

In most felony cases, the defense's initial discovery request can be prepared and ready to serve on the prosecution at the time of the defendant's arraignment. Paralegals working for prosecutors and defense attorneys are frequently called upon to draft these discovery requests.

1. Pattern Discovery Requests

Like most other court documents, discovery requests typically include the following components:

- Caption
- Introductory paragraph
- Body
- Signature
- Address block/preparer's data
- Proof of service

Pattern discovery Model discovery requests that use generic, boilerplate language to request all of the information allowable under the applicable criminal discovery rules.

Boilerplate language Model sentences that include standardized legal terms and phrases.

As in the drafting of other types of commonly used court documents, **pattern discovery** requests usually involve customizing **boilerplate language** to reflect the facts of the specific case. See Chapter 5, pages 151-152, for instructions on

Caption
The section of a court document containing the names of the parties, case number, name of the court in which it is being filed, and a title that identifies the type of document being filed.

drafting the **caption** section of court documents. Because there are variations from court to court, you should look at other documents filed in your jurisdiction for guides to the custom and practice used. Exhibit 8.2 provides an example of a discovery request for *United States v. Edwards* (*see* hypothetical case on page xxxviii).

Notice how the requested material closely tracks FRCrP 16. Although this form includes separate citations to each relevant subparagraph of the rule, most forms simply cite the rule as a whole in the introductory paragraph. This

Exhibit 8.2: Pattern Discovery Request from Defendant in *United States v. Edwards*

THE UNITED STATES DISTRICT COURT
FOR THE NORTHERN DISTRICT OF
INDIANA HAMMOND DIVISION

UNITED STATES OF AMERICA	)	Case No. 20 CR XXX
vs	)	
WILLIAM EDWARDS,	)	
Defendant.	)	

DEFENDANT'S INITIAL DISCOVERY REQUEST

Now comes Defendant WILLIAM EDWARDS, by CHARLES HOVEY, his attorney, and as his initial discovery request, brought pursuant to Rule 16 of the Federal Rules of Criminal Procedure and *Brady v. Maryland*, 373 U.S. 83 (1963), asks the UNITED STATES OF AMERICA to disclose and produce the following materials and information:

1. *Defendant's Oral Statements*: The substance of any relevant oral statement made by the defendant, before or after arrest, in response to interrogation by a person the defendant knew was a government agent if the government intends to use the statement at trial. [FRCrP 16(a)(1)(A).] In the event that the government intends to use such an oral statement at trial, Defendant requests that it be reduced in writing and produced. This request includes the substance of the Defendant's response to *Miranda* warnings.
2. *Defendant's Written or Recorded Statements:*
   a. Any relevant written or recorded statement by the defendant if the statement is within the government's possession, custody, or control; and the attorney for the government knows—or through due diligence could know—that the statement exists;
   b. The portion of any written record containing the substance of any relevant oral statement made before or after arrest if the defendant made the statement in response to interrogation by a person the defendant knew was a government agent; and
   c. The defendant's recorded testimony before a grand jury relating to the charged offense. [FRCrP 16(a)(1)(B).]
3. *Defendant's Prior Record*: The defendant's prior criminal record that is within the government's possession, custody, or control if the attorney for the government knows—or through due diligence could know—that the record exists. [FRCrP 16(a)(1) (D).]

This request includes the Defendant's entire criminal record, including all arrests along with offenses regardless of conviction or severity. It includes all matters that may affect the Defendant's criminal history score pursuant to the United States Sentencing Guidelines.

4. *Documents and Objects Material to Preparing the Defense:* Inspection and copying or photographing books, papers, documents, data, photographs, tangible objects, buildings or places, or copies or portions of any of these items if they are within the government's possession, custody, or control and the item is material to preparing the defense. [FRCrP 16(a)(1)(E)(i).]
5. *Documents and Objects to be Used in Government's Case-in-Chief:* Inspection and copying or photographing books, papers, documents, data, photographs, tangible objects, buildings or places, or copies or portions of any of these items if they are within the government's possession, custody, or control and the government intends to use the item in its case-in-chief at trial. [FRCrP 16(a)(1)(E)(ii).]
6. *Documents and Objects that Belong to the Defendant:* Inspection and copying or photographing books, papers, documents, data, photographs, tangible objects, buildings or places, or copies or portions of any of these items if they are within the government's possession, custody, or control and the item was obtained from or belongs to the defendant. [FRCrP 16(a)(1)(E)(iii).]
7. *Reports of Examinations and Tests:* Inspection and copying or photographing the results or reports of any physical or mental examination and of any scientific test or experiment when (i) the item is within the government's possession, custody, or control; (ii) the attorney for the government knows—or through due diligence could know—that the item exists; and (iii) the item is material to preparing the defense or the government intends to use the item in its case-in-chief at trial. [FRCrP 16(a)(1)(F).]
8. *Expert Witnesses:* A written summary of any expert testimony that the government intends to use under the Federal Rules of Evidence, the grounds and bases for such opinion testimony, and the qualifications of the expert. [FRCrP 16(a)(1)(G).]
9. *Brady v. Maryland Disclosure*: Any exculpatory evidence material to guilt or punishment, including but not limited to impeachment evidence.

Respectfully submitted,

WILLIAM EDWARDS,
Defendant

By________________________

CHARLES HOVEY, his attorney

Charles Hovey
Attorney for Defendant
1857 Bone Street
Normal, IL 61617
(309) 555-1857

Certificate of Service

I hereby certify that a true and accurate copy of the foregoing Defendant's Initial Discovery Request was served upon ______, Assistant U.S. Attorney by depositing the same in the U.S. Post Office mailbox in Chicago, Illinois in an envelope, postage fully prepaid, addressed to: Office of the United States Attorney [Address of U.S. Attorney] on the day of _______, 20 _____ at or about the hour of _____ p.m.

document is specifically drafted for *United States v. Edwards*. If you were to use this form as guide for another case, you should review FRCrP 16 in light of the facts involved in your case and adapt the form accordingly. For instance, if the defendant in your case is an organization, you would seek discovery of statements of agents, officers, and employees.[27] The *United States v. Edwards* form does not include a request for this information because Edwards is an individual defendant rather than an organizational defendant.

In jurisdictions in which court approval is needed to initiate discovery, the parties must file a motion. As in the case with pattern discovery requests, motions for leave to take discovery contain boilerplate language taken from the jurisdiction's applicable discovery rules. Exhibit 8.3 includes a motion for discovery in an Illinois felony case. The motion closely tracks Illinois Supreme Court Rule 412, which lists the disclosures that the state must make upon motion of the defense.

Exhibit 8.3: Pattern Discovery Request from Defendant in *Illinois v. Cook*

IN THE CIRCUIT COURT OF
THE ELEVENTH JUDICIAL CIRCUIT
MCLEAN COUNTY, ILLINOIS

PEOPLE OF THE STATE OF ILLINOIS	)	
v.	)	Case No. 20 CF XXX
BUD COOK,	)	
Defendant.	)	

Motion for Supreme Court Rule 412 Discovery

Now comes Defendant BUD COOK, by CHARLES HOVEY, his attorney, and moves that the court order the State to provide the Defendant with discovery pursuant to Illinois Supreme Court Rule 412. In support of this motion, seeks the following discovery:

1. The names and last known addresses of persons whom the State intends to call as witnesses, together with their relevant written or recorded statements, memoranda containing substantially verbatim reports of their oral statements, and a list of memoranda reporting or summarizing their oral statements. [412(a)(i)]

[27]FRCrP 16(a)(1)(C) concerns discovery of oral statements from certain representatives of an organizational defendant.

2. Any written or recorded statements and the substance of any oral statements made by the accused or by a co-defendant, and a list of witnesses to the making and acknowledgment of such statements. [412(a)(ii)]
3. A transcript of those portions of grand jury minutes containing testimony of the accused and relevant testimony of persons whom the prosecuting attorney intends to call as witnesses at the hearing or trial. [412(a)(iii)]
4. Any reports or statements of experts, made in connection with the particular case, including results of physical or mental examinations and of scientific tests, experiments, or comparisons, and a statement of qualifications of the expert. [412(a)(iv)]
5. Any books, papers, documents, photographs or tangible objects which the prosecuting attorney intends to use in the hearing or trial or which were obtained from or belong to the accused. [412(a)(v)]
6. Any record of prior criminal convictions, which may be used for impeachment, of persons whom the State intends to call as witnesses at the hearing or trial. [412(a)(vi)]
7. Disclosure of any electronic surveillance (including wiretapping) of conversations to which the accused was a party, or of his premises. [412(b)]
8. Any material or information within the State's possession or control which tends to negate the guilt of the accused as to the offense charged or which would tend to reduce his punishment therefor. [412(c)]

Defendant, BUD COOK, prays that this court order the State to provide the him with the above-listed discovery pursuant to Illinois Supreme Court Rule 412.

Respectfully submitted,

WILLIAM EDWARDS, Defendant

By______________________
CHARLES HOVEY, his attorney

Charles Hovey
Attorney for Defendant
1857 Bone Street
Normal, IL 61617
(309) 555-1857

2. ELECTRONIC DISCOVERY

Electronic discovery (e-discovery) The discovery of documents created, disbursed, and stored electronically.

Electronic discovery, also known as "e-discovery," is the discovery of documents created, disbursed, and stored electronically. Among other things, the types of documents sought and produced in e-discovery include e-mails, word-processed documents, spreadsheets, databases, and audio and video files.

Although the Federal Rules of Civil Procedure (FRCP) sets forth standards for electronic discovery,[28] there are no federal discovery rules for criminal cases. Likewise, most state rules of criminal procedure do not address

[28]See FRCP 16(b), 26, 33, 34, 37, & 45.

electronic discovery. Despite this absence, there is no dispute that electronically stored information (ESI) is discoverable in criminal prosecutions.

APPLICATION EXERCISES

6. Contact a local criminal defense attorney or prosecutor's office to find out what criminal law formbooks are customarily used in the jurisdiction. Make a copy of a form used to seek discovery.

7. Prepare federal and state court requests for discovery directed to the prosecution for the *Turner* case (*see* hypothetical case on pages xxxvii-xxxviii). Assume that your instructor is the defense attorney and that the instructor's address and telephone numbers are those of your school.
   a. For the federal prosecution, assume that the case was the first case filed this calendar year in the federal district in which your college is located.
   b. For the state prosecution, assume that Brandon Turner was charged with the lowest-class felony for possession of cocaine. If your state requires that the defense must first get leave of court to conduct discovery, also draft a motion for leave to take discovery. This also was the first case filed by the prosecutor this calendar year.

At one time, only complex, white-collar crime cases involved voluminous e-discovery. It is not uncommon today for street crime prosecutions to involve cell phone data and other ESI.[29] Therefore, both prosecutors and defense attorneys must be able to digest and understand e-discovery to prepare for trial and enter informed plea negotiations.

Although Rule 16 provides that a party may request the opposing side to produce "data," it makes no mention of ESI or the method of producing this data. Hence, federal district court judges have discretion to order e-discovery in the manner they deem to be appropriate. Two U.S. magistrate judges have used Rule 34 of the FRCP for guidance in administering e-discovery in criminal cases, whereas a federal court of appeals has rejected the argument that courts should apply Rule 34 to criminal e-discovery.[30]

---

[29]E.g., *Carpenter v. United States*, 138 S. Ct. 2206 (2018) (cell-site location information in robbery case); *Riley v. California*, 573 U.S. 373, (2014) (cell phone's digital information in illegal possession of firearms case); *United States v. Jones*, 565 U.S. 400 (2012) (global positioning system (GPS) tracking data in drug trafficking case).

[30]*Compare United States v. Warshak*, 631 F.3d 266 (6th Cir. 2010) *with United States v. O'Keefe*, 537 F. Supp. 2d 14 (D.D.C. 2008) *and United States v. Briggs*, No. 10CR184S, 2011 WL 4017886 (W.D.N.Y. Sept. 8, 2011).

To provide comprehensive, national e-discovery guidance to the criminal bar, a group of Department of Justice and criminal defense attorneys developed *The ESI Protocol*.[31] Several U.S. District Courts have adopted protocols for ESI discovery.[32] The Protocol makes the following general recommendations for the production of ESI discovery:

> a. The parties should discuss what formats of production are possible and appropriate, and what formats can be generated. Any format selected for producing discovery should, if possible, conform to industry standards for the format.
>
> b. ESI received from third parties should be produced in the format(s) it was received or in a reasonably usable format(s). ESI from the government's or defendant's business records should be produced in the format(s) in which it was maintained or in a reasonably usable format(s).
>
> c. Discoverable ESI generated by the government or defense during the course of their investigations (e.g., investigative reports, witness interviews, demonstrative exhibits, etc.) may be handled differently than in . . . (a) and (b) above because the parties' legal discovery obligations and practices vary according to the nature of the material, the applicable law, evolving legal standards, the parties' policies, and the parties' evolving technological capabilities.
>
> d. When producing ESI discovery, a party should not be required to take on substantial additional processing or format conversion costs and burdens beyond what the party has already done or would do for its own case preparation or discovery production. For example, the producing party need not convert ESI from one format to another or undertake additional processing of ESI beyond what is required to satisfy its legal disclosure obligations. If the receiving party desires ESI in a condition different from what the producing party intends to produce, the parties should discuss what is reasonable in terms of expense and mechanics, who will bear the burden of any additional cost or work, and how to protect the producing party's work product or privileged information. Nonetheless, with the understanding that in certain instances the results of processing ESI may constitute work product not subject to discovery, these recommendations operate on the general principle that where a producing party elects to engage in processing of ESI, the results of that processing should, unless they constitute work product, be produced in discovery along with the underlying ESI so as to save the receiving party the expense of replicating the work.[33]

---

[31]Department of Justice and Administrative Office of the U.S. Courts Joint Working Group on Electronic Technology in the Criminal Justice System, "Recommendations for Electronically Stored Information (ESI) Discovery Production in Federal Criminal Cases" https://www.uscourts.gov/sites/default/files/finalesiprotocolbookmarked.pdf (last checked September 10, 2022).

[32]K & L Gates, Local Rules, Forms and Guidelines of United States District Courts Addressing E-Discovery Issues, https://www.ediscoverylaw.com/local-rules-forms-and-guidelines-of-united-states-district-courts-addressing-e-discovery-issues/ (last accessed September 10, 2022).

[33]Id. at Strategies, pp. 6-10.

3. RESPONSES TO DISCOVERY REQUESTS

When responding to discovery requests, you must first note the date on which the discovery response is due. Failure to comply in a timely manner can prompt a motion from the opposing side and the imposition of sanctions—including the inability to use some types of the evidence at trial.

In gathering the requested documents, be sure to identify all references to any confidential information. For example, prosecutors' offices ordinarily receive reports, statements, and other investigation documents from the law enforcement agency that conducted the investigation. Such materials frequently contain confidential information, such as the identity of an informant or the address of a witness whose safety may be in jeopardy. Paralegals need to bring this information to the attention of their supervisors for direction on how these references should be handled. A paralegal's inadvertent disclosure of privileged information may have serious consequences to law enforcement or to the client. The supervising attorney may either file a formal objection to disclosing the confidential material or **redact** the sensitive information before releasing the documents in question.

Redaction
The process of masking some part of the content of a document before making it available for inspection.

After it has been determined how confidential information is to be handled, a paralegal is usually assigned to number and index the materials being turned over. Different offices may use different systems for labeling documents. One of the most common is the **Bates numbering** system. A Bates number is a number that is given to a document to identify it. Ordinarily, sequential Arabic numbers are used to identify each page of the discovery. As additional documents are acquired, each page is given a number. Some offices use labels that are affixed to each page; others use a sequential stamp. Bates numbers typically are placed on the same corner of each document. Paralegals may also prepare a Bates document index that identifies each document. Typically, there is not as much information for the defendant to organize and index at the beginning of a case because most prelitigation information is part of the police investigation.

Bates numbering
An organizational method used to label documents by assigning a number (or alphanumeric designation) to each document (or page), thereby creating a unique identifier for each

Materials being sent in response to a formal discovery request should be accompanied by a formal court document identified as a response to a request for production. This is a captioned document that provides a preview of the information being produced. Like other court documents, it contains a caption, introductory paragraph, body, attorney signature, and preparer's data. A sample face sheet of the response is depicted in Exhibit 8.4.

The body of this document should reiterate the requests made by the opposing side. Each individual request should then be followed by a response to that specific request. These responses can include:

- a list of the titles of the document(s) being produced;
- the name of the item(s) or document(s) that you are making available for inspection;
- (if required by rule) a narrative answer to the inquiry; or
- an objection to the request.

It is best to use a different type font or boldface for your responsive information for easier reading of the document. Also, cite the page numbers of the documents.

Exhibit 8.4: Face Sheet of Government Response to Production Request

THE UNITED STATES DISTRICT COURT
FOR THE NORTHERN DISTRICT OF
INDIANA HAMMOND DIVISION

UNITED STATES OF AMERICA	)	
vs	)	Case No. 20 CR XXX
WILLIAM EDWARDS,	)	
Defendant.	)	

GOVERNMENT'S FIRST RESPONSE TO DEFENDANT'S INITIAL DISCOVERY REQUEST

Now comes the UNITED STATES OF AMERICA, by the U.S. ATTORNEY, and as its first response to the defendant's initial discovery request, states as follows:

1. *Defendant's Oral Statements*: The substance of any relevant oral statement made by the defendant, before or after arrest, in response to interrogation by a person the defendant knew was a government agent if the government intends to use the statement at trial. [FRCrP 16 (a)(1)(A).] In the event that the government intends to use such an oral statement at trial, Defendant requests that it be reduced in writing and produced. This request includes the substance of the Defendant's response to *Miranda* warnings.

   Tape recording of November 23, 2018 interview between William Edwards and FBI agent Justin Colby, dated August 3, 2019, is available for inspection at a mutually convenient time during business hours at the office of the United States Attorney. A verbatim transcript of the interview does not exist at this time.

2. *Defendant's Written or Recorded Statements:*
   a. Any relevant written or recorded statement by the defendant if the statement is within the government's possession, custody, or control; and the attorney for the government knows—or through due diligence could know—that the statement exists;
   b. The portion of any written record containing the substance of any relevant oral statement made before or after arrest if the defendant made the statement in response to interrogation by a person the defendant knew was a government agent; and
   c. The defendant's recorded testimony before a grand jury relating to the charged offense. [FRCrP 16 (a)(1)(B).]

   Copies of the following documents are produced:
   Signed statement of William Edwards prepared by FBI agent Justin Colby on November 23, 2019.

[Bates Nos. 1-9]
Form letter to clients from William Edwards, dated August 3, 2018.
[Bates No.10]
Form letter to clients from William Edwards, dated September 13, 2018.
[Bates No. 11]
Grand jury transcript [Bates Nos. 11-39]

3. *Defendant's Prior Record:* The defendant's prior criminal record that is within the government's possession, custody, or control if the attorney for the government knows—or through due diligence could know—that the record exists. [FRCrP 16 (a)(1)(D).] This request includes the Defendant's entire criminal record, including all arrests along with offenses regardless of conviction or severity. It includes all matters that may affect the Defendant's criminal history score pursuant to the United States Sentencing Guidelines.
   Copies of the following documents are produced: Abstract of criminal record of William Edwards [Bates Nos. 40-43]

* * *

[Attorney Signature]

[Address Block]

Motion for entry of a protective order
A formal request to the court to protect either the opposing party or a third party from an unreasonable or invasive request for discovery.

Attorney work product
Trial preparation materials consisting of the attorney's mental impressions, conclusions, opinions, and legal theories about a case.

When a party does not have the information necessary to answer the discovery request, the proper response is "None." If responsive information is later discovered, there is a duty to supplement the response with that information. The prosecution cannot refuse to disclose information simply because the material is in the custody of law enforcement officers but not in the actual physical possession of the prosecutor's office. There is a duty on the part of the various law enforcement agencies to share information with each other. Likewise, the defense is not excused from making a disclosure if the information is the custody of the defendant's employee or agent.

When the information requested should not be disclosed due to an evidentiary privilege or otherwise, the party should object and set forth the basis of the objection in the response to the request. Either side may also file a **motion for a protective order.**[34] There are several bases to object to disclosure. Both parties can claim the information sought is **attorney work product.** Attorney work product consists of trial preparation materials containing the attorney's mental impressions, conclusions, opinions, and legal theories about a case. The government also can object on the basis that disclosure would breach national security or compromise the identity of a confidential informant. The defense may raise attorney-client privilege or the Fifth Amendment privilege against self-incrimination.

[34]Motions for protective orders are discussed later in this chapter.

The paralegal will provide copies of responsive documents themselves, along with the face sheets. Originals of the documents will be kept in the office. The paralegal also should prepare a proof of service to accompany each response.

APPLICATION EXERCISE

8. In the *Turner* case, the police had been provided information by a confidential source before the officer made the traffic stop. The defense is seeking the identity of the source, as well as his address. The prosecution does not intend to call the informant as a witness. The police are continuing to use the informant. Draft a motion for a protective order on behalf of the prosecution for the jurisdiction in which your school is located. Assume that your supervising attorney is Terry Law, 123 Main Street, Anytown (555-1234). This was the first felony case filed by the prosecutor this calendar year.

4. INFORMATION ON EXPERT WITNESSES

In addition to producing documentary and tangible items, some criminal rules of procedure impose a duty on the parties to provide a summary of **expert testimony,** along with a list of the expert's qualifications.[35] Often, forensic experts prepare reports that show their findings, bases and reasons for their conclusions, and their opinions. When this is the case, you may satisfy this discovery request by attaching copies of the report, along with the expert's **curriculum vitae (CV).** On the other hand, if the report is not sufficient to meet the obligation imposed under the rules, you may need to draft the summary. Your draft should fairly and accurately reflect the expert's anticipated testimony. Because the opponent could use the summary to cross-examine the expert, the expert should assist in preparing the statement to prevent any possibility of inconsistency between the statement and the trial testimony. Ask the expert to furnish you with a current CV.

Expert testimony
Testimony that is given by a witness who the court determines to be expert on the topic upon which the testimony is to be given. Once accepted as an expert witness, the person is allowed to state his or her opinion on relevant matters.

Curriculum vitae (CV)
A written description of a person's work experience, educational background, and skills.

APPLICATION EXERCISE

9. Using the Internet as a resource, locate experts on fingerprints and blood spatter. Provide copies of the experts' curriculum vitaes.

[35] FRCrP 16(a)(1)(G) requires the government to disclose this information upon the defendant's request. Once the defense makes this request, there is a reciprocal obligation on the defense to make the same disclosures. FRCrP 16(b)(1)(C).

5. SUPPLEMENTAL DISCOVERY

It is important to note that there is a duty to supplement discovery. Therefore, as the defense gathers information during the course of its investigation and law enforcement officers continue to build their case, the attorneys need to furnish supplemental reports to the opposing side. The format of a supplemental discovery response is essentially the same as that of the original.

When supplemental materials are involved, a new face sheet should describe the type of response in the title (e.g., Defendant's First Supplemental Response to the State's Rule 413 Request). The body of the supplemental response should restate the request that you are supplementing. As in the case of the original discovery reply, the description of the supplemental materials being provided should appear after the request in a different font style. You will send copies of the new documents to the opponent along with the face sheet. Another proof of service denoting the date of mailing or delivery should also be prepared and served.

6. WRITTEN DISCOVERY AGREEMENTS

Before we close our discussion of responses to discovery requests, it is worth noting that in federal court, the prosecution may react to the defendant's discovery request with a proposal to enter into a written discovery agreement. Typical provisions of this agreement include the following:

- The government will provide a timely response to a Rule 16(a) request, on the condition that the defendant produces reciprocal discovery pursuant to Rule 16(b).
- The government will provide statements of prospective witnesses prior to trial, on the condition that the defendant produces reciprocal discovery.
- The government will furnish *Brady v. Maryland* material in a timely manner.
- The government will give notice of its intent to use evidence of other crimes or wrong acts of the defendant.
- The government will reserve its right to produce further discovery if the prosecution believes that disclosure presents a security risk to the witness.
- The agreement is void if the defendant files a discovery motion.[36]

If the government has a practice of routinely suggesting the use of an agreement, a paralegal employed by the prosecutor's office may be required to draft the cover letter and the proposed discovery agreement.

Figure 8.2 summarizes the paralegal's role as it relates to these written discovery requests.

[36] B. Boss & E. R. Marek, *Federal Criminal Practice* (James Publishing 2006), at 10-48 through 10-49.

Discovery Requests	Discovery Responses
1. Prepare discovery request a. Adapt request from other cases b. Alternatively, use formbook	1. Note the due date
2. Arrange for service of request	2. Review documents in file
3. Prepare proof of service	3. Identify sensitive documents
4. Note the due date	4. Obtain direction as to sensitive matters
5. Review response to ascertain compliance	5. Label documents (e.g., Bates)
6. File response	6. Prepare face sheet of response
7. Prepare draft enforcement motion	7. Serve response
	8. Prepare proof of service
	9. Prepare motion for protective order
	10. Prepare supplemental responses

Figure 8.2 Paralegal's Written Discovery Responsibilities

Application Exercise

10. Draft a letter directed to the defense attorney in the *Turner* case proposing that the United States and the defendant enter into a written discovery agreement

E. Depositions

1. FUNCTIONS OF DEPOSITIONS

A **deposition** is testimony taken under oath and subject to cross-examination before a trial begins. It may also be preserved on video or in writing. Those present at the deposition include the parties' attorneys, a court reporter, and the witness being deposed (the **deponent**). The parties themselves have a right to be present, but they do not have to be there.

Deposition
Testimony taken before trial under oath, subject to cross-examination, and preserved in writing.

Deponent
The witness being questioned under oath at a deposition.

Depositions are used in criminal cases as a means of gathering additional information about the alleged crime, as well as assessing the strengths and weaknesses of potential trial witnesses, and potentially impeaching witnesses who change their stories. A discovery deposition reveals the witness's appearance and demeanor prior to trial. Often, it elicits spontaneous, unanticipated information. It is, however, an expensive and time-consuming method of gathering information. Indeed, a court reporter must be hired to take the deposition and transcribe it. Although depositions are widely used in civil cases, their use is severely restricted in most criminal litigation. Only 20 percent of the states permit depositions as a basic discovery mechanism.[37] The federal courts and the rest of the states only allow **depositions to perpetuate testimony**. This type of deposition preserves the witness's statement so that it can be presented at a later time as evidence at trial.

Deposition to perpetuate testimony
A deposition that preserves the witness's statement so it can be presented at a later time as evidence at trial.

To take such a deposition, a party must file a motion with the court for leave to do so. Generally, the party that wishes to take the deposition must make a showing that the deponent is a prospective material witness and is likely not to be available to testify at trial. The deponent's age, sickness, infirmity, or imprisonment are justifications for taking the witness's deposition. In most jurisdictions, the court will permit the deposition when there is a substantial possibility that relevant testimony would be unavailable at the time of trial.

Nevertheless, the presentation of a witness by means of deposition testimony is disfavored by the courts. Federal Rule 15(a)(1) illustrates the reluctance of the federal criminal justice system to permit depositions. The rule provides: ". . . A party may move that a prospective witness be deposed in order to preserve testimony for trial. The court may grant the motion because of *exceptional circumstances* and in the interest of justice" (emphasis added). A judge or jury is in a better position to evaluate the credibility of a witness if the witness appears in person.

2. ROLE OF PARALEGALS RELATED TO DEPOSITIONS

Figure 8.3 lists some of the tasks that paralegals perform in the deposition process. Many of these tasks relate to drafting motions and subpoenas. Paralegals often play an important role in contacting the participants and scheduling the room, time, and other elements of the meeting. Although paralegals cannot actually conduct a deposition, they may be present to take notes and observe the proceedings.

Although the use of video depositions is becoming more widespread, ordinarily the transcript of the deposition to perpetuate testimony is presented through a public reading of the document. The defense and prosecution attorneys each read their questions aloud, while a third person sits on the witness stand and reads the deponent's answers. Paralegals often play the role of the witness during this presentation. If you are asked to read from a deposition transcript, you should:

- Familiarize yourself with the pronunciation of the words.
- Become comfortable with the witness's speech pattern.
- Know the script well enough to maintain eye contact with the jury.
- Act as if you actually are the witness.

---

[37]W. LaFave, J. Isreal, & N. King, *Criminal Procedure* 928 (4th ed., West 2004).

1. Draft motion for leave to take	7. Prepare witness, if appropriate
2. Schedule motion with court	8. Prepare deposition exhibits
3. Notice motion for hearing	9. Confirm deposition
4. Schedule deposition	10. Take notes at deposition
5. Draft notice of deposition	11. Abstract or summarize deposition
6. Draft deposition subpoena	12. Read deposed witnesses' answers aloud at trial when the witness is unavailable

Figure 8.3 Paralegal's Tasks Related to Depositions

APPLICATION EXERCISE

11. After reviewing your notebook materials on the *Turner* case (*see* hypothetical case on pages xxxvii-xxxviii, along with facts and exhibits included in previous chapters), take note of the following additional facts:

> When the local prosecuting attorneys' office decides to prosecute Turner for the possession of cocaine, Brandon contends that he was unaware of the presence of the narcotic. It turns out that the car in which the cocaine was found was jointly owned by both Turner and Dennis Watterson. Watterson is a drug dealer who is in the hospital for injuries caused by a gunshot wound and is not expected to be released from the hospital until after Turner's trial. Brandon, who is in custody, has not spoken to Watterson since his arrest, but he believes that Watterson will testify that the drugs were his and not Brandon's.

Illinois Supreme Court Rule 414(a) provides as follows:

> If it appears to the court in which a criminal charge is pending that the deposition of any person other than the defendant is necessary for the preservation of relevant testimony because of the substantial possibility it would be unavailable at the time of hearing or trial, the court may, upon motion and notice to both parties and their counsel, order the taking of such person's deposition under oral examination or written questions for use as evidence at a hearing or trial.

a. What do you think Turner's attorney should do under these circumstances?
b. Explain why you think this is what the attorney should do.

3. DRAFTING THE MOTION FOR A DEPOSITION

Motion
An application made to a court for the purpose of getting a ruling on an issue in favor of the moving party.

In most jurisdictions, the party seeking to take a deposition must get leave of the court to do so. This requires preparing a motion and "noticing" it for hearing. A **motion** is an application made to a court for the purpose of getting a ruling on an issue in favor of the moving party.

One approach to preparing a motion is to gather the basic facts first. Ordinarily, your supervising attorney will be able to provide this information. You may be directed to the client or others so that you can gain this knowledge from an interview. Thereafter, you should refer to the criminal code of procedure of the jurisdiction in which the case has been filed. In many cases, this will give you the statutory basis for the relief that you are seeking. Statutory annotations may reveal factual scenarios similar to your case. If the case involves more than procedural matters, then you will also need to research all substantive issues at stake. Once you have completed your legal research, you may need to gather additional facts. Thereafter, you can write the body of the motion.

The body of the motion can be presented as a logical argument. Set forth the facts. Sometimes you may have to attach documents that are supporting proof of the facts that you cite in the motion, such as affidavits. If there are many facts, you should offer them in multiple paragraphs. Then present the law. If you are relying on a procedural rule, consider quoting the relevant portion. Thereafter, present your analysis. In other words, show the court how the facts warrant the relief that you are seeking under the law.

Noticing a motion
The process of sending a written notice to the other party informing the party that the motion will be argued in front of the judge on a particular date at a specific time.

The body section of a motion differs from the discovery request body. Instead of simply listing the information being sought, the body of a motion presents an argument in support of the relief sought. Relevant facts in addition to legal authority are presented in this part of the motion. Although there are many ways to present effective motions, most are organized in concise, consecutively numbered paragraphs. The pertinent facts, as well as citations to authorities, are set forth to provide a basis for the court to grant the motion.

See Exhibit 8.5 for an example of a motion to take a deposition in the *Turner* case.

4. NOTICING THE DEPOSITION

Movant
The party filing a motion with the court.

Respondent
The party who receives the motion from the opposing side of a case.

Prayer for relief
A short, unnumbered paragraph near the end of a motion in which the moving party presents the relief being sought from the court.

Once you have drafted your motion for leave to take the deposition, you need to notice it for hearing. **Noticing a motion** means sending a written notice to the other party that the motion will be argued in front of the judge on a particular date at a specific time. The party filing the motion is referred to as the **movant**, and the opposing party that receives the motion is called the **respondent**. Motions contain the same components that are included in most court documents, plus a **prayer for relief**, which is a short, unnumbered paragraph near the end of a motion in which the moving party presents the relief being sought from the court.

Although there is no requirement that you communicate with the opposing party before scheduling a motion, a professional paralegal will contact the opponent to choose a mutually convenient date. This type of courtesy does not undermine the client's interests and promotes civility in the legal community.

Exhibit 8.5: Motion for Order to Take Deposition to Preserve Testimony

Now comes Defendant BRANDON TURNER, by CHARLES HOVEY, his attorney, and pursuant to Illinois Supreme Court Rule 414(a), moves that the court order the taking of Dennis Watterson's deposition under oral examination. In support of this motion, Defendant states as follows:

1. Defendant is charged with unlawful possession of cocaine.
2. The report of the reporting officer disclosed in discovery that a package of a substance believed to be cocaine was found on the front seat of the vehicle that Defendant had been driving. A copy of the report is attached hereto and incorporated herein as Exhibit "A."
3. The car in which the cocaine was found was jointly owned by Defendant and Dennis Watterson. A copy of the vehicle registration is attached hereto and incorporated herein as Exhibit "B."
4. On information and belief, Defendant believes that if called as a witness, Watterson will testify that he sells narcotics and that the drugs found in the car were not Defendant's drugs but were his.
5. The doctrine of constructive possession requires the state to establish the defendant's knowledge of the presence of contraband and his immediate and exclusive control of it. *People v. Williams*, 98 Ill. App. 3d 844, 424 N.E.2d 1234 (3d Dist. 1981).
6. Defense counsel has learned that Dennis Watterson is currently hospitalized at Dunbarton Hospital in Joliet, Illinois for injuries suffered from a gunshot. Watterson is not expected to be released for weeks, well after this case is scheduled to go to jury trial.
7. Supreme Court Rule 414(a) provides as follows:

   > If it appears to the court in which a criminal charge is pending that the deposition of any person other than the defendant is necessary for the preservation of relevant testimony because of the substantial possibility it would be unavailable at the time of hearing or trial, the court may, upon motion and notice to both parties and their counsel, order the taking of such person's deposition under oral examination or written questions for use as evidence at a hearing or trial.

8. The expected testimony of Watterson is relevant to the defense's case. The State's case is based upon the doctrine of constructive possession of cocaine. Indeed, the alleged contraband was not found on Defendant's person but rather in a car to which another person had access. Watterson is expected to testify that he was an owner of the car; that he is a drug dealer; and that the drugs found in the car were his.
9. Because Watterson is not expected to be released from the hospital until after the trial, the court should order the taking of his deposition to preserve relevant testimony.

WHEREFORE, Defendant BRANDON TURNER prays that the court order the taking of Dennis Watterson's deposition under oral examination.

Scheduling a motion for a time that the opposing party is unable to attend not only breeds bad will but usually leads to unnecessary court appearances. To notice a hearing, you call the clerk of the judge assigned to the case, who will set it in the judge's calendar. Some federal courts do not allow the parties to set motions and instead set the matters themselves. You should consult local rules for guidance.

Notice of hearing
A court document that states the time, the date, and the judge who will hear arguments on a particular motion.

After you get a court date, send a written notice of hearing to the opposing party. A **notice of hearing** is a court document that states the time, the date, and the judge who will hear arguments on a particular motion. When both the motion and the notice of hearing are sent at the same time, the notice references a hearing on the "attached" motion. Alternatively, if the motion has already been filed with the clerk, then the notice references the motion by name. There must be written proof of service for the notice of hearing. If the notice and motion are sent together, one proof of service can be used. If the motion is not noticed up, there will be no ruling on it. In some jurisdictions, you must notice the motion within a set number of days. If the motion is not noticed during this time frame, the motions will be stricken by the court. You should check the local rules. See Exhibit 8.6 for a sample of a notice of hearing.

Both the motion and notice of hearing are filed with the clerk of the court. You should present the original for filing and a copy to be stamp-filed by the court. This is your record that the document has been filed and the date on which it was filed. When the document returns to your office you can include it in a file that should mirror the court's file of the case. If the clerk of the court is located outside of your locale, you can file the document by mail. The best practice for this type of filing is to do so by certified mail, return receipt requested. This should provide your office with proof of filing in the event the document is lost by the clerk's office.

If the court grants the motion for the order to take deposition to preserve testimony, you will need to schedule the deposition. You should contact the opposing party, the witness, and the court reporter before you set the deposition. If you plan a videotaped deposition, you will also need to line up a videographer. Often, the court reporter can refer you to an experienced videographer. Depositions typically take place at the attorney's office or the office of the court reporter. However, circumstances may dictate that they take place at a hotel room, the home of the witness, a hospital room, or a prison.

Noticing the deposition
The process of sending a written notice to the other party informing the opposing party of the time, date, and place of a deposition of a named witness, along with the method of recording testimony, such as stenography or audio recording.

After you confirm a date, time, and place, you will be **noticing the deposition**. The notice of deposition should give reasonable notice to the other party of the date, time, and place for taking the deposition, along with the method of recording testimony, such as stenography or audio recording. It also should specify whether the deposition is going to be videotaped. You should direct the notice to the opposing party. Although it is not required, a practice that can eliminate confusion is to also direct the notice to the court reporter who will be taking the deposition. Once you serve a copy of the notice on the opposing side, file the original with the clerk of the court. A sample notice of deposition is depicted in Exhibit 8.7.

At the time you prepare the notice of deposition, you also should prepare a deposition subpoena for the deponent. The clerk of the court will provide you with blank subpoena forms that have been issued under seal of the court. You must fill in the blanks and take steps to have the witness served with this

Exhibit 8.6: Notice of Motion with Proof of Service

IN THE CIRCUIT COURT OF
THE 12th JUDICIAL CIRCUIT
WILL COUNTY, ILLINOIS

PEOPLE OF THE	)	
STATE OF ILLINOIS	)	
v.	)	Case No. 20 CF XXXX
BRANDON TURNER,	)	
Defendant.	)	

NOTICE OF HEARING

To: [Name and Address of opposing counsel]

On February 1, 20 at 9:00 a.m., or as soon after as counsel may be heard, the undersigned will appear before the Honorable Susan Horton, or any judge sitting in her stead, in the courtroom usually occupied by her in the Will County Courthouse located in Joliet, Illinois, and then and there present a Motion for Order to Take Deposition to Preserve Testimony, a copy of which is attached hereto, at which time and place you may appear if you so desire and request an immediate hearing.

____
CHARLES HOVEY, Attorney for Defendant

CERTIFICATE OF SERVICE

UNDER PENALTIES OF PERJURY and pursuant to the provisions of 735 ILCS 5/1-109, the undersigned, hereby certifies that he/she served the foregoing attached Notice of Motion by depositing a copy thereof into a U.S. Post Office mailbox in Normal, Illinois in an envelope, postage fully prepaid, addressed to:

[Name & Address of Opposing Counsel]

on the ________ day of ________, 20___ at or about the hour of 5:00 p.m.

____

CHARLES HOVEY
Attorney for Defendant
1857 Bone Street
Normal, IL 61761
(309)-555-1857

Exhibit 8.7: Notice of Deposition

IN THE CIRCUIT COURT OF
THE 12th JUDICIAL CIRCUIT WILL
COUNTY, ILLINOIS

PEOPLE OF THE STATE OF ILLINOIS	))	
v.	)	Case No. 20 CF XXXX
BRANDON TURNER,	)	
Defendant.	)	

NOTICE OF DEPOSITION

TO: [Opposing Party's Name and Address] [Optional: Court Reporter's Name and Address]

You are hereby notified that pursuant to the provisions of Supreme Court Rules 202 and 414(a), the evidence deposition of Dennis Watterson will be taken by court stenographer for the purpose of preserving evidence for trial, before a Notary Public in the County of Will, State of Illinois, at the hour of 2:00 p.m., on March 15, 20__, at the Office of Charles Hovey, 185 Bone Street, Normal, IL 61716.

CERTIFICATE OF SERVICE

UNDER PENALTIES OF PERJURY and pursuant to the provisions of 735 ILCS 5/1-109, the undersigned, hereby certifies that he/she served the foregoing attached Notice of Deposition by depositing a copy thereof into a U.S. Post Office mailbox in Normal, Illinois in an envelope, postage fully prepaid, addressed to:

[Name and Address of Opposing Counsel]

on the _________ day of _________, 20_________ at or about the hour of 5:00 p.m.

____

CHARLES HOVEY
Attorney for Defendant
1857 Bone Street
Normal, IL 61761
(309)-555-1857

document. The subpoena can simply require the witness to appear or to appear and bring documents to the deposition.[38]

Application Exercises

12. Prepare a notice of deposition for the *Cook* sample case (see hypothetical case on pages xxxvii-xxxviii). The deposition will take place on the first day of next month, at 1:30 p.m., in the conference room of the courthouse closest to your school. The witness is Jeffrey Z. Braden, who lives at 9008 Elm Road, Anytown, USA. You work for the defense attorney, Charles Hovey, 228 Fifteen Ave., Anytown, USA. The opposing counsel is the prosecuting attorney for the district in which your school is located. The deposition will be taken by a court reporter by stenography. It will not be videotaped. Assume that this case was the 55th felony case filed this year.

13. Prepare a notice of hearing (and proof of service) in the *Cook* case on the state's motion to bar deposition of Jeffrey Z. Braden. You work for the local prosecutor. The motion is to be served upon Charles Hovey. The motion should be set for the business day before the deposition of Braden. Judge Susan Bunk will hear the motion at 9 a.m. in courtroom 100 at the state courthouse located closest to your school. Use the information in paragraph 11 to prepare the notice.

5. PREPARING FOR THE DEPOSITION

In situations in which a friendly witness is going to be deposed, paralegals may participate in preparing the witness. This preparation involves explaining to the witness the purpose and format of the deposition and the types of questions likely to be asked. Figure 8.4 provides an example of the type of guidelines that should be given as part of this preparation.

If the attorney taking the deposition plans to show the witness documents, photographs, or physical objects, the paralegal may be asked to mark them as **exhibits**. When the deposition is for the purpose of preserving testimony, the exhibits may become "trial exhibits," which ultimately are shown to the jury if the judge admits them into evidence. (See the discussion of preparation of exhibits in Chapter 11.) If your office does not have the exhibits needed for the deposition and there is reason to believe that they are in the possession of a third party, your attorney should ask for permission from the court to subpoena these items prior to taking the deposition. (We discuss third-party subpoenas in Section F of this chapter.)

Exhibit
A tangible item that is marked for identification for purpose of being used as evidence at a trial or deposition.

A day or two before the deposition, your office should contact the opposing side, the witness, and the court reporter to verify that the deposition will

[38]The methods of serving subpoenas on witnesses will be discussed in Section F of this chapter.

- Tell the truth.
- Speak slowly, clearly, and out loud.
- Do not interrupt the questioner.
- Use words to answer; avoid answering with "uh huh" or using body language.
- Bring nothing with you except what you are ordered to bring by the subpoena.
- Listen carefully to the questions.
- If you don't understand a question, let the questioner know.
- Read any documents presented to you carefully.
- Do not guess or speculate.
- Do not volunteer information.

Figure 8.4 Instructions for Witnesses Being Deposed

still move forward as scheduled. In situations in which a witness does not speak English, arrangements must be made for a translator to be present as well.[39] Paralegals often sit in on depositions to take notes and assist with the exhibits.

6. DRAFTING SUMMARIES AND ABSTRACTS

Following the deposition, the party noticing the deposition usually orders a transcript. The original goes to the party noticing the deposition, and a copy goes to the other party. The transcript contains a verbatim record of the questions and answers presented during the deposition. Each page and line of the transcript is numbered.

Transcripts often are lengthy and cumbersome. For this reason, attorneys may have their paralegals prepare **deposition summaries or deposition abstracts**. There are various styles and formats, and your supervising attorney can give you direction as to the way to lay out the abstract or summary. These documents are substantially shorter than the deposition transcript. The rule of thumb is that for every five pages of transcript, there is one page of summary or abstract.

Deposition summary
A written summary of the transcript of the witness's responses to the questions asked in a deposition.

Deposition abstract
A special type of deposition summary that presents the witness's statements as one- or two-sentence bits of information accompanied by page and line references to the deposition transcript.

A deposition summary captures the thrust of what the witness said and is prepared as a narrative. One possible format is as follows:

- Caption
- Introductory information (the name of witness; persons present; date of deposition)
- Witness personal information (job; relation to the defendant or victim)
- Background of experts (education, training, experience)
- Incident
- Conversations with parties
- Credibility issues (bias, etc.)
- Other matters

[39] Court reporters and local universities can be good sources for locating competent interpreters.

If the deposition is used to preserve testimony, a summary may be useful in the preparation of the opening statement and closing argument.

If the deposition is a discovery deposition, an abstract can be more helpful than a summary if the attorney wants to use it at trial to impeach the witness by showing contradictions between trial testimony and deposition testimony. Because an abstract has pinpoint citations to the line and page of the transcript, it is an effective tool to identify inconsistent statements.

Unlike a summary, which is written as a narrative, the abstract presents the witness's statements as one- or two-sentence bits of information that are accompanied by the page and line reference. The body of the abstract should be organized into segments based upon the type of examination (direct, cross, re-direct, re-cross). The name of the questioner for each examination should be included in the subtitles. A possible format for a deposition abstract follows:

- Caption
- Introductory information (name of witness; persons present; date of deposition)
- Direct examination
- Cross-examination
- Redirect examination
- Recross examination

Although most depositions taken to preserve testimony are presented at trial, sometimes the witness is available and presents live testimony. When this occurs, the deposition can be used for impeachment. Accordingly, an abstract of the deposition may be a useful trial aid. Exhibit 8.8 provides a side-by-side comparison between a deposition transcript and the body of the abstract of that deposition.

You also can also draft summaries and abstracts of a variety of other documents. If there is a preliminary hearing, the police officers who testify often are witnesses at trial. An abstract can be helpful from the defense side of the case to impeach the officer's trial testimony. From the government's point of view, a summary of preliminary hearing testimony can assist the prosecutor or the paralegal in preparing the officer for trial. Other relevant transcribed proceedings also can be abstracted or summarized, such as a coroner's inquest for a homicide victim, a civil trial stemming from the circumstances that gave rise to criminal charges.

F. Subpoenas Directed to Third Parties

A subpoena is a tool that can be used at various stages of a case to assist the parties in procuring evidence. In addition to being used to require someone to appear in court to testify or in front of some other government entity, subpoenas can be used to gather non-testamentary information to prepare for trial. A subpoena that seeks the production of documents or other tangible items is referred to as a **subpoena *duces tecum***. Unlike civil pretrial subpoenas *duces tecum,* which are returnable to the party requesting the subpoena, pretrial criminal subpoenas *duces tecum* are returnable to the court itself. Material procured through the use of a subpoena *duces tecum* that was not sanctioned by and returnable to the court generally is inadmissible at trial.

Subpoena *duces tecum*
A special form of the subpoena used to compel the witness to produce documents or other tangible items to the court or to a grand jury.

Exhibit 8.8: Comparison Between Deposition Transcript and Abstract

	Transcript	**Body of Abstract**
	Page 1	
	DIRECT EXAMINATION	**DIRECT EXAMINATION**
	BY MR. HOVEY	**BY MR. HOVEY**
		Page, Line
Q	What is your name?	
A	Dennis Watterson.	
Q	Now, we are at Dunbarton Hospital in Joliet, Illinois right now?	
A	Yes.	**1, 6-10 Witness is patient at Dunbarton Hospital.**
Q	And you are a patient here?	
A	Yes.	
Q	What is your current physical condition?	
A	Paralyzed.	
Q	You're paralyzed?	**1, 13-14 He is paralyzed.**
A	Yes.	
Q	And do you expect to remain in the hospital throughout the month of April of this year?	**1, 15-17 He will be in hospital through April, YY.**
A	Yes.	
Q	Mr. Watterson, do you know a man by the name of Brandon Turner?	
A	Yes.	
Q	How do you know him?	
A	Through a relationship; we're friends.	**1,18-22 He's friends with defendant.**
Q	All right. How long have you and Mr. Turner known each other?	
	Page 2	
A	About five years.	
Q	Do you and Mr. Turner own any property	

together?

A Yes, a car.

2, 2-4 He owns a car with defendant.

MR. HOVEY: I'd like to have this marked, Ms. Reporter, as Defendant's Exhibit No. 1.

(Defendant's Exhibit No. 1 was marked for identification as of 3/15/--)

2, 5-22 Witness identifies title application for car.

[DEFEN DANT'S EXHIBIT 1]

Q I'm handing you what's been marked as Defendant 's Exhibit No. 1 and ask you to take a look at that that piece of paper. Do you recognize your signature on that piece of paper?

A Yes.

Q Do you recognize any other signatures?

A Yes, the other one in Brandon's.

Q Do you mean Brandon Turner?

A Yes.

Q This document is the title application for the car that you and Brandon own together?

A Yes.

Q What kind of car is it?

Page 3

A A 1995 Buick.

2, 24-3, 1 Car was 1995 Buick.

Q When did you buy it? You can look at the exhibit.

A October 30 of last year.

Q Now after you and Mr. Turner bought the

3, 1-9 After 10/30/YY, both the witness

	car, who used the car?		**and defendant used the car.**
A	Me and him.		
Q	Both of you?		
A	Yes.		
Q	Would the car stay at one particular place?		
A	At Brandon's house.		
Q	All right. I'd like to direct your attention to November 29 of last year. Do you remember that particular day, the day that Brandon was arrested?		
A	Not too clearly, but I remember parts of it.		
Q	On the morning of November 29 do you remember who had the car?	**3, 16-20**	**On morning of 11/29/YY, witness used the car to take his girlfriend to the grocery store.**
A	Yeah, I used the car.		
Q	Where did you go?		
A	I took my girlfriend to the grocery store.		
Q	Which store?		
A	Goodman's in Joliet.		
Q	Where is that located?		
A	I think it's on Wright Street near Haney.		

Note that the actual transcript testimony does not appear in the abstract as it is depicted in this figure; only the digested information with pinpoint citations is presented. When you prepare a deposition abstract, you should skip one line between each abstracted piece of information. Additional space appears between each entry here so that you can see the testimony that was digested and compare it to the abstract.

The first step in obtaining a subpoena for documents is to file a motion with the court. In *United States v. Nixon*,[40] the U.S. Supreme Court held that under FRCrP 17, the movant must show the following:

> (1) that the documents are evidentiary and relevant; (2) that they are not otherwise procurable reasonably in advance of trial by exercise of due diligence; (3) that the party cannot properly prepare for trial without such production and inspection in advance of trial, and that the failure to obtain such inspection may

---

[40]418 U.S. 683 (1974).

> tend unreasonably to delay the trial; and (4) that the application is made in good faith and is not intended as a general "fishing expedition."[41]

State court standards may be different. Accordingly, you should research the law of your state before you prepare the motion. An example of a motion for issuance of subpoenas *duces tecum* is set forth in Exhibit 8.9. It is from a widely publicized case in which three Duke University lacrosse players were charged with the rape and kidnapping of an exotic dancer who claimed that she was assaulted at a team party.

Each court system has preprinted subpoena forms; many are available online.[42] When drafting a subpoena, be sure to include a clause that directs the custodian to produce the documents at a specific courtroom rather than at your office. To have the subpoena issued by the clerk of the court, it must be presented to the clerk's office before it is served upon the custodian of the documents or other tangible property.

After the subpoena *duces tecum* is prepared and sealed by the court, your office must make arrangements to have it served. In most jurisdictions, the person serving the subpoena does not have to be a law enforcement officer, although there may be circumstances when an officer is the best choice to deliver the subpoena. In federal cases, any non-party who is at least 18 years old is authorized to serve a subpoena. This is the situation in many states; however, you must check the law of the jurisdiction where the case is pending to make sure that your subpoena server is qualified.

Because most adults are qualified, you may be asked to serve the subpoena yourself. A list of duties a paralegal may be required to perform to obtain documents from third parties appears in Figure 8.5. If you are the subpoena server, you need to act in a professional manner. Be prepared to let the witness know that he or she is ordered to produce the items specified on the subpoena at a particular time and date. Emphasize that the items are to be delivered to the court, not to the lawyer's office. It is not your role to discuss the facts of the case with this individual. If the person served asks a question that you either are unable to answer or do not feel comfortable answering, direct that person to your supervising attorney.

In some jurisdictions, including federal court, the recipient of the subpoena must be given a fee. FRCrP 17(d) provides that the server must "tender to the witness one day's witness-attendance fee and the legal mileage allowance." On the other hand, Illinois does not require the tender of fees at the time of service of a subpoena in a criminal case. You, therefore, must find out the fee requirements of the jurisdiction. The clerk of the court may be able to direct you to the current fee/mileage schedule. A fee check is typically stapled to the copy of the subpoena that is delivered to the custodian.

After the subpoena is delivered, the server then prepares a proof of service, or affidavit of service. This is a document in which the server attests under penalty of perjury or under oath when he or she served the witness with the

---

[41]418 U.S. at 699-700.

[42]There are three federal forms for subpoenas in a criminal case. Form A0 089 is the subpoena to testify at a hearing or trial. Form A0 89B is a subpoena to produce documents, information, or objects, and Form A0 90 is a subpoena to testify at a deposition. These forms are located online at https://www.uscourts.gov/forms/criminal-forms.

Exhibit 8.9: Motion for Issuance of Subpoenas *Duces Tecum*

NORTH CAROLINA — IN THE GENERAL COURT OF JUSTICE
SUPERIOR COURT DIVISION
DURHAM COUNTY — FILE NOS. 06 CRS 4334-356

STATE OF NORTH CAROLINA)
)
vs.)
)
READE WILLIAM SELIGMANN,)
Defendant.)

RITCHIE MOTION FOR PRODUCTION AND INSPECTION OF RECORDS OF MENTAL DISABILITY, HOSPITAL COMMITMENT, DRUG ABUSE HISTORY EDUCATIONAL HISTORY, DEPARTMENT OF SOCIAL SERVICE RECORDS, JUVENILE RECORDS, PROBATION AND PAROLE RECORDS, CHILD PROTECTIVE SERVICES RECORDS, AND VICTIM'S ADVOCACY RECORDS

NOW COMES the Defendant, READE WILLIAM SELIGMANN, through counsel, and respectfully moves this Honorable Court pursuant to the Fifth, Sixth, Eighth and Fourteenth Amendments to the United States Constitution, Article I, §§ 19, 23 & 27 of the North Carolina Constitution, and *Pennsylvania v. Richie,* 480 U.S. 39, 59-61 (1987) and its progeny, for orders directing the appropriate agencies to provide to the Court copies of all records of the complaining witness, [redacted], regarding Mental Disability, Hospital Commitments, Drug Abuse History, Educational Records, Probation and Parole Record, and Department of Social Service Records. This request is based on the fact that the complaining witness has a history of criminal activity and behavior which includes alcohol abuse, drug abuse, and dishonesty, all conduct which indicate mental, emotional and/or physical problems which affect her credibility as a witness. Since these problems do not occur overnight, they probably began in her teenage years and continue to exist. The Defendant requests that these orders include directing both Hillside High School and North Carolina Central University to provide to this Court her entire educational records including any disciplinary action and that the State make affirmative inquiry of the complaining witness as to any and all hospitalizations, treatment at mental centers, involvement with the Department of Social Services Agencies, Probation and Parole, Juvenile Agencies, Child Protective Services Agencies, Victims' Advocacy Agencies or Organizations, or any other agencies providing services for mental, emotional, drug or alcohol problems.

* * *

WHEREFORE, Defendant respectfully requests the Court to issue orders to accompany subpoenas to produce documents (subpoena duces tecum) to all hospital, agencies, treatment centers, including the Durham County Office of Probation and Parole, Durham Department of Social Services, Juvenile Agencies, Child Protective Services Agencies, Victims' Advocacy Agencies or Organizations, Hillside High School, North Carolina Central University, and any other institution or agency which may have housed or treated the complaining witness in this matter and any other agency identified by the District Attorney's Office pursuant to an inquiry ordered by this Court.

After this material is produced, counsel for the Defendant request a pretrial "reliability hearing" in which to review the following in addition to the materials provided pursuant to this Motion to determine if the complaining witness is even credible enough to provide reliable testimony:

1. The complaining witness' complete criminal history;

2. Any deal, promise, inducement, or benefit the State has made or may make in the future to her;

3. The time, place, and manner of any specific statements the complaining witness has made in this case;

4. All other cases in which the complaining witness has testified or offered statements against an individual but was not called;

5. Whether the complaining witness has recanted testimony or statements in this case or any other case and a transcript or copy of the recantation; and

6. Any other information relevant to her credibility.

RESPECTFULLY SUBMITTED this the 24th day of April, 2006.

J. Kirk Osborn

J. KIRK OSBORN
ATTORNEY FOR THE DEFENDANT

1. Research law
2. Prepare motion to issue subpoena duces tecum
3. Draft motion for issuance of subpoena duces tecum
4. Obtain subpoena duces tecum form from clerk of court or online
5. Complete subpoena duces tecum form
6. Have clerk of court issue subpoena duces tecum
7. Attach copy of the fee check for the subpoena duces tecum
8. Arrange for subpoena server
9. Prepare a proof of service
10. File original along with proof of service with clerk of court

Figure 8.5 Paralegal's Responsibilities for Obtaining Documents or Other Items from Third Parties

subpoena and tendered fees. Most subpoenas provided by the clerk's office have a fill-in-the-blank form as part of the document. The original of the subpoena along with the proof of service is filed with the clerk of the court. You should retain a copy of the subpoena and proof of service to be file-stamped by the clerk of the court.

Discussion Questions

1. What type of subpoena was being sought in Exhibit 8.9?

2. How significant is the complaining witness to the prosecution in this case?

3. In what ways could the enumerated items sought at the conclusion of the motion be used to assist the defense in preparing the case for trial?

Application Exercise

14. Prepare a subpoena *duces tecum* in the Turner case that is directed to Dennis Watterson, 357 Magee Drive, Anytown, USA, requiring production of the vehicle title of the 1995 Buick automobile owned by Watterson and Brandon Turner. Use the information contained in Application Exercise 11.

a. For the federal prosecution, have the subpoena returned to the federal court located closest to your college at 9 a.m. on the first business day of next month. Use Form A089 located at https://www.uscourts.gov/forms/criminal-forms.

b. For the state prosecution, have the subpoena returned to the state court located closest to your college at 9 a.m. on the first business day of next month. Obtain the appropriate form from the Internet or from the clerk's office.

G. Disclosure of the Person

In addition to disclosing written material, the defendant may be required to present his or her person for discovery. Illinois Supreme Court Rule 413(a) is illustrative of this type of discovery. The rule provides as follows:

> [A] judicial officer may require the accused, among other things, to:
> (i) Appear in a lineup;
> (ii) Speak for identification by witnesses to an offense;
> (iii) Be fingerprinted;
> (iv) Pose for photographs not involving reenactment of a scene;
> (v) Try on articles of clothing;
> (vi) Permit the taking of specimens of material under his fingernails;
> (vii) Permit the taking of samples of his blood, hair and other materials of his body which involve no unreasonable intrusion thereof;
> (viii) Provide a sample of his handwriting; and
> (ix) Submit to a reasonable physical or medical inspection of his body.

Usually, the attorney will escort the defendant to this procedure, but it is possible that a paralegal might accompany the client instead of or in addition to the attorney. The primary role of the law firm's representatives is to provide support to the client, who is going through an unfamiliar and uncomfortable situation.

Although a criminal defendant may be requested to give basic information, such as name and address, the client should not discuss the case with anyone. If you have any doubt about disclosure, contact your supervising attorney. The meeting with the government's representative will be professional.

Application Exercise

15. What type of disclosure of one's body must a defendant make in your state? What is the citation for the authority requiring this production?

H. Other Discovery Tools for the Defense

Defendants can also gain pertinent information through a number of mechanisms that are not specifically designed for discovery. The bail hearing, the preliminary hearing, and hearings on pretrial motions, such as a motion to suppress, will reveal some of the prosecution's evidence. Court reporters typically record the proceedings through stenography or audio recordings. Both sides can obtain transcripts of the testimony provided at the hearings through the court's administrator or clerk's office.

The defense can also obtain information by filing a **motion for bill of particulars**. The federal rules, along with many state codes, permit the defendant

Motion for bill of particulars
A defense motion that requests the court to order the prosecution to file a supplementary document that gives the specifics of a charge that were not set forth in the original charge.

to file a motion to seek specifics of a charge. Federal Rule 17(f) allows the defendant to file a motion for bill of particulars before arraignment, within ten days after the arraignment, or at a later date with permission of the court. States, such as Illinois, allow the defense to make the motion before or within a reasonable time after arraignment.[43]

The purpose of the bill of particulars is to provide sufficient information so that the defendant is apprised of the nature of the charges and is in a position to prepare for trial. The court may allow the motion when the information, indictment, or charge fails to allege essential information, such as the time, date, or place of the alleged offense. This information is paramount when the defense is claiming an alibi or that the charge was filed after the statute of limitations expired.

Although most criminal law formbooks contain sample motions for a bill of particulars, you should customize the motion to address the specific deficiencies of the charging instrument. In preparing your draft, you should not only point out what information is missing but also explain how the defendant is prejudiced by the omission. Courts have a great deal of discretion in ruling on these motions, so it is important that the motion present particularized reasons for allowing the request.

Both the prosecution and the defense can use information from related cases in preparing for the criminal case. Indeed, some cases have parallel proceedings. For example, victims may file civil tort actions against defendants—for battery, wrongful death, sexual assault, personal injury caused by persons driving under the influence, and so on. A coroner's office often convenes a coroner's jury to consider evidence in deciding the cause of a victim's death.

Although the district attorney's office had knowledge of sexual assault allegations against comedian/actor Bill Cosby, it was not until the prosecution received a copy of Cosby's deposition given in a civil case that the matter was brought to a grand jury. In his deposition, Cosby testified that he obtained seven prescriptions for Quaaludes. An excerpt of the deposition transcript states:

> Q: When you got the Quaaludes, was it in your mind that you were going to use these Quaaludes for women you wanted to have sex with?
> A: Yes.

When Cosby was asked about his sexual encounter with the victim, this exchange took place:

> Q: So, you're not telling us that you verbally asked her for permission?
> A: I didn't say it verbally, I said. The action is my hand on her midriff, which is skin. I'm not lifting any clothing up. This is, I don't remember fully what it is, but it's there and I can feel. I got her skin and it's just above the hand and it's just above where you can go under the pants.
> Q: Then what happens?
> A: I don't hear her say anything. And I don't feel her say anything. And so I continue and I go into the area that is somewhere between permission and rejection. I am not stopped.

[43] 725 ILCS 5/114-2.

A Pennsylvania jury found Cosby was guilty of three counts of drugging and sexually assaulting a woman. The judge sentenced him to 3 to 10 years in state prison and fined $25,000.[44]

I. Discovery Variations

We have noted throughout this text that specific procedures and formats for documents will vary from one state to another and between state and federal courts. More complex criminal litigation may have a more diverse set of rules than the procedures that are generally applied. In addition, misdemeanor discovery may differ from felony discovery.[45]

1. DISCOVERY IN MISDEMEANOR CASES

An example of differences between discovery procedures for misdemeanor and felony cases can be illustrated by reference to Illinois Supreme Court Rule 411, which defines the scope of the criminal discovery rules as being expressly limited to felony prosecutions. There are no rules addressing discovery in other criminal cases. This absence of a parallel procedure for misdemeanor cases gave rise to the decision in *People v. Schmidt*, a case in which the Illinois Supreme Court held that defendants in misdemeanor driving under the influence (DUI) prosecutions are entitled to the following discovery from the prosecution:

> [A] list of witnesses, any confession of the defendant, evidence negating the defendant's guilt, and, in this particular case, the results of the breathalyzer test. Additionally, the report which the defendant seeks will be available at trial for use in impeachment of the prosecution witness who prepared it.[46]

In 2011, the Illinois Supreme Court ruled that the prosecution must also furnish a defendant charged with a misdemeanor with the squad car video camera recording of the incident resulting in the arrest.[47]

You should therefore carefully review the criminal discovery rules of procedure of your jurisdiction to determine whether they apply to misdemeanor and petty offenses. If the rules are inapplicable, research the case law to determine whether there are common law standards that govern discovery for cases other than felonies. Ordinarily, you can use standard forms containing boilerplate language for requests and responses in misdemeanor cases.

---

[44]The Pennsylvania Supreme Court reversed Cosby's conviction in *Commonwealth v. Cosby*, 252 A.3d 1092 (PA 2021). Excerpts of this decision appears in Chapter 4.

[45]The FRCrP do not distinguish between felonies and misdemeanors. FRCrP 1 states that the "rules govern the procedure in all criminal proceedings in the Unites States district courts. . . ."

[46]56 Ill. 2d 572, 575 (1974).

[47]*People v. Kladis*, 960 N.E.2d 1104 (Ill. 2011).

APPLICATION EXERCISE

16. In the Clay Marshall case (*see* hypothetical case on pages xxxviii-xxxix), Randy Jefferson and Madison Pickering filed charges with the state fair employment practices commission (FEPC) claiming that they were sexually harassed. Before the criminal case goes to trial, the FEPC ordered Marshall, Jefferson, and Pickering to appear for a conciliation conference in an effort to settle the sexual harassment claims. Your supervising attorney, who will attend the hearing with Clay, plans to direct the client to refrain from answering questions because of the pending criminal charges, but plans to question the complainants.

a. Draft a set of questions that would be helpful in preparing for the client's defense in the criminal case.
b. Find out whether the existence of pending criminal charges is a valid basis for the client to refuse to testify in a parallel civil proceeding. Draft a memo to your supervising attorney presenting your analysis.

2. DISCOVERY IN COMPLEX CRIMINAL CASES

There is a movement toward requiring more extensive discovery in certain types of serious cases. For instance, in federal death penalty cases, the government is required to disclose the identities of its witnesses at least three days prior to trial.[48] This responsibility is not conditioned upon the defendant's request.

Discovery may be more extensive in complex non-capital cases. For instance, in Illinois cases in which a party intends to use deoxyribonucleic acid (DNA) evidence, a mandatory disclosure requirement is imposed upon that party to furnish all pertinent information and testing data involving the DNA results.[49]

APPLICATION EXERCISE

17. How does misdemeanor discovery differ from felony discovery in your state? What, if any, differences are there in felony discovery when the defendant faces capital punishment? Give citations to authority for your answer.

---

[48] 18 U.S.C. §3432.

[49] Illinois Supreme Court Rule 417.

J. The Court's Role in Discovery Disputes

There are two general categories of dispute that arise in the course of discovery: (1) one party seeks material that should not be disclosed, and (2) a party does not provide what should be tendered. In both situations, the court may be asked to resolve the dispute. Courts have a great degree of discretion in regulating discovery, so these types of disputes are determined on a case-by-case basis.

1. PROTECTIVE ORDERS

When a party requests some item or information for which there is a legitimate basis to withhold disclosure, such as attorney work product, the party receiving the request can object to the discovery request. In addition, the party from whom discovery is sought may apply to the court for a **protective order.** A protective order is a decree issued by a court that is issued to shield a party or witness from unreasonable or invasive discovery requests. The party filing a motion for entry of a protective order must make a showing of good cause in order to obtain a protective order.

Protective order
A court order commonly used to protect a party or witness from unreasonable or invasive discovery requests.

The federal courts, as well as most state courts, have the authority to enter this type of order. FRCrP 16(d)(1) provides that a party may file a motion with the district court for an order to delay, restrict, or deny pretrial discovery. Some jurisdictions require that the parties meet and confer prior to the filing of the motion. Paralegals may be asked to prepare a draft letter asserting the basis for the order and inviting a conference between the attorneys. Sometimes the motion may ask the court to review materials at issue in the absence of the parties to determine whether the information should be released. This type of proceeding is referred to as an ***in camera* review.** Many times, this procedure is needed to avoid disclosure of the information for which protection is sought. The movant must make a showing of good cause in order to obtain a protective order. In some jurisdictions, the court on its own initiative may enter a protective order. If the motion is granted, the record of the materials that were reviewed ***in camera*** is sealed and made available to the appellate court on review.

***In camera* review**
A judge's review of materials in chambers outside of the presence of the parties and the public.

In camera
In a judge's chambers, outside the presence of a jury and the public.

A non-party can also apply to the court for protection against unwarranted discovery. Specifically, the custodian of records who has been served with a subpoena *duces tecum* can seek a protective order. The party making the original discovery request can file a response. In view of the burden of proof obligation faced by the movant, a respondent can argue that the motion must articulate specific facts to justify the entry of the order. Respondents also can argue that the basis enunciated in the motion does not justify non-disclosure. Defendants objecting to the entry of a protective order often maintain that the information sought is necessary to prepare a defense and the material should be disclosed under *Brady v. Maryland*.

2. DISCOVERY ENFORCEMENT

When discovery is not produced in a timely fashion or is provided in an inadequate manner, the requesting party can appeal to the court through a motion to compel compliance. The court also can impose sanctions upon a party that fails to abide by a discovery request or a court order.

The first step in response to the opponent's failure to comply is for the attorney to contact the opponent. If you are responsible for tracking the due date of discovery, you will alert your supervisor of the other party's lack of diligence. You may be required to draft the letter alerting the other side of its failure to respond or the inadequacy of the response.

Motion to compel
A formal request to the court to order either the opposing party or a third party to take some action. Typically, this motion is filed in connection with discovery disputes.

If conferring with opposing counsel does not result in compliance, the matter can be brought before the court through a **motion to compel,** which asks the court to order either the opposing party or a third party to take some action. The motion should give the factual basis for the relief sought. Specifically, the motion should tell the court about the material requested and why your side is entitled to it. If the opponent failed to provide any discovery, attach a copy of the discovery request as an exhibit to the motion. If the opponent declined to fully respond to portions of the request, you should quote the requests in the body of the motion. The body of the motion should also set forth in chronological order the dates of the request and all follow-up contacts with the opponent. You also should cite the authority under which the material is sought. The motion for compliance can seek an order compelling compliance as well as a prayer for sanctions.

If the respondent is objecting to disclosure on a legitimate basis, the respondent may file a response that discusses the basis for the lack of disclosure. In addition, the respondent may file a motion for a protective order.

FRCrP 16(d)(2) provides that when a party fails to comply with the discovery rules, the court may order the discovery, grant a continuance, prohibit a party from introducing the undisclosed evidence, or enter any other order that is just under the circumstances. State courts have similar authority. When pretrial discovery is incomplete, courts will often compel the offending party to respond and reserve judgment on the request for more severe sanctions to see if there is compliance. Thereafter, if the court order is disobeyed, the judge will impose sanctions. When the discovery violation becomes apparent at trial, the offended party can move for sanctions at that time.

Read the following excerpts from two Ohio courts that reached opposite results concerning the question of sanctions against the prosecution for failing to provide the defendant with body-cam video before trial.

Toledo v. Strickland
Court of Appeals of Ohio, Sixth District
72 N.E.3d 668 (2016)

OSOWIK, J.

This is a state appeal from a December 28, 2015 judgment of the Toledo Municipal Court, striking the testimony of appellant's sole witness in response to the commission of a fundamental discovery violation by appellant. For the reasons set forth below, this court affirms the judgment of the trial court.

. . .

The following undisputed facts are relevant to this appeal. On October 7, 2015, defendant

Dwayne Strickland was operating a motor vehicle in the vicinity of Central Avenue and Stickney Avenue in Toledo. The defendant encountered a Toledo police officer at that location. The Toledo police officer was wearing a body camera equipped with both video and audio at the time of the incident. The officer's equipment recorded the interaction with the defendant. The recordings have not been reviewed and are not part of the record in this matter. The fact that the independent recordings, which reflect the truth of what transpired, are not part of the record constitutes the fundamental issue in this case.

The defendant maintains that he was subjected to police brutality during the incident. Conversely, the officer maintains that the defendant resisted arrest. Again, the incident was captured and recorded, with both audio and video, by the officer's body camera. The content of the recordings remains unknown.

On October 7, 2015, defendant was charged with one count of carrying a concealed weapon, . . . one count of resisting arrest, . . . along with several minor traffic offenses.

On October 14, 2015, counsel was appointed to represent defendant on the above-described pending cases. On December 1, 2015, counsel for defendant filed a written request with appellant for discovery to be provided pursuant to the discovery rules . . .

In response to the defendant's official discovery request, appellant provided a copy of the written Toledo police report of the incident reflecting that the arresting officer was wearing a body camera at the time of the arrest. No further discovery materials were provided or offered to be made available for review and/or copying by appellant.

On December 16, 2015, the matter proceeded to trial. Appellant furnished the testimony of a single witness, the arresting officer who had worn the body camera that recorded the events.

Given the failure of the discovery process to enable counsel for the defendant to access and review the body cam video and audio to evaluate the proper defense based upon the recordings, the defendant took the stand himself to refute the testimony of the officer. During his testimony, the defendant stated to the court that the officer had been wearing a body camera at the time of the incident and that the court could discover the truth by reviewing the recordings.

Following this revelation at trial by defendant, the trial court recessed to determine the proper course of action. Ultimately, the trial court determined that appellant had committed a discovery violation by failing to furnish the body cam video to counsel for the defendant or take any actions which would have enabled the review of the video by counsel for defendant prior to the defendant electing to take the witness stand in his own defense. The trial court held in pertinent part, "The purpose of the criminal rules is to prevent unfair surprise or trial by ambush. Even unintentional discovery violations have adverse effect. And, in this case, the court feels compelled to strike the testimony of the state's sole witness. No other remedy would mitigate the harm done." This appeal ensued.

In the sole assignment of error, appellant maintains that the trial court erred in striking the testimony of the arresting officer. In support, appellant suggests that the fact that a copy of the police report reflecting that a body camera was worn by the officer was provided in reply to defendant's Crim.R. 16 discovery motion somehow negates the possibility of a discovery violation in this case. We do not concur.

Crim.R. 16(B)(1) clearly mandates that any written or recorded statement by a defendant *shall* [emphasis added] be provided or permission furnished for it to be copied or photographed to counsel for the defendant. It is undisputed that this discovery mandate did not occur in this case. It was not provided or made available to counsel for defendant prior to trial. Accordingly, the defendant elected to testify on his own behalf to refute the officer's testimony.

. . .

In applying these relevant principles to this matter, we find that although the record does not reflect that appellant's failure to comply with Crim.R. 16 was intentional, given the mention of the body camera in the written report that was drafted by appellant's sole witness and the fact that it was subsequently in appellant's possession, it can certainly be construed as neglectful.

Regardless, the record does reflect the determinative importance to the defendant of having foreknowledge of the content of the video and audio recordings in preparation for trial and the resultant prejudice to the defendant of taking the witness stand in his own defense without benefit of the foreknowledge of the content of the video and audio recordings.

Lastly, we note that it is not persuasive for appellant to suggest that requiring appellant to have taken some action in either providing a copy of the video to the defense or offering arrangements for the video to be inspected and copied by the defense somehow constitutes mandating appellant to conduct "hand holding" of appellee in a scenario in which the recordings were made by appellant's sole witness, were referenced in the report created by that witness, is the property of appellant and appellant's witness, and is fundamental to the truth of the matter.

Given these facts and circumstances, we find that appellant has failed to demonstrate that the disputed trial court discovery sanction in response to appellant's Crim.R. 16 violation was arbitrary, unreasonable or unconscionable. As such, we find appellant's sole assignment of error not well-taken.

Wherefore, the judgment of the Toledo Municipal Court is hereby affirmed. . . .

Judgment affirmed.

MARK L. PIETRYKOWSKI, ARLENE SINGER, and THOMAS J. OSOWIK, JJ., concur.

State v. McGuire
Court of Appeals of Ohio, Eighth District
2018 WL 1778588 (2018)

TIM McCORMACK, P.J.:

Defendant-appellant David McGuire ("McGuire") appeals from his convictions following a jury trial. For the reasons that follow, we affirm.

On March 16, 2016, between 7:00 p.m. and 8:00 p.m., McGuire and his cousin Mac McGuire ("Mac") were arguing outside of McGuire's home at 1237 East 146th Street in East Cleveland.

Mac was sitting in the passenger seat of a car that was backed into the driveway with the door open. McGuire went upstairs to his third floor apartment, retrieved a gun, returned to the driveway and fired four shots into Mac's legs and groin.

Sultan Muhammad, who was renting the second-floor apartment from McGuire, witnessed the incident from a second-floor window and instructed his girlfriend, Kristen Angel, to call 911. Angel did so, and two East Cleveland police officers responded to the scene, but not before McGuire fled the scene. Medical personnel also responded to the scene and transported Mac to the hospital, where he died as a result of gunshot wounds.

Responding officer Kenneth Bolton secured the scene, and Officer Elshawn Williams spoke to Muhammad, Angel, and a neighbor who had heard gunshots and saw McGuire standing near the car with his hands on his head several minutes later.

McGuire was arrested on March 28, 2016. On April 12, 2016, a Cuyahoga County grand jury indicted McGuire on Count 1, aggravated murder; Count 2, murder in violation; Count 3, felonious assault; and Count 4, having weapons while under disability. . . .

McGuire pleaded not guilty to all four counts. A jury trial began on March 28, 2017.

During the trial, it became apparent during the defense's cross-examination of Officer Williams, one of the responding officers, that he had been wearing a body camera at the time he responded to the incident.

Upon learning this information, McGuire's counsel discussed making an oral motion for mistrial based on two alleged *Brady* violations by the state. The court noted that a complete record on the issue of body camera evidence had not been developed, and it declined to consider such a motion at that time.

. . . While there was uncontroverted testimony that the responding officers, including Bolton, were wearing body cameras when they responded to the crime scene, the state did not turn over any of the body camera footage, and the record reveals that the East Cleveland Police Department either lost or destroyed any body camera evidence that had existed.

. . .

At a later point in [the] trial, defense counsel informed the court that after discussing the matter at length with McGuire, they would not be making another oral motion for mistrial based on the state's failure to turn over body camera evidence. Instead, defense counsel moved for a sanction for the discovery violation in the form of an additional jury instruction, asking the court to instruct the jury that they may infer from the state's failure to preserve body camera evidence that the evidence was relevant to the case and favorable to McGuire.

Ultimately, the court instructed the jury on the issue as follows:

> You have also heard evidence that two East Cleveland Police officers who arrived first at the crime scene used body worn cameras. The East Cleveland Police Department was required to preserve the images and audio from those cameras. The State of Ohio was obligated to provide all of those recordings to counsel for the defendant. Those obligations were not met. You may consider these failures and draw any reasonable inference from them when deciding whether the State of Ohio has proved the charges beyond a reasonable doubt.

Following deliberations, the jury returned a verdict of guilty on all counts and corresponding specifications.

. . .

In his sole assignment of error, McGuire argues that the state of Ohio violated his right to a fair trial by deliberately withholding exculpatory evidence. Specifically, McGuire argues first that without the body camera footage, he was unable to put forth a self-defense argument at trial without this evidence of the position of Mac's body as he lay dying in the car. . . .

Due process requires that the state provide criminal defendants with any evidence that is material to either their guilt or punishment. *Brady v. Maryland,* 373 U.S. 83 (1963). Evidence is considered material "if there is a reasonable probability that, had the evidence been disclosed to the defense, the result of the proceeding would have been different." [Citation omitted]

The defendant carries the burden to prove a *Brady* violation rising to the level of a denial of due process. There are three elements of a *Brady* violation: "(1) evidence at issue must be favorable to the accused because it is exculpatory or impeaching; (2) evidence must have been willfully or inadvertently suppressed by the State; and (3) prejudice ensued." [Citations omitted]

. . .

McGuire also argues that his due process rights were violated by the state's failure to turn over the body camera footage from the responding officers, as this was crucial to his defense and could have supported a theory of self-defense. Specifically, McGuire argues that if the position of Mac's body appeared in the video to be even slightly altered from how it was described by Officer Williams, the state's entire theory of the case would have been disrupted. This assertion is without merit.

Applying the *Brady* analysis laid out above, McGuire's claim here fails. Courts have consistently rejected *Brady* claims that are too speculative, requiring defendants to substantiate claims that the evidence in question was favorable and material. [Citations omitted]. . . .

Not only is McGuire's assertion that the body camera evidence might have supported a claim of self-defense speculative, it also ignores other evidence in the record that would refute such a theory—specifically, the location of the bullet wounds and the path of the bullets through Mac's body. The bullets entered Mac's body through the back of his thighs and pelvis and traveled up and across his body, with one bullet reaching his liver and another piercing his lung. The medical examiner explained in his testimony that this was consistent with the victim laying down in the vehicle with his legs up in a defensive posture. Such a position is also consistent with the eyewitness testimony of Sultan Muhammad.

Finally, McGuire made statements to the police from the time of his arrest and through trial that he did not possess a gun and was not at the crime scene when Mac was shot. Therefore, even if body camera evidence existed that supported a self-defense theory of the case, McGuire is unable to show how he was prejudiced by this alleged *Brady* violation.

Although McGuire's claim fails under the three-prong test discussed above, we note that this case is different than a traditional *Brady* case because the body camera footage did not exist at the time of trial. The state argues that it "cannot be faulted for failing to disclose evidence it did not have." [Citation omitted] This statement is generally accurate, but it does not account for cases in which the state loses, destroys, or otherwise fails to preserve evidence. The state argues that there is no evidence suggesting that the state ever possessed body camera footage from Officers Bolton and Williams from March 16, 2016. While the record contains no evidence that the prosecutor ever possessed body camera evidence, the same cannot be said of the East Cleveland Police Department.

The record shows that the parties stipulated that "a thorough search was made on March 30, 2017 for body camera video of Bolton and Williams from March 16th or even the 17th, and none can be located."...

"[W]hen potentially exculpatory evidence requested by a defendant is permanently lost, 'courts face the treacherous task of divining the import of materials whose contents are unknown and, very often, disputed.'" In light of this difficulty, a different analysis is required when dealing with the state's failure to preserve evidence of an uncertain exculpatory value, "of which no more can be said than that it could have been subjected to tests, the results of which might have exonerated the defendant." "Unless a criminal defendant can show bad faith on the part of the police, failure to preserve potentially useful evidence does not constitute a denial of due process of law." [Citations omitted]

The defendant bears the burden of showing that the government acted in bad faith. "'The term "bad faith" generally implies something more than bad judgment or negligence.'" "It imports a dishonest purpose, moral obliquity, conscious wrongdoing, breach of a known duty through some ulterior motive or ill will partaking the nature of fraud." [Citations omitted]

... Based on the East Cleveland Police Department policy articulated on the record at trial, we know that the failure to preserve the body camera evidence constitutes a breach of a known duty. We cannot, however, conclude that it was done through some ulterior motive or ill will as required for a finding of bad faith. There is nothing in the record indicating bad faith as alleged by McGuire. In fact, the record reveals a thorough, though ultimately fruitless, effort by the prosecutor to procure body camera evidence.

In light of the foregoing, we overrule McGuire's assignment of error and affirm his conviction and sentence.

LARRY A. JONES, SR., J., and KATHLEEN ANN KEOUGH, J., CONCUR.

Case Discussion Questions

1. What levels of court in the Ohio judicial system decided each of these two cases?
2. Should *Toledo v. Strickland* (2016) serve as controlling precedent for the court deciding *State v. McGuire* (2018)? Why or why not?
3. What facts are substantially the same in both decisions?
4. What facts differ in the two cases?
5. Explain how opposite outcomes for the two cases can be reconciled.

SUMMARY

This chapter presented the two major discovery models, along with the principles underlying disclosure in criminal prosecutions. In addition to discovery requirements imposed by various rules of criminal procedure, the government has a constitutional duty under *Brady v. Maryland* to disclose exculpatory evidence to the accused.

As a paralegal, you may be required to draft written discovery requests, respond to the requests tendered by the opposing side, prepare discovery motions, notice depositions and motions, and subpoena documents. We showed you how to prepare these documents in this chapter. We also presented how to object to a discovery request and seek a protective order to counter an inappropriate request for information.

In addition, this chapter discussed the role of the paralegal with respect to depositions. The deposition to perpetuate testimony can be an important part of a criminal case. The discovery deposition is becoming an increasingly significant discovery tool in a number of jurisdictions. You were shown how to abstract and summarize depositions and how to prepare witnesses for them.

Rules of discovery vary from one jurisdiction to another. Even in the same jurisdiction there may be separate rules for discovery in different types of cases. You will always need to check the applicable court rules to see what rules apply to the cases assigned to you.

REVIEW QUESTIONS

1. What is the purpose of criminal discovery?
2. In *Brady v. Maryland,* the U.S. Supreme Court ruled that the Due Process Clause requires prosecutors to turn over all exculpatory evidence to the defense. What is exculpatory evidence?
3. What is impeachment evidence, and when is it considered to be material?
4. Which part of the U.S. Constitution contains the right to be free from self-incrimination? What is the nature of this constitutional right?
5. What are the major criticisms of Rule 16 of the FRCrP?
6. What are the components of a pattern discovery request?
7. How should a paralegal who is preparing a response to a discovery request address sensitive information that is contained in the documents requested by the other side?
8. What is the face sheet of a discovery response, and what are its component parts?
9. What are the types of appropriate responses that can be made on the face sheet of the response in reaction to individual discovery requests?
10. What is attorney work product, and what bearing does it have on discovery?
11. List and explain the use of the types of depositions that are used in criminal cases. There are two types of criminal depositions: discovery depositions and depositions to perpetuate testimony.
12. How do you notice a deposition and notice a motion for hearing?
13. How does a paralegal prepare a witness for a deposition?
14. How do deposition summaries and abstracts differ from one another?
15. What is a subpoena *duces tecum,* and how does it differ from other written discovery requests?

16. What is the purpose of a bill of particulars, and when can a defendant make a motion to seek it?
17. Why do courts conduct *in camera* reviews when deciding whether to grant a motion for protective order?
18. What remedies are available to a federal judge for sanctioning a party that fails to comply with discovery rules?

Chapter 9

Pretrial Motions and Plea Bargaining

Chapter Objectives

After reading this chapter, you should be able to:

- Identify the most commonly filed pre-trial motions and discuss why they are filed.
- Explain the difference between a motion to suppress evidence and a motion *in limine*.
- Compare and contrast the motions related to potential bias in judges or juries.
- Explain how plea bargaining works and why it is used.
- Discuss the positive and negative aspects of plea bargaining.

Introduction

In Chapter 8 we saw how both prosecuting attorneys and defense counsel use pre-trial discovery to develop the information they need to present their case, evaluate its strengths and weaknesses, identify witnesses, and gather documents and electronically stored information (ESI) that they may be able to use at trial. In this chapter we discuss the types of motions that attorneys file regarding such issues as

- The competence of a defendant to stand trial
- Whether co-defendants will be tried together or separately
- The place where the trial will occur
- Whether a particular judge should preside over the case
- Whether evidence should be suppressed because it was illegally gathered

Although plea bargaining can take place at any time before the rendering of the verdict, many plea agreements are not reached until after the court has ruled on these motions. Later in this chapter, we will discuss the pros and cons of this practice, as well as the procedures used.

Because the nature of the punishment is an important aspect of discussions held during plea bargaining, we end the chapter with an overview of optional programs designed to reduce taxpayer costs by providing educational and treatment options for selected types of defendants.

A. Pre-Trial Motions

1. MOTIONS RELATING TO DISCOVERY

We have already discussed motions related to discovery in Chapter 8. As more information is revealed, additional discovery motions may be filed.

2. MOTIONS RELATING TO THE FORUM

As we saw in Chapter 5, a criminal case officially begins when the prosecutor's office files formal charges in a particular court. For example, if a violation of the state criminal code took place in Normal, Illinois, the McLean County State Attorney's Office would file charges with the McLean County Circuit Court in the 11th Judicial Circuit of Illinois. On the other hand, if there was a violation of federal law, it would be up to the U.S. Attorney's Office to decide to file charges, and the charging document would be filed in the U.S. Clerk's Office for the Peoria Division of the U.S. District Court for the Central District of Illinois.

As pointed out in Chapter 7, the constitutional protection against double jeopardy does not prohibit trial in both a state and a federal court for the same act when that action violates both state and federal laws. However, such situations are rare, and one jurisdiction will usually hold off on its prosecution until the other is completed. In addition, state prosecutors sometimes decline to pursue charges against certain types of offenders, such as drug traffickers, to clear the way for the U.S. Attorney's Office to pursue charges because federal offenses carry greater penalties or the federal government may have greater resources at its disposal.

Motion for a change of venue
A formal request to the court to move the trial to a different location.

A **motion for a change of venue** is made when one of the parties wants to change the location of the trial so that the case is heard in some other city, county, or judicial district rather than where the case originally was filed. (*Venue* is Latin for "a place where people gather.") A change of venue might be requested if one of the parties believes that either the current venue is improper under the court's procedural rules or an alternative location would be more appropriate. These motions for a change of venue are most common in highly publicized cases where the defense argues that the trial must be moved to another community to be able to impanel an impartial jury. To justify a venue change, the defense must prove that the prejudice against the defendant is so great that the defendant cannot obtain a fair and impartial trial in the current venue.[1]

---

[1]FRCrP 21(a).

Newspaper articles, transcripts of radio and television broadcasts, and commissioned public opinion polls are often used as evidence to show the predisposition of potential jurors against the defendant. Paralegals may be called upon to research media coverage to support a motion for change of venue.

An excerpt from a motion for change of venue is displayed in Exhibit 9.1. This motion was filed by the attorney representing Drew Peterson on charges that he killed his third wife, Kathleen Savio.[2] Prior to the indictment, Peterson appeared on CNN's *Larry King Live*, NBC's *Today Show*, Fox News, the *Dr. Phil Show*, and a number of local Chicago media outlets. Peterson moved for a change of venue on the basis of prejudicial pretrial publicity. The judge in the case denied the motion, and in 2012, Peterson was convicted of premeditated murder.[3]

Exhibit 9.1: Excerpts from Motion for Change of Venue

DEFENDANT'S MOTION FOR CHANGE OF VENUE

NOW COMES the above named Defendant, Drew Peterson, and hereby files this Motion for Change of Venue, and further states as follows:

* * *

18. In the present case, there is no reasonable dispute that this matter has received saturated media attention. For example, but not by way of limitation:

a. A Google search for "Drew Peterson" returned about 2,950,000 results.[1] This is almost double the amount of results of a Google search for "Rod Blagojevich.[2]

b. An article about Drew Peterson entitled "Ex-cop arrested on murder charges in '04 death of third wife" was the most viewed article on the Chicago Tribune Website for the week of May 3-10, 2009.[3]

19. In addition, numerous articles have been prejudicial toward the Defendant and have prejudiced the jury pool toward him. For example, but not by way of limitation:

* * *

The judge denied the motion.

[2]Peterson, a former Bolingbrook, Illinois, police sergeant, was indicted in 2009 for a crime that allegedly took place in 2003. The indictment was based on an investigation that was started after the mysterious disappearance of Peterson's fourth wife in 2007.

[3]Peterson's conviction was upheld by the Illinois Supreme Court in 2017.

In addition to requesting a change of venue to avoid the effects of pre-trial publicity, the motion can be brought on the basis that a different venue would be more convenient for the parties, the witnesses, or both if the trial were held in an alternative location.

Change of venire
The process of selecting jurors from a different area than the place of the trial.

A limited number of states have enacted statutes providing for a **change of venire** to provide defendants an alternative remedy for prejudicial pre-trial publicity. Under this scheme, the trial takes place in the venue where the charge was filed, but the jury is selected from another judicial district.[4]

In cases in which there has been extensive pre-trial publicity, the defense attorney may have filed a pre-trial motion seeking either a change of venue or change of venire. However, since either alternative involves additional costs and greater inconvenience for some of the participants, judges are reluctant to grant these requests and instead rely on *voir dire* to eliminate individuals who might be affected by such coverage. In high profile cases, a public opinion pollster may be employed to determine the effect of pre-trial publicity on potential jurors. Exhibit 9.2 displays an excerpt of a pollster's report that was appended to a motion for change of venue.

3. MOTIONS RELATED TO THE PARTICIPANTS

a. *Motions for Substitution of Judges*

In most state courts, cases are randomly assigned to a pool of judges who hear specialized types of cases (major felonies, misdemeanors, traffic, juvenile, family). If more than one judge is assigned to a particular call, the luck of the draw usually determines which member of the bench will hear a particular case. However, in smaller jurisdictions, there may be only one judge handling a specific type of case. Therefore, when a case is assigned to a judge who appears to favor the government in criminal cases or has had personal conflicts with the defense attorney, the attorney may file a **motion for substitution of judges**.

Motion for substitution of judges
A formal request to the court to substitute a different judge for the one that is currently assigned to the case.

The circumstances under which such a motion may be granted differ from one jurisdiction to the next. Some states provide a statutory right to change judges at least once, without cause. For instance, in Illinois both the prosecutor and the defendant can move for substitution of judges as a matter of right so long as the motion to substitute is made within ten days of the assignment of the judge to the case. When an Illinois defendant is charged with a Class X felony or a crime punishable by death or life imprisonment, the defendant may name two judges in the motion for substitution.[5] There is no provision in the federal courts for substitution of judges without cause.

Substitution for cause can be for any bias a judge may have in the case, such as an association with a party (family, friendship, or even stock ownership), having made vocal comments in the past on the topic at trial, or other indications of prejudice or conflict of interest. Ordinarily, the basis for the

---

[4]W. LaFave, J. Isreal, & N. King, *Criminal Procedure* 1092 (4th ed., Thomson West 2004).

[5]725 ILCS §114-5. Even though the provision mentions the death penalty, the Illinois legislature abolished capital punishment in 2011.

Exhibit 9.2: Public Opinion Report in Support of Venue Change

The Justice Department filed income tax evasion charges against actor Wesley Snipes in the Middle District of Florida. Snipes filed a motion to change venue to the Southern District of New York. His motion was supported by the report of a public opinion pollster. The court denied the motion. A central Florida jury found Snipes guilty of income tax evasion. Here are excerpts of the report.

Methodology and Data

Overview

The Bernhoft Law Survey project obtained telephone interviews with 353 registered voters in the Ocala Division of the Middle District of Florida, and 226 in the Southern District of New York. The survey was conducted by the Public Opinion Research Laboratory at the University of North Florida. The interviews were done in English and Spanish from October 23 to October 31, 2007. Analysis is not weighted in Ocala or the Southern District of New York since demographic discrepancies do not exist between the sample and the known population of registered voters. (On the Southern District of new York sample, it is slightly low on African Americans (about 3%). Further data collection may correct that. The margin of sampling error for the Ocala set of data is ±5.2%. The margin of sampling error for the Southern District of New York set of data is ±6.5%. A further 147 responses in the Ocala Division and 124 in the Southern District of New York are being collected beginning November 1 and will appear in a supplemental report.

Sample Design

The telephone samples were provided by Survey Sampling International, LLC (SSI). These samples were drawn using standard list-assisted random digit dialing (RDD) methodology. The Ocala Division of the Middle District of Florida covers four counties (Marion, Lake, Sumter, and Citrus). The Ocala sample covers these four counties. The Southern District of New York covers eight counties (New York, Bronx, Westchester, Putnam, Dutchess, Sullivan, Orange, and Rockland). The Southern District sample covers these eight counties.

Procedure

Interviews were conducted from October 23- October 31, 2007. As many as 6 attempts were made to contact every sampled telephone number. The sample is released in replicates- representative subsamples of the larger sample. As many as six callbacks were attempted per number.

Analysis

Weighting was not used on the either sample. The Ocala and the Southern District of New York sets of data do not have discrepancies with the demographic composition of registered voters in that location.

Sample Disposition

The below table illustrates the disposition coding for all sampled callback telephone numbers ever dialed in Ocala Division of the Middle District and the Southern District of New York.

motion must be set forth with particularity and shown through affidavit or live testimony. The defendant bears the burden of proving bias. Generally, these motions are heard by a different judge since the judge from whom the defendant is seeking a change is not likely to believe that there is bias.

Sometimes judges will remove themselves from a case without a motion for substitution of judges having been filed. When judges determine on their own that they are biased, they announce that they are **recusing** themselves from the case. The Judicial Conference of the United States[6] enacted the Code of Conduct for United States Judges (see Canon 3C(1) on page 297). The Code lists various circumstances in which recusal is required.[7]

Recusal
The judge's voluntary departure from a case because of bias or the appearance of impropriety created if continuing to preside over the case.

It is important to note that if the motion to substitute judges is granted, the attorney filing the motion does not get to select the new judge. Rather, a random assignment is usually made from among the remaining judges hearing those kinds of cases. If a substitution takes place in a jurisdiction with no other available judges, a retired judge or one from a neighboring jurisdiction may be assigned to the case.

Discussion Questions

1. Why should it make any difference who the judge is?
2. What factors does an attorney need to evaluate when deciding whether to seek a substitution for a judge?
3. Recently, there have been calls for Supreme Court Justices to recuse themselves from particular cases; e.g., Clarence Thomas because of his wife's involvement in the January 6 insurrection; Ruth Bader Ginsberg because of her personal attacks of President Trump. Should the Ethical Code for U.S. Judges apply to Supreme Court Justices?

---

[6]The Judicial Conference serves as the policymaking body for the federal courts. It is composed of the Chief Justice of the United States, the chief judge of each judicial circuit, the chief judge of the Court of International Trade, and a district judge from each regional judicial circuit The Conference considers administrative and policy issues affecting the federal court system.

[7]The Code of Conduct for United States Judges does not apply to U.S. Supreme Court justices.

b. Joinder and Severance

Rule 8 of the Federal Rules of Criminal Procedure provides for **joinder of offenses and defendants.** Specifically, joinder of offenses is proper when the offenses are "of the same or similar character or are based on the same act or transaction or on two or more acts or transactions connected together or constituting parts of a common scheme or plan."[8] Co-defendants may be charged in the same indictment if they have participated in the same series of acts constituting the offense. "Defendants may be charged in one or more counts together or separately, and all of the defendants need not be charged in each count."[9]

Joinder of offenses
A process whereby a defendant is tried on multiple charges at the same time.

Joinder of defendants
A process whereby individual defendants who are alleged to have committed the same offenses are tried together at the same time.

Canon 3 C (1) of the Code of Conduct for United States Judges

A judge shall disqualify himself or herself in a proceeding in which the judge's impartiality might reasonably be questioned, including but not limited to instances in which:

(a) The judge has a personal bias or prejudice concerning a party, or personal knowledge of disputed evidentiary facts concerning the proceeding;

(b) The judge served as a lawyer in the matter in controversy, or a lawyer with whom the judge previously practiced law served during such association as a lawyer concerning the matter, or the judge or lawyer has been a material witness;

(c) The judge knows that the judge, individually or as a fiduciary, or the judge's spouse or minor child residing in the judge's household, has a financial interest in the subject matter in controversy or in a party to the proceeding, or any other interest that could be affected substantially by the outcome of the proceeding;

(d) The judge or the judge's spouse, or a person related to either within the third degree of relationship, or the spouse of such a person is:

(i) a party to the proceeding, or an officer, director, or trustee of a party;

(ii) acting as a lawyer in the proceeding;

(iii) known by the judge to have an interest that could be substantially affected by the outcome of the proceeding; or

(iv) to the judge's knowledge likely to be a material witness in the proceeding;

(e) The judge has served in governmental employment and in that capacity participated as a judge (in a previous judicial position), counsel, advisor, or material witness concerning the proceeding or has expressed an opinion concerning the merits of the particular case in controversy.

The Code of Conduct for United States Judges was initially adopted by the Judicial Conference in 1973 and was last revised in 2009. It can be found at http://www.uscourts.gov/Viewer.aspx?doc=/uscourts/RulesAndPolicies/conduct/Vol02A-Ch02.pdf.

---

[8]FRCrP 8(a).

[9]FRCrP 8(b).

An example of the joining of charges would be the government's charging one defendant with a series of separate drug trafficking offenses in a single indictment. A joinder of defendants would occur when the government tries several defendants who had all been charged with conspiracy to distribute illegal drugs, even though some of them had not also been charged with money laundering. Even if initial joinder is proper, Federal Rule of Criminal Procedure 14 authorizes a court to order separate trials of counts if it appears that a defendant is prejudiced by the joinder. In order to seek such an order, the defense attorney would file a **motion to sever**. The same procedure is used in state court.

Motion to sever
A formal request to the court to require separate trials for individual defendants who are scheduled to be tried together, or for individual charges against a specific defendant.

It is important to emphasize that the decision to sever is up to the discretion of the judge. Federal and state law generally favors joint trials of defendants who are charged together and allows severance only upon a showing of real prejudice to an individual defendant.[10] To be successful, a defense motion for severance must show that concerns for the defendant's right to a fair trial outweigh the goals of judicial economy and efficiency. Trial courts are thus reluctant to grant severance, and rarely do appellate courts overturn a lower court decision to refuse severance. One of the most successful grounds for seeking severance arises when a defendant wishes not to testify on all charges in a trial and chooses to claim a Fifth Amendment privilege on one or more counts.

Application Exercises

1. A state grand jury in the Clay Marshall Hypothetical Case (*see* hypothetical case on pages xxxviii-xxxix), in the county where your school is located, returned a two-count indictment against the client. The first count alleges sexual contact with Randy Jefferson, and the second count asserts sexual abuse of Madison Pickering. Prepare a motion to sever.
2. For the Brandon Turner Hypothetical Case (*see* hypothetical case on page xxxvii), draft the body of a motion to sever Count I (sexual assault) from Count II (possession of crack cocaine with intent to deliver) and Count III (possession of a firearm in connection with a drug trafficking crime). Assume that the sexual assault allegedly occurred on January 1 of last year and that the two other charges were alleged to have taken place September 1 of last year. All occurrences took place in the state where your school is located. The charges were brought in a state court bill of indictment.

Discussion Questions

After reviewing the facts of the Brandon Turner Hypothetical Case, answer the following questions:

4. If both Brandon Turner and Dennis Watterson (the co-owner of the car driven by Turner at the time of arrest) were charged with possession of

[10] *Zafiro v. United States*, 506 U.S. 534, 537 (1993).

illicit drugs with the intent to distribute, how do you think a judge would rule on Turner's motion to sever the counts against him from the charges against Watterson?

5. If Turner was also charged with a sexual assault that allegedly occurred nine months prior to his drug arrest, how successful would a motion be to sever the sexual assault charge from the other charges?

After reviewing the facts of the Clay Marshall Hypothetical Case, answer the following question:

6. If the local prosecutor files charges against Clay Marshall in one document concerning his alleged sexual assaults of Randy Jefferson and Madison Pickering, what arguments can he raise in a motion to sever Jefferson's charge from Pickering's charges?

c. *Motion for a Competency Hearing*

In addition to being important to the determination of a person's legal responsibility for criminal actions, the mental condition of the defendant is relevant to the government's ability to put the accused on trial and to enter into a plea agreement. (See the discussion of the insanity defense in Chapter 7.) Therefore, if there are serious questions about the defendant's mental ability to adequately assist his or her attorneys in preparing a defense, the defense attorney should consider filing a **motion for a competency hearing.** In some jurisdictions, instead of seeking a competency hearing, the defense moves for a continuance on the ground that the defendant is incompetent.[11] In determining whether the motion should be allowed, the court conducts a competency hearing.

Motion for a Competency Hearing
A formal request to the court to hold a hearing to determine if the defendant is competent to stand trial.

If the motion is granted, a special hearing will be held, prior to the trial, at which evidence will be presented relating to the defendant's ability to make informed decisions about trial strategy. The U.S. Supreme Court has defined competency in this context to mean the defendant has the ability to understand the charges and consult rationally with an attorney to aid in his or her own defense.[12] Customarily, the court relies on psychiatric expert testimony to decide whether the defendant should stand trial. Prior to the hearing, both the government and the defense will have the defendant undergo a psychological assessment. (See Exhibit 9.3 for an excerpt of the government psychiatrist's report on a defendant's competency to stand trial.) Although the statutes addressing competency vary from state to state, they generally reflect these same elements. A judge may also rule a defendant incompetent to stand trial even though neither side files a motion to determine competency.

4. MOTIONS INVOLVING THE EVIDENCE

a. *Motion to Suppress Evidence*

One of the most common and perhaps most important pretrial motions filed by the defendant in a criminal case is a **motion to suppress.** This is a

Motion to Suppress
A request that the court prohibit specified material from being admitted into evidence at a trial because it was gathered in an illegal manner.

---

[11]For instance, in Illinois, the judge may allow a motion for continuance based on the defendant's inability to stand trial due to physical or mental incompetency. 725 ILCS 5/114-4(b)(4).

[12]*Dusky v. United States,* 362 U.S. 402 (1960).

Exhibit 9.3: Excerpt of Report of Defendant's Competency to Stand Trial

In 2007 after a jury trial, José Padilla, an alleged Al Qaeda operative, was found guilty of federal terrorism charges and sentenced to seventeen years in prison. Before trial, a federal judge determined that Padilla was competent. Defense counsel contended the defendant was suffering from post-traumatic stress syndrome and therefore incompetent to stand trial. In contrast, the government maintained that Padilla was not suffering from a severe mental disorder. The first page of the government doctor's report appears below.

U.S. DEPARTMENT OF JUSTICE
FEDERAL BUREAU OF PRISONS
FEDERAL DETENTION CENTER
MIAMI, FLORIDA

FORENSIC REPORT

DEFENDANT NAME: Padilla, Jose **REGISTRATION NUMBER:** 20796-424
DATE OF BIRTH: October 18, 1970 **DATE OF REPORT:** February 5, 2007
CASE NUMBER: 04-60001-CR-COOKE/Brown
DATE OF EVALUATION: December, 2006 to February, 2007

IDENTIFICATION AND REASON FOR REFERRAL:

Mr. Jose Padilla, also known as (AKA) Jose Rivera, Julio Rodriguez, Jose Ortiz, Ibrahim, Abu Abdullah the Puerto Rican, and Abu Abdullah Al Mujahir, is a 36-year-old, Caucasian-Hispanic male who has been charged with the following offenses: Conspiracy to Murder, Kidnap, and Maim Persons in a Foreign Country; Conspiracy to Provide Material Support for Terrorists; and Material Support for Terrorists, all in violation of Title 18, United States Code (USC), Sections 956(a)(1), 371, 2339A(a) and 2.

On December 18, 2006, the Court ordered the Federal Bureau of Prisons (BOP) to examine the defendant and determine if he is suffering from a mental disease that would preclude his ability to participate in the court process or assist his attorney. The tests of competency involve determining whether or not the defendant is suffering from a mental illness that precludes his ability to understand the nature and consequences of the proceedings against him, and to properly assist in his own defense.

Mr. Padilla was admitted on January 5, 2006, to the Federal Detention Center (FDC), Miami, Florida as a pre-trial inmate, and designated on December 21, 2006, for the evaluation. This evaluation was conducted under the provisions of Title 18, USC Section 4241.

ASSESSMENT PROCEDURES:

During the initial interview, it was explained to Mr. Padilla that the purpose of the examination was to determine if he is competent to stand trial. He was also informed of the limits of confidentiality and advised that the usual client/doctor privilege would not be in effect. It was explained to him that anything he discussed with the examiner might be relayed to the Court. Mr. Padilla was informed that a written report summarizing test results and clinical findings would be provided to the Court, to his attorney, and to the prosecuting attorney. Mr. Padilla indicated that he understood; however, he indicated that he did not intend to cooperate with the parameters set forth by the examination procedures.

formal request to have the judge prohibit the use of certain kinds of evidence on the basis that it was collected in a manner that violated the defendant's constitutional or statutory rights. For example, if the evidence was seized during an illegal search or an incriminating statement was made under conditions that violated the defendant's right to counsel, the **exclusionary rule**[13] prohibits this evidence from being used during the trial.

Exclusionary Rule
The doctrine that evidence obtained in violation of a defendant's constitutional rights cannot be used against the defendant in a criminal prosecution.

A **motion *in limine*** is another type of motion that is also designed to prohibit the admission of certain types of evidence, but since these motions aren't usually made until the pre-trial conference stage, we will wait until Chapter 11 to discuss them in greater detail.

Motion *in limine*
A formal request to the court to prohibit mention of specified information because it is not sufficiently relevant to the issues being tried and would have a prejudicial effect on the jury.

A defense counsel's first step in determining whether a motion to suppress should be filed is to review the police reports and witness statements furnished by the prosecution in discovery. Motions to suppress seek to prevent the use at trial of either statements made by the defendant or evidence discovered through a search. If there appears to be reason to suspect illegal conduct by law enforcement officers in either one of these situations, the defense should immediately launch its own investigation.

The next step is for counsel to develop a constitutional law theory for suppressing the evidence. A defendant's incriminatory statements are subject to suppression under the Fifth Amendment Self-Incrimination Clause when the police either coerced him or her into making a statement or obtained a confession without first giving the defendant the *Miranda* warnings. Recent Supreme Court decisions have diminished the protection the Fifth Amendment Self-Incrimination Clause affords to suspects being interrogated by the police. Hence, defense attorneys experience few victories when they move for the suppression of incriminating statements.[14]

Defendants have been more successful in suppressing physical evidence and electronic data on Fourth Amendment grounds because the Supreme Court has expanded the constitutional protections in this area of law in a number of respects.

First, the Court now bases its search-and-seizure jurisprudence on two alternative theories. Until the mid-twentieth century, the Court analyzed searches in terms of common law trespass principles. Under this approach, a defendant had to have a property interest in the item that was seized in order to have standing to assert a Fourth Amendment right. Thus, wiretaps could be conducted without a search warrant or probable cause because the target of the eavesdropping did not own the telephone wires. In the late 1960s, the Court replaced this approach with the "reasonable expectation of privacy"

---

[13] See the discussion in Chapter 7, pp. 229-233.

[14] E.g., *Salinas v. Texas*, 570 U.S. 178 (2013) (self-incrimination clause does not protect a defendant's refusal to answer questions in a non-custodial police interview even though he was not given his *Miranda* rights); *Howes v. Fields*, 565 U.S. 499 (2012) (Self-Incrimination Clause does not require that *Miranda* warnings be given before questioning incarcerated prisoner about issues unrelated to the case for which the prisoner is in custody). ***But see***, e.g., ***Missouri v. Seibert***, 542 U.S. 600 (2004) (*Miranda* warnings given mid-interrogation, after defendant gave confession without being first given *Miranda* rights, were ineffective, even though the defendant repeated the confession after *Miranda* warnings were given).

test.[15] Under this analysis, individuals were protected from government intrusion into matters they wanted to keep private if this expectation of privacy was something society is prepared to recognize as reasonable. The Supreme Court continues to use this test.[16]

The Roberts Supreme Court resurrected the common law trespassory test in *United States v. Jones,* a case in which the Court held that a global positioning system (GPS) device attached to a suspect's vehicle to monitor his vehicle's movements constituted a "search" because the government physically occupied private property for the purpose of obtaining information.[17] After the *Jones* decision, the Court applied the common law trespass analyses in cases involving warrantless searches of the immediate area outside a suspect's home, known as the "curtilage."[18]

If warranted by the facts, motions to suppress, based on the Fourth Amendment, should argue that the defendant's "reasonable expectation of privacy" was violated and that the officers violated the defendant's property interests. If the motion does not raise one of these grounds, the argument is considered "forfeited" which bars the defendant from presenting this argument later.[19]

Second, the Supreme Court has expanded Fourth Amendment protection to new technologies. In *Riley v. California*, the Court held that the Fourth Amendment does not permit a warrantless search of digital information on a cell phone seized from an individual who has been arrested.[20] The Supreme Court in *Carpenter v. United States* held that the warrantless seizure and search of historical cell phone records revealing the location and movements of a cell phone user over the course of 127 days is not permitted by the Fourth Amendment.[21]

Third, motorists stopped by the police have greater rights under the Fourth Amendment. For example, the Supreme Court now requires the police to secure a warrant before a suspected drunk driver is required to submit to a blood draw.[22] In addition, the Court ruled that absent reasonable suspicion, a

---

[15]In *Katz v. United States*, 389 U.S. 347 (1967), the Court said that "the Fourth Amendment protects people, not places," and found that officers violated the Fourth Amendment by attaching an eavesdropping device to a public telephone booth. Later cases applied the analysis of Justice John Marshall Harlan's *Katz* concurrence, in which he stated that a violation occurs when government officers intrude on a person's "reasonable expectation of privacy."

[16]E.g., *Carpenter v. United States*, 138 S. Ct. 2206 (2018); *Byrd v. United States* 138 S. Ct. 1518 (2018).

[17]565 U.S. 400 (2012).

[18]*See*, e.g., *Florida v. Jardines*, 569 U.S. 1 (2013) (porch); *Collins v. Virginia*, 138 S. Ct. 1663 (2018) (driveway).

[19]*See*, e.g., *Byrd v. United States*, 138 S. Ct. 1518 (2018); Carpenter v. United States, 138 S. Ct. 2206 (2018)(Gorsuch dissent).

[20]573 U.S. 373 (2014).

[21]138 S. Ct. 2206 (2018).

[22]*Birchfield v. North Dakota*, 579 U.S. 438 (2016). Although the Court also held that motorists can be compelled to submit to a breathalyzer test, the officer must first have probable cause to make the traffic stop. If the defense shows there was no probable cause, the trial judge will suppress evidence such as the officer's reports of the defendant's slurred speech, lack of coordination, and the odor of alcohol as well as the results of blood and breath tests.

police extension of a traffic stop in order to conduct a dog sniff is an unreasonable search.[23]

Most states apply federal constitutional law in interpreting their own constitutional protections. In jurisdictions where state constitutional law is not in lockstep with U.S. constitutional law, there may be dual standards for suppression of evidence. In any event, a careful defense attorney will always cite both the federal and the state constitutional provisions in support of a motion to suppress.

Once the defense attorney determines that there is a good faith basis for suppressing the evidence, the attorney or paralegal will prepare a written motion to suppress. It must contain specific facts evidencing a constitutional violation. Boilerplate language that simply asserts conclusions that the government violated constitutional law is not sufficient. State or local court rules may require that the motion be supported by affidavit or verified under penalties of perjury. Unless the motion is sufficiently definite, specific, and not based on conjecture, the court may reject it without even conducting an evidentiary hearing.

The components of the motion are: caption, introductory paragraph (citing specific statutory and constitutional provisions), body, prayer for relief, attorney's signature, and address block. The body of the motion may be written in narrative format or in numbered paragraphs, depending upon local custom. Often, the motion is accompanied by a memorandum of law, also known as points and authorities.

When the court conducts a suppression hearing, the defendant has the burden of presenting evidence to support the claim that the government acted illegally. Although the prosecutor generally has to prove by a preponderance of evidence that the government obtained evidence properly, there are a few limited situations in which the defendant has the burden of persuasion.[24] Because the rules of evidence are relaxed at suppression hearings, hearsay testimony is routinely considered by the judge. Although defendants testifying at suppression hearings do not waive their Fifth Amendment right against self-incrimination,[25] their testimony at the hearing may be used to impeach any inconsistent statements they may make at trial.

The success of a motion to suppress often has a great impact on plea bargaining because the exclusion of evidence often makes it more difficult for the prosecution to meet its burden of proving guilt beyond a reasonable doubt. This in turn may motivate the prosecution attorney to offer to reduce the charges or request a lighter sentence. Likewise, when the court denies a motion to suppress, a defendant may be more likely to enter into a plea agreement, knowing that the prosecutor will be able to use the contested evidence at the trial. On some occasions, the prosecution may dismiss the charges if the court suppresses key evidence. *See* Exhibit 9.4.

---

[23] *Rodriguez v. United States*, 135 S. Ct. 1609 (2015).

[24] The defendant has the burden of persuasion on issues such as defendant's standing to assert a constitutional violation (*Rawlings v. Kentucky*, 448 U.S. 98, 104 (1980)) and due process challenges of suggestive identification of the defendant (*Stovall v. Denno*, 388 U.S. 293 (1967)).

[25] *Simmons v. United States*, 390 U.S. 377, 394 (1968).

Exhibit 9.4: Dismissal of Charges After Evidence Is Suppressed

After the judge granted the defense motion for suppression of evidence, a Florida prosecutor dropped all twelve counts of possession of child pornography filed against singer R. Kelly. The Florida prosecutor's notice of dismissal of the charges (*nolle prosequi*) appears below. An Illinois jury in Chicago acquitted him of similar charges several years later. In 2022, a Chicago federal jury found him guilty on child pornography charges.

IN THE CIRCUIT COURT OF THE TENTH JUDICIAL CIRCUIT
IN AND FOR POLK COUNTY, FLORIDA

STATE OF FLORIDA,
vs
ROBERT S. KELLY

CASE NO.: 53-2003-CF-000196-01XX-XX
AGENCY CASE # :

CHARGES:
POSSESSION OF CHILD PORNOGRAPHY
(TWELVE COUNTS)

NOTICE OF NOLLE PROSEQUI [NP]

BRADFORD H COPLEY as Assistant State Attorney, gives notice that the above-styled cause is hereby **TERMINATED AND DISMISSED** for the following principal reason, to-wit:

THE DEFENDANT IN THIS CASE IS CHARGED WITH TWELVE COUNTS OF POSSESSION OF CHILD PORNOGRAPHY BASED ON 12 PICTURES OF AN UNDERAGE GIRL INVOLVED IN SEXUAL SITUATIONS WITH THE DEFENDANT, MR. KELLY, AND WITH AN UNIDENTIFIED WOMAN. THESE PICTURES THAT WERE FOUND IN MR. KELLY'S POSSESSION HAVE BEEN SUPPRESSED BY THE COURT AND THE STATE CANNOT PROVE THIS CASE WITHOUT THE EVIDENCE.

CERTIFICATE OF SERVICE

I HEREBY CERTIFY that a true copy of the foregoing has been furnished to MR. RON TOWARD, POST OFFICE BOX 1772, BARTOW FL 33830-1772 AND MS DIANE BUERGER, 766 E MAIN STREET, BARTOW FL 33830-4832 this 17th day of March, 2004.

Bradford H Copley
BRADFORD H COPLEY
Assistant State Attorney
Bar Number:0437662
Drawer SA. Box 9000
Bartow, Florida 33831

Application Exercise

3. After reviewing the facts of the *Turner* case (*see* hypothetical case on pages xxxvii-xxxviii), take note of the following additional facts about the case:
   - Brandon Turner was pursued by the police for an alleged traffic violation. He traveled one block, left his car and entered a restaurant, and went into the public restroom for less than one minute. A baggie of what appeared to be cocaine was left on the front seat of the car. The police officer recovered a handgun from the restroom.

     After he was arrested for possession of cocaine and use of a firearm during a drug felony, Brandon Turner was taken to the local county jail. During processing, a local drug enforcement unit police officer took information without first advising Turner of his rights. Officer Manfred Chester obtained biographical information from him. Sgt. Hugh Ett, the supervising officer of the drug enforcement unit, then joined the conversation and began talking to Turner. The government's discovery included a police report that stated, in part, as follows:

     > The suspect was interviewed by Sergeant Hugh Ett after his arrest. He told Sergeant Ett that the reason he attempted to hide his gun and not the cocaine was because he had current firearms charges pending against him.

   After researching your jurisdiction's criminal code to locate the provision governing motions to suppress evidence, draft a motion to suppress evidence in the *Turner* case. Your draft should cite the applicable statutes and constitutional provisions. (Assume that the case is the first felony filed this year by the local prosecuting authority in the jurisdiction in which your school is located. The attorney for the defendant is Charles Hovey. Hovey's address and telephone numbers are those of your school.)

b. Motion in Limine

A motion *in limine* asks the court to limit the issues or evidence presented in the trial. For example, the defendant might ask the court to exclude certain inflammatory allegations that are not related to the charges against him, evidence of a prior conviction that occurred a long time ago, or hearsay statements contained in a police report. Since these motions aren't usually made until the pre-trial conference stage, we will cover them in more detail in Chapter 11.

5. MOTION TO DISMISS

Motion to dismiss
A formal request to the court to drop a pending criminal charge against the defendant.

A **motion to dismiss** asks the court to dismiss charges against the defendant. At the federal level, these motions fall under Rule 12, which authorizes parties to raise by motion any defense, objection, or request that the court can determine without a trial of the general issue. It can be used in criminal cases to seek dismissal of charges on the basis that there were procedural defects in the indictment or information.[26]

States also authorize defendants to move for dismissal. For example, the Illinois Code of Criminal Procedure lists the following grounds to dismiss charges:

> (1) The defendant has not been placed on trial in compliance with [the Speedy Trial Act].
>
> (2) The prosecution of the offense is barred by [the statute of limitations or the defendant's double jeopardy rights were violated].
>
> (3) The defendant has received immunity from prosecution for the offense charged.
>
> (4) The indictment was returned by a Grand Jury which was improperly selected and which results in substantial injustice to the defendant.
>
> (5) The indictment was returned by a Grand Jury which acted contrary to [statute] and which results in substantial injustice to the defendant.
>
> (6) The court in which the charge has been filed does not have jurisdiction.
>
> (7) The county is an improper place of trial.
>
> (8) The charge does not state an offense.
>
> (9) The indictment is based solely upon the testimony of an incompetent witness.
>
> (10) The defendant is misnamed in the charge and the misnomer results in substantial injustice to the defendant.
>
> (11) [The indictment was not returned or a preliminary hearing was not held in a timely manner in accordance with statute.][27]

Statute of limitations
A law that sets forth a maximum time limit between the occurrence or discovery of a crime and the date at which formal charges must be filed.

Speedy Trial Act
A law that sets forth a maximum time limit between the time that formal charges are filed and the start of a trial on those charges.

Nolle prosequi
The formal entry of record by the prosecutor declaring no interest in prosecuting the case.

Although grounds for dismissal vary from state to state, defendants typically can seek dismissal when the charges were filed after the **statute of limitations** expired or when the case is not brought to trial soon enough in violation of the state's **Speedy Trial Act**.

There are a variety of reasons why a prosecutor may choose to dismiss a case voluntarily. This type of dismissal of a charge is called ***nolle prosequi***, a Latin term meaning "not wish to prosecute." For instance, when a domestic battery victim reconciles with the perpetrator, the victim may refuse to cooperate with the prosecution. Other circumstances include the unavailability of a police officer, the death of a key witness, and a witness's invocation of the Fifth Amendment right not to incriminate oneself. *See* Exhibit 9.5.

---

[26] FRCrP 12(a)(3)(B).

[27] 725 ILSC 5/114-1.

Exhibit 9.5: Dismissal of Charges After Complaining Witness Invokes Fifth Amendment Rights

Prosecutors have dropped felony charges of indecent assault and battery against the actor Kevin Spacey (whose legal name is Kevin Spacey Fowler) after the alleged victim invoked his Fifth Amendment right not to testify. The Massachusetts prosecutor's *nolle prosequi* of the case appears below.

COMMONWEALTH OF MASSACHUSETTS

Nantucket, ss

Nantucket District Court
Docket No. 1888CR000598

Commonwealth)
)
vs.) Nolle Prosequi
)
Kevin S. Fowler)

Now comes the Commonwealth, by and through its District Attorney, Michael O'Keefe, and hereby files a Nolle Prosequi in the above matter due to the unavailability of the complaining witness.

Respectfully Submitted,

Michael O'Keefe
District Attorney

Dated: July 17, 2019

FILED
JUL 17 2019
NANTUCKET DISTRICT COURT

6. MOTION FOR A CONTINUANCE

Motion for continuance
A formal request to the court to postpone the date of an upcoming court proceeding.

Continuance
The postponement of a scheduled court proceeding, such as a hearing or the trial.

One of the most common pre-trial motions is a **motion for a continuance.** A **continuance** is the postponement of a scheduled court proceeding, such as a hearing or the trial. Lawyers typically request continuances either because they have a schedule conflict before a different judge or because they need more time to prepare for the scheduled proceeding. Other reasons could include the absence of key witnesses or important pieces of evidence. In rare cases, a judge might grant a continuance where there has recently been a great deal of prejudicial publicity in the local press[28] or when the defendant is not competent to stand trial.[29]

In some jurisdictions, motions for continuance must be accompanied by a supporting affidavit, whereas in others, the attorney need only recite the basis for the delay in the motion itself. An example of a federal motion for continuance appears in Exhibit 9.6.

Many times, motions for continuance are unopposed. Sometimes this is due to the exercise of professional courtesy. An attorney may not object to the opposing counsel's request for more time to prepare, knowing that he or she may ask for the same accommodation later. Other times, an advocate, in choosing his or her battles, may not challenge a motion that the court will most likely allow. Finally, the attorney may need a continuance at the same time.

In response to delays in bringing cases to trial, some states have adopted "fast-track" rules that sharply limit the ability of judges to grant continuances. However, a motion for continuance may be granted when necessitated by unforeseeable events, or where the court deems it necessary and prudent in the "interest of justice."

Under most speedy trial statutes, the granting of a defense motion for a continuance "stops the clock" on the time limits within which the defendant must be brought to trial. Even the delay resulting from a prosecution motion for continuance may be charged to the defense if the defendant fails to object to the motion.

B. PLEA BARGAINING

Plea bargain
An agreement whereby the defendant pleads guilty to a criminal charge in exchange for a reduction in the charges, the number of counts, or a lesser sentence.

Like it or not, our modern criminal justice system has become dependent upon the widespread use of plea bargaining. A **plea bargain** is an agreement between the prosecutor and the defendant in which the defendant pleads guilty to a criminal charge in exchange for a benefit in the eventual disposition of the case. Typical benefits received by defendants include the dismissal of one or more charges, the reduction of a charge to a lesser offense, and a lesser penalty as part of the sentence. While the numbers vary from one jurisdiction to the next, it is widely accepted that more than 90 percent of all felony convictions are the result of plea-bargaining agreements. The discussions and negotiations that

---

[28]In cases where prejudicial press coverage is involved, attorneys might also file a motion for a change of venue. See the discussion of this topic earlier in this chapter, on pp. 290-294.

[29]For instance, in Illinois, the judge may allow a motion for continuance based on the defendant's inability to stand trial due to physical or mental incompetence. 725 ILCS 5/114-4(b)(4).

Exhibit 9.6: Motion for Continuance in Federal Court

Three weeks prior to this tax evasion trial, actor Wesley Snipes fired his legal team and moved to continue the case. In the order denying this motion, the federal judge stated, "This series of events would any reasonable person to suspect that the defendant's dismissal of able counsel is nothing more than a ploy designed to force a continuance of the trial." Here is the motion for continuance.

At his jury trial, Snipes was convicted of three counts of willfully failing to file income tax returns.

UNITED STATES DISTRICT COURT
MIDDLE DISTRICT OF FLORIDA
OCALA DIVISION

UNITED STATES, Plaintiff, v. WESLEY SNIPES, Defendant.	Case No. 5:06-cr-00022-WTH-GRJ

DEFENDANT'S EMERGENCY MOTION TO CONTINUE TRIAL

Wesley Trent Snipes ("Snipes"), the defendant in the above-captioned matter, by and through counsel of record, Robert G. Bernhoft, hereby respectfully moves this Court to continue the currently scheduled trial date of October 22, 2007, to give new counsel adequate time to prepare for trial. Snipes' fundamental right to the effective assistance of counsel compels a continuance to ensure a fair trial.

Grounds for this motion are two-fold. First, Snipes' concerns over Attorney Meachum's health, which were previously conveyed to the Court, may preclude Attorney Meachum's meaningful involvement in the trial at this time. Second, and most importantly, Snipes' former lead trial counsel, William R. Martin, was responsible for discovery review, pre-trial investigation, and motion practice. It is abundantly apparent, however, from the defense's discovery motion practice and this Court's recent orders relating thereto, that there are fundamental deficiencies in Mr. Martin's pre-trial preparation in this matter, involving lack of diligence in reviewing hundreds of thousands of pages of discovery documents that form the core of this case. It is also undisputed that Attorney Martin failed to timely raise critical issues of venue, and furthermore, failed to seek remedy for serious grand jury abuse of which he should have known with the exercise of reasonable diligence. The scope and prejudicial effect of this pervasive ineffective assistance of counsel only recently came to Snipes' attention, causing an irreparable breach in the attorney-client relationship with his former attorneys, and precipitating their discharge by Snipes, and the hiring of new trial counsel.

Of particular import here, these deficiencies have rendered Snipes wholly unprepared for trial. Consequently, Snipes' fundamental right to effective assistance of counsel is violated, and he is axiomatically prejudiced, without a continuance for new counsel to perform and discharge these tasks. *See Williams v. Taylor*, 529 U.S. 362, 371 (2000); *Wiggins v. Smith*, 539 U.S. 510

* * *

For the foregoing reasons, Snipes respectfully requests a trial continuance so that his new attorneys may obtain the voluminous discovery documents from former counsel; review, index, and incorporate those documents into necessary trial preparation; conduct the necessary pre-trial investigations; protect Mr. Snipes' right to raise all issues concerning venue, including those not previously raised and all issues improperly waived through ineffective assistance of counsel;

* * *

Respectfully submitted on October 3, 2007.

THE BERNHOFT LAW FIRM, S.C.
Attorneys for the Defendant

By: /s/ Robert G. Bernhoft
Robert G. Bernhoft
Wisconsin State Bar No. 1032777

207 East Buffalo Street, Suite 600
Milwaukee, Wisconsin 53202
(414) 276-3333 telephone
(414) 276-2822 facsimile
rgbernhoft@bernhoftlaw.com

* * *

At his jury trial, Snipes was convicted of three counts of willfully failing to file income tax returns.

are an essential part of the plea-bargaining process are often going on at the same time as the motions discussed above are being filed and argued in court. Therefore, the judge's rulings on these motions typically have a significant impact on the terms of any potential plea bargain.

1. BENEFITS OF PLEA BARGAINING

The extent to which the criminal justice system currently uses plea bargaining is probably best explained by noting the cost savings that it provides for taxpayers. If everyone (not just the current 5 to 10 percent) had to go to trial, it would require roughly nine times as many judges, prosecutors, public defenders, jurors, bailiffs, court reporters, etc., and the costs of their salaries and fees would have to be paid by the taxpayers. Plea bargaining is a far more efficient and less expensive way of obtaining convictions and ensuring some degree of punishment.

Plea bargaining also reduces the lost productivity that businesses incur when jurors have to take time off from their jobs to sit around the courthouse waiting to be called, sitting through hours (sometimes even weeks and months) of testimony and jury deliberations. In addition to the time witnesses have to spend waiting to be called and then actually testifying, victims are often forced to relive traumatic events and face emotionally unsettling, public examinations by attorneys. This is especially true in cases involving murder, rape, and sexual abuse of minors.

Another advantage of plea bargaining is that it replaces the uncertainty of the trial process with a guarantee that guilty defendants will be punished for their actions. Even when the prosecutor has strong evidence of guilt, it is always possible that key witnesses may not be available at the time of the trial or may change their testimony. Police departments have been known to lose or contaminate evidence, and there is always the possibility that at least one juror will have what he or she considers to be a "reasonable" doubt. Therefore, the prosecutor would rather settle for a guaranteed five-year sentence for manslaughter than risk having the defendant go free on a murder charge.

In some cases, plea bargains secure a defendant's assistance in building a case against other wrongdoers. For instance, Illinois governor George Ryan's former chief of staff and campaign manager, Scott Fawell, agreed to a plea agreement that reduced the prison time for him and his fiancée in exchange for his testimony against his former boss. Fawell's testimony helped prosecutors convict the ex-governor of multiple counts of political corruption. Likewise, Tony Taylor pleaded guilty to his role in a brutal dog fighting ring and agreed to cooperate with the U.S. Attorney's Office in the prosecution of National Football League (NFL) star Michael Vick. Taylor received a two-month sentence for his role in the conspiracy, whereas Vick was sentenced to twenty-three months in prison.

There are also instances in which prosecutors may negotiate a plea bargain because they sincerely believe that there are extenuating circumstances that make the mandatory minimum sentence for the crime more severe than it should be.

Defendants often enter into plea bargains to avoid the "trial penalty," a concept that suggests that defendants receive harsher sentences if they are found guilty after a trial than if they plea bargain. Although this theory has intuitive appeal, empirical analysis casts doubt on it.[30]

2. CRITICISMS OF PLEA BARGAINING

Although plea bargaining increases the probability that criminals will end up with a conviction on their record and at least some form of punishment for their crime, it also creates greater inequalities in the system and the possibility of innocent defendants being punished for crimes they did not commit.

One obvious inequity is that those who plead guilty may end up with a lesser punishment than they would have had if they had been found guilty in a trial. By rewarding those who speed up the process by accepting a plea bargain, the system penalizes those who choose to use their constitutional right to a trial. Thus, two people who commit the same crime receive very different punishments.

Even more disturbing is the fact that the plea-bargaining system sometimes pressures innocent men and women to plead guilty to crimes they did not commit. In general, prosecutors with weaker cases are more likely to offer better deals to defendants. Thus, defendants with a stronger defense are forced to choose between risking years in prison (perhaps even death) by going to trial, or pleading to a crime they didn't commit and serving a relatively short time in jail. The situation is especially tough for indigent defendants who are represented by overworked public defenders and cannot afford bail while their case is pending. In these types of situations, accepting the plea bargain may mean immediate release from jail for time already served as opposed to remaining in jail for many more months waiting for the case to come to trial. Defendants prefer to enter a "no-contest" plea as part of their plea bargains rather than plead guilty. A no contest plea, also known as a ***nolo contendere* plea,** is a plea in which the defendant does not admit or deny criminal responsibility but agrees to accept punishment; also known

***Nolo contendere* plea**
A plea in which the defendant does not admit or deny criminal responsibility but agrees to accept punishment; also known as a "no-contest" plea.

When a jurisdiction does not permit *nolo contendere* pleas, a **plea of convenience**, or "***Alford* plea**," involves a situation in which a defendant pleads guilty to a crime the defendant did not commit in order to end the case in a way that the defendant perceives to be in his or her long-term best interests.[31] Authorities are divided as to whether this practice is appropriate. Florida Criminal Procedure expressly recognizes that some defendants plead guilty to crimes they did not commit. Rule 3.172(d) provides:

Plea of convenience
A guilty plea for a crime the defendant does not acknowledge committing that is made in order to conclude the case on terms the defendant feels are in his or her best interest; also known as an *Alford* plea.

> Before the trial judge accepts a guilty or *nolo contendere* plea, the judge must determine that the defendant either (1) acknowledges his or her guilt or (2) acknowledges that he or she feels the plea to be in his or her best interest, while maintaining his or her innocence.

[30] David S. Abrams, *Is Pleading Really a Bargain?* 8 Journal of Empirical Legal Studies 200 (2011).

[31] This type of plea was approved by the U.S. Supreme Court in *North Carolina v. Alford,* 400 U.S. 25 (1970). A defendant asserting an *Alford* plea maintains his or her innocence but admits there is sufficient evidence for a conviction.

When Pee-wee Herman (the stage name of actor Paul Reubens) entered into a plea agreement in a case in which he was charged with exposure of a sexual organ, his attorney declared: "Mr. Reubens continues to insist upon his innocence—it was a plea of convenience. It was a fair resolution for everyone concerned."[32] In contrast, the form used in Minnesota courts to petition for approval of a plea bargain requires the defendant to acknowledge commission of the crime. A Minnesota defendant must concede:

> 24. My attorney has told me and I understand that a judge will not accept a plea of guilty from anyone who claims to be innocent.
> 25. I now make no claim that I am innocent.[33]

Another criticism of plea bargaining is that prosecutors give the rich and famous preferential treatment. An example of such a plea agreement involved the actor Jussie Smollett, who had reported to the police that he had been the victim of a hate crime. After conducting an extensive investigation, the Chicago police superintendent announced that Smollett had staged his own assault and falsely reported the incident. After Smollett was indicted, the State's Attorney's office entered into a deal in which it agreed to dismiss all 16 felony counts in return for Smollett's agreement to forfeit his $10,000 bond and complete community service. The last page of the redacted investigative detective's final report appears in Exhibit 9.7.

Unlike most plea bargains, which get little public attention, in this case the Chicago police superintendent and Chicago mayor Rahm Emanuel held a joint press conference criticizing the plea agreement that had been negotiated by the prosecutors' office and claiming that it had circumvented the judicial system. In addition to filing a civil suit against Smollett for $130,106.15 (for reimbursement of overtime pay paid to officers due to his false statements), a Cook County judge ruled that while it had been appropriate for State's Attorney Kim Fox to remove herself from personally handling the Smollett case,[34] it was not appropriate for her to appoint her top assistant as a "special prosecutor" to handle the case.[35]

An example of preferential plea bargaining at the federal level can be found in the prosecution of Congressman Aaron Schock. After the former member of the House of Representative from Illinois was indicted on 22 felony counts (including fraud, filing false reports, and theft), federal prosecutors agreed to defer all charges against him in exchange for his agreement to repay more than

---

[32] *Pee-wee's Big Plea Bargain*, The Free-Lance Star A3 (Nov. 8, 1991). Under the terms of the plea, Reubens agreed to pay a $50 fine plus $85 court costs and produce and pay for a nationally distributed antidrug commercial to fulfill a 75-hour community service requirement. The court placed him on six months of court supervision.

[33] Minn. R. Crim P. 15, Appendix A.

[34] She stated that she informally recused herself because of her relationship with Smollett's family.

[35] In July 2019, an Illinois judge appointed a special prosecutor to independently investigate the State's Attorney's handing of the case. Following his investigation, the special prosecutor revived the case. A jury found Smollett guilty of felony disorderly conduct for staging a fake hate crime. The court sentenced him to thirty months of felony probation, including 150 days in jail. The judge also ordered Smollett to pay a $25,000 fine and over $120,000 in restitution to reimburse the City of Chicago for the cost of its investigation.

Exhibit 9.7: Excerpt of Chicago Detective's Investigative Report

Smollett reported to the police that he had been brutally assaulted by two men who yelled racist and homophobic slurs at him. He claimed they poured a chemical solution on him and wrapped a rope around his neck. The police investigation revealed that the incident may have been a hoax. Cook County State's Attorney Kim Fox "removed herself from the decision making" in case and turned the matter over to her first assistant. Police then received authority from the State's Attorney's Office to charge Smollett with filing a false police report. Smollett was indicted, and the police were instructed to end the investigation.

JC133190
DETECTIVE SUP. APPROVAL COMPLETE

The meeting ended quickly with CPD stating they needed to talk to SMOLLETT and his defense team stating they would talk to their client and let CPD know.
On the afternoon of February 20, 2019 R/D and Detective Vogenthaler brought [redacted] and [redacted] to the Grand Jury where they testified. As soon as [redacted] and [redacted] had finished testifying the CCSAO told R/D to call in for approval of charges against SMOLLETT. R/D made the phone call and the Cook County State?s Attorney?s Office approved charges of Disorderly Conduct against SMOLLETT at 6:10 PM on February 20, 2019.
On February 21, 2019 a little after 5:00 AM SMOLLETT turned himself in at the First District of the Chicago Police Department and was placed into custody. After SMOLLETT's arrest processing was completed he was transferred by CPD to Cook County Department of Corrections at 26th St. and California.
R/D was informed by the CCSAO that CPD would no longer be able to use Grand Jury subpoena's in their investigation.
R/D was notified by the CCSAO that R/D would be testifying before the Grand Jury to indict SMOLLET on February 28, 2019. Once SMOLLETT was indicted by the Grand Jury on February 28, 2019 CPD was informed by the CCSAO that they could no longer investigate the crime. R/D and Det. Vogenthaler met with Risa Lanier, the Chief of the Criminal Bureau for the CCSAO, and turned over all items that were left on the Detectives TODO list for this case. At this time ASA Lanier informed detectives that she felt the case would be settled with SMOLLETT paying the City of Chicago $10,000 in restitution and doing community service. ASA Lanier stated that she would handle the TODO list and would likely be requesting all evidence in the case by Monday, March 11, 2019. As of the writing of this progress the CCSAO has not requested any evidence items from R/D.
Based on the above information R/D requests this case be reclassified as CLEAR CLOSED ARREST AND PROSECUTION.

Detective Michael Theis
Detective Michael Vogenthaler
Area Central Detective Division

$100,000 in misappropriated funds. As part of the deal, his campaign committee pleaded guilty to a misdemeanor charge of improperly reporting expenses and agreed to pay a fine. The U.S. Attorney's Office deviated from its own guidelines when it agreed to pre-trial diversion (PTD) for a former public official accused of an offense arising out of an alleged violation of the public trust.[36]

[36]*Department of Justice U.S. Attorneys Manual,* §9-22.100-Eligibility Criteria, states: "The U.S. Attorney, in his/her discretion, may divert any individual against whom a prosecutable case exists

3. THE PLEA-BARGAINING PROCESS

a. Timing

In state court, the plea-bargaining process can take place anytime between the arraignment and the end of the trial. In traffic cases, many plea agreements are made at the defendant's first court appearance. Even some misdemeanor cases are resolved by plea bargain at the first appearance. However, in more serious cases, plea negotiations do not usually take place until the government produces discovery and pre-trial conferences are held.

In federal court, plea agreements may be reached at any time during an investigation or prosecution of a case. This means that some defendants reach agreements with the government before charges are even filed against them. Ordinarily, these deals involve the defendant's promise to cooperate in the investigation and prosecution of other persons for criminal activity.

b. Participants

Prosecutors are generally expected to begin the plea-bargaining process by making an offer. An example of a prosecutor's offer of a plea agreement appears in Exhibit 9.8. This offer may involve reducing the charges or agreeing to recommend a lighter sentence than would normally be given for the offense in question. For example, the prosecutor can offer to settle for a guilty plea on a robbery charge where the original charge was for the more serious offense of armed robbery, or to drop related counts. So, if the original indictment included three counts of burglary, the prosecutor might agree to drop two of them in return for a guilty plea to the third. When it comes to sentencing, the prosecutor can recommend the minimum authorized sentence, probation, or suspending the sentence. Once the prosecutor puts an initial offer on the table, negotiations involve a series of counteroffers that go on until an agreement is reached between the two attorneys. If an agreement is reached, it will then be up to the defendant and the judge to decide if it will be formalized and implemented.

After having negotiated the best possible deal, the defense attorney must present the offer to the client. Clients must then decide whether they want to accept the deal or roll the dice on the outcome of a trial. As mentioned in our discussion of the negative aspects of plea bargaining, there are significant pressures on defendants to accept these bargains, even when they may not have committed the crimes with which they are being charged.

The other key participant in the plea-bargaining process is the judge. The nature of the judge's involvement varies widely among jurisdictions, though in most, the plea agreement must be entered into the record and the judge can reject agreements that are deemed to be against the public interest. In some localities, the defense attorney and the prosecutor can meet with the judge prior to the formal presentation of a plea bargain to find out whether the court will approve the tentative plea agreement.[37] In federal court, the judge

---

and who is **NOT** . . . [a] public official or former public official accused of an offense arising out of an alleged violation of a public trust" (emphasis added), https://www.justice.gov/jm/jm-9-22000-pretrial-diversion-program#22.100#9-22.100.

[37]For example, Illinois Supreme Court Rule 402(d)(2).

Exhibit 9.8: Prosecution Offer of a Plea Agreement

STATE'S ATTORNEY
1857 Bloomington Street
Normal, Illinois 61761

Mr. Charles Hovey
Attorney at Law
1857 Bone Street
Normal, IL 61761

In re: People v. Bud Cook

Dear Charlie:

I have reviewed the file, and am prepared to make you the following offer. If your client pleads guilty to either count of reckless homicide, I will offer 5 years in the Illinois Department of Corrections. As you are aware, this is a class 2 felony carrying a prison term of 3-14 years.

If your client is unwilling to accept the above offer, as an alternative, I will agree to "cap" a sentencing recommendation at 7 years in exchange for an open plea to one count of reckless homicide.

If you have questions, please call me.

Yours truly,

Mark O. Union, ASA

is not permitted to participate in the plea-bargaining discussions.[38] You will need to check your jurisdiction's rules to determine what the practices in your locale are.

4. TYPES OF DEALS

Charge bargaining
A plea bargain in which the prosecution dismisses a more serious charge in exchange for the defendant's pleading guilty to a lesser offense.

There are three major types of plea agreements: charge bargaining, count bargaining, and sentence bargaining. **Charge bargaining** occurs when the prosecution agrees to dismiss the crime charged, in exchange for the defendant's plea of guilty to a less serious offense. For instance, a defendant might plead guilty to voluntary manslaughter in return for the prosecutor's agreement to dismiss a first-degree homicide charge. Although charge bargaining is common in state courts, it is not typically used in federal court.[39]

---

[38] FRCrP 11(c)(1).

[39] FRCrP 11(c)(1) lists the possible approaches that the government can take in entering plea agreements. Reduction of charges to less serious offenses is not listed.

Count bargaining occurs when the defendant agrees to plead guilty to one or more of the counts for which he or she is charged in exchange for the government's agreement to dismiss the remaining counts charged. For example, where someone is charged with three separate counts of fraud (each involving a different transaction) the prosecutor might agree to dismiss two of the counts in return for the defendant pleading guilty to the third.

Count bargaining
A plea bargain in which the prosecution drops one or more related charges in exchange for the defendant's pleading guilty to at least one of the counts originally charged.

In federal court, these agreements are governed by Department of Justice Policy and the Federal Sentencing Guidelines.[40] The federal prosecutor must pursue the most serious, readily provable charge consistent with the nature and extent of the defendant's criminal conduct.[41] Only under limited circumstances may the prosecutor dismiss the most serious provable charge and allow a lesser charge to remain.

The third type of plea negotiations is **sentence bargaining**, in which the defendant pleads guilty in exchange for a lighter sentence. It saves the prosecution the necessity of going through a trial and proving its case, while it provides the defendant with an opportunity for a lighter sentence.

Sentence bargaining
A plea bargain in which the defendant enters a plea of guilty in exchange for a lighter sentence.

Sentencing bargaining can take several forms. First, the parties negotiate an agreed-upon sentence. This sentence may take the form of an agreed range of sentences or an agreed-upon sentencing guideline range. Under this scenario, the parties set a "floor" and a "ceiling" that define the perimeters of the eventual sentence. For example, the parties can enter an agreement limiting the sentence to 36 to 48 months of incarceration. If the court does not accept the agreement, the defendant can withdraw the plea of guilty.[42]

Another variation of sentence bargaining focuses on the prosecutor's sentencing recommendation. The prosecutor can agree not to oppose the defendant's request for a particular sentence or to make no recommendation. However, with this type of agreement, the defendant is not permitted to withdraw the plea of guilty if the court imposes a sentence that is not acceptable to the defendant.

Often, the negotiated agreement is a combination of charge, count, and/or sentence bargaining. When a count bargain or a charge bargain is not accompanied by a sentence bargain, the guilty plea is known as an **open plea**.[43] In this situation, the judge decides the appropriate sentence without a joint recommendation from the parties.

Open plea
A plea agreement under which the defendant pleads guilty and the judge determines the sentence without a joint recommendation from the parties.

5. FORMALIZING THE PLEA

When the prosecutor makes an offer, the defense attorney must convey it to the defendant. In doing so, the defense attorney must provide sufficient information for the client to be able to make an intelligent, informed decision. The decision should be based on the potential evidence that both sides will present

---

[40]The Federal Sentencing Guidelines will be discussed in detail in Chapter 13.

[41]*Department of Justice U.S. Attorneys Manual*, §9-27.430, https://www.justice.gov/jm/jm-9-27000-principles-federal-prosecution#9-27.430.

[42]FRCrP 11(d)(2)(A).

[43]Defendants can also make a "blind plea" in which they plead guilty without any promise of leniency from the prosecution.

at trial, the applicable sentencing statutes and/or guidelines, and the sentences imposed historically by the judge. Defense paralegals may be asked to research sentences ordered in similar cases.[44]

In federal court, the Assistant U.S. Attorney typically prepares a written plea agreement. Among other things, this document includes the defendant's voluntary waiver of constitutional rights, a plea of guilty to specified charge(s), a recitation of the proposed penalties for such charge(s), the factual basis for the charge(s), and an acceptance of the agreement by the government, defendant, defense counsel, and the court. The practice in state court varies.

Once a bargain is struck, the plea agreement is presented by the prosecution and defense to the judge in open court. At that time, the prosecutor gives the factual basis for the plea. This can either be accomplished through the defendant's admissions in open court or the prosecutor's proffer of the evidence the government expects to present if the case goes to trial. Depending on the jurisdiction, either the prosecutor or the judge will question the defendant to make sure he or she is entering into the plea agreement knowingly and voluntarily.

Plea colloquy
The in-court examination of a criminal defendant entering a guilty plea to determine whether the defendant is entering the plea intelligently, knowingly, and voluntarily.

This questioning process is often referred to as a **plea colloquy**. In most state courts, this examination is recorded by a court reporter and documented by a formal order or docket entry. Even in misdemeanor and traffic cases, defendants are examined to assure that they are freely and consciously enter the plea bargain.

Although it appears tedious, this line of questioning is typical of proceedings on the presentation of pleas. During the colloquy, the court must advise the defendant of the nature of the charge; the potential penalties that might result from the plea, including any mandatory minimum sentence; and the constitutional rights the defendant is waiving by pleading guilty. Exhibit 9.9 is an example of a plea colloquy. In 1977, the acclaimed film director Roman Polanski, charged with unlawful sexual intercourse with a minor, entered into a plea bargain with the Los Angeles District Attorney's Office. In the passages included in this exhibit, there are questions designed to make sure the defendant intelligently, knowingly, and voluntarily entered into the plea agreement.[45]

Note that the plea agreement reached in the Polanski case did not cover the nature of the sentence. After presentation of the plea, but before sentencing, Polanski reportedly learned that the judge was going to send him to prison. He then fled to Europe to escape incarceration. In 2010, the California Superior Court ruled that he must return to the United States to be sentenced. Courts in Switzerland and Poland have denied requests by the United States to extradite Polanski. In 2018, the Academy of Motion Pictures and Sciences expelled him from its membership because of the case.

---

[44]Although most court systems provide this type of information online, in some localities this investigation must take place at the courthouse.

[45]*People of the State of California v. Roman Raymond Polanski*, Case No. A-334139, August 8, 1977, Report of Proceedings, 8-15.

Exhibit 9.9: Excerpts from Plea Colloquy in the Roman Polanski Case

[Prosecutor]: Do you realize that by pleading guilty, you give up your right to a jury trial?
[Defendant]: Yes.
[Prosecutor]: Do you have any questions about your right to a jury trial?
[Defendant]: No.
[Prosecutor]: Do you then give up your right to a jury trial?
[Defendant]: Yes.
[Prosecutor]: Do you realize that by pleading guilty, you give up your right to be confronted by the witnesses against you?
[Defendant]: Yes.
[Prosecutor]: Do you realize that by pleading guilty, you give up your right of cross examination; to have your attorney ask those witnesses questions?
[Defendant]: Yes.
[Prosecutor]: Do you give up your right to confrontation and your right to cross examination of the witnesses?
[Defendant]: Yes.
[Prosecutor]: Do you know that you have a right against self-incrimination? That is, the right to remain silent, and to require the prosecution to prove a case against you beyond a reasonable doubt?
[Defendant]: Yes.
[Prosecutor]: Do you realize that by pleading guilty, you give up this right and admit the commission of the crime charged?
[Defendant]: Yes.
[Prosecutor]: Do you have any questions about your right to remain silent?
[Defendant]: No.
[Prosecutor]: Do you give up your privilege against self-incrimination?
[Defendant]: Yes.

. . .

[Prosecutor]: Mr. Polanski, before you can plead guilty, you have to understand the charges against you, and there must be a factual basis for your plea.
[Defendant]: Yes.
[Prosecutor]: Do you know what the charges are against you?
[Defendant]: Yes.
[Prosecutor]: And what is the nature of the charge to which you want to plead guilty?
[Defendant]: Unlawful Sexual Intercourse.
[Prosecutor]: What does the person have to do to be guilty of that charge?
[Defendant]: He has to—the person has to have sexual intercourse with the female person not his wife, under the age of 18.
[Prosecutor]: Are you in fact guilty of this charge?
[Defendant]: Yes.
[Prosecutor]: What did you do in this case?
[Defendant]: I had sexual intercourse with a female person not my wife, under the age of 18.
[Prosecutor]: And was this female person the complaining witness in this case?
[Defendant]: That's correct.
[Prosecutor]: And was it in the evening at 12850 Mulholland Drive?
[Defendant]: Mulholland Drive, yes.
[Prosecutor]: And that was in Los Angeles County?
[Defendant]: Yes.

[Prosecutor]: Mr. Polanski, before you can plead guilty, you must understand the possible direct consequences of your plea. Do you understand you are pleading guilty to a felony?
[Defendant]: Yes.
[Prosecutor]: What is the maximum sentence for unlawful sexual intercourse?
[Defendant]: It's one to fifteen–twenty years in State Prison.
[Prosecutor]: Do you understand it is also possible that you could be placed on probation, with or without being required to serve up to one year in the County Jail?
[Defendant]: Yes.
[Prosecutor]: . . . Mr. Polanski, who do you believe will decide what your sentence will be in this matter?
[The Defendant]: The Judge.
[The Prosecutor]: Who do you think will decide whether or not you will get probation?
[Defendant]: The Judge.
[Prosecutor]: Who do you think will determine whether the sentence will be a felony or a misdemeanor?
[Defendant]: The Judge.

. . .

[Prosecutor]: Do you understand that the Judge has not made any decision?
[Defendant]: Yes.

. . .

[Prosecutor]: Has anyone threatened you or threatened any one near and dear to you, in order to get you to plead guilty?
[Defendant]: No.
[Prosecutor]: The District Attorney will make a motion to dismiss the remaining pending charges after sentencing. Other than that promise, has anyone made any promises to you, such as a lesser sentence or probation, or reward? Immunity? A Court recommendation to the Immigration and Naturalization Service, or anything else, in order to get you to plead guilty?
[Defendant]: No.
[Prosecutor]: Do you have any questions about your plea?
[Defendant]: No.
[Prosecutor]: Are you pleading guilty freely and voluntarily?
[Defendant]: Yes.

Application Exercise

4. After reviewing the information you have been given on the Cook Hypothetical Case (*see* hypothetical case on page xxxvii), take note of the following additional information Before trial, defense attorney Charles Hovey asked the prosecutor for an offer to conclude the case that did not include incarceration. In support of this position, he pointed out the following facts:

- The area lacked overhead lighting, making it difficult for any driver to see a bicyclist at 10 p.m.

- The bicyclist was difficult to see for a number of reasons. First, she was wearing non-reflective clothes. Next, the bicycle did not have a headlamp or rear taillights, as required under state law. Finally, the bike itself was black.
- The bicyclist was riding two feet into the lane of traffic, even though there was a two-foot-wide, paved shoulder she could have used.
- The bicyclist was legally intoxicated, as shown by a toxicology report reflecting a blood alcohol concentration greater than 0.08.
- The accident reconstruction report indicated that the Cook vehicle was traveling no less than 38 mph in a 45 mph zone and did not conclude that the speed of the Cook vehicle was a contributing cause to the fatality.

Several days later, Hovey received the written offer shown in Exhibit 9.8.

a. What steps need to be taken to analyze the state's offer?
b. What type of plea bargain is the state offering to the defendant? Explain your answer.
c. Based upon defense counsel's original argument and the prosecutor's offer, what disposition do you think is just for the defendant? What is a just result for the prosecutor? What is just for the victim's family? What is just for the public at large?
d. What do you think the prosecutor's offer would be if the judge had already ruled on the motion to suppress all statements that Cook made to the police following his arrest?
e. What, in your opinion, would be a just outcome in terms of the charges that Cook would plead guilty to and the type of sentence to be served?

6. ENFORCEMENT OF PLEA BARGAINS

Because plea bargains are treated as enforceable contracts, it is important to get the terms in writing and documented in court records. If a plea agreement includes provisions requiring the defendant to cooperate in an ongoing investigation or testify against a co-defendant, the prosecutor can cancel the agreement if the defendant does not fulfill these promises. If the prosecutor fails to follow through on his or her promises, the defendant may be able to either withdraw the guilty plea or have the judge force the prosecutor to comply with its terms. Read *Santobello v. New York* to see how the U.S. Supreme Court has approached these issues.

Santobello v. New York
Supreme Court of the United States
404 U.S. 257 (1971)

MR. CHIEF JUSTICE BURGER delivered the opinion of the Court (joined by JUSTICES DOUGLAS, WHITE, and BLACKMUN).

We granted certiorari in this case to determine whether the State's failure to keep a commitment concerning the sentence recommendation on a guilty plea required a new trial.

The facts are not in dispute. The State of New York indicted petitioner in 1969 on two felony counts, Promoting Gambling in the First Degree, and Possession of Gambling Records in the First Degree, N.Y. Penal Law §§225.10, 225.20. Petitioner first entered a plea of not guilty to both counts. After negotiations, the Assistant District Attorney in charge of the case agreed to permit petitioner to plead guilty to a lesser-included offense, Possession of Gambling Records in the Second Degree, N.Y. Penal Law §225.15, conviction of which would carry a maximum prison sentence of one year. The prosecutor agreed to make no recommendation as to the sentence.

On June 16, 1969, petitioner accordingly withdrew his plea of not guilty and entered a plea of guilty to the lesser charge. Petitioner represented to the sentencing judge that the plea was voluntary and that the facts of the case, as described by the Assistant District Attorney, were true. The court accepted the plea and set a date for sentencing. . . .

Petitioner's new counsel moved immediately to withdraw the guilty plea. In an accompanying affidavit, petitioner alleged that he did not know at the time of his plea that crucial evidence against him had been obtained as a result of an illegal search. . . .

. . . On January 9 petitioner appeared before a different judge, the judge who had presided over the case to this juncture having retired. Petitioner renewed his motions, and the court again rejected them. The court then turned to consideration of the sentence.

At this appearance, another prosecutor had replaced the prosecutor who had negotiated the plea. The new prosecutor recommended the maximum one-year sentence. In making this recommendation, he cited petitioner's criminal record and alleged links with organized crime. Defense counsel immediately objected on the ground that the State had promised petitioner before the plea was entered that there would be no sentence recommendation by the prosecution. He sought to adjourn the sentence hearing in order to have time to prepare proof of the first prosecutor's promise. The second prosecutor, apparently ignorant of his colleague's commitment, argued that there was nothing in the record to support petitioner's claim of a promise, but the State, in subsequent proceedings, has not contested that such a promise was made.

. . .

The judge then imposed the maximum sentence of one year.

. . .

This record represents another example of an unfortunate lapse in orderly prosecutorial procedures, in part, no doubt, because of the enormous increase in the workload of the often understaffed prosecutor's offices. The heavy workload may well explain these episodes, but it does not excuse them. The disposition of criminal charges by agreement between the prosecutor and the accused, sometimes loosely called "plea bargaining," is an essential component of the administration of justice. Properly administered, it is to be encouraged. If every criminal charge were subjected to a full-scale trial, the States and the Federal Government would need to multiply by many times the number of judges and court facilities. Disposition of charges after plea discussions is not only an essential part of the process but a highly desirable part for many reasons. It leads to prompt and largely final disposition of most criminal cases; it avoids much of the corrosive impact of enforced idleness during pretrial confinement for those who are denied release pending trial; it protects the public from those accused persons who are prone to continue criminal conduct even while on pretrial release; and, by shortening the time between charge and disposition, it enhances whatever may be the rehabilitative prospects of the guilty when they are ultimately imprisoned. See *Brady v. United States*.

However, all of these considerations presuppose fairness in securing agreement between an accused and a prosecutor. It is now clear, for example, that the accused pleading guilty must be counseled, absent a waiver. Fed. Rule Crim. Proc. 11, governing pleas in federal courts, now makes clear that the sentencing judge must develop, *on the record*, the factual basis for the plea, as, for example, by having the accused describe the conduct that gave rise to the charge. The plea must, of course, be voluntary and knowing and if it was induced by promises, the essence of those promises must in some way be made known. There is, of course, no absolute right to have a guilty plea accepted. Fed. Rule Crim. Proc. 11. A court may reject a plea in exercise of sound judicial discretion.

This phase of the process of criminal justice, and the adjudicative element inherent in accepting a plea of guilty, must be attended by safeguards to insure the defendant what is reasonably due in the circumstances. Those circumstances will vary, but a constant factor is that when a plea rests in any significant degree on a promise or agreement of the prosecutor, so that it can be said to be part of the inducement or consideration, such promise must be fulfilled.

On this record, petitioner "bargained" and negotiated for a particular plea in order to secure dismissal of more serious charges, but also on condition that no sentence recommendation would be made by the prosecutor. It is now conceded that the promise to abstain from a recommendation was made, and at this stage the prosecution is not in a good position to argue that its inadvertent breach of agreement is immaterial. The staff lawyers in a prosecutor's office have the burden of "letting the left hand know what the right hand is doing" or has done. That the breach of agreement was inadvertent does not lessen its impact.

We need not reach the question whether the sentencing judge would or would not have been influenced had he known all the details of the negotiations for the plea. He stated that the prosecutor's recommendation did not influence him and we have no reason to doubt that. Nevertheless, we conclude that the interests of justice and appropriate recognition of the duties of the prosecution in relation to promises made in the negotiation of pleas of guilty will be best served by remanding the case to the state courts for further consideration. The ultimate relief to which petitioner is entitled we leave to the discretion of the state court, which is in a better position to decide whether the circumstances of this case require only that there be specific performance of the agreement on the plea, in which case petitioner should be resentenced by a different judge, or whether, in the view of the state court, the circumstances require granting the relief sought by petitioner, *i.e.*, the opportunity to withdraw his plea of guilty. [If the state court decides to allow withdrawal of the plea, the petitioner will, of course, plead anew to the original charge on two felony counts.] We emphasize that this is in no sense to question the fairness of the sentencing judge; the fault here rests on the prosecutor, not on the sentencing judge.

The judgment is vacated and the case is remanded for reconsideration not inconsistent with this opinion.

MR. JUSTICE DOUGLAS, concurring.

I join the opinion of the Court and add only a word. I agree both with THE CHIEF JUSTICE and with MR. JUSTICE MARSHALL that New York did not keep its "plea bargain" with petitioner and that it is no excuse for the default merely because a member of the prosecutor's staff who was not a party to the "plea bargain" was in charge of the case when it came before the New York court. The staff of the prosecution is a unit and each member must be presumed to know the commitments made by any other member. . . .

However important plea bargaining may be in the administration of criminal justice, our opinions have established that a guilty plea is a serious and sobering occasion inasmuch as it constitutes a waiver of the fundamental rights to a jury trial, to confront one's accusers, to present witnesses in one's defense, to remain silent, and to be convicted by proof beyond all reasonable doubt . . . this Court has recognized that "unfairly obtained" guilty pleas in the federal courts ought to be vacated. . . .

State convictions founded upon coerced or unfairly induced guilty pleas have also received increased scrutiny as more fundamental rights have been applied to the States. . . . Under these circumstances it is clear that a guilty plea must be vacated.

But it is also clear that a prosecutor's promise may deprive a guilty plea of the "character of a voluntary act." The decisions of this Court have not spelled out what sorts of promises by prosecutors tend to be coercive, but in order to assist appellate review in weighing promises in light of all the circumstances, all trial courts are now required to interrogate the defendants who enter guilty pleas so that the waiver of these fundamental rights will affirmatively appear in the record. The lower courts, however, have uniformly held that a prisoner is entitled to some form of relief when he shows that the prosecutor reneged on his sentencing agreement made in connection with a plea bargain, most jurisdictions preferring vacation of the plea on the ground of "involuntariness," while a few permit only specific enforcement. . . .

. . .

I join the opinion of the Court and favor a constitutional rule for this as well as for other pending or oncoming cases. Where the "plea bargain" is not kept by the prosecutor, the sentence must be vacated and the state court will decide in light of the circumstances of each case whether due process requires (a) that there be specific performance of the plea bargain or (b) that the defendant be given the option to go to trial on the original charges. One alternative may do justice in one case, and the other in a different case. In choosing a remedy, however, a court ought to accord a defendant's preference considerable, if not controlling, weight inasmuch as the fundamental rights flouted by a prosecutor's breach of a plea bargain are those of the defendant, not of the State.

MR. JUSTICE MARSHALL, with whom MR. JUSTICE BRENNAN and MR. JUSTICE STEWART join, concurring in part and dissenting in part.

I agree with much of the majority's opinion, but conclude that petitioner must be permitted to withdraw his guilty plea. This is the relief petitioner requested, and, on the facts set out by the majority, it is a form of relief to which he is entitled.

There is no need to belabor the fact that the Constitution guarantees to all criminal defendants the right to a trial by judge or jury, or, put another way, the "right not to plead guilty," . . . This and other federal rights may be waived through a guilty plea, but such waivers are not lightly presumed and, in fact, are viewed with the "utmost solicitude." Given this, I believe that where the defendant presents a reason for vacating his plea and the government has not relied on the plea to its disadvantage, the plea may be vacated and the right to trial regained, at least where the motion to vacate is made prior to sentence and judgment. In other words, in such circumstances I would not deem the earlier plea to have irrevocably waived the defendant's federal constitutional right to a trial.

Here, petitioner never claimed any automatic right to withdraw a guilty plea before sentencing. Rather, he tendered a specific reason why, in his case, the plea should be vacated. His reason was that the prosecutor had broken a promise made in return for the agreement to plead guilty. When a prosecutor breaks the bargain, he undercuts the basis for the waiver of constitutional rights implicit in the plea. This, it seems to me, provides the defendant ample justification for rescinding the plea. Where a promise is "unfulfilled," *Brady v. United States* specifically denies that the plea "must stand." Of course, where the prosecutor has broken the plea agreement, it may be appropriate to permit the defendant to enforce the plea bargain. But that is not the remedy sought here. Rather, it seems to me that a breach of the plea bargain provides ample reason to permit the plea to be vacated.

It is worth noting that in the ordinary case where a motion to vacate is made prior to sentencing, the government has taken no action in reliance on the previously entered guilty plea and would suffer no harm from the plea's withdrawal. More pointedly, here the State claims no such harm beyond disappointed expectations about the plea itself. At least where the government itself has broken the plea bargain, this disappointment cannot bar petitioner from withdrawing his guilty plea and reclaiming his right to a trial.

I would remand the case with instructions that the plea be vacated and petitioner given an opportunity to re-plead to the original charges in the indictment.

Case Discussion Questions

1. Why does Justice Burger think that plea bargaining is an essential component of the administration of justice?
2. What does Rule 11 of the Federal Rules of Criminal Procedure require, and how is it relevant to this case?
3. Was the breach of the plea agreement intentional, and how does the answer to this question affect the Court's decision?
4. Was the sentencing judge influenced by knowledge of the details of the negotiations for the plea, and to what degree does the answer to this question affect the Court's decision?
5. How would you summarize the issue before the Court, and what was the Court's decision with respect to this issue?
6. With which part of the Opinion of the Court did Justice Douglas agree, and what additional points did he make in his concurring opinion?
7. With which part of the Opinion of the Court did Justice Marshall agree, and what additional points did he make in his concurring opinion?

C. Pre-Trial Diversion Programs

In addition to bargaining for reduced charges or shorter periods of incarceration, some plea bargains involve **pre-trial diversion (PTD)**. Designed to relieve some of the demands on and to reduce the costs of the criminal justice system, this alternative to prosecution diverts certain types of lawbreakers (typically, first offenders and persons involved in lesser crimes) away from the traditional criminal justice system and into a program of supervision and services. PTD has become an important option in the plea-bargaining process. Whereas a plea bargain is part of the official court record and ordinarily involves a criminal conviction, under PTD, the prosecutor refers the defendant to an agency that is not part of the court proceedings. Successful completion of the PTD program's requirements often will lead to dismissal or reduction of the charges, whereas failure will return the matter to the criminal courts.

Pre-trial diversion (PTD): An alternative to prosecution that seeks to divert certain offenders from traditional criminal justice processing into a program of supervision and services.

In addition to reducing the costs associated with criminal prosecutions and incarceration, PTD programs are designed to educate and rehabilitate minor offenders so they will not repeat the behavior that led to their arrests. The federal government, the District of Columbia, and 48 states all have PTD in some form.[46]

At the federal level, the U.S. Probation Service supervises and administers the services provided to offenders. The U.S. Attorney may use PTD for most first-time offenders.[47]

[46]National Conference of State Legislatures, http://www.ncsl.org/research/civil-and-criminal-justice/pretrial-diversion.aspx.

[47]The following offenders are ineligible for PTD:

1. One accused of an offense which, under existing Department guidelines, should be diverted to the State for prosecution;
2. A person with two or more prior felony convictions;
3. A public official or former public official accused of an offense arising out of an alleged violation of a public trust; or
4. One accused of an offense related to national security or foreign affairs. 9-22.100—Eligibility Criteria.

Frequently, state prosecutors recommend PTD for misdemeanor and traffic offenders. Drivers who commit minor violations may be given court supervision and required to attend traffic school. Motorists who were driving while intoxicated may be required to undergo alcohol abuse treatment. After being charged with driving under the influence (DUI), Tiger Woods pleaded guilty to reckless driving and entered a PTD program rather than losing his driver's license and serving jail time. The program consisted of one year of probation, DUI school, community service, and fines. The prosecutor's office entered into the standard agreement for first-time offenders, which Woods was. Thus, Woods's celebrity status played no role in the disposition of the case.

Specialty court
A court that focuses on one type of offense or offender with the objective of addressing the underlying causes of the offender's criminal behavior by working collaboratively with outside agencies to provide counseling treatment or education in an effort to prevent recidivism. Also known as "treatment court."

Certain categories of offenders and offenders charged with particular types of crimes are often directed to **specialty courts** (also known as "treatment courts") as part of a state court's PTD protocol. The purpose of specialty courts is to provide treatment, instead of punishment, in an attempt to reduce the offender's contact with the criminal justice system. This court focuses on one type of offense or offender, with the objective of addressing the underlying causes of the offender's criminal behavior by working collaboratively with outside agencies to provide counseling treatment or education.

Almost 80 percent of the states have treatment courts for persons charged with drug- or alcohol-related offenses and defendants identified as addicts. Nearly half of the states offer PTD for persons identified as needing mental health treatment. And about half of the states have veterans' court to address the needs specific to veterans or active members of the military. Other specialty courts exercise authority over persons charged with domestic violence, writing worthless checks, and prostitution. Still others focus on homeless offenders.

Most PTD agreements allow prosecutors to reinstate the original criminal charges if the defendant does not complete all the conditions of the program or commits another crime within an established time limit. In addition to the requirements for participating in educational programs or performing public service activities, defendants may be required to compensate any victims of their criminal activity or refrain from having any further contact with the victims.

Although it appears there are no specialty courts there, Limestone County, Alabama, has formalized a PTD program. The District Attorney's Office's website describes the program as follows:

> The Pre-trial Diversion Program is designed for individuals who are first-time offenders. These individuals want to take responsibility for their actions, pay their debt to society, and rehabilitate themselves through individualized treatment plans. Defendants will make application to the program and will only be accepted after a thorough application packet is reviewed and approved by the District Attorney's Office. The program team consists of the Judge presiding over the case, the community prosecutor from the District Attorney's Office, the Defendant and his/her attorney, the program counselor, and treatment professionals.[48]

The application for the Limestone County diversion program is displayed in Exhibit 9.10.[49]

---

[48]See Limestone County District Attorney's Office website, https://www.limestonecountyda.org/community-service/pre-trial-diversion (accessed June 27, 2022).

[49]Application for Admission found at https://www.limestonecountyda.org/images/PDFs/ApplicationforAdmission.pdf (accessed June 27, 2022).

Exhibit 9.10: Diversion Program Application

Limestone County Pretrial Diversion Program
Office of Brian C. T. Jones, District Attorney
39th Judicial Circuit

Application for Admission
PTD-F01c

IN THE ______________ COURT OF LIMESTONE COUNTY, ALABAMA

STATE OF ALABAMA,	)	
	)	
Plaintiff,	)	
	)	
vs.	)	CASE NO: ____________________
	)	
	)	
______________________,	)	
	)	
Defendant.	)	

APPLICATION FOR ADMISSION INTO THE LIMESTONE COUNTY PRETRIAL DIVERSION PROGRAM

DEFENDANT'S NAME: ____

ADDRESS: ____

TELEPHONE NUMBER(S): ____

SOCIAL SECURITY NUMBER: _______________ DATE OF BIRTH: ___________

CHARGE(S): ____

DEFENDANT'S ATTORNEY: ____

Comes now the Defendant and hereby makes request to enter the Pretrial Diversion Program of the 39th Judicial Circuit. I understand that my acceptance into program is expressly conditioned upon the approval of the Limestone County District Attorney's Office and acceptance of the application for admission. By entering into this program, I freely and voluntarily waive my constitutional rights concerning self-incrimination and search and seizure to the extent necessary for the consideration of this request and for participation in this program. My attorney has explained these rights to me, and I understand these rights. I hereby state that no threats, promises, or inducements of any kind have been made to force me to waive these rights, except the provisions of any plea agreement entered into herein. I agree to provide all information requested in the application packet for determination as to whether I qualify for participation in the program, as well as to be subjected to any and all assessments for treatment as recommended by the District Attorney's Office and the Program Counselor.

Limestone County Pretrial Diversion Program
Office of Brian C. T. Jones, District Attorney
39th Judicial Circuit

Application for Admission
PTD-F01c

I understand that my application into this program is entirely voluntary. Upon acceptance into the program, I understand that I will be waiving my right to a trial and entering a plea of guilty. I understand that the issue of probation will be at the discretion of the Judge. I further understand that after actual entry into the program, my participation and compliance with the Pretrial Diversion Program demands and the Court's orders will be required. If I fail to comply with the program requirements, I understand that I will be subject to sanctions, including dismissal from the program and imposition of the sentence.

Upon successful completion of the program as determined by the District Attorney's office and program counselor, I understand that my guilty plea will be set aside and that the case will be dismissed.

During my participation in the pretrial diversion program, my case will be assigned to the Honorable ____________________, Judge. Judge_________________ will be reviewing my case with the program's community prosecutor and program counselor, and will be presiding over my review hearings. I acknowledge that during the course of my participation in the program, the Judge will be provided with information about my participation from my program counselor, treatment team, and others who are actively involved with my case. In the event of my failure to successfully complete the program, the Judge will also preside over the revocation and sentencing proceedings.

I acknowledge that I will be assessed by the program counselor and I will have an individualized treatment plan developed for me.

I further acknowledge that in order to successfully complete the pretrial diversion program, I must comply with all terms and conditions of the pretrial diversion court order attached hereto and incorporated herein by reference.

I have read and understand the application packet and the Court order. I have reviewed it with my attorney, and acknowledge my understanding of the requirements of said Order.

_______________________________ Defendant

_______________________________ Defendant's Attorney

Date:____________________________

Date:____________________________

In addition to turning in the application, individuals seeking PTD in Limestone County must submit a detailed personal data sheet. The District Attorney's Office processes the application, completes a criminal background check, and consults the victim in the case before approving a defendant's entry into the program. If approved, the defendant enters into a contract for services in the diversion program.

APPLICATION EXERCISE

5. Contact the clerk's office for the jurisdiction in which your school is located to find out whether there are any specialty courts. If there are, prepare a memorandum to your instructor, as your supervising attorney, that presents the following information:
   a. The qualifications a defendant must meet to be diverted to the court.
   b. The term and conditions the defendant must satisfy in order to successfully complete diversion.
   c. The outcome for a defendant who successfully completes the diversion requirements.
   d. The outcome for a defendant who does not successfully complete the diversion requirements.
   e. Is there any leniency granted to a defendant who has trouble meeting the requirements? Is so, explain how the judge addresses this situation.

SUMMARY

Based on the defense they plan to use and the information gathered in the discovery process, defense attorneys will file pre-trial motions designed to seek judicial rulings on where and when the trial will take place, which judge should not preside, and what evidence should not be admitted if the case goes to trial. How the judge rules on these motions typically influences the plea-bargaining process.

Most cases conclude with a plea agreement. When plea bargains are reached, they are often structured to include PTD that requires the defendant to participate in education, treatment, counselling, and community service.

INTERNET RESOURCES

General Information on the Criminal Justice System

- Court Rules and Forms: **http://www.llrx.com/courtrules**
- List of Resources on Plea Bargaining: **http://www.pbs.org/wgbh/pages/frontline/shows/plea/etc/links.html**

- Information on Drug Courts: **https://nij.ojp.gov/topics/articles/overview-drug-courts**
- Diversion Programs for Juveniles: **http://www.ncjrs.gov/html/ojjdp/9909-3/contents.html**

REVIEW QUESTIONS

1. Why would state prosecutors decline to pursue charges against some offenders and allow the U.S. Attorneys' Office to be the prosecuting agency?
2. What steps must a defendant take to change the location of the case to some other city, county, or judicial district from where the case originally was filed?
3. What is the difference between a change of venue and a change of venire?
4. Under what circumstances is a judge substituted out of a case, and in what situations does the judge "recuse" himself or herself from a case?
5. What are the differences and similarities between joinder of offenses and joinder of defendants?
6. How would a defendant attack an improper joinder of offenses or defendants? What is the likelihood of success?
7. What does the term "competent to stand trial" mean?
8. What is the purpose of a motion to suppress?
9. What are the components of a motion to suppress?
10. What impact does the judge's grant or denial of a motion to suppress have on the progression of the case?
11. What relief is sought in a motion to dismiss?
12. For what reasons would an attorney choose not to object to the opponent's motion for continuance?
13. What benefits do defendants receive from entering into a plea bargain?
14. What benefit does society receive from plea bargains?
15. Why do innocent men and women plead guilty to crimes they did not commit? What is the name of this type of plea?
16. At what stage of a case can the parties enter into a plea bargain?
17. List and define the three major types of plea agreements.
18. What is a plea colloquy?
19. What are the purposes of PTD programs?

PART 3

Criminal Procedure: Trials and Their Aftermath

Chapter 10

The Nature of Criminal Trials

Chapter Objectives

After reading this chapter, you should be able to:

- Identify and discuss the constitutional rights that apply to the conduct of criminal trials.
- Discuss the role of juries and the way they are selected in criminal trials.
- Explain how the rules of evidence affect what can be presented in court.
- Identify the different types of evidence and discuss the various ways of laying a foundation for the admission of these different types of evidence.

Introduction

In Part 2, we followed the development of criminal cases from the detection of a crime through the bringing of formal charges, pre-trial discovery, plea bargaining, and diversion. In Part 3, we cover trials, sentencing, appeals, and additional proceedings.

Our coverage of trials begins in this chapter, with a look at their basic functions and roles of key participants. We then move on to examine the constitutional principles governing criminal trials and the rules concerning the introduction of evidence at trials. Chapter 11 covers how attorneys and paralegals prepare for trials. Chapter 12 discusses what actually goes on during a criminal trial and what paralegals do to assist the attorneys during these trials. Chapter 13 will cover issues related to sentencing, while Chapter 14, deals with appeals. Finally, Chapter 15 presents collateral remedies, pardons, and commutations, as well as the expungement and sealing of criminal records.

A. Functions of the Courts in Criminal Cases

In Chapter 2, we discussed the importance of the concept of the "rule of law" and noted how it involved three basic principles:

- The government must follow its own rules.
- The government must apply the law impartially.
- The government must provide due process for those accused of breaking the rules.

In our legal system, it is the responsibility of the courts to ensure that government officials impartially follow the law and that those accused of breaking the law receive due process of law. Judges are responsible for ensuring due process, and trials are the mechanism used to determine if the government can prove, beyond a reasonable doubt, that someone has done something that the government has designated a crime.[1] The rules used to conduct the trial must comport with the constitutional protections considered to be essential to the "due process of law," and if the defendant is found guilty, either the judge or sometimes a jury plays an important role in determining what the punishment will be.

B. Constitutional Rights Related to the Conduct of Trials

Figure 2.2 (page 25) listed 16 constitutional rights that apply to applications of criminal law. Some, such as the right to indictment by a grand jury and the prohibition against unreasonable searches and seizures, were discussed in Part 2, where they were related to actions taken prior to the start of a criminal trial. In this section, we will focus on the constitutional rights that are directly related to what goes on at the trial itself.

1. RIGHT TO COUNSEL

In order to help defendants take advantage of their constitutional rights, the Sixth Amendment includes a provision creating a right to counsel. It declares: "In all criminal prosecutions, the accused shall enjoy the right . . . to have the Assistance of Counsel for his defense."[2]

Back in Chapter 4, we discussed how the right to counsel has been interpreted to apply to the criminal investigation stage, and in Chapter 6, we discussed the appointment of counsel for people who couldn't afford to hire an attorney on their own. Chapters 6 through 9 covered various activities that defense attorneys undertake to prepare a defense and attempt to negotiate

[1] At the federal level and in most states, an action must be formally prohibited by a valid statute or regulation. There are a few states, however, that still recognize common law crimes.

[2] The drafters of the Constitution used the British spelling for "defense."

favorable plea agreements. In the remaining chapters of this section, we will cover their roles in the trial process, sentencing, and appeals.

2. RIGHT TO A PUBLIC TRIAL

The Sixth Amendment declares: "In all criminal prosecutions, the accused shall enjoy the right to a speedy and **public trial**."[3] This provision, along with several others in the Bill of Rights, was designed to prevent the type of star-chamber proceedings that had taken place in England from the 15th into the 17th centuries, whereby someone was seized in the middle of the night and secretly tried, convicted, and punished without relatives or the general public ever knowing what happened to the person. The provision for public trials was clearly designed to be a check against the abuse of governmental power.

Public trial
A trial open to the public.

Although the U.S. Supreme Court has allowed judges to close some types of pre-trial hearings to protect privacy rights and to avoid prejudicial publicity, it ruled in *Richmond Newspapers, Inc. v. Virginia* that criminal trials had to be open to the public, and the public included representatives of the press.[4]

Note, however, that trials related to juvenile offenses are typically not open to the public. Although the U.S. Supreme Court has ruled that the Due Process Clause required juveniles be given the right to notice of charges, the right to counsel, the privilege against self-incrimination, and the right to confront and cross-examine witnesses, it does not require that trials of juveniles be open to the public.

3. RIGHT TO A JURY TRIAL

There are three references to jury trials in the U.S. Constitution. The first appears in Article III, which states in part: "The Trial of all Crimes . . . shall be by Jury; and such Trial shall be held in the State where the said Crimes shall have been committed." The other two references are part of the Bill of Rights: the Sixth Amendment establishes a right to a trial "by an impartial jury of the State and district wherein the crime shall have been committed," and the Seventh Amendment establishes a right to a jury trial in many types of civil cases.

a. Functions of Juries

The basic function of the jury is to resolve the factual, as opposed to the legal, questions raised in the case. **Factual questions** relate to the determination of who did what and when, where, and how they did it. Was the defendant the person who witnesses claim they saw robbing the gas station? Did the blow struck by the defendant cause the victim's death? The resolution of factual issues usually comes down to which witnesses the jurors choose to believe. On

Factual questions
Issues related to the determination of who did what and when, where, and how they did it.

[3] The speedy aspect of the trial was covered in Chapter 8.

[4] 448 U.S. 555 (1980). In *Presley* v. *Georgia*, 558 U.S. 209 (2010) (*per curiam*), the Court ruled that the *voir dire* selection process also had to be open to the public.

Legal questions
Issues related to the interpretation of the meaning of the law, including procedures used in the trial and the admissibility of different kinds of evidence, as well at the type of behavior that is covered by the terms of the statutes being applied.

the other hand, **legal questions** relate to the procedures used in the trial, the admissibility of different kinds of evidence, and the interpretation of the statutes being applied. These legal issues are handled by the judge, rather than the jury, because they require special legal training and experience. When a case is tried by a judge alone (known as a "bench trial"), the judge decides both questions of law and questions of fact.

b. Justifications for the Use of Juries

Juries are an important part of our English common law heritage. They developed as a means of limiting the powers of the English monarchy and safeguarding citizens against corrupt or biased judges and prosecutors. In addition to serving as a check on potential abuses of power and political corruption, an argument in favor of the jury system is that a representative group of common, ordinary people from the local community is better situated to judge the credibility of the witnesses than a single judge would be. This is especially true in smaller communities, where jurors may be more apt to have had personal dealings with the defendant and/or the witnesses and may have knowledge of their reputations for truth and veracity.

c. A Jury of One's Peers

All of you have probably heard the phrase "jury of one's peers," but you will not find it in the Constitution. There is no legal requirement that a jury be made up of people like the defendant. The Sixth Amendment, however, does require "an impartial jury of the State and district wherein the crime shall have been committed." Thus, it is the demographics of the community, rather than the characteristics of the defendant, that must be represented in the jury.[5]

Jury selection is a two-step process: The first involves identifying people who are eligible to serve on juries in general, and the second involves selection of individuals to be jurors in a specific case. Usually in the first stage, public officials with titles like jury commissioner collect names and addresses from public records, such as lists of registered voters and licensed drivers. Questionnaires are then sent to a random sampling of people on these lists to collect data relating to their age, occupation, citizenship, disabilities, ability to understand the English language, and the existence of any conditions that would excuse them from being a juror.

Local practices vary with respect to exempting certain classes of people from jury duty. Historically, people would be excused if they could convince jury commissioners that jury service would be a personal hardship or a hardship for their employer. In many jurisdictions, mothers of small children were routinely excused; however, that practice is becoming far less common today. Attorneys and judges have also been typically excused, but many jurisdictions are now requiring them to serve as well. People with certain types of physical and mental disabilities may also be excused.

---

[5] An exception to this general practice would be a change of venire. See the discussion in the next section, on impartial juries. In addition, when the court grants a motion for change of venue, the venue to which the case is transferred may have a different demographic composition that the original venue. See Chapter 9 for a discussion on motions for change of venue.

Based on the information gathered from questionnaires and other sources, the public officials develop a list of people they will call for jury duty on specific dates. Typically, individuals are sent a summons that requires them to be available to report for a period of a week. During that period, they are required to call a special phone number or check a special website to learn the specific dates and times at which they will have to report to the courthouse for duty.

d. An Impartial Jury

The Sixth Amendment specifically states that juries should be "impartial." In other words, the members of the jury should not be biased or prejudiced toward either the government or the defendant. Note that this requirement of impartiality may be somewhat at odds with the justifications for the jury system discussed above. The more knowledge jurors have about the reputation of the defendant and key witnesses, the more likely it is that the jurors have already formed opinions that may bias their conclusions about the credibility of the testimony they hear. When these types of situations arise, the impartiality requirement is supposed to supersede the advantages of prior knowledge.

The court relies on the ***voir dire*** process to determine if an individual will be considered sufficiently impartial to qualify to serve on the jury in a specific case. Prior to the actual start of the trial, people who were called in for jury duty are brought into the courtroom to be questioned by the judge, and in many cases by the attorneys, about what they know of the case and if there are any factors that might bias their judgment.[6] We will discuss how attorneys prepare for *voir dire* in detail in Chapter 11.

Voir dire
An examination of prospective jurors to see if they are fit to serve on a jury in a specific case.

Based on the answers given during *voir dire*, the attorneys may raise one of two types of challenges to keep a potential juror from serving in that specific case. The first line of attack is usually a **challenge for cause.** To exercise this challenge, the attorney must convince the judge that something about the juror's background or answers demonstrates that the person has some type of bias. If unsuccessful at removing a juror for cause, an attorney usually can achieve the same result by using a **peremptory challenge.** Whereas the decision to excuse a juror for cause ultimately rests with the judge, a peremptory challenge is ordinarily within the sole discretion of the attorney who exercises it. Therefore, the attorney need not even give a reason for having used a peremptory challenge.

Challenge for cause
A method of removing a prospective juror based on a finding by the judge that the juror has some sort of bias or other factors that should disqualify him or her from serving on this specific case.

However, there are two important restrictions on the use of these peremptory challenges. The first is that the number of peremptory challenges is strictly limited.[7] The second restriction relates to the use of peremptory challenges to remove prospective jurors on the basis of race or sex. We will discuss this topic more fully in Chapter 12.

Peremptory challenge
A method that an attorney can use to remove a prospective juror without being required to state a reason.

---

[6] To stop attorneys from using *voir dire* questions to begin indoctrinating the jurors, and to simply reduce the time taken up by *voir dire*, some jurisdictions require the attorneys submit their questions to the judge, who presents them to the potential jurors.

[7] The number allowed sometimes varies with the severity of the charges that the defendant is facing.

Discussion Question

1. While these challenges are generally thought to be sufficient to weed out biased jurors in most trials, some observers have suggested that additional actions need to be taken in cases that have received so much pre-trial publicity that it is nearly impossible to find jurors who do not know about things that will not be admissible at the trial. With this in mind, a judge handling one of the R. Kelly cases (*see* Exhibit 5.10 in Chapter 5) placed a gag order on attorneys to prevent them from divulging any new evidence that had not already been made public from being publicized.

a. Do you think this type of gag order is appropriate?

b. Defense attorneys in the Kelly case objected on the basis that alleged victims had already appeared on television talk shows and an unfavorable "documentary" film had already been released. Does this information change your opinion regarding the appropriateness of the judge's order?

e. *Types of Trials Covered*

At the beginning of this section, we identified the provisions of the U.S. Constitution specifically mentioning juries. Although the Bill of Rights was originally interpreted as applying only to the federal government, the Supreme Court has ruled that the Fourteenth Amendment's Due Process Clause makes the right to a jury trial in criminal cases applicable to the states.[8] Furthermore, most state constitutions also grant a right to a trial by jury in most criminal matters.

Several key court cases, however, have limited the application of the Sixth Amendment right to a jury trial in cases involving "minor offenses." In *Duncan v. Louisiana*,[9] the U.S. Supreme Court overturned a conviction for simple battery because the state trial court had denied defendant's request for a jury trial. The Court ruled that although the offense was classified as a misdemeanor, it was serious enough to entitle the defendant to a jury trial because it carried a penalty of up to two years' incarceration. In the majority opinion, the justices stated that a person accused of any crime punishable by more than six months' imprisonment was entitled to demand trial by jury, but that when the punishment involved imprisonment for six months or less, it was up to the states to choose whether to permit a defendant to have a jury trial.

In *Apprendi v. New Jersey*[10] and *Blakely v. Washington*,[11] the Supreme Court held that a criminal defendant has a right to a jury trial not only on the question of guilt or innocence, but any time facts were used to increase a defendant's sentence beyond the maximum otherwise allowed by statutes or sentencing guidelines. These rulings invalidated the procedures used in many states and the federal courts that allowed sentencing enhancement based on "a preponderance of evidence," where enhancement could be based on the judge's findings alone.

---

[8]See the discussion in Chapter 4 on the application of the Bill of Rights to the states.

[9]391 U.S. 145 (1968).

[10]530 U.S. 466 (2000).

[11]542 U.S. 296 (2004).

As with most other rights, a legally competent defendant can choose to voluntarily waive the right to be tried by a jury. Defendants typically choose to waive this right in cases that have received a great deal of prejudicial publicity, that involve a community perceived as prejudiced against members of the defendant's racial or ethnic group, or that involve a particularly gruesome crime. In cases where a jury is not used, the judge takes over the jury's function and decides the guilt or innocence of the defendant as well as questions of law.

f. The Number of Jurors Required

Under the common law, a jury consisted of 12 people. However, to cut costs and expedite the legal process, federal and state courts have sometimes used smaller juries in civil and sometimes even in criminal cases. The U.S. Supreme Court has ruled that there is nothing that is constitutionally significant about having 12 jurors and has permitted 6-person juries in civil cases at both the federal and the state levels. While 12 jurors are required in federal criminal trials,[12] *Williams v. Florida*[13] approved the use of 6-person juries in state criminal cases. Then in *Ballew v. Georgia*, the Court held that criminal juries composed of fewer than 6 members do not meet Sixth and Fourteenth Amendment standards.[14]

Whatever the number of jurors required to serve on a jury, it is common practice to select one or two extra jurors as alternates—especially when the trial is expected to last for more than a few days. These alternates sit in the jury box with their fellow jurors throughout the trial and are used as substitutes if regular jurors are unable to continue. An alternate does not participate in the deliberations, however, unless he or she has replaced one of the original jurors.

g. Requirement for a Unanimous Verdict

Just as common law tradition called for 12 jurors, it also required that verdicts be unanimous. If all 12 jurors could not agree with either a guilty or a not guilty verdict, the judge would declare a mistrial, and the prosecution had to either retry the case or drop the charges against the defendant. Although the Constitution has required unanimous jury verdicts in federal criminal trials for decades, it was not until 2020 that the Supreme Court held that the Constitution grants defendants the right to a unanimous jury verdict in state criminal cases.[15]

h. Jury Nullification

Jury nullification refers to a situation in which a jury votes to acquit a defendant even though the facts clearly establish a violation of the letter of the law. In these types of cases, the jury is in effect refusing to apply a law because

Jury nullification
A term used to describe a situation in which a jury votes to acquit a defendant even though the facts clearly establish a violation of the letter of the law.

[12] *Rassmussen v. United States*, 197 U.S. 516 (1905) (invalidating a conviction by a 6-man jury in a federal territorial court in Alaska).

[13] 399 U.S. 78 (1970).

[14] 435 U.S. 223 (1978). In this case, the defendant was convicted by a 5-person jury of two misdemeanor counts for violating Georgia obscenity statutes.

[15] *Ramos v. Louisiana*, 140 S. Ct. 1390 (2020).

the jurors believe that the law itself is unjust, or because they believe that it is unjust to apply it to the defendant in the specific circumstances presented in the case they are deciding. An example might be where an elderly spouse assists in the suicide of a partner who is suffering from terminal cancer.

In some situations, nullification can become a means by which the public expresses its opposition to an unwanted legislative enactment. When such a pattern of verdicts exists, it can have the de facto effect of invalidating the statute because prosecutors decide not to use it. An historical example of nullification would be the American revolutionaries' refusal to convict under English laws. Although the legal system permits jury nullification, legal ethics do not permit defense attorneys to explicitly ask the jurors to disregard the law.

Discussion Questions

2. What is the justification for requiring a public trial? Should public trials also be required in juvenile cases or those involving rape or incest?

3. On what basis should authorities decide who gets to be present at a trial where there is more demand for seats than there are seats available in the courtroom?

4. What are the pros and cons of allowing video cameras in the courtroom? Do you think they should be allowed? Why or why not?

5. What are the pros and cons of having lawyers serve as jurors?

6. Under what circumstances, if any, should there be a requirement that minorities be represented on the jury when the defendant is a member of a racial minority? Should the minority jurors be from the same racial group as the defendant? Should the same principles apply to sex and religion?

7. In the 2010 federal trial of the former Illinois governor Rod Blagojevich, the jury found him guilty of lying to the Federal Bureau of Investigation (FBI) but could not persuade the single holdout juror to vote for any of the other 23 counts of corruption and fraud. Since federal criminal juries are required to reach unanimous verdicts, the judge declared a mistrial on these remaining counts.

   a. Do you think it is right that a single juror should be able to stand in the way of a conviction? Why?

   b. If you were the U.S. Attorney in this situation, what factors would you consider in deciding whether to retry Blagojevich on some or all of the other 23 counts?

8. Should judges have the authority to throw out jury verdicts when they reflect a form of jury nullification?

Application Exercises

1. Look through the archive files of a newspaper in the community where your college/university is located and identify a local criminal case that received a lot of publicity in that paper. Then, make a list of the information disclosed in the newspaper that might be prejudicial to the defendant or defendants.

2. In the clerk's office, review the files that apply to the case you used in Exercise 1. Did the defense attorney file any motions to either delay or move the trial? If so, how did the judge rule on those motions?
3. Were there any motions or orders in the case that were designed to limit what the attorneys could say to the press?
4. Based on your review, do you think the press account of the defendant and the crime could have prevented the defendant from receiving a fair trial? What is the basis for your opinion?

4. PRESUMPTION OF INNOCENCE

The presumption of innocence is one of the most basic elements of due process. It is reflected in the fact that the prosecution is assigned the burden of proving the defendant's guilt **beyond a reasonable doubt**.[16] Furthermore, the defense is not required to put the defendant, or any other witnesses, on the stand, and if the defendant chooses not to testify, the prosecution cannot comment or otherwise draw attention to it during any part of the trial.

Beyond a reasonable doubt
The standard of proof used in criminal trials. The evidence presented must be so conclusive and complete that all reasonable doubts regarding the facts are removed from the jurors' minds.

Judges usually explain the "beyond a reasonable doubt" standard to jurors as the degree of doubt that exceeds the doubt that a reasonable person would have after considering all of the evidence. The proof must be so conclusive and complete that all reasonable doubts regarding the facts are removed from the jurors' minds.

It should be noted, however, that even though the prosecution must meet this high standard of proof, it does not have to establish guilt beyond *any* doubt or beyond a *shadow of a doubt*.

5. PRIVILEGE AGAINST SELF-INCRIMINATION

The presumption of innocence is enhanced by the privilege against self-incrimination. Not only does the prosecution bear the burden of proving a defendant's guilt, but it must be able to do so without requiring the defendant to incriminate himself or herself. Specifically, the Fifth Amendment declares: "No person shall be . . . compelled in any criminal case to be a witness against himself." Back in Chapter 4, we discussed how this privilege against self-incrimination applies to police investigations, and in Chapter 9, we pointed out how violations of this right can result in the suppression of evidence that was illegally gathered. At the trial stage, it means that the prosecution cannot call the defendant as a witness as part of its "case in chief."[17]

Defendants can, of course, choose to waive this privilege and testify as a defense witness on their own behalf. However, if defendants do testify, the prosecution has the right to cross-examine them. They cannot pick and choose which questions they wish to respond to or refuse to discuss topics, such as a criminal record, if the judge rules that they are relevant.

---

[16] In contrast to the preponderance of the evidence and the clear and convincing standards used in civil cases.

[17] The part of the trial during which the prosecution presents evidence to prove its case.

6. RIGHT TO CONFRONT AND CROSS-EXAMINE WITNESSES

You can probably relate to the frustration that comes from having false or misleading rumors spread, in a way that allows you neither to know what exactly is being alleged nor to explain why they are false or misleading. To prevent this happening in criminal trials, the Sixth Amendment includes the following: "In all criminal prosecutions, the accused shall enjoy the right . . . to be confronted with the witnesses against him."

Although it isn't specifically stated in the Sixth Amendment, the right to confront witnesses includes the right to cross-examine them. After the prosecuting attorney has questioned the witness, the defense has the opportunity to elicit further testimony that either supports the defendant's position or challenges the witness's credibility.

Justice Antonin Scalia authored a series of early twenty-first-century opinions that redefined the way that the Supreme Court analyzes issues arising under the Confrontation Clause. In *Crawford v. Washington*,[18] a defendant who had been charged with assault and attempted murder claimed self-defense. His wife did not testify because of the marital privilege. In the State of Washington, this privilege does not extend to a spouse's out-of-court statements admissible under a hearsay exception, so the prosecutor sought to introduce the wife's tape-recorded statements to the police as evidence that the stabbing was not in self-defense. The Court held that the Sixth Amendment Confrontation Clause barred the admission of the wife's statement. It reasoned that a "testimonial" out-of-court statement against a defendant in a criminal prosecution is barred under the Confrontation Clause unless (1) the declarant is unavailable to testify in court and (2) the defendant has had a prior opportunity to cross-examine the declarant.

Some statements are easy to classify as testimonial, such as sworn testimony given before a grand jury, in a preliminary hearing, or in a deposition. Likewise, statements made in affidavits or in police interrogations are testimonial. Non-testimonial statements include informal remarks made in conversations to friends, family, or co-workers. The Supreme Court clarifies this distinction in the consolidated cases of *Davis v. Washington* and *Hammon v. Indiana*, presented below.

Davis v. Washington
consolidated with *Hammon v. Indiana*
United States Supreme Court
547 U.S. 813 (2006)

Justice Scalia delivered the opinion of the Court.

These cases require us to determine when statements made to law enforcement personnel during a 911 call or at a crime scene are "testimonial" and thus subject to the requirements of the Sixth Amendment's Confrontation Clause.

The relevant statements in *Davis v. Washington* were made to a 911 emergency operator on

[18] 541 U.S. 36 (2004).

February 1, 2001. When the operator answered the initial call, the connection terminated before anyone spoke. She reversed the call and Michelle McCottry answered. In the ensuing conversation, the operator ascertained that McCottry was involved in a domestic disturbance with her former boyfriend Adrian Davis, the petitioner in this case:

> 911 Operator: Hello.
> Complainant: Hello.
> 911 Operator: What's going on?
> Complainant: He's here jumpin' on me again.
> 911 Operator: Okay. Listen to me carefully. Are you in a house or an apartment?
> Complainant: I'm in a house.
> 911 Operator: Are there any weapons?
> Complainant: No. He's usin' his fists.
> 911 Operator: Okay. Has he been drinking?
> Complainant: No.
> 911 Operator: Okay, sweetie. I've got help started. Stay on the line with me, okay?
> Complainant: I'm on the line.
> 911 Operator: Listen to me carefully. Do you know his last name?
> Complainant: It's Davis.
> 911 Operator: Davis? Okay, what's his first name?
> Complainant: Adrian
> 911 Operator: What is it?
> Complainant: Adrian.
> 911 Operator: Adrian?
> Complainant: Yeah.
> "911 Operator: Okay. What's his middle initial?
> Complainant: Martell. He's runnin' now."

As the conversation continued, the operator learned that Davis had "just r[un] out the door" after hitting McCottry, and that he was leaving in a car with someone else. McCottry started talking, but the operator cut her off, saying, "Stop talking and answer my questions." She then gathered more information about Davis (including his birthday), and learned that Davis had told McCottry that his purpose in coming to the house was "to get his stuff," since McCottry was moving. McCottry described the context of the assault, after which the operator told her that the police were on their way. "They're gonna check the area for him first," the operator said, "and then they're gonna come talk to you."

The police arrived within four minutes of the 911 call and observed McCottry's shaken state, the "fresh injuries on her forearm and her face," and her "frantic efforts to gather her belongings and her children so that they could leave the residence."

The State charged Davis with felony violation of a domestic no-contact order. "The State's only witnesses were the two police officers who responded to the 911 call. Both officers testified that McCottry exhibited injuries that appeared to be recent, but neither officer could testify as to the cause of the injuries." McCottry presumably could have testified as to whether Davis was her assailant, but she did not appear. Over Davis's objection, based on the Confrontation Clause of the Sixth Amendment, the trial court admitted the recording of her exchange with the 911 operator, and the jury convicted him. . . .

In *Hammon v. Indiana,* police responded late on the night of February 26, 2003, to a "reported domestic disturbance" at the home of Hershel and Amy Hammon. They found Amy alone on the front porch, appearing "'somewhat frightened,'" but she told them that "'nothing was the matter.'" She gave them permission to enter the house, where an officer saw "a gas heating unit in the corner of the living room" that had "flames coming out of the . . . partial glass front. There were pieces of glass on the ground in front of it and there was flame emitting from the front of the heating unit."

Hershel, meanwhile, was in the kitchen. He told the police "that he and his wife had 'been in an argument' but 'everything was fine now' and the argument 'never became physical.'" By this point Amy had come back inside. One of the officers remained with Hershel; the other went to the living room to talk with Amy, and "again asked [her] what had occurred." Hershel made several attempts to participate in Amy's conversation with the police but was rebuffed. The officer later testified that Hershel "became angry when I insisted that [he] stay separated from Mrs. Hammon so that we can investigate what had happened." After hearing Amy's account, the officer "had her fill out and sign a battery affidavit." Amy handwrote the following: "Broke our Furnace & shoved me down on the floor into the broken glass. Hit me in the chest and threw me down. Broke our lamps & phone. Tore up my van where I couldn't leave the house. Attacked my daughter."

The State charged Hershel with domestic battery and with violating his probation. Amy was subpoenaed, but she did not appear at his subsequent bench trial. The State called the officer who had questioned Amy, and asked him to recount what Amy told him and to authenticate the affidavit. Hershel's counsel repeatedly objected to the admission of this evidence. At one point, after hearing the prosecutor defend the affidavit because it was made "under oath," defense counsel said, "That doesn't give us the opportunity to cross-examine [the] person who allegedly drafted it. Makes me mad." Nonetheless, the trial court admitted the affidavit as a "present sense impression," and Amy's statements as "excited utterances" that "are expressly permitted in these kinds of cases even if the declarant is not available to testify." The officer thus testified that Amy "informed me that she and Hershel had been in an argument. That he became irrate [sic] over the fact of their daughter going to a boyfriend's house. The argument became . . . physical after being verbal and she informed me that Mr. Hammon, during the verbal part of the argument was breaking things in the living room and I believe she stated he broke the phone, broke the lamp, broke the front of the heater. When it became physical he threw her down into the glass of the heater.

. . . "She informed me Mr. Hammon had pushed her onto the ground, had shoved her head into the broken glass of the heater and that he had punched her in the chest twice I believe."

The trial judge found Hershel guilty on both charges,. . .

The Confrontation Clause of the Sixth Amendment provides: "In all criminal prosecutions, the accused shall enjoy the right . . . to be confronted with the witnesses against him." In *Crawford v. Washington*, (2004), we held that this provision bars "admission of testimonial statements of a witness who did not appear at trial unless he was unavailable to testify, and the defendant had had a prior opportunity for cross-examination." A critical portion of this holding, and the portion central to resolution of the two cases now before us, is the phrase "testimonial statements." Only statements of this sort cause the declarant to be a "witness" within the meaning of the Confrontation Clause. It is the testimonial character of the statement that separates it from other hearsay that, while subject to traditional limitations upon hearsay evidence, is not subject to the Confrontation Clause.

Our opinion in *Crawford* set forth "[v]arious formulations" of the core class of " 'testimonial' " statements but found it unnecessary to endorse any of them, because "some statements qualify under any definition." Among those, we said, were "[s]tatements taken by police officers in the course of interrogations." The questioning that generated the deponent's statement in *Crawford*—which was made and recorded while she was in police custody, after having been given Miranda warnings as a possible suspect herself—"qualifies under any conceivable definition" of an " 'interrogation.' " We therefore did not define that term, except to say that "[w]e use [it] . . . in its colloquial, rather than any technical legal, sense," and that "one can imagine various definitions . . . and we need not select among them in this case." Ibid. The character of the statements in the present cases is not as clear, and these cases require us to determine more precisely which police interrogations produce testimony.

Without attempting to produce an exhaustive classification of all conceivable statements—or even all conceivable statements in response to police interrogation—as either testimonial or nontestimonial, it suffices to decide the present cases to hold as follows: Statements are nontestimonial when made in the course of police interrogation under circumstances objectively indicating that the primary purpose of the interrogation is to enable police assistance to meet an ongoing emergency. They are testimonial when the circumstances objectively indicate that there is no such ongoing emergency, and that the primary purpose of the interrogation is to establish or prove past events potentially relevant to later criminal prosecution.

. . .

The question before us in *Davis*, then, is whether, objectively considered, the interrogation that took place in the course of the 911 call produced testimonial statements. When we said in *Crawford,* that "interrogations by law enforcement officers fall squarely within [the] class" of testimonial hearsay, we had immediately in mind (for that was the case before us) interrogations solely directed at establishing the facts of a past crime, in order to identify (or provide evidence to convict) the perpetrator. The product of such interrogation, whether reduced to a writing signed by the declarant or embedded in the memory (and perhaps notes) of the interrogating officer, is testimonial. It is, in the terms of the 1828 American dictionary quoted in *Crawford,* " '[a] solemn declaration or affirmation made for the purpose of establishing or proving some fact.' " . . . A 911 call, on the other hand, and at least the initial interrogation conducted in connection with a 911 call, is ordinarily not designed primarily to "establis[h] or prov[e]" some past fact, but to describe current circumstances requiring police assistance.

The difference between the interrogation in *Davis* and the one in *Crawford* is apparent on the face of things. In *Davis,* McCottry was speaking about events as they were actually happening, rather than "describ[ing] past events." Sylvia Crawford's interrogation, on the other hand, took place hours after the events she described had occurred. Moreover, any reasonable listener would recognize that McCottry (unlike Sylvia Crawford) was facing an ongoing emergency. Although one might call 911 to provide a narrative report of a crime absent any imminent danger, McCottry's call was plainly a call for help against bona fide physical threat. Third, the nature of what was asked and answered in *Davis,* again viewed objectively, was such that the elicited statements were necessary to be able to resolve the present emergency, rather than simply to learn (as in *Crawford*) what had happened in the past. That is true even of the operator's effort to establish the identity of the assailant, so that the dispatched officers might know whether they would be encountering a violent felon. And finally, the difference in the level of formality between the two interviews is striking. Crawford was responding calmly, at the station house, to a series of questions, with the officer-interrogator taping and making notes of her answers; McCottry's frantic answers were provided over the phone, in an environment that was not tranquil, or even (as far as any reasonable 911 operator could make out) safe.

We conclude from all this that the circumstances of McCottry's interrogation objectively indicate its primary purpose was to enable police assistance to meet an ongoing emergency. She simply was not acting as a witness; she was not testifying.

. . .

This is not to say that a conversation which begins as an interrogation to determine the need for emergency assistance cannot, as the Indiana Supreme Court put it, "evolve into testimonial statements," once that purpose has been achieved. In this case, for example, after the operator gained the information needed to address the exigency of the moment, the emergency appears to have ended (when Davis drove away from the premises). The operator then told McCottry to be quiet, and proceeded to pose a battery of questions. It could readily be maintained that, from that point on, McCottry's statements were testimonial, not unlike the "structured police questioning" that occurred in *Crawford.* This presents no great problem. Just as, for Fifth Amendment purposes, "police officers can and will distinguish almost instinctively between questions necessary to secure their own safety or the safety of the public and questions designed solely to elicit testimonial evidence from a suspect," trial courts will recognize the point at which, for Sixth Amendment purposes, statements in response to interrogations become testimonial. Through in limine procedure, they should redact or exclude the portions of any statement that have become testimonial, as they do, for example, with unduly prejudicial portions of otherwise admissible evidence. Davis's jury did not hear the complete 911 call, although it may well have heard some testimonial portions. We were asked to classify only McCottry's early statements identifying Davis as her assailant, and we agree with the Washington Supreme Court that they were not testimonial. That court also concluded that, even if later parts of the call were testimonial, their admission was harmless beyond a reasonable doubt. Davis does not challenge that holding, and we therefore assume it to be correct.

Determining the testimonial or nontestimonial character of the statements that were the product of the interrogation in Hammon is a much easier task, since they were not much different from the statements we found to be testimonial in *Crawford*. It is entirely clear from the circumstances that the interrogation was part of an investigation into possibly criminal past conduct—as, indeed, the testifying officer expressly acknowledged. There was no emergency in progress; the interrogating officer testified that he had heard no arguments or crashing and saw no one throw or break anything. When the officers first arrived, Amy told them that things were fine, and there was no immediate threat to her person. When the officer questioned Amy for the second time, and elicited the challenged statements, he was not seeking to determine (as in Davis) "what is happening," but rather "what happened." Objectively viewed, the primary, if not indeed the sole, purpose of the interrogation was to investigate a possible crime—which is, of course, precisely what the officer should have done.

It is true that the *Crawford* interrogation was more formal. It followed a Miranda warning, was tape-recorded, and took place at the station house. While these features certainly strengthened the statements' testimonial aspect—made it more objectively apparent, that is, that the purpose of the exercise was to nail down the truth about past criminal events—none was essential to the point. It was formal enough that Amy's interrogation was conducted in a separate room, away from her husband (who tried to intervene), with the officer receiving her replies for use in his "investigat[ion]." What we called the "striking resemblance" of the *Crawford* statement to civil-law *ex parte* examinations is shared by Amy's statement here. Both declarants were actively separated from the defendant—officers forcibly prevented Hershel from participating in the interrogation. Both statements deliberately recounted, in response to police questioning, how potentially criminal past events began and progressed. And both took place some time after the events described were over. Such statements under official interrogation are an obvious substitute for live testimony, because they do precisely what a witness does on direct examination; they are inherently testimonial.

. . . For the reasons we find the comparison to *Crawford* compelling, we find the comparison to *Davis* unpersuasive. The statements in *Davis* were taken when McCottry was alone, not only unprotected by police (as Amy Hammon was protected), but apparently in immediate danger from Davis. She was seeking aid, not telling a story about the past. McCottry's present-tense statements showed immediacy; Amy's narrative of past events was delivered at some remove in time from the danger she described. And after Amy answered the officer's questions, he had her execute an affidavit, in order, he testified, "[t]o establish events that have occurred previously."

Although we necessarily reject the Indiana Supreme Court's implication that virtually any "initial inquiries" at the crime scene will not be testimonial, we do not hold the opposite—that no questions at the scene will yield nontestimonial answers. We have already observed of domestic disputes that "[o]fficers called to investigate . . . need to know whom they are dealing with in order to assess the situation, the threat to their own safety, and possible danger to the potential victim." Such exigencies may often mean that "initial inquiries" produce nontestimonial statements. But in cases like this one, where Amy's statements were neither a cry for help nor the provision of information enabling officers immediately to end a threatening situation, the fact that they were given at an alleged crime scene and were "initial inquiries" is immaterial.

. . .

We affirm the judgment of the Supreme Court of Washington in No. 05-5224. We reverse the judgment of the Supreme Court of Indiana in No. 05-5705, and remand the case to that court for proceedings not inconsistent with this opinion.

It is so ordered.

Case Discussion Questions

As noted in the title of this case opinion, it covers two closely related cases that were consolidated into a single opinion.

1. With respect to *Davis v. Washington*:
   a. What statement did the prosecution want to put into evidence?
   b. Why couldn't the prosecutor call the declarant to testify?
   c. Did the Supreme Court determine that the statement was testimonial or non-testimonial? What was the basis of the Court's determination?
2. With respect to *Hammon v. Indiana*:
   a. What statement did the prosecution want to put into evidence?
   b. Why couldn't the prosecutor call the declarant to testify?
   c. Did the Supreme Court determine that the statement was testimonial or non-testimonial? What was the basis of the Court's determination?
3. Based on this consolidated opinion, what factors should a judge be taking into account in deciding whether an out-of-court statement is testimonial or non-testimonial?

The Supreme Court has decided other cases that clarify the distinction between testimonial and non-testimonial statements. The Court held in *Michigan v. Bryant*[19] that a statement was non-testimonial when its primary purpose is to enable police assistance in an ongoing emergency. In *Ohio v. Clark*,[20] the Court held that a pre-school student's statement to his teacher that his mother's boyfriend caused facial injuries was not testimonial. The Supreme Court held that a teacher's obligation to report suspected child abuse does not make the teacher a law enforcement agent for purposes of the Confrontation Clause.

Application Exercise

5. After reviewing the information you have been given on the Clay Marshall Hypothetical Case (*see* hypothetical case on pages xxxviii-xxxix), take note of the following additional facts: Madison Pickering, one of the complaining witnesses, has left the country for a study-abroad semester. Because of the defense's demand for an immediate trial, the Speedy Trial Act requires that the case be tried prior to Ms. Pickering's return. The prosecutor plans to have the jury hear a 911 tape in lieu of the witness's testimony. The transcript of the tape appears as Exhibit 10.1. Prepare a legal memorandum that analyzes whether the 911 tape should be barred under the Confrontation Clause. After you present the arguments in favor of finding that the statement was testimonial as well as the factors supporting the argument that it was not testimonial, reach a conclusion.

[19] 562 U.S. 344 (2011).
[20] 135 S. Ct. 2173 (2015).

Exhibit 10.1: 911 Tape

Madison Pickering called 911 on her cell phone the morning she claimed she was groped by Clay Marshall. A transcript of her conversation with the 911 dispatcher follows:

Dispatcher: This is 911. Do you need police, fire, or medical?
911 Caller: Police.
Dispatcher: What's the address?
911 Caller: I'm in my office, my boss forced himself on me. He touched and kissed me. I told him to stop and ran into my office to call you.
Dispatcher: What's the address, ma'am?
911 Caller: I don't remember the street number. We're on Main Street.
Dispatcher: What's your name?
911 Caller: Madison Pickering.
Dispatcher: Okay, ma'am, what's the emergency?
911 Caller: Mr. Marshall kissed me and rubbed my vagina through my clothes.
Dispatcher: Are you injured?
911 Caller: No.
Dispatcher: Does he have a weapon?
911 Caller: No.
Dispatcher: Do you need medical attention?
911 Caller: No.
Dispatcher: Is this an emergency?
911 Caller: I just want to make a report.
Dispatcher: What's the name of the business that operates out of the office?
(Silence)
Dispatcher: Are you still there, ma'am? . . . Are you there, ma'am?
(Dial tone)

7. RIGHT TO COMPEL WITNESSES TO TESTIFY

In addition to the right to confront the prosecution's witnesses, the Sixth Amendment gives the defendant the right to compel the testimony of other witnesses who may have information relevant to the trial. It declares: "In all criminal prosecutions, the accused shall enjoy the right . . . to have compulsory process for obtaining witnesses in his favor." To enforce this right, the defense must place the name of the persons on the official witness list and have the court issue subpoenas requiring the witnesses' attendance.

It is important to note, however, that although witnesses can be compelled to appear, they may be able to claim their own privilege against self-incrimination as a legitimate reason for not answering all the questions that are asked. In some cases, this problem can be overcome by a grant of immunity, but in others it cannot.[21]

[21]See discussion on severance and joinder on pp. 297-298 in Chapter 9.

Discussion Questions

9. If your client chose not to testify at the criminal trial, would you want the judge to give the jury an instruction about there being a constitutional right not to testify and that the jury should not allow its verdict to be influenced by the defendant's failure to testify? Why or why not?

10. Even though he had made frequent public statements about how he looked forward to telling his side of the story at his trial, and his attorney had declared in his opening statement that his client would testify on his own behalf, former Illinois governor Rod Blagojevich chose not to testify at his federal criminal trial on corruption charges. What factors do you think went into this decision? Given the fact that the jury found him guilty on 1 of 24 counts and failed to reach a unanimous verdict on the other 23 counts, what can you conclude about the wisdom of this decision?

11. Should someone on trial for child molestation have the right to be in the courtroom when the victim is testifying about the alleged molestation? Why or why not?

C. The Use of Evidence

In the previous section, we discussed how the presumption of innocence makes the prosecution responsible for proving the defendant's guilt beyond a reasonable doubt. It must meet this burden of proof by presenting legally admissible **evidence** at trial. This evidence can take the form of testimony by witnesses, relevant documents, physical objects, stipulations, and judicial notice.

Evidence
Witness testimony, documents, physical objects, and stipulations that are presented in court for the purpose of determining the facts of the case.

The specific rules governing the presentation of evidence in federal courts are set forth in the Federal Rules of Evidence. Each state has a similar set of rules that apply to trials in their courts. The sources of state rules of evidence may include case law, statutory enactments, and court rules. Figure 10.1 presents an overview of the organization and topics covered in the Federal Rules of Evidence.

ARTICLE I. GENERAL PROVISIONS
ARTICLE II. JUDICIAL NOTICE
ARTICLE III. PRESUMPTIONS IN CIVIL ACTIONS AND PROCEEDINGS
ARTICLE IV. RELEVANCY AND ITS LIMITS
ARTICLE V. PRIVILEGES
ARTICLE VI. WITNESSES
ARTICLE VII. OPINIONS AND EXPERT TESTIMONY
ARTICLE VIII. HEARSAY
ARTICLE IX. AUTHENTICATION AND IDENTIFICATION
ARTICLE X. CONTENTS OF WRITINGS, RECORDINGS, AND PHOTOGRAPHS
ARTICLE XI: MISCELLANEOUS RULES

Figure 10.1 Federal Rules of Evidence

Testimonial evidence Verbal statements that are given under oath at a trial for the purpose of helping the jury and/or judge to understand the facts of the case.

Physical evidence Tangible physical objects that can be picked up and handled.

Demonstrative evidence Physical objects, such as photos, maps, x-rays, and diagrams, used to illustrate or aid in the understanding of verbal testimony.

Documentary evidence Legal instruments such as contracts, leases, wills, and deeds and other written documents used to support claims made in court.

Direct evidence Evidence that establishes a direct link to the fact or event that a party seeks to prove.

Circumstantial evidence Evidence that permits the inference of the existence or nonexistence of a fact or event that a party seeks to prove

Cumulative evidence Evidence that does not add any new information but confirms facts that already have been established.

Corroborative evidence Evidence supporting other evidence that has already been admitted but that is presented in a different form.

1. TYPES OF EVIDENCE

a. *Based on Format*

Evidence is often categorized as being either testimonial or physical. **Testimonial evidence** consists of verbal statements that witnesses give under oath at a trial in response to appropriate questions from the attorneys or the judge; **physical evidence** involves tangible physical items. Examples include items such as guns, knives, shell casings, drugs, stolen jewelry, counterfeit money, etc. See Exhibit 10.2.

Physical evidence can also take the form of photos, maps, x-rays, and diagrams that are used to illustrate or aid in the understanding of witness testimony. These are categorized as **demonstrative evidence**. Written documents such as contracts, leases, wills, and deeds are categorized as legal instruments, and along with other written documents such as estimates, letters, and e-mails, are referred to as **documentary evidence**.

b. *Based on How It Is Used*

Evidence can also be classified on the basis of how it contributes to proving the case. **Direct evidence** establishes a direct link to a fact or event that a party seeks to prove. For example, a witness's testimony that "I saw the defendant shoot the victim" would be direct evidence of a key event in a homicide case. **Circumstantial evidence**, on the other hand, provides information that permits the inference of the existence or nonexistence of a fact or event that a party seeks to prove. An example would be testimony given by a police officer who did not witness the crime, but who testifies that the defendant was found at the scene with powder burns on his hands consistent with having recently fired a handgun. Although the powder burns do not directly prove the defendant shot the victim in question, this information is logically consistent with a conclusion that the defendant did. This bit of information by itself would be insufficient to gain a criminal conviction, but it could be combined with other pieces of circumstantial evidence that together might be sufficient to meet the prosecution's burden of proof.

Cumulative evidence is evidence that confirms facts that already have been established by previously admitted evidence. For example, if two people both testify that they saw the defendant fire a handgun at the victim, the second witness would be providing cumulative evidence. Such evidence may be excluded if the judge believes that the facts that it proves have already been sufficiently established. This is especially true if the other party is not contesting the particular fact in question.

The concept of **corroborative evidence** is very similar, in that this evidence also supports previous testimony, but it comes in a different form. For example, if a second person testified that he had seen the defendant make a phone call shortly before leaving the scene of an accident, that would be classified as cumulative evidence. On the other hand, the introduction of telephone company records showing the defendant made a call to a certain party on a certain date and time would be corroborative evidence.

Exhibit 10.2: Photographs of Explosive Materials

Below are FBI evidence photographs of copper tubing, wiring, various chemicals, electrical components, and other bomb-making materials recovered from the home of Theodore Kaczynski, the "Unabomber." The items themselves are physical evidence. The photographs are demonstrative evidence.

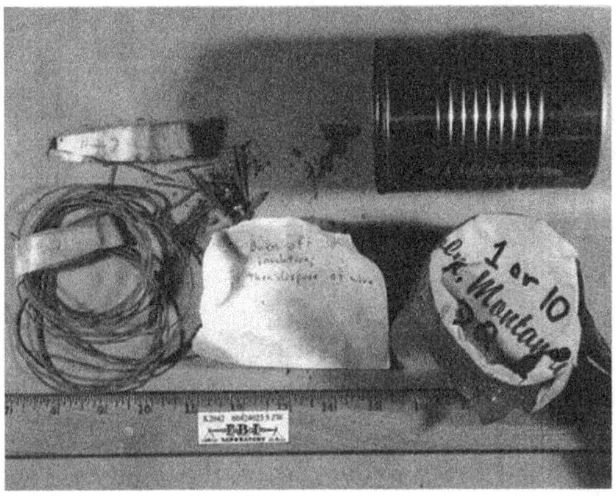

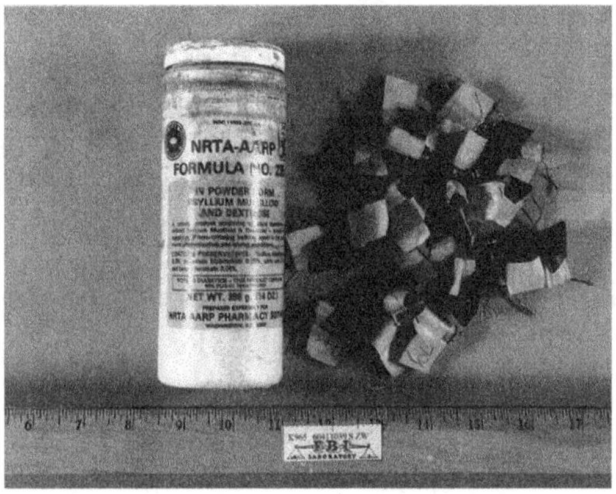

Discussion Question

12. Can you think of a situation in which circumstantial evidence alone would be sufficient to justify returning a guilty verdict in a murder case? If so, what would that evidence have to be?

2. ADMISSIBILITY OF EVIDENCE

a. Relevance and Materiality

In order for anything (witness testimony, documents, physical objects, etc.) to be used as evidence in a criminal trial, it must be relevant and material to determining the defendant's guilt or innocence.

Relevance refers to the "probative value" of the evidence. **Relevant evidence** is defined in Rule 401 as: "[E]vidence having any tendency to make the existence of any fact that is of consequence to the determination of the action more probable or less probable than it would be without the evidence." For example, the fact that the defendant had a tattoo on his shoulder would be relevant if the store clerk had testified that because the robber had been wearing a sleeveless tank top, she had noticed that he had a tattoo on his shoulder. However, if the clerk had reported that the robber was wearing a long-sleeved hoodie, the existence of the defendant's tattoo would not be relevant to determining if the defendant had been the robber.

Relevant evidence
Evidence that leads one to logically conclude that an asserted fact is either more or less probable.

Material evidence Evidence that is more probative than prejudicial.

Materiality is usually thought of as either a subcategory of relevancy or simply another word for relevancy. Often, it is stated as requiring that the evidence be more probative than prejudicial. This concern is reflected in Rule 403:

> Although relevant, evidence may be excluded if its probative value is substantially outweighed by the danger of unfair prejudice, confusion of the issues, or misleading the jury, or by considerations of undue delay, waste of time, or needless presentation of cumulative evidence.

Thus, a gruesome photograph of the condition of the victim of a mutilation murder may be relevant and yet be excluded because of the probability that it would inflame the jury.

Character evidence Evidence of a person's reputation in the community as to a particular trait, such as honesty or chastity.

One of the most complex areas of evidence law involves the handling of "character evidence." This area of the law involves the admissibility of information about a person's reputation within the community for moral behavior. Rule 404 states:

> (a) Evidence of a person's character or a trait of character is not admissible for the purpose of proving action in conformity therewith on a particular occasion, except:
>
> (1) Character of accused—*In a criminal case, evidence* of a pertinent trait of character offered by an accused, or by the prosecution to rebut the same, or if evidence of a trait of character of the alleged victim of the crime is offered by an accused and admitted under Rule 404 (a)(2), evidence of the same trait of character of the accused offered by the prosecution;
>
> (2) Character of alleged victim—*In a criminal case, and subject to the limitations imposed by Rule 412, evidence* of a pertinent trait of character of the alleged victim of the crime offered by an accused, or by the prosecution to rebut the same, or evidence of a character trait of peacefulness of the alleged victim offered by the prosecution in a homicide case to rebut evidence that the alleged victim was the first aggressor;
>
> (b) Evidence of other crimes, wrongs, or acts is not admissible to prove the character of a person in order to show action in conformity therewith. It may, however, be admissible for other purposes, such as proof of motive, opportunity, intent, preparation, plan, knowledge, identity, or absence of mistake or accident, provided that upon request by the accused, the prosecution in a criminal case shall provide reasonable notice in advance of trial, or during trial if the court excuses pretrial notice on good cause shown, of the general nature of any such evidence it intends to introduce at trial.

Other rules relating to the admissibility of various types of character evidence include:

- Rule 410: Inadmissibility of Pleas, Plea Discussions, and Related Statements
- Rule 412: Sex Offense Cases; Relevance of Alleged Victim's Past Sexual Behavior or Alleged Sexual Predisposition
- Rule 413: Evidence of Similar Crimes in Sexual Assault Cases
- Rule 415: Evidence of Similar Acts in Civil Cases Concerning Sexual Assault or Child Molestation
- Rules 608 and 609: Evidence Related to the Character of Witnesses

b. Testimonial Evidence

As previously mentioned, testimonial evidence consists of verbal statements given under oath[22] by **competent** witnesses. Rule 603 states:

> Before testifying, every witness shall be required to declare that the witness will testify truthfully, by oath or affirmation administered in a form calculated to awaken the witness' conscience and impress the witness' mind with the duty to do so.

Competency
The ability of a witness to testify; generally, the witness must be capable of being understood by the jury; must understand the duty to tell the truth; and have knowledge of the facts to which he or she is testifying.

According to the Advisory Committee on the Federal Rules, this requirement is designed to afford the flexibility required in dealing with religious adults, atheists, conscientious objectors, mental defectives, and children. Affirmation is simply a solemn undertaking to tell the truth and no special formula is required. Witnesses must be old enough and have enough mental competency to understand the questions and the duty to tell the truth. Where language might be a barrier, the court will provide an interpreter.

The nature of the testimony witnesses can give is determined by whether they are testifying as **lay witnesses** or **expert witnesses**. Lay witnesses are limited to testifying about events they personally observed through their own senses and statements they heard with their own ears. They are not allowed to speculate about things for which they lack personal knowledge. On the other hand, **expert witnesses** are brought in to supply scientific, technical, or other specialized knowledge that will help the jury or judge evaluate the facts that have been presented. In this capacity, they may speculate as to the reasonable probability of certain things having occurred if they have properly been recognized as experts[23] on the subject and limit their opinions to their area of recognized expertise. Prior to having someone be recognized as an expert witness, the examining attorney must ask preliminary questions designed to qualify the witness as an expert in the field on which the witness will be testifying.

Lay witness
A witness who is called to testify about things personally observed through his or her senses.

Expert witness
A witness who is called to supply scientific, technical, or other specialized knowledge that will help the jury and/or judge evaluate the facts that have been presented.

Article VII of the Federal Rules of Evidence is devoted to sorting out when different types of witnesses can give opinions and what it means to be an "expert witness." Rule 701 states:

> If the witness is not testifying as an expert, the witness' testimony in the form of opinions or inferences is limited to those opinions or inferences which are (a) rationally based on the perception of the witness, and (b) helpful to a clear understanding of the witness' testimony or the determination of a fact in issue, and (c) not based on scientific, technical, or other specialized knowledge within the scope of Rule 702.

This rule allows witnesses who have not been qualified as experts to give opinions on matters such as the similarity of a person's voice or handwriting to that of someone's with whom they are familiar or whether a person appeared to be angry or intoxicated. Most courts have permitted the owner or officer of a business to testify to the value or projected profits of the business without the necessity of qualifying the witness as an accountant, appraiser, or similar expert. Such opinion testimony is admitted not because of experience, training or specialized knowledge

---

[22]The witness swears or affirms, under penalty of perjury, "to tell the truth, the whole truth or nothing but the truth."

[23]To be recognized as an expert, the judge must find that the witness has special skills or knowledge that exceed those of the average person.

within the realm of an expert, but because of the particularized knowledge that the witness has by virtue of his or her position in the business.

Rule 702 spells out the role of expert testimony:

> If scientific, technical, or other specialized knowledge will assist the trier of fact to understand the evidence or to determine a fact in issue, a witness qualified as an expert by knowledge, skill, experience, training, or education may testify thereto in the form of an opinion or otherwise, if (1) the testimony is based upon sufficient facts or data, (2) the testimony is the product of reliable principles and methods, and (3) the witness has applied the principles and methods reliably to the facts of the case.

While expert witnesses are allowed to give their opinions and are frequently asked hypothetical questions, they are not limited only to giving opinions. Rule 702 recognizes that an expert witness may also testify about scientific facts and theories relevant to the case. It leaves it up to the judge to decide whether the opinion evidence is reasonably reliable, whether it will substantially assist the trier of fact, and whether the proposed witness has sufficient expertise to express such opinions in court.[24]

Although witnesses are not permitted to express their opinions as to the guilt or innocence of the defendant, Rule 704 does permit experts to give opinions that embrace ultimate issues. However, this rule explicitly prohibits opinion testimony as to whether the defendant was legally insane at the time the crime was committed. The Rule provides:

> (b) No expert witness testifying with respect to the mental state or condition of a defendant in a criminal case may state an opinion or inference as to whether the defendant did or did not have the mental state or condition constituting an element of the crime charged or of a defense thereto. Such ultimate issues are matters for the trier of fact alone.

Application Exercises

6. Based on the Federal Rules of Evidence, should a judge allow a lay witness to testify that a substance appeared to be a narcotic?
7. Locate and read what the U.S. Supreme Court has said about assessing the reliability of scientific expert testimony in *Daubert v. Merrell Dow Pharmaceuticals, Inc.*, 509 U.S. 579 (1993) and *Kumho Tire Co. v. Carmichael*, 526 U.S. 137 (1999).
   a. Based on the *Daubert* opinion, make a checklist of factors that a judge should use in assessing the reliability of scientific expert testimony.
   b. How does the *Kumho Tire Co.* opinion affect the way in which the *Daubert* decision should be applied?

[24] In *Daubert v. Merrell Dow Pharmaceuticals, Inc.*, 509 U.S. 579 (1993), the Court charged trial judges with the responsibility of acting as gatekeepers to exclude unreliable expert testimony, and the Court in *Kumho Tire Co. v. Carmichael*, 526 U.S. 137 (1999) clarified that this gatekeeper function applies to all expert testimony, not just testimony based in science.

c. *Hearsay Evidence*

One of the most important limitations on the presentation of evidence is the rule against **hearsay evidence** (the **hearsay rule**). Rule 801(c) defines hearsay as "a statement, other than one made by the declarant while testifying at the trial or hearing, offered in evidence to prove the truth of the matter asserted." Rule 801(a) defines a statement as "(1) an oral or written assertion or (2) non-verbal conduct of a person, if it is intended by the person as an assertion." Rule 801(b) defines a **declarant** as "a person who makes a statement." In nontechnical terms, hearsay is secondhand information about an event that the witness got from someone else rather than having observed it with his or her own senses. For example, it would be hearsay for a witness to testify that a friend had told him that the friend had seen the defendant near the scene of the crime, or that the friend had overheard the defendant bragging about having robbed a liquor store Tuesday night.

Hearsay evidence
A statement, other than one made by the declarant while testifying at the trial or hearing, offered in evidence to prove the truth of the matter asserted.

Hearsay rule
The general rule of evidence providing that hearsay evidence is not admissible at trial or hearing.

Declarant
The person who made the out-of-court statement.

The general principle, stated in Rule 802, is: "Hearsay is not admissible except as provided by these rules or by other rules prescribed by the Supreme Court pursuant to statutory authority or by Act of Congress." Hearsay is generally excluded because the witnesses cannot personally attest that what someone else told them had actually occurred and because the original source of the information is not there to be cross-examined. In the examples given above, the witness has personal knowledge of what somebody else claimed to have seen or heard but cannot offer proof that the defendant had in fact been at the scene of the crime or that the defendant had in fact bragged about having committed the robbery.

Two types of out-of-court statements routinely permitted into evidence are (1) admissions by party opponents and prior statements by a witness. Under Federal Rule 801(d), these types of statements are considered as non-hearsay and therefore are not barred by the hearsay rule. In most states, however, prior witness statements and admissions by party opponents are admissible as exceptions to the hearsay rule. Although the underlying legal theories differ, the practical effect is the same—these types of out-of-court statements are admitted into evidence.

Prior statements can be used to impeach the credibility of a witness. If a key witness testifies at the trial that the robber drove off in a red car but had previously told someone that it had been a white car, the defendant could have that other person testify as to what the witness had previously told her about the color of the getaway vehicle in order to create doubt about the reliability of the prosecution witness's identification. Admissions by a party opponent can be particularly important to the prosecution. Virtually anything the defendant tells the police, his friends, his girlfriend, or his cellmate potentially can be presented at trial by the prosecutor. For example, when a defendant brags to someone that he robbed a liquor store, the people who heard this admission can testify as to what the defendant had said. Furthermore, a statement by a co-conspirator made in furtherance of the conspiracy can be used against everyone in the conspiracy.

Rules 803 and 804 list 24 general exceptions and 6 that apply only when the declarant is not available. See Figure 10.2 for a listing of these exceptions.

Rule 803: Hearsay Exceptions; Availability of Declarant Immaterial

The following are not excluded by the hearsay rule, even though the declarant is available as a witness:

(1) Present sense impression

(2) Excited utterance

(3) Then existing mental, emotional, or physical condition

(4) Statements for purposes of medical diagnosis or treatment

(5) Recorded recollection

(6) Records of regularly conducted activity

(7) Absence of entry in records kept in accordance with provision (6)

(8) Public records and reports

(9) Records of vital statistics

(10) Absence of public record or entry

(11) Records of religious organizations

(12) Marriage, baptismal, and similar certificates

(13) Family records

(14) Records of documents affecting an interest in property

(15) Statements in documents affecting an interest in property

(16) Statements in ancient documents

(17) Market reports, commercial publications

(18) Learned treatises

(19) Reputation concerning personal or family history

(20) Reputation concerning boundaries or general history

(21) Reputation as to character

(22) Judgment of previous conviction

(23) Judgment as to personal, family or general history, or boundaries

(24) Other exceptions covered in Rule 807

Rule 804. Hearsay Exceptions; Declarant Unavailable

The following are not excluded by the hearsay rule if the declarant is unavailable as a witness:

(1) Former testimony

(2) Statement under belief of impending death

(3) Statement against interest

(4) Statement of personal or family history

(5) Other exceptions covered in Rule 807[25]

(6) Forfeiture by wrongdoing

Figure 10.2 Federal Rules of Criminal Procedure Rules 803 and 804 on Hearsay Exceptions

---

[25]FRE 807(a) provides: "Under the following conditions, a hearsay statement is not excluded by the rule against hearsay even if the statement is not admissible under a hearsay exception in Rule 803 or 804:

(1) the statement is supported by sufficient guarantees of trustworthiness–after considering the totality of circumstances under which it was made and evidence, if any, corroborating the statement; and

(2) it is more probative on the point for which it is offered than any other evidence that the proponent can obtain through reasonable efforts."

According to Rule 804, a declarant is considered to be "unavailable as a witness" if he or she

(1) is exempted by ruling of the court . . . ; or
(2) persists in refusing to testify . . . despite an order of the court to do so; or
(3) testifies to a lack of memory. . . . or
(4) is unable to be present or to testify at the hearing because of death or then existing physical or mental illness or infirmity; or
(5) is absent from the hearing and the proponent of a statement has been unable to procure the declarant's attendance . . . by process or other reasonable means.

A declarant is not unavailable as a witness if exemption, refusal, claim of lack of memory, inability, or absence is due to the procurement or wrongdoing of the proponent of a statement for the purpose of preventing the witness from attending or testifying.

Although many states follow the federal rules of evidence, in many situations there are differences. You should check the case law, statutes, and court rules for your jurisdiction when you research an evidentiary issue.

3. AUTHENTICATING EVIDENCE

Although physical and documentary evidence is supposed to speak for itself, witnesses are needed to **authenticate** it before it can be introduced. Before a business record can be introduced, an appropriate official of the company must take the witness stand to identify the document, explain what it is, and tell how it is used in the ordinary course of the business. Before an alleged weapon can be used as evidence, appropriate law enforcement officials have to take the witness stand to identify the object as being one that was found at the scene of the crime or in the defendant's possession and establish the "**chain of custody**."

Articles IX and X of the Federal Rules of Evidence lay out specific guidelines for authenticating different types of evidence. Certain types of official public documents can be "self-authenticated"; other types of evidence require specific types of testimony. Authentication is accomplished through a practice commonly referred to as **laying a foundation,** in which attorneys ask witnesses a series of preliminary questions designed to identify the evidence they want to introduce and explain how it relates to the issues involved in the trial. Prior to giving testimonial evidence about what he or she saw or heard, the attorney must ask preliminary questions designed to establish where the witness was and who else may have been present at the time of the witness's observations.

Proper testimony must establish that a document being presented is in fact what it is purported to be. Under some circumstances, however, a copy may be considered admissible. Public records (official governmental documents as well as private deeds and mortgages that are officially recorded with the government) can be presented through the use of certified copies. In addition to presenting a copy showing an official seal and signature, an affidavit from the record's custodian usually is presented explaining what the record shows and attesting that it is an accurate copy of the one on file. According to the **best evidence rule**, the original document itself usually must be produced at the trial.

Authentication of evidence
The process of establishing that the objects being introduced into evidence are what they are claimed to be.

Chain of custody
A record of who possessed an object being presented as evidence from the time it came into the possession of government agents until it is presented in court.

Laying a foundation
A process by which an attorney asks a witness a series of preliminary questions designed to identify potential evidence and explain how it relates to the issues involved in the trial.

Best evidence rule
An evidentiary rule requiring that the original document be produced at trial.

However, copies of documents may be allowed when the original no longer exists, is in the hands of an adverse party who refuses to produce it, or is held by a third party who is outside the jurisdiction of the court's subpoena power. In cases where the original is so voluminous that it is impractical to produce it in its entirety, the litigant is usually allowed to produce a summary.

The rules governing the authentication of photographs differ from one jurisdiction to the next. Most courts simply require that a witness who is familiar with an object or a scene in the photograph testify that it is an accurate representation of that object or scene as it appeared at the time of the incident. On the other hand, a few courts require that the person who actually took the photograph testify about the type of camera and the settings used. Some require testimony relating to the chain of possession of the photograph.

There is a trend in the federal courts to require the parties to address issues of authenticity of exhibits prior to trial. Under this practice, the parties list all of the exhibits in a joint pre-trial memorandum. Any objections to authenticity are included in the document. This approach streamlines the trial of the case.

4. STIPULATIONS AND JUDICIAL NOTICE

Stipulation
An agreement by the parties to accept something as being true without the need to present formal proof.

Judicial notice
An action taken by a judge to formally recognize something as being a fact without requiring the attorneys to prove it through the introduction of other evidence.

As alternatives to providing witness testimony to introduce exhibits into evidence, attorneys can submit a **stipulation** or request that the judge take **judicial notice** of certain types of adjudicative facts. For example, a judge could take judicial notice that a city lies within a particular county or that July 9, 2019 fell on a Tuesday. In effect, the judge acknowledges that the information is so well known that specific proof is not required.

Judicial notice is covered in Article II of the Federal Rules of Evidence. Rule 201 declares: "A judicially noticed fact must be one not subject to reasonable dispute in that it is either (1) generally known within the territorial jurisdiction of the trial court or (2) capable of accurate and ready determination by resort to sources whose accuracy cannot reasonably be questioned." It also states: "In a criminal case, the court shall instruct the jury that it may, but is not required to, accept as conclusive any fact judicially noticed."

SUMMARY

Criminal trials are the mechanism used to determine if the government can prove, beyond a reasonable doubt, that someone has done something that the government has designated a crime. The rules used to conduct the trial must comport with the constitutional protections considered to be essential to the due process of law.

The most important constitutional rights impacting the conduct of criminal trials are the right to a public trial, the right to a jury trial, the presumption of innocence, the privilege against self-incrimination, the right to confront and cross-examine witnesses, the right to compel witnesses to testify, and the right to counsel. The nature of each of these rights was explained in this chapter.

At the end of the trial, the judge or jury is supposed to decide the guilt or innocence of the defendant based on the information that was admitted into evidence during the trial. This evidence can take the form of witness testimony, documents, physical objects, and stipulations. Lay witnesses can testify as to what they personally observed, and expert witnesses are called upon to provide specialized knowledge (usually scientific/technical information) relevant to a better understanding of the facts being presented.

Regardless of the source, only evidence that is relevant and material can be used for reaching a verdict in the case. One of the most confusing parts of the rules of evidence involves the hearsay rule. Not only is the definition of hearsay hard to grasp, Rules 803 and 804 list a total of thirty exceptions to the basic rule.

INTERNET RESOURCES

Handbooks for Jurors

- Judicial Conference of the United States: **https://www.uscourts.gov/topics/judicial-conference-united-states**
- *Petit Juror Handbook:* **https://ilcourtsaudio.blob.core.windows.net/antilles-resources/resources/b04f7ab8-31c2-40bd-9bf2-a87b404075c2/Jury.pdf**
- Jury nullification *Cornell Law School, Legal Information Institute:* **https://www.law.cornell.edu/wex/jury_nullification**

REVIEW QUESTIONS

1. What does the Sixth Amendment right to a public trial encompass?
2. What are the three references to jury trials in the U.S. Constitution?
3. In a jury trial, who decides factual questions? Who decides legal questions?
4. What is the difference between legal questions and factual questions?
5. What are the two steps of jury selection?
6. Name and describe the two types of challenges attorneys can assert during the *voir dire* process.
7. What is the minimum potential sentence of incarceration that gives rise to the Sixth Amendment right to trial by jury?
8. In what types of situations would criminal defendants ordinarily choose to waive their right to be tried by a jury?
9. What is the minimum number of jurors required in federal and in state felony cases?
10. What is jury nullification?
11. How does the presumption of innocence affect each side's obligations at trial?
12. What part of the Sixth Amendment gives criminal defendants the right to cross-examine witnesses against them?
13. Besides witness testimony, what are the typical forms of evidence used to prove facts at trial?
14. What is the difference between testimonial and physical evidence?
15. What evidence can expert witnesses present that fact witnesses cannot?

16. What is hearsay, and is it ever admissible in a criminal trial?
17. How are cumulative evidence and corroborative evidence similar? How are they different?
18. Before an exhibit is introduced into evidence, identify and explain the process that the attorney must follow.
19. Other than the parties' stipulation of facts, what other method authorizes a judge to inform the jury that certain facts are to be accepted as true without any proof?
20. According to the Federal Rules of Evidence, under what circumstances can relevant evidence be inadmissible because it is not material?

Chapter 11

Preparation for Trial

Chapter Objectives

After reading this chapter, you should be able to:

- Explain how paralegals can help attorneys prepare for *voir dire*.
- Prepare motions and pocket briefs concerning the admissibility of evidence.
- Discuss how attorneys and paralegals prepare witnesses (defendants, other lay witnesses, and expert witnesses) for trial.
- Explain how to organize materials for trial.
- Prepare a computer-based opening statement.

Introduction

In one sense, pre-trial preparation begins as soon as the government receives the police reports or when the defense attorney begins representation of the client. From this point forward, both prosecutors and defense attorneys are gathering information that not only influences the plea bargaining process but is also used in evaluating potential witnesses and other evidence that can be used at a trial. The discovery process, discussed in Chapter 8 and the motions, discussed in Chapter 9, are designed to gather information that will minimize surprises at the trial.

In this chapter, we discuss the preparations that generally don't take place until after the case has been set for trial. This is the point at which the parties must notify the opposition the witnesses who will be called to testify and identify the exhibits that will be offered as evidence. Activities taking place during this period usually include preparing for *voir dire*, meeting with witnesses, preparing trial subpoenas, conducting further factual research, preparing exhibits, creating slide presentations, organizing the file for trial, and preparing motions and briefs on evidentiary issues.

A. Jury Trials

1. THE DECISION TO USE A JURY

In Chapter 10, we noted that the right to be tried by a jury varies between the federal and state courts, and depends upon the severity of the crimes being charged. In situations in which the right to a jury trial applies, state court defendants ultimately decide whether to exercise this right or to waive it and leave the verdict in the hands of the judge.

It is the defense attorney's obligation to carefully discuss the pros and cons associated with this decision. As a general rule, defendants typically choose to be tried by a jury because they think at least some of the jurors will be more sympathetic and more likely to identify with their situation than a judge would. Since jury verdicts must either be unanimous or require a supermajority to convict, the odds of avoiding a conviction usually seem better with a jury. On the other hand, in cases where there has been a great deal of prejudicial publicity, the community is perceived as being prejudiced against members of the defendant's racial or ethnic group, or the crime was particularly gruesome, some defendants believe that they are better off being tried by a professional who is committed to following the letter of the law and less likely to be influenced by these prejudicial factors. The procedure is different in federal court because Rule 23(a) requires felonies to be tried by a jury unless the defendant files a written waiver, the prosecutor consents, and the court approves.[1]

2. PREPARATION FOR *VOIR DIRE*

If a jury will be used, both prosecution and defense begin preparation for the *voir dire* examinations that will occur during the process of seating the jury. These examinations are supposed to uncover factors that might prevent the person being questioned from being a fair and impartial juror.

The combination of challenges for cause and peremptory challenges (which we discussed in Chapter 10) is designed to eliminate jurors who are not deemed to be impartial. However, there is no guarantee that they will successfully achieve that result, and much depends on the extent to which each side has researched the background of the potential jurors, how skillful their questioning is, how well they listen to inflections in their answers, and how well they read the potential juror's body language.

The preparation for this questioning typically begins by examining the list of people who have been summoned for jury duty during the time that the trial is expected to begin. In addition to having names and addresses, it may list the

---

[1]F.R.Cr.P. 23(a).

potential juror's date of birth. If juror questionnaires are available, the attorneys can also learn other information about jury candidates. This information includes such matters as educational and employment background, marital and family status, whether they have previously been victims of a crime, and whether they have friends or relatives who are crime victims, police officers, or attorneys.

If the financial resources are available, attorneys for both sides may actually have their paralegals or outside investigators do further research to find out as much as they can about the people on the list. Public records frequently give indications of the potential juror attitudes. Voter registration lists may reveal party affiliation. Real estate and vehicle ownership records may indicate financial wherewithal and self-image. Court documents often show detailed information about financial status, criminal background, and relationships with others. Sources such as the *Haines Directory*, the *City Directory*, and *Who's Who* are available in most public libraries. These reference books provide information as to occupation, neighborhood income level, and family members.

In addition, the internet is an excellent source of information. Social media sites like Facebook, LinkedIn, and Twitter reveal personal data and give insight into the personality, emotions, interests, and attitudes of the author. Instagram, blogs, and personal websites also can be productive sources of information. People seem to be less guarded in communicating on the Internet than in person.

Search engines, such as Google, can yield fruitful information, as well. When you conduct this type of research, use more than one search engine. Using Bing, for instance, may yield different results than using Google. Although Google and Bing are excellent places to begin, don't limit yourself to one or two search engines. Yahoo and DuckDuckGo are also popular search engines. There also are a multitude of websites that can be used to acquire information about people.

In high-profile cases, either or both sides may contract with special jury consultants to collect and review this background information. Jury consultants may even organize and evaluate focus groups and mock trials to identify characteristics that are correlated with different views about the type of crimes or the type of defendants involved. While this information is unlikely to convince a judge to remove a juror for cause, it may well become the basis for exercising peremptory challenges.

In addition to collecting background information, paralegals can help attorneys draft questions to either be submitted to the judge or for the attorneys to ask themselves. Good *voir dire* questions should be designed to uncover potential conflicts of interest or biases that might work against your client's interests. Sample *voir dire* questions appear in Figure 11.1.

Discussion Questions

1. If you were an attorney for the defense, in what types of situations would you recommend having a bench trial rather than a jury trial?

2. Do you think that attorneys should be allowed to ask their own questions during *voir dire*, as opposed to having the judge read the attorney's questions to the jurors? Why?

1. As the Court has just stated, my client is an African-American Chicago Police Department patrolman. Is there anything about him being an African-American male that would prejudice you for or against him in connection with your obligation to hear all of the evidence, listen to all arguments given by counsel, and carefully consider all of the instructions and law provided by the Court before making a decision as to whether my client, Officer Isaac Berry Innocent, is guilty of the crimes charged?
2. Is there anything about my client's status as a Chicago police officer that would unfairly bias or prejudice your own opinion concerning the Defendant's guilt or innocence based on his occupational status?
3. Have you ever been involved in any law enforcement work whatsoever?
4. Do you have any family members or close friends who are currently or who have been previously involved in law enforcement?
5. Have you had any adverse encounters with African American males under any circumstances whatsoever? If so, describe those experiences.
6. Have you had any adverse encounters with any African American law enforcement personnel on any level whatsoever? If so, describe those experiences.

Source: William H. Hooks, *Trial Issues*, Defending Illinois Criminal Cases (IICLE, 2003, Supp. 2007) at 11S-65.

Figure 11.1 Proposed *Voir Dire* Questions from the Defense

APPLICATION EXERCISES

1. List five biographical resources or community directories available at your school's library.
2. Conduct an Internet search of your instructor for this course and then prepare a list of all facts about the instructor's professional life, along with the web address for the source for each fact.
3. Conduct an Internet search of the mayor of your community, list four attitudes and beliefs of the mayor and cite the web addresses for this information.
4. Prepare six *voir dire* questions concerning alcoholic beverages that would be appropriate to use in *People v. Bud Cook* (*see* hypothetical case on page xxxvii).
5. Prepare six *voir dire* questions concerning "experiencing financial troubles" to use in *United States v. William Edwards* (*see* hypothetical case on page xxxviii).
6. Prepare six *voir dire* questions concerning Clay Marshall's participation in marital counseling, history of consensual relationships with women outside his marriage, and his reputation for making sexual innuendos to use in *People v. Clay Marshall* (*see* hypothetical case on pages xxxviii-xxxix).

B. Preparation of Exhibits

To be entered into evidence at a trial, an item, or **exhibit**, must be properly labeled and marked by the side that presents it. For instance, the knife used as a weapon in an aggravated battery case may be designated "People's Exhibit 1," whereas a ticket stub corroborating the defendant's alibi could be labeled "Defendant's Exhibit 3." The parties should determine what exhibits they plan to present before the case goes to trial, and paralegals are often charged with organizing and compiling the trial exhibits that their supervising attorneys plan to submit at trial.

Exhibit
A tangible item presented by the parties at trial to supplement the testimony of witnesses.

In some courts, the parties prepare a formal exhibit list which is attached to the final pre-trial memorandum. The format of this exhibit list is usually set forth in the local court rules governing pre-trial memoranda. Often, the rules require the parties to state whether there are foundation objections to the exhibits.

In many state courts, a less formal procedure is followed. In these jurisdictions, parties still prepare exhibit lists so they are organized for trial but are not required to share them with the opponent. Because the other side does not share its list, one of the functions a paralegal assisting trial counsel is to keep an ongoing list of the opposing side's trial exhibits. The paralegal also may track the court's ruling on admission into evidence of both side's exhibits.

Once the trial attorney has finalized the exhibit list, defense paralegals may be asked to compile and mark the exhibits. Marking is accomplished through a number of methods. The labeler may affix stickers to the exhibits. Documents may be marked by hand, stamped, or imprinted with computer-generated labels. Each item has a separate identifier. Examples of stickered and stamped/handwritten labeled trial exhibits are shown in Exhibits 11.1 and 11.2. In addition to preparing and properly labeling each potential exhibit, it is important to identify which witnesses will be used to properly authenticate the exhibits[2] and to prepare the witnesses to discuss these exhibits.

If an exhibit is comprised of multiple parts, it may be presented as a **group exhibit**. For instance, a package containing a number of bullet casings found at the scene of the crime could be labeled "Government's Group Exhibit 19." For multiple paged documentary exhibits, each page may have a label (e.g., "Exhibit 12, page 5 of 7 pages.")

Group exhibit
A trial exhibit comprised of multiple components.

If the court holds that a portion of a documentary exhibit is inadmissible, it may order that the exhibit is redacted. **Redaction** is the deletion of the objectionable portion of an exhibit. Although blackening out the objectionable work does eliminate objectionable material, it also draws attention to the objection. Therefore, you may have to white out the problematic portion and copy the document so that your exhibit looks clean and unaltered. There are software programs that permit the electronic redaction of documents. These programs make clean erasures.

Redaction
The deletion of the objectionable portion of an exhibit.

Sexual assault victims' statements are often redacted to protect their identity. Exhibit 11.3 shows the redacted statement of the resort employee who claimed that she was sexually assaulted by the National Basketball Association (NBA) star Kobe Bryant.

---

[2]For more on this topic, see Chapter 10 at pp. 357-358.

Exhibit 11.1: Transcript of Cockpit Voice Recorder

The exhibit below, presented in *United States v. Zacarias Moussaoui,* is marked by a sticker. Government Exhibit 01-455-A is the transcript of the last half hour of United Airlines Flight 93, as captured by the cockpit voice recorder on September 11, 2001.

GOVERNMENT EXHIBIT P200056T 01-455-A (ID)

United Airlines Flight #93 Cockpit Voice Recorder Transcript

Key:
Bolded text = English translation from Arabic

Time (EDT)	Transcript
09:31:57	*Ladies and Gentlemen: Here the captain, please sit down keep remaining seating. We have a bomb on board. So sit.*
09:32:09	*Er, uh . . . Calling Cleveland Center . . . You're unreadable. Say again slowly.*
09:32:10	*Don't move. Shut up.*
09:32:13	*Come on, come.*
09:32:16	*Shut up.*
09:32:17	*Don't move.*
09:32:18	*Stop.*
09:32:34	*Sit, sit, sit down.*
09:32:39	*Sit down.*
09:32:41	Unintelligible . . . **the brother.**
09:32:54	*Stop.*
09:33:09	*No more. Sit down.*
09:33:10	**That's it, that's it, that's it,** *down, down.*
09:33:14	*Shut up.*
09:33:20	Unintelligible.
09:33:20	*We just, we didn't get it clear . . . Is that United Ninety Three calling?*
09:33:30	**Jassim.**
09:33:34	**In the name of Allah, the Most Merciful, the Most Compassionate.**
09:33:41	Unintelligible.
09:33:43	*Finish, no more. No more.*
09:33:49	*No. No, no, no, no.*
09:33:53	*No, no, no, no.*

1

Exhibit 11.2: Evidence Envelope and Bullet

This exhibit shows the marked evidence envelope and the mangled bullet that killed Malcolm X. The state presented the bullet as Exhibit 68 in the murder prosecution of the assailants. This exhibit is marked by an ink stamp and handwriting.

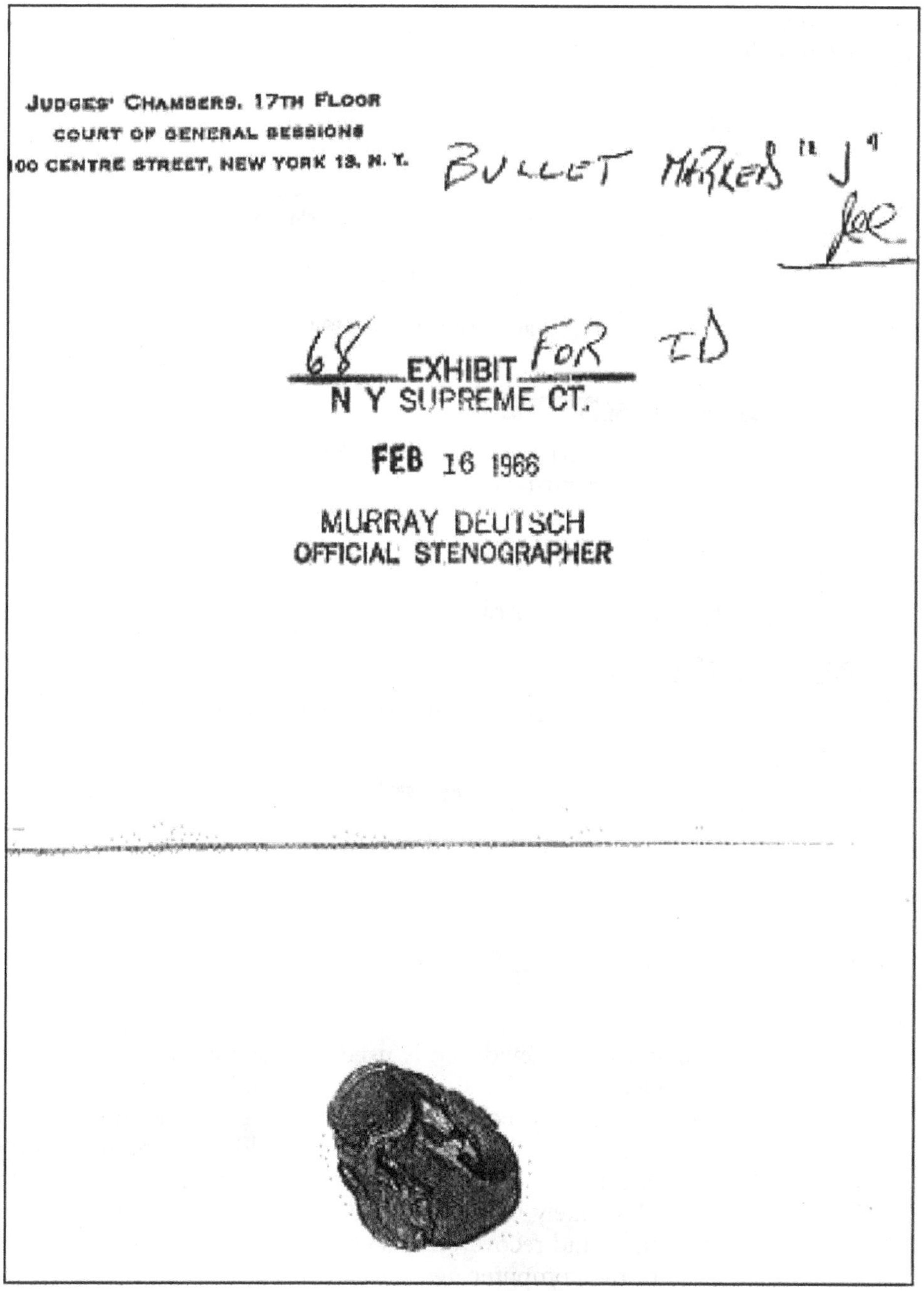

Exhibit 11.3: Redacted Transcript of Witness Statement

Sexual assault victims' statements are often redacted to protect their privacy. Below is the redacted statement of the resort employee who claimed she was sexually assaulted by NBA star Kobe Bryant.

FINAL COPY
Kobe Bryant S03-1169 Videotape transcribed

Detective Winters
Deputy Marsha Rich
Nicole Shanor – victim advocate

Det. W: This is Detective Winters of the Eagle County Sheriff's office in Eagle, Colorado. Present with me is Deputy Marsha Rich, the Eagle County Sheriff's Office.

N: Nicole Shanor of the advocates against assault and resource center of Eagle County.

Det W: Ok. Go ahead and state your name, spell your last name and give your date of birth.

[redacted]

Det W: 6/18/84. With the air conditioner going here its kinda loud so when I'm talking to you, we are video taping the interview, I'll need you to speak up, you have kinda of a soft voice.

[redacted] Ok.

Det W: [redacted] how do spell your first name?

[redacted]

Det W: Ok. Can you kinda of explain to me um, why we're here and what happened last night?

[redacted] Last night I was at work and I was sexually assaulted.

Det W: Ok. And when you mean, well where do you work at?

[redacted] Cordillera Lodge and Spa.

Demonstrative evidence is used to illustrate a key point. Demonstratives include videotapes, DVDs, photographs, blowups, charts, scale models, and diagrams. Juries appreciate visual aids. There is no reason for a witness to have difficulty describing the layout of a building without the aid of a diagram, photographs, DVD, or computer-assisted blueprint. By using these exhibits, the jury is less likely to be confused or misunderstand testimony. Exhibit 11.4 depicts contraband recovered at a crime scene.

Before the computer age, litigators used large art boards as the primary mode of demonstrative evidence. These boards typically displayed enlargements of photographs or other trial exhibits, timelines, and brief commentaries.

Exhibit 11.4: Photograph of Contraband

During a traffic stop, Louisiana State Police recovered baggies of cannabis and a bag of mushrooms during a search of singer Willie Nelson's tour bus. An officer photographed the drugs on the hood of a police cruiser. This photo could be used by the government in the prosecution of an illegal possession charge.

Today, more and more demonstrative exhibits are presented in electronic format, although printed demonstratives, hard-copy charts, and models are still commonly used. Ordinarily, enlargements are outsourced to specialty shops. However, a paralegal can prepare a text-based demonstrative by pasting passages printed in extremely large typeface onto art boards.

C. Preparation for Evidentiary Disputes

Exhibits can be used in a trial only if the judge trying the case enters them into evidence. Therefore, attorneys must be prepared to defend their admissibility. Conversely, lawyers wishing to keep exhibits from being admitted have to be ready to attack the admissibility of evidence that the other side plans to present at trial. Indeed, the outcome of a case is often determined by the evidentiary rulings of the judge. Two commonly disputed types of evidence are items seized during a warrantless search and references to the defendant's prior bad acts and poor character. Two commonly disputed types of evidence are items seized during a warrantless search and references to the defendant's prior bad acts and character. Some evidentiary issues are decided in pre-trial hearings, but others may not be settled until the trial is actually under way. Therefore, good litigators try to anticipate these issues in advance of trial and draft motions *in limine* or pocket briefs to address them.

1. MOTIONS TO SUPPRESS EVIDENCE AND MOTIONS *IN LIMINE*

Back in Chapter 7, we discussed the exclusionary rule and how motions to suppress illegally seized evidence are used to prevent evidence seized in illegal searches from being admitted in criminal prosecutions. Typically, judges set a cutoff date for the filing of motions to suppress before setting the case for trial.

Unlike motions to suppress, which ask for the exclusion of evidence that was illegally collected, motions *in limine* typically seek to exclude lawfully gathered evidence that violates the rules of admissibility. Motions in *limine* seek not only to prohibit the admission of specified evidence, but also to prohibit any verbal references to the information in question in the presence of the jury. Even though motions *in limine* are usually used to bar evidence, they also can be used to obtain a formal pre-trial ruling from the court that certain evidence will be admissible.

For example, the defendant might ask the court to exclude certain inflammatory allegations that are not related to the charges against him, evidence of a prior conviction that occurred a long time ago, or hearsay statements contained in a police report. In reaching a decision on the motion, the judge must determine if the material in question is admissible under the rules of evidence. If the judge decides that it is inadmissible, the motion is granted.

The motion is made and acted upon either before the trial or during a recess when the jury is not present, because it is designed to head off the possibility of the jury learning about the challenged material. It is based on the well-founded assumption that once jurors are exposed to the prejudicial information, they will be influenced by it even when the judge instructs them not to be. A violation of an order not to mention prejudicial material can result in the court declaring a mistrial, finding the attorney who violated it in contempt, or both.

There are numerous approaches to drafting these motions *in limine*. Some attorneys draft one comprehensive motion addressing all potentially objectionable matters. (*See* Exhibit 11.5.) Other litigators prepare individual motions for each objectionable matter. Sometimes motions *in limine* merely ask the court to exclude the evidence without giving the basis for the exclusion. (*See* Exhibit 11.6.) These motions are supported by memoranda of law which cite law and analysis in support of the motion. (*See* Exhibit 11.7.) If you are asked to draft a motion *in limine*, find out the preference of your supervising attorney. Your supervisor may also be able to refer you to the appropriate form book.

Exhibit 11.5: Motion *in Limine* in State Reckless Homicide Prosecution

IN THE CIRCUIT COURT OF THE 11th JUDICIAL CIRCUIT
McLEAN COUNTY, ILLINOIS

PEOPLE OF THE	)	
STATE OF ILLINOIS	)	
v.	)	Case No. 20 CF XXXX
BUD COOK,	)	
Defendant.	)	

MOTION IN LIMINE

Now comes Defendant, BUD COOK, by CHARLES HOVEY, his attorney, and prior to the selection of the jury in this case, respectfully moves this court *in limine* to enter an order directing the McLean County State's Attorney, her assistants, and any witnesses called by the prosecution to refrain from making any direct or indirect mention, whatsoever, at the trial, before the jury or potential jurors, of the matters hereinafter set forth without first obtaining the express permission from this court, outside the presence and hearing of the jury:

1. Numerous photographs of the alleged victim.
   a. The Defendant does not dispute the cause of death or the identity of the victim.
   b. It is error to admit gruesome photographs of a corpse when it is not relevant to any fact in issue and has no real purpose other than to horrify the jurors and arouse their emotions against the Defendant. *People v. Coleman*, 116 Ill. App. 3d 28, 451 N.E.2d 973, 978 (3d Dist. 1983).
2. Any statement that either the Defendant's attorney advised him not to make a statement or that the Defendant himself exercised his right to remain silent.
   a. The 5th Amendment to the U.S. Constitution grants the right to remain silent.
   b. The right of the accused to remain silent is violated when a police officer is permitted to testify that, after advising the accused of his rights, the accused stated that he did not want to speak to the officer any further. *People v. Hughes,* 11 Ill. App. 3d 224, 296 N.E.2d 643, 649 (2d Dist. 1973).
3. Statements or opinions made by the State's accident reconstruction expert that the Defendant's alleged intoxication was a cause of the alleged victim's death.
   a. Expert accident reconstruction testimony should be permitted where it is needed to rely on knowledge and application of principles of physics, engineering, and other sciences beyond the ken of the average juror. *People v. Rushtin,* 254 Ill. App. 3d 156, 626 N.E.2d 1378, 1385 (2d Dist. 1993).
   b. Expert opinions on matters of common knowledge are not admissible unless the subject is difficult to comprehend or explain. *Thacker v. UNR Industries, Inc.,* 151 Ill. 2d 343, 603 N.E.2d 449, 460 (1992).

c. Opinion testimony by the State's accident reconstruction expert in a reckless homicide case, that alcohol consumption by the Defendant was a contributing cause of a fatal accident, is inadmissible. *People v. Reding,* 191 Il. App. 3d 424, 547 N.E.2d 1310, 1320-21 (2d Dist. 1989).

4. Any statement directly or indirectly suggesting that the Defendant's alleged intoxication alone establishes recklessness. *People v. Pomkala,* 203 Ill. 2d 198, 784 N.E.2d 784, 787 (2003).

5. The Defendant's convictions for driving while suspended and other minor traffic offenses.

a. The only purpose for which a prior criminal conviction can be used is to attack the credibility of the witness. *People v. Williams,* 72 Ill. App. 2d 96, 218 N.E.2d 771, 774 (1st Dist.1996).

b. Convictions are not admissible to impeach a defendant unless the crime is punishable by death or more than one year imprisonment or under a law involving dishonesty or false statement. *People v. Montgomery,* 47 Ill. 2d 510, 268 N.E.2d 695, 698 (1971).

WHEREFORE, Defendant BUD COOK, respectfully requests this court to enter an order directing the People of the State of Illinois, through its counsel, not to mention, refer to or interrogate concerning, or voluntarily answer or attempt to convey before the jury, at any time during these proceedings, in any manner, either directly or indirectly, the subject matters as stated above without first informing the court and obtaining permission of the court, outside the presence and hearing of the jury; and further, to instruct the People, through its counsel, not to make and reference or inference to the fact that this motion has been filed, argued or ruled upon by this court, and further, that each respective counsel be instructed to warn and caution each and every witness appearing in their phase of this litigation to strictly comply with this rule of the court.

Respectfully submitted,

BUD COOK, Defendant

By________________________

CHARLES HOVEY, his attorney

CHARLES HOVEY
Attorney for Defendant
1857 Bone Street
Normal, IL 61761
(309)-555-1857

Exhibit 11.6: Excerpts from a Motion *in Limine* in Federal Court

This is an excerpt of a motion in limine filed by the U.S. Attorney in an antitrust case. The motion sought exclusion of a number of items of evidence. The motion was supported by a separate memorandum of law, which appears in Exhibit 11.7.

UNITED STATES DISTRICT COURT
SOUTHERN DISTRICT OF TEXAS
HOUSTON DIVISION

UNITED STATES OF AMERICA,	)	
v.	)	Criminal No.: H-97-93
MARK ALBERT MALOOF,	)	15 U.S.C. § 1
Defendant.	)	18 U.S.C. § 371
		FILED 6/11/97

UNITED STATES' MOTION IN LIMINE

Pursuant to Fed. R. Crim. P. 12(b), and for the reasons set forth in the accompanying Memorandum, the United States hereby moves that the Court enter an Order:

Prohibiting the defendant from offering or commenting on the following evidence on the grounds that it is irrelevant to the charges against him and the fact-finding duties of the jury:

a. Evidence related to the punishment that may be provided by law for a violation of the Sherman Act (15 U.S.C. § 1); and conspiracy to commit wire fraud (18 U.S.C. § 371); and
b. Evidence of the potential direct or indirect effects of a conviction of the defendant.

* * *

Respectfully submitted,

____

MARK R. ROSMAN
Attorney-in-Charge
Florida State Bar No. 0964387
U.S. Department of Justice
Antitrust Division
1601 Elm Street, Suite 4950
Dallas, Texas 75201-4717
(214) 880-9401

Exhibit 11.7: Excerpts from a Memorandum in Support of a Motion *in Limine*

UNITED STATES DISTRICT COURT
SOUTHERN DISTRICT OF TEXAS
HOUSTON DIVISION

UNITED STATES OF AMERICA,	)	
v.	)	
	)	Criminal No.: H-97-93
MARK ALBERT MALOOF,	)	
Defendant.	)	15 U.S.C. § 1
	)	18 U.S.C. § 371
	)	
	)	

MEMORANDUM IN SUPPORT OF UNITED STATES' MOTION IN LIMINE

Pursuant to Rule 12(b) of the Federal Rules of Criminal Procedure, the United States has filed a Motion *in limine* with the Court that addresses certain matters that are capable of resolution prior to trial. This Memorandum sets forth the reasons for the relief sought and the supporting legal authority.

I

INADMISSIBILITY OF EVIDENCE REGARDING PUNISHMENT OR COLLATERAL CONSEQUENCES OF CONVICTION

In a federal criminal prosecution, the jury's sole function is to determine guilt or innocence. Evidence regarding punishment or the effects of conviction is thus irrelevant and inadmissible before the jury. The punishment provided by law upon conviction of a criminal violation is a matter exclusively in the province of the Court and should never be considered by the jury in any manner in arriving at their verdict as to guilt or innocence. *See, e.g., Beavers v. Lockhart*, 755 F.2d 657, 662 (8th Cir. 1985) ("Historically, the duty of imposing sentence has been vested in trial judges. . . .") (citing *United States v. Hartford*, 489 F.2d 652, 654 (5th Cir. 1974)); *United States v. Brown*, 744 F.2d 905, 909 (2d Cir.), *cert. denied*, 469 U.S. 1089 (1984) ("[T]he fact finding necessary for sentencing is the responsibility of the sentencing judge. . . ."); *Turnbough v. Wyrick*, 551 F.2d 202, 203 (8th Cir.), *cert. denied*, 431 U.S. 941 (1977) (defendant has no constitutional right to have punishment assessed by a jury). *See also* Pattern Jury Instr., Crim., 5th Cir., Instruction No. 1.21 (1990).

It is recognized that, when the pertinent statute does not vest responsibility for sentencing in the jury, the jury's duty is to find facts without consideration of the potential punishment:

The authorities are unequivocal in holding that presenting information to the jury about possible sentencing is prejudicial. Breach of this standard has often been grounds for reversal. A jury is obligated to "reach its verdict without regard to what sentence might be imposed." [Citations omitted.] Absent a statutory requirement that the jury participate in the sentencing decision, nothing is left "for jury determination beyond the guilt or innocence of an accused." *United States v. Greer,* 620 F.2d 1383, 1385 (10th Cir. 1980). *Accord United States v. McCracken,* 488 F.2d 406, 423 (5th Cir. 1974); *United States v. Davidson,* 367 F.2d 60, 63 (6th Cir. 1966); *Lyles v. United States,* 254 F.2d 725, 728 (D.C. Cir. 1957), *cert. denied,* 356 U.S. 961 (1958).

Evidence that relates to the issue of punishment upon conviction of a criminal offense has no bearing on the only question the jury in this case will be called upon to decide—that of the guilt or innocence of the defendant. As the Fifth Circuit held in *McCracken,* "[e]xcept where a special statutory provision mandates a jury role in assessment or determination of penalty, the punishment provided by law for offenses charged is a matter exclusively for the court and should not be considered by the jury in arriving at a verdict as to guilt or innocence." 488 F.2d at 423. Evidence dealing with possible fines or other collateral consequences of conviction is not probative of the issue of guilt or innocence. Since such evidence would not tend to prove or disprove any fact of consequence to the jury's determination of guilt or innocence, such evidence is not "relevant," as that term is defined by Fed. R. Evid. 401. Such evidence should, therefore, be excluded under Fed. R. Evid. 402, which specifically provides that evidence which is not relevant is inadmissible.

Punishment evidence is inadmissible not only during the parties' examination of witnesses, but also in closing argument. If the issue of punishment is raised during closing argument, the trial court should instruct the jury not to consider the matter of punishment in arriving at their verdict. *Gretter v. United States,* 422 F.2d 315, 319 (10th Cir. 1970). It is error to tell the jury the probable or potential consequences resulting from a particular verdict. *United States v. McCracken,* 488 F.2d at 424-25. The disposition of the defendant is "not a matter for the jury's concern." *Pope v. United States,* 372 F.2d 710, 731 (8th Cir. 1967), *cert. denied,* 401 U.S. 949 (1971).

Therefore, for the reasons discussed above, the United States respectfully requests that this Court enter an order that any evidence or argument relating to possible punishment upon, or collateral consequences of, conviction be excluded from the trial of this case.

* * *

The first part of the motion is the caption, including the title, "Motion *in Limine*." Next is an introductory paragraph that identifies the party bringing the motion and the authority under which it is brought, as well as that a motion *in limine* is being presented. This is followed by the body of the motion. In many courts, the body is presented in a series of short, numbered paragraphs. Approaches to drafting the body vary from court to court and from lawyer to lawyer. One approach for drafting the body of a motion *in limine* seeking to exclude evidence follows:

- Identify the potentially prejudicial fact expected to be presented by the opponent.
- State the rule of evidence that bars the prejudicial fact. If the legal principle is embodied in a statute or court rule, quote the relevant rule. If the principle is part of the common law, cite caselaw, along with the applicable black letter rule.
- Present your analysis by applying the rule of evidence to the facts in the case at bar.
- If a court of review has decided a closely analogous case, then present the facts of the analogous case and compare them to the facts of the case at hand.
- Conclude that under the rule of evidence, the prejudicial fact is inadmissible.

The prayer for relief, attorney's signature, and address block follow the body of the motion.

The following excepts from *United States v. Harper* illustrate the manner in which judges go about reaching decisions as to whether they will grant motions *in limine*.

United States v. Harper
United States District Court, for the Eastern District of Wisconsin
2010 WL 1507869

Decision and Order

LYNN ADELMAN, District Judge.

The government charged defendant Adrian Harper with possessing a firearm as a felon, contrary to 18 U.S.C. §922(g)(1), and the case is currently scheduled for trial. Before me is the government's motion in limine seeking a ruling on the admissibility of certain evidence. First, the government seeks permission to introduce the hearsay statement of an unidentified bystander-witness. Second, if defendant testifies, the government seeks permission to impeach him with his prior felony convictions. Defendant opposes both requests.

I. Bystander Statement

A. Background

According to the government, on September 17, 2008, at about 1:50 a.m., two Milwaukee police officers conducting surveillance outside a nightclub heard multiple gunshots. One of the officers saw smoke emanating from the window of a truck about fifteen feet away. The truck took off at a high rate of speed, and as the officers made a u-turn to follow, a woman yelled at the officers, "There they go right there; that's the one," as she pointed to the truck. The woman was walking in the middle of the street, right behind where the truck was stopped when the shots were fired.

The government seeks admission of the woman's statement as either a present sense impression, Fed.R.Evid. 803(1), or an excited utterance, Fed.R.Evid. 803(2). Defendant responds that the statement is not relevant, qualifies as neither a present sense impression nor an excited utterance, and that its admission would violate his confrontation rights.

B. Analysis

1. *Relevance*

Defendant argues that the bystander's statement is not relevant because the purpose of the trial is not to determine whether the police had grounds to stop the truck. He indicates that he will stipulate that a firearm was found in the truck; the only issue for trial is whether he possessed that gun; and the bystander's statement has no tendency to make the existence of that disputed fact more or less probable. See Fed.R.Evid. 401 ("'Relevant evidence' means evidence having any tendency to make the existence of any fact that is of consequence to the determination of the action more probable or less probable than it would be without the evidence.").

The government indicates that its theory in this case is that defendant possessed the gun when he fired shots out the window of the truck. The government does not intend to prove its case simply by establishing that the gun was in the truck. The bystander's statement helps to prove, not that there was a firearm in the truck, but that someone (defendant or the driver) fired shots from the truck. This, in turn, helps to establish that defendant actually possessed the firearm.

To be relevant, evidence need not conclusively decide the ultimate issue in a case, nor make the proposition appear more probable; it need only to some degree advance the inquiry. *Thompson v. City of Chicago,* 472 F.3d 444, 453 (7th Cir.2006). "This is not a difficult standard to meet." *United States v. Brisk,* 171 F.3d 514, 525 (7th Cir.1999). I find that the bystander's statement has a tendency to prove that defendant possessed the gun by firing it from the truck. *Cf. United States v. Canady,* 578 F.3d 665, 671 (7th Cir.2009) ("[I]f the parties contest whether Canady possessed the gun in the SUV, evidence that he was seen with (and may have used) the gun minutes beforehand increases the likelihood that he possessed the gun in the car.").

2. *Hearsay Exceptions*

A. Present Sense Impression

Federal Rule of Evidence 803(1) permits the introduction of a hearsay statement "describing or explaining an event or condition made while the declarant was perceiving the event or condition, or immediately thereafter." A statement may be admitted under this Rule if: (1) the statement describes an event or condition without calculated narration; (2) the speaker personally perceived the event or condition described; and (3) the statement was made while the speaker was perceiving the event or condition, or immediately thereafter. *United States v. Ruiz,* 249 F.3d 643, 646 (7th Cir.2001).

The bystander's statement may be admitted under this Rule. The proffered facts indicate that the woman, who was standing right behind the truck, made the statement immediately after she observed the shots being fired, and her brief statement contains no "calculated narration." Defendant argues that the statement does not describe "the event," i.e. the shots being fired, but rather pertained to what happened afterward. But the woman described her present perception of the shots by stating "that's the one," and her perception of the truck from which they came by stating "there they go right there" as she observed the vehicle driving away.

In any event, courts have not demanded the sort of strict contemporaneousness defendant would require. For example, in *United States v. Thomas,* 453 F.3d 838 (7th Cir.2006), the court admitted under Rule 803(1) a 911 call, in which the caller stated "[t]here's a dude that just got shot," and "the guy who shot him is still out there." Later in the call, the caller stated that "[t] here is somebody shot outside, somebody needs to be sent over here, and there's somebody runnin' around with a gun, somewhere." *Id.* at 844. In *United States v. Campbell,* 782 F.Supp. 1258 (N.D.Ill.1991), a 911 caller told a police dispatcher that a shooting just occurred in a drug store and described the general appearance and clothing of the alleged assailant. The court admitted the statement, even though it occurred after the shooting was complete. The court noted that "precise contemporaneity" often is impossible and that a slight time lapse between the event and the statement is allowable. *Id.* at 1260-61; *see also United States v. Mejia-Valez,* 855 F.Supp. 607, 613 (E.D.N.Y.1994) (admitting two 911 calls indicating that there had been a shooting and providing the location and a description of the alleged assailant).

B. EXCITED UTTERANCE

Federal Rule of Evidence 803(2) permits the introduction of a hearsay statement "relating to a startling event or condition made while the declarant was under the stress of excitement caused by the event or condition." A statement may be admitted under this Rule if: (1) a startling event occurred; (2) the declarant made the statement while under the stress of excitement caused by the startling event; and (3) the declarant's statement relates to the startling event. *United States v. Wesela,* 223 F.3d 656, 663 (7th Cir.2000).

The bystander's statement may also be admitted under this Rule. The shots fired from the truck on a public street qualify as a startling event. The government indicates that the officer will testify that the woman gestured excitably towards the truck, spoke in an almost frantic tone, and her facial expression was one of surprise and fear. Defendant again argues that the statement does not relate to the event (the shots) but rather to what occurred thereafter. His analysis is again too cramped. The woman's statement "that's the one" relates to the shooting, and her statements "there they go right there" relates to the truck from which the shots emanated.

It is also worth noting in this regard that the "excited utterance exception allows a broader scope of subject matter coverage than does the present sense impression exception." *United States v. Moore,* 791 F.2d 566, 572 (7th Cir.1986). Under Rule 803(2), if the subject matter of the statement would likely be evoked by the event, the statement may be admitted, even if it goes beyond a mere description of the event. *Id.* Courts have admitted similar statements under the excited utterance exception. *See, e.g., Thomas,* 453 F.3d at 844 (admitting as an excited utterance a 911 call indicating that someone had been shot and that the shooter was outside running around with a gun); *Reid v. Fischer,* No. 00-CV-3054, 2003 WL 23185754, at *13 (E.D.N.Y. Oct. 24, 2003 (Weinstein, J.) (holding that the trial court properly admitted as an excited utterance a witness statement implicating the defendant in a shooting made immediately after the shooting and virtually while the witness was fleeing the scene of the shooting); *Mejia-Valez,* 855 F.Supp. at 614 (admitting as excited utterances 911 calls reporting shooting and describing assailant); *Campbell,* 782 F.Supp. at 1262 (admitting under the excited utterance exception a tape recording of a police officer's statements to the dispatcher during his attempt to apprehend shooting suspect); *see also United States v. Harper,* No. 05-CR-6068L, 2009 WL 140125, at *3 (W.D.N.Y. Jan.20, 2009) (collecting cases).

3. *Confrontation Clause*

Having concluded, based on the government's proffer, that the bystander's statement is relevant and admissible, I turn to the issue of whether admission of the statement would nevertheless violate defendant's rights under the Sixth Amendment's Confrontation Clause. The Clause forbids admission of out-of-court, testimonial statements, unless the declarant is unavailable and the defendant had a prior opportunity for cross-examination. *Crawford v. Washington,* 541 U.S. 36, 53-54, 124 S. Ct. 1354, 158 L.Ed.2d 177 (2004). The crucial issue here is whether the bystander's statement is "testimonial."

In *Davis v. Washington,* 547 U.S. 813, 822, 126 S. Ct. 2266, 165 L.Ed.2d 224 (2006), the Court explained that:

> Statements are non-testimonial when made in the course of police interrogation under circumstances objectively indicating that the primary purpose of the interrogation is to enable police assistance to meet an ongoing emergency. They are testimonial when the circumstances objectively indicate that there is no such ongoing emergency, and that the primary purpose of the interrogation is to establish or prove past events potentially relevant to later criminal prosecution.

Under this test, the bystander's statement is non-testimonial. She made the statement spontaneously, rather than in response to police questioning, and it appears that her purpose in making the statement was to assist the officers responding to the ongoing emergency presented by a fleeing suspect who just fired shots on a crowded public street.

Defendant contends that the emergency situation presented by the shots being fired had ended when the bystander identified the truck containing the shooter; he argues that her statement instead proved a past event relevant to a later criminal prosecution. I disagree. At the time the bystander spoke, the shooter was still on the scene; it was certainly possible that he might fire again; and the truck then started to flee at a high rate of speed, creating further danger. Further, the statement—"there they go right there"—pertained to events as they were happening. *See Davis,* 547 U.S. at 827 (finding non-testimonial statements to a 911 operator describing events as they were actually happening, rather than describing past events).

Defendant cites no case finding similar statements testimonial, and I have found none.... Therefore, I will grant the government's motion pertaining to the bystander statement.

II. Defendant's Prior Convictions

Under Fed.R.Evid. 609(a)(1), a defendant may be impeached by evidence of his prior felony convictions "if the court determines that the probative value of admitting this evidence outweighs its prejudicial effect to the accused." Rule 609(b) generally imposes a ten-year time limit on such convictions, measured from the date of the conviction or of the release of the defendant from the confinement imposed for that conviction, whichever is later, to the start of the trial. *See United States v. Watler,* 461 F.3d 1005, 1008-09 (8th Cir.2006) (collecting cases).

In the present case, the parties stipulate that defendant has four prior felony convictions: (1) battery by a prisoner on August 23, 1995, for which he was sentenced to five years in prison and released on May 11, 1999; (2) manufacture/delivery of cocaine on August 30, 2001; (3) vehicle operator flee/elude police officer on September 25, 2006; and (4) possession of THC-second offense on November 23, 2006. If defendant testifies, the government indicates that it wishes to attack his credibility with evidence of these convictions. I first note that, according to the parties' stipulation, defendant was released from the battery sentence more than ten years prior to the commencement of this trial. Thus, absent the presentation of specific facts and circumstances demonstrating that the probative value of this conviction "substantially outweighs its prejudicial effect," Fed.R.Evid. 609(b); *see United States v. Redditt,* 381 F.3d 597, 601 (7th Cir.2004) (explaining that the purpose of Rule 609(b) is to ensure that convictions over ten years old will be admitted very rarely and only in exceptional circumstances), this conviction will not be admitted. However, I will permit the government to impeach defendant with evidence of the other three felony convictions.

The Seventh Circuit has established a five-part test to guide the district court in the exercise of its discretion in determining whether the probative value of a conviction outweighs its prejudicial effect: (1) the impeachment value of the prior crime; (2) the point in time of the conviction and the defendant's subsequent history; (3) the similarity between the past crime and the charged crime; (4) the importance of the defendant's testimony; and (5) the centrality of the credibility issue. *United States v. Montgomery,* 390 F.3d 1013, 1015 (7th Cir.2004) (citing *United States v. Mahone,* 537 F.2d 922 (7th Cir.1976)). Although none of defendant's prior convictions go directly to his truthfulness (e.g., they do not involve fraud or false statements), the remaining *Mahone* factors favor admission.

The convictions are all fairly recent in time, occurring in 2001 and 2006. None are similar to the charged crime; thus, admission of defendant's prior convictions for drug possession and delivery, and fleeing an officer will not suggest to the jury that defendant has a propensity to possess firearms. Further, it appears that defendant's credibility will be a significant issue in this case. Presumably, he will testify that he never possessed the firearm found in the truck, which is the ultimate issue for the jury to decide. Thus, the value of impeachment evidence is increased. Finally, I note that the prejudice to defendant is decreased by the nature of the charge; because he is charged with being a felon-in-possession of a firearm, the jury will learn that he is a felon whether or not the government impeaches him with his prior convictions. *See Montgomery,* 390 F.3d at 1015. It is true that this case involves three prior convictions, which may increase the possibility of prejudice. However, given the importance of the credibility issue, the probative value outweighs the prejudicial effect. I will, in order to reduce the possibility of prejudice, give an appropriate limiting instruction to the jury. *See id.* at 1015-16 (affirming use of six prior convictions to impeach the defendant in a felon-in-possession case where credibility was important and the district court gave a limiting instruction); *United States v. Nururdin,* 8 F.3d 1187, 1192 (7th Cir.1993) (admitting four prior convictions for impeachment purposes in a felon-in-possession case given the importance of the defendant's testimony and the centrality of the credibility issue, where the court gave a limiting jury instruction); *see also United States v. Smith,* 131 F.3d 685, 687 (7th Cir.1997) (admitting evidence of prior convictions for robbery, armed robbery, kidnapping and attempted sexual assault in a bank robbery case).

Defendant argues that his prior convictions did not involve acts of dishonesty and thus say little about his veracity. The nature of the prior conviction is just one factor for the court to consider; Rule 609(a)(1) allows the introduction of any prior felony conviction so long as the probative value outweighs the prejudicial effect; it is not limited to crimes involving dishonesty or deceit. *See United States v. Wolf,* 561 F.2d 1376, 1381 (10th Cir.1977). Defendant further argues that admission of his 2006 fleeing conviction would be prejudicial because it is similar to the facts of this case. But defendant is charged here with possessing a firearm, not fleeing from the police. And, based on the proffered facts, the government will not argue that defendant operated the truck and fled from the police; rather, he was the passenger. Thus, I see no significant similarity between that case and this one. Finally, defendant argues that admitting his 2006 marijuana conviction would be prejudicial because one of the AUSA's assigned to this case sentenced him in that case while serving as a state court trial judge. The identity of the sentencing judge will not be presented to the jury, so there is no danger that the jury will come to believe that this prosecution carries a judicial imprimatur. See *United States v. Smith,* 454 F.3d 707, 716 (7th Cir.2006) (indicating that the government should limit its inquiry to the name, the date and the disposition of the prior felony).

III. Conclusion

THEREFORE, IT IS ORDERED that the government's motion in limine is granted.

Case Discussion Questions

1. What was the government attempting to accomplish through its motion *in limine*?
2. What hearsay statement made by a bystander did the prosecutor seek to admit into evidence?
3. Identify and explain the exceptions to the hearsay rule the court discussed as its bases for the admission of the bystander's statement.
4. Which provision of the U.S. Constitution gives a defendant the right to confront his or her accusers?
5. The district judge held that the bystander's statement was "non-testimonial," and therefore admissible under the Confrontation Clause. What is meant by the term *non-testimonial statement*?
6. On what basis did the court rule that some of the defendant's convictions may be presented, but one was inadmissible?
7. Which of the Federal Rules of Evidence did the court rely on in its decision and order?

Application Exercises

7. After reviewing the information that you have been given on the Clay Marshall Hypothetical Case (*see* hypothetical case on pages xxxviii-xxxix), take note of the following additional information: one of the complaining witnesses, has engaged in consensual sexual relations with many partners, some of whom were "one-night stands." Using caselaw from the state in which your school is located, draft a motion *in limine* on behalf of the local prosecutor seeking to bar the defense from mentioning this witness's past sexual conduct. Assume that the case was filed in the state court jurisdiction in which your school is located as the fiftieth case filed this year.
8. After referring to Application Exercise 5 and Exhibit 10.1 in Chapter 10 (pages 347-348), prepare a motion *in limine* on behalf of Clay Marshall, in which you seek to exclude the 911 tape of the conversation that Madison Pickering had with the 911 dispatcher. Assume that your instructor is the defense attorney. Use your instructor's professional address. Also, assume that the case was filed in the state court jurisdiction in which your school is located as the 50th case filed this year.
9. Prepare a motion *in limine* on behalf of the defense in Hypothetical Case 2, *United States v. Brandon Turner,* to exclude evidence of the defendant's nine-year-old felony conviction for aggravated driving under the influence of alcohol. The case is filed in the U.S. District Court in which your school is located and docketed as case number [CURRENT YEAR]-666. List your instructor as the attorney representing the defendant. Use your instructor's professional address.

2. POCKET BRIEFS

Pocket brief
A short memorandum of law used to advise the court on a discrete point of law.

Just as your side will attempt to prevent prejudicial evidence from being heard by the jury, the opposing side will try to keep facts harmful to its client from being admitted into evidence. In anticipation of the opponent's challenge, your litigation team can prepare a **pocket brief,** a short legal memorandum used to advise the court on a discrete point of law. Often, the opposing side will not prepare pocket briefs, so your litigation team's brief may be the only argument shown to the judge. It is, therefore, extremely important to use an objective tone in drafting this document. Although motions *in limine* are the preferred method of seeking exclusion of evidence, pocket briefs may also be used to support an argument against the admission of evidence. Pocket briefs may also be used to address procedural matters arising at trial.

Typically, a pocket brief addressing an evidentiary question begins with a caption, including a title headlining the application of the rule of evidence at issue. After an introductory paragraph, the body of the document should present pertinent facts, the rule of evidence, and the application of the rule to the facts. You can use a pocket brief to give support for the admission of evidence favoring your side or in opposition to unfavorable evidence. A possible approach for the body of a pocket brief seeking to admit evidence is set forth as follows:

- Identify the facts that your side wants admitted into evidence.
- State the applicable rule of evidence. If the legal principle is embodied in a statute or court rule, quote the relevant rule. If the principle is part of the common law, cite caselaw, along with the applicable black letter rule.
- Present your analysis by applying the rule of evidence to the facts in the case at bar.
- If a court of review has decided a closely analogous case, then present and compare the facts of that case to the facts of the case at hand.
- Conclude that under the rule of evidence, the facts are admissible.

The prayer for relief, attorney's signature, and address block follow the body of the motion.

APPLICATION EXERCISE

10. Prepare a pocket brief on behalf of the U.S. Attorney for Hypothetical Case 4, *United States v. Brandon Turner,* on the admissibility of evidence as to witness Police Officer Steve Milner's reputation in the community of telling lies. The case is filed in the U.S. District Court in which your school is located and docketed as case number [CURRENT YEAR]-987. List the U.S. Attorney for the federal district as the person subpoenaing the witness on behalf of the government.

D. Witness Preparation

Witnesses play a central role in most trials. Their testimony is typically needed to establish the facts that are essential to the decisions made by a judge and/or jury. In addition to their being the source of testimonial evidence, they are used to lay the foundation for the admission of physical, demonstrative, and documentary evidence. It is, therefore, important to establish what type of information each witness will be testifying about and preparing questions that will elicit the testimony that your side needs to establish to obtain the verdict it wants. This applies not only to the witnesses that your side will be calling to the stand, but also to those that the other side is likely to be using.

1. PREPARING YOUR LAY WITNESSES

As a result of having reviewed written summaries and transcripts of interviews and discovery documents, the attorneys handling the case will decide who they want to testify at the trial. That judgment will be made on the basis of what they can testify to and the type of impression that they think the witness will make on the judge or jury.

As you should recall from Chapter 10, lay witnesses are used to present information about what they personally did or personally observed others doing, while expert witnesses are allowed to provide background information and express opinions about such things as matching bullets found at the scene of a crime with a gun found in the defendant's possession, or whether a child's injuries were the result of a typical fall or the result of physical abuse of a parent or caregiver.

Lay witnesses are typically very nervous and often reluctant to give testimony at a trial. Even though attorneys have the power to require them to appear, they typically try to get witnesses to testify voluntarily. Attorneys will attempt to make them feel more at ease and will review with them the types of questions that will asked on direct examination and cross-examination. This preparation is designed to put the witness at ease and to help make the testimony as effective as possible. Many times, the paralegal may participate in witness preparation.

To make the witnesses feel more comfortable, they should be educated about the trial proceeding. Explain where their testimony fits into the trial schedule and about the uncertainty of maintaining a rigid timetable. Let them know how direct examination, cross-examination, and redirect examination work and that they must stop talking when an **objection** is made and wait until the judge rules before continuing with their answer. Define the terms **sustained** and **overruled**. Discuss the setup of the courtroom, the exclusion of witnesses from the courtroom when they are not testifying, and the importance of following the directions of the judge. If possible, witnesses should visit the courtroom where the trial will take place so they can become comfortable with the courtroom environment.

You should also preview the types of questions they will be asked on direct examination and cross-examination. If the witnesses will be used to discuss a

Objection
A formal protest raised in court, asking the judge to disallow an opposing attorney's question or a witness's answer on the grounds that it violates the rules of evidence or procedure.

Sustained objection
The judge's favorable ruling on an evidentiary objection.

Overruled objection
The judge's unfavorable ruling on an evidentiary objection.

particular exhibit, make sure that they understand the nature of the questions they will be asked about it.

Also, emphasize the importance of telling the truth. While it is unethical to put words into the witness's mouth, it is acceptable to refresh the witness's recollection. This is usually accomplished by showing witnesses their police statements. If they gave prior testimony, transcripts of what was said are also excellent ways to help them remember what took place.

Witnesses should be forewarned that the opposing side may ask whether they have discussed their testimony with anyone. Let them know that there is nothing wrong with talking to the lawyer's staff about their testimony and that they should acknowledge talking to you if they are asked about discussing their testimony with anyone.

Moreover, you should teach them how to respond to questions. Emphasize that they should not volunteer information. Their role is to answer the questions presented, not to offer information that was not elicited. They should be especially careful not to speculate or offer testimony not within their personal knowledge. Explain that the witness will be answering questions posed by both sides and to listen carefully to the whole question, regardless of which lawyer is asking the question. Instruct the witness to ask for the question to be rephrased if he or she truly does not understand it. Remind witnesses that this is not a test to see how smooth they are, but rather an opportunity to make an accurate record of the testimony. Finally, advise the witness to speak to the jury when testifying.

It is also important to discuss with witnesses how they should act during cross-examination. Sometimes witnesses who are identified with one side of a case tend to respond in a confrontational or sarcastic manner on cross-examination. Instruct witnesses to treat the cross-examiner in the same manner that they treat the favorable attorney on direct examination and not to get angry or act discourteously toward the opposing attorney. Alert witnesses that if they are impeached by use of their prior statements, they must be able to explain the inconsistency. A string of "I don't remember" answers on cross-examination diminishes the witness's credibility. Furthermore, tell witnesses not to look at your attorney during cross-examination, as it gives the impression that answers are being fed to them.

Finally, good witness preparation covers not only what they say and how they say it, but their appearance and dress as well. One size does not fit all, and the clothes worn should fit the personality and occupation of the witness. Think of it in the way that a director would dress an actor for a performance. The witness should look the part because a landscaper dressed like an attorney will be less credible than one dressed like the public image of a landscaper. If the witness doesn't feel comfortable with the outfit, he or she will appear uneasy to the jury.

While local customs vary, there are a still a few universal guidelines. The witness should wear clean clothes, not ones they have been wearing all day on the job. A witness, such as a police officer or nurse, may wear a uniform if it is customary dress. A person who works with his hands all day, for example, probably would not be comfortable wearing a suit and tie. Emphasize the need for the witness to act appropriately at the courthouse, to respond to questions respectfully, and not to chew gum.

At the close of the meeting, the witness should be given a trial subpoena and the required fees. The trial attorney will probably conduct a dress rehearsal of the direct examination of the witness. If you have done your job in witness preparation, this should be smooth.

2. PREPARING THE DEFENDANT

Although the Fifth Amendment privilege against self-incrimination protects defendants from being forced to testify, there are several potentially negative consequences that can accompany the use of that right. Despite a judicial admonition to the contrary, many jurors expect defendants to assert their innocence and are more inclined to convict them if they don't. However, if defendants do choose to take the stand, they become subject to cross-examination and to having past criminal activities brought out. Although defense attorneys must inform and should advise their clients with respect to their testifying, it is ultimately up to the defendant to make this critical decision.

If the defendant chooses to testify the defense team has to go through the same type of preparation that is given to other witnesses it will call. But, regardless of whether the defendant testifies, the client will sit at the defense table where the judge and the jury will be observing their demeanor in the courtroom. The defendant must be instructed to maintain self-control and show respect for the prosecutor and the judge.

In addition, the defense team may take a greater role in directing the client's courtroom appearance. Excessive jewelry or makeup should be avoided. Both women and men should avoid overtly sexually suggestive apparel. In conservative communities, clients should cover their tattoos. Likewise in these venues, other than ear piercings, body piercings should not be on display. If the defendant presents a distracting characteristic of dress or hairstyle, consider having this quality toned down without converting the witness into a phony.

An attorney representing Richard Rodriguez, a gang member who was allegedly attacked by a California police officer at the end of a televised, high-speed chase, had his client undergo a significant transformation for trial. Rodriguez's attorney instructed him to grow a moustache to cover the name of his street gang, which is inked on his upper lip, and to grow out his hair on his shaved head to hide the tattoos on his scalp. He also directed Rodriguez to wear a conservative suit at trial.[3] While an extreme makeover strategy can present the client in a better light, it can also backfire if jurors believe they are being deceived.

3. PREPARING YOUR EXPERT WITNESSES

Expert witnesses include a variety of professions, including medical doctors, forensic experts, and accident reconstruction experts. Most have testified in similar

[3]"Makeover Advised for Gang Member Kicked by El Monte Officer," *LA Times,* July 24, 2009, http://articles.latimes.com/2009/jul/24/local/me-elmonte24.

cases, and many have published articles in peer-reviewed professional journals. Since they will already be familiar with the facts and issues involved in the case, it is not necessary to go over the general orientation types of matters that are discussed with lay witnesses. You should educate them about the local courthouse customs and tell them about the experts lined up to testify for the other side.

Make sure that the expert has copies of all relevant documents, including their reports and statements containing facts on which their opinions are based. If they have given sworn statements, such as testimony in a prior hearing or in a deposition, you should provide them with a copy. Likewise, ensure that the expert has given you an up-to-date résumé or curriculum vitae (CV).

If the expert witness rehearses testimony with you, pay attention to the expert's manner and word choices. If the expert comes off as a know-it-all, the jury may not want to believe the testimony. In a non-judgmental tone, you should let the expert know that some of the jurors may not be high school graduates so the expert will be more effective by speaking to these jurors. If technical terms are used, the expert needs to explain them in a non-condescending manner.

Often, experts use demonstrative exhibits to explain their testimony. Make sure that your rehearsal includes the staging of this part of the testimony. An unrehearsed use of a demonstrative aid or item of physical evidence may lead to unanticipated disastrous results. For instance, in the O. J. Simpson murder trial, one of the prosecutors asked the defendant to put on a glove that was presumably worn by the murderer. When it became obvious that the glove was too small and did not fit Simpson, the prosecution lost tremendous credibility with the jury.

While expert witnesses are familiar with the subject matter of their expertise, they may not be familiar with the courtroom and trial procedure. Depending upon the extent to which they have testified in other cases, they may already be familiar with court proceedings and how to handle cross-examination, but if they aren't, it is important to give them the same type of orientation that is given to non-expert witnesses.

4. PREPARING FOR OPPOSING WITNESSES

In addition to preparing the witnesses that their own side plans to call, attorneys and paralegals must prepare to cross-examine the witnesses called by the other side. This is usually done by reading witness statements and police reports, conducting background checks, and interviewing their witnesses when possible.

Prosecutors have access to this information and routinely run criminal background checks. For the defense bar, there are a variety of online services that enable subscribers to conduct criminal background checks. If your employer does not have one of these subscriptions, you may investigate a witness by reviewing the criminal file index maintained by the clerk of the court. This information often is available on public access computer terminals. Cases in which a witness is a party may reveal criminal convictions and relationships of the witness with others. This is most cost-effective way to obtain background information.

In addition, you can interview witnesses. Law enforcement officers and agents typically perform this task for the government. Private investigators do this on behalf of the defense. Sometimes, however, paralegals may conduct these interviews for the defense team.

If you are given this assignment, identify yourself and your supervising attorney, along with the identity of the defendant. If the witness declines to talk to you, leave a business card so the witness can contact you later if there is a change of heart. Write down your favorable and unfavorable impressions of the witness. Even if a witness is against the defendant, that does not mean that the witness is an adversary. When you make your evaluation, try to place yourself in the witness's position to reenact the situation from the witness's point of view. This may assist you in objectively evaluating the testimony. Your report will be helpful to your supervising attorney in developing cross-examination.

5. PREPARING TRIAL SUBPOENAS

To ensure that a witness will appear in court, the party who intends to call the witness must subpoena that individual. **Trial subpoenas** are often prepared by a paralegal employed by the attorney seeking the attendance of the witness. In federal court, as well as a growing number of state courts, the attorney can issue a subpoena by signing it. In more traditional jurisdictions, the clerk of the court must impress the seal of the court on the document before it is issued under authority of law. Exhibit 11.8 is the subpoena form used in South Carolina criminal cases.

Trial subpoena
A document prepared under the authority of the court used to compel a non-party to an action to appear for trial.

Although a law office can generate its own subpoenas, most criminal litigators use the standard forms provided by the clerk of the court. The forms are generally available at the clerk's office in hard copy and online at the clerk's website. The subpoena must be accompanied by the payment of a witness fee and mileage to be enforceable. Although some jurisdictions may not require this payment, most do. Check the applicable rules in your court to find out what is required, along with the payment to be tendered. The subpoena must be served on the witness prior to the date that he or she is to appear in court. Unlike summons, in most jurisdictions, any competent person who is not a party to the action may serve as a witness. When a witness resides a great distance from the place of trial, the subpoenaing party must pay the witness's travel expenses. For instance, in the sexual assault prosecution of Michael Jackson, the California District Attorney's office subpoenaed the New York City journalist whose documentary led to the criminal investigation of the defendant. The proof of payment of these expenses is presented in Exhibit 11.9.

The person serving the subpoena must complete under oath a **return of service**. The return is a document that verifies the witness was served with the subpoena along with the applicable witness fee and mileage. Often, the return of service appears on the reverse side of the subpoena. Exhibit 11.10 is the return of service appearing on the back side of the South Carolina criminal subpoena form. As noted above, in the case of "friendly witnesses," the attorney or paralegal may serve the trial subpoena when meeting with witnesses to prepare them for trial.

Return of service
The written verification establishing that a document has been served.

Sometimes subpoenas are served by certified or registered mail, return receipt requested. This type of service is spelled out in the criminal rules or code. There are express time limits governing this service by mail. If service is accomplished this way, the server must furnish an affidavit showing that the mailing was prepaid and was addressed to the witness, restricted delivery, with a check or money order for the fee and mileage enclosed.

When the party wants the witness to bring objects, documents, or other tangible items to court, the party serves the witness with a subpoena *duces*

Exhibit 11.8: South Carolina Trial Subpoena

SUBPOENA IN A CRIMINAL CASE SOUTH CAROLINA ____ COURT	COUNTY
V.	CASE NO.
	SUBPOENA FOR PERSON DOCUMENT(S) OR OBJECT(S)
TO:	
YOU ARE HEREBY COMMANDED to appear in the above-named court at the place, date, and time specified below to testify in the above-entitled case.	
PLACE	COURTROOM
	DATE AND TIME
YOU ARE ALSO COMMANDED to bring with you the following document(s) or object(s).	
LIST DOCUMENT(S) OR OBJECT(S)	
This subpoena shall remain in effect until you are granted leave to depart by the court or by an officer acting on behalf of the court.	
CLERK OF COURT	DATE
(BY) DEPUTY CLERK	
THIS SUBPOENA IS ISSUED UPON APPLICATION OF THE: SOLICITOR DEFENDANT	ATTORNEY'S NAME AND ADDRESS
SCCA 253 (JULY 1, 1993)	

Exhibit 11.9: Proof of Travel Expenses for Subpoenaed Witness

By: Patrick J. McKinley
Assistant District Attorney
State Bar #44297
1105 Santa Barbara Street
Santa Barbara, CA 93101
Telephone: (805) 568-2300
Attorneys for Plaintiff

DEC 2 1 2004
GARY M. BLAIR, Executive Officer
BY Carrie L. Wagner
CARRIE L. WAGNER, Deputy Clerk

SUPERIOR COURT OF THE STATE OF CALIFORNIA
FOR THE COUNTY OF SANTA BARBARA
COOK STREET DIVISION

~~FILED UNDER SEAL~~
Unsealed per order dated 1/10/05

PEOPLE OF THE STATE OF CALIFORNIA, Plaintiff, vs. MICHAEL JOE JACKSON, Defendant.	Case No. 1133603 DECLARATION OF VICTIM/WITNESS ASSISTANT

I, SHAMRA LIMON, am employed by the Santa Barbara County District Attorney's Office.

In accordance with the California Penal Code section 1434.3, I shall make the following travel arrangements in the name of MARTIN BASHIR, for the date of March 1, 2005, and to return when his testimony is complete, plane reservations (for which tickets are prepaid) from a convenient airport in New York to Santa Maria and back; lodging reservations (which are to be billed to Santa Barbara County District Attorney's Office) for the above-stated dates at an appropriate hotel in Santa Maria.

Ground transportation between airport, place of lodging, and courthouse while in Santa Maria, will be provided by this office. Reimbursement for ground transportation between a convenient airport in New York and place of residence in New York City is enclosed (at twenty cents per mile x miles round trip). I am informed and believe that the cost of a taxi ride to either of the New York City airports is approximately $50.00 from Manhattan.

Witness fees of $20.00 per day for 10 days of travel and days of testimony, have also been enclosed.

A check in the total amount is being forwarded. This is the total amount of the above-listed expenditures.

I declare under penalty of perjury that the foregoing is true and correct.

Executed December 20, 2004, at Santa Maria, California.

Shamra Limon
Victim Witness Assistant

Exhibit 11.10: South Carolina Criminal Subpoena Return of Service

PROOF OF SERVICE

SERVED	DATE	PLACE
SERVED ON (PRINT NAME)		MANNER OF SERVICE
SERVED BY (PRINT NAME)		TITLE

DECLARATION OF SERVER

I certify that the foregoing information contained in the Proof of Service is true and correct.

Executed on ______________ ______________________________

DATE SIGNATURE OF THE SERVER

____

ADDRESS OF THE SERVER

____

Subpoena *duces tecum*
A special form of subpoena that is used to compel the witness to bring documents or other tangible items to court.

tecum. As you will recall from our discussion of this document in Chapter 8, a **subpoena *duces tecum*** is a special form of subpoena used to compel the witness to bring documents or other tangible items to court. Other than the requirement that the witness bring something to court, the rules regarding trial subpoenas and subpoenas *duces tecum* are the same.

You should be mindful that most people do not want to be witnesses in criminal cases. This experience can be stressful for many, and downright frightening for others. This is especially true for children. Moreover, participation in court proceedings disrupts work, school, or other obligations. Seasoned litigators are careful not to alienate their witnesses. These attorneys give their witnesses a cover letter with the subpoena to explain the expected timetable for the case and ask the witnesses to call at specified times to learn exactly when they need to show up in court. Generally, these attorneys subpoena all of the witnesses to appear on the first day of trial and have the court continue the subpoenas from day to day.

Application Exercises

11. Use the Internet to find a CV of an accident reconstruction expert and a forensic pathologist located in your state.
12. Prepare a trial subpoena directed to the president of your school in Hypothetical Case 3, *United States v. William Edwards.* Assume that (a) the trial will take place the first Tuesday of next month, beginning at 10:00 A.M., in courtroom 201 at the federal courthouse for the U.S. District and division in which your school is located; (b) the case number is [CURRENT YEAR]-1857; (c) the witness is to bring all educational records concerning the defendant to court; and (d) the president will be served at his or her office at the school. List the U.S. Attorney for the federal district as the person subpoenaing the witness on behalf of the government. Use U.S. Courts form AO89 found at: https://www.uscourts.gov/sites/default/files/ao089.pdf.
13. Prepare a trial subpoena on behalf of the defense directed to the president of your school in Hypothetical Case 1, *People v. Bud Cook.* Assume that (a) the trial will take place the last Thursday of next month, beginning at 9:30 A.M., in courtroom 400 at the state courthouse exercising jurisdiction over events occurring in the community where your school is located; (b) the case number is [CURRENT YEAR]-123; and (c) the president will be served at his or her office at the school. List your instructor as the attorney representing the defendant along with the instructor's professional address.
14. Cite the court rule or statute applicable to the state where your school is located that sets the amount of the witness fee and the rate of mileage to which a subpoenaed witness is entitled in a criminal case.

E. Organizing File Materials for the Trial

To be an effective member of the litigation team, a paralegal must be able to review and produce critical documents during various stages of the trial. These documents can include charging instruments, police reports, witness statements, and lab reports. Prior to the use of laptop computers in courtrooms, many attorneys used **trial notebooks** to organize these types of materials. Others simply brought in expandable, accordion-style folders filled with manila files. Today, however, increasing numbers of attorneys keep this kind of information on laptop computers and in flash drives. They use eDiscovery software programs such as Relativity or Abacus to manage high volumes of documents, and CaseMap to organize the facts, witnesses, and issues of the case. Regardless of which method is used, paralegals typically play a key role in collecting, organizing, and retrieving these trial materials.

Trial notebook
A three-ring notebook with appropriately tabbed sections containing materials required for a specific trial.

The three basic components of any trial file are a court filings folder, witness folders, and discovery folders. The court filings folder contains copies of the documents filed with the clerk of the court for the case. These filings should be organized in either chronological or reverse chronological order. An index should be prepared to make it possible to identify each document by title and the date it was filed with the clerk.[4]

The largest part of the case file is the witness section. It contains individual subfiles for each witness expected to testify. The first step in preparing witness folders is to outline the evidence expected to be presented by both sides at trial. The outline initially should list all of the witnesses for the prosecution, along with a brief statement of each witness's direct testimony and the exhibits expected to be introduced through the witness. Next, the same information should be set forth for each of the defense's witnesses. Similarly, witness and exhibit information should be included for the government's rebuttal and the defendant's surrebuttal.

The outline should also include references to the pertinent documents on which direct and cross-examination are based. Typically, this means citations of police reports, witness statements, and transcripts. Once the basic information is compiled for the direct examination for each witness, you should expand the treatment of each witness with the topics and documents required for cross-examination.

In addition to this summary information, the witness section should include subfiles for each witness. Each witness's file should include copies of all documents related to that witness. It also should have an outline of the particular facts expected to be discussed during the witness's testimony, accompanied by references to exhibits or other documents. There should be pinpoint citations to the page, paragraph and line number of each document. If witness files are voluminous, an individual index should be prepared for each file. If you are not using a computer program to manage documents, many witness files will include copies of documents already included in other witness files.

The third component of the case file is the discovery section. The discovery file contains separate subfiles for the government's discovery, as well as the discovery tendered by the defense. The discovery file duplicates documents already included in the witness subfiles, but this redundancy aids the attorney in reacting to the unexpected.

F. Preparation of Computer-Based Presentation

U.S. district courtrooms are now wired for electronic presentations, and most of the attorneys who regularly practice in these courtrooms routinely use this technology to present cases. The use of this technology in state courts varies from state to state, and from county to county within a state. Where it is available, witnesses will usually handle hard copies of documentary exhibits as the judge and the jury view electronic copies on courtroom monitors.

There is also increasing use of presentation software in opening statements and closing arguments. While the attorney's speaking skills continue to play a key role, the integration of visual images can increase the effectiveness of the presentation. Opening-statement slide presentations may include the photographs of witnesses, and closing-argument presentations often include copies

[4]Often, the court's docket sheet can be used as the index. If you are using a hard-copy organizer, make sure that each document is separately stapled. The documents should be collected in a binder or held together with a paper fastener.

of documents used to impeach a witness, such as written statements and transcripts of testimony given on prior occasions.

To use this technology, someone (usually a paralegal) has to scan the documents and save them on a laptop computer's hard drive, a flash drive, or a removable disk prior to the trial. The Portable Document Format (PDF) file format is preferred for use in federal courts.) The electronic information can be incorporated into slide presentations, such as Microsoft PowerPoint, Sanction, or Trial Director, so that attorneys can reference the exhibits during opening statements or closing arguments.

In addition to scanning exhibits, paralegals can assist attorneys in selecting materials to be included in opening statements and closing arguments. Even though they may be excellent in crafting a theme of the case based upon a legitimate legal theory, many litigators do not have the technical expertise to create the slides for these productions. Generally, they will turn to the paralegal to produce these slide presentations.

Slide presentations may be linear or non-linear. Linear presentations move in a fixed chronological order from slide to slide to slide. Once a slideshow begins, the order of the slides cannot change. PowerPoint is an example of a linear presentation. On the other hand, non-linear presentations allow users to jump from exhibit to exhibit as the needs of a trial develop, without having to follow a predetermined order of slides. Sanction and Trial Director are examples of non-linear presentation platforms. When preparing an opening-statement presentation, make sure that each slide should be designed to not only educate the jury, but also to promote the theme of the case. (*See* Figure 11.2 for preparation guidelines.) The text should be kept to a minimum so as not to distract the viewer from listening to what the attorney is saying. Avoid using long quotes and, wherever possible, limit each slide to one point.

Create attractive slides. Pictures are better than words. Incorporate photographs of witnesses and scenes. Google Map images, simple timelines, and easy-to-follow charts may also be incorporated into the presentation. If there is footage of actual events, you may include concise video clips. Design the slides with visually appealing backgrounds with contrasting lettering. Avoid red and green lettering because some jurors may not be able to differentiate the lettering from the background. Do not use glitzy transitions from slide to slide.

Proper setup and operation of the electronic presentation equipment are other important tasks that are often assigned to paralegals. If you are going to be using courthouse equipment, you need to check it in advance to make sure that there are no compatibility problems with the program or operating systems being used. If you are given this responsibility, make sure to get permission from the court personnel before you inspect, test, and use their equipment.

In a courtroom that is not set up for computer-based presentations, you will need to bring a laptop computer, projector, and projection screen with you. You will again need to visit the courtroom in advance to determine where to set up your equipment and to make sure that it performs adequately in that courtroom. You need to experiment with the placement of the equipment. Use duct tape to indicate where the equipment should be set up. (Let court personnel know what you are doing so that the tape is not removed.) You also should use duct tape to tape down cables so that persons in the courtroom will not trip over them. Position the monitor/projection screen in places where the jury, judge, the opponent, and your side all can see.

1. **Concise:** Each slide should be concise; presentation is not repetitive.
2. **Educational:** Each slide must inform; every slide must present important information; the presentation as a whole tells a story; the theme is well thought out and drives the entire slideshow.
3. **Attractive:** Variety of visuals is used; appropriate slide backgrounds; wise color choices; readable text.

Figure 11.2 Guidelines for Preparing PowerPoint Slides for Opening Statements and Closing Arguments

Application Exercises

15. Exhibit 11.11 shows the narrative portions of the police reports detailing the arrest of the Harvard University professor Henry Gates, Jr., for disorderly conduct. After reading the reports, review the following elements of the Massachusetts crime of disorderly conduct:

> A person is guilty of disorderly conduct if, with purpose to cause public inconvenience, annoyance or alarm, or recklessly creating a risk thereof, he:
> (a) engages in fighting or threatening, or in violent or tumultuous behavior; or. . .
> (c) creates a hazardous or physically offensive condition by any act which serves no legitimate purpose of the actor.[5]

Now answer the following questions:

1. What theme could the government use for this criminal prosecution?
2. What theme could the defense use for this case?
3. What story would each side tell to fit the favorable facts within its theme?
4. What photographs should each side collect to prepare a slideshow presentation to accompany their opening statements?
5. Other than pictures of persons, what other photographs would be helpful components of a slideshow presentation?

Based on these answers, prepare the following presentations:

A. A PowerPoint slideshow of seven to nine slides to accompany the prosecutor's opening statement in a criminal prosecution for disorderly conduct against Professor Gates.
B. A PowerPoint slideshow of seven to nine slides to accompany the defense's opening statement in a criminal prosecution for disorderly conduct against Professor Gates.

[5]In *Alegata v. Commonwealth*, 353 Mass. 287, 231 N.E.2d 201, 211 (1967), the Massachusetts Supreme Judicial Court adopted the Model Penal Code's offense of disorderly conduct. The court struck down subsection (b) of the Model Penal Code version as unconstitutionally overbroad and held that subsections (a) and (c) must only be construed as covering conduct, not activities involving the "lawful exercise of a First Amendment right." *See Commonwealth v. A Juvenile*, 368 Mass. 580, 334 N.E.2d 617, 628 (1975).

Exhibit 11.11: Incident Reports Documenting Disorderly Conduct Arrest

CAMBRIDGE POLICE DEPARTMENT
CAMBRIDGE, MA

Incident Report #9005127

Report Entered: 07/16/2009 13:21:34

Narrative

On Thursday July 16, 2009, Henry Gates, Jr. ([redacted], of [redacted] Ware Street, Cambridge, MA) was placed under arrest at [redacted] Ware Street, after being observed exhibiting loud and tumultuous behavior, in a public place, directed at a uniformed police officer who was present investigating a report of a crime in progress. These actions on the behalf of Gates served no legitimate purpose and caused citizens passing by this location to stop and take notice while appearing surprised and alarmed.

On the above time and date, I was on uniformed duty in an unmarked police cruiser assigned to the Administration Section, working from 7:00 AM-3:30 PM. At approximately 12:44 PM, I was operating my cruiser on Harvard Street near Ware Street. At that time, I overheard an ECC broadcast for a possible break in progress at [redacted] Ware Street. Due to my proximity, I responded.

When I arrived at [redacted] Ware Street I radioed ECC and asked that they have the caller meet me at the front door to this residence. I was told that the caller was already outside. As I was getting this information, I climbed the porch stairs toward the front door. As I reached the door, a female voice called out to me. I turned and looked in the direction of the voice and observed a white female, later identified as Lucia Whalen. Whalen, who was standing on the sidewalk in front of the residence, held a wireless telephone in her hand and told me that it was she who called. She went on to tell me that she observed what appeared to be two black males with backpacks on the porch of [redacted] Ware Street. She told me that her suspicions were aroused when she observed one of the men wedging his shoulder into the door as if he was trying to force entry. Since I was the only police officer on location and had my back to the front door as I spoke with her, I asked that she wait for other responding officers while I investigated further.

As I turned and faced the door, I could see an older black male standing in the foyer of [redacted] Ware Street. I made this observation through the glass paned front door. As I stood in plain view of this man, later identified as Gates, I asked if he would step out onto the porch and speak with me. He replied "no I will not". He then demanded to know who I was. I told him that I was "Sgt. Crowley from the Cambridge Police" and that I was "investigating a report of a break in progress" at the residence. While I was making this statement, Gates opened the front door and exclaimed "why, because I'm a black man in America?". I then asked Gates if there was anyone else in the residence. While yelling, he told me that it was none of my business and accused me of being a racist police officer. I assured Gates that I was responding to a citizen's call to the Cambridge Police and that the caller was outside as we spoke. Gates seemed to ignore me and picked up a cordless telephone and dialed an unknown telephone number. As he did so, I radioed on channel 1 that I was off in the residence with someone who appeared to be a resident but very uncooperative. I then overheard Gates asking the person on the other end of his telephone call to "get the chief" and "what's the chief's name?". Gates was telling the person on the other end of the call that he was dealing with a racist police officer in his home. Gates then turned to me and told me that I had no idea who I was "messing" with and that I had not heard the last of it. While I was led to believe that Gates was lawfully in the residence, I was quite surprised and confused with the behavior he exhibited toward me. I asked Gates to provide me with photo identification so that I could verify that he resided at [redacted] Ware Street and so that I could radio my findings to ECC. Gates initially refused, demanding that I show him identification but then did supply me with a Harvard University identification card. Upon learning that Gates was affiliated with Harvard, I radioed and requested the presence of the Harvard University Police.

With the Harvard University identification in hand, I radioed my findings to ECC on channel two and prepared to leave. Gates again asked for my name which I began to provide. Gates began to yell over my spoken words by accusing me of being a racist police officer and leveling threats that he wasn't someone to mess with. At some point during this exchange, I became aware that Off. Carlos Figueroa was standing behind me. When Gates asked a third time for my name, I explained to him that I had provided it at his request two separate times. Gates continued to yell at me. I told Gates that I was leaving his residence and that if he had any other questions regarding the matter, I would speak with him outside of the residence.

As I began walking through the foyer toward the front door, I could hear Gates again demanding my name. I again told Gates that I would speak with him outside. My reason for wanting to leave the residence was that Gates was yelling very loud and the acoustics of the kitchen and foyer were making it difficult for me to transmit pertinent information to ECC or other responding units. His reply was "ya, I'll speak with your mama outside". When I left the residence, I noted that there were several Cambridge and Harvard University police officers assembled on the sidewalk in front of the residence. Additionally, the caller, Ms. Walen and at least seven unidentified passers-by were looking in the direction of Gates, who had followed me outside of the residence.

As I descended the stairs to the sidewalk, Gates continued to yell at me, accusing me of racial bias and continued to tell me that I had not heard the last of him. Due to the tumultuous manner Gates had exhibited in his residence as well as his continued tumultuous behavior outside the residence, in view of the public, I warned Gates that he was becoming disorderly. Gates ignored my warning and continued to yell, which drew the attention of both the police officers and citizens, who appeared surprised and alarmed by Gates's outburst. For a second time I warned Gates to calm down while I withdrew my department issued handcuffs from their carrying case. Gates again ignored my warning and continued to yell at me. It was at this time that I informed Gates that he was under arrest. I then stepped up the stairs, onto the porch and attempted to place handcuffs on Gates. Gates initially resisted my attempt to handcuff him, yelling that he was "disabled" and would fall without his cane. After the handcuffs were properly applied, Gates complained that they were too tight. I ordered Off. Ivey, who was among the responding officers, to handcuff Gates with his arms in front of him for his comfort while I secured a cane for Gates from within the residence. I then asked Gates if he would like an officer to take possession of his house key and secure his front door, which he left wide open. Gates told me that the door was un securable due to a previous break attempt at the residence. Shortly thereafter, a Harvard University maintenance person arrived on scene and appeared familiar with Gates. I asked Gates if he was comfortable with this Harvard University maintenance person securing his residence. He told me that he was.

After a brief consultation with Sgt. Lashley and upon Gates's request, he was transported to 125 6th. Street in a police cruiser (Car 1, Off's Graham and Ivey) where he was booked and processed by Off. J. P. Crowley.

CAMBRIDGE POLICE DEPARTMENT
CAMBRIDGE, MA

Incident Supplement #9005127 - 1

Report Entered: 07/16/2009 13:52:50

Narrative

On July 16, 2009 at approximately 12:44 PM, I Officer Figueroa#509 responded to an ECC broadcast for a possible break at [redacted] Ware St. When I arrived, I stepped into the residence and Sgt. Crowley had already entered and was speaking to a black male.
As I stepped in, I heard Sgt. Crowley ask for the gentleman's information which he stated "NO I WILL NOT!". The gentleman was shouting out to the Sgt. that the Sgt.. was a racist and yelled that "THIS IS WHAT HAPPENS TO BLACK MEN IN AMERICA!" As the Sgt. was trying to calm the gentleman, the gentleman shouted " You don't know who your messing with!"
I stepped out to gather the information from the reporting person, WHALEN, LUCIA. Ms. Whalen stated to me that she saw a man wedging his shoulder into the front door as to pry the door open. As I returned to the residence, a group of onlookers were now on scene. The Sgt., along with the gentleman, were now on the porch of [redacted] Ware St. and again he was shouting, now to the onlookers (about seven) ,"THIS IS WHAT HAPPENS TO BLACK MEN IN AMERICA"! The gentleman refused to listen to as to why the Cambridge Police were there.
While on the porch, the gentleman refused to be cooperative and continued shouting that the Sgt. is racist police officer.

SUMMARY

If it appears that a case will not be concluded through plea bargaining, each side must prepare to try it in court. This preparation involves making decisions as to whether to use a jury trial or bench trial and what witnesses should be called. Both decisions depend upon the nature of the charges, the nature of the evidence, and the nature of the defendant. Preparation also involves the development of a coherent theory of the case around which the attorneys will organize their opening statements, the questions that they will ask the witnesses, and the arguments that they will make to the judge or jury.

If it is going to be a jury trial, the attorneys and their support staffs should research the backgrounds of the potential jurors and prepare appropriate questions to ask during the *voir dire*.

Regardless of which type of trial it is, though, the attorneys need to determine who they wish to call as witnesses and to prepare the exhibits they want to introduce. In an attempt to exclude certain types of evidence, the attorneys frequently file additional motions to suppress and motions *in limine*.

In addition to lining up expert witnesses and subpoenaing lay witnesses, the attorneys and their staffs should meet with the witnesses to explain their role in the trial and discuss the types of questions that they are likely to be asked during both direct examination and cross-examination.

Pre-trial preparation also involves the numbering of exhibits and the development of trial notebooks. As courts continue to expand their use of technology, paralegals have begun to play increasingly important roles in organizing databases of documents and developing slide show presentations to enhance opening statements and closing arguments.

REVIEW QUESTIONS

1. When does pre-trial preparation begin?
2. What type of information does the clerk's office collect on prospective jurors?
3. What public records are helpful to review in order to gain insight into prospective jurors' attitudes?
4. What private sources of information are available to conduct background searches of prospective jurors?
5. Why do trial attorneys prepare their own *voir dire* questions?
6. What are the three types of trial exhibits?
7. What methods are used to mark trial exhibits?
8. Give examples of demonstrative exhibits.
9. What are the two documents that are prepared in advance of trial to address evidentiary questions?
10. What are the basic components of a motion *in limine*?
11. What is the purpose of a pocket brief?
12. What are the guidelines for witness appearance at trial?
13. How can you refresh a witness's recollection during pre-trial preparation?
14. What does it mean when an objection is sustained or overruled?

15. What must accompany a trial subpoena when it is served on the witness?
16. What is the purpose of a subpoena *duces tecum*?
17. What is the risk of having a client undergo an extreme makeover in order to make a better impression at trial?
18. What are the basic components of the trial file?
19. What is the difference between linear and non-linear slide presentations?
20. What three qualities make individual slides effective in an opening-statement presentation?
21. What sources are available for obtaining photographs of opposing witnesses?
22. If the courtroom is not designed for computer-based presentations, what advance work must be carried out to prepare for the presentation?

Chapter 12

The Conduct of the Trial

Chapter Objectives

After reading this chapter, you should be able to:

- Describe what takes place during each of the stages of a criminal trial.
- Discuss the manner in which jurors are selected and how paralegals assist in this process.
- Explain the differences between direct examination and cross-examination, and how paralegals can assist attorneys at this stage of a trial.
- Discuss the importance of jury instructions and how paralegals can assist attorneys at this stage of a trial.
- Prepare post-verdict and post-trial motions.

Introduction

Having discussed the purpose of trials and the roles played by attorneys, judges, and juries in Chapter 10, and the ways in which lawyers and paralegals prepare for trials in Chapter 11, this chapter takes a closer look at how trials are typically conducted. Although paralegals are not authorized to directly represent clients at a trial, they can be an important part of the litigation team, and they often sit at the counsel table with the attorneys.

Prior to the arrival of the Covid pandemic in early 2020, trials were held in formal courtrooms in federal, state, and local buildings and were open to the public and representatives of the press.[1] During the Covid pandemic period,

---

[1]In some jurisdictions, cameras are allowed in the courtroom, and in others, they are not. National television networks gave live coverage of the trials of Minneapolis police officer Derek Chauvin

some trials and other hearings took place virtually (with judge, attorneys, witnesses, and jurors in different locations), while others took place in courtrooms with plexiglass partitions between participants. Some courts allowed a limited numbers of masked observers practicing appropriate social distancing. Many courts continue to conduct virtual hearings for arraignments, status calls, and arguments on motions as the pandemic comes to an end.

A. The Order of Events

An overview of the various stages of a typical jury trial of a criminal case is presented in Figure 12.1. Look at it now and then refer to it as you read through this chapter.

B. Rules of Criminal Procedure

The procedures used in federal criminal trials are spelled out in Section VI of the Federal Rules of Criminal Procedure (FRCrP). Each state has its own, similar rules governing criminal trials. Both federal and state rules can generally be found online and are often supplemented by "local" rules. At both the federal and state levels, it is the trial judge's responsibility to see that they are enforced.

Application Exercise

1. Using the FRCrP and those of your state, develop a table that:
   a. Compares and contrasts the portions of these two sets of rules that apply to the conduct of criminal trials.
   b. Compares and contrasts the portions of these two sets of rules that apply to the conduct of juvenile court proceedings.

C. Calling the Case for Trial

We begin our discussion of trial procedures at the point at which the case is formally called for trial. At this juncture, the judge takes up preliminary matters, such as scheduling and ruling on pre-trial motions. Neither witnesses nor prospective jurors are present.

The prosecutor, defense counsel, and the defendant typically report to the courtroom on the day and time that the case is scheduled. Once the case is called for trial, the judge will address preliminary matters, including the trial schedule. Because paralegals are often the liaison between the attorney and the

(accused and later convicted of manslaughter in the death of George Floyd) and the three Georgia men involved in killing of Ahmaud Arbery, a Black jogger.

Items that occur only in jury trials are in italics; non-italicized items apply to both jury and non-jury criminal trials

- Case called for trial: Initial hearing before judge
  - Scheduling decisions made
  - Judge rules on pre-trial motions
- *Selection of the jury*
  - *Judge's welcome to jurors and swearing in*
  - *Voir dire*
  - *Rulings on challenges for cause*
  - *Exercise of peremptory challenges*
  - *Seating of jurors and alternates*
- Opening statements
  - Prosecution's opening
  - Defense's opening
- Presentation of the prosecution's case-in-chief
  - Prosecution's first witness takes the stand and is sworn in
    - Direct examination of prosecution witness 1
    - Cross-examination of prosecution witness 1
    - Re-direct examination of prosecution witness 1
    - Re-cross examination of prosecution witness 1
  - Additional prosecution witnesses called and examined.
- Consideration of defense's motion for judgment of acquittal/motion for directed verdict
- Presentation of defense's case-in-chief
  - Defense's first witness takes the stand and is sworn in
    - Direct examination of defense witness 1
    - Cross-examination of defense witness 1
    - Re-direct examination of defense witness 1
    - Re-cross examination of defense witness 1
  - Additional defense witnesses called, sworn, and examined.
- Presentation of rebuttal witnesses (following same format)
- Presentation of surrebuttal witnesses (following same format)
- Consideration of renewal of defense motion for judgment of acquittal or motion for directed verdict
- *Jury instructions conference*
- Closing arguments
  - Prosecution's closing argument
  - Defense's closing argument
  - Prosecution's rebuttal argument
- *Judge's instructions to the jury*
- *Jury deliberations*
- Announcement of verdict
- Post-verdict actions
  - Filing of post-trial motions
  - Preparation and filing of pre-sentence investigation report (PSR)
  - Sentencing hearing
  - Imposition of sentence
- Filing of notice of appeal

Figure 12.1 Stages in a Typical Criminal Trial

witnesses, the day-to-day trial schedule that the judge sets at this court date is of particular importance for paralegals. If they haven't already done so, the parties provide the judge with their lists of witnesses, any stipulation of facts not in dispute, and exhibit lists.[2] Paralegals are often involved in the preparation of these documents.

Exhibit and witness lists are relatively easy to prepare. Usually, a case caption appears at the top of each document. The document title next appears (e.g., Defendant's Exhibits, Government's List of Witnesses), and a short introductory sentence follows. The body of the exhibit list is a chronological listing of the numbered trial exhibits along with a description of each (*see* Exhibit 12.1). The witness list consists of an alphabetical listing of the witnesses (*see* Exhibit 12.2). The attorney's signature and the address block follow the body in both types of lists.

The stipulations lists vary in format. When the stipulation is presented at the time the case is called for hearing, it is usually formatted as a standard captioned document (*see* Exhibit 12.3). When the parties reach a stipulation after testimony has begun, it may be handwritten on a sheet from a legal pad. In either instance, attorneys from each side typically sign the document.

Motions *in limine* may also be presented and decided at this juncture.[3] Once the court rules on the motions *in limine* and addresses any other preliminary matters needing attention, the jury selection process begins.

Application Exercises

2. Prepare a list of prosecution witnesses for the *Turner* hypothetical case (*see* pages xxxvii-xxxviii). Assume that (1) all the faculty members of your instructor's department are the government's witnesses; (2) the case is the 30th felony case of the year filed in the federal district in which your school is located; and (3) the U.S. Attorney for your federal district is the prosecutor.

3. Draft the body of a stipulation of facts in the *Marshall* hypothetical case (*see* pages xxxviii-xxxix). The stipulation should be based on the undisputed facts: Clay Marshall is the office manager of the Van Buren Insurance Agency in the city where your school is located. He supervised Randy Jefferson and Madison Pickering, two clerks for the firm. Jefferson continues to work for the agency. Pickering used to work part time at Van Buren Insurance Agency but no longer does.

In cases in which there has been extensive pre-trial publicity, the defense attorney may decide to file a pre-trial motion seeking either a change of venue

---

[2]In some jurisdictions, including federal court, many of these documents may have already been submitted prior to the case being called for trial.

[3]See Chapter 11, pp. 370-376, for a discussion of how to prepare motions *in limine*.

Exhibit 12.1: Exhibit List

IN THE CIRCUIT COURT OF THE ELEVENTH JUDICIAL CIRCUIT
MCLEAN COUNTY, ILLINOIS

PEOPLE OF THE STATE OF ILLINOIS	)	
	)	
v.	)	Case No. 20 CF XXX
	)	
BUD COOK	)	
Defendant.	)	

EXHIBIT LIST

Now comes the Defendant BUD COOK, by CHARLES HOVEY, his attorney, and states that he will present the following exhibits at trial in his case-in-chief:

Defendant's Exhibit No. 1	Coroner's Inquest Report
Defendant's Exhibit No. 2	Toxicology Report
Defendant's Exhibit No. 3	State Police Accident Reconstruction Report (redacted)
Defendant's Exhibit No. 4	Aerial map of Sumner Drive
Defendant's Group Exhibit No. 5	Photographs of scene of automobile/ bicycle accident
Defendant's Group Exhibit No. 6	Photographs of decedent's clothing
Defendant's Group Exhibit No. 7	Photographs of decedent's bicycle

Respectfully submitted,

BUD COOK, Defendant

By____________________________

CHARLES HOVEY, his attorney

Charles Hovey
Attorney for Defendant
1857 Bone Street
Normal, IL 61617
(309) 555-1857

Exhibit 12.2: Excerpt from Prosecution Witness List

UNITED STATES OF AMERICA, Plaintiff, v. ANTHONY PELLICANO, et al., Defendants.	No. CR 05-1046(E)-DSF GOVERNMENT'S WITNESS LIST Date: March 5, 2008 Time: 8:30 a.m.

Plaintiff United States of America intends to call the following witnesses in its case-in-chief at trial of the above-captioned matter:

1. Pedro Tenoch Aguilar
2. Thomas Ashley
3. R.T. Ballard III
4. Heidi Binford
5. Laura Buddine
6. Diane Burns
7. Anita Busch
8. Richard Campau
9. Sandra Carradine
10. Keith Carradine
11. Ricardo Cestero
12. Wayne Chen
13. Patrick Coffin
14. Kissandra Cohen
15. Mark Cohn
16. Stephen Corso
17. Jill Cossman
18. Daniel Davis
19. Frederick DeMann
20. Pilar DeMann
21. Jane Doe #2
22. Jane Doe #8
23. Linda Doucett
24. Gregory Dovel
25. Jeffrey Edwards
26. Robert Ellis
27. Elizabeth Eurich
28. Farrah Fawcett

Exhibit 12.3: Stipulation of Undisputed Facts

IN THE CIRCUIT COURT OF THE 12th JUDICIAL CIRCUIT
WILL COUNTY, ILLINOIS

PEOPLE OF THE	)	
STATE OF ILLINOIS	)	
v.	)	Case No. 20 CF XXX
BRANDON TURNER,	)	
Defendant.	)	

STIPULATION

Now come the parties by their respective attorneys and enter into the following stipulation of undisputed fact:

When the Defendant, Brandon Turner, was stopped by Officer Steve Milner, he was driving a 1995 Buick automobile registered to Brandon Turner and Dennis Watterson as co-owners.

____________________	____________________
CHARLES HOVEY	Will County State's Attorney
Attorney for Defendant	Attorney for the People of the State of Illinois
1857 Bone Street	First Illinois University Plaza
Normal, IL 61761	Joliet, IL 60089
(309)-555-1857	(815)-123-4567

or change of venire.[4] However, since either alternative involves additional costs and greater inconvenience for some of the participants, judges are reluctant to grant these requests and instead rely on *voir dire* to eliminate individuals who might be affected by such coverage. In high-profile cases, defense counsel may employ a public opinion pollster to determine the effect of pre-trial publicity on potential jurors.

D. Jury Selection

Back in Chapter 10, we discussed the constitutional basis for the right to a jury trial and how the *voir dire* process is designed to select an impartial jury. In this chapter, we go into greater detail about how the jury selection process works.

[4]See the discussion on motions relating to the forum in Chapter 9, pages 292-294.

1. SELECTION OF JURY POOL

Prior to being selected to serve on a trial jury, people are randomly selected from lists of registered voters, licensed drivers, property taxpayers, and other public records. They are screened by a local jury commissioner who determines if they meet statutory criteria for serving on a jury.

Judges set jury trials during time periods when the jury commission will summon a pool of potential jurors to report to the courthouse for duty. Many jurisdictions now use telephone call-in numbers to inform jurors as to the specific days and times they need to report within a week or two-week period. The entire array of prospective jurors called during a specific court calendar is known as the **venire.**

Once prospective jurors have arrived at the courthouse, a court official sends them to a jury assembly room, where a judge or clerk swears them in and gives them general instructions about their role in the process. Court officials distribute badges or name tags to the jurors that identify them by juror number. Depending on the number of jury trials taking place, some or all of these individuals are then taken to the courtroom being used for a specific trial that is about to begin.

Venire
A panel of prospective jurors.

Jury box
The specific location in the courtroom where the jury sits during the trial.

Jury box system
A method of jury selection in which prospective jurors fill the jury box in the order of the numbers they drew. As individual jurors are stricken, they are replaced by other prospective jurors, until everyone left in the box is acceptable to both sides or all peremptory challenges by both sides are exhausted.

Challenge for cause
A method for removing a prospective juror based on a finding by the judge that the juror has some sort of bias or has another disqualifying factor for serving on the jury for this specific case.

Peremptory challenge
A method whereby an attorney can remove a prospective juror without being required to state a reason.

Back strike
A practice that allows a party's attorney to exercise a peremptory challenge of a juror who was part of a panel that had previously been accepted.

2. THE *VOIR DIRE* PROCESS

When potential jurors arrive in the courtroom, they are usually seated in the audience section, while the judge gives a brief welcoming speech and explains how the questioning will be done. Although the process varies from one courtroom to the next, the judge frequently starts by using a show-of-hands procedure to obtain responses to some very general questions. After this introduction, the judge will usually call out the numbers of a smaller group that will then take seats in the **jury box**.

There are two primary methods employed for selecting a jury: the first is the **jury box system**. When courts use the jury box system, the initial members of the array are placed in the jury box and then questioned by the judge. Then when jurors are excused, they are individually replaced by other members of the venire, also chosen by lot. In this system, prospective jurors are often interviewed in panels of four. After a juror is stricken, another juror in the jury box changes seats and becomes a member of the four-person panel under consideration. The prosecutor initially is given the opportunity to pose **challenges for cause** or **peremptory challenges**. The prosecutor may also accept the panel as constituted. If the prosecution removes jurors from the panel, the court then questions the replacements. The prosecution again may challenge the new members of the panel. Once the panel is accepted by the government, it is tendered to the defense. The defense can exercise peremptory challenges, ask that juror to be removed for cause, or accept the panel. If the defense replaces a prospective juror, the panel is tendered to the prosecution.

In some courts, if a panel is tendered back, a party can exercise a **back strike**, which is the practice of a party's exercise of a peremptory challenge to dismiss a juror who was part of a panel that it had previously accepted. Many courts, however, do not permit back strikes. Once a panel is accepted by both sides, it is then sworn and seated as jurors by the court. The same process is followed until the entire jury is chosen.

An alternative procedure for selecting jurors is called the **struck jury method.** In this system, the judge randomly selects a subgroup of the venire in a number equal to the sum of the total number of jurors required, the total number of peremptory challenges, the number of alternates, and a few extras. After the lawyers exercise all of their challenges, those remaining in the box are the jurors and alternates. Because the parties know the sequence in which the members of the jury pool are seated, they strike jurors with the knowledge of the identities of those remaining. The manner in which the struck method is carried out varies. Some judges have the attorneys alternate exercising peremptory challenges until all the challenges are exhausted. Other judges have the parties submit a list of unacceptable jurors without revealing their selections to the other side. In either situation, the jurors remaining in the box become the jury in the order in which they were seated. The next two usually are named as alternate jurors. The remaining prospective jurors are discharged by the court.

Struck jury method
A process in which the judge randomly selects the number of jurors required for the case plus a few extra, and after the lawyers exercise all of their challenges, those remaining in the jury box are the jurors and alternates.

In both systems, the judge oversees the process and does much of the actual questioning. However, there is a great deal of variation in the extent to which attorneys participate in the *voir dire* process. In federal court, attorney participation is typically limited to follow-up questions after the venire men and women answer the questions posed by the court. Some federal judges allow the lawyers to ask these questions, whereas other judges require the attorneys to submit written questions which in turn are asked by the judge.[5] In some state courts, attorneys get a chance to ask their own questions; in others, the judge will read questions submitted by the attorneys in advance. Attorneys prefer asking their own questions because it gives them more flexibility and a chance to start connecting with the jurors. It also gives them a chance to word the questions in a way that begins to subtly indoctrinate the jury with either the prosecution or defense point of view. Courts exercise broad discretion to modify or decline supplemental *voir dire* or questionnaire inquires. If an attorney's question is rejected, the attorney can make an **objection on the record,** along with the basis for the objection.

Objection on the record
A challenge to a judge's ruling that is memorialized either by the electronic or stenographic capture of a verbal objection or a written notation of the objection by docket entry or otherwise.

While this questioning is going on, paralegals working as trial assistants take notes on the potential juror's responses. When professional jury consultants are involved, they will carefully observe the body language the potential jurors exhibit during *voir dire.*

3. EXERCISING CHALLENGES

The point at which the prosecution and defense attorneys get to raise their challenges for cause and peremptory challenges depends on which of the abovementioned *voir dire* systems is being used. Since the number of peremptory challenges available to each side is limited, attorneys prefer to remove potential jurors by using challenges for cause, for which there is no limit. If an attorney is unsuccessful at disqualifying a juror for cause, he or she can still remove the juror with a peremptory challenge.

[5]FRCrP 24(a)(2)(B) provides that the attorneys may submit proposed *voir dire* questions.

Challenges for cause are used to excuse jurors after showing good reason that they will not or cannot serve in a satisfactory manner. Ordinarily, this means that the candidates express a bias that would prevent them from fairly and impartially hearing the case. Factors such as present professional relationships with one of the attorneys, racial or ethnic bias, preconceived attitudes about the case, or rigid attitudes about the death penalty in capital cases are among the causes that warrant discharge of a prospective juror. Sometimes jurors are disqualified for cause when they do not meet the statutory qualifications for jury service, such as age and citizenship.

Sometimes judges act on their own initiative to remove a juror, and sometimes they wait for one of the attorneys to raise a challenge. Although potential jurors sometimes give responses that clearly show a prejudice toward one side or the other, it is usually necessary to show some potential conflict of interest based on occupation or past experiences with the law. If the judge agrees, the person will not be seated. Some examples of situations in which a potential juror would probably be disqualified are a personal relationship with a party in the case or with one of the attorneys involved, having been a victim of a similar crime, or answers indicating prejudice based on race, religion, or some other characteristic relevant to the trial.

Another basis for dismissal for cause would be a situation in which the potential jurors' answers indicated that they had been influenced by what they had read in newspapers or seen on television about the case. While some potential jurors will state that they have been influenced in order to purposely avoid having to serve, others will declare that they are capable of setting aside what they read or heard in the news, because they want to be on the jury. If an attorney is unsuccessful in removing a juror for cause, the attorney may be able to use a peremptory challenge to achieve the same result.[6]

Sidebar conference
A discussion between the judge and the attorneys that takes place during the trial outside the hearing of the jury. Typically, attorneys stand in front of the bench when they participate in this conference.

Attorneys exercise challenges for cause by asking for a hearing outside the presence of the jurors, known as a **sidebar conference** (or simply "sidebar"), and presenting the specific reason they believe the prospective juror should not serve. If the judge is persuaded that the juror should not serve, the juror will be excused following the sidebar. There is no limit to the number of challenges for cause available to both sides.[7] The party asserting the challenge bears a heavy burden to convince the court that either the juror is unqualified to serve or cannot be fair and impartial.

If an attorney is unsuccessful in getting someone removed for cause, that person can be removed by using a peremptory challenge *if the attorney has not already exhausted the number authorized for the case.* The number of peremptory challenges that each party can exercise is defined by statute and is based on the nature of the offense charged. In federal court, each side receives 20 in capital felonies. In non-capital felonies, the government has 6 and the defendants collectively have 10. Each side has 3 peremptory challenges in misdemeanors.[8]

Similarly, in state court, more peremptory challenges are provided as the severity of the offense increases. For example, in Illinois, each side is afforded

---

[6] However, an attorney who loses a challenge for cause is unable to eliminate a potential juror if he or she has exhausted the limited number of peremptory challenges allowed in that case.

[7] See 28 U.S.C. §1866(c)(2).

[8] FRCrP 24(b).

10 peremptory strikes in felonies, with a guarantee of 6 for each defendant if there are multiple defendants. Each side has 5 in all other cases, with 3 for each defendant in multiple-defendant cases.[9]

Because the number of peremptory challenges is limited, attorneys are faced with having to decide between accepting a questionable juror in order to preserve a peremptory challenge for later use on what may turn out to be a worse juror. To help them decide when to use their peremptory challenges, attorneys often rely on generalized stereotypes. Prosecutors generally look for persons who place a high value on the enforcement of the laws and protecting the status quo. The defense favors non-judgmental, sympathetic persons who may be skeptical of the police. Some attorneys employ jury consultants to identify desirable and undesirable juror profiles for specific types of cases. In some cases, these experts are present during *voir dire* to observe and interpret body language and voice stressors.

Although the general rule is that attorneys do not need to give a justification for exercising a peremptory challenge, but they cannot be used to strike a juror on the basis of race or sex. The U.S. Supreme Court first wrestled with this dilemma in *Batson v. Kentucky* where it held that the systematic exclusion of jurors on the basis of race is unconstitutional.[10]

Batson v. Kentucky
Supreme Court of the United States
476 U.S. 79 (1986)

JUSTICE POWELL delivered the opinion of the Court, in which Brennan, White, Marshall, Blackmun, Stevens, and O'Connor, JJ. joined.

This case requires us to reexamine that portion of *Swain v. Alabama*, 380 U.S. 202 (1965), concerning the evidentiary burden placed on a criminal defendant who claims that he has been denied equal protection through the State's use of peremptory challenges to exclude members of his race from the petit jury.

Petitioner, a black man, was indicted in Kentucky on charges of second-degree burglary and receipt of stolen goods. On the first day of trial in Jefferson Circuit Court, the judge conducted *voir dire* examination of the venire, excused certain jurors for cause, and permitted the parties to exercise peremptory challenges. The prosecutor used his peremptory challenges to strike all four black persons on the venire, and a jury composed only of white persons was selected.

Defense counsel moved to discharge the jury before it was sworn on the ground that the prosecutor's removal of the black veniremen violated petitioner's rights under the Sixth and Fourteenth Amendments to a jury drawn from a cross section of the community, and under the Fourteenth Amendment to equal protection of the laws. Counsel requested a hearing on his motion. Without expressly ruling on the request for a hearing, the trial judge observed that the parties were entitled to use their peremptory challenges to "strike anybody they want to." The judge then denied petitioner's motion, reasoning that the cross-section

[9] 725 ILCS 5/115-4.

[10] 476 U.S. 79 (1986).

requirement applies only to selection of the venire and not to selection of the petit jury itself.

The jury convicted petitioner on both counts. On appeal to the Supreme Court of Kentucky, petitioner pressed, among other claims, the argument concerning the prosecutor's use of peremptory challenges. . . . The Supreme Court of Kentucky affirmed. . . . We granted certiorari, and now reverse.

In *Swain v. Alabama*, this Court recognized that a "State's purposeful or deliberate denial to Negroes on account of race of participation as jurors in the administration of justice violates the Equal Protection Clause." This principle has been "consistently and repeatedly" reaffirmed, in numerous decisions of this Court both preceding and following *Swain*. We reaffirm the principle today.

More than a century ago, the Court decided that the State denies a black defendant equal protection of the laws when it puts him on trial before a jury from which members of his race have been purposefully excluded. *Strauder v. West Virginia*. That decision laid the foundation for the Court's unceasing efforts to eradicate racial discrimination in the procedures used to select the venire from which individual jurors are drawn. In *Strauder*, the Court explained that the central concern of the recently ratified Fourteenth Amendment was to put an end to governmental discrimination on account of race. Exclusion of black citizens from service as jurors constitutes a primary example of the evil the Fourteenth Amendment was designed to cure.

In holding that racial discrimination in jury selection offends the Equal Protection Clause, the Court in *Strauder* recognized, however, that a defendant has no right to a "petit jury composed in whole or in part of persons of his own race." . . . But the defendant does have the right to be tried by a jury whose members are selected pursuant to nondiscriminatory criteria. The Equal Protection Clause guarantees the defendant that the State will not exclude members of his race from the jury venire on account of race, or on the false assumption that members of his race as a group are not qualified to serve as jurors.

. . .

Accordingly, the component of the jury selection process at issue here, the State's privilege to strike individual jurors through peremptory challenges, is subject to the commands of the Equal Protection Clause. Although a prosecutor ordinarily is entitled to exercise permitted peremptory challenges "for any reason at all, as long as that reason is related to his view concerning the outcome" of the case to be tried, . . . the Equal Protection Clause forbids the prosecutor to challenge potential jurors solely on account of their race or on the assumption that black jurors as a group will be unable impartially to consider the State's case against a black defendant.

The principles announced in *Strauder* never have been questioned in any subsequent decision of this Court. Rather, the Court has been called upon repeatedly to review the application of those principles to particular facts. A recurring question in these cases, as in any case alleging a violation of the Equal Protection Clause, was whether the defendant had met his burden of proving purposeful discrimination on the part of the State. . . .

Swain required the Court to decide, among other issues, whether a black defendant was denied equal protection by the State's exercise of peremptory challenges to exclude members of his race from the petit jury. The record in Swain showed that the prosecutor had used the State's peremptory challenges to strike the six black persons included on the petit jury venire. While rejecting the defendant's claim for failure to prove purposeful discrimination, the Court nonetheless indicated that the Equal Protection Clause placed some limits on the State's exercise of peremptory challenges.

. . . While the Constitution does not confer a right to peremptory challenges, those challenges traditionally have been viewed as one means of assuring the selection of a qualified and unbiased jury. To preserve the peremptory nature of the prosecutor's challenge, the Court in *Swain* declined to scrutinize his actions in a particular case by relying on a presumption that he properly exercised the State's challenges.

The Court went on to observe, however, that a State may not exercise its challenges in contravention of the Equal Protection Clause. It was impermissible for a prosecutor to use his challenges to exclude blacks from the jury "for reasons wholly unrelated to the outcome of the particular case on trial" or to deny to blacks "the same right and opportunity to participate in the administration of justice enjoyed by the white population." Accordingly, a black defendant could make out a prima facie case of purposeful discrimination on proof that the peremptory challenge system was "being perverted" in that manner. For example, an inference of purposeful discrimination would be raised on evidence that a prosecutor, "in case after case, whatever the circumstances, whatever the crime and whoever the defendant or the victim may be, is responsible for the removal of Negroes who have been selected as qualified jurors by the jury commissioners and who have survived challenges for cause, with the result that no Negroes ever serve on petit juries." Evidence offered by the defendant in *Swain* did not meet that standard. While the defendant showed that prosecutors in the jurisdiction had exercised their strikes to exclude blacks from the jury, he offered no proof of the circumstances under which prosecutors were responsible for striking black jurors beyond the facts of his own case.

A number of lower courts following the teaching of *Swain* reasoned that proof of repeated striking of blacks over a number of cases was necessary to establish a violation of the Equal Protection Clause. Since this interpretation of *Swain* has placed on defendants a crippling burden of proof, prosecutors' peremptory challenges are now largely immune from constitutional scrutiny. For reasons that follow, we reject this evidentiary formulation as inconsistent with standards that have been developed since *Swain* for assessing a prima facie case under the Equal Protection Clause.

. . .

The standards for assessing a prima facie case in the context of discriminatory selection of the venire have been fully articulated since *Swain*. . . . To establish such a case, the defendant first must show that he is a member of a cognizable racial group, and that the prosecutor has exercised peremptory challenges to remove from the venire members of the defendant's race. Second, the defendant is entitled to rely on the fact, as to which there can be no dispute, that peremptory challenges constitute a jury selection practice that permits "those to discriminate who are of a mind to discriminate." Finally, the defendant must show that these facts and any other relevant circumstances raise an inference that the prosecutor used that practice to exclude the veniremen from the petit jury on account of their race. This combination of factors in the empaneling of the petit jury, as in the selection of the venire, raises the necessary inference of purposeful discrimination.

In deciding whether the defendant has made the requisite showing, the trial court should consider all relevant circumstances. For example, a "pattern" of strikes against black jurors included in the particular venire might give rise to an inference of discrimination. Similarly, the prosecutor's questions and statements during *voir dire* examination and in exercising his challenges may support or refute an inference of discriminatory purpose. These examples are merely illustrative. We have confidence that trial judges, experienced in supervising *voir dire*, will be able to decide if the circumstances concerning the prosecutor's use of peremptory challenges creates a prima facie case of discrimination against black jurors.

Once the defendant makes a prima facie showing, the burden shifts to the State to come forward with a neutral explanation for challenging black jurors. Though this requirement imposes a limitation in some cases on the full peremptory character of the historic challenge, we emphasize that the prosecutor's explanation need not rise to the level justifying exercise of a challenge for cause. But the prosecutor may not rebut the defendant's prima facie case of discrimination by stating merely that he challenged jurors of the defendant's race on the assumption—or his intuitive judgment—that they would be partial to the defendant because of their shared race. Just as the Equal Protection Clause forbids the States to exclude black persons from the venire on the assumption that blacks as a group are unqualified to serve as jurors, supra, so it forbids the States to strike black veniremen on the assumption that they will be biased in a particular case simply because the defendant is black. The core guarantee of equal protection, ensuring citizens that their State will not discriminate on account of race, would be meaningless were we to approve the exclusion of jurors on the basis of such assumptions, which arise solely from the jurors' race. Nor may the prosecutor rebut the defendant's case merely by denying that he had a discriminatory motive or "affirm[ing] [his] good faith in making individual selections." If these general assertions were accepted as rebutting a defendant's prima facie case, the Equal Protection Clause "would be but a vain and illusory requirement." The prosecutor therefore must articulate a neutral explanation related to the particular case to be tried. The trial court then will have the duty to determine if the defendant has established purposeful discrimination.

The State contends that our holding will eviscerate the fair trial values served by the peremptory challenge. Conceding that the Constitution does not guarantee a right to peremptory challenges and that *Swain* did state that their use ultimately is subject to the strictures of equal protection, the State argues that the privilege of unfettered exercise of the challenge is of vital importance to the criminal justice system.

While we recognize, of course, that the peremptory challenge occupies an important position in our trial procedures, we do not agree that our decision today will undermine the contribution the challenge generally makes to the administration of justice. The reality of practice, amply reflected in many state- and federal-court opinions, shows that the challenge may be, and unfortunately at times has been, used to discriminate against black jurors. By requiring trial courts to be sensitive to the racially discriminatory use of peremptory challenges, our decision enforces the mandate of equal protection and furthers the ends of justice. In view of the heterogeneous population of our Nation, public respect for our criminal justice system and the rule of law will be strengthened if we ensure that no citizen is disqualified from jury service because of his race.

Nor are we persuaded by the State's suggestion that our holding will create serious administrative difficulties. In those States applying a version of the evidentiary standard we recognize today, courts have not experienced serious administrative burdens, and the peremptory challenge system has survived. We decline, however, to formulate particular procedures to be followed upon a defendant's timely objection to a prosecutor's challenges.

In this case, petitioner made a timely objection to the prosecutor's removal of all black persons on the venire. Because the trial court flatly rejected the objection without requiring the prosecutor to give an explanation for his action, we remand this case for further proceedings. If the trial court decides that the facts establish, prima facie, purposeful discrimination and the prosecutor does not come forward with a neutral explanation for his action, our precedents require that petitioner's conviction be reversed.

It is so ordered.

CHIEF JUSTICE BURGER, joined by JUSTICE REHNQUIST, dissenting.

Today the Court sets aside the peremptory challenge, a procedure which has been part of the common law for many centuries and part of our jury system for nearly 200 years.

. . .

Permitting unexplained peremptories has long been regarded as a means to strengthen our jury system in other ways as well.

. . .

Instead of even considering the history or function of the peremptory challenge, the bulk of the Court's opinion is spent recounting the well-established principle that intentional exclusion of racial groups from jury venires is a violation of the Equal Protection Clause. I too reaffirm that principle, which has been a part of our constitutional tradition since at least *Strauder v. West Virginia*. But if today's decision is nothing more than mere "application" of the "principles announced in *Strauder*," as the Court maintains, some will consider it curious that the application went unrecognized for over a century. The Court in *Swain* had no difficulty in unanimously concluding that cases such as *Strauder* did not require inquiry into the basis for a peremptory challenge. More recently we held that "[defendants] are not entitled to a jury of any particular composition. . . ."

A moment's reflection quickly reveals the vast differences between the racial exclusions involved in *Strauder* and the allegations before us today:

> Exclusion from the venire summons process implies that the government (usually the legislative or judicial branch) . . . has made the general determination that those excluded are unfit to try *any* case. Exercise of the peremptory challenge, by contrast, represents the discrete decision, made by one of two or more opposed *litigants* in the trial phase of our adversary system of justice, that the challenged venireperson will likely be more unfavorable to that litigant in that *particular case* than others on the same venire.
>
> Thus, excluding a particular cognizable group from all venire pools is stigmatizing and discriminatory in several interrelated ways that the peremptory challenge is not. The former singles out the excluded group, while individuals of all groups are equally subject to peremptory challenge on any basis, including their group affiliation. Further, venire-pool exclusion bespeaks *a priori* across-the-board total unfitness, while peremptory-strike exclusion merely suggests potential partiality in a particular isolated case. Exclusion from venires focuses on the inherent attributes of the excluded group and infers its *inferiority*, but the peremptory does not. To suggest that a particular race is unfit to judge in any case necessarily is racially insulting. To suggest that each race may have its own special concerns, or even may tend to favor its own, is not.

. . .

The Court also purports to express "no views on whether the Constitution imposes any limit on the exercise of peremptory challenges by *defense* counsel." But the clear and inescapable import of this novel holding will inevitably be to limit the use of this valuable tool to both prosecutors and defense attorneys alike. Once the Court has held that *prosecutors* are limited in their use of peremptory challenges, could we rationally hold that defendants are not? "Our criminal justice system 'requires not only freedom from any bias against the accused, but also from any prejudice against his prosecution.' " . . .

Rather than applying straightforward equal protection analysis, the Court substitutes for the holding in *Swain* a curious hybrid. The defendant must first establish a "prima facie case," of invidious discrimination, then the "burden shifts to the State to come forward with a neutral explanation for challenging black jurors." . . .

While undoubtedly these rules are well suited to other contexts, particularly where (as with Title VII) they are required by an Act of Congress, they seem curiously out of place when applied to peremptory challenges in criminal cases. Our system permits two types of challenges: challenges for cause and peremptory challenges. Challenges for cause obviously have to be explained; by definition, peremptory challenges do not. "It is called a peremptory challenge, because the prisoner may challenge peremptorily, on his own dislike, *without showing of any cause*." Analytically, there is no middle ground: A challenge either has to be explained or it does not. . . .

Confronted with the dilemma it created, the Court today attempts to decree a middle ground. To rebut a prima facie case, the Court requires a "neutral explanation" for the challenge, but is at pains to "emphasize" that the "explanation need not rise to the level justifying exercise of a challenge for cause." I am at a loss to discern the governing principles here. A "clear and reasonably specific" explanation of "legitimate reasons" for exercising the challenge will be difficult to distinguish from a challenge for cause. Anything short of a challenge for cause may well be seen as an "arbitrary and capricious" challenge. . . . Apparently the Court envisions permissible challenges short of a challenge for cause that are just a little bit arbitrary—but not too much. . . .

The effect of the Court's decision, however, will be to force the defendant to come forward and "articulate a neutral explanation" for his peremptory challenge, a burden he probably cannot meet. This example demonstrates that today's holding will produce juries that the parties do not believe are truly impartial. This will surely do more than "disconcert" litigants; it will diminish confidence in the jury system.

. . .

JUSTICE REHNQUIST, with whom THE CHIEF JUSTICE joins, dissenting.

. . .

I cannot subscribe to the Court's unprecedented use of the Equal Protection Clause to restrict the historic scope of the peremptory challenge, which has been described as "a necessary part of trial by jury." *Swain*. In my view, there is simply nothing "unequal" about the State's using its peremptory challenges to strike blacks from the jury in cases involving black defendants, so long as such challenges are also used to exclude whites in cases involving white defendants, Hispanics in cases involving Hispanic defendants, Asians in cases involving Asian defendants, and so on. This case-specific use of peremptory challenges by the State does not single out blacks, or members of any other race for that matter, for discriminatory treatment. Such use of peremptories is at best based upon seat-of-the-pants instincts, which are undoubtedly crudely stereotypical and may in many cases be hopelessly mistaken. But as long as they are applied across-the-board to jurors of all races and nationalities, I do not see—and the Court most certainly has not explained—how their use violates the Equal Protection Clause.

. . .

CASE DISCUSSION QUESTIONS

1. To what extent does this decision alter the definition we gave for a peremptory challenge? How would you modify the definition to take this decision into account?
2. What procedure is the trial judge supposed to use to determine if the prosecutor's peremptory challenge was based on race? Do you think this procedure is appropriate? Can you think of a better way for the judge to determine if a peremptory challenge was based on race?
3. What negative consequences do Chief Justice Burger and Justice Rehnquist think will occur as a result of this decision? Do you think they were right?
4. This case was limited to the use of peremptory challenges by the prosecution to eliminate Black jurors in a Black defendant's trial. Should the holding be extended to the exercise of peremptory challenges by a defense attorney? Why or why not? Should it extend to jurors' religious affiliation? Why or why not?

In 1994, the Supreme Court extended its ruling to also apply to exclusions based on gender.[11] In 2016 and 2019, the Court overturned murder convictions of African American defendants in trials in which the prosecutors systematically used peremptory challenges to remove prospective jurors who were Black.[12]

The procedure for *Batson* objections is initiated by one side making the objection in a sidebar. The opponent then must justify every peremptory challenge exercised against jurors who possess the characteristic on which the

[11] *J.E.B. v. Alabama*, 511 U.S. 127 (1994).

[12] *Flowers v. Mississippi*, 139 S. Ct. 2228 (2019); *Foster v. Chapman*, 136 S. Ct. 1737 (2018).

objection is based. In other words, the opponent must show that the jurors were struck for a reason other than race or sex. Although this is done in a sidebar or in chambers, a court reporter usually is present so that there is a record of the discussion. The defendant and the struck juror do not have to be of the same race or gender to raise this objection.

4. SELECTION OF ALTERNATE JURORS

In trials that are expected to go on for more than a day or two, it is common practice to select a few alternate jurors to be ready to step in if one of the regular jurors gets sick or is unable to continue for some other reason.[13] In federal court, the judge may empanel up to six alternates.[14] Alternate jurors sit in the jury box with the regular jurors and listen to all the same testimony. However, they do not participate in jury deliberations unless they have been chosen to replace one of the original jurors.

5. INSTRUCTIONS TO JURORS AND SEQUESTERING JURIES

Once the jurors, and any alternates, have been chosen, the judge will instruct them not to discuss the case, either among themselves or with anyone else—including family and friends. The judge will usually also instruct them not to read any newspaper articles or watch or listen to any news broadcasts about the trial. During lunch breaks, the jurors eat together under the watch of a bailiff or other court officer.

In highly publicized cases, the court may **sequester a jury**. This is a procedure for isolating jurors so they are not exposed to outside influences. Generally, this means that the court houses the jury members in a hotel and blocks access to newspaper, television, radio, and Internet content related to the trial. However, due to the added expense and the resentment it evokes in the jurors, judges are reluctant to use this option.

Sequestering a jury
A procedure for isolating jurors in order to prevent them from being exposed to outside influences such as media coverage or internet discussion of the case.

APPLICATION EXERCISES

4. Research the number of peremptory challenges given to each side in non-capital felony and misdemeanor cases in the state in which your school is located. Give the citation to the statute or rule.
5. Visit a local court during jury selection in a criminal case. Write a report to your instructor that includes your observations of the following:

[13]Other reasons could include situations in which a juror has a family emergency, is shown to have withheld or lied about key information during *voir dire,* or has acted improperly during the course of the trial.

[14]FRCrP 24(c)(1).

a. The system used to select a jury (jury box or struck jury)
b. The extent to which the attorneys got to question jurors directly
c. Whether prospective jurors were dismissed
d. If jurors were dismissed for cause, what the reason was for their dismissal
e. If jurors were dismissed through a peremptory challenge, what you speculate the reason was for their dismissal

Include the names of the judge, attorneys, and defendant in your report, along with the date and time that you visited the court.

E. OPENING STATEMENTS

Opening statements Remarks made by prosecutors and defense attorneys at the start of a trial, which are designed to provide a framework for understanding the witnesses and documents that will be part of their cases.

Most criminal trials begin with **opening statements** from the attorneys representing the prosecution and the defense. An attorney for the prosecution speaks first because the government carries the burden of proof. The prosecution's opening statements usually provide a framework that explains the nature of the alleged crimes and helps the decision maker (either a jury or the judge) understand how the evidence to be presented will prove the elements of the crimes being charged. After describing how the prosecution thinks the crime happened, the prosecutor will usually highlight some of the key witnesses that will be called and what their testimony is expected to contribute to the prosecution's case.

The defense's opening statement typically follows the prosecutor's, and it explains the defendant's theory of the case, highlights what key defense witnesses are expected to contribute, and encourages the jurors to keep an open mind until the defense has had a chance to present its witnesses.[15] Note that these remarks are called opening "statements," while the remarks made at the end of the trial are referred to as closing "arguments." This distinction in terminology reflects the fact that attorneys are not supposed to be able to argue the guilt or innocence of defendants at this stage of the trial. These opening remarks are supposed to be limited to providing a framework or context in which to place the evidence that will be presented during the trial. The attorneys can describe what a specific witness will be testifying about but cannot argue that some witnesses are more credible than others. Many litigators use their opening statements to introduce the theme of their case. Exhibit 12.4 includes excerpts of the opening statements made by both sides in the trial of the former Brooklyn Center, Minnesota, police officer Kimberly Potter, who killed Daunte Wright, a young Black man, when she mistakenly shot him with her revolver rather than a taser. The jury found Potter guilty of manslaughter. The judge sentenced her to 16 months in prison, followed by supervised release.

[15]In some jurisdictions, the defense has the choice of deferring their opening statement until after the prosecution has finished its case in chief. However, most prefer to begin to raise doubts in the jurors' minds from the very beginning of the trial.

Exhibit 12.4: Excerpts from Opening Statements

Prosecution

This case is about an officer who knew not to get it dead wrong, but she failed to get it right. This case is about the defendant Kimberly Potter betraying her badge, betraying her oath, and betraying her position of public trust. And on April 11 of this year, she betrayed a 20-year-old kid. She pulled out her firearm. She pointed it at his chest, and she shot and killed Daunte Wright. . . . She was trained on the differences between her gun and a taser. She was also trained on the risks of pulling the wrong weapon, and that drawing and firing the wrong weapon could kill someone.

Defense

She said "I'll tase you. I'll tase you." The language was direct. It was clear. It was unmistakable. All Mr. Wright had to do was stop. He was told he was arrested on a warrant. He resisted; she said "I'll tase you." . . . What she is seeing is that her partner, Sergeant Johnson, is in the car . . . restraining the gearshift so that Mr. Wright can't escape. . . . Mr. Wright can stop; he goes. She can't let him leave because he's going to kill her partner. So she goes, "Taser, taser, taser" and pulls the trigger believing it was a taser, or why else would she say it? And immediately, upon pulling the trigger a single time. . ., she realized what has happened, much to her everlasting and unending regret.

F. Presentation of the Evidence

The heart of the trial process involves putting people on the stand to provide testimonial evidence about what took place and lay the foundation for the admission of written documents, test results, and various types of physical objects like weapons, illicit drugs, and stolen goods.[16]

1. PROSECUTION'S CASE-IN-CHIEF

Just as the prosecution side gets to make the first opening statement, it gets to present its witnesses and exhibits first.[17] This section of the trial is referred to as being the prosecution's "case-in-chief." For each witness called, whether that witness is called as part of the prosecution's case-in-chief, the defense's case-in-chief, or as a rebuttal witness, the questioning will follow the pattern of direct, cross, re-direct, re-cross, re-re-direct, re-re-cross, etc.

---

[16]See Chapter 10 for a discussion of evidence (pp. 349-358) and Chapter 11 for a discussion on the selection and preparation of witnesses (pp. 383-386).

[17]As was the case with opening statements, the prosecution goes first because it has the burden of proof.

The complexity of the case will determine the number of witnesses called, the exhibits presented, and the length of the trial itself. In a traffic case, the prosecutor may only need to call the police officer operating the radar gun to prove beyond a reasonable doubt that the defendant was speeding. In contrast, in the illegal wiretapping trial of Los Angeles celebrity private investigator Anthony Pellicano, U.S. Attorneys listed 127 witnesses they intended to call, including the actors Keith Carradine and Farrah Fawcett. (*See* Exhibit 12.2 on page 404 for the first part of the prosecution's witness list.)

a. *Direct Examinations*

Direct examination
The initial questioning conducted by attorneys for the side that called the witnesses.

Direct examinations begin with a brief ceremony in which witnesses raise their hand and take an oath to answer the questions truthfully.[18] This procedure is designed to impress upon the witnesses the importance of telling the truth while they are on the stand. Failure to tell the truth can, but seldom does, result in perjury charges being brought against the witness.

They are usually pretty much scripted and rehearsed[19] because the witnesses are usually cooperative and supportive of the side that called them. After some introductory questions designed to put the witness at ease and to provide relevant background information about the witness, the prosecuting attorney will ask questions designed to bring out the facts needed to describe the nature of the crime and establish the nature of the defendant's involvement.

Leading questions
Questions worded in such a way as to suggest what the answer should be.

Perhaps the most important thing to keep in mind about direct examination is that the attorney conducting the examination is generally prohibited from using **leading questions.** This type of question is worded in such a way as to suggest what the answer should be. An example would be a prosecutor asking: "Wouldn't you say the defendant appeared to be very angry at that time?" The form of the question in effect suggests what the attorney wants the witness to say. Another example is: "Is it true that you saw the defendant pull a knife and stab the victim?" Instead of using these leading questions, the attorney must ask such questions as: "Where were you when the victim was attacked?" "Please describe to the court what you saw." "Can you identify the person you saw?"

Adverse witness
A witness who is either the opposing party in the case or a witness who is closely affiliated with the opposing party.

Hostile witness
A witness who manifests great hostility or prejudice against the side that called him or her to testify.

There are, however, some important exceptions to the general prohibition against asking leading questions on direct. For example, attorneys are allowed to lead witnesses through background information about where they live or what their educational background is. Leading questions are also allowed in situations where the witness may be very young or be mentally disabled. These exceptions are justified in terms of saving time in situations where such questioning isn't expected to disadvantage the other side. There are also exceptions for examinations of adverse and hostile witnesses.

An **adverse witness** is either the opposing party in the case or a witness closely affiliated with the opposing party, whereas a **hostile witness** is a witness who shows great hostility or prejudice against the side calling him or her to

---

[18]Because some people have religious objections to "solemnly swearing," they are given the alternative of "affirming" or "declaring."

[19]The attorneys or their paralegals have often gone over the questions and answers with the witness in advance of their appearance in court.

testify. In the criminal context, the arresting officer is an adverse witness to the defendant. The defendant's family members or someone who was also involved in criminal endeavors are hostile witnesses when called by the government. By allowing leading questions in these situations, the attorney can prevent the witness from wasting the court's time and giving overly ambiguous answers.

At this point, we also want to remind you about the differential treatment given to those accepted as "expert" witnesses.[20] Attorneys are allowed to pose hypothetical questions to expert witnesses that they could not ask of regular witnesses. Although expert witnesses were not present at the scene of the crime or have not seen the defendant, they can give an informed opinion as to the probability of something occurring in a situation similar to that of the defendant.

b. Introduction of Exhibits

Although testimonial evidence is extremely important in most criminal cases, physical and documentary evidence is often critical. To get things like weapons, test results, medical records, and photographs admitted into evidence, attorneys need to use witness testimony to lay a proper foundation.[21]

As mentioned in Chapter 11, paralegals are often assigned the task of organizing and labeling each exhibit so that each is associated with the witness needed to lay the proper foundation. In addition, attorneys may have their paralegals keep track of the exhibits during the trial. Figure 12.2 presents the typical protocol paralegals follow with respect to trial exhibits. The attorney doing the direct examination is responsible for seeing that the right questions are asked. For example, to properly authenticate physical evidence, law enforcement officers are typically called to testify that they either kept the object in their exclusive personal control from the time it was found until the time it is presented in court or maintained a complete record of everyone involved in the chain of custody (i.e., everyone who handled the object from the time it was found to the time it was presented in court). In both situations, officers give testimony that they marked the object in a way that will make it easily distinguishable at a later time.

Once the proper foundation has been laid, the party calling the witness who identified the exhibit will move for its admission into evidence. The opposing side may object to its admission on the basis of one of the rules of evidence.

1. Mark exhibits before testimony begins.
2. Chart the use of exhibits at trial:
   a. Marked for identification
   b. Motion to admit
   c. Admit/deny
3. Before resting, verify that all exhibits have been offered and the court has ruled.
4. Before the case goes to the jury, make sure that the court has all the exhibits.

Figure 12.2 Handling Exhibits at Trial

[20]See Chapter 10, pp. 353-354.

[21]See Chapter 10, pp. 357-358.

If the objection is overruled, the exhibit is admitted. Conversely, if the objection is sustained, the exhibit is not admitted into evidence.

> **APPLICATION EXERCISE**
>
> **6.** Create a five-column Microsoft Excel spreadsheet to display defense trial exhibits by number and description, along with whether they were offered into evidence, subjected to objection, and admitted by the judge. Insert the number and description of the exhibits referenced in Exhibit 12.1 in the *Cook* case.

c. Objections

Objection
A request to the judge to disallow specific questions to a witness, comments by opposing counsel, or responses from witnesses.

During direct examination, opposing attorneys are limited to taking notes and making **objections**. The ability to make effective objections is one of the greatest skills that an attorney can have because the timely use of appropriate objections can keep damaging evidence out and throw opposing attorneys "off their game."

When it comes to making objections, timing is critical. Rule 103(1) of the Federal Rules of Evidence states:

> In case the ruling is one admitting evidence, a timely objection or motion to strike appears of record, stating the specific ground of objection, if the specific ground was not apparent from the context.

Thus, if the objection comes too late, it will be rejected on that basis alone. If the objection is to the type of question being asked or the way in which it is worded, it must be raised as soon as the question is asked, rather than waiting until after the witness has answered. If the objection is to something the witness said in response to a legitimate question, the objection must be raised as soon as it is clear that the answer being given is objectionable. Then if the objection is sustained, the attorney must request to have the witness's answer stricken from the record. When the judge sustains an objection to a question, the attorney conducting the examination must either reword the question to make the inquiry in a less objectionable way or get the same information from another witness in an acceptable way.

d. Preserving the Record

Attorneys will make objections even when they do not expect the trial judge to sustain them. This "objecting for the record" is sometimes called "protecting the record" or "making a record for appeal." Not only are attorneys required to raise appropriate objections at the proper times during the trial, they are also expected to preserve a proper record for a possible appeal. When attorneys fail to object during trial, they cannot complain later to an appellate court about something that was admitted into evidence during the trial. In addition, the judge must overrule the objection in order to preserve the error on review. If the judge does not rule on an objection, it is waived.

When the judge sustains an objection to the admission of testimonial evidence, the attorney who sought to have the testimony admitted should make an **offer of proof** to make a record for appeal. This is a procedure whereby the attorney either (1) tells the judge what the witness would have testified to if the judge had not sustained the objection to admitting it or (2) elicits the challenged testimony from the witness. In either event, the court reporter records the offer of proof. The contested testimony is taken outside the presence of the jury, so the jury won't be influenced by what the judge excluded.

Offer of proof
A procedure whereby excluded testimony is placed into the record for possible appellate review of the judge's decision to exclude it.

e. *Cross-Examinations*

After the attorney who called the witness finishes a direct examination, the opposing attorney gets an opportunity to **cross-examine** that witness. This is a very important right guaranteed by the Sixth and Fourteenth Amendments to the U.S. Constitution.[22] It provides the opportunity to clarify potentially misleading statements and half-truths, as well as to bring out additional favorable information not touched on by the opponent's attorney. Although cross-examination is limited to the scope of the topics considered on direct examination, judges give cross-examiners broad latitude in exploring these topics, as well as any potential bias or prejudice of the witness.

Cross-examination
The questioning of a witness called by the opposing side.

An important objective in many cross-examinations is to attack the credibility of the witness. In most trials, there are conflicts between the testimonies of different witnesses. One says that the defendant was at the scene of the crime; another says that the defendant was across town playing poker with his buddies. One says that the robber had dark hair; another says that it was blond. To help jurors resolve these conflicts in their favor, attorneys attempt to bring out possible biases or the inability of the witness to have seen clearly what he or she claims to have seen.

Another key way to attack credibility is to confront the witnesses with inconsistencies between their trial testimony and their written statements. In most states, written statements are provided to the opposing side through discovery. In the federal courts and some states, there is no requirement to furnish witness statements until after direct examination. FRCrP 26.2(a) states:

> After a witness other than the defendant has testified on direct examination, the court, on motion of a party who did not call the witness, must order an attorney for the government or the defendant and the defendant's attorney to produce, for the examination and use of the moving party, any statement of the witness that is in their possession and that relates to the subject matter of the witness's testimony.

You should check your jurisdiction's requirements for witness statement production. Impeachment is usually more effective when the prior statements are available prior to trial.

---

[22]See Chapter 10, pp. 342-347.

Re-direct
The portion of a witness's testimony during which the side that conducted the initial direct examination has an opportunity to ask additional questions designed to clarify issues raised during cross-examination.

Re-cross
The portion of a witness's testimony during which the side that conducted the initial cross-examination has an opportunity to ask additional questions designed to clarify issues raised during the re-direct.

Resting the case
A phrase used by attorneys to announce that they have presented all of the evidence that they intend to present at the current stage of the trial.

Motion for judgment of acquittal or motion for directed verdict
A request to have the judge enter a verdict of not guilty on the basis that the prosecution failed to present enough evidence to establish a *prima facie* case of guilt. In some jurisdictions, it is called a motion for directed verdict.

***Prima facie* case**
Evidence that, if not contradicted by other evidence, is sufficient to meet the burden of proof required for that type of case.

The process of drawing potentially negative information out of the other side's witnesses is made much easier by the fact that leading questions are allowed in cross-examinations. So, on cross, the attorney can dramatically ask: "Isn't it true that you used to date . . . ," or "Isn't it true that you recently were fired by. . . ."

APPLICATION EXERCISE

7. Research when witness statements must be provided in the state in which your school is located.
   a. Give the citation to the statute or rule.
   b. Is the rule more liberal or more restrictive than FRCrP 26.2?

f. Re-Direct and Re-Cross

After the defense has taken its best shot at undercutting the impact of the prosecution's witness, the prosecution gets a chance to rehabilitate its witness's credibility during the **re-direct** phase of the testimony. However, re-direct questions are limited to issues that were raised by the cross-examination of that witness. They cannot be used to raise new issues or to explore subjects that were not covered as part of the cross.

Although the questioning of the witness usually ends with the re-direct, there are occasions in which a re-direct will be followed by a **re-cross**. Re-crosses are limited to issues that were raised in the re-direct. In very rare cases, there could be a re-redirect and a re-re-cross, etc., but in each case, the questions must be within the scope of the examination that preceded it.

g. Resting the Case-in-Chief

After the prosecution has finished with all of its planned witnesses, it **rests its case**. This signals the end of the first stage of the presentation of the evidence and leads to the start of the defendant's case-in-chief. The prosecution still retains the right to present additional evidence at the rebuttal stage of the trial.

2. DEFENDANT'S MOTION FOR JUDGMENT OF ACQUITTAL OR MOTION FOR DIRECTED VERDICT

Following the resting of the prosecution's case, the defense attorney will often make a **motion for judgment of acquittal**. This is a request to the judge to enter a verdict of not guilty on the basis that the prosecution failed to present enough evidence to establish a ***prima facie* case** of guilt. In many state courts, this motion may also be referred to as a motion for directed verdict.[23]

[23]A motion for directed verdict brought in a bench trial is referred to as a "motion for directed finding." The motion typically is presented orally and may be written and supported by a legal memorandum.

Although it is rarely granted, defense attorneys have nothing to lose by making this motion immediately after the prosecution rests its case-in-chief. If the judge agrees that the prosecution has not met its burden of presenting a *prima facie* case that the defendant committed the crime charged, the judge must enter a not-guilty verdict, and there is no need for the defense to call any witnesses. In federal court, the judge may enter a judgment of acquittal on his or her own motion.[24] If the judge grants the motion, the trial is over. However, judges rarely grant such motions.

3. DEFENDANT'S CASE-IN-CHIEF

The presentation of the defendant's case-in-chief generally follows the same pattern and rules as that of the prosecution. Witnesses are called to give testimonial evidence and lay the foundation for documentary and physical evidence. The defendant's direct examinations are followed by prosecution cross-examinations, defendant re-directs, and prosecution re-crosses.

The defendant's attorney uses this opportunity to offer evidence in support of a defense or in opposition to the prosecution's evidence. The most effective theory that the defendant can present is one that completely explains all of the facts supporting the hypothesis of innocence. Under this approach, the defendant will explain, impeach, or refute every fact that may contradict the theory of innocence.

Even if the theory completely explains all of the evidence, it must make sense to the jury in order to acquit a defendant. The Jussie Smollett case is an example of a complete defense theory that was rejected because it didn't add up to the jury. The prosecution claimed that the defendant hired two men to stage an attack that he falsely reported to the police as a racist, homophobic assault. At trial, Smollett testified that the men put a noose around this neck, and after the attack, he returned home and put the noose back around his neck so the police could see it. Andre Hope, the sole Black juror in the case, didn't find Smollett's testimony credible. "As an African American person, I'm not putting that noose back on at all," Hope explained.[25]

The defense can also present character witnesses to establish that the defendant possesses qualities that are inconsistent with the commission of the crime charged. Although the defendant cannot be forced to testify, if the defendant takes the stand, on cross the prosecutor may ask questions beyond the scope of direct and explore facts surrounding the offenses for which the defendant is charged.

4. REBUTTAL AND SURREBUTTAL

Rebuttal evidence
Evidence presented to explain, counteract, or disprove facts given in evidence after a party had rested its case.

After both sides have presented their cases-in-chief, the prosecution gets a chance to bring in **rebuttal evidence** to counter information presented by the

[24] FRCrP 29(a).

[25] "Only Black Juror in Jussie Smollett Case Couldn't Get Past Ex-'Empire' Actor's Reaction to Noose," *USA Today* (December 14, 2021), https://www.usatoday.com/story/entertainment/2021/12/14/jussie-smollett-case-black-juror-confused-reaction-noose/8894592002/.

1. Preparing witnesses and trial exhibits (pre-trial)
2. Preparing witness list (pre-trial)
3. Preparing witness files with impeachment material (pre-trial)
4. Preparing draft *motions in limine* (pre-trial)
5. Preparing pocket briefs on questions of evidence (pre-trial)
6. Preparing stipulations (pre-trial)
7. Preparing stipulations, exhibit list (pre-trial)
8. Preparing list of witnesses (pre-trial)
9. Exhibit management
   a. Charting both sides' exhibits
   b. Acting as custodian of exhibits
   c. Reminding attorney of exhibits not offered into evidenced. Reminding attorney of exhibits not offered into evidence
10. Keeping track of evidentiary rulings taken under advisement
11. Keeping witnesses updated as to when they are expected to testify
12. Taking notes during direct and cross-examinations
13. Highlighting opposition witnesses' statements for use against them on cross-examination.

Figure 12.3 Paralegals' Roles in the Evidence Phase of Trials

Rebuttal
The phase of the trial in which the prosecution calls witnesses to dispute the evidence presented by the defense in its case-in-chief.

Surrebuttal
The phase of a trial in which the defense calls witnesses to dispute the rebuttal evidence offered by the prosecution.

defense. This section of the trial is referred to as the **rebuttal.** During this phase of the trial, the prosecutor may either call additional witnesses, or recall witnesses, who have already testified, for the purpose of countering evidence presented in the defense's case-in-chief.

Following the prosecution's rebuttal, the defense has the opportunity to present **surrebuttal** witnesses. In this part of the trial, the defense recalls witnesses who previously testified or calls new witnesses to counter evidence presented during the prosecution's rebuttal.

Figure 12.3 lists the different ways in which paralegals can assist attorneys during the evidence phase of a trial.

5. RENEWED MOTION FOR DIRECTED VERDICT

After all the evidence has been presented, the defendant may renew the motion for a directed verdict (or acquittal). In this context, the defense attorney is arguing that all of the evidence, taken in the light most favorable to the prosecution and resolving all the credibility issues in favor of the government, is insufficient to establish the defendant's guilt beyond a reasonable doubt. However, this motion is rarely granted at this stage of the case, either. The government cannot appeal the granting of the motion. This would place the defendant in double jeopardy in violation of the Fifth Amendment.[26]

[26]See *Smalis v. Pennsylvania*, 476 U.S. 140 (1986).

APPLICATION EXERCISE

8. For the state in which your school is located, research the type of motion filed when the prosecution does not meet its burden of establishing a *prima facie* case.

a. Where did you find the answer?

b. How do the requirements of the motion compare to motions brought pursuant to FRCrP 29(a)?

G. Jury Instructions

It is the role of the jury to apply the law to the facts that were presented in the trial and then determine whether the prosecution proved, beyond a reasonable doubt, that the defendant violated specific statutes. However, the statutes and court rules they are supposed to apply are written in "legalese" and are often very confusing to lay jurors. Therefore, instructions are given to the jurors on the laws that they are supposed to apply, as well as the procedures that they should follow in their deliberations.

Jury instructions are written directions given by the judge to the jury pertaining to the controlling principles of law in the case. They also let the jury know the theories of the case proposed by each party and advise them of the standards they must apply to make their decision. There are two types of these instructions: pattern and non-pattern.

Jury instructions
Written directions given by the judge to the jury pertaining to the controlling principles of law in the case.

1. Pattern Jury Instructions

Since it is grounds for reversal if a judge fails to give the proper instructions, judges usually rely on **pattern jury instructions.** These are a set of basic instructions that have been prepared by committees of judges, lawyers, and scholars for use by the trial courts in their jurisdictions. A total of 48 states and most federal circuits[27] make pattern criminal jury instructions available. Although trial courts are not required to use them, most judges do so because they generally are upheld by appellate courts in their jurisdiction.

Pattern jury instructions
Uniform basic jury instructions typically prepared by committees of judges, lawyers, and scholars for use by the trial courts in a specific jurisdiction.

Two of the jury instructions given in the Derek Chauvin murder prosecution appear in Exhibits 12.5 and 12.6. Exhibit 12.5 displays the elements the government had to prove. Exhibit 12.6 presents a description of a police officer's use of force.

[27]Pattern criminal jury instructions are available in the D.C., First, Third, Fourth, Fifth, Sixth, Seventh, Eighth, Ninth, Tenth, and Eleventh Circuits.

Exhibit 12.5: Elements of Offense Jury Instruction

COUNT I

The Defendant is charged in Count I with Murder in the Second Degree in connection with the death of George Floyd.

Definition

Under Minnesota law, a person causing the death of another person, without intent to cause the death of any person, while committing or attempting to commit a felony offense is guilty of the crime of Murder in the Second Degree.

The Defendant is charged with committing this crime or intentionally aiding the commission of this crime.

Elements

The elements of the crime of Murder in the Second Degree while committing a felony are:

First Element: The death of George Floyd must be proven.

Second Element: The Defendant **caused the death** of George Floyd.

Third Element: The Defendant, at the time of **causing the death** of George Floyd, was committing or **attempting** to commit the felony offense of Assault in the Third Degree. It is not necessary for the State to prove the Defendant had an **intent to** kill George Floyd, but it must prove that the Defendant committed or **attempted** to commit the underlying felony of Assault in the Third Degree.

There are two elements of Assault in the Third Degree:

(1) Defendant assaulted George Floyd.

"Assault" is the intentional infliction of **bodily harm** upon another or the attempt to inflict **bodily harm** upon another. The intentional infliction of **bodily harm** requires proof that the Defendant **intentionally** applied unlawful force to another person without that person's consent and that this act resulted in **bodily harm**.

(2) Defendant inflicted **substantial bodily harm** on George Floyd. It is not necessary for the State to prove that the Defendant **intended** to inflict **substantial bodily harm**, or **knew** that his actions would inflict **substantial**

bodily harm, only that the Defendant **intended** to commit the assault and that George Floyd sustained **substantial bodily harm** as a result of the assault.

Fourth Element: The Defendant's act took place on or about May 25, 2020 in Hennepin County.

If you find that each of these elements has been proven beyond a reasonable doubt, the Defendant is guilty of this charge. If you find that any of these elements has not been proven beyond a reasonable doubt, the Defendant is not guilty of this charge, unless you find the State has proven beyond a reasonable doubt that the Defendant is liable for this crime committed by another person or persons according to the instruction below on page 8 under the heading "Liability for Crimes of Another."

Exhibit 12.6: Defense of Authorized Force by Police Officer

Defense: Authorized Use of Force by a Police Officer

No crime is committed if a **police officer's** actions were justified by the **police officer's** use of reasonable force in the line of duty in effecting a lawful arrest or preventing an escape from custody.

The kind and degree of force a **police officer** may lawfully use in executing his duties is limited by what a reasonable **police officer** in the same situation would believe to be necessary. Any use of force beyond that is not reasonable. To determine if the actions of the **police officer** were reasonable, you must look at those facts which a reasonable officer in the same situation would have known at the precise moment the officer acted with force. You must decide whether the officer's actions were objectively reasonable in light of the totality of the facts and circumstances confronting the officer and without regard to the officer's own subjective state of mind, intentions, or motivations.

The Defendant is not guilty of a crime if he used force as authorized by law.

To prove guilt, the State must prove beyond a reasonable doubt that the Defendant's use of force was not authorized by law.

2. NON-PATTERN JURY INSTRUCTIONS

Non-pattern jury instructions
Jury instructions that were not created as part of the uniform pattern instructions for the jurisdiction.

When a case presents facts or circumstances that are not covered by the pattern jury instructions for the jurisdiction, the court may present **non-pattern instructions** to the jury. For instance, when a defendant is prosecuted under a newly enacted statute, there typically is no pattern instruction to fit the case, so a non-pattern jury instruction must be produced. Often attorneys and paralegals draft their non-pattern jury instructions using formbooks for guidance.[28] Other times, non-pattern instructions are created for a particular case by the attorneys based on legal authority, such as a statute or appellate case.

While jury instructions are designed to give greater direction to jurors as to the meaning of the law, there are some concepts that the courts prefer to leave undefined. Perhaps the most controversial of these is "reasonable doubt." In a long line of cases, the courts have repeatedly avoided attempts to instruct jurors how they should define it, because such definitions are likely to "confuse juries more than the simple words themselves."[29]

3. JURY INSTRUCTIONS CONFERENCE

Jury instructions conference
A meeting with the judge in which the attorneys discuss the content of the instructions that the judge will give to jurors.

Following the end of the evidence phase of a jury trial, the judge will hold a **jury instructions conference** with the attorneys to discuss the instructions that the judge will give to the jury. It may take place in either the courtroom or the judge's chambers.

During the conference, the judge and each attorney will review the proposed instructions, which are usually numbered and marked with the name of the party offering them. Each pattern instruction lists the pattern instruction number. Non-pattern instructions are referenced to a legal authority, such as case law or statutes. In some courts, the judge prepares the proposed instructions; in others, the attorneys draft them. In either event, the attorneys for each side are given an opportunity to raise objections, offer additional instructions, and propose modifications.

On the record
Statements made in court that are recorded by either a court reporter or by the clerk of the court as a written entry in the case file.

Usually, the judge goes through each proposed instruction one at a time, allowing the attorneys to either accept or object to each instruction. The objections and bases for the objections generally are presented **on the record;** that is, before a court reporter and/or recorded on the court's docket sheet.

If neither side's submission is acceptable, the judge may order the preparation of an alternative version of an instruction. By the end of the conference, the judge will have approved a complete set of jury instructions, as well as the order in which the instructions will be given. The judge also approves the verdict forms to be distributed to the jury. Before the instructions are presented to the jury, a clean set is prepared, which is not marked with pattern instruction numbers, case or statute citations, or the name of a party. Sample pattern and non-pattern instructions appear in Exhibits 12.7 and 12.8.

---

[28]Among the jury instruction formbooks used in the U.S. District Court are: E. Devitt, C. Blackmar & K. O'Malley, *Federal Jury Practice & Instructions* (West Publishing, 6th ed., 2019); W. Loughlin et al., *Modern Federal Jury Instructions* (LexisNexis, 2019).

[29]*United States v. Blackburn*, 992 F.2d 666, 668 (7th Cir.), *cert. denied*, 510 U.S. 949 (1993).

Exhibit 12.7: Marked Pattern Jury Instruction

The format of proposed jury instructions varies from court to court. The following is a pattern instruction in a format used in many federal courts. Notice the instruction number at the top and the Seventh Circuit Pattern Instruction Number at the bottom. These features are deleted from the clean copy that goes to the jury.

JURY INSTRUCTION NO. 31

The verdict must represent the considered judgment of each juror. Your verdict, whether guilty or not guilty, must be unanimous.

You should make every reasonable effort to reach a verdict. In doing so, you should consult with each other, express your own views, and listen to your fellow jurors' opinions. Discuss your differences with an open mind. Do not hesitate to re-examine your own view and change your opinion if you come to believe it is wrong. But you should not surrender your honest beliefs about the weight or effect of evidence solely because of the opinions of your fellow jurors or so that there can be a unanimous verdict.

The twelve of you should give fair and equal consideration to all the evidence. You should deliberate with the goal of reaching an agreement that is consistent with the individual judgment of each juror.

You are impartial judges of the facts. Your sole interest is to determine whether the government has proved its case beyond a reasonable doubt.

7th Cir. 7.03

Exhibit 12.8: Marked Non-Pattern Jury Instruction

The following is a hypothetical non-pattern instruction based on a format used in some state courts. The bottom-right corner includes the name of the tendering party, the instruction number, and the legal authority for the instruction. Like the pattern instruction depicted in Exhibit 12.6, these references are deleted from the clean copy.

"Agent" means any officer, director, servant or employee of the corporation or any other person authorized to act on behalf of the corporation.

Prosecution Instruction No. 13

Non-Pattern: *State v. Jenny*, 867 N.E.2d 53 (N.J. 2009)

In federal court and some state courts, judges may dispense with an instruction conference. When this happens, the judge may ask the attorneys to submit proposed instructions before the trial begins or at a certain stage of the trial, such as the close of the government's case-in-chief. Even when this procedure is used, an attorney may request a jury instruction conference.

Application Exercises

9. Determine whether there are pattern jury instructions in the state in which your school is located.
   a. In what form and where are they published?
   b. Who (occupations, organizations) drafted and approved these instructions?

10. Prepare a marked copy of your state's pattern criminal jury instruction concerning the reasonable doubt burden of proof. (Assume that this will be the prosecution's tenth proposed instruction.) If there is more than one reasonable doubt instruction, prepare all of them and continue the numbering (10, 11, 12, etc.).

11. Prepare a non-pattern instruction for the defendant based on a hypothetical Union Supreme Court case of *Union v. Accused*, 800 Union Rpts. 3d 12 (2010) in which the Court, in overruling a conviction, ruled that "under the Due Process Clause of the State of Union Constitution, persons accused of crimes cannot be convicted of a crime unless the prosecution disproves beyond a reasonable doubt any legitimate hypothesis of innocence."

12. Is there a pattern jury instruction in the jurisdiction in which your school is located that is used to encourage a jury to break its deadlock? If so, provide a copy of this instruction and a citation as to where you found it.

13. In the *Turner* hypothetical case (see Hypothetical Case section), the defendant was charged with the felony offense of possession of crack cocaine with the intent to deliver.
   a. Under your state's criminal code, what are the lesser included offenses of drug possession?
   b. List the quantity of illicit drugs for each lesser offense, along with a citation to the appropriate statutes.

Closing argument
An oral presentation made to the jury, after all of the evidence has been presented, for the purpose of convincing the jury to find in favor of the side that is presenting the argument.

H. Closing Arguments

Whereas opening statements are supposed to create a framework for viewing the case, **closing arguments** are designed to convince jurors to either convict (if your side represents the prosecution) or acquit (if you represent the defendant).

As with opening statements, the prosecution makes its presentation first. In its closing argument, the prosecution seeks to show how the evidence presented was sufficient to prove each element of the various counts that were charged in the indictment or information. The prosecutor will highlight the specific testimony of witnesses, documents, test results, and other elements of the case and explain how each helps provide a basis for a guilty verdict.

The defense's closing argument usually begins with a reminder that it is the prosecution's obligation to prove the defendant guilty and that the defendant has no duty to prove innocence. The presentation will then go on to respond to points made by the prosecution, attack the credibility of the prosecution's witnesses, and attempt to show why it was insufficient to prove the defendant committed the alleged crimes. The defense attorney will emphasize the testimony of particular witnesses, documents, and other exhibits that support the defendant's version of what is supposed to have taken place. The attorney will usually end with a discussion of the meaning of "beyond a reasonable doubt" and an emotional appeal to avoid a potential miscarriage of justice.

If the defense presents a closing argument, the prosecutor is then given the opportunity to present a rebuttal argument. This gives the prosecution the chance to counter key points made in the defense close and allows the prosecutor to have the last word.[30] The rebuttal usually ends with an emotional appeal for justice to be served by punishing the defendant for the harm done to the victims.

I. Charging the Jury

Traditionally, the judge reads the instructions to the jury immediately following closing arguments. However, U.S. District Court judges and many state judges have discretion to charge the jury prior to the closings. In federal court, the judge may give selected instructions throughout the course of the trial to fit the individual circumstances of the case.

Before sending them to a special conference room to begin their deliberations, judges instruct the jury on the meaning of the laws that they are supposed to apply, as well as the procedures they should follow in their deliberations. The process of delivering these instructions is called **charging the jury**. The judge accomplishes this task by reading to the jury the instructions approved at the jury instruction conference. The jury is given a set of the instructions before it is dismissed from the courtroom to begin its deliberations.

Charging the jury
A process in which the judge instructs the jurors as to their responsibilities and presents the laws that they are supposed to apply.

J. Jury Deliberations

Once the jury gets settled in the deliberations room, the first item of business is the selection of a foreperson to preside over the deliberations and serve as the official spokesperson for the jury in communications to the judge and, in some

[30] Unlike witness examinations, where there are multiple opportunities for each side to come back with rebuttals and surrebuttals, the defense gets only one closing argument and no rebuttal.

courtrooms, to announce the verdict. Since this selection, like the deliberations over guilt, are held in secret, there is no systematic, empirical data regarding how criminal juries actually reach their decisions.[31] Based on scattered tales of jurors' self-reported experiences, there is reason to believe that many are chosen simply because they were the first to volunteer for the job.

Perhaps the most famous of all jury deliberations was that portrayed in *Twelve Angry Men.* In this classic movie, the jurors' initial vote is 11-1 in favor of conviction, but as they discuss the evidence in greater detail, the lone dissenting juror gradually wins over all the others, and the jury returns with a verdict of not guilty. While this made for a great movie, Hollywood's vision of a single juror being so persuasive is not consistent with the experience of most courthouse observers. Indeed, Professors Kalven and Zeisel's research conducted as part of the University of Chicago Jury Project showed that whichever side has the majority on the first vote usually ends up winning over the minority. Furthermore, they found that people in the minority on the first vote were successful in winning over their fellow jurors only when there was a core group of at least three or four jurors dissenting on the first round of votes.[32]

There is no set length of time that a jury can deliberate, and when juries report that they are deadlocked, the judge will often give a special instruction displayed in Exhibit 12.9. In federal court, this type of jury instruction is referred to as an "*Allen* charge," named for the 1896 U.S. Supreme Court case of *Allen v. United States.*[33]

If this type of instruction doesn't produce a verdict, it is common practice for the judge to send a stern message to the effect that the jurors have to try harder because they will not go home until they do. If the hour is late at night, they will be required to return early the next morning and to continue to deliberate "for as long as it takes." This type of direction obviously places great social pressure on the holdout jurors to get on board with the majority so they can resume their normal lives. On occasion, the judge will even sequester the jurors during deliberations so that they will be denied outside contact until they achieve a verdict.

In most cases, the social pressure to go along with the crowd and to get back to one's regular life is sufficient to lead to some sort of compromise verdict. The potential for compromise arises when there is more than one simple guilty or not-guilty verdict to be reached for a single crime. As we saw in earlier chapters, there are often multiple counts related to the same basic event. After having concluded that the defendant caused someone else's death, the jurors often have to go on to make a determination as to the defendant's intent at

---

[31]There is, however, empirical data that examines the deliberative process in civil cases. The Arizona Supreme Court sanctioned a study in Pima County in which all phases of 50 civil jury trials, including deliberations, were videotaped and studied. See Supreme Court of Arizona Administrative Order 98-10. The results of the study were published in S. Diamond & N. Vidmar, *Juror Discussions during Civil Trials: A Study of Arizona's Rule 39(f) Innovation,* 45 Arizona Law Rev. 1 (April 2002). http://www.law.northwestern.edu/faculty/fulltime/diamond/papers/arizona_civil_discussions.pdf.

[32]H. Kalven, Jr. & H. Zeisel, *The American Jury,* 488 (Little, Brown, 1966).

[33]164 U.S. 492 (1896).

Exhibit 12.9: Deadlocked Jury Instruction (United States Court for the Ninth Circuit)

Members of the jury, you have reported that you have been unable to reach a unanimous verdict in this case. I have decided to suggest a few additional thoughts to you.

As jurors, you have a duty to discuss the case with one another and to deliberate in an effort to reach a unanimous verdict if each of you can do so without violating your individual judgment and conscience. Each of you must decide the case for yourself, but only after you consider the evidence impartially with your fellow jurors. During your deliberations, you should not hesitate to reexamine your own views and change your opinion if you become persuaded that it is wrong. You should not, however, change an honest belief as to the weight or effect of the evidence solely because of the opinions of your fellow jurors or for the mere purpose of returning a verdict.

I also remind you that in your deliberations you are to consider the instructions that I have given you as a whole. You should not single out any part of any instruction, including this one, and ignore others. They are all equally important.

What I have just said is not meant to rush you or pressure you into agreeing on a verdict. Take as much time as you need to discuss things. There is no hurry.

I ask that you now return to the jury room and continue your deliberations with these additional comments in mind.

the time the act was committed. So, for example, they are required to decide if the defendant was guilty of homicide, voluntary manslaughter, or involuntary manslaughter. The existence of these types of multiple options opens the door for possible compromise verdicts where a group of jurors that favors a guilty verdict for first-degree murder agrees to a guilty verdict on voluntary manslaughter, while jurors who were holding out for a not-guilty verdict agree to go along with a conviction on the lesser charge.

Sometimes the defense will ask the judge to give the jury an instruction on a **lesser included offense** when some, but not all, of the elements of the crime charged against the defendant are a separate crime. This allows the jury to enter a guilty verdict on the lesser crime but find the defendant not guilty of the more serious one. For instance, the jury can reject an aggravated battery charge but convict on simple battery. Many criminal defense attorneys view the conviction on the lesser included defense as a victory because the defendant will receive a lighter sentence. Moreover, the conviction may be for a misdemeanor rather than for a felony. When the jury is deadlocked, a conviction on the lesser included defense often forms the basis of a compromise.

Lesser included offense
A crime that shares some, but not all, of the elements of a more serious criminal offense. Thus, the greater offense cannot be committed without committing the lesser crime.

K. Announcement of the Verdict

When the jury reaches its verdict, the foreperson will fill out a verdict form that reflects the jury's decision as to all charges. A sample jury verdict form appears in Exhibit 12.10. The foreperson then notifies the bailiff, who in turn notifies the judge. Calls then go out to the attorneys so that they and the defendant can assemble for the public reading of the verdict.

Once the court has reconvened, the judge asks if the jury has reached a verdict, and the foreperson responds that they have. The verdict form is then given to the judge for review. In some courtrooms, the judge will then read the verdict; in others, the judge will direct the foreperson to read it. In some cases, the parties will request the judge to **poll the jury**. This requires the jurors to individually acknowledge in open court their agreement or disagreement with the verdict that was read.

Polling the jury
A procedure in which the judge asks the jurors to individually confirm their votes.

If the defendant is found not guilty on all charges, the defendant and the defense attorneys celebrate as the prosecutors try to quickly and quietly exit the courtroom. On the other hand, in many cases if the jury returns at least one guilty verdict, the defense attorneys try to console the defendant and emphasize that they have prepared for the sentencing and potential appeals. In cases in which a compromise verdict is struck, neither side has cause to celebrate.

L. Mistrials

Mistrial
The early termination of a trial because of extraordinary circumstances, such as a deadlocked jury, prejudicial trial error, or the illness or death of a trial participant.

In extraordinary circumstances, the judge may declare a **mistrial**. When a mistrial occurs, it is then up to the prosecutors to decide whether they want to have another trial, negotiate a plea agreement, or just drop the prosecution completely.

In deciding whether to declare a mistrial, the judge must determine whether a trial error is so prejudicial and fundamental that the continuation of the proceedings would be pointless. Some of the reasons for declaring a mistrial include significant misconduct by one of the parties, the judge, or a witness; improper juror selection; outside influence on the jury; significant procedural error; the illness or death of a juror, judge, or attorney; and a hopelessly deadlocked jury. A mistrial can be declared until the jury reaches a verdict.

A mistrial may be declared by the judge on the court's own motion or on the motion of one of the parties. Probably the most common reason for declaring a mistrial is a jury deadlocked without reaching a verdict after lengthy deliberation. This is commonly referred to as a **hung jury**.

Hung jury
A jury that is unable to reach a verdict after lengthy deliberation.

M. Post-Trial Motions

Post-trial motion
A defense motion filed after a guilty verdict that seeks court action on various case-related matters.

After a finding of guilt, the defendant has the right to file various types of **post-trial motions** (also referred to as "post-verdict motions"). Since the Fifth Amendment Double Jeopardy Clause prohibits a retrial once the defendant has been acquitted, the prosecution does not have the right to file post-trial motions where there was a finding of not guilty. The prosecutor, of course, does have the opportunity to respond to arguments made by the defense in support of

Exhibit 12.10: Jury Verdict Form

A jury convicted entrepreneur and media personality Martha Stewart of conspiracy, obstruction of an agency proceeding, and giving false statements to federal investigators arising from her use of insider information that she received from Peter Bacanovic, her broker. The completed jury verdict form appears below.

<u>UNITED STATES OF AMERICA v. MARTHA STEWART AND PETER BACANOVIC</u>

03 Cr. 717 (MGC)

<u>JURY VERDICT FORM</u>

DEFENDANT MARTHA STEWART

<u>COUNT ONE</u>: Guilty ✓ or Not Guilty ____

If and only if you find the defendant guilty on Count One, please check the objects of the conspiracy which you found:

Obstruction of an Agency Proceeding	✓
False Statements	✓
Perjury	✓

<u>COUNT THREE:</u> Guilty ✓ or Not Guilty ____

If and only if you find the defendant guilty on Count Three, please check each of the specifications which you found:

Specification One:	
Specification Two:	✓
Specification Three:	✓
Specification Four:	✓
Specification Five:	✓
Specification Six:	✓
Specification Seven:	✓

these types of motions. Note that some of these motions are filed before or during the sentencing phase of the trial, and they are filed with the court that tried the case rather than in an appellate court.

Motion for a new trial
A request to have the judge order a new trial on the basis of errors that were made in the pre-trial and trial stages.

Motion for judgment of acquittal
A formal request to have the judge acquit the defendant, notwithstanding the jury's verdict to the contrary.

Delayed motion for a new trial
A request to have the judge order a new trial on the basis of errors that were discovered long after the trial ended.

The most common post-trial motion is a **motion for a new trial.** It lists specific errors that the defendant claims were made in the pre-trial and trial stages of the case. Often the defense will point to evidentiary rulings, prosecutorial misconduct, or the denial of a motion to suppress in support of the prayer for a new trial. In some jurisdictions, the defendant does not file a separate **motion for judgment of acquittal** and instead seeks a judgment of acquittal as part of the motion for a new trial. A motion for judgment of acquittal is a request to have the judge acquit the defendant even though the jury returned a guilty verdict. Although it is routinely filed, it is rarely granted. In federal court, the defendant may file a motion for a new trial if is required in the "interest of justice." In federal court, a motion for a new trial must be filed within 14 days of the verdict.[34]

If the alleged errors in the conduct of the trial are discovered after the end of the trial, it is possible to file what is known as a **delayed motion for a new trial**. In federal court, FRCrP 33 sets a three-year deadline for filing this type of motion. Time limits in state courts vary significantly across the nation. If the motion is premised upon the government's failure to disclose exculpatory evidence pursuant to *Brady v. Maryland*,[35] the defense must show that there is a reasonable probability that, had the evidence been disclosed to the defendant, the outcome of the trial would have been different.[36] If the motion is not based on the prosecution's failure to comply with *Brady*, the defense must show that the evidence was discovered after trial, it could not have been discovered early through the use of due diligence, the evidence is material and not merely cumulative and impeaching, and the evidence would likely produce an acquittal if the case were retried.[37]

With the obvious exception of the delayed motion for a new trial, the judge will ordinarily rule on the defendant's post-verdict motions before proceeding to sentencing. If the motion is allowed, there is no need for a sentencing hearing, of course. Most of the time, however, the judge denies the motion and sentences the defendant at the same court hearing.

SUMMARY

In this chapter, we walked through the various stages of a typical criminal jury trial, from the judge's call of the case for trial through post-trial motions. Although attorneys are the most visible members of the prosecution and defense teams, paralegals can play important roles during the course of these trials.

---

[34]FRCrP 33(b)(2).

[35]373 U.S. 83 (1963). See Chapter 7 for a discussion of *Brady v. Maryland.*

[36]*United States v. Bagley*, 473 U.S. 667, 682 (1985).

[37]See *United States v. Barlow* 693 F.3d 954, 966 (6th Cir. 1982).

Given the requirement for unanimous verdicts in most criminal cases, the selection of the jury can be one of the most important parts of the trial. In addition to doing background research on potential jurors, paralegals can help evaluate the nature of people's answers to the *voir dire* questions and the body language they exhibit during the process.

As the trial progresses, paralegals can assist their attorneys by keeping witnesses informed of schedule changes and updating them as to the time at which they are expected to be called to testify.

During direct examination and cross-examination, paralegals are often asked to take notes about the answers given and to organize the exhibits their attorneys will be referring to. They can also highlight parts of the opposition witnesses' statements that can be used against them on cross.

Once the judge has ruled on the jury instructions, the paralegal can assist the attorney in putting together Microsoft PowerPoint presentations to be used during the closing arguments.

Jury deliberations can result in convictions, acquittals, or a mistrial on each count. If the case is a bench trial, the judge must choose among the same three verdicts. When the defendant is convicted, paralegals may assist in drafting post-verdict motions and memoranda in support (for the defense) or opposition (for the prosecution.)

REVIEW QUESTIONS

1. What typically takes place at the time the judge calls a jury case for trial?
2. Who is present in court when the case is called?
3. What documents are presented to the judge?
4. What is the difference between venire and *voir dire*?
5. Describe the two primary methods employed by the courts for jury selection.
6. Describe the two types of challenges used during jury selection to eliminate jurors.
7. What relief is sought when a defendant moves for a change of venue?
8. What relief is sought when a defendant moves for a change of venire?
9. What is the holding of *Batson v. Kentucky*?
10. Why are alternate jurors selected?
11. Which side gives the first opening statement? Why?
12. What limitations are placed on the content of opening statements?
13. State the evidentiary stages of the case, beginning with the prosecution's case-in-chief.
14. State the progression of the examination phases of a witness's testimony, beginning with direct examination.
15. What is the difference between adverse witnesses and hostile witnesses? What benefit does the examiner gain during the direct examination of these types of witnesses?
16. What type of testimony must a law enforcement officer give to authenticate physical evidence properly?
17. What is an offer of proof, and why is it made?
18. What is the purpose of a motion for a directed verdict in a criminal case, and how does this motion differ from a motion for judgment of acquittal?
19. What is the purpose of jury instructions?
20. Who creates pattern jury instructions?
21. Which side gets the last opportunity to argue its position to the jury? Why?
22. How long may a jury deliberate?

23. What happens when a jury is deadlocked?
24. What is a lesser included offense? Give an example of a lesser included offense of the felony of theft in excess of $500.
25. What circumstances may prompt a judge to declare a mistrial?
26. What term describes a hopelessly deadlocked jury?
27. What is the difference between a post-verdict motion and a post-trial motion?
28. What are the three most common types of post-verdict motions?

Chapter 13

Sentencing

Chapter Objectives

After reading this chapter, you should be able to:

- Describe the variety of different sentencing options available in the federal and state legal systems.
- Discuss the use of sentencing guidelines and the degree to which judges are given discretion in determining an individual's sentence.
- Explain the difference between probation and parole.
- Discuss the arguments for and against the imposition of the death penalty.
- Explain the differences among federal, state, and local detention facilities, and between publicly and privately run prisons

Introduction

This chapter covers the nature of the punishments that judges can impose and the process used in determining what those penalties will be. In Chapters 14 and 15, we will cover appeals, post-conviction relief, pardons, and other related procedures.

In cases in which the defendant is found not guilty on all counts, the defendant will be released from custody (if incarcerated at the time of the trial) or otherwise free to go, and funds that were posted for bail will be refunded.[1] The Fifth Amendment double jeopardy clause prevents the government from reprosecuting the defendant on those same charges.[2]

---

[1]In some jurisdictions (e.g., Illinois), the defendant forfeits a small percentage of the posted bail.

[2]See Chapter 2, pages 32-35.

In those relatively rare cases in which the jury could not agree on a verdict for one or more of the counts, the prosecutor has the option of either retrying the defendant on some or all of the charges related to those counts or dismissing the charges.[3] On the other hand, when a defendant is found guilty and post-verdict motions have been denied, the case moves on to the sentencing and appeals stages.

A. Types of Punishment

The severity of punishment generally varies in proportion to the seriousness of the offense. For minor infractions, such as simple traffic citations, ordinance violations, and lesser misdemeanors, the penalty is typically a small fine. In cases involving more serious crimes, the punishment usually involves incarceration, and in some jurisdictions, even death.

Sentence
A judgment formally pronouncing the punishment to be imposed on a person who has been convicted of a crime.

Before discussing the sentencing process, it is useful to identify the wide range of sentences that are authorized for different type of offenses. A **sentence** is a judgment formally pronouncing the punishment to be imposed on a person who has been convicted of a crime.

In the federal system, the sentencing judge is authorized to impose fines, restitution, imprisonment, and probation.[4] State court judges have these options as well as a variety of additional sentencing alternatives, such as court supervision, traffic school, and substance abuse treatment.

1. Fines, Restitution, Assessments, Surcharges, and Costs

Fine
The monetary penalty imposed upon a defendant as punishment for committing an illegal act.

All jurisdictions authorize judges to impose **fines** in misdemeanor cases, and most also allow it in felonies.[5] Fines often are the only penalty available for ordinance violations, minor traffic offenses, and misdemeanors.

The statute or local ordinance creating the offense usually establishes an upper limit for the fine but leaves the actual dollar amount up to the judge's discretion. Sometimes the amount of the fine is defined in terms of multipliers of the amount of the defendant's financial gain or the victim's loss. Judges will often take the defendant's financial resources into account before imposing large fines, so someone who is wealthy may be ordered to pay a much larger fine than an indigent defendant. For instance, former vice president Dick Cheney's

---

[3]For example, in a political corruption trial involving the former Illinois governor Rod Blagojevich, the jury was unable to reach a decision on 23 of 24 charges against him and all 4 of the charges against his brother. The U.S. Attorney chose to drop the case against the brother but retry the charges against the ex-governor. The ex-governor was convicted on 17 charges on retrial and sentenced to 14 years in prison. President Donald Trump commuted the sentence in 2020, after Blagojevich had served nearly 8 years.

[4]Federal judges may impose several types of sentences: fines [18 U.S.C. §3571]; restitution [18 U.S.C. §3663]; imprisonment [18 U.S.C. §3581]; and probation [18 U.S.C. §3561].

[5]W. LaFave, J. Israel & N. King, Criminal Procedure (West 4th ed. 2004) at 1216.

chief of staff, Scooter Libby, was ordered to pay the maximum fine of $250,000 as part of his sentence for perjury and obstruction of justice.[6]

Restitution is money paid to the victims of the crime to compensate them for their losses. Judges consider several factors in deciding whether to order restitution, such as the amount of victim's loss resulting from the crime; the defendant's financial resources; and the defendant's earning ability and financial needs.[7] In the federal system, the judge must order restitution when the defendant is convicted of certain offenses, such as violent crimes, crimes against property, drug offenses, consumer product offenses, sexual abuse of children, and telemarketing fraud.[8]

Restitution
A component of a sentence entered against a defendant to be used to compensate the victims of the crime for their losses.

The restitution amount can be staggering in some white-collar crime cases. For instance, the district judge ordered the ex-congressional aide Michael Scanlon to pay his victims over $19 million as part of a plea agreement in a fraud and corruption case, and the New York financier Bernard Madoff agreed to make restitution in the sum of $171 billion to the victims of his Ponzi scheme. Unfortunately, the victims don't always receive all the money that the judge orders. Despite the U.S. District judge's forfeiture order requiring Madoff to turn over all of his assets, the victims probably will never be fully compensated for their losses.

In addition to fines and restitution orders, the sentencing judge usually orders the defendant to pay court costs and various assessments.[9] The **court costs** are monetary reimbursements for such things as the expenses of subpoenaing witnesses, providing probation services, and conducting drug testing. **Assessments** are payments to fund court-connected programs related to the crime.

Court costs
Fees, charged to the defendant, that are designed to pay for the operating expenses of the court system.

2. SUPERVISION, PROBATION, AND PAROLE

Assessment
The charge imposed upon a specified group (i.e., users of the court system) for the purpose of funding specified services (e.g., women's shelters or legal aid programs).

In the context of sentencing, there are situations in which criminal offenders are not incarcerated but do have special limitations placed on what they can do. Some of these judicial dispositions are non-convictions, whereas others are criminal convictions.

a. Court Supervision

For less serious offenses and infractions, such as traffic tickets and minor offenses, the violators may be eligible for **court supervision**. With court supervision, the judge imposes conditions on the defendant and **takes the case under advisement** for a fixed period. If the conditions are satisfied, the case is dismissed and the defendant is not convicted. Typical conditions include refraining from committing other offenses while on supervision, payment of fines and costs, performing public service work, undergoing substance abuse treatment, and completing traffic school. Courts do not give court supervision for felonies

Court supervision
A sentencing option used for minor offenses in which the defendant is not convicted if he or she complies with the judge's conditions during a specific period of time.

Taking case under advisement
The judge's deferral of a decision on a case or issue raised in a case.

[6] He paid the fine in full shortly after he was sentenced.

[7] See 18 U.S.C. §3663(A)(1)(b).

[8] 18 U.S.C. §3663(A).

[9] Defendants are not required to pay costs if they are indigent.

or to chronic offenders, and the supervision period usually ranges from 3 to 24 months.

b. Probation

Probation
A criminal sentence discharging the defendant to the community subject to conditions, which may include reporting to a probation officer.

Petition to revoke probation (PTR)
A motion filed by the prosecutor seeking to revoke probation and resentence the offender.

Probation is a sentencing alternative to incarceration in which the offender is allowed to continue to live in the community but must abide by certain conditions set by the judge. Unlike court supervision, the offender is first convicted of the crime.[10] Furthermore, the conditions of probation are much more imposing than those of court supervision. The defendant may be ordered to stay away from the victim, consent to random drug testing, and refrain from possessing a firearm. The individual is also required to regularly report to a probation officer. An example of a state court probation order appears in Exhibit 13.1.

If a defendant either commits another crime or violates one of the conditions of probation, the prosecutor will file a **petition to revoke probation (PTR).** Usually, the government takes this action when the offender commits a crime, flunks a random drug test, or chronically fails to report to the probation officer. If this petition is granted, the judge may revoke probation and resentence the defendant.

3. INCARCERATION

Incarceration
Mandatory confinement in a facility that limits one's ability to move around as the person wishes.

Jail
A facility controlled by a local governmental authority to hold criminal defendants awaiting trial and offenders convicted in state court of misdemeanors.

Prison (also known as a penitentiary)
A facility controlled by the state or federal government to house convicted state court felons and federal offenders.

Incarceration, mandatory confinement in a facility that limits one's ability to move around as the person wishes, is the penalty that comes to most people's minds when they think of a criminal sentence. **Jails** are facilities controlled by a county or another local governmental authority to hold criminal defendants awaiting trial and offenders convicted in state court of misdemeanors. **Prisons,** also known as **penitentiaries,** are facilities controlled by the state or federal government to house convicted felons. Federal misdemeanor offenders also may be sentenced to prison.

There are many variations of prison facilities. They range from maximum-security adult prisons to minimum-security juvenile "boot camps." Some are run by the federal government, some by state governments, and some by private, for-profit corporations. Within the same prison, there often are separate cells and cell blocks for different levels of offenders.

To protect them from being molested or otherwise negatively influenced by adult criminals, juveniles typically are held either in separate juvenile detention facilities or in special, separate sections of local jails. In some jurisdictions, younger adults may be sentenced to serve their time in a boot camp in lieu of prison. These boot camps are frequently set up in remote rural areas, house their residents in tents or cabins, and maintain a military type of training and atmosphere. This sentence is usually imposed on first-time offenders who are physically capable of withstanding the rigors of the program. In jurisdictions

---

[10] Some states provide for probation without a conviction for first- time offenders in limited circumstances. For example, Illinois offers some defendants 710-1410 probation, TASC probation, Second Chance Probation, and enrollment in the Offender Initiative Program. Persons who successfully complete these programs do not have convictions on their record.

Exhibit 13.1: Order of Probation

Wisconsin college student Anthony Scholfield was convicted of felony burglary after a search of his apartment uncovered more than 850 pairs of stolen women's underwear. The judge sentenced him to ninety days' periodic jail incarceration so he could attend school and work. He also was ordered to stay away from his female victims and pay $8,873.04 in restitution. Released after two years' probation, Scholfield committed a similar offense two years later. The court's judgment of conviction and sentencing order appears below.

STATE OF WISCONSIN CIRCUIT COURT BRANCH 2 DUNN COUNTY *For Official Use Only*

State of Wisconsin vs. Anthony Allen Scholfield

Date of Birth: 02-15-1981

Judgment of Conviction

Sentence Withheld, Probation Ordered

Case No.: 2003CF000099

FILED
DEC 2 6 2003
DUNN COUNTY
CLERK OF COURT

The defendant was found guilty of the following crime(s):

Ct.	Description	Violation	Plea	Severity	Date(s) Committed	Trial To	Date(s) Convicted
1	Burglary-Building or Dwelling	943.10(1)(a)	No Contest	Felony C	11-01-2002		12-22-2003

IT IS ADJUDGED that the defendant is guilty as convicted and sentenced as follows:

Ct.	Sent. Date	Sentence	Length	Concurrent with/Consecutive to/Comments	Agency
1	12-22-2003	Probation, Sent Withheld	3 YR		Department of Corrections

Conditions of Sentence or Probation

Obligations: (Total amounts only)

Fine	Court Costs	Attorney Fees	Restitution	Other	Mandatory Victim/Wit. Surcharge	5% Rest. Surcharge	DNA Anal. Surcharge
	20.00		8873.04		70.00		

Conditions:

Ct.	Condition	Length	Agency/Program	Begin Date	Begin Time	Comments
1	Jail Time	90 DA	County	12-22-2003	05:00 pm	huber allowed for work and school

Ct.	Condition	Agency/Program	Comments
1	Restitution		Restitution Hearing at 01/21/04 at 10:15am
1	Costs		Defend to pay through Prob.
1	Prohibitions		No contact with any victims- Jessica M, Sara K, Lindsey H, Kristina B, Katie L.

IT IS ADJUDGED that 1 days sentence credit are due pursuant to § 973.155, Wisconsin Statutes

IT IS ORDERED that the Sheriff execute this sentence.

BY THE COURT:

Rod Smeltzer, Judge
Kristine A Cusick, District Attorney
Julie Smith, Defense Attorney

Vera M Berg Deputy clerk
Court Official

12-26-2003
Date

where this option is offered, it is in high demand because the duration of incarceration is significantly shorter than the prison term that the offender would likely receive. Some inmates are given jobs in the prison laundry or kitchen, and some are even trained to assist other inmates do legal research in the library.

Discussion Question

1. What are the advantages and disadvantages of private, for-profit prisons?

a. Periodic Imprisonment

Periodic imprisonment
A probation option which permits a defendant sentenced to imprisonment to leave custody for work or school.

Sometimes probation is combined with incarceration in what is known as **periodic imprisonment.** In this situation, the convicted defendant is sentenced to jail but is permitted to leave the jail during specified hours or days to work at a job or attend school. Other conditions of confinement may include halfway houses and home detention.

b. Parole

Parole
A conditional release from incarceration after actually serving part of the sentence.

After a certain percentage of their sentence has been served, and often dependent upon both their good behavior and the degree of overcrowding in the prison system, some prisoners are released to serve the balance of their sentence on **parole**, a conditional release under which the prisoner is monitored to ensure that they abide by special conditions for a specified period of time. Among other thing, the parolee must report to a public official, maintain employment, and submit to random drug tests. The major difference between probation and parole is that parole occurs after a convict has served a set amount of time in prison, while probation is a substitute for incarceration.

While there is no parole at the federal level, U.S. District judges typically impose a term of supervised release when the defendant is sentenced to at least a year of imprisonment.

B. Capital Punishment

Capital crimes
Crimes for which the death penalty is an authorized punishment.

Capital punishment
Punishment by death.

The most severe punishment that the government can impose for a convicted criminal is the death penalty. Criminal offenses that authorize a death sentence are classified as **capital crimes**. Both the use of **capital punishment** and the means of execution are areas of continuing controversy in the United States.

1. VIEWS ON CAPITAL PUNISHMENT

Over the last several decades capital punishment has been a controversial and highly debated topic. Figure 13.1 summarizes the most common arguments raised on both sides of the issue.

In Support of Capital Punishment	Counterarguments
Fear of the death penalty deters potential criminals	Death penalty is not an effective deterrent because potential criminals either don't stop to think about the consequences or don't think they will get caught.
Justice demands that a killer be killed based on the biblical command of "an eye for an eye."	Retribution is not valid justification because the Bible stresses forgiveness rather than revenge.
It gives closure to the victim's families.	Life imprisonment also gives closure.
It ensures that the criminal won't commit any future crimes.	Life imprisonment with adequate security can achieve the same result.
It saves taxpayers money.	This point is not actually true when additional legal costs are considered, and even if it were true, the negative aspects of capital punishment outweigh any added costs.
It gives prosecutors a bargaining chip in plea bargaining.	This may be true, but this tactic is not fair to the defense.
Life in prison adequately protects the public and makes criminal suffer longer.	A criminal may escape or harm others while in prison. Death is worse than life imprisonment.
Capital punishment leads to innocent people being killed for things they didn't do.	More use of modern deoxyribonucleic acid (DNA) testing and better system of defense representation will avoid mistakes.
It violates the Eighth Amendment prohibition against "cruel and unusual punishment" and the Fourteenth Amendment Equal Protection Clause.	A majority of the Supreme Court has rejected these interpretations.
It shows that the United States is out of step with the standards of human dignity accepted by the majority of the world's countries.	It is not appropriate for the United States to base its public policy on the views of other countries.
It brings added suffering to innocent members of the criminal's family.	This may be true, but it doesn't outweigh the perceived advantages of having capital punishment.

See Balanced Politics.org at http://www.balancedpolitics.org/death_penalty.htm for a listing of more arguments for and against capital punishment.

Figure 13.1 Arguments Relating to the Imposition of Capital Punishment

Discussion Questions

2. Which of the arguments in support of capital punishment included in Figure 13.1 do you find most convincing? Why?

3. Which of the arguments against capital punishment included in Figure 13.1 do you find most convincing? Why?

4. Can you think of any persuasive arguments, either for or against capital punishment, that are not included in Figure 13.1? If so, what are these arguments?

For many people, the possibility of executing an innocent man or woman, is one of the strongest arguments against the death penalty. A 1993 staff report to the House Judiciary Subcommittee on Civil & Constitutional Rights, more than 160 people have been released from death row between 1973 and 1993 based on evidence of their innocence that came to light after their conviction.

2. CONSTITUTIONALITY OF THE DEATH PENALTY

In addition to the ethical and pragmatic arguments, the death penalty raises a constitutional issue involving the interpretation of the Eighth Amendment prohibition against "cruel and unusual punishment" and the Fourteenth Amendment Equal Protection Clause. In 1972, the U.S. Supreme Court ruled in *Furman v. Georgia*[11] that the Georgia capital punishment statute that existed at that time violated the Eighth and Fourteenth Amendments to the U.S. Constitution.

However, four years later, the court upheld a newly revised death penalty statute in the state of Georgia, on the basis that the new law had been written in such a way as to reduce the chance for "wanton and freakish" punishment.[12] Under this revised statute, guilt or innocence was to be determined in the first stage of a bifurcated trial (and, if the trial is by jury, the trial judge must charge lesser included offenses if they are supported by any view of the evidence). Upon a guilty verdict (or a guilty plea), a presentence hearing is held, in which the judge or jury hears additional extenuating or mitigating evidence, as well as evidence in aggravation of punishment if made known to the defendant before trial. At least 1 of 10 specified aggravating circumstances must be found to exist beyond a reasonable doubt and designated in writing before a death sentence can be imposed. In jury cases, the trial judge is bound by the recommended sentence. In its review of a death sentence (which is automatic), the state supreme court must consider whether the sentence was influenced by passion, prejudice, or any other arbitrary factor; whether the evidence supports the finding of a statutory aggravating circumstance; and whether the death sentence "is excessive or disproportionate to the penalty imposed in similar cases, considering both the crime and the defendant." If the court affirms the death sentence, it must include in its decision reference to similar cases that it has considered.

---

[11]408 U.S. 238.

[12]*Gregg v. Georgia*, 428 U.S. 153 (1976).

3. MODERN USE OF THE DEATH PENALTY

Prior to the mid-1800s, the federal government and all of the states authorized and carried out the death penalty. However, starting with Michigan in 1847, 17 states abolished its use. Although death penalty statutes are still on their books, 4 states currently have a moratorium on carrying out executions.[13]

The federal government has carried out the death penalty from the time of its creation until the 1972 *Furman* decision. Unlike many of the states, it didn't reinstate the death penalty until 1988. It currently authorizes the death penalty for about 60 offenses.[14]

Although capital punishment remains constitutional, the U.S. Supreme Court has rendered a number of decisions further narrowing the circumstances under which it can be used. For example, it cannot be used in situations involving mentally retarded criminals[15] or when the crime was committed by someone who was younger than 18 when the crime was committed,[16] In 2008, the Court overturned a death sentence for someone who had been convicted of the rape of a child.[17]

Some states, such as Illinois, have taken steps to provide additional procedural safeguards to capital defendants. For instance, the legislature created the Capital Litigation Trust Fund to pay investigative costs and employ independent forensic experts in death penalty cases.[18] Illinois Supreme Court Rules require special training for judges assigned to try death penalty cases, establish minimum qualifications for attorneys representing capital defendants, and create ethical standards for prosecutors in capital cases.[19]

Federal statutes authorize the use of capital punishment for treason, espionage, murder, piracy, large-scale drug trafficking, and attempted murder of a witness, juror, or court officer in certain cases. From 2004 until 2019, no federal executions were carried out. During the Trump administration, there were 13. And in 2021, the Joe Biden administration announced a moratorium on federal executions. But just months later, the Justice Department asked the Supreme Court to uphold capital punishment for Dzhokhar Tsarnaev, one of the two Boston Marathon bombers, and the Court did so.[20] To date, the Biden administration has not acted to either execute Tsarnaev or commute his death sentence.

State procedures concerning the death penalty vary. However, there must be an individualized sentencing process before the penalty is imposed. In the sentencing phase of the case, the jury will consider mitigating and aggravating factors to determine whether the defendant should be sentenced to death.

---

[13]This trend appears to have been in response to a troubling number of instances in which DNA evidence has been used to establish the innocence of people who had been convicted of murder and in some cases sentenced to death.

[14]See the Death Penalty Information Center website, https://deathpenaltyinfo.org.

[15]*Atkins v. Virginia*, 536 U.S. 304 (2002).

[16]*Roper v. Simmons*, 543 U.S. 551 (2005).

[17]*Kennedy v. Louisiana*, 554 U.S. 407 (2008).

[18]30 ILCS 105/5.519 was repealed after Illinois abolished capital punishment.

[19]Illinois Supreme Court Rules 3.8(a); 43, and 714 became moot following the abolition of the death penalty in Illinois.

[20]*United States v. Tsarnaev*, 142 S. Ct. 1024 (2022).

Mitigating factors may include impaired capacity, duress, and the absence of a prior criminal record. Aggravating facts may include a prior violent felony conviction, the heinous or cruel manner of committing the offense, and the vulnerability of the victim.

APPLICATION EXERCISES

1. Research the death penalty statute in the state where your school is located and list the aggravating and mitigating facts that are considered in cases in which capital punishment may be imposed.
2. If the state in which your school is located has capital punishment, find out how many times a defendant has been executed in the last ten years.

4. METHODS USED IN EXECUTIONS

The Supreme Court has also decided several cases challenging the manner of carrying out executions. At the time that the Eighth Amendment was adopted, the death penalty was typically carried out by either hangings or firing squads. In the years that followed, these methods were replaced with the electric chair and the gas chamber. Many of the states that still employed the death penalty switched to administering lethal drugs. In 2008, the Supreme Court in *Baze v. Rees* considered the constitutionality of this practice and ruled that Kentucky's drug protocol did not constitute cruel and unusual punishment.[21]

However, since the *Baze* decision, a shortage of the drugs used in executions and several botched executions during which the inmate suffered terribly before finally dying forced states to change the formula that had been used in *Baze*, and it also led to a challenge to a second Supreme Court decision that upheld (by a 5-4 vote) a different drug formula in an Oklahoma case.[22]

DISCUSSION QUESTIONS

5. Which, if any, of the methods of execution used today (hanging, firing squad, electric chair, gas chamber, or lethal drugs), do you think constitute "cruel and unusual" punishment? Why?

6. Can you think of a better way of executing criminals? If so, what would it be?

---

[21] *Blaze v. Rees*, 553 U.S. 35 (2008).

[22] *Glossip v. Gross*, 576 U.S. 863 (2015).

C. Discretion in Sentencing

One of the most prominent controversies in the criminal law field involves the amount of discretion that judges should have in determining the sentences to be given to those convicted of criminal offenses. Traditionally, federal, state, and local legislatures have established broad ranges, within which judges were to exercise their own discretion in designating a sentence that would best serve the interests of justice. Within the broad range of options established by the criminal code, judges could select from various fines, types of supervision, and jail or prison terms.

1. DETERMINATE AND INDETERMINATE SENTENCING

There are two general types of sentencing: indeterminate and determinate. **Indeterminate sentencing** occurs when the defendant is sentenced to a range of imprisonment, with the actual release date determined by a parole board. When offenders are released into the community on parole, they continue to serve a sentence under the supervision of the parole authorities. **Determinate sentencing** involves a judge imposing a specific sentence. The federal government abolished parole in the Sentencing Reform Act of 1984 as a way to attain uniform determinate sentencing.[23] Most states continue to punish felons with indeterminate sentencing and maintain parole boards to decide whether offenders should be released from prison into the community.

Indeterminate sentencing
A form of punishment in which the defendant is sentenced to a range of imprisonment, with the actual release date determined by a parole board.

Determinate sentencing
A form of punishment in which the defendant is sentenced to a specific term of imprisonment.

Whether determinate or indeterminate sentencing is employed, the statute creating the offense ordinarily specifies the minimum and maximum terms of incarceration. Instead of spelling out the particular sentence range for each individual offense, the statute will assign the crime to a class of crimes that share a specific range of punishments. In these situations, you must refer to another section of the statutes that specifies the range of punishments for all crimes in that class. Figure 13.2 provides an example of how punishments vary depending how the crime was classified in the Illinois system.

2. EXTENDED TERM SENTENCES

Under certain circumstances, the judge can subject an offender to an **extended term sentence** (sometimes called an "enhanced sentence"), which is a sentence beyond the statutory maximum of the basic range of penalties that otherwise could be imposed for the crime charged. A common circumstance is the fact of a prior conviction. Other representative circumstances include brutal or heinous behavior; commission of a felony against a senior citizen, disabled person, or young child; torture of a victim as part of a gang ceremony or rite; and participation in a gang rape of a single victim.

Extended term sentence
A sentence beyond the statutory maximum of the basic range of penalties that otherwise could be imposed for the crime charged; also known as an "enhanced sentence."

---

[23] 18 U.S.C. §3500 *et seq.*

Offense Class	Basic Range
First-degree murder	20–60 years
Class X	6–30 years
Class 1	4–15 years
Class 2	3–7 years
Class 3	2–5 years
Class 4	1–3 years

Note: These basic ranges do not apply to all crimes within each class. Illinois sentencing law is extremely complex and filled with enhancements, add-ons, extended terms, and other exceptions.

Figure 13.2 Illinois Felony Incarceration Terms

However, in *Apprendi v. New Jersey*,[24] the U.S. Supreme Court held that any fact (other than a prior conviction) that increases the defendant's sentence above the otherwise applicable statutory maximum must be submitted to a jury and proven beyond a reasonable doubt. Following this ruling, states reacted by modifying their extended term sentencing statutes. For instance, in Illinois, extended sentences are not permitted (except when based on prior convictions) unless the sentence enhancing facts "are included in the charging instrument or otherwise provided to the defendant through a written notification before trial"; submitted to the trier of fact as an aggravating factor; and proven beyond a reasonable doubt.[25]

Often, the use of a firearm during the commission of the offense is an enhancement that can extend the standard term of the sentence. Other times, it is merely an aggravating factor that can serve the basis of a longer term within the basic sentencing range for the offense.

3. CONCURRENT VERSUS CONSECUTIVE SENTENCES

Concurrent sentences Sentences that are served simultaneously rather than one after the other.

Consecutive sentences Sentences that must be served one after the other rather than simultaneously.

Another type of discretion that a judge can exercise arises when an offender is convicted of multiple counts. When this situation occurs, the judge can order either **concurrent** or **consecutive sentences.** Concurrent sentences are served simultaneously, so the total duration of the sentence is that of the longest sentence. The sentencing of ex-police officer Derek Chauvin illustrates how the two types of sentencing can create dramatic outcomes for the convicted offender. In 2021, a Minnesota trial judge sentenced Chauvin to 22½ years imprisonment for the homicide of George Floyd. A year later, a federal judge sentenced Chauvin to 21 years in federal prison for violating Floyd's civil rights, to run

[24] 530 U.S. 466 (2000).

[25] 725 ILCS 5/111-3.

concurrently with the Minnesota sentence. Had the federal court ordered the sentence to run consecutively, Chauvin's total prison time would have been 43½ years—nearly twice as much as his actual sentences imposed.[26]

Some statutes specifically state that the judge is required to impose consecutive sentencing for certain crimes. In other legislation, the judge is granted discretion to impose consecutive sentences. In this instance, the judge considers the seriousness and circumstances of the crimes, along with the history, character, and the prospect for rehabilitation of the defendant, when deciding whether to order consecutive sentences.

Unless a statute specifically provides for either mandatory or discretionary consecutive sentencing, the judge will order concurrent sentences. The approach taken in North Carolina is typical. N.C.G.S. §15A- 1354(a) provides:

> (a) Authority of Court.—When multiple sentences of imprisonment are imposed on a person at the same time or when a term of imprisonment is imposed on a person who is already subject to an undischarged term of imprisonment, including a term of imprisonment in another jurisdiction, the sentences may run either concurrently or consecutively, as determined by the court. *If not specified or not required by statute to run consecutively, sentences shall run concurrently.* (Emphasis added.)

Mandatory sentence
A statutory requirement that the judge must impose a minimum prison term for a specified crime.

Habitual offender laws
Mandatory sentencing laws that require judges to give extended terms of imprisonment to persons the third time that they are convicted of a serious criminal offense, without the possibility of parole, for life or an extended period of time. Also known as "three strikes and you're out" laws.

Sentencing guidelines
A uniform set of standards used to calculate the range of punishments to be given to people convicted of specific crimes.

4. MANDATORY VERSUS DISCRETIONARY SENTENCING

In response to the perception that the judiciary was soft on crime, many legislatures have enacted statutes that mandated certain sentences for specific crimes. Proponents contend that **mandatory sentences** deter certain crimes, while opponents argue that judicial discretion is needed to account for the particular circumstances of the crime and the offender. They further claim that mandatory sentences unnecessarily crowd the prisons.

Among the most controversial mandatory sentencing schemes are **habitual offender laws,** which require judges to give extended terms of imprisonment to persons the third time that they are convicted of a serious criminal offense, without the possibility of parole, for life or an extended period. A majority of the states, along with the federal government, have enacted these "three strikes and you're out" statutes. The U.S. Supreme Court held in *Ewing v. California*[27] that habitual offender sentences do not violate the Eighth Amendment prohibition against cruel and unusual punishment.

5. SENTENCING GUIDELINES

In what appeared to be an attempt to establish a middle ground between mandatory and discretionary sentencing, many states and the federal government developed **sentencing guidelines,** a uniform set of standards used to calculate

---

[26]When a person is given concurrent federal and state sentences, it must also be determined if the incarceration will take place in a state or federal prison. In Derek Chauvin's case, the parties agreed to have him serve his time in the federal prison system.

[27]538 U.S. 11 (2003).

the range of punishments to be given to people convicted of specific crimes. These guidelines give judges limited discretion within a range between a statutory minimum and a maximum punishment.

a. *Federal Sentencing Guidelines*

At the federal level, concerns about disparities in sentencing prompted the creation of the U.S. Sentencing Commission, an independent agency in the judicial branch. Its primary purpose is to "establish sentencing policies and practices for the federal courts, including guidelines to be consulted regarding the appropriate form and severity of punishment for offenders convicted of federal crimes."[28] The commission was designed to respond to the lack of uniform structure in sentencing, the need for certainty in administering punishment, and the necessity to target specific offenders with more serious penalties.

The Federal Sentencing Guidelines created by this commission went into effect November 1, 1987. They apply to federal defendants convicted of felonies or Class A misdemeanors, not to lesser misdemeanors. They attempt to ensure that sentences are uniformly based on the seriousness of the criminal activity and the defendant's criminal history by establishing mandatory sentencing ranges based on these two factors. Although the Guidelines do include a procedure for departing from the range, such departures are rare.

Shortly after the Guidelines went into effect, defense attorneys challenged the constitutionality of the act creating the commission. In *Mistretta v. United States,*[29] the Supreme Court held that Congress did not violate separation of powers by creating the commission as a judicial branch agency. A challenge to the constitutionality of the Guidelines themselves made it to the Supreme Court in *United States v. Booker,*[30] and in 2005, the Court held that the mandatory nature of the Guidelines violated the Sixth Amendment right to trial by jury. The Court struck two specific provisions of the act creating the guidelines, but left the remainder in place. As a result, federal judges were expected to take the Guidelines into consideration in setting the sentence but were not required to stay within the range specified there.

Discussion Question

7. Within limits established in the criminal statutes, the judge may either have a great deal of discretion or very little discretion in determining the nature of the punishment that the offender will receive. How much discretion should the judge have?

In 2007, the Supreme Court returned two more decisions dealing with the now-advisory Federal Sentencing Guidelines. In *Kimbrough v. United States,*

---

[28]The U.S. Sentencing Commission webpage at https://www.ussc.gov/about-page.

[29]488 U.S. 361 (1989).

[30]543 U.S. 220 (2005).

the Court ruled that judges were not bound by Federal Sentencing Guidelines that punished crack-cocaine crimes more harshly than similar crimes involving powdered cocaine.[31] Three months later, the U.S. Sentencing Commission amended the Guidelines to retroactively reduce the penalties for crack-cocaine crimes.

In *Gall v. United States*, the Court considered how much deference should be given under the "abuse of discretions standard." The defendant had been a second-year college student at the University of Iowa, when he joined an ongoing enterprise distributing a controlled substance called 3,4-Methylenedioxymethamphetamine, popularly known as "ecstasy." A month or two later, he stopped using ecstasy and withdrew from the conspiracy. He had not sold illegal drugs of any kind since then and had, in the words of the district court, "self-rehabilitated." After graduating from the University of Iowa in 2002, he obtained a job in the construction industry and later became a master carpenter. Federal drug agents learned of his earlier involvement with ecstasy and brought charges against him. He entered into a plea agreement. The pre-sentence report recommended a sentencing range of 30 to 37 months of imprisonment, but the district judge sentenced the man to probation for a term of 36 months. The court of appeals reversed and remanded for resentencing. The Supreme Court ruled, however, that the court of appeals should have given due deference to the district court's reasoned and reasonable sentencing decision.[32]

Even though the Guidelines are no longer binding, the sentencing judge still must determine the range that they specify before imposing a sentence. Figure 13.3 displays the Guidelines chart pertaining to the length of incarceration.[33] The left side of the chart is the offense level, and the top of the sentencing chart is the criminal history. The chart displays different shading for each zone of sentencing ranges. Zone A presents sentencing ranges of 0–6 months. Zone B presents sentencing ranges greater than Zone A but with a maximum penalty of no more than 15 months. Zone C presents sentencing ranges greater than Zone B but whose maximum penalty is 18 months or less. Zone D presents sentencing ranges greater than Zone C.

There are 43 offense levels. The *Federal Sentencing Guidelines Manual*[34] provides the base offense level for every federal crime. The greater the seriousness of the crime, the greater the offense score. The base-level offense entails more than the crime of which the defendant was convicted. Relevant conduct consists of acquitted acts, all activity committed or aided and abetted by the defendant;[35] and all reasonably foreseeable acts of others in furtherance of jointly taken criminal conduct.

---

[31] 552 U.S. 85 (2007).

[32] 552 U.S. 38 (2007).

[33] There is also a Guidelines chart for the range of fines to be levied.

[34] https://www.ussc.gov/guidelines/2021-guidelines-manual-annotated.

[35] *United States v. Watts*, 519 U.S. 148, 149 (1997).

		Criminal History Category (Criminal History Points)					
Offense level		I (0 or 1)	II (2 or 3)	III (4, 5, 6)	IV (7, 8, 9)	V (10, 11, 12)	VI (13 or more)
ZONE A	1	0-6	0-6	0-6	0-6	0-6	0-6
	2	0-6	0-6	0-6	0-6	0-6	1-7
	3	0-6	0-6	0-6	0-6	2-8	3-9
	4	0-6	0-6	0-6	2-8	4-10	6-12
	5	0-6	0-6	1-7	4-10	6-12	9-15
	6	0-6	1-7	2-8	6-12	9-15	12-18
	7	0-6	2-8	4-10	8-14	12-18	15-21
	8	0-6	4-10	6-12	10-16	15-21	18-24
ZONE B	9	4-10	6-12	8-14	12-18	18-24	21-27
	10	6-12	8-14	10-16	15-21	21-27	24-30
	11	8-14	10-16	12-18	18-24	24-30	27-33
ZONE C	12	10-16	12-18	15-21	21-27	27-33	30-37
	13	12-18	15-21	18-24	24-30	30-37	33-41
ZONE D	14	15-21	18-24	21-27	27-33	33-41	37-46
	15	18-24	21-27	24-30	30-37	37-46	41-51
	16	21-27	24-30	27-33	33-41	41-51	46-57
	17	24-30	27-33	30-37	37-46	46-57	51-63
	18	27-33	30-37	33-41	41-51	51-63	57-71
	19	30-37	33-41	37-46	46-57	57-71	63-78
	20	33-41	37-46	41-51	51-63	63-78	70-87
	21	37-46	41-51	46-57	57-71	70-87	77-96
	22	41-51	46-57	51-63	63-78	77-96	84-105
	23	46-57	51-63	57-71	70-87	84-105	92-115
	24	51-63	57-71	63-78	77-96	92-115	100-125
	25	57-71	63-78	70-87	84-105	100-125	110-137
	26	63-78	70-87	78-97	92-115	110-137	120-150
	27	70-87	78-97	87-108	100-125	120-150	130-162
	28	78-97	87-108	97-121	110-137	130-162	140-175
	29	87-108	97-121	108-135	121-151	140-175	151-188

30	97-121	108-135	121-151	135-168	151-188	168-210
31	108-135	121-151	135-168	151-188	168-210	188-235
32	121-151	135-168	151-188	168-210	188-235	210-262
33	135-168	151-188	168-210	188-235	210-262	235-293
34	151-188	168-210	188-235	210-262	235-293	262-327
35	168-210	188-235	210-262	235-293	262-327	292-365
36	188-235	210-262	235-293	262-327	292-365	324-405
37	210-262	235-293	262-327	292-365	324-405	360-life
38	235-293	262-327	292-365	324-405	360-life	360-life
39	262-327	292-365	324-405	360-life	360-life	360-life
40	292-365	324-405	360-life	360-life	360-life	360-life
41	324-405	360-life	360-life	360-life	360-life	360-life
42	360-life	360-life	360-life	360-life	360-life	360-life
43	life	life	life	life	life	life

Figure 13.3 Federal Sentencing Guidelines

The sentencing range is determined by locating the intersection of the offense level with the six criminal history categories. There are 258 sentence ranges displayed on the chart. Most are shown in months, starting at 0–6 months. However, several go up to life imprisonment.

Each of the 258 ranges appears in one of four sentencing zones, labeled A, B, C, and D. The 23 sentences appearing in Zone A include ranges of 0–6 months. The 19 sentences in Zone B consist of ranges greater than those of Zone A but do not exceed 12 months. Zone C consists of 10 sentences harsher than those of Zone B, but with a minimum incarceration period of less than 12 months. The remaining 206 sentences are included in Zone D.

Under the Advisory Guidelines, Zone A defendants are eligible for probation without a term of imprisonment. Defendants in Zone B are also probation-eligible if the court also imposes a condition or combination of conditions requiring intermittent confinement, community confinement, or home detention, so long as the defendant serves at least 1 month of the sentence in prison. Zone C defendants qualify for similar treatment but must serve at least half of their sentence in prison.

Prior to the sentencing hearing, a probation officer provides the U.S. Attorney and the defense counsel with the **Presentence Investigation Report (PSR)**, which includes a calculation of the appropriate Guidelines range for presentation to the judge. The parties advise the judge whether they agree with the probation officer's calculations. Excerpts from the government's sentencing memorandum appear in Exhibit 13.2. Take a look at the Guidelines chart

Presentence Investigation Report (PSR)
The document which reports the results of the probation officer's post-trial investigation of a convicted defendant, including all factors the court should take into account when determining the sentence.

Exhibit 13.2: Excerpts of Prosecution Sentencing Memorandum

Michael Barrett was convicted in federal court of stalking the ESPN reporter Erin Andrews. Barrett removed the peephole device from her hotel room doors on three separate occasions without Andrews's knowledge, videotaped her naked in her room, and posted ten nude videos of her on the Internet. The judge sentenced him to 30 months in federal prison. Excerpts of the government's sentencing memorandum appear below.

amount of $334,808.27, and a special assessment of $100. The government also requests that the Court remand defendant to the custody of the Bureau of Prisons ("BOP") at the conclusion of his sentencing hearing.

II.

ARGUMENT

A. THE GOVERNMENT CONCURS IN THE ADVISORY GUIDELINES CALCULATIONS SET FORTH IN DEFENDANT'S PSR

With respect to the presentence investigation report ("PSR"), the government requests that the Court adopt its advisory Sentencing Guidelines calculation. This calculation is as follows: a base offense level of 18 (U.S.S.G. § 2A6.2(a)); +2 for a pattern of activity involving stalking, threatening, harassing or assaulting the same victim (U.S.S.G. § 2A6.2(b)(1)(D)); and -3 for acceptance of responsibility--for a total adjusted offense level of 17. The parties stipulated to this calculation in the plea agreement. (Plea Agt. ¶ 13.)

The government also respectfully submits that the PSR correctly calculated defendant's criminal history to be Category I and asks that the Court adopt that calculation. Thus, the government requests that the Court adopt an advisory Guidelines range of 24 to 30 months.

B. A SENTENCE OF 27 MONTHS IMPRISONMENT IS SUFFICIENT, BUT NOT GREATER THAN NECESSARY, TO PUNISH DEFENDANT FOR HIS CONDUCT

In addition to the advisory Guidelines range, of course, the Court must consider the factors set forth under 18 U.S.C. § 3553(a). The government respectfully submits that application to see if you can follow how the government reached its conclusion as to the Guidelines sentencing range.

The Advisory Guidelines provide for departure from the sentencing ranges. However, the circumstances warranting departure are extremely limited. The most common reason is the prosecutor's recommendation for a lesser sentence based on the defendant's "substantial assistance to authorities."[36] Another basis for departure is an early disposition program (a "fast track") authorized by the U.S. Justice Department.[37] This program is employed in the border states for drug and immigration cases. The prosecutor must request "substantial assistance" and "fast-track" departures, and the judge determines whether to grant the request. The defendant cannot request either departure. Although they are not as common, there are also other bases for departure based on policy rationales. For example, there may be justification for a downward departure when the victim contributed significantly to the defendant's conduct. Conversely, there may be an upward departure when the victim suffered extreme psychological injury or the crime significantly disrupted governmental functions.

APPLICATION EXERCISES

Apply the Federal Sentencing Guidelines to each of the following examples. State the offense level, crime history, and sentencing range.

3. A jury convicted Jane Doe, a first-time offender, of kidnapping, level 32. Because the defendant injured the victim through the use of a dangerous weapon, the offense level increased by 4.
4. Joe Smith was found guilty of a minor assault, level 7. During the assault, Smith hit the 21-year-old victim in the face causing severe bruising and injuries. The nature of the victim's injuries increased the offense level by 2. This is Joe Smith's third offense.
5. Owen Black was convicted of trespass, a level 4 offense. He was found guilty of an invasion of a protected computer with a loss of $3,000, an increase of 1. This is Black's third conviction of this nature, so there are 2 criminal history points for each prior conviction.
6. A jury found Vivian White guilty of obstructing or impeding officers, a level 10 offense. She has five previous convictions of 60 days or more, with 2 criminal history points for each offense.

[36] *Federal Sentencing Guidelines 2009 Manual*, §5K1.1, provides: "Upon motion of the Government stating that the defendant has provided substantial assistance in the investigation or prosecution of another person who has committed an offense, the court may depart from the guidelines."

[37] *Federal Sentencing Guidelines 2009 Manual*, §5K3.1, provides: "Upon motion of the Government, the court may depart downward not more than 4 levels pursuant to an early disposition program authorized by the Attorney General of the United States and the United States Attorney for the district in which the court resides."

7. John Roe was found to have committed involuntary manslaughter involving criminally negligent conduct, a level 12 offense. He is currently on probation that gives him 2 criminal history points. He also has six previous convictions with sentences of incarceration over 60 days that amount to 2 criminal history points each.

8. Seth Owen was found guilty of burglary of a residence, a level 17 offense. The judge determined the property loss to be $10,000, level increase of 2 and found Owen to have clearly demonstrated acceptance of responsibility, an offense level decrease of 2. This is the first time that Seth Owen has gotten into trouble with the law.

9. Jean Green was convicted of robbery, level 20. Because she robbed a financial institution, the offense-level increased by 2. During the robbery, she shot the security guards, who sustained life-threatening injuries, thereby increasing the offense level by 6 and 7. Although authorities apprehended her, they never recovered the $5 million that she stole, which increases the offense level by 7. Green has five prior criminal convictions, four of which did not involve incarceration (1 criminal history point each) and the other resulted in a three-year sentence (3 criminal history points).

10. Hannah Brown was found guilty of robbery, a level 20 offense. No weapons were used, and no one was hurt. She stole $250,000, which was never recovered (add 2 levels). The judge found that the defendant was only a minor participant in the robbery, which decreases the offense level by 2. Brown has two other criminal convictions, neither involving incarceration.

In the aftermath of *Booker*, Congress enacted 18 U.S.C. §3553. U.S. District Court judges now must consider a number of factors, including the Guidelines range. Section 3553(a) provides that the sentencing judge consider:

> (1) the nature and circumstances of the offense and the history and characteristics of the defendant;
> (2) the need for the sentence imposed—
>   (A) to reflect the seriousness of the offense, to promote respect for the law, and to provide just punishment for the offense;
>   (B) to afford adequate deterrence to criminal conduct;
>   (C) to protect the public from further crimes of the defendant; and
>   (D) to provide the defendant with needed educational or vocational training, medical care, or other correctional treatment in the most effective manner;
> (3) the kinds of sentences available;
> (4) the kinds of sentence and the sentencing range established [by the Sentencing Guidelines];
> (5) any pertinent policy statement [issued by the Sentencing Commission];

(6) the need to avoid unwarranted sentence disparities among defendants with similar records who have been found guilty of similar conduct; and
(7) the need to provide restitution to any victims of the offense."

In light of Booker and §3553, most sentencing courts apply a three-step approach to determining the sentence. First, the judge must determine the appropriate Guideline sentencing range. Second, the judge decides whether to depart from the Guidelines. If so, the judge must specifically state the reasons for departure. Third, the judge considers the §3553 factors to determine whether the defendant should be given a non-Guideline sentence, referred to as a **variance**. In the appropriate case, defendants can argue for both a Guidelines departure and a variance.

Variance
A federal sentence that is not within the Federal Guidelines or based on a departure from the Guidelines.

In the aftermath of *Booker*, a growing number of federal judges have begun imposing sentencing outside the Guidelines range. The percentage of sentences within the Guidelines in 2020 was 50.4 percent, and in 2021 it was 42.8 percent.

It is anticipated that this trend will continue in certain types of cases. A 2010 survey of U.S. District Court judges reveals that more than two-thirds of the respondents believed that the Guidelines were too strict with regard to trafficking of crack cocaine, receipt of child pornography, and possession of child pornography. Although most respondents believed that the Guideline ranges should be broadened, they also thought that the Guidelines were generally appropriate for most offenses.[38]

Application Exercises

11. Develop a chart that shows the range of fines associated with different types of drug possession felonies and misdemeanors in your state.

12. Report whether the statutes in your state authorize the death penalty. If so:
a. For what crimes is it authorized?
b. What, if any, special rules apply to capital cases in your state?

13. Report whether your state utilizes determinate or indeterminate sentencing.

14. Report whether your state has any habitual offender statutes. If so, how is habitual offender defined, and what sentence is required?

15. Develop a chart that shows the range of incarceration times associated with different types of illegal drug offenses in your state.

[38]United States Sentencing Commission, 2012 Report to the Congress: Continuing Impact of United States v. Booker on Federal Sentencing, Part F, Appendix, p. 54 found at https://www.ussc.gov/sites/default/files/pdf/news/congressional-testimony-and-reports/booker-reports/2012-booker/Part_F.pdf.

16. Report whether your state has a parole board. If it does, how many members does it have and how are they selected? How often do they meet?
17. Report whether your state uses any type of sentencing guidelines. If it does, state who developed them and how they differ from the federal guidelines.
18. Research your own state's statutes and court rules to determine what, if any, sentencing guidelines have been established for handing out sentences in your state.

D. Sentencing Procedures

Except in capital cases, the judge rather than the jury sentences the defendant.[39] For minor misdemeanors and traffic citations, the judge ordinarily will sentence the defendant immediately after trial. At that time, the prosecutor will let the court know the offender's prior record. Both sides will offer sentencing proposals. The judge will then impose a sentence.

In more serious cases, the judge directs the probation department to prepare a pre-sentence investigation report. After the parties have an opportunity to review the report, the judge conducts a sentencing hearing.

1. PRE-SENTENCE INVESTIGATION REPORT

The pre-sentence investigation (PSI) report is the most important document for sentencing the defendant. The judge uses it to identify and limit issues decided at a sentencing hearing. The report contains information about the offender's social background, criminal history, and financial circumstances. In federal court and in states with sentencing guidelines, the probation officer also includes a calculation of the sentencing range in the report. In states in which aggravating and mitigating circumstances are to be taken into account, the report will discuss the applicable circumstances.

The probation officer usually begins the pre-sentence investigation by conducting an extensive interview with the defendant. The defense attorney often attends the interview to advise the client concerning responses to questions, counsel the client not to discuss certain topics, or aid the probation officer in

[39]There are a few jurisdictions in which the jury determines the sentence in non-capital cases. The Supreme Court has ruled that defendants have a right to a jury determination of eligibility for the death penalty. *Ring v. Arizona*, 536 U.S. 584 (2002). However, in a few states, judges play a role in imposing capital punishment. See the Death Penalty Information website for a listing of the state of the law in each state. https://deathpenaltyinfo.org/stories/u-s-supreme-court-ring-v-arizona (last checked September 15, 2022).

the disclosure of accurate information. A defense paralegal may accompany the attorney.

Because of the Fifth Amendment privilege against self-incrimination, the defendant does not have to submit to an interview with the probation officer.[40] In the federal system, the main reason for a defendant to talk about the offense after a guilty plea is to get the offense level reduced two or three levels in the Guideline calculations by clearly demonstrating acceptance of responsibility for the offense. However, even if the defendant limits comments to the offense of conviction, there may be a risk to being open with the probation department. For instance, if the defendant admits to taking a leadership role in the commission of the crime, the Guidelines offense level may increase. There are other reasons for the defendant to cooperate, such as making a record of the defendant's substance abuse when the defense plans to seek treatment as part of the sentence. If the defendant tells the probation officer about a drug or alcohol problem, this issue will be included in the pre-sentence report.

In addition to speaking to the defendant, the probation officer will contact the prosecutor and the investigating law enforcement agents to get their versions of the defendant's conduct. The probation officer may also contact members of the defendant's family and past and present employers, the victims of the crimes at issue, and institutions having had contact with the defendant, such as medical, military, and financial entities.

In federal court, both sides are entitled to know in advance about the grounds on which the judge plans to rely to depart upward or downward from the sentencing guideline range, including variances. This means that the attorneys must provide the probation officer with information to support a Guidelines departure or variance so the other party is aware of this possible ground before the sentencing hearing.

Following the investigation, a PSR is prepared and shared with the parties. The report discusses the defendant's background, criminal history, and personal characteristics and includes an analysis of the relevant statutory factors.[41] In sentencing guidelines jurisdictions, the PSR will include a calculation of the sentencing range. In non-guidelines jurisdictions, it discusses each of the aggravating and mitigating statutory factors pertinent to the offense.

The report also presents the range of possible sentences, as well as the probation officer's recommended sentence. If a departure from or variance to the guidelines range is proposed, the PSR states the applicable guidelines sentence, as well as the extent of the departure or variance. In addition, it may recommend imprisonment, fines, restitution, costs and assessments, supervised release, or a combination of these options. Typically, the terms and conditions of the proposed sentence are set forth in detail.

Most jurisdictions require the probation officer to provide the PSR to the attorneys prior to the sentencing hearing. In federal cases, disclosure must be made no later than 35 days before the hearing.[42]

---

[40]The defendant retains the privilege against self-incrimination prior to sentencing after a guilty plea or jury verdict. *Mitchell v. United States*, 526 U.S. 314, 326 (1999).

[41]*See, e.g.*, 18 U.S.C. §3553.

[42]F.R.Cr.P. 32.

2. OBJECTIONS AND MEMORANDA

Under Federal Rule 32, the parties must submit written objections or additions to the PSR to the probation officer within 14 days after their receipt of the report. They also have to send their objections to the opposing side. The probation officer then must submit a revised PSR to the judge and the parties within 7 days before sentencing. The revised report will include an addendum listing the unresolved objections, the grounds for the objections, and the probation officer's analysis of the objections.

After reviewing the PSR and the prosecution's objections and additions, defense counsel may renew their *Brady* request for exculpatory evidence. At this time, the request will specifically seek information pertaining to sentencing.

If either side intends to request a departure from the Guidelines that is not mentioned in the PSR, it should send a letter to the opposing counsel and the probation officer. The letter should give the grounds for the departure or variance and ask that the proposed departure or variance be included in the PSR. Without advance notice of intent to depart from the sentencing range, the court may lack the authority to deviate from the Guidelines.[43]

In addition to submitting objections and proposed additions to the PSR, parties may file a sentencing memorandum with the court. The memorandum should discuss each relevant factor and explain how the factors justify the sentence that your side is proposing. In federal cases, the parties will analyze the Section 3553 factors, including the Guidelines calculations. The memo should be drafted to help the judge prepare written findings of fact in support of the sentence. If the judge finds your attorney's memorandum persuasive, the judge may use this language in the court's written findings. It is, therefore, important that the memo systematically analyze all of the §3553 factors.

3. THE HEARING

Often the judge will rule on the post-verdict motion and then proceed to sentencing if the motion is denied. The judge will give great weight to the PSR. If the probation officer has not resolved objections to the report, the judge will have to come to a decision on the controversy. In federal court, the judge must make written findings as to disputed guidelines factors. Although the parties may or may not have the opportunity to present live witnesses at a sentencing hearing, both sides have the right to state their positions. Ordinarily, the parties can present evidence regarding objections to the PSR and to disputed sentencing factors. Moreover, the defendant will have the opportunity to rebut hearsay information offered at sentencing. Many states and the federal criminal justice systems allow the victim of an offense to provide a statement at sentencing. Some jurisdictions permit the submission of written statements only; others give the victim the right to speak at the sentencing hearing.[44]

The prosecution bears the burden of proving factors that enhance the sentence, including aggravating factors. The defendant has the burden of proving

---

[43]*Burns v. United States*, 501 U.S. 129 (1991).

[44]*See, e.g.*, 18 U.S.C. §3771.

mitigating factors. Usually, the standard of proof for both sides is a showing by a preponderance of the evidence. Hearsay evidence is generally admissible at sentencing, so long as there is a minimal indication that the information is reliable.

Before entering a sentence, the judge will give the defendant the opportunity to make a statement and present information in mitigation of the sentence. The defendant's statement at sentencing is known as the right of **allocution**. After the defendant makes this statement, the judge announces the sentence. The judge then advises the defendant of the right to appeal both the judgment of conviction and the sentence. The court also will let the defendant know of the right to be represented by counsel on appeal, and if the defendant is unable to pay the cost of an attorney on appeal, the defendant has the right to be provided counsel at public expense.

Allocution
The defendant's statement in mitigation of the sentence.

Read the transcript of the sentencing of the convicted investment advisor Bernard Madoff (Exhibit 13.3) and answer the Discussion Questions.

Discussion Questions

8. What conclusions does the judge reach as to the nature of Madoff's crime?

9. What is it about the nature of the crime, besides the amount of money that victims lost, that the judge focuses on in this statement?

10. Where does Madoff's crime fall on the Federal Sentencing Guidelines chart? Why should this matter?

11. What did the judge have to say about the impact of Madoff having turned himself in to the Federal Bureau of Investigation (FBI)?

12. How did Madoff's crime compare to similar "white collar" crimes?

13. What did the judge note to be lacking from the evidence submitted in mitigation?

14. How did Madoff's age affect the judge's sentencing decision?

15. What is the judge's response to Madoff's attorneys' plea that he (the judge) not succumb to "mob vengeance"?

16. How many separate counts was Madoff sentenced on, and did the judge order that the sentences on those counts be served concurrently or consecutively? All told, how many years was Madoff sentenced to serve?

17. What fine did the judge impose, and what was his justification for his decision?

18. What actions did the judge take at this hearing with regard to supervised release, restitution, and assessments?

19. To what extent do you agree or disagree with the judge's decision in this case?

E. Modification of Sentences

1. POST-SENTENCE MOTIONS TO CORRECT ERRORS

If the judge enters an erroneous sentence, there are several ways to challenge it. First, either party may move to correct a clear error in sentencing. Federal Rule 35(a) authorizes the judge to correct a sentence imposed as a result of arithmetic, technical, or other clear error. The U.S. District judge must act within seven days of the imposition of the sentence.

Exhibit 13.3: Excerpts of Transcript of Sentencing in White-Collar Crime

The judge in *United States v. Madoff* conducted a sentencing hearing. He considered victim statements and testimony as well as arguments made by counsel. At the conclusion of the hearing, the judge discussed the relevant factors and announced the sentence. Excerpts of the judge's statements follow.

I take into account what I have read in the presentence report, the parties' sentencing submissions, and the e-mails and letters from victims. I take into account what I have heard today. I also consider the statutory factors as well as all the facts and circumstances in the case.

***

Objectively speaking, the fraud here was staggering. It spanned more than 20 years.

***

The fraud reached thousands of victims.

***

As for the amount of the monetary loss, there appears to be some disagreement. Mr. Madoff disputes that the loss amount is $65 billion or even $13 billion. But Mr. Madoff has now acknowledged, however, that some $170 billion flowed into his business as a result of his fraudulent scheme.

***

Moreover, the offense level of 52 is calculated by using a chart for loss amount that only goes up to $400 million. By any of these measures, the loss figure here is many times that amount. It's off the chart by many fold.

Moreover, as many of the victims have pointed out, this is not just a matter of money. The breach of trust was massive. Investors -- individuals, charities, pension funds, institutional clients -- were repeatedly lied to, as they were told their moneys would be invested in stocks when they were not. Clients were sent these millions of pages of account statements that the government just alluded to confirming trades that were never made, attesting to balances that did not exist. As the victims' letters and e-mails demonstrate, as the statements today demonstrate, investors made important life decisions based on these fictitious account statements -- when to retire, how to care for elderly parents, whether to buy a car or sell a house, how to save for their children's college tuition. Charitable organizations and pension funds made important decisions based on false information about fictitious accounts. Mr. Madoff also repeatedly lied to the SEC and the regulators, in writing and in sworn testimony, by withholding material information, by creating false documents to cover up his scheme.

***

Mr. Madoff argues a number of mitigating factors but they are less than compelling. It is true that he essentially turned himself in and confessed to the FBI. But the fact is that with the turn in the economy, he was not able to keep up with the requests of customers to withdraw their funds, and it is apparent that he knew that he was going to be caught soon.

***

largely, if not entirely, symbolic.

But the symbolism is important, for at least three reasons. First, retribution. One of the traditional notions of punishment is that an offender should be punished in proportion to his blameworthiness.

***

The symbolism is important because

the message must be sent that in a society governed by the rule of law, Mr. Madoff will get what he deserves, and that he will be punished according to his moral culpability.

Second, deterrence. Another important goal of punishment is deterrence, and the symbolism is important here because the strongest possible message must be sent to those who would engage in similar conduct that they will be caught and that they will be punished to the fullest extent of the law.

Finally, the symbolism is also important for the victims.

***

A substantial sentence will not give the victims back their retirement funds or the moneys they saved to send their children or grandchildren to college. It will not give them back their financial security or the freedom from financial worry. But more is at stake than money, as we have heard. The victims put their trust in Mr. Madoff. That trust was broken in a way that has left many -- victims as well as others -- doubting our financial institutions, our financial system, our government's ability to regulate and protect, and sadly, even themselves.

I do not agree that the victims are succumbing to the temptation of mob vengeance. Rather, they are doing what they are supposed to be doing -- placing their trust in our system of justice. A substantial sentence, the knowledge that

Mr. Madoff has been punished to the fullest extent of the law, may, in some small measure, help these victims in their healing process.

Mr. Madoff, please stand.

It is the judgment of this Court that the defendant, Bernard L. Madoff, shall be and hereby is sentenced to a term of imprisonment of 150 years, consisting of 20 years on each of Counts 1, 3, 4, 5, 6, and 10, 5 years on each of Counts 2, 8, 9, and 11, and 10 years on Count 7, all to run consecutively to each other. As a technical matter, the sentence must be expressed on the judgment in months. 150 years is equivalent to 1,800 months.

Although it is academic, for technical reasons, I must also impose supervised release. I impose a term of supervised release of 3 years on each count, all to run concurrently.

***

I will not impose a fine, as whatever assets Mr. Madoff has, as to whatever assets may be found, they shall be applied to restitution for the victims.

As previously ordered, I will defer the issue of restitution for 90 days.

Finally, I will impose the mandatory special assessment of $1,100, $100 for each count.

Second, either side can file a motion to correct a clerical mistake. Federal Rule 36 permits the court to modify the record so it reflects the actual rulings of the judge. Third, in most jurisdictions, a party can appeal the sentence to a higher court. (We will discuss the steps needed to perfect the appeal in Chapter 14.)

Finally, a defendant may make a collateral attack of a sentence through a post-conviction relief petition.[45]

2. REDUCTION OF A SENTENCE BY A JUDGE

There are a few additional circumstances where the trial judge may reduce the original sentence of imprisonment. The most common occurs when the appellate court reverses a sentence and remands the case back to the trial court to modify the sentence or to conduct a new sentencing hearing.

In federal court, the Bureau of Prisons can move for a reduction in hardship cases involving elderly persons serving life terms for serious, violent felonies. Also, the U.S. Attorney may move for a reduction when the defendant assists the government in the investigation or prosecution of another person. Further, the federal district court is authorized to modify a fine at the request of the prosecution or terminate probation or supervised release after one year. Circumstances for reduction under state law vary from jurisdiction to jurisdiction.

3. REDUCTION OF A SENTENCE BY CORRECTIONS OFFICIALS

A defendant's sentence of imprisonment may be reduced due to a variety of factors outside the court system. Many jurisdictions release prisoners for "good time" served. Depending on the nature of the crime, this reduction can be substantial or minimal. For instance, in Illinois, many prisoners are given day-for-day credit for good time served. In contrast, federal prisoners are given only 54 days at the end of each year of a prison term.[46] Federal and state prisoners may get a reduction of time for residential drug treatment. Successful completion of boot camp can also reduce the length of a sentence.

---

[45]*See, e.g.*, 28 U.S.C. §2000 (1) 55.

[46]In *Barber v. Thomas*, 560 U.S. 474 (2010), federal prisoners contended that federal statutes required a straightforward calculation based on the length of the term of imprisonment that the sentencing judge imposed, rather than on the length of time that the prisoner actually served. The U.S. Supreme Court interpreted the language of §3624(b) as supporting the practice of awarding a specific number of days of credit at the end of each full year of imprisonment. The justices noted that basing the award of credit on the sentence imposed rather than served, as the prisoners suggested, would have resulted in the prisoners receiving good-time credit for a portion of the sentence that was not actually served with good behavior. Further, the government's method of calculation served as a proper incentive for the prisoners to comply with institutional disciplinary rules by awarding credit at the end of the year, after good behavior was demonstrated for a readily identifiable period.

4. REDUCTION OF A SENTENCE BY LEGISLATION

The First Step Act of 2018,[47] enacted with bipartisan support during the Trump presidency, created a variety of sentencing reforms. For example, it allows inmates earn "time credits" by participating in job training and other programs, which will permit them to be released earlier. It minimizes the "three strikes" rule so that people with three or more convictions automatically get sentences of 25 years rather than life. It also creates a safety valve that judges can use so that they are not obligated to impose mandatory minimum sentences.

The act also makes retroactive the reforms included in the Fair Sentencing Act of 2010, which reduced the disparity between crack cocaine and powder cocaine sentences. Since the law was enacted, nearly 1,700 people convicted of crack cocaine offenses also have received sentence reductions.

In July 2019, the Bureau of Prisons released 3,100 inmates in accordance with the act. Most were drug offenders although the group also included persons convicted of robbery, sex offenses, weapons crimes, and national security-related crimes.

SUMMARY

The criminal justice system provides a variety of options for punishing individuals convicted of violations of the law. These punishments include various types of financial penalties (such as fines, court-ordered restitution, assessments, surcharges, and court costs), incarceration (in local jails, state prisons, or special juvenile detention facilities), and, in a limited number of cases, even death.

There are also situations in which offenders are not incarcerated, so long as they abide by special limitations that don't apply to ordinary citizens. These limitations are imposed as part of court supervision, probation, or parole and can include such things as having to attend special classes, not associating with specific types of people, or not consuming alcohol or drugs.

One of the most controversial topics in sentencing involves the amount of discretion judges should have in determining the nature of the sentences given out. Should the offender receive the minimum or the maximum sentence allowed, and should the sentence be for a predetermined length of time or left to a parole board to determine when the prisoner will actually be released? When someone is convicted on more than one charge, should the offender serve multiple sentences consecutively or concurrently? How strictly do judges have to apply sentencing guidelines?

For minor misdemeanors and traffic citations, the judge ordinarily will sentence the defendant immediately after trial, but in more serious cases the judge directs the probation department to prepare a PSR. After the parties have an opportunity to review the report, the judge conducts a sentencing hearing that usually focuses on aggravating and mitigating circumstances that should be taken into consideration in determining what the proper sentence should be.

---

[47] PL 115-391, December 21, 2018, 132 Stat 5194.

INTERNET RESOURCES

U.S. Sentencing Guidelines

- U.S. Sentencing Commission: **http://www.ussc.gov/**
- Sentencing.us: **http://www.sentencing.us/**

Federal Prisons:

- Federal Bureau of Prisons: **http://www.bop.gov/**

REVIEW QUESTIONS

1. In the federal system, what types of sentences is the judge authorized to impose?
2. Generally, what punishment is imposed by the courts for ordinance violations, minor traffic offenses, and insignificant misdemeanors?
3. What types of factors are taken into account by the judge in imposing a large fine?
4. In what types of cases must federal judges order a convicted defendant to pay restitution?
5. What is the difference between court costs and assessments?
6. What governmental bodies typically operate jails, prisons, and penitentiaries?
7. What are typical conditions attached to court supervision??
8. What circumstances would prompt a prosecutor to file a PTR?
9. What is the major difference between probation and parole?
10. What are the main arguments in favor of and against the death penalty?
11. What is the difference between determinate and indeterminate sentencing?
12. How does an enhanced sentence differ from an extended-term sentence?
13. How long is an offender's total sentence when she or he is given sentences of 8 years, 6 years, and 5 years when the sentences are to be served concurrently? How long is the total term of imprisonment when the sentences are to be served consecutively?
14. What are the main arguments in favor of and against mandatory sentences?
15. Why did Congress create the U.S. Sentencing Commission?
16. What are the two variables shown in the Guidelines chart that come into play in determining the appropriate sentence range when applying the Federal Sentencing Guidelines?
17. What is the most common basis justifying a departure from the Federal Sentencing Guidelines?
18. What factors does 18 U.S.C. §3553 require a federal judge to take into account when imposing a sentence?
19. What is the three-step-approach that most sentencing courts apply to determining the sentence?
20. What type of information typically appears in a PSR?
21. In federal court, what is the time frame given to the parties to submit objections or additions to the PSR?
22. In federal court, in addition to filing an appeal, what means are available to the defendant to challenge an improper sentence?
23. What length of time is given to federal defendants for good time served?

Chapter 14

Appeals

Chapter Objectives

After reading this chapter, you should be able to:

- Explain the differences between trial and appellate courts and which appellate courts have jurisdiction in which types of cases.
- Explain the differences between trial and appellate courts and the types of cases over which appellate courts have jurisdiction.
- Compare and contrast interlocutory appeals with other types of appeals.
- Discuss the content, use, and importance of the record.
- Identify and distinguish between the various types of error and explain why these differences are important.
- Compare and contrast the concepts of "proof beyond a reasonable doubt" and "clearly erroneous."

Introduction

Due to the Fifth Amendment's prohibition against double jeopardy, prosecutors cannot appeal a not-guilty verdict, so criminal appeals can be initiated only by individuals who have been convicted in a state or federal court. However, some states permit the prosecution to appeal dismissals of indictments and informations, orders that quash arrests or suppressing evidence, and sentencing orders. In this chapter, we provide an overview of the appeals process, an analysis of the decision to appeal, and a discussion of the steps that should be taken to prepare for an appeal. We focus on the preservation of issues for review, the types of errors presented to the appellate court, the standard of review, and the steps involved in filing an appeal.[1]

A. The Right to Appeal Criminal Convictions

Appeal
A formal request for review of an order or judgment entered by another court that seeks to reverse or modify the other court's decision.

The term "appeal" is most commonly used to refer to a request to reconsider a decision or intended action. Thus, a student may appeal to an instructor to raise a grade on a paper or a test.[2] In the legal context, it is an attempt to have a legal decision reviewed and overturned by a higher-ranking legal authority. Most criminal appeals involve lower-level state appellate courts reviewing decisions of trial court judges in their state or, in the case of the federal courts, a U.S. Circuit Court of Appeals reviewing decisions of U.S. District Court judges within their circuit. There are also criminal appeals in which decisions of lower-level state appellate courts are reviewed by higher-level appellate courts (usually, but not always, called "supreme courts"), and the decisions of U.S. Circuit Courts of Appeals are reviewed by the U.S. Supreme Court. Finally, there are a limited number of situations in which decisions by the highest state court are reviewed by the U.S. Supreme Court. In the context of this chapter, we will define the term **appeal** as referring to a formal request for review of an order or judgment entered by a court, which seeks to reverse or modify another lower court's decision.[3]

When most people think about criminal appeals, they imagine a case where the defendant was convicted after a trial, is sentenced to prison, and then looks to a higher court for relief. While this is the most common scenario, there are other types of situations in which cases end up in appellate courts. For instance, defendants sometimes appeal orders approving plea agreements. In many jurisdictions, defendants may appeal misdemeanor convictions that did not result in a prison term.

Although there is no constitutional right to an appeal in a criminal case,[4] all states and the federal government provide some type of appellate review for people who are convicted in criminal cases. Furthermore, several constitutional provisions protect defendants' ability to effectively present their appeal. For instance, indigent convicted felons are entitled to a free transcript[5] and appointed counsel for their first appeal.[6] In misdemeanor cases, defendants

---

[1]We will not get into the details of the preparation of appellate briefs, motions prepared for the courts of review, or the nature of oral arguments made in appellate courts.

[2]The term "appeal" can also be used to refer to the basis upon which the decision should be made. For example, in asking for a favor, one might appeal to the decision maker's sense of fairness, morality, or loyalty.

[3]Collateral proceedings, initiated through petitions for post-conviction relief or for habeas corpus, are not technically considered appeals. However, since these remedies are used by defendants to challenge their convictions, we will discuss these actions in Chapter 15 (see pp. 494-495).

[4]See *McKane v. Durston*, 153 U.S. 684 (1894).

[5]*Griffin v. Illinois*, 351 U.S. 12 (1956).

[6]*Douglas v. California*, 372 U.S. 353 (1963).

commonly have a right of review in the general trial court, followed by discretionary appellate review.[7]

B. Matters That Can Be Appealed

An appeal of a judge's or jury's decision cannot be successfully made solely on the basis of not liking the outcome. One cannot appeal on the basis that the judge or jury came to the wrong conclusion about the defendant's guilt. Rather, an appeal must allege that one or more significant legal errors were made at trial involving things like the types of evidence that were admitted or the instructions the judge gave to the jury.

Furthermore, these mistakes must be sufficiently serious to have affected the outcome of the case. Errors that do not meet this standard are classified as **harmless errors** and cannot be used as a basis for overturning a lower court's action. Examples of harmless errors include (1) a mistake in the pleadings if the facts can be determined at trial; (2) errors in jury instructions unless there is reason to believe that they actually misled the jury; and (3) the failure to strictly follow the rules of evidence in a bench trial, as it is assumed a judge is unlikely to be affected by incompetent evidence. In contrast, errors that could have changed the result in the case are classified as **reversible errors**. Examples of reversible errors would include the failure to exclude evidence that was illegally obtained or to allow testimony from a competent witness when the testimony was relevant and material.

Harmless error
A mistake that is not considered prejudicial enough to justify overturning the court's decision/action.

Reversible error
A mistake that is considered sufficiently prejudicial to warrant reversing the trial court's decision.

In situations in which several "minor errors"[8] were found to have occurred in the trial, the appellate court may conclude that **cumulative error** prevented the defendant from receiving a fair trial. In these circumstances, the court of review will reverse the verdict and remand the case to the lower court to conduct a new trial.

Cumulative error
The prejudicial impact of a series of two or more trial errors that do not warrant reversal of a case when viewed separately but collectively amount to reversible error.

C. Standards Used in Appellate Review

At the trial court level, the defendant is presumed to be innocent, and the prosecution has the burden of proving guilt beyond a reasonable doubt. But when the case proceeds to the appellate level, the burdens and standards of proof change. At the appellate level, the appellant carries the burden of proving that a reversible error occurred at the trial court level. Furthermore, the standard of proof used in appellate courts depends on whether the decision being reviewed involves the facts of the case or the interpretation and application of the law.

Appellate judges will generally defer to the findings made by trial judges and juries with regard to factual issues. Unless the appellant can prove that the trial court's findings of fact were **clearly erroneous**, they will not overturn them. This deference is based on the fact that the judge and jury were in the better position to reach these judgments about the facts because they, as the

Clearly erroneous
The standard used by appellate courts when reviewing a trial court's findings of fact, in which appellate judges defer to conclusions reached by the trial judge or jurors unless the appellant demonstrates that those findings were clearly unreasonable.

---

[7] W. LaFave, J. Isreal & N. King, *Criminal Procedure* 1273 (4th ed., West 2004).

[8] These would be errors that individually would not be sufficient to warrant reversal.

triers of fact, personally observed the demeanor, body language, and other characteristics of the witnesses.

Appellate judges also give great deference to the trial judge's case management decisions, such as permission to amend a complaint or a denial of a request for a continuance. They will reverse in these types of situations only if the appellant can prove that the judge committed a clear error of judgment, lacked the authority to act, or acted with prejudice or malice.

On the other hand, if it is reviewing a decision involving the interpretation or application of a statute or court decision, such as a trial judge's ruling on the admissibility of evidence, the appropriateness of a line of questioning, or the nature of the jury instructions, the appellate judges will make their own independent review without giving any deference to the trial judge's decision.

Situations can also arise where the resolution of a legal issue requires the court to review the facts. For example, when a party appeals based on the trial judge's decision to deny a motion for a directed verdict, the appellant is arguing that the evidence was so one-sided that it could support only one conclusion. Because the appellate judges are ruling on a motion, this is a legal question. However, before they can reach a decision on this issue, they must make their own judgment about the strength of the evidence itself. In these mixed law and fact situations, the appellate court judges may end up making an independent review of the facts.

It is important to remember that even where the appellant has met the stiff burden of convincing an appellate court that legal errors were made, the previously convicted defendant may still wind up with the same, or even a worse, sentence. Not only can a lower-level appellate court be reversed by a higher-level appellate court, but an appellate reversal also may lead to a re-do, in which the conviction or sentence is reinstated after the remaining "appropriate evidence" is reheard.

D. Filing the Appeal

After ruling on the post-trial motions and imposing the sentence, the trial judge will inform the defendant as to the right of appeal. The judge will also instruct the defendant about the rights to counsel and to be furnished with a free transcript if the defendant cannot afford an attorney and the transcript.[9] The defendant then has a narrow window of time within which to decide whether to appeal the case to a higher court. The specific filing requirements for each court can be found on their websites, as well as in the published rules of the pertinent court of review.

Appellant
The party initiating the appeal.

Appellee
The party defending the trial court's decision on appeal.

A defendant who initiates an appeal is called the **appellant** in the court of review, and the prosecution, as the party defending the trial court's decision on appeal, is called the **appellee.**[10] In some jurisdictions, the appealing party is known as the "petitioner" or "applicant" and the defending party is known as

---

[9]If the defendant lacks the financial resources to appeal, the court will either assign the case to a state or federal appellate defender's office or appoint counsel to represent the indigent defendant. Except in cases involving the death penalty, the constitutional right to an appeal applies only to a single appeal to the lowest-level appellate court.

[10]When the prosecution files an interlocutory appeal, it is referred to as the "appellant," and the defendant is called the" appellee." See discussion of interlocutory appeals on p. 478.

the "respondent." The procedures governing appeals are found in court rules or statutes.

While the prosecution cannot appeal a guilty verdict, it can seek review of additional aspects of the case once the matter is before the appellate court. Whereas the defense may contend that guilt was not proved beyond a reasonable doubt, the government may object to the sentence that was given to the defendant. In situations like this, the prosecution's request for review is called a **cross appeal**. The parties are then referred to as the **appellant-cross appellee** and the **appellee-cross appellant**.

Cross appeal
An appeal filed by the appellee of an existing appeal.

Appellant-cross appellee
The party defending the trial court's decision on appeal and initiating the cross appeal.

Appellee-cross appellant
The party initiating the appeal and defending the trial court's decision on appeal.

Nunc pro tunc
A Latin term meaning "now for then;" in the courts, this refers to the modification of an order or record retroactively to show what actually happened at the time.

After an appeal has been filed, the trial court may take only ministerial actions,[11] such as approving a bystander's report[12] or staying the sentence. For the most part, the trial court loses jurisdiction, and the appellate court is the only court with authority to act on the merits of the case. Although a trial court may not modify a judgment or otherwise make a decision on the merits of the case once a notice of appeal has been filed, it may correct the record to reflect the judgment actually entered. For instance, the trial judge is authorized to correct typographical mistakes by modifying the record ***nunc pro tunc***.

Generally, the court reviewing a judicial decision is made up of at least three judges from a higher court for a particular geographic area. The reviewing court does not conduct a new trial. There are no new witnesses or additional evidence presented. Instead, the appellate panel simply reviews the record of the proceedings at the trial court and the legal arguments raised in the briefs that are filed as part of the appeals process. The outcome of the appeal is then determined by a majority vote of the judges who were assigned to review the case.

At the federal level, appeals from the U.S. district courts are decided by three-judge panels from the circuit in which the district court is located. The appellate jurisdiction of each U.S. circuit is displayed in Figure 14.1.

The Federal Rules of Appellate Procedure (FRAP) govern the filing and processing of appeals taken from the U.S. district courts. Appeals to the decisions of the federal circuit courts of appeal go to the U.S. Supreme Court and are governed by the Rules of the Supreme Court of the United States.

Most, but not all, states have a similar three-tiered judicial system consisting of trial courts, intermediate appeals courts, and then a single state "supreme court."[13] The procedural rules governing the use of these courts of review usually contain the words "Rules of Appellate Procedure" somewhere in their title. Ordinarily, review of intermediate appellate court decisions is discretionary; that is, the state supreme court does not have to accept appeals from the appellate court.[14] If an appeal involves a "federal issue," the party losing in the state's highest court may petition for review in the U.S. Supreme Court. Figure 14.2 displays the path of an appeal through the state and federal court systems.

Because there are variations among the states, appellants should check the jurisdiction's statutes and rules of appellate procedure to determine the proper

---

[11]Procedural actions mandated by law that do not involve the exercise of discretion.

[12]See the discussion of the bystander's report on p. 492.

[13]Most states call their highest appeals court the supreme court, but in New York, trial courts are called "Supreme Courts," the first level of appellate courts is the "Appellate Division of the Supreme Court," and the highest-level appellate court is simply the "Court of Appeals."

[14]The one major exception is when the defendant is sentenced to death.

Circuit	States and Territories Within Circuit's Jurisdiction
First	Maine, Massachusetts, New Hampshire, Rhode Island, and Puerto Rico
Second	Connecticut, New York, and Vermont
Third	Delaware, New Jersey, Pennsylvania, and U.S. Virgin Islands
Fourth	Maryland, North Carolina, South Carolina, Virginia, and West Virginia
Fifth	Louisiana, Mississippi, and Texas
Sixth	Kentucky, Michigan, Ohio, and Tennessee
Seventh	Illinois, Indiana, and Wisconsin
Eighth	Arkansas, Iowa, Minnesota, Missouri, Nebraska, North Dakota, and South Dakota
Ninth	Alaska, Arizona, California, Hawaii, Idaho, Nevada, Montana, Oregon, Washington, Northern Mariana Islands, and Guam
Tenth	Colorado, Kansas, New Mexico, Oklahoma, Utah, and Wyoming
Eleventh	Alabama, Florida, and Georgia
D.C.	District of Columbia

Note: There is also a U.S. Court of Appeals for the Federal Circuit, which has nationwide jurisdiction in a number of subject areas, such as international trade, government contracts, intellectual property, veterans' benefits, and public safety officers' benefits claims.

Figure 14.1 Regional U.S. Circuit Courts of Appeals

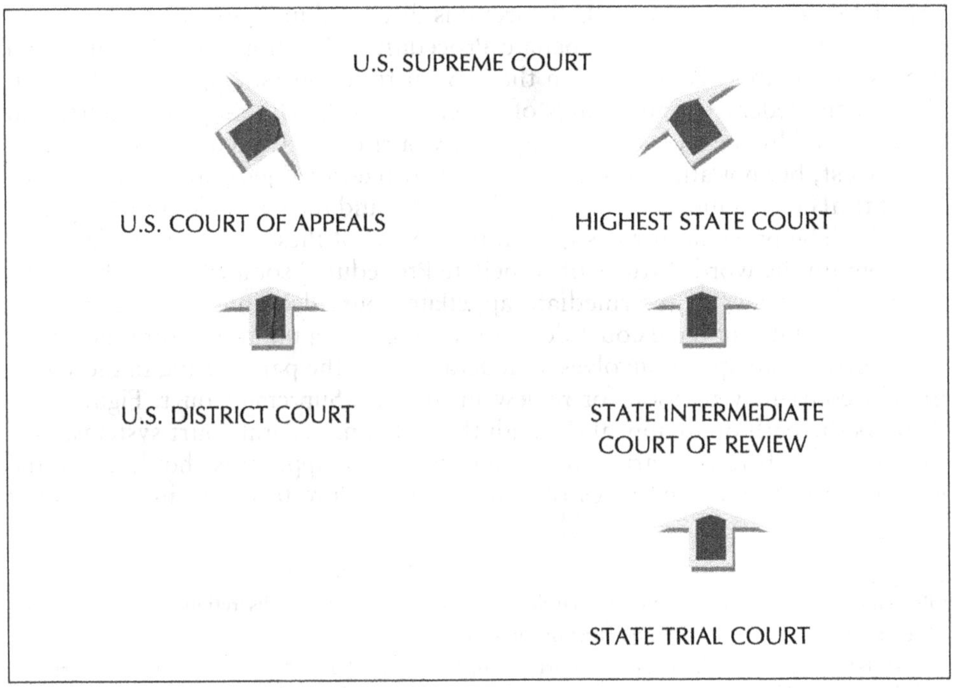

Figure 14.2 Path of Appeals in the Courts of Review

court for reviewing an adverse decision. Sometimes a defendant convicted in a capital case may appeal directly to the state's highest court rather than to an intermediate court.

Once an appeal is filed, the appellant is responsible for having the clerk of the trial court and the court reporters prepare the record for transmittal to the appellate court. Typically, the clerk of the reviewing court will notify the parties of the deadlines for filing the record. There is also a time limit within which the appellant must file a written brief with the court of review. This brief presents arguments, based on facts disclosed in the record and relevant law, as to why the trial court's decision should be overturned.

The opposing side then has a specified amount of time within which to file the appellee's brief that counters the arguments contained in the appellant's brief. It will typically suggest different interpretations of the case law and often include additional cases that contradict, or at least undercut, the cases referenced by the appellant. Following the submission of the appellee's brief, the appellant gets a specified amount of time within which to file a reply brief that responds to the arguments and cases included in the appellee's brief.

Ordinarily, the reviewing court will give the attorneys an opportunity to present oral argument. Following oral argument, the court takes the case under advisement and later renders a written decision or order. The reviewing court's decision usually is subject to discretionary review by a higher court. However, the U.S. Supreme Court is extremely selective when it comes to reviewing cases and declines more than 80 percent of all appeals directed its way.[15]

Application Exercise

1. Based on where your school is located, find and report on the following:
   a. Where would you file an appeal for a criminal case that was tried in your local state court? (Include both the name of the court and the address of the clerk's office.)
   b. What are the time limits within which the appealing party has to file its case?
   c. What, if any, provisions are made for extending any of these deadlines?
   d. What is the time line for both the appellant and the appellee for filing copies of the record, briefs, and other necessary documents?
   e. Where would you file an appeal for a criminal case that was tried in your local federal court? (Include both the name of the court and the address of the clerk's office.)
   f. What are the time limits within which the appealing party has to file its case?
   g. What is the time line for both the appellant and the appellee for filing copies of the record, briefs, and other necessary documents?
   h. What, if any, provisions are made for extending any of these deadlines?

[15]Even prominent political figures like former Illinois governor George Ryan have their appeals rejected by the U.S. Supreme Court. When Ryan lost his appeal in the Seventh Circuit by a 2–1 vote of the panel, the Supreme Court declined to review his case.

The general rule is that only final decisions can be appealed. That is, there can be no appeal from any order until the case has been completed in the trial court. For instance, if the trial judge sustains a hearsay objection to a question asked by the defense attorney, this ruling cannot be immediately appealed. Instead, the defendant must wait to appeal the ruling until the judge denies the post-trial motion and sentences the defendant. This approach promotes efficiency by requiring a party to raise all trial errors in one appeal without disrupting the completion of the trial.

Interlocutory appeal
An appeal from an order by a trial court that does not conclude the case.

In many jurisdictions, the appellate rules of procedure permit an exception to the final decision rule and provide for **interlocutory appeals** from nonfinal orders. For instance, in Illinois, the prosecution may appeal an order that suppresses evidence even though the case has not been concluded.[16] In some jurisdictions, defendants are permitted to bring interlocutory appeals to challenge a bail order.

Although the procedures vary from state to state, the types of orders that the government can appeal are limited. Many jurisdictions permit the prosecution to appeal dismissals of indictments and informations, orders quashing arrests, and sentencing orders. The Fifth Amendment Double Jeopardy Clause forbids the government to appeal the defendant's acquittal. On the other hand, the defense in most jurisdictions can assert on appeal pre-trial rulings, trial errors, and the sentence imposed.

1. NOTICE OF APPEAL

Notice of appeal
A formal document filed with the clerk of the trial court stating that a party is appealing the decision of the trial court.

The filing process begins with the appellant filing a **notice of appeal** with the clerk of the trial court within the established deadline. The trial court clerk then transmits the notice of appeal to the clerk of the appellate court. Exhibit 14.1 displays the official form used by defendants in Colorado criminal cases. Notice of appeal templates also appear in formbooks. Exhibit 14.2 is the template for the U.S. Attorney's notice of appeal form used in criminal cases.

---

[16]Illinois Supreme Court Rule 604(a)(1) provides:

> *When State May Appeal.* In criminal cases the State may appeal only from an order or judgment the substantive effect of which results in dismissing a charge for any of the grounds enumerated in section 114-1 of the Code of Criminal Procedure of 1963; arresting judgment because of a defective indictment, information or complaint; quashing an arrest or search warrant; suppressing evidence; decertifying a prosecution as a capital case on the grounds enumerated in section 9-1 (h-5) of the Criminal Code of 1961; or finding that the defendant is mentally retarded after a hearing conducted pursuant to section 114-15(b) of the Code of Criminal Procedure.

Exhibit 14.1: State Court Notice of Appeal Form for Defendant

<table>
<tr><td>☐ County Court ☐ District Court
______________County, Colorado
Court Address:

____
State of Colorado/Appellee:

v.

Defendant/Appellant:</td><td>▲ ▲

COURT USE ONLY</td></tr>
<tr><td>Attorney or Party Without Attorney (Name and Address):

Phone Number: E-mail:

FAX Number: Atty. Reg. #:</td><td>Case Number:

Division Courtroom</td></tr>
<tr><td colspan="2">NOTICE OF APPEAL AND DESIGNATION OF RECORD - CRIMINAL</td></tr>
</table>

The Defendant hereby files an appeal in ________________ (County Court case number) for the following reason(s):

____

____

____

☐ At this time, I request a stay of execution. I understand that as a condition of the stay of execution, I may be required to post a bond or deposit the amount of fines and costs assessed.

Current information about the Appellant/Defendant:

Full Name: ______________________________

Mailing Address: ______________________________

City & Zip: ______________________________

Home Phone #:______________ Work Phone #: __________ Cell #: ________________

Designation of Record:

The clerk of court will prepare the record on appeal, pursuant to Rule 37, Rules of Criminal Procedure and will include the following items:

- ☐ The county court case file, including all pleadings, motions, reports, exhibits, orders of the court, and jury instructions, if applicable.
- ☐ The original transcript: (identify proceedings).

  ____

  ____

☐ By checking this box, I am acknowledging I am filling in the blanks and not changing anything else on the form.

☐ By checking this box, I am acknowledging that I have made a change to the original content of this form.

Date: ____________________

________________________	________________________
Signature of Defendant/Appellant	Signature of Attorney for Defendant/Appellant, if applicable

Exhibit 14.2: Federal Notice of Appeal Form for Government

UNITED STATES DISTRICT COURT

FOR THE DISTRICT OF ________

UNITED STATES OF AMERICA,	)	
Plaintiff	)	
v.	)	Case No. _________
[NAME OF DEFENDANT],	)	
Defendant.	)	

NOTICE OF APPEAL

Notice is hereby given that the United States of America, plaintiff in the above-captioned case, hereby appeals to the United States Court of Appeals for the Circuit from the order of this Court [*describe order appealed from*], entered on *[date order was entered*]. [If the order appealed from is an order suppressing or excluding evidence or requiring the return of seized property, include the following language: "I hereby certify that the appeal is not taken for purpose of delay and that the evidence is a substantial proof of a fact material in the proceeding."].

[SIGNATURE BLOCK]

Source: United States Attorneys' Manual (USAM), Title 9 Criminal Resource Manual 22 Notice of Appeal Form *http://www.justice.gov/usao/eousa/foia_reading_room/usam/title9/crm00022.htm*

The party filing the notice of appeal must send a copy of the notice to the other party in the case. Customarily, the appellant will also send the appellee **a notice of filing notice of appeal**. The notice of filing will inform the opposing party of the date on which the notice of appeal was filed. This notice is filed with the clerk of the trial court. An example of a notice of filing notice of appeal is displayed in Exhibit 14.3.

Notice of filing notice of appeal
A document filed with the clerk and served on the opposing party stating the date on which the appellant filed a notice of appeal.

Exhibit 14.3: Notice of Filing Notice of Appeal

THE UNITED STATES DISTRICT COURT

FOR THE NORTHERN DISTRICT OF INDIANA

HAMMOND DIVISION

UNITED STATES OF AMERICA	)	
vs.	)	Case No. 20 CR XXX
WILLIAM EDWARDS,	)	
Defendant.	)	

NOTICE OF FILING NOTICE OF APPEAL

Now comes Defendant WILLIAM EDWARDS, by CHARLES HOVEY, his attorney, and hereby gives notice that on the XXth day of XXXXXXXX, 20XX, he filed a notice of appeal with the office of the U.S. District Clerk before the hour of 4:30 p.m.

Respectfully submitted,

WILLIAM EDWARDS, Defendant

By________________________________

CHARLES HOVEY, his attorney

Charles Hovey
Attorney for Defendant
1857 Bone Street
Normal, IL 61617
(309) 555-1857

Certificate of Service

I hereby certify that a true and accurate copy of the foregoing Defendant's Initial Discovery Request was served upon ________, Assistant U.S. Attorney by depositing the same in the U.S. Post Office mailbox in Chicago, Illinois in an envelope, postage fully prepaid, addressed to: Office of the United States Attorney [Address of U.S. Attorney] on the ________ day of ______, 20 ________ at or about the hour of p.m.

Application Exercises

2. Prepare a notice of appeal in the *Turner* case (*see* hypothetical case on pages xxxvii-xxxviii) using the appropriate form for the state in which your school is located. Assume the following: The trial court's decision became final five days before your assignment is due; the basis of the appeal is that the government presented evidence of a domestic violence order of protection entered against the defendant 15 years ago over the objection of the defense; the case was heard by the felony judge who customarily decides cases stemming from crimes committed in the place where your school is located; the defense attorney is Charles Hovey, and his contact information is listed in Exhibit 14.1; and the defendant currently lives at your address.
3. Prepare a notice of filing notice of appeal in the *Turner* case using the appropriate form for the state in which your school is located. Assume the facts set forth in Exercise 2.

The deadline for filing a notice of appeal varies from jurisdiction to jurisdiction. In some states, parties may have as long as 60 days in which to file their appeal. The federal deadlines are much shorter. FRAP 4 (b)(1) provides:

> (A) In a criminal case, a defendant's notice of appeal must be filed in the district court within 14 days after the later of:
>
> (i) the entry of either the judgment or the order being appealed; or
>
> (ii) the filing of the government's notice of appeal.
>
> (B) When the government is entitled to appeal, its notice of appeal must be filed in the district court within 30 days after the later of:
>
> (i) the entry of the judgment or order being appealed; or
>
> (ii) the filing of a notice of appeal by any defendant.

Generally, the time for filing the notice of appeal is computed from the date on which the trial judge rules on any post-trial motion. It is extremely important to check a state's filing deadline because the reviewing court may not acquire jurisdiction if the notice is filed late. In some jurisdictions, there are safety net provisions for extreme circumstances when the notice of appeal was not filed by the deadline. For instance, Illinois Supreme Court Rule 606(c) creates 30-day and six-month safety nets. On the other hand, failure to file the notice of appeal on time may result in a dismissal of the appeal. This, in turn, will eliminate the client's prospects for overturning the trial court's decision and may lead to a malpractice case against the lawyer who failed to act diligently. The Texas appellate court's decision in *Strange v. Texas* is typical of the way in which these deadlines are enforced.

Strange v. Texas
Appellate Court of Texas
258 S.W.3d 184 (Tex. App. 2007)

OPINION BY: CHIEF JUSTICE RADACK, joined by JUSTICES ALCALA and BLAND.

On November 6, 2007, this Court considered the State's motions to dismiss these appeals for lack of jurisdiction. The State contends that appellant, Mark Allen Strange, did not timely perfect his appeals. Appellant does not dispute that his notices of appeal were file-marked beyond the deadline imposed by the Rules of Appellate Procedure, but contends that the late filing resulted from clerical error. We grant the State's motions and dismiss the appeals for lack of jurisdiction.

Background

Appellant, Mark Allen Strange, waived a jury trial and was convicted of two first-degree felony offenses of misapplication of fiduciary property. *See* TEX. PEN. CODE ANN. § 32.45(c)(7) (Vernon Supp. 2006). The trial court assessed punishment at 15 years' confinement for each offense, to run concurrently, and signed the judgments on November 10, 2005. No party filed a motion for new trial.

Jurisdiction

Ascertaining whether this Court has jurisdiction is a threshold issue in every case. . . .We have no authority to dispose of a pending controversy unless our jurisdiction has been invoked. . . .

Article 44.02 of the Code of Criminal Procedure codifies a convicted defendant's right to appeal his criminal conviction. . . . Rule 25.2 of the Rules of Appellate Procedure restricts a defendant's right of appeal in certain cases, none of which applies here. . . .

Our jurisdiction over a criminal appeal derives from Article V, section 1 of the Texas Constitution and the Code of Criminal Procedure. . . .

A. Prerequisites to Invoking This Court's Jurisdiction

Rules 25.2 and 26.2 impose the procedural prerequisites by which a defendant may invoke the criminal appellate jurisdiction vested in this Court by the Texas Constitution and the Code of Criminal Procedure. . . .

1. *Deadline to File Notices of Appeal — Rules 25.2(b), (c)(1), 26.2(a)*

Rule 25.2(b) applies to all non-death-penalty cases. TEX. R. APP. P. 25.2(b). Pursuant to this rule, appellant had to perfect his appeals by "timely filing a sufficient notice of appeal" for each trial-court cause. . . . A notice of appeal must be in writing and must be filed with the clerk of the trial court. . . .

No motion for new trial was filed in either trial-court cause. Therefore, to meet rule 25.2(b)'s timeliness requirement and to invoke this Court's jurisdiction, appellant had to file his notices of appeal with the clerk of the trial court within the 30 days after the trial court signed the judgments. . . .

In this case, the trial court signed the judgments in both causes on Thursday, November 10, 2005. Accordingly, appellant's notices of appeal were due to be filed by Monday, December 12, 2005. . . .

2. *Alternative Deadline to File Motion to Extend Deadline — Rule 26.3*

This Court may extend a deadline for filing a notice of appeal, provided an appellant complies with rule 26.3. . . . But this rule, too, imposes a time limit. . . . To have invoked our rule 26.3 authority, appellant had to (1) file notices of appeal for both trial-court causes in the trial court and (2) file motions requesting an extension of time with this Court within the 15 days after the notices of appeal were due . . . Because the notices of appeal were due on Monday, December 12, 2005, appellant had to invoke our rule 26.3 authority by Tuesday, December 27, 2005. The limited, 15-day extended time period applies to both the notice and the motion for extension; both must be filed within the 15-day time period.

B. Prerequisites to Exercise of Jurisdiction Not Met

Appellant directs our attention to the preliminary steps he took to appeal his convictions on November 30, 2005, when the trial court signed the judgments. On that day, appellant filed and presented to the trial court a single-page document pertaining to both trial-court cause numbers. This document contained (1) appellant's pauper's oath, in which (2) he also requested that counsel be appointed for appeal and (3) that the reporter's record be prepared. On that same day, November 30, 2005, the trial court endorsed appellant's oath and signed orders that appointed counsel for appeal and ordered the court reporter to prepare the reporter's record.

Appellant did nothing further to perfect his appeal until January 10, 2006, when the district clerk filed appellant's notices of appeal. Appellant neither filed his notices of appeal by the December 12, 2005 deadline, nor moved to extend the December 12, 2005 deadline pursuant to rule 26.3. Appellant did not, therefore, comply with rule 26.2's mandate that the "written notice of appeal must be filed with the clerk's office within thirty days of sentencing" in a case in which no motion for new trial has been filed. . . . Accordingly, this Court never acquired jurisdiction over the appeals.

Appellant does not dispute the January 10, 2006 filing dates stamped on his notices of appeal by the Harris County District Clerk. January 10, 2006 was 29 days after December 12, 2005, when the notices were initially due to be filed, pursuant to rule 26.2(a), and 14 days after December 27, 2005, the last possible date for a timely rule 26.3 motion in this Court.

C. Filing Error by District Clerk?

Appellant's response to the State's motion to dismiss his appeals acknowledges that his notices of appeal were not marked "filed" until January 10, 2006, but he contends that the file mark constitutes a "clerical error" by the district clerk. Appellant explains the late file marking on the face of the notice as a mere "discrepancy" between actual *presentment* of the notice to the trial court, which occurred on November 30, 2005, and *receipt* of the notice by the district clerk, which did not occur until January 10, 2006.

Appellant's contentions disregard that he had to invoke this Court's jurisdiction by *filing* his notice of appeal *timely* with the clerk of the trial court. *See Few v. State,* 230 S.W.3d 184, 189 (Tex. Crim. App. 2007). ("In a criminal case, appeal is perfected by timely filing a sufficient notice of appeal.") (quoting TEX. R. APP. P. 25.2(b)); . . . Appellant has not provided us any authority—and we know of none—on which we may rely to support exercise of our appellate jurisdiction based solely on timely "presentment" of a notice of appeal to a trial court, despite late filing with the clerk.

Appellant relies on the following recital in the late-filed notices of appeal: "On *November 30, 2005,* [appellant] *gives* NOTICE OF APPEAL of his conviction." (Emphasis added.) But rules 25.2(b) and (c)(1) do not address either "giving" or "presenting" the notice of appeal, but, rather, unequivocally require that notices be "*filed*" with the clerk in order to perfect an appeal and vest jurisdiction with this Court." . . . A document is "filed" "when it is placed in the custody or control of the clerk." . . . As filed with this Court, the record on appeal shows that appellant's notices were not marked as filed until January 10, 2006 and, thus, too late.

In addition to reaffirming the filing requirement in *Stansberry v. State,* No. PD-0867-06, 239 S.W.3d 260, 2007 Tex. Crim. App. LEXIS 861, 2007 WL 1828901, the Court of Criminal Appeals also recognized that "a litigant who properly pursues his right to appeal should not be prejudiced by a clerk's error that prevents the timely filing of a notice of appeal. . . ." Accordingly, "[i]f a document would have been timely filed but for an error by an employee of the court, then the document is considered to be timely filed." The exception to the filing requirement recognized in *Stansberry* does not apply.

In this case, the notices of appeal appear in the record and were undisputedly filed late. In *Stansberry,* the record did not contain a "tangible, written notice of appeal" from which a filing date might be determined. . . . In this case, appellant contends that clerical error is the only possible means of explaining the late file-marking on the notices of appeal. But in *Stansberry,* in contrast to this case, the claim of clerical error was well-founded in the record, not disputed by the State, and supported by express findings by the trial court that the notice had been filed, all of which circumstances compelled the conclusion that clerical error had occurred. In this case, appellant's claim lacks any evidentiary support in the record. Indeed, the record contravenes appellant's claim.

At Stansberry's plea hearing, his trial counsel stated on the record that he would be filing a notice of appeal, and that the notice would be filed as soon as the hearing concluded. . . . There are no similar oral pronouncements in this case. When Stansberry's newly appointed appellate counsel could not locate a notice of appeal in the clerk's file, he filed a motion asking to amend any notice that might exist and also contacted Stansberry's trial counsel, who provided affidavits attesting that the notice had been timely filed. Appellate counsel filed these affidavits with the trial court, which conducted a hearing on the timeliness issue, during which the State did not challenge either the affidavits or appellate counsel's assertions. The hearing concluded with "an express finding" by the trial court that Stansberry had timely filed his notice of appeal. . . .

Though acknowledging the significance of lack of a "tangible, written notice of appeal" in the clerk's record, the Court of Criminal Appeals held that the "circumstances demonstrated by the record" compelled holding that (1) "a clerical error occurred at some point in time between the moment the notice was tendered to the clerk['s] custody and the moment the omission was discovered" and, therefore, (2) that Stansberry had satisfied rule 25.2. . . .

In this case, we have neither findings by the trial court that would support a claim of clerical error, nor any proof that would have supported such findings and, thus, no circumstances like those in *Stansberry* that would warrant our holding that clerical error thwarted appellant's compliance with rule 25.2(b). In contrast to the lack of a "tangible, written" and filed notice of appeal in *Stansberry*, the clerk's records in both of appellant's attempted appeals contain tangible, written, and filed notices of appeal, each of which demonstrates on its face that appellant did not comply timely with rule 25.2(b) and (c)(1) when the notices were "placed in the custody or control of the clerk" on January 10, 2006.

By arguing that clerical error occurred without offering evidence to support that argument, appellant seemingly contends that the notices of appeal he "presented" to the trial court on November 30, 2005 were either lost, overlooked, or somehow misplaced, in dereliction of the clerk's duties imposed by TEX. R. APP. P. 25.2(e), until they were discovered and marked as filed on January 10, 2006. We disagree, because appellant's notices of appeal contain additional, adverse information that precludes applying *Stansberry*'s rule of clerical error to this case.

Based solely on the file stamps placed on the notices of appeal by the district clerk, the notices of appeal were not "tendered" to and thus not "filed" until January 10, 2006. . . . In addition, however, each notice contains a paragraph by appellant's "undersigned attorney," in which appellant's counsel reported to the trial court that (1) he would continue to represent appellant on appeal and that (2) appellant was indigent. In addition to signing this portion of the notices of appeal, appellant's counsel recorded the date on which he made these representations to the trial court. The date counsel provided is January 10, 2006, specifically, the same date on which the district clerk marked the notices filed.

Because the date on which appellant's counsel provided the additional information in the notices is the same date on which the clerk marked the notices as filed, the record of this case compels the conclusion that appellant's counsel did not tender the notices for filing any earlier than January 10, 2006. In contrast to the record in *Stansberry*, which compelled a conclusion of clerical error, the record of this case negates that claim.

We also reject appellant's reliance on the trial court's having certified appellant's right to appeal both causes, as required by rule 25.2(e). . . . Appellant contends that, by certifying his right to appeal, the trial court "clearly recognized" the clerk's clerical error. Nothing in the certification by the trial court supports this contention. In certifying appellant's right to appeal, the trial court stated only that, appellant's case "is not a plea-bargain case, and [appellant] has the right of appeal."

For the reasons stated in this opinion, we grant the State's motions to dismiss the appeals.

Conclusion

We dismiss the appeals for lack of jurisdiction.

Case Discussion Questions

1. What actions did Strange take to appeal his case, and why weren't they considered adequate?
2. What does it take to file an appeal in the Texas courts? How does "filing" differ from "giving notice"?
3. What was the *Stansberry v. State* about, and why didn't it apply to Strange's situation?
4. What was the significance of the fact that the trial court "certified" appellant's right to appeal?
5. To what extent do you think Strange, rather than his appointed attorney, should be held responsible for the late filing?

Once the reviewing court receives the notice of appeal from the trial court, it will notify the parties of the appellate case number. From that point forward, all documents concerning the appeal, such as docketing statements and briefs, are filed with the clerk of the court of review. The trial court usually will only handle motions to stay enforcement of the sentence and other ministerial matters until the reviewing court makes its decision.

2. STAYING ENFORCEMENT OF SENTENCE

When a defendant appeals a judgment of conviction, the defense will move to stay enforcement of the sentence during the appeal. The motion is made first to the trial court. If allowed, the defendant is required to post post-conviction bail.

Although there is no constitutional right to bail after conviction pending appeal,[17] the Federal Bail Reform Act of 1984[18] does permit a defendant

[17] *McKane v. Durston*, 153 U.S. 684 (1894).

[18] 18 U.S.C. §3141 *et seq.*

Exhibit 14.4: State Court Order Granting Motion to Stay Sentence

A jury found the actor Jussie Smollett guilty of felony disorderly conduct for staging a fake hate crime. In addition to a fine, Smollett's sentence included 150 days in jail. Although the trial judge denied his motion to stay the sentence, the court of appeals granted the motion.

IN THE
APPELLATE COURT OF ILLINOIS
FIRST DISTRICT- FIFTH DIVISION

THE PEOPLE OF THE STATE OF ILLINOIS, Plaintiff-Appellee, v. JUSSIE SMOLLETT, Defendant-Appellant.	No. 1-22-0322

ORDER

This cause having come on for hearing on the motion of the defendant. Jussie Smollett, to stay his sentence of incarceration and to grant him a bond pending the disposition of his appeal; and the court being advised in the premises:

FINDING that the defendant has been convicted on non-violent offenses and that this Court will be unable to dispose of the instant appeal before the defendant would have served his entire sentence of incarceration:

IT IS HEREBY ORDERED THAT:

1. The motion of the defendant Jussie Smollett, to stay his sentence of incarceration and to grant him a bond pending the disposition of his appeal or until further order of this Court is GRANTED; and
2. The defendant, Jussie Smollett, shall be released from the custody of the Cook County Sheriff upon the posting of a personal recognizance bond (I Bond) in the amount of $150,000.

ORDER ENTERED

MAR 1 6 2022

APPELLATE COURT FIRST DISTRICT

ENTER:

Justice

Justice

Justice

I dissent and would deny the defendant's motion.

Justice

who has filed an appeal to request post-conviction bail. The process varies in the states across the nation. The seriousness of the offense and the likelihood that the defendant would flee are important factors considered by the trial court in deciding whether to grant the defendant's request. The likelihood of a court ordering bail after conviction is diminished because the presumption of innocence and the right of the defendant to participate in the preparation of a defense are no longer present.

If the trial court denies the motion to stay the sentence pending appeal, the defendant can present the motion to the appellate court. Exhibit 14.4 is an order of an appellate court staying an appellant's sentence of incarceration pending disposition of his appeal.

3. ORDERING THE RECORD

In addition to alleging that errors have been made, the appellant must provide documentation that the alleged errors did indeed occur. This is done by referencing specific parts of the official court records for the case.

Appellants are required to provide the appellate court with what is commonly referred to as the **record on appeal** (commonly referred to as "the record"). It consists of three parts:

- The original papers and exhibits filed in the trial court
- The docketing sheet accompanying the court file
- The transcripts of court proceedings

The first two parts are collectively referred to as the **common law record**, whereas the transcripts of witness testimony and the statements made by the judge or lawyers about the case in court are called the **report of proceedings**. (*See* Figure 14.3 for a listing of the typical components of the record on appeal.)

Record on appeal
The common law record and the report of proceedings; also known as "the record."

Common law record
All documents contained in the case file in the trial court, including the docketing statement, exhibits, and jury instructions.

Report of proceedings
The transcripts of testimony, as well as any other oral statements made in the trial court.

Illinois Supreme Court Rule 608(a) lists the required parts of the record on appeal as follows:

(1) a cover sheet showing the title of the case;
(2) a certificate of the clerk showing the impaneling of the grand jury if the prosecution was commenced by indictment;
(3) the indictment, information, or complaint;
(4) a transcript of the proceedings at the defendant's arraignment and plea;
(5) all motions, transcript of motion proceedings, and orders entered thereon;
(6) all arrest warrants, search warrants, consent to search forms, eavesdropping orders, and any similar documents;
(7) a transcript of proceedings regarding waiver of counsel and waiver of jury trial, if any;
(8) the report of proceedings, including opening statements by counsel, testimony offered at trial, and objections thereto, offers of proof, arguments and rulings thereon, the instructions offered and given, and the objections and rulings thereon, closing argument of counsel, communications from the jury during deliberations, and responses and supplemental instructions to the jury and objections, arguments and rulings thereon;

(9) in cases in which a sentence of death is imposed, a transcript of all proceedings regarding the selection of the jury, . . . ;
(10) exhibits offered at trial and sentencing, along with objections, offers of proof, arguments, and rulings thereon; except that physical and demonstrative evidence, other than photographs, which do not fit on a standard size record page shall not be included in the record on appeal unless ordered by a court upon motion of a party or upon the court's own motion;
(11) the verdict of the jury or finding of the court;
(12) post-trial motions, including motions for a new trial, motions in arrest of judgment, motions for judgment notwithstanding the verdict and the testimony, arguments and rulings thereon;
(13) a transcript of proceedings at sentencing, including the presentence investigation report, testimony offered and objections thereto, offers of proof, argument, and rulings thereon, arguments of counsel, and statements by the defendant and the court;
(14) the judgment and sentence; and
(15) the notice of appeal, if any.

Figure 14.3 Components of Record on Appeal

Application Exercises

4. Prepare a letter directed to the official court reporter in the *Turner* case requesting the preparation of the transcripts of all proceedings. Assume the following: The case was heard by the felony judge who customarily decides cases stemming from crimes committed in the place where your school is located; your supervisor is the prosecutor for the state court jurisdiction in which your school is located; the case was the first felony case filed last year in that jurisdiction; and the office of the court reporter, Lee Eastgate, is located at the local courthouse.

5. Prepare a letter directed to the clerk of the court in the *Turner* case requesting the preparation of the common law record for all proceedings. Assume the following: Your supervisor is the prosecutor for the state court jurisdiction in which your school is located and the case was the first felony case filed last year in that jurisdiction.

On the record
Statements made in court that are recorded by either a court reporter or by the clerk of the court as written entries in the case file.

As discussed in Chapter 12, attorneys must make sure that the record reflects the various motions and objections made, even if they don't expect the judge to grant them. If they fail to file their motions or make their objections at the appropriate times, they lose their chance to raise these issues on appeal. All objections must be made **on the record;** that is, either stenographically recorded by a court reporter or written on the docket sheet. If the error is not on the record, the appellate court will not be able to determine whether the trial court made a mistake. This is because appellate courts do not hear from witnesses but instead examine the documents before them.

For example, to make a successful *Batson* claim of systematic exclusion of African Americans from a jury,[19] the record must reveal the races of the jurors selected, as well as the races of the prospective jurors who were subject to the prosecution's peremptory challenges. If this information is absent, the appellate court cannot conclude that African Americans were systematically excluded from the jury. Similarly, if the trial judge sustains an objection to a question asked of a witness, the attorney must make an **offer of proof** in order to show the expected testimony. This is a procedure whereby the attorney either (1) tells the judge what the witness would have testified to if the judge had not sustained the objection to admitting it or (2) elicits the challenged testimony from the witness. In either event, the court reporter records the offer of proof. The contested testimony, if it is given, is taken outside the presence of the jury so the jury won't be influenced by what the judge excluded. This procedure allows the appellate court to decide whether the absence of the testimony harmed the appellant's case. Without the offer of proof, the reviewing court cannot conclude that the trial judge's ruling prejudiced the appellant.

Offer of proof
A procedure whereby excluded testimony is placed into the record for possible appellate review of the judge's decision to exclude it.

As we noted in Chapter 13, following the trial, attorneys present all trial and pre-trial errors in the post-trial motion. Although redundant, this action not only protects the record but also gives the trial judge one last opportunity to review and correct mistakes in a less pressured environment than the heat of trial. If an issue is not presented in the trial court or is omitted from the post-trial motion, it is considered to have been waived or forfeited and cannot be argued on appeal. A party's intentional abandonment of a claim is a **waiver**, whereas the inadvertent failure to present a claim in a timely manner is a **forfeiture.**[20]

Waiver
The rule of appellate procedure that a party's intentional abandonment of an issue in the lower court cannot be argued on appeal.

Forfeiture
The rule of appellate procedure that a party's inadvertent abandonment of an issue in the lower court cannot be argued on appeal.

However, when a mistake made at trial is a highly prejudicial error affecting the fundamental rights of the defendant, appellate courts create an exception to the general rules of waiver and forfeiture. This highly prejudicial error is referred to as **plain error**. Since courts of review are reluctant to characterize a mistake as "plain error," careful litigators will present the issue in pre-trial motions, make timely objections at trial, and include all issues for a second time in their post-trial motions.[21]

Plain error
The exception to the waiver rule that permits an appellant to raise on appeal a mistake that was not preserved in the trial court because it was a highly prejudicial error that affected the fundamental rights of the defendant.

The appellant is charged with the responsibility of requesting the clerk of the trial court to prepare the record. Usually, the clerk must be asked to prepare the common law record and the court reporter to prepare the report of proceedings. Some courts provide fill-in-the-blank forms for this purpose. The Colorado notice of appeal form (reproduced in Exhibit 14.1) includes a

[19]See the discussion in Chapter 12, pp. 409-414 of *Batson v. Kentucky*, 476 U.S. 79 (1986).

[20]The distinction between waiver and forfeiture has developed in recent years. Previously, any failure to raise an issue in a lower court was called a "waiver" whether the party's omission was intentional or inadvertent.

[21]In two 2018 cases decided by the U.S. Supreme Court, defendants failed to raise common law trespass as a basis for their motions to suppress evidence, thereby forfeiting this argument on appellate review. *Byrd v. United States*, 138 S. Ct. 1518 (2018); *Carpenter v. United States*, 138 S. Ct. 2206 (2018) (Gorsuch dissent). See the discussion of motions to suppress evidence in Chapter 9.

section in which the appealing party makes this request. In other jurisdictions, the appellants do not submit standard forms but must certify to the appellate court that the record has been ordered.[22] It is best to make the requests in writing, even if the attorney has a trusting relationship with the clerk and the court reporters. Indeed, if the attorney needs to file a motion for extension of time to file the record, the written request for the record is helpful documentation.

If no court reporter was present and the docket sheet does not completely reflect what took place in court, the attorney may need to reconstruct what occurred so that the appellate court has a sufficient record to consider all of the issues. This can be accomplished through a **bystander's report**. The procedure for obtaining the bystander's report varies from jurisdiction to jurisdiction. Customarily, the appellant's attorney prepares a proposed report that reflects what he or she recalls took place in court on specified dates. The appellant then notices a motion for approval of the proposed report. Sometimes, the appellee will present an alternative proposed report. The trial judge conducts a hearing to determine what should be included in the bystander's report. The report approved by the judge is forwarded to the appellate court as part of the record on appeal.

Bystander's report
A statement, reflecting what court proceedings, approved by the trial judge as to what happened in court.

SUMMARY

In the context of this chapter, appeals are formal legal requests for review of an order or judgment entered by a trial court that are designed to reverse or modify the trial court's decision. While they most frequently occur after the defendant has been convicted and sentenced, there are some situations in which an interlocutory appeal can be made on the basis of such things as an order suppressing evidence or a challenge to a bail order.

Appeals from state criminal court decisions must proceed through that state's appellate court system; federal convictions are appealed to the regionally designated circuit of the U.S. Circuit Court of Appeals. Where an issue of federal law is involved, state court decisions may be brought to the federal courts after the state appeals have been exhausted. Appeals must be filed within strict time limits.

It is particularly important to remember that, to be successful, appeals must identify and document reversible errors in the official court record. Furthermore, the standard of review utilized by appellate courts depends upon whether the court is dealing with questions of fact or questions of law. Appellate judges are much more likely to defer to the judgment of trial court judges on factual issues and much more likely to make an independent judgment as to the way in which the law should be applied to those facts.

Paralegals are most likely to be involved in drafting the notice of appeal, ordering the record, tracking the filing deadlines for appeal documents, and researching supporting case law.

[22]See, for example, Illinois Supreme Court Rule 606(g).

INTERNET RESOURCES

- U.S. Court of Appeals: **https://www.uscourts.gov/about-federal-courts/court-role-and-structure/about-us-courts-appeals**

REVIEW QUESTIONS

1. What are the designations for the parties initiating an appeal and defending an appeal?
2. When there is a right to appeal, what constitutional rights are afforded to indigent criminal defendants?
3. After a notice of appeal is filed, what type of authority remains in the trial court?
4. In federal non-capital cases, what court of review considers the appeal of a trial court's decision?
5. In what federal circuit is the state in which your school is located?
6. What is the three-tiered judicial system?
7. What types of tasks associated with appealing a case have deadlines?
8. How do interlocutory appeals differ from other appeals in criminal cases?
9. What is the first step in the appellate process?
10. When a defendant decides to appeal the decision of the trial court, in which courts will the parties file documents?
11. What is the purpose of a bystander's report?
12. What are the components of the record?
13. Why is it important that objections be made on the record?
14. What are the two ways in which an attorney can make an offer of proof?
15. Generally, what is the consequence of a party's failure to raise an objection or other issue to the trial judge?
16. Explain the difference between plain error and harmless error.
17. What is the relationship between reversible errors and cumulative errors?
18. How are the concepts of "proving guilt beyond a reasonable doubt" and showing that findings of fact were "clearly erroneous" related to each other?

Chapter 15

Related Proceedings

Chapter Objectives

After reading this chapter, you should be able to:

- Explain the two types of collateral remedies available to convicted defendants.
- Discuss the different types of clemency and the process that someone must use to request clemency.
- Explain the steps that must be taken to expunge or seal a criminal record.
- Prepare a petition to discontinue sex offender registration.
- Discuss the police seizure of a person's assets that were allegedly connected to criminal activity and the process that can be used to recover those assets.
- Discuss the process for challenging the summary suspension of the driver's license of a motorist arrested for driving under the influence (DUI).

Introduction

While the appeals process ends what is technically considered criminal law, there are several related administrative and civil legal actions that are used to assist clients who either have participated in or have been affected by the criminal justice system. Paralegals employed by attorneys in a general criminal practice may work on habeas corpus actions and post-conviction relief petitions, requests for clemency, expungement and sealing of criminal records, and civil suits to recover seized assets. Paralegals working on DUI cases may assist attorneys handling civil and administrative proceedings involving the suspension of driving privileges.

A. Collateral Remedies

As we have seen, direct appeals must take place within specific, often very limited time periods after the completion of the trial. But what about situations in which new evidence of the defendant's innocence, such as deoxyribonucleic acid (DNA) test results that weren't available at the time of the trial or a confession from the real killer, doesn't come to light until after this limited time frame has expired? Actions such as petitioning for a writ of habeas corpus or post-conviction relief petitions can be used to gain justice for people who have been wrongly convicted are examples of **collateral remedies**.

Collateral remedies
Actions designed to challenge judgments of conviction that have otherwise become final in the normal appellate review process.

1. POST-CONVICTION RELIEF

Many states allow a defendant to file a motion for **post-conviction relief** after a direct appeal. In most cases, this remedy is open only to claims that the trial court had no jurisdiction to convict the defendant, that the sentence exceeds the maximum possible for the crime, or that the conviction or sentence violates constitutional or state law.

Post-conviction relief
A statutory collateral challenge to a judgment of conviction.

2. HABEAS CORPUS ACTIONS

Writ of habeas corpus
A court order to bring someone being detained by government agents to court so that a neutral judge can determine if the government agents involved have a legal right to detain that person.

One of the most commonly used collateral remedies is the **writ of habeas corpus**. This writ is a court document ordering public officials (usually a state correctional agency) to produce the person (named in the writ) in court so that a neutral judge can determine if there is a lawful basis for detaining that person. These writs of habeas corpus date back to the English common law.

Article I, Section 9, Clause 2 of the U.S. Constitution declares: "The Privileges of the Writ of Habeas Corpus shall not be suspended unless when in Cases of Rebellion or Invasion the public Safety may require it."[1] In modern times, most petitions for collateral remedies are filed by prisoners incarcerated after they were convicted of committing a state crime, such as murder. Typically, their petitions argue that the state deprived them of a fundamentally fair trial by violating their constitutional rights. For example, a defendant could argue that his trial lacked fundamental fairness because the judge was biased or the attorney was incompetent.

Because a petition for a writ of habeas corpus is a new civil action by the incarcerated individual, it can indirectly result in the overturning of an existing criminal conviction. Petitioners who are in state custody must first file for the writ in the state trial court. If the petitioner is unsuccessful at the trial level, the

[1]Congress enacted the Habeas Corpus Suspension Act, 12 Stat. 775 (1863) which permitted the president to suspend the writ of habeas corpus so long as the Civil War was ongoing. However, in *Ex Parte Milligan*, 71 U.S. 2 (1866), the Supreme Court decided this act did not empower the president to try citizens before military tribunals where the civil courts were open and operational. During World War II, the Supreme Court selectively suspended right to habeas corpus with regard to Japanese Americans interned in the United States during World War II. *See Korematsu v. U.S.*, 323 U.S. 214 (1944) *abrogated by Trump v. Hawaii*, 138 S.Ct. 2392 (2018).

individual may appeal the rejection through the state appellate system. After exhausting all appeals in the state system, the inmate can seek a writ in the federal system.

Discussion Questions

1. What factors do you think can explain why the Supreme Court would have allowed the writ of habeas corpus to be suspended during the Civil War, and for people of Japanese descent during World War II, but not for terrorist suspects following the attack on the World Trade Center in 2001? Do you agree with any of these decisions? Why?

2. How should appellate judges go about determining if an attorney failed to provide a competent defense or just chose a reasonable legal strategy that just didn't work?

3. Do you think it would make a difference if the defense attorney at the trial or sentencing level had had an ethics complaint filed against him or her for misuse of a different client's funds? Should it make a difference?

4. What do you think the standard of review should be when judges are considering appeals based on claims of new evidence? Why?

B. Clemency

Whereas a successful petition for a collateral remedy provides the defendant with another trial, the grant of **clemency** concludes the case more favorably than the original outcome. While this authority is sparingly used, the president and the states (usually the governor) have the power to grant **pardons** (which cancel a conviction for a crime *and* the penalty that was associated with it), **commutations** (which reduce the penalty imposed by the court), and **reprieves** (which temporarily postpone the imposition of the punishment).

It is important to note, however, that governors may use this authority only in connection with violations of the laws of their own state. Because the United States and the states are "separate sovereigns,"[2] the president can exercise this power for persons convicted of federal crimes, but not for state convictions.[3] The Attorney General provides advice on federal pardon policy and makes recommendations to the president on all applications for pardon and commutations.[4] Offenders seeking presidential pardons apply to the Office of the Pardon Attorney (OPA) in the U.S. Department of Justice using an approved form. After the OPA investigates the application, it makes a recommendation.[5] There is no hearing.

Clemency
The power to pardon a crime, commute a sentence, or grant a reprieve.

Pardon
An official action that cancels a conviction for a crime as well as the penalty associated with it.

Commutation
An official action that lessens the penalty without changing the conviction.

Reprieve
An official action that temporarily postpones the punishment until some future point in time where some other authority can review the sentence.

---

[2]The U.S. Supreme Court has held that because of the dual-sovereignty doctrine, an individual may be convicted under both federal and a state law for the same criminal conduct without violating the Fifth Amendment's Double Jeopardy Clause. *Gamble v. United States*, 139 S. Ct. 1960 (2019). Therefore, a presidential pardon does not prevent a defendant from being convicted for conduct under state law for which he or she was pardoned by the president.

[3]The U.S. Constitution specifically grants the president the power to pardon. U.S. Constitution, art. II, sec. 2.

[4]28 C.F.R., Part 1.

[5]Unlike his predecessors, President Donald Trump granted pardons without first receiving recommendations from the OPA.

One of the best-known and most controversial instances of federal clemency was President Gerald Ford's pardon of his predecessor, Richard Nixon, in 1974. Within hours of Nixon's resignation from the presidency to avoid being impeached for crimes related to the Watergate scandal, Ford (who had been the vice president prior to Nixon's resignation) pardoned Nixon for any crimes he may have committed while he had been president.

At one time, federal commutations and pardons were rare. However, in his second term, President Barack Obama commuted the sentences of hundreds of non-violent drug offenders to reduce the impact of harsh federal sentencing laws. In 2022, President Joe Biden pardoned thousands who had been convicted of marijuana possession under federal law.

Parallel to the federal process, the states typically maintain an administrative office that receives and reviews applications for clemency. Most of these entities make recommendations to the governor, who then decides whether to pardon or commute a sentence. However, there are exceptions. For instance, the Alabama constitution grants its legislature pardon power, which it carries out through an independent board.

Although clemency policy and application processes differ from state to state, you can use the same general approach on behalf of clients who are seeking either a pardon or commutation. First, verify whether the client's offense is eligible under your state's law, because there is no national uniformity. For instance, New Mexico does not permit its governor to pardon persons convicted of committing violent crimes against children. In many states, the governor may not be authorized to pardon a defendant convicted of violating a municipal ordinance.

Some states require a waiting period to apply for a pardon. For example, the governor in California will not consider pardon requests until the offender has been discharged from the parole or probation system for at least ten years.

The number of pardons granted widely varies from jurisdiction to jurisdiction. Figure 15.1 displays pardoning frequencies.

Once you determine that the client and the offense qualify for clemency, you can complete the application. In most states, the governor's office can provide you with the pardon application, which is usually a fill-in-the-blank form. An example of the face sheet of a pardon petition appears in Exhibit 15.1. If permitted, you should include information listing the client's educational, employment, and civic accomplishments following the conviction.

Discussion Questions

5. In 1991, Troy Davis was convicted of murder and sentenced to death for killing a police officer. At the trial, several witnesses stated they saw Davis shoot the officer. No gun or other physical evidence tied Davis to the murder. Davis then began a series of appeals and habeas corpus actions based on affidavits from ten witnesses in the case in which they recanted their testimony and claimed that police had coerced them into falsely implicating him. The Georgia Board of Pardons and Paroles received more than 663,000 signatures on petitions to spare his life, and such prominent people as Jimmy Carter, Pope Benedict XVI, and Desmond Tutu publicly supported his appeals. After a last-minute appeal to the U.S. Supreme Court was denied, he was executed by lethal injection in 2011.

Frequent and Regular (grants a significant percentage of applications)						
Alabama	Arkansas	California*	Connecticut	Delaware	Georgia	Idaho
Illinois	Louisiana	Nebraska	Nevada	Oklahoma	Pennsylvania	South Carolina
South Dakota	Virginia	Utah				
Sparing (process regular, grants a small percentage of applications)						
Florida	Iowa	Minnesota	Ohio	Texas	Washington	
Infrequent/Uneven (pardoning depends on incumbent governor)						
Colorado	Hawaii	Indiana	Iowa	Kentucky	Maine	Maryland
Missouri	New Mexico	New York	Oregon	Tennessee	Washington	Wisconsin
Wyoming						
Pardons Rare (small percentage/no pardons in past 20 years)						
Alaska	Arizona	D.C.	Kansas	Massachusetts	Michigan	Mississippi
Montana	New Hampshire	New Jersey	Montana	North Carolina	North Dakota	Rhode Island
Vermont	West Virginia					

*California is included on the "Frequent and Regular" list even though only a small percentage of applicants are successful, because of the regularity of the pardon process and the unusually large number of pardons granted by the two most recent governors Jerry Brown and Gavin Newsom.

Source: Restoration of Rights Project website, https://ccresourcecenter.org/state-restoration-profiles/50-state-comparisoncharacteristics-of-pardon-authorities-2/ (accessed September 17, 2022).

Figure 15.1 Pardoning Frequencies

a. What does this case indicate about the efficiency of the criminal justice process?

b. What does this case indicate about the ability of the system to reach a "just" result?

c. To what extent do you think a pardon and parole board or a governor should consider petitions from members of the public in determining whether to grant clemency?

6. At one time, some members of Congress considered including an impeachment count against President Donald Trump related to allegations that President Trump promised to pardon current and former staff members to encourage them not to cooperate with law enforcement officers who were investigating conduct that might have been impeachable offenses. If President Trump had indeed made these promises, do you think his actions constituted "obstruction of justice"?

C. Removing or Limiting Access to Criminal Records

Whereas a successful attempt to get a pardon might keep someone from having to serve time in prison or having to pay a fine, it does not remove the stigma associated with the conviction or clear the person's criminal record. Therefore, if a record can be expunged, it is a better to petition for expungement of the

Exhibit 15.1: Massachusetts Pardon Petition

In 2014, the actor Mark Wahlberg petitioned Massachusetts governor Deval Patrick for a pardon for offenses that he committed when he was almost 17 years old. He received adult felony convictions as a result of a plea agreement he entered. The first page of the petition appears below. Wahlberg withdrew his petition before it was considered by the Massachusetts Parole Board, so the felonies remain on his record.

THE COMMONWEALTH OF MASSACHUSETTS
PARDON PETITION

November 26, 2014
DATE YEAR

TO HIS EXCELLENCY, THE GOVERNOR:

I, Mark Wahlberg
(NAME OF PETITIONER)

ADDRESS [redacted]
(Street Address, City, State, Zip code)

DATE OF BIRTH [redacted]

HAVING BEEN CONVICTED OF THE CRIME(S) OF Criminal Contempt (Violation of a Prior Civil Injunction), Assault & Battery, Assault & Battery by a Dangerous Weapon (two counts), and Possession of a Class D Controlled Substance, all such offenses arising out of a single episode that occurred on the evening of April 8, 1988, prior to my 17th birthday,

FOR WHICH I WAS SENTENCED ON October 13 and October 14, 1988

IN THE Suffolk Superior Court and Dorchester District Court

TO SERVE A TERM OF 2 years in the house of corrections, 21 months suspended,

(IF NECESSARY, USE ADDITIONAL PAPER)

DO HEREBY PETITION FOR A PARDON OF SAID CRIME(S), EITHER ABSOLUTE OR UPON SUCH CONDITIONS AND LIMITATIONS AS MAY BE DEEMED PROPER.

- RETURN TO: -

GOVERNOR'S EXECUTIVE COUNCIL
ROOM 184
STATE HOUSE
BOSTON, MA 02133

records than to apply for clemency. With the expansion of technology, the public has easy access to criminal records that are available online in most jurisdictions. If the case goes to court, there will be a public record of the formal criminal charge, the judicial proceedings, and the disposition of the case. This means that anyone can go to the court clerk's office to look at the record. This information is routinely accessed by employers, landlords, and newspapers.

1. CONSEQUENCES OF HAVING A CRIMINAL RECORD

There is a direct effect of an arrest when a judge or jury finds someone guilty or approves a plea bargain in that the defendant is sentenced or fined as part of the court proceedings. There also are collateral effects of a conviction. The **collateral consequences of a conviction** are the "legal and regulatory sanctions and restrictions that limit or prohibit people with criminal records from accessing employment, occupational licensing, housing, voting, education, and other opportunities."[6] Other types of benefits that may be affected include parental rights, education, public aid, voting privileges, military service, and student financial aid. There are nearly 48,000 laws, rules, and regulations across the nation that impose collateral consequences of convictions.

Collateral consequences of a conviction
The legal and regulatory sanctions and restrictions that limit or prohibit people with criminal records from accessing employment, occupational licensing, housing, voting, education, and other opportunities.

An estimated 10,000 to 12,000 names of persons arrested in the United States are added daily to the master criminal database of the Federal Bureau of Investigation (FBI).[7] Whenever someone is arrested, the arresting law enforcement agency creates a record of it. Even if no charges are filed or the person is found not guilty, the record continues to exist.

Furthermore, there is an entire industry of "data harvesters" that has emerged, which allows people to view these records online. Data harvesters go to courthouses and police record centers to compile information on individuals who have been arrested and formally charged with a crime in the jurisdiction. Nearly 90 percent of employers, 80 percent of landlords, and 60 percent of university admissions offices conduct background searches for applicants.

Some collateral consequences serve legitimate public purposes, such as prohibiting violent offenders from possessing firearms or forbidding convicted sex abusers from working with children. Collateral consequences for people convicted of serious traffic offenses may include driver's license suspensions and revocations. However, there are some collateral consequences that do not seem to bear a relationship between the crime and restricted activity, such as the denial of the right to vote or the revocation of a business license after conviction of a felony.

When the defense attorney conveys a plea offer to the client, the attorney should present collateral consequences of any plea bargain that includes a conviction as part of the deal. Most practitioners use the National Inventory of the Collateral Consequences of Conviction (NICCC) to research this issue.

---

[6]National Reentry Resource Center, National Inventory of Collateral Consequences of Conviction website, https://niccc.csgjusticecenter.org/.

[7]The FBI's Criminal Databse is Filling Up with Non-Criminals and No One in Law Enforcement Seems to Care, August 14, 2014 found at https://www.techdirt.com/2014/08/22/fbis-criminal-database-is-filling-up-with-non-criminals-no-one-law-enforcement-seems-to-care/.

The NICCC, which was created by the American Bar Association (ABA), is an online searchable database that identifies and categorizes the statutes and regulations imposing collateral consequences in every state, territory, the federal system, and the District of Columbia. The Council of State Governments (CSG) Justice Center maintains and updates the NICCC data to account for statutory and regulatory changes.

2. TYPES AND CONTENT OF CRIMINAL RECORDS

There are two primary types of criminal records: police records and court records. Police records are generated when a law enforcement officer arrests an individual. Police records are kept by the local arresting agency, the state police, and the FBI. Court records consist of the files maintained by the court clerk. Each file includes the charging document (criminal complaint, information, or bill of indictment) along with the filings made by both sides and the case disposition. Favorable and unfavorable dispositions of the case are matters of public record.

Even though a non-conviction is a favorable outcome, there is a police record of the arrest, in addition to a court record if the prosecuting authority filed charges. Non-conviction dispositions include release without being charged with a crime, an acquittal following a trial, the dismissal of the charges, the striking of the charges with leave to reinstate, or a *nolle prosequi*. Sometimes defendants who successfully satisfy the conditions set by the judge are not convicted of a crime. For example, Illinois defendants are not convicted if they successfully complete court supervision, Treatment Alternatives for Safe Communities (TASC) probation,[8] 1410 probation,[9] or second chance probation.[10]

Another type of criminal record is the listing of a defendant's name on a sex offender registry. In 1994, Congress enacted the Sex Offender Registration and Notification Act (SORNA).[11] Under this act, persons who meet the definition of a "sex offender"[12] must provide their name, address, and certain

---

[8]TASC is an Illinois not-for-profit organization that provides treatment services for adults who have substance abuse issues. TASC probation is a type of sentence available to offenders who have substance abuse issues and choose to receive treatment for their addiction. TASC probation is available to offenders charged with drug offenses, as well as non-drug-related crimes.

[9]1410 probation is a type of sentence for some first-time felony drug offenders in Illinois. This sentencing option is available for defendants found guilty of the possession of a Schedule I or II controlled substance, such as heroin, methamphetamine, opiates, cocaine, barbiturates, and ecstasy as well as for possession of an unauthorized prescription form.

[10]Under second chance probation, Illinois offenders are placed on probation for a minimum of two years, with no prison time. If they successfully complete all the probation terms, the case will be dismissed, and they will have no felony conviction on their record. However, if they violate any of the probation terms, they will be convicted on the original charge.

[11]34 U.S.C. §§20901 *et seq.*

[12]Under SORNA, a "sex offender" is defined as "an individual who was convicted of" specified criminal offenses: all offenses "involving a sexual act or sexual contact" and other offenses "against a minor." 34 U.S.C §§20911(1), (5)(A), (7).

other information in every state where they reside, work, or study. They must keep the registration current and periodically report to police departments for a period between 15 years and life.[13] Jurisdictions that do not meet SORNA's standards lose federal grant money.[14] Among jurisdictions that have substantially implemented SORNA, registration and notification laws vary. Failure to register as a sex offender is a crime at both the state and federal levels. In *Gundy v. United States*, the U.S. Supreme Court held that offenders are required to register even if their sex offense conviction occurred before SORNA became law.[15]

Sex offender registration is conducted at the local level. Every jurisdiction determines who is required to register, the information offenders must furnish, and the information posted on the its public registry website. In some states, many details are not listed on the public registry website, thus leading many people to draw negative conclusions without even considering the specifics of the offense or the age of the offender at the time the offense was committed. Other websites display extensive information including multiple photographs of each offender. The Department of Justice created the National Sex Offender Public Website (NSOPW) to provide the public with access to sex offender registries across the nation.[16] Jurisdictions link their sex offender registries to NSOPW jurisdictions' websites to permit access to information that is publicly listed on a jurisdiction's public sex offender registry website.

SORNA does not establish residency restrictions. However, states and localities have enacted legislation limiting registered sex offenders from residing within a certain distance from schools, day care centers, and parks. Several courts have found that some of these residency limitations are unconstitutional.[17] However, most residency restrictions have survived court challenges.[18]

---

[13]34 U.S.C. §§20915, 20918. In some circumstances, offenders who maintain a clean record for 10 years are permitted to reduce their registration period from 15 years to 10 years.

[14]They stand to lose 10 percent of its Edward R. Byrne Justice Assistance Grant funds. As of March 1, 2018, 18 states, 4 territories, and more than 125 Indian tribes have substantially implemented SORNA. U.S. Department of Justice, *Sex Offender Registration and Notification in the United States* (March 2018), at 1, found at https://www.smart.gov/caselaw/Case-Law-Update-2018-Compiled.pdf.

[15]139 S. Ct. 2116 (2019).

[16]This website (www.nsopw.gov) is administered by the Office of Sex Offender Sentencing, Monitoring, Apprehending, Registering, and Tracking.

[17]E.g., *Doe v. Cooper*, 842 F.3d 833 (4th Cir. 2016) (prohibition on being present at "any place where minors gather for regularly scheduled educational, recreational, or social programs" is impermissibly vague); *In re William Taylor*, 343 P.3d 867 (Cal. 2015) (residency requirements violate Due Process Clause); *Murphy v. Raoul*, 2019 WL 1437880 (N.D. IL 2019) (law governing mandatory supervised release for indigent sex offenders violates Fourteenth Amendment Equal Protection Clause and Eighth Amendment Cruel and Unusual Punishment Clause).

[18]U.S. Department of Justice, *Sex Offender Registration and Notification in the United States*, at 13.

APPLICATION EXERCISES

1. After reviewing the facts in the Cook case (*see* page xxxvii), consider the following facts: The prosecutor in the jurisdiction where your school is located has offered Bud Cook a plea agreement under which the motor vehicular homicide charge is dropped in exchange for a plea of guilty to driving under the influence of alcohol (DUI), serving six months in jail, and payment of fines and costs totaling $2,500.
   a. Use the NICCC Collateral Consequences Inventory (https://niccc.csgjusticecenter.org/), to research this issue and then prepare a memorandum that presents the collateral consequences of vehicular homicide and DUI convictions.
   b. Prepare an addendum to your memorandum that presents the potential range of a sentence for a motor vehicle homicide conviction.
2. After reviewing the facts in the Marshall case (*see* pages xxxviii-xxxix), consider the following facts: The prosecutor in the jurisdiction where your school is located has offered Clay Marshall a plea agreement under which the two sexual assault charges are reduced from felonies to misdemeanors in exchange for a plea of guilty and payment of fines and costs totaling $1,500.
   a. Use the NICCC Collateral Consequences Inventory (https://niccc.csgjusticecenter.org/), to research this issue and then prepare a memorandum that compares the collateral consequences of two misdemeanor sexual abuse convictions with two felony sexual assault convictions.
   b. Prepare an addendum to your memorandum that presents the potential range of the sentence for two sexual assault convictions.

Expungement
The process of physically eliminating the record of an individual's arrest and conviction.

Sealing
The process of preventing an individual's criminal records from being accessed by the public.

3. CLEARING CRIMINAL RECORDS

Paralegals often conduct the research and prepare the documents to request that a client's criminal records be cleared. There are three ways to clear a criminal record: clemency (discussed in Section B of this chapter), expungement, and sealing. The key difference between **expunging** a person's criminal record and **sealing** it is that a sealed record still exists in both a legal and physical sense, while expungement results in the deletion of any record that an arrest or criminal charge ever occurred.

In most states, records of juvenile criminal proceedings are automatically sealed when the juvenile reaches age 18. However, the records are still in existence and can be opened by court order.

Discussion Question

7. In recent years, many states have made major changes in laws relating to marijuana use and distribution.

a. Should the criminal records of people who were convicted of violating the old laws prohibiting the use of marijuana be able to have those records expunged? Why?

b. Should the states that changed their marijuana laws automatically purge their criminal records of people who were convicted of violating the old laws? Why?

a. Researching Criminal Records

The first step in the process of clearing criminal records is to obtain the client's arrest records. Individuals typically can request their arrest records from the state police and the local agencies that arrested them. In some jurisdictions, such as Illinois, licensed Live Scan[19] vendors can provide persons with a transcript of their arrest record.

Next, you must gather the client's court records in all of the jurisdictions where the client was arrested. In many locales, these records are available online. If the court clerk's office does not provide online access to records, you need to go to the court clerk's office where the client's case was filed to get copies of the court dispositions. You should only examine criminal cases; civil matters, such as civil orders of protection and evictions, are ineligible for clearing.

Once the records have been received, the paralegal should review them and prepare a summary report that includes the following information:

1. Arrest date and name of arresting department
2. Charge
3. Case disposition
4. Sentence
5. Date that the sentence was completed

This information is vital to determining whether expungement or sealing is appropriate to seek clearance of the client's criminal record under the laws of that state.

These state laws for expungement vary tremendously. Some states permit expungements only in cases in which the charge is dismissed before the entry of a plea, such as through successful completion of pre-trial diversion. Other states allow a defendant to expunge convictions for minor infractions or misdemeanors. Generally, felony convictions are not eligible for expungement. Check your state's law to determine the criteria for expungement eligibility.[20]

---

[19]LiveScan is an inkless, digital fingerprinting process that submits your fingerprints electronically law enforcement authorities, such as the state police or FBI.

[20]The Restoration of Rights Project website (http://ccresourcecenter.org/restoration) is an excellent resource that you can use to find out a state's approach to expungement, record sealing, and clemency.

Illinois permits expungement for the following types of cases:

- Arrests for misdemeanors and felonies that did not result in a conviction.
- Convictions for misdemeanors and felonies only if:
    - The conviction was either reversed or vacated; or
    - The defendant received a pardon from the Governor allowing expungement of all convictions on the defendant's record; or
    - An honorably discharged veteran received a Certificate of Eligibility for Expungement from the Prisoner Review Board allowing expungement of all convictions.
- Sentences for court supervision only if:
    - 2 years have passed since successful competition of court supervision, except for certain offenses; or
    - 5 years have passed since successful competition of court supervision for:
        - Domestic battery
        - Criminal sexual abuse (victim was 18 or older)
        - Operation of an uninsured motor vehicle
        - Operation of a motor vehicle when registration is suspended for not having insurance
        - Display of false insurance card
        - Scrap processors to keep records
    - For defendants 25 or older, whose reckless driving supervision occurred when they were under 25, and have no other convictions.
- Sentences of qualified probation, only if 5 years have passed since successful completion of qualified probation.[21]

Illinois offenses that cannot be expunged:

- Minor traffic offenses, unless the motorist was released without being charged.
- Convictions for misdemeanors and felonies unless they were reversed, vacated, pardoned by the Governor, or approved by the Prisoner Review Board.
- Court supervision or qualified probation that was not successfully completed.
- Court supervision for the following offenses:
    - Reckless driving (if driver was 25 or older at the time)
    - Driving under the influence
    - Sexual offenses against a minor under age 18
- Convictions include a finding of guilt resulting in a sentence of: probation (other than qualified probation, successfully completed), jail or prison time, conditional discharge, time considered served, fines (with no other sentence), and supervisions or qualified probations that are not successfully completed.[22]

Illinois offenses that can be sealed:

- Convictions for most Illinois felonies and misdemeanors can be sealed if at least three years have passed since successful completion of the last sentence. Convictions of defendants who have met certain educational goals are eligible for sealing before the end of the waiting period.*

---

[21]State of Illinois, Instruction Booklet for Expunging and Sealing Court Forms, p. 3 located at www.illinoiscourts.gov/Forms/approved/expungement/ExpungementSealing_Instructions_Approved.pdf.

[22]*Id.* at pp. 3-4.

Illinois offenses that cannot be sealed:

- Minor traffic offenses,
- DUI, reckless driving (unless under age 25),
- Domestic battery,
- Violation of an order of protection,
- Sexual offenses (except prostitution and misdemeanor public indecency),
- Animal offenses (e.g., dog fighting), and
- New felony convictions (following prior sealing of felony conviction).

* The educational goals that accelerate eligibility for sealing are: high school diploma, associate's degree, career certificate, vocational or technical certification, bachelor's degree, and passing the high school GED test. *Id.* at p. 4.

Figure 15.2 Illinois Rules on Expungement

For example, Illinois has one of the more liberal expungement and records sealing laws in the country. See Figure 15.2.

b. Requesting a Court to Clear Criminal Record

After you determine that a record qualifies for either expungement or sealing, draft a petition seeking the appropriate relief[23] from the court of the jurisdiction where the arrest occurred. In some jurisdictions, such as Illinois, this simply requires you to insert information in a fill-in-the-blank form.[24] If the client was arrested in multiple venues, separate petitions must be filed in each venue.

Ordinarily, the person petitioning to clear the criminal record must provide copies of the petition to the police department and prosecutor. The prosecutor and law enforcement agency will be given a specific amount of time to object. The case then goes before a judge. In some places, the petitioner always must schedule a specific time and date for the petition to be heard. In other venues, the petitioner does not need to set the matter for hearing if no objection is filed. Check with the court clerk to find out how you should proceed. In some states, the petitioner is entitled to relief if the conditions of the statute are satisfied. In other states, the judge has discretion to grant or deny petitions seeking expungement or record sealing. When there is judicial discretion, the petitioner should present evidence at the hearing as to the defendant's educational and employment history and the positive effect the granting of the petition will have on the defendant's future.

Some categories of offenders may be subject to different procedures. For instance, juveniles typically can get their records expunged or records sealed more easily than adults. In some jurisdictions, juvenile records are automatically

[23]The court document seeking expungement or the sealing of criminal records is referred to by different names in different places, such as "petition," "request," or "motion."

[24]The Illinois Supreme Court approved a form entitled "Request to Expunge & Impound and/or Seal Criminal Records" which is required to be accepted in all trial courts. *See* http://www.illinoiscourts.gov/Forms/approved/expungement/expungement.asp.

sealed. In states that have legalized recreational marijuana, persons who were found guilty of cannabis possession under drug possession laws may be entitled to automatic expungement.

APPLICATION EXERCISES

3. After reviewing the facts in the Cook case (*see* page xxxvii), consider the following facts: On the second Monday of this year, Bud Cook entered into a plea agreement under which the motor vehicular homicide charge was dismissed in exchange for his plea of guilty to driving under the influence of alcohol. He has paid all fines and costs. He is currently serving a six-month jail term, which will be completed in early July.
   a. Determine whether the client is eligible for expungement or record sealing in the jurisdiction in which your school is located.
   b. If so, how long does he have to wait before applying for this relief?

4. After reviewing the facts in the Marshall case (*see* pages xxxviii-xxxix), consider the following facts: On the third Tuesday of this year, the prosecutor in the jurisdiction where your school is located dismissed the charges against Clay Marshall because neither victim appeared for trial and cannot be located.
   a. Determine whether the client is eligible for expungement or record sealing in the jurisdiction in which your school is located.
   b. If so, how long does he have to wait before applying for this relief?

c. Removal from Sex Offender Registries

A 1996 Act of Congress requires the U.S. Attorney General to establish a national database at the FBI to track the whereabouts and movements of certain convicted sex offenders.[25] The National Crime Information Center retains the offender's current registered address and dates of registration, conviction, and residence. The legislation also made it a criminal offense for a registered sex offender to move to another state and knowingly fail to notify the FBI and authorities in the new state. Notification to the FBI and state authorities must be made within ten days upon moving to a new state and/or establishing residence following release from prison or being placed on parole, supervised release, or probation.

Procedures for removing a name from a sex offender registry vary from one state to another. For instance, in Illinois, there is no procedure for removal of the name of an adult convicted offender. The registry automatically deletes

---

[25] See the Pam Lychner Sexual Offender Tracking and Identification Act of 1996, 42 U.S.C. §14072 (Lychner Act).

Exhibit 15.2: Petition to Discontinue Sex Offender Registration

Approved, SCAO

Original - Court
1st copy - Defendant/Juvenile

2nd copy - Prosecuting official
3rd copy - Return

STATE OF MICHIGAN JUDICIAL DISTRICT JUDICIAL CIRCUIT COUNTY	PETITION TO DISCONTINUE SEX OFFENDER REGISTRATION	(A) CASE NO.

(B) ORI MI- | Court address | Court telephone no.

(C) THE PEOPLE OF ☐ The State of Michigan ☐ ______ v Defendant's name, address, and telephone no.

CTN	SID	DOB

In the Matter of ______
Juvenile name, DOB, alias(es)

(D) 1. On ______ I was convicted of the following offense ______.
☐ I was not confined for this offense. ☐ I completed the term of confinement for this offense on ______.

(E) 2. a. ☐ I am a Tier I offender and at least 10 years have passed since I was convicted or since I was released from confinement for the conviction. OR
☐ I am a Tier III offender and at least 25 years have passed since I was adjudicated or since I was released from confinement for the adjudication. AND
1) I have not been convicted of any felony or any offense listed in MCL 28.722(s), (u), or (w) since the date of my conviction or the date of my release from any confinement for this conviction.
2) I have successfully completed my assigned period of supervised release, probation, or parole without revocation at any time of that supervised release, probation, or parole.
☐ 3) I was ordered to complete a sex offender treatment program and I successfully completed that program.
☐ b. I was convicted of an offense listed in MCL 28.722(s), (u), or (w), and the conviction was for an offense that was the result of a consensual sexual act between me and the victim, and the victim was 13 years of age or older but less than 16 years of age at the time of the offense and I was not more than 4 years older than the victim.
☐ c. I was convicted of a violation of MCL 750.158, 750.338, 750.338a, 750.338b, or 750.520c(1)(i) as a result of a consensual act and the victim was 16 years of age or older and not under my custodial authority at the time of the violation.
☐ d. I was registered under the Sex Offenders Registration Act before July 1, 2011 for an offense that required registration and the offense no longer requires registration.
☐ e. I was adjudicated as a juvenile for an offense listed in MCL 28.722(s), (u), or (w), and I was less than 14 years of age at the time of the offense.

3. I request that the court issue an order to discontinue sex offender registration as provided by law.

(F) ______
Petitioner Signature

(G) Subscribed and sworn to before me on ______ (Date), ______ County, Michigan.

My commission expires: ______ (Date) Signature: ______ (Deputy clerk/Notary public)

Notary public, State of Michigan, County of ______

NOTICE OF HEARING NOTE: If you require special accommodations to use the court because of a disability or if you require a foreign language interpreter to fully participate in court proceedings, please contact the court immediately to make arrangements.

(H) A hearing will be held on the above petition to discontinue registration on ______ (Date) at ______ (Time)

at ______ (Location) before ______ (Bar no.)

NOTE: The victim has the right to attend this hearing and to make a written or an oral statement to the court before any decision regarding this petition is made. The victim is not required to appear at this hearing against his or her will.

CERTIFICATE OF MAILING
I certify that on this date I served a copy of this petition and notice of hearing on the prosecuting official by first-class mail addressed to his/her last-known address as defined by MCR 2.107(C)(3).

(I) ______ (Date) ______ (Petitioner/Attorney signature)

MC 406a (6/18) PETITION TO DISCONTINUE SEX OFFENDER REGISTRATION MCL 28.728c the names of certain classifications of offenders after they complete their ten-year registration period. In contrast, Michigan has an approved form to petition for discontinuation of registration. *See* Exhibit 15.2. You need to research the law in your own state to determine the steps to take to petition for this relief.

Defense attorneys will advise clients who are required to register as sex offenders to stay out of trouble; to complete all required incarceration, treatment, parole, probation, and supervision required by their sentence; to promptly notify the appropriate authorities if they move; and to take concerted steps to improve themselves (in the family, professional, educational, or religious area). If the client follows this advice, the odds of successfully petitioning for discontinuation of registration are improved.

Application Exercises

5. After reviewing the facts in the Marshall case (*see* pages xxxviii-xxxix), consider the following facts: After Clay Marshall was convicted of two sexual assaults, he was required to register as a sex offender. Answer the following questions for the jurisdiction in which your school is located:

a. What information must Clay report? To whom should he provide this information?
b. How long must he continue to register as a sex offender?
c. As a registered sex offender, does Clay have restrictions as to where he can reside or places that he can visit? If so, what are these restrictions?
d. What process, if any, is available to discontinue registration? When can Clay begin this process?

6. Assume that a Michigan jury found Clay Marshall guilty of two counts of criminal sexual conduct in the fourth degree. The judge sentenced him to probation. The pertinent law provides as follows:

MCL Sec. §520e. (1) A person is guilty of criminal sexual conduct in the fourth degree if he or she engages in sexual contact with another person and if any of the following circumstances exist:

. . .

(b) Force or coercion is used to accomplish the sexual contact. Force or coercion includes, but is not limited to, any of the following circumstances:

(i) When the actor overcomes the victim through the actual application of physical force or physical violence.

MCL §750.520a(q) defines "sexual contact" as follows: the intentional touching of the victim's or actor's intimate parts or the intentional touching of the clothing covering the immediate area of the victim's or actor's intimate parts, if that intentional touching can reasonably be construed as being for the purpose of sexual arousal or gratification, done for a sexual purpose . . ."

a. Is Clay required to register as a sex offender in Michigan? If so, where does he register, and how long must registration continue?

b. If he moves to the state in which your school is located, will he have to register in that state?
c. What steps, if any, will Clay need to take to end his obligation to register in the state in which your school is located?
d. Using the petition template in Exhibit 15.1, prepare a petition to discontinue registration for the client. Assume that 15 years have transpired since the conviction and that Clay has not had any other problems with the law. If information requested in the form is unknown, leave the spaces blank.

D. Recovery of Seized Assets

During an arrest or through executing a search warrant, police officers may seize property that they suspect was obtained either through criminal activities or purchased with money generated from a specific crime. For instance, if officers arrest someone for selling drugs, they may confiscate the money used for the drug purchase. Defense attorneys often represent clients whose assets were taken by the police, under these and other types of seizures.

When an officer takes possession of an item of property, the property has been "seized," although legal title has not been transferred. To transfer title, the prosecutor will use a process called **asset forfeiture**. In criminal forfeiture, the prosecution seeks ownership of property owned by the person convicted of a crime.

Asset forfeiture
The process used by law enforcement officers to keep and take ownership of seized property that was obtained either through criminal activities or purchased with money generated from a specific crime.

Law enforcement officers also can use civil forfeiture to pursue property that they believe was used in the commission of a crime or is related to that crime. In contrast to criminal forfeiture, the owner of the property need not be charged with a crime. Instead, civil asset forfeiture proceedings are against the property itself. In civil forfeiture cases, the owners of the seized assets do not have the rights provided to persons accused of crimes, such as an indigent person's right to a court-appointed attorney.

The federal government and almost every state have civil forfeiture laws. Procedures vary from state to state, so you need to check your state's statute to learn the civil forfeiture process in your community. Typically, the process begins with the law enforcement authorities sending notice to the property owner informing the owner that the property was seized. The next step is the claim period in which the owner must submit a claim to the authorities for the return of the property. If the law enforcement agency chooses not to return the property, it will file a civil complaint in court. The property owner is required to file an answer, and the case is heard by a judge. There are strict time limits for giving notice, submitting claims, and filing documents in court.

There are several defenses in civil forfeiture proceedings. One of the most common is the lack of probable cause to make the seizure. The government must prove a connection between the seized asset and a specific crime. This proof is based on the facts known to the officer at the time of the seizure. This defense may be raised by either the person accused of the underlying crime or the person whose property was confiscated.

Field sobriety test
A series of tasks a driver is directed to perform in front of a police officer to help the officer determine whether the motorist was driving under the influence of alcohol or drugs.

Breathalyzer
A device that measures the percentage of alcohol in a driver's system by analyzing a breath sample.

Blood alcohol concentration (BAC)
The percentage of alcohol in a person's bloodstream.

Implied consent law
A state statute providing that persons who are issued driver's licenses consent to field sobriety tests and chemical tests to determine impairment while operating a vehicle.

Summary suspension
The automatic cessation of driving privileges of an individual who has a specified blood alcohol concentration percentage in his or her bloodstream, as shown by a blood or breathalyzer test. A driver may also have his or her license suspended by refusing to submit to a breathalyzer test.

Another defense is disproportionality of the value of the seized asset in comparison to the crime. The Eighth Amendment's prohibition of excessive fines applies to both federal and state asset forfeitures.[26] The owners of expensive cars seized by the police may have the best prospects of raising the disproportionality defense.

Finally, the innocent owner defense is available in most states to innocent third-party owners who can show that they own the seized asset and prove that they were unaware of or did not consent to the illegal use of their property.

E. Challenging Summary Suspensions of Driver's Licenses

As discussed in Chapter 4, when a police officer has reason to believe that a motorist is intoxicated, the officer may administer a **field sobriety test**, and if the field test results lead the officer to conclude that the driver is impaired, the officer can ask the driver to take a **breathalyzer** test at the scene.

If the results of a breathalyzer test indicate that the driver's **blood alcohol concentration** (BAC) exceeds the legal limit, the officer will arrest and transport the driver to the station, where the police will ask the driver to submit to a second breathalyzer test. Whereas the results of the portable breathalyzer are inadmissible at trial, the results of the test taken at the station can be introduced as evidence at a trial.

All states have **implied consent laws**[27] that require motorists to consent to undergo field sobriety and chemical tests to determine whether they are driving while impaired as a condition of getting a license to drive. In most jurisdictions, if the driver refuses the test, the state automatically suspends the motorist's license for 3 to 12 months, and drivers with a history of DUIs are subject to even longer suspensions or revocations. According to the National Highway Traffic Safety Administration, about 20 percent of drunk driving suspects refuse to submit to BAC testing.[28]

Even when drivers submit to testing, their licenses will be suspended or revoked if their BAC exceeds the lawful limit. Drivers arrested for DUI usually face a summary suspension of their driver's license. A **summary suspension** is the automatic cessation of driving privileges of an individual who has a specified BAC in his or her bloodstream as shown by a blood test or a breathalyzer.

---

[26]In *Austin v. United States,* 509 U.S. 602 (1993), the Supreme Court of held that the Eighth Amendment's Excessive Fines Clause applies to federal civil forfeiture cases. The Court ruled in *Timbs v. Indiana*, 139 S. Ct. 682 (2019) that the Excessive Fines Clause applies to state asset forfeiture.

[27]Two states make refusal to submit to such testing a crime.

[28]A 2005 NHTSA study of data collected in 37 states, the District of Columbia, and Puerto Rico placed the average refusal rate at 22.4 percent, and the median refusal rate was 17.4 percent. The weighted mean of the refusal rates based on the jurisdictions' populations was almost 21 percent. A. Bening, et al., *Refusal of Intoxication Testing: A Report to Congress*, Report DOT HS 811 098, found at https://www.nhtsa.gov/sites/nhtsa.dot.gov/files/811098_1.pdf.

Summary suspensions come into play when a driver refuses to take a breathalyzer test or if the driver has a BAC over the legal limit.

While there are variations in the procedures used to challenge summary suspensions, in some states[29] they are civil proceedings in which the motorist, rather than the prosecution, has the burden of proof. Paralegals who work for defense attorneys representing DUI clients may be involved in preparing for these hearings.

Because this is a civil proceeding rather than a criminal case, the defense can use civil discovery tools to prepare for the hearing, such as a request to produce[30] or a request for admissions.[31] Typical grounds for the petition to rescind include the officer's misleading or improper statements concerning the consequences of refusing testing, lack of probable cause to make the traffic stop, and invalid testing results.

When the challenge to the summary suspension is unsuccessful,[32] the motorist may qualify for a judicial driving permit or restricted driver's license. These items permit the suspended motorist to drive to and from work and to substance abuse treatment until their driving privileges are restored.

SUMMARY

After being found guilty, criminal defendants in some cases may be able to successfully challenge their convictions by filing collateral actions. These remedies include requests for issuance of a writ of habeas corpus and a petition for post-conviction relief.

If they are unable to convince a court to overturn their conviction through direct appeals or collateral actions, defendants may apply for clemency. For federal crimes, they must seek a pardon or commutation from the president. Defendants convicted of state offenses typically apply to the governor's office or a state clemency board. In limited circumstances, persons convicted of sex offenses can petition to discontinue their obligation to register as sex offenders.

Paralegals may be involved in cases in which the client's assets were taken by the police because the assets were allegedly connected to criminal activity. Whereas criminal asset forfeiture is the process used when a convicted defendant is the owner, civil forfeiture is used when either the defendant is not convicted or the assets are owned by persons not accused of breaking the law.

---

[29] In Illinois, a motorist served with a notice of summary suspension can challenge it by filing a petition to rescind.

[30] A request to produce is a written civil discovery demand made upon the opposing party to obtain documents, objects, and electronic data in the opposing party's possession or control.

[31] A request for admissions is a written civil discovery tool that requires the opposing party to either admit or deny the truth of statements of fact. If a party fails to respond in a timely manner, the fact is deemed admitted.

[32] After a driver's license is suspended or revoked, the motorist must submit a formal application to the state to have it reinstated. If a suspension is for a first offense, the state will process the request without conducting a hearing. In other cases, the state will conduct a hearing. Consult the statutes in your jurisdiction to learn your state's process.

Motorists accused of DUI often have their driving privileges summarily suspended because of the implied consent law. In some jurisdictions, paralegals may help their attorney challenge the summary suspension in a civil proceeding.

INTERNET RESOURCES

- Inventory National Reentry Resource Center, National Inventory of Collateral Consequences of Conviction (NICCC): **https://niccc.csgjusticecenter.org/**
- State of Illinois, Instruction Booklet for Expunging and Sealing Court Forms: **www.illinoiscourts.gov/Forms/approved/expungement/ExpungementSealing_Instructions_Approved.pdf**
- National Sex Offender Public Website (NSOPW): **www.nsopw.gov**
- Restoration of Rights Project: **http://ccresourcecenter.org/restoration/**

REVIEW QUESTIONS

1. Identify and define two major alternatives to a direct appeal from conviction.
2. What are the steps involved in petitioning for a writ of habeas corpus?
3. What is the difference between a pardon and a commutation?
4. In most states, what public official has the authority to issue a pardon?
5. For what types of crimes can the president issue a pardon?
6. What is the process for requesting a commutation?
7. What type of benefits and opportunities do defendants lose because of a conviction?
8. What are the two primary types of criminal records kept on a person who was arrested?
9. Is expungement available to defendants who were acquitted at trial of criminal charges?
10. What is SORNA?
11. How do expungement and record sealing differ?
12. When researching an individual's criminal record, what information should be recorded to prepare a petition to expunge the records?
13. What Internet website can be used to find out a state's approach to expungement, record sealing, and clemency?
14. What is the difference between criminal asset forfeiture and civil asset forfeiture?
15. What are the key defenses that can be raised in civil forfeiture proceedings?
16. What is implied consent?
17. What are the consequences of a motorist's refusal to take a breathalyzer test?

Glossary

Accessory A person who assisted in the preparation of the crime but was not present when it was actually carried out.

Accessory after the fact A person who first aided the principal after the commission of the crime.

Accomplice A person who assists the principal with the crime or with the preparation of the crime.

Actus reus A Latin term referring to a person's wrongful conduct that resulted in an illegal act.

Address block The portion of a court document that identifies the attorney responsible for the preparation of the document, the party that the attorney represents, the address, and the telephone number. The address block is also known as the preparer's data.

Administrative law Rules and regulations created by administrative agencies.

Adversary system A judicial system in which judges are supposed to act as passive, neutral decisionmakers, while the attorneys for the litigants are responsible for presenting the evidence and arguments that favor their clients.

Adverse witness A witness who is either the opposing party in the case or a witness who is closely affiliated with the opposing party.

Affiant The person who signs an affidavit under oath or under penalty of perjury.

Affidavit A voluntarily written declaration of facts signed under oath or under penalty of perjury.

Alibi defense A criminal defense requiring proof that the defendant could not have been at the scene of the crime.

Allocution The defendant's statement in mitigation of the sentence.

American Bar Association The largest voluntary association of attorneys in the United States. As the national representative of the legal profession, the ABA's stated mission is to serve the public and the profession by promoting justice, professional excellence, and respect for the law.

Appeal A formal request for review of an order or judgment entered by another court that seeks to reverse or modify the other court's decision.

Appellant The party initiating the appeal.

Appellant-cross appellee The party defending the trial court's decision on appeal and initiating the cross appeal.

Appellee The party defending the trial court's decision on appeal.

Appellee-cross appellant The party initiating the appeal and defending the trial court's decision on appeal.

Application for search warrant A motion presented to the court that specifies the reasons that a search warrant should be issued. The application for search warrant is typically in affidavit form or accompanied by an affidavit.

Arraignment The court proceeding at which the judge informs the defendant of the charges filed by the government.

Arrest The act of physically apprehending and taking into custody a person who is suspected of committing a crime,

Arrest warrant A court order issued at the request of the prosecutor and/or law enforcement that authorizes the arrest and detention of an individual.

Arson An act of starting a fire or causing an explosion with the purpose of destroying or damaging the property of another; or to collect insurance for such loss.

Assault An act that causes or attempts to cause serious bodily harm to another individual.

Assessment The charge imposed upon a specified group (i.e., users of the court system) for the purpose of funding specified services (e.g., women's shelters or legal aid programs).

Asset forfeiture The process used by law enforcement officers to keep and take ownership of seized property that was obtained either through criminal activities or purchased with money from a specific crime.

Assigned counsel A lawyer in private practice appointed by the court to handle an indigent client's criminal case.

Attorney A lawyer; a person licensed by a state to practice law.

Attorney-client privilege The rule of evidence that forbids an attorney, or the attorney's employees, from testifying about communications with the client.

Attorney's trust fund A special account holding money on behalf of the client.

Attorney work product Trial preparation materials consisting of the attorney's mental impressions, conclusions, opinions, and legal theories about a case.

Authentication of evidence The process of establishing that the objects being introduced into evidence are what they are claimed to be.

Back strike A practice that allows a party's attorney to exercise a peremptory challenge of a juror who was part of a panel that had previously been accepted.

Bail Money or something else of value that is pledged to guarantee that the accused will appear in court for scheduled proceedings.

Bailiff A court employee who is responsible for maintaining order in the courtrooms and watching over juries when they are in recess or when they have been sequestered.

Bates numbering An organizational method used to label documents by assigning a number (or alphanumeric designation) to each document (or page), thereby creating a unique identifier for each.

Battered woman's or spouse's syndrome A syndrome of being the victim of repeated attacks; self-defense is sometimes allowed to the victim even when the victim is not in immediate danger.

Battery An act of intentional physical contact that is either offensive or harmful to another person.

Bench trial A non-jury trial at which the judge decides all questions of fact.

Bench warrant A court order that authorizes the arrest of someone for failing to show for a court appearance.

Best evidence rule An evidentiary rule requiring that the original document be produced at trial.

Beyond a reasonable doubt The standard of proof used in criminal trials. The evidence presented must be so conclusive and complete that all reasonable doubts regarding the facts are removed from the jurors' minds.

Bill of Attainder A law that imposes criminal penalties on a single person or small, select group of people.

Bill of particulars A supplementary document that gives the specifics of a charge that were not set forth in the original charge.

Black letter law Widely used, generally accepted, basic legal principles.

Blood alcohol concentration (BOC) The percentage of alcohol in a person's blood.

Boilerplate language Model sentences that include standardized legal terms and phrases.

Burglary An act of entering into a building for the purpose of committing a crime.

Bystander's report A statement approved by the trial judge as to what happened in court.

Capital crimes Crimes for which the death penalty is an authorized punishment.

Capital offense A special type of felony that is punishable by death.

Capital punishment Punishment by death. It is also referred to as the death penalty.

Caption The section of a court document containing the names of the parties, case number, name of the court it is being filed in, and a title that identifies the type of document being filed.

Chain of custody A record of who possessed an object being presented as evidence from the time it came into possession of government agents until it is presented in court.

Challenge for cause A method for removing a prospective juror based on a finding by the judge that the juror has some sort of bias or has another disqualifying factor for serving on the jury for this specific case.

Change of venire The process of selecting jurors from a different location than the place of the trial.

Change of venue An action taken by the judge to move a trial to an alternative location.

Character evidence Evidence of a person's reputation in the community as to a particular trait, such as honesty or chastity.

Charge bargaining A plea bargain in which the prosecution dismisses a more serious charge in exchange for the defendant's pleading guilty to the lesser offense.

Charging the jury A process in which the judge instructs the jurors as to their responsibilities and presents the laws that they are supposed to apply.

Chilling effect doctrine A principle of constitutional law that invalidates statutes that are worded in such a way as to make people fearful of engaging in legitimate, constitutionally protected First Amendment activities.

Circumstantial evidence Evidence that permits the inference of the existence or nonexistence of a fact or event that a party seeks to prove.

Civil law The body of law defining actions for which individuals can use the courts to seek remedies for violations of their private rights, establishing procedural requirements for using the courts, and establishing remedies for violations of those rights.

CJA panel attorney An attorney in private practice who is appointed in federal cases to represent indigent defendants for a fixed hourly fee.

Clearly erroneous The standard used by appellate courts when reviewing a trial court's findings of fact, in which appellate judges defer to conclusions reached by the trial judge or jurors unless the appellant demonstrates that those findings were certainly unreasonable.

Clemency The power to pardon a crime, commute a sentence, or grant a reprieve.

Closing argument An oral presentation made to the jury, after all of the evidence has been presented, for the purpose of convincing the jury to find in favor of the side that is presenting the argument.

Code A compilation of statues, ordinances, or administrative regulations that is organized by subject matter rather than by the date of its enactment.

Collateral consequences (of a conviction) The legal and regulatory sanctions and restrictions that limit or prohibit people with criminal records from accessing employment, occupational licensing, housing, voting, education, and other opportunities.

Collateral remedies Actions designed to challenge judgments of conviction that have otherwise become final in the normal appellate review process.

Common law Legal principles that have evolved over time from the analysis of court decisions made in the absence of constitutional, statutory, and administrative law.

Common law record All documents contained in the case file in the trial court, including the docketing statement, exhibits, and jury instructions.

Commutation An official action that lessens the penalty without changing the conviction.

Competency The ability of a witness to testify; generally, the witness must be capable of being understood by the jury; must understand the duty to tell the truth; and have knowledge of the facts to which he or she is testifying.

Complainant The person who signs a criminal complaint under oath attesting that the allegations of the complaint are true.

Complete defense A defense that, if proven, relieves the defendant of all criminal responsibility. [Contrast with partial defense]

Concurrent sentences Sentences that are served simultaneously rather than one after the other.

Conflict of interest A situation in which an attorney's representation of one client is either directly adverse to another client or materially limits the attorney's duties to another client, a former client or third party, or the personal interest of the attorney.

Conflicts check The process of verifying whether the acceptance of a new case would result in a conflict of interest for the attorney.

Consecutive sentences Sentences that must be served one after the other rather than simultaneously.

Conspiracy An agreement between two or more persons to commit an unlawful act.

Constitutional law Laws and legal principles derived from constitutions through judicial interpretation.

Content neutrality Laws may not limit free expression on the basis of whether the speech's content supports or opposes any particular position.

Contingent fee The lawyer fee owed by the client if the attorney is successful. There is no fee if the client does not prevail.

Continuance The postponement of a scheduled court proceeding, such as a hearing or the trial.

Contract lawyer An attorney who enters into an agreement with the government to furnish legal services to indigent clients.

Corroborative evidence Evidence supporting other evidence that has already been admitted but that is presented in a different form.

Count A subsection of the body of a charging document that alleges the defendant's commission of a crime and sets out all of the required elements of an offense.

Count bargaining A plea bargain in which the prosecution drops one or more related charges in exchange for the defendant's pleading guilty to at least one of the counts originally charged.

Court clerk A court employee who is responsible for maintaining the court files in proper order as well as ensuring that the various motions submitted by lawyers are properly filed and the actions taken by judges accurately docketed.

Court costs Fees, charged to the defendant, that are designed to pay for operating expenses of the court system.

Court reporter (person) The court employee who prepares verbatim transcripts of courtroom proceedings.

Court reporters (books) Books that contain decisions and opinions of courts.

Court supervision A sentencing option used for minor offenses in which the defendant is not convicted if he or she complies with the judge's conditions during a specific period of time.

Crime control model An approach to evaluating the criminal justice system on the basis of how efficiently it suppresses crime.

Criminal complaint A charge of the commission of a crime, made under oath.

Criminal justice system A collection of institutions and individuals that are typically involved in the processing of criminal cases.

Criminal law The body of law defining offenses against the community at large, regulating how suspects are investigated, charged and tried, and establishing punishments for convicted offenders.

Criminal summons A document issued under a court order that directs the accused to appear in court to answer the charges made against him or her.

Cross appeal An appeal filed by the appellee of an existing appeal.

Cross-examination The questioning of a witness called by the opposing side.

Cumulative error The prejudicial impact of a series of two or more trial errors that do not warrant reversal of a case when viewed separately but collectively amount to reversible error.

Cumulative evidence Evidence that does not add any new information but confirms facts that already have been established.

Curriculum vitae (CV) A written description of a person's work experience, educational background, and skills.

Damages The monetary compensation awarded to the wronged party in a civil case.

Deadly force A force that would cause serious bodily injury or death.

Declarant The person who made the out-of-court statement.

Defendant The party who is defending against either a criminal prosecution or a civil lawsuit. In a criminal case, the defendant is the person accused of committing a crime.

Defense attorney The lawyer who represents a defendant in criminal court.

Delayed motion for a new trial A request to have the judge order a new trial on the basis of errors that were discovered long after the trial ended.

Demonstrative evidence Physical objects, such as photos, maps, x-rays, and diagrams, used to illustrate or aid in the understanding of verbal testimony.

Deponent A witness being questioned under oath at a deposition.

Deposition Testimony taken before trial under oath that is subject to cross-examination and preserved in writing.

Deposition abstract A special type of deposition summary that presents the witness's statements as one- or two-sentence bits of information accompanied by page and line references to the deposition transcript.

Deposition summary A written summary of the transcript of the witness's responses to the questions asked in a deposition.

Deposition to perpetuate testimony A deposition that preserves the witness's statement so that it can be presented at a later time as evidence at trial.

Determinate sentencing A form of punishment in which the defendant is sentenced to a specific term of imprisonment.

Dicta Statements made in a court's opinion that go beyond the facts necessary to decide the case and therefore are not binding legal precedent in subsequent cases.

Direct evidence Evidence that establishes a direct link to the fact or event that a party seeks to prove.

Direct examination The initial questioning conducted by attorneys for the side that called the witnesses.

Disclosure The revealing of information.

Discovery A legal procedure by which a party in the case can obtain information about the case from other parties prior to the start of the trial.

Diversion program An educational and/or social service program operated by public and private agencies outside of the criminal justice system to which criminal defendants are sent as an alternative to getting a criminal conviction on their record and/or serving time in an official government corrections program.

Documentary evidence Legal instruments such as contracts, leases, wills and deeds, and other written documents used to support claims made in court.

Domestic violence Physical abuse, harassment, or intimidation of a victim by a family or household member.

Double jeopardy The Fifth Amendment prohibition against prosecuting or punishing a defendant twice for the same crime.

Due process of law Legal procedures that enforce basic rights that are considered necessary for fairness and justice.

Due process model An approach to evaluating the criminal justice system on the basis of how well it protects people from being charged and/or convicted of crimes they didn't commit.

DUI The offense of driving under the influence of alcoholic beverages. Some states refer to the violation as **DWI**.

Duress A defense requiring proof that force or a threat of force was used to cause a person to commit a criminal act.

Duty of confidentiality An attorney's ethical duty to maintain the confidences of the client.

DWI Driving while intoxicated.

Electronic discovery (e-discovery) The discovery of documents created, disbursed, and stored electronically.

Entrapment A defense requiring proof that the defendant would not have committed the crime but for police trickery.

Espionage The act of disclosing information with intent to interfere with the operation or success of the U.S. armed forces or to promote the success of enemies of the United States.

Evidence Witness testimony, documents, physical objects, and stipulations that are presented in court for the purpose of determining the facts of the case.

Excessive force Any force greater than the level of force that a reasonable and prudent law enforcement officer would use under the circumstances.

Exclusionary rule The doctrine that evidence obtained in violation of a defendant's constitutional rights cannot be used against the defendant in a criminal prosecution.

Exculpatory evidence Evidence that either tends to establish the defendant's innocence or is favorable to the accused on the question of punishment.

Execution of a warrant Police, or other law enforcement officers searching for the objects identified in the warrant in the locations specified in the warrant.

Executive order A directive issued by the president or a governor, enforceable by members of the executive branch of government, that has the force of law.

Exhibit A tangible item that is marked for identification for purpose of being used as evidence at a trial.

Exigent circumstances Conditions that excuse an officer from obtaining a warrant in order to protect a life, preserve evidence, or prevent a suspect from escaping.

Expert testimony Testimony that is given by a witness who the court determines to be expert on the topic upon which the testimony is to be given. Once accepted as an expert witness, the person is allowed to state his or her opinion on relevant matters.

Expert witness A witness who is called to supply scientific, technical, or other specialized knowledge that will help the jury and/or judge evaluate the facts that have been presented.

Ex post facto law A law that imposes criminal penalties for actions that were taken prior to the passage of the law.

Expungement The process of physically eliminating the record of an individua's arrest and conviction.

Extended term sentence A sentence beyond the statutory maximum of the basic range of penalties that otherwise could be imposed for the crime charged; also known as an "enhanced sentence."

Extortion The practice of obtaining money, property, or services from an individual or institution, through coercion.

Extradition The procedure by which one state formally requests another state to turn over the custody of a fugitive for criminal prosecution or punishment.

Factual questions Issues related to the determination of who did what and when, where, and how they did it.

Fact witness A person who has first-hand knowledge of the events at issue in a case.

Federal defender An attorney appointed to represent persons who are unable to afford private counsel in federal prosecutions.

Federal Rules of Criminal Procedure (FRCrP) The rules that govern the procedure in all criminal proceedings in the U.S. District Courts, the U.S. Courts of Appeals, and the Supreme Court of the United States.

Federal Rules of Evidence (FRE) The rules of evidence that govern proof in all civil and criminal proceedings in the U.S. district courts.

Federal Sentencing Guidelines The uniform sentencing standards used to calculate the sentencing range for federal defendants convicted of felonies or Class A misdemeanors.

Felony A major crime that is punishable by a year or more in a state prison.

Felony murder The unintended killing of a human being that occurs during the commission of another felony. The intent to commit the felony transfers to the killing to give rise to first degree murder.

Field sobriety tests A series of tasks a driver is directed to perform in front of a police officer to help the officer determine whether the motorist was driving under the influence of alcohol or drugs.

Fifth Amendment privilege against self-incrimination An individual's constitutional right to refuse to answer questions or to otherwise provide statements that could be used as evidence against himself.

Fine The monetary penalty imposed upon a defendant as punishment for committing an illegal act.

Flat fee A pre-established amount that the client must pay for representation in the case.

Forfeiture The rule that appellate procedure that a party's inadvertent abandonment of an issue in the lower court cannot be argued on appeal.

Fraud An act of using deception to commit a theft.

Friendly witness A fact witness who knows something about the underlying occurrence and holds a favorable impression of the client.

Fruit of the poisonous tree doctrine Evidence that is derived from an illegal search or interrogation is inadmissible.

Fugitive from justice A person who has fled a jurisdiction to escape criminal prosecution or punishment.

Grand jury A court-appointed panel composed of 16 to 23 citizens that considers evidence presented by prosecutors and determines whether there is probable cause to bring formal criminal charges.

Group exhibit A trial exhibit comprised of multiple components.

Guilty but mentally ill A verdict finding that the defendant is guilty of a crime although the defendant lacked the mental capacity to commit it.

Habitual offender laws Mandatory sentencing laws that require judges to give extended terms of imprisonment to persons the third time that they are convicted of a serious criminal offense, without the possibility of parole, for life or an extended period of time. Also known as "three strikes and you're out" laws.

Harmless error A mistake that is not considered prejudicial enough to justify overturning the court's decision/action.

Hate crime A prejudice-motivated crime in which the offender intentionally targets the victim because of the victim's membership in a particular social or demographic group.

Hate speech Speech directed at a particular group or classification of people that involves expressions of hate or intimidation.

Hearsay evidence A statement, other than one made by the declarant while testifying at the trial or hearing, offered in evidence to prove the truth of the matter asserted.

Hearsay rule The general rule of evidence providing that hearsay evidence is not admissible at trial or hearing.

Homicide An act by one human being that causes the death of another human being. To be considered a crime, the act must have been done purposely, knowingly, recklessly, or negligently.

Hostile witness A witness who manifests great hostility or prejudice against the side that called him or her to testify.

Hourly fee The rate of compensation earned by an attorney based on the time devoted to the case.

Hung jury A jury that is unable to reach a verdict after lengthy deliberations.

Immunity An exemption from prosecution given to a witness so that the witness can be compelled to give self-incriminating testimony.

Impeachment The challenge to a witness's credibility.

Impeachment by omission The challenge to a witness's credibility based on what the witness failed to state on a prior occasion.

Impeachment evidence Evidence that tends to undermine the credibility of the opponent's witnesses.

Implied consent law A state statute providing that persons who are issued driver's licenses consent to field sobriety tests and chemical tests to determine impairment while operating a vehicle.

In camera In a judge's chambers, outside the presence of a jury and the public.

In camera review A judge's review of materials in the absence of the parties and the public

Incarceration Mandatory confinement in a facility that limits the ability to move around as the person wishes.

Inchoate crimes A crime that was planned but not completed.

Inculpatory evidence Evidence tending to show that a person committed a crime.

Indeterminate sentencing A form of punishment in which the defendant is sentenced to a range of imprisonment with the actual release date determined by a parole board.

Indictment The formal criminal charge against a defendant returned by a grand jury. It is also referred to as "a bill of indictment."

Indictment jurisdictions Jurisdictions in which defendants accused of committing felonies have the right to be indicted by a grand jury.

Information The formal written charge presented by the prosecution without a grand jury indictment.

Information jurisdictions Jurisdictions in which prosecutors are authorized to initiate felony charges by either indictment or information.

Initial appearance The first time a person charged with a crime appears before a judge. This is also referred to as a "first appearance."

Inquisitorial system A judicial system in which judges are supposed to play an active role in bringing out all relevant information related to reaching the appropriate decision in a case.

Insanity defense A defense that relieves people who are legally insane from criminal responsibility for their actions.

Insurrection/rebellion An organized, and usually violent, act of revolt against an established governmental entity or its leaders.

Interlocutory appeal An appeal from an order by a trial court that does not conclude the case.

Intimidation An act which involves putting someone in fear of something bad happening to them, their loved ones, or their property.

Involuntary intoxication The consumption of alcohol and/or drugs without knowledge or consent.

Irresistible impulse test A test that provides that the defendant is not guilty due to insanity if, at the time of the killing, the defendant could not control his or her actions.

Jail A facility controlled by a local governmental authority to hold criminal defendants awaiting trial and offenders convicted in state court of misdemeanors.

Joinder of defendants A process whereby individual defendants who are alleged to have committed the same offense(s) are tried together at the same time.

Joinder of offenses A process whereby a defendant is tried on multiple charges at the same time.

Judge A governmental official who presides at court proceedings. The judge decides all legal issues presented and determines the facts in non-jury cases.

Judicial notice An action taken by a judge to formally recognize something as being a fact without requiring the attorneys to prove it through the introduction of other evidence.

Judicial precedent An earlier judicial decision that is relied upon by judges in deciding a case.

Judicial review The legal doctrine that courts have the power to strike down statutes and void other government actions that are not consistent with the court's interpretation of the constitution.

Jurisdiction The geographic area within which a political entity has the right to exercise authority. Jurisdiction also refers to a court's power to decide a case or issue an order.

Jury box The specific location in the courtroom where the jury sits during the trial.

Jury box system A method of jury selection in which prospective jurors fill the jury box in the order of the numbers they drew. As individual jurors are stricken, they are replaced by other prospective jurors, until everyone left in the box is acceptable to both sides or all peremptory challenges by both sides are exhausted.

Jury instruction conference A meeting with the judge in which the attorneys discuss the content of the instructions that the judge will give to jurors.

Jury instructions Written directions given by the judge to the jury pertaining to the controlling principles of law in the case.

Jury nullification A term used to describe a situation in which a jury votes to acquit a defendant even though the facts clearly establish a violation of the letter of the law.

Juvenile A young person who has not yet attained the age at which persons are legally considered to be adults under criminal law.

Juvenile courts Special courts established to deal with juveniles who commit acts that are violations of criminal law or who are adjudged to be abused or neglected.

Juvenile delinquent A juvenile who has been adjudicated to have committed acts that are violations of criminal law.

Knowingly Not intending to cause a specific harm, but being aware that such harm would be caused.

Larceny A crime that involves the taking away of the goods or property of another without the consent and against the will of the owner or possessor and with a criminal intent to convert the property to the use of someone other than the owner.

Law A rule of conduct promulgated and enforced by the government.

Laying a foundation A process by which an attorney asks a witness a series of preliminary questions designed to identify potential evidence and explain how it relates to the issues involved in the trial.

Lay witness A witness who is called to testify about things personally observed through his or her senses.

Leading questions Questions worded in such a way as to suggest what the answer should be.

Legal defense A set of facts or legal arguments that, if accepted by the court, relieves a person of criminal liability for having committed an act that is defined as a crime.

Legal questions Issues related to the interpretation of the meaning of the law, including procedures used in the trial and the admissibility of different kinds of evidence, as well at the type of behavior that is covered by the terms of the statutes being applied.

Lesser included offense A crime whose elements are all included among the elements of the more serious crime being charged.

Magistrate A judicial officer vested with limited authority to administer and enforce the law.

Making false statements to federal investigators The act of lying to or concealing information from a federal official.

Malice aforethought The level of intent shown by the actor's premeditation, the cruelty or conscious disregard for the safety of others or the intent to commit another felony.

Mandatory sentence A requirement, by the legislature, that the judge impose a minimum prison term for a specified crime.

Manslaughter A homicide where the act was committed recklessly or under the influence of extreme mental or emotional disturbance.

Marshal A court officer who serves summonses and other court documents, collects money as required by court judgments, provides security for the courthouse, and otherwise helps in carrying out the court's orders.

Material evidence (For purposes of determining the prosecution's disclosure obligations under *Brady*), evidence is material if there is a reasonable probability that had the evidence been disclosed to the defense, the result of the proceeding would have been different.

Materiality A requirement that the evidence be more probative than prejudicial.

Mens rea A Latin term referring to what was going on in someone's mind at the time he or she committed an illegal act.

Misdemeanor A minor crime that is punishable by a fine and/or less than a year in jail.

Mistrial The early termination of a trial because of extraordinary circumstances such as a deadlocked jury, prejudicial trial error, or the illness or death of a trial participant.

M'Naghten test A test that provides that the defendant is not guilty due to insanity if, at the time of the killing, the defendant suffered from a defect or disease of the mind and could not understand whether the act was right or wrong.

Model Penal Code A model criminal code prepared by the American Law Institute (ALI) to promote improvements in and greater consistency among state criminal codes.

Model Rules of Professional Conduct A set of recommended ethics standards for attorneys promulgated by the American Bar Association. Most of the states have adopted some or all of the model rules.

Motion An application made to a court for the purpose of getting a ruling on an issue in favor of the moving party.

Motion for a new trial A request to have the judge order a new trial on the basis of errors that were made in the pre-trial and trial stages.

Motion for bill of particulars A defense motion that requests the court to order the prosecution to file a supplementary document that gives the specifics of a charge that were not set forth in the original charge.

Motion for change of venire A formal request to the court to select jurors from a different location than the place of trial.

Motion for change of venue A formal request to the court to move the trial to a different location.

Motion for competency hearing A formal request to the court to hold a hearing to determine if the defendant is competent to stand trial.

Motion for continuance A formal request to the court to postpone the date of an upcoming court proceeding.

Motion for entry of a protective order A formal request to the court to protect either the opposing party or a third party from an unreasonable or invasive request for discovery.

Motion for judgment of acquittal/motion for directed verdict A formal request to have the judge acquit the defendant, notwithstanding the jury's verdict to the contrary.

Motion for substitution of judges A formal request to the court to substitute a different judge for the one that is currently assigned to the case.

Motion *in limine* A formal request to the court to prohibit mention of specified information because it is not sufficiently relevant to the issues being tried and would have a prejudicial effect on the jury.

Motion to compel A formal request to the court to order either the opposing party or a third party to take some action. Typically, this motion is filed in connection with discovery disputes.

Motion to dismiss A formal request to the court to drop a pending criminal charge against the defendant.

Motion to sever A formal request to the court to require separate trials for individual defendants who are scheduled to be tried together, or for individual charges against a specific defendant.

Motion to suppress A formal request that the court prohibit specified material from being admitted into evidence at a trial because it was gathered in an illegal manner.

Movant The party filing a motion with the court.

Murder A homicide that was committed purposefully, knowingly, or where the person acted recklessly with extreme indifference to the value of human life.

Necessity A defense requiring proof that the defendant was forced to take an action to avoid a greater harm.

Negligence A failure to act reasonably under the circumstances.

Negligent homicide A homicide based on a negligent act.

Neutral witness A witness who has no relationship with either the defense or the prosecution.

No bill The grand jury's determination that there is no probable cause that an individual committed a crime.

No-knock warrant A special type of search warrant that authorizes police to break into a house/apartment without first knocking on the door and waiting to be let in.

Nolle prosequi The formal entry of record by the prosecutor declaring no interest in prosecuting the case.

Nolo contendere plea (also known as a "no contest" plea) A plea in which the defendant does not admit or deny criminal responsibility but agrees to accept punishment.

Non-pattern jury instructions Jury instructions that were not created as part of the uniform pattern instructions for the jurisdiction.

Not guilty by reason of insanity A verdict finding that the defendant carried out the actions constituting a crime but lacked the mental capacity to have intended to commit the crime.

Notice of appeal A formal document filed with the clerk of the trial court stating that a party is appealing the decision of the trial court.

Notice of filing notice of appeal A document filed with the clerk and served on the opposing party stating the date on which the appellant filed a notice of appeal.

Notice of hearing A court document that states the time, the date, and the judge who will hear arguments on a particular motion.

Notice to appear A notice informing a party that he or she must appear in court or risk losing the matter set for hearing.

Noticing a motion The process of sending a written notice to the other party informing the party that the motion will be argued in front of the judge on a particular date at a specific time.

Noticing the deposition The process of sending a written notice to the other party informing the opposing party of the time, date, and place of a deposition of a named witness along with the method of recording testimony, such as stenography or audio recording.

Nunc pro tunc A Latin term meaning "now for then," in the courts, this refers to the modification of an order or record retroactively to show what actually happened at the time.

Objection A request to the judge to disallow specific questions to a witness, comments by opposing counsel, or responses from witnesses.

Objection on the record A challenge to the judge's ruling that is memorialized either by the electronic or stenographic capture of a verbal objection or a written notation of the objection by docket entry or otherwise.

Obstruction of justice An act that intentionally interferes with the work of police, prosecutors, and other government officials.

Offer of proof A procedure whereby excluded testimony is placed into the record for possible appellate review of the judge's decision to exclude it.

On the record Statements made in court that are recorded by either a court reporter or by the clerk of the court as a written entry in the case file.

Opening statement Remarks made by prosecutors and defense attorneys, at the start of a trial, which are designed to provide a framework for understanding the witnesses and documents that will be part of their cases.

Open plea A plea agreement under which the defendant pleads guilty and the judge determines the sentence without a joint recommendation from the parties.

Order of protection A court order entered to forbid an individual from harassing, abusing, or otherwise interfering with the liberty of a particular person. Typically, the order protects a victim from a household or family member.

Ordinance A form of law that is created by local legislative bodies such as city councils.

Overbreadth A reason for invalidating a statute that criminalizes constitutionally protected activities along with those that it can legally prohibit.

Overbreadth doctrine A principle of constitutional law that any regulation of expression must be narrowly tailored to meet the government's legitimate object.

Overruled objection The judge's unfavorable ruling on an evidentiary objection.

Own recognizance The defendant's promise to appear in court without posting a bond. This is also referred to as "O.R." or and "personal recognizance."

PACER The acronym for Public Access to Court Electronic Records, an online public-access service that permits users to retrieve case and docket information from the federal courts and the U.S. Party/Case Index.

Paralegal A person qualified by education, training, or work experience who is employed by a lawyer, law office, corporation, governmental agency, or other entity who performs specifically delegated substantive legal work for which a lawyer is responsible.

Pardon An official action that cancels a conviction for a crime as well as the penalty associated with it.

Parole A conditional release from incarceration after actually serving part of the sentence.

Partial defense A defense that reduces a crime to a lesser included offense.

Pattern discovery Model discovery requests that use generic, boilerplate language to request all of the information allowable under the applicable criminal discovery rules.

Pattern jury instructions Uniform basic jury instructions typically prepared by committees of judges, lawyers, and scholars for use by the trial courts in a specific jurisdiction.

Penalty enhancement statute A law providing for a stiffer penalty for the violation of a criminal statute due to the presence of an aggravating factor, such as the age or race of the victim, the heinous nature of the offense, or other circumstances.

Peremptory challenge A method that an attorney can use to remove a prospective juror without being required to state a reason.

Periodic imprisonment A probation option that permits a defendant sentenced to imprisonment to leave custody for work or school.

Perjury The act of lying or knowingly making false statements while under oath in court or in affidavits or depositions.

Personal recognizance bond (PR) (also known as Own recognizance (OR)) A defendant's promise to appear in court without posting cash or other security.

Petition to revoke (PTR) A motion filed by the prosecutor seeking to revoke probation and resentence the offender.

Petit jury A court-appointed panel of citizens who consider the evidence presented by both sides at trial and determine the facts in dispute.

Petty offense A violation of the law that is considered less serious than a misdemeanor.

Physical evidence Material objects related to the case.

Plain error The exception to the waiver rule that permits an appellant to raise on appeal a mistake that was not preserved in the trial court because it was a highly prejudicial error affecting the fundamental rights of the defendant.

Plaintiff The party who initiates a civil lawsuit.

Plain view doctrine The legal theory that law enforcement officials have the right to seize contraband items or evidence of a crime when they see such items in public or from a location where there is no reasonable expectation of privacy.

Plea bargain An agreement whereby the defendant pleads guilty to a criminal charge in exchange for a reduction in the charges, the number of counts, or a lesser sentence.

Plea colloquy The in-court examination of a criminal defendant entering a guilty plea to determine whether the defendant is entering the plea intelligently, knowingly, and voluntarily.

Plea of convenience A guilty plea for a crime the defendant does not acknowledge committing that is made in order to conclude the case on terms the defendant feels are in his or her best interest; also known as an "*Alford* plea."

Pocket brief A short memorandum of law used to advise the court on a discreet point of law.

Polling the jury A procedure in which the judge asks each the jurors to individually confirm their votes.

Post-conviction relief A statutory collateral challenge to a judgment of conviction.

Post-verdict motion (also known as post-trial motion) A defense motion filed after a guilty verdict that seeks court action on various case-related matters.

Prayer for relief A short, unnumbered paragraph near the end of a motion in which the moving party presents the relief being sought from the court.

Preliminary hearing The initial hearing by a judge to determine whether there is probable cause for the charge against the defendant.

Presentence Investigation Report (PSR) The document which reports the results of the probation officer's post-trial investigation of a convicted defendant, including all factors the court should take into account when determining the sentence.

Pre-trial diversion programs An alternative to prosecution that seeks to divert certain offenders from traditional criminal justice processing into a program of supervision and services.

Prima facie case Evidence that, if not contradicted by other evidence, is sufficient to meet the burden of proof required for that type of case.

Principal A person who actually commits the crime.

Prison (also known as a penitentiary) A facility controlled by the state or federal government to house convicted state court felons and federal offenders.

Private practice A form of legal practice in which attorneys charge their clients fees for the legal services being provided.

Privilege against self-incrimination An individual's constitutional right to refuse to answer questions or to otherwise provide statements that could be used as evidence against the individual.

Probable cause The reasonable belief based on specific facts that a person committed a crime or that something will be found in a specific location.

Probation A criminal sentence discharging the defendant to the community subject to conditions, which may include reporting to a probation officer.

Pro bono A Latin term translated as "for the good," is used to identify legal work performed for free, or at a reduced rate.

Procedural due process The series of procedures that federal and state government are constitutionally required to follow before they can deny anyone life, liberty, or property.

Proof of service A sworn statement by a member of the attorney's office attesting to the service of the document on the opposing side by mail, personal delivery, or other means.

Prosecutor The lawyer authorized to represent a particular unit of government in criminal court.

Prosecutor's rebuttal case The phase of the trial in which the prosecution calls witnesses to dispute the evidence presented by the defense in its case-in-chief. This is also referred to as "the rebuttal."

***Pro se* party** A party to litigation who is unrepresented by counsel.

Protective order A court directive to protect a party or witness from unreasonable or invasive discovery requests.

Public defender An attorney paid by the government to represent indigent persons accused of committing crimes.

Public trial A trial open to the public.

Purposeful Intending to cause a specific harm.

Rape Traditionally defined as non-consensual sexual intercourse between a male and a female who was not his wife. (Exceptions for forced intercourse with a wife no longer apply in some states.)

Reasonable force The amount of force necessary to protect oneself or one's property.

Reasonable suspicion A reasonable belief in the context of the specific facts of the situation. This standard is greater than a mere hunch but less than a probable cause.

Rebuttal The phase of the trial in which the prosecution calls witnesses to dispute the evidence presented by the defense in its case-in-chief; also known as the "prosecution's rebuttal case."

Rebuttal evidence Evidence presented to explain, repel, counteract, or disprove facts given in evidence after a party had rested its case.

Recklessness Disregarding a substantial and unjustifiable risk that harm will result.

Record on appeal The common law record and the report of proceedings; also known as "the record."

Re-cross The portion of a witness's testimony during which the side that conducted the initial cross-examination has an opportunity to ask additional questions designed to clarify issues raised during the re-direct.

Recusal The judge's voluntary removal of himself or herself from a case because of bias or the appearance of impropriety if he or she continues to preside over the case.

Redaction The process of masking some part of the content of a document before making it available for inspection.

Re-direct The portion of a witness's testimony during which the side that conducted the initial direct examination has an opportunity to ask additional questions designed to clarify issues raised during cross-examination.

Relevant evidence Evidence that leads one to logically conclude that an asserted fact is either more or less probable.

Report of proceedings The transcripts of testimony as well as any other oral statements made in the trial court.

Reprieve An official action that temporarily postpones the punishment until some future point in time where some other authority can review the sentence.

Respondent The party who receives the motion from the opposing side of a case.

Resting the case A phrase used by attorneys to announce that they have presented all of the evidence that they intend to present at the current stage of the trial.

Restitution A component of a sentence entered against a defendant to be used to compensate the victims of the crime for their losses.

Retreat exception The rule that in order to claim self-defense there must have been no possibility of retreat.

Return of search warrant A court document that specifies when a search warrant was executed and lists the items of the property seized.

Return of service The written verification establishing that a document has been served.

Reversible error A mistake that is considered sufficiently prejudicial to warrant reversing the trial court's decision/action.

Robbery A crime in which someone uses force or fear to take something of value from the possession of another against that person's wishes.

Rule of law A collection of legal principles that all relate to the placement of limitations on the exercise of political power and the operation of government. These principles include: (1) government must follow its own rules; (2) government must apply the law impartially; and (3) government must provide due process for those accused of breaking the rules.

Sealing criminal records The process of preventing an individual's criminal records from being accessed by the public.

Search warrant A written court order that authorizes an officer to search a specific place for specific objects. A neutral judge must determine that there is probable cause in order to issue a search warrant.

Sedition Conduct or speech that incites individuals to violently rebel against the authority of the government.

Self-defense The justified use of force to protect oneself or others from being injured.

Sentence A judgment formally pronouncing the punishment to be imposed on a person who has been convicted of a crime.

Sentence bargaining A plea bargain in which the defendant enters a plea of guilty in exchange for a lighter sentence.

Sentencing guidelines A uniform set of standards used to calculate the range of punishments to be given to people convicted of specific crimes,

Sequestering a jury A procedure isolating jurors in order to prevent them from being exposed to outside influences such as media coverage or internet discussion of the case.

Sidebar conference The discussion between the judge and the attorneys that takes place during the trial outside of the hearing of the jury. Typically, attorneys stand in front of the bench when they participate engage in this conference standing in front of the bench.

Solicitation The crime of encouraging someone to commit a crime.

Specialty court A court that focuses on one type of offense or offender with the objective of addressing the underlying causes of the offender's criminal behavior by working collaboratively with outside agencies to provide counseling treatment or education in an effort to prevent recidivism. Also known as "treatment court."

Speedy Trial Act A law that sets forth a maximum time limit between the time that formal charges are filed and the start of a trial on those charges.

Stalking The act of following another person or placing them under surveillance when these actions place that person in reasonable apprehension of bodily harm, sexual assault, confinement, or restraint.

Statute of limitations A law that sets forth a maximum time limit between the occurrence or discovery of a crime and the date at which formal charges must be filed.

Statutes A form of written law that is enacted by federal and state legislative bodies.

Statutory law A form of law that is created by legislative bodies in the form of statutes and ordinances.

Statutory rape An act of sexual intercourse (even if consensual) with a person under a certain age.

Stipulation An agreement by both sides to accept something as being true so as to simplify and expedite the trial by dispensing with the need to present formal proof.

Street crime A crime that usually involves violence and is typically carried out by a person considered to be from a low socioeconomic class.

Struck jury method The jury selection process in which the judge randomly selects the number of jurors required for the case plus those numbering the total of peremptory challenges and a few extras. After the lawyers exercise all of their challenges, those remaining in the jury box are the jurors and alternates.

Subpoena An order issued by the authority of a court that commands an individual to appear to testify or produce documents at a judicial event such as a trial or grand jury proceeding.

Subpoena *duces tecum* A special form of subpoena that is used to compel the witness to bring documents or other tangible items to court.

Substantial capacity test (Part of the Model Penal Code) A test that provides that the defendant is not guilty due to insanity if, at the time of the killing, the defendant lacked either the ability to understand the act was wrong or the ability to control the behavior.

Substantive due process The constitutional limitation placed on the federal and state governments barring the deprivation of anyone's life, liberty, or property by means of a law found to be arbitrary and/or unreasonable.

Suicide The deliberate termination of one's own life.

Summary suspension The automatic cessation of driving privileges of an individual who has a specified blood alcohol concentration percentage in his or her bloodstream, as shown by a blood or a breathalyzer test. A driver may also have his or her license suspended by refusing to submit to a breathalyzer test.

Summons An official notice issued under seal of the court informing a party that he or she must appear in court or risk losing the case.

Surrebuttal The phase of the trial in which the defense calls witnesses to dispute the rebuttal evidence offered by the prosecution.

Suspect A person that law enforcement officials think may have committed a crime.

Sustained objection The judge's favorable ruling on an evidentiary objection.

Taking case under advisement The judge's deferral of a decision on a case or issue raised in a case.

Temporary insanity The defense that the accused was momentarily insane when the crime was committed and therefore was incapable of understanding the nature of his or her actions.

***Terry* stop** A law enforcement officer's stop of a person for a brief period of time to ask a few questions when the officer has "reasonable suspicion" that the person has committed, is in the process of committing, or is about to commit a crime.

Testimonial evidence Verbal statements that are given under oath at a trial for the purpose of helping the jury and/or judge to understand the facts of the case.

Theft A crime involving taking property without the owner's consent.

Transactional immunity Prosecutorial immunity that protects a witness from prosecution for the offense revealed in his or her testimony.

Transferred intent doctrine The concept that when an actor who intends to injure one victim unintentionally harms another, the *mens rea* from the original offense is transferred to the crime involving the unintended victim.

Treason An attempt to overthrow the government of one's country or to assist its enemies in war.

Treatment Courts Courts that focus on one type of offense or offender with the objective of addressing the underlying causes of the offender's criminal behavior by working collaboratively with outside agencies to provide counseling treatment or education in an effort to prevent recidivism.

Trespass An unauthorized intrusion onto private land or into a building that belongs to someone else.

Trial notebook A three-ring notebook with appropriately tabbed sections containing materials required for a specific trial.

Trial subpoena A document prepared under the authority of the court that commands a witness to appear at a trial to give testimony.

True bill A grand jury's determination that the evidence before it constitutes probable cause that an individual committed a crime.

U.S. Attorney The chief federal law enforcement officer of the judicial district to which he or she is assigned. The U.S. Attorney is responsible for prosecuting persons accused of committing federal crimes.

Use immunity Prosecutorial immunity that bars the government from using the testimony in the prosecution of the witness, except on charges of perjury. Use immunity is also known as "derivative use immunity."

U.S. Magistrate Judge A federal trial judge appointed by the life-tenured federal judges of a district court. Magistrates often try misdemeanor and petty offense cases and handle felony preliminary proceedings.

Variance A federal sentence that is not within the Federal Guidelines or based on a departure from the Guidelines.

Venire A panel of prospective jurors.

Victim impact statement A written or oral statement made by the victim of a crime (or the family members of a deceased victim) that is presented at the sentencing hearing for the convicted offender.

Void for vagueness defense A principle of constitutional law that requires penal statutes be written so that they fairly inform ordinary people as to what is commanded or prohibited.

Voir dire An examination of prospective jurors to see if they are fit to serve on a jury in a specific case.

Voluntary intoxication The knowing and voluntary consumption of alcohol and/or drugs.

Waiver rule The rule of appellate procedure that an issue not presented in the trial court is waived and cannot be argued on appeal.

White-collar crime A non-violent crime characterized by deceit, concealment, or violation of trust that is committed by an individual in the course of his or her occupation or by a company in the course of its business.

Writ of habeas corpus A court document ordering public officials to produce the person named so that a neutral judge can determine if there is a lawful basis for detaining that person.

Index